THE
BRUCE B. LAWRENCE
READER

The Bruce B. Lawrence Reader

Islam beyond Borders

Edited and with an Introduction by

ALI ALTAF MIAN

DUKE UNIVERSITY PRESS · *Durham and London* · 2021

© 2021 Duke University Press
All rights reserved
Designed by Matt Tauch
Typeset in Huronia Latin Pro by Westchester Book Group

Library of Congress Cataloging-in-Publication Data
Names: Lawrence, Bruce B., author. | Mian, Ali Altaf, [date]
editor., writer of the introduction.
Title: The Bruce B. Lawrence reader : Islam beyond borders /
Bruce B. Lawrence ; edited and with an Introduction by
Ali Altaf Mian.
Other titles: Islam beyond borders
Description: Durham : Duke University Press, 2021. |
Includes bibliographical references and index.
Identifiers: LCCN 2020017613 (print) | LCCN 2020017614 (ebook) |
ISBN 9781478010241 (hardcover) |
ISBN 9781478011293 (paperback) |
ISBN 9781478012825 (ebook)
Subjects: LCSH: Islam.
Classification: LCC BP163 .L397 2021 (print) |
LCC BP163 (ebook) | DDC 297—dc23
LC record available at https://lccn.loc.gov/2020017613
LC ebook record available at https://lccn.loc.gov/2020017614

CONTENTS

ix PREFACE · *Bruce B. Lawrence*
xiii ACKNOWLEDGMENTS · *Bruce B. Lawrence*

1 INTRODUCTION · *Ali Altaf Mian*

25 **Part I. Theorizing Islam in World History**

29 ONE · Introduction to *Shattering the Myth: Islam beyond Violence* | 1998

54 TWO · Islam in Afro-Eurasia: A Bridge Civilization | 2010

78 THREE · Muslim Cosmopolitanism | 2012

90 FOUR · Genius Denied and Reclaimed: Hodgson's *The Venture of Islam* | 2014

99 **Part II. Revaluing Muslim Comparativists**

103 FIVE · Al-Biruni: Against the Grain | 2014

113 SIX · Shahrastani on Indian Idol Worship | 1973

124 SEVEN · Introduction to Ibn Khaldun's *Muqaddimah* | 2005/2015

141 EIGHT · Mystical and Rational Elements in the Early Religious Writings of Sir Sayyid Ahmad Khan | 1979

161   **Part III. Translating Institutional Sufism**

165   NINE · Can Sufi Texts Be Translated? Can They Be Translated from Indo-Persian to American English? | 1990

176   TEN · "What Is a Sufi Order? 'Golden Age' and 'Decline' in the Historiography of Sufism," from *Sufi Martyrs of Love: The Chishti Order in South Asia and Beyond* | 2002, Coauthored with Carl W. Ernst

191   ELEVEN · Sufism and Neo-Sufism | 2010

218   TWELVE · "Allah Remembered: Practice of the Heart," from *Who Is Allah?* | 2015

229   **Part IV. Deconstructing Religious Modernity**

233   THIRTEEN · "Fundamentalism as a Religious Ideology in Multiple Contexts" and Conclusion, from *Defenders of God: The Fundamentalist Revolt against the Modern Age* | 1989

255   FOURTEEN · "The Shah Bano Case," from *On Violence: A Reader* | 2007

262   FIFTEEN · Introduction to *Messages to the World: The Statements of Osama bin Laden* | 2005

274   SIXTEEN · Muslim Engagement with Injustice and Violence | 2013

305   **Part V. Networking Muslim Citizenship**

307   SEVENTEEN · Preface and Conclusion, from *New Faiths, Old Fears: Muslims and Other Asian Immigrants in American Religious Life* | 2002

327   EIGHTEEN · "W. D. Mohammed: Qur'an as Guide to Racial Equality," from *The Qur'an: A Biography* | 2006

333   NINETEEN · Introduction to *Muslim Networks from Hajj to Hip Hop* | 2005, coauthored with miriam cooke

345   TWENTY · "AIDS Victims and Sick Women: Qur'an as Prescription for Mercy," from *The Qur'an: A Biography* | 2006

351   **Part VI. Reflecting the Divine Other in Words and Images**

353   TWENTY-ONE · Approximating *Sajʿ* in English Renditions of the Qur'an: A Close Reading of *Sura* 93 (*al-Ḍuḥā*) and the *Basmala* | 2005

370   TWENTY-TWO · Epilogue to *The Qur'an: A Biography* | 2006

374   TWENTY-THREE · A Metaphysical Secularist? Decoding M. F. Husain as a Muslim Painter in Exile | 2011

395   TWENTY-FOUR · Conclusion, from *Who Is Allah?* | 2015

409   TWENTY-FIVE · The Future of Islamic Studies: Bruce B. Lawrence Interviewed by Ali Altaf Mian | 2018

432   AFTERWORD · *Yasmin Saikia*
441   BRUCE B. LAWRENCE'S WRITINGS
451   INDEX
463   CREDITS

PREFACE

Bruce B. Lawrence

I never imagined that my life would unfold as an academic, much less one focused on the Islamic world. I did major in Near Eastern studies, along with History, when I was an undergraduate at Princeton. I was convinced that I would become a foreign service officer, after first serving a term in the US Navy as a junior officer. The Navy stint inspired me to think about religion, not least because President Kennedy was assassinated while I was serving in DC. I anticipated a gloomy period in world history better served by meditation than mediation. Three years at the Episcopal Divinity School launched me as an Episcopal priest but also made me interested in the life of the mind beyond the boundaries of the church. I was admitted to Yale as a Ph.D. student, intent on exploring Abrahamic roots for Judaism, Christianity, and Islam. Hinduism, however, displaced Judaism on my agenda, as I became fascinated with the Vedas and ancient Indian thought. I had not yet finished my Yale Ph.D., relating Islamic thought to Indian subjects, when I was hired at Duke. A first job became a lifetime career. I never left Duke, though I did travel to many parts of Muslim Asia during forty years on the Duke faculty. Especially formative were two years I spent in India as a visiting scholar at Aligarh Muslim University. I felt a great affinity for Sufism, not least for medieval Indian exemplars related to a South Asian order, the Chishtiyya. Alas, international catastrophes redefined my academic labor. First, the Iranian Revolution in 1979 shifted me to thinking comparatively about extremist religion, or fundamentalism, across the Abrahamic spectrum, and then the 2001 attacks on the United States compelled me to revisit Islam at its roots, in the Qur'an as scripture, in order to find the different threads of belief that could produce both Sufism and terrorism.

In all these labors I have been assisted by a companion who exceeds me in her zest for travel and her passion for writing. miriam cooke has accompanied me on research/teaching forays that stretch from North Africa to Southeast

Asia, from Morocco to Indonesia, and many other places in between. She has also read nearly everything I have written since 1980, improving the argument as well as the accessibility of all my literary output as a scholar of Islam.

I have also had the benefit of extraordinary colleagues, both at Duke and elsewhere. Carl Ernst heads the list, having been my collaborator, co-teacher, and catalyst since the early 1990s, when he moved from Pomona College to the University of North Carolina. We co-wrote a book on Chishti Sufism that is among the selections in this volume, and we also co-edited a series of monographs, "Islamic Civilization and Muslim Networks," for the University of North Carolina Press. I should also mention the late Richard C. Martin, from Emory, who helped on numerous publication ventures, including the volume coedited with Carl Ernst that marked my retirement from Duke, *Rethinking Islamic Studies: From Orientalism to Cosmopolitanism*. Among numerous others are two former Duke colleagues, Vincent Cornell (now at Emory) and Ebrahim Moosa (now at Notre Dame). I learned from them about different forays of scholarship and also the beauty of collaboration.

Of equal benefit to me have been loyalty and inspiration from many former students. I esteem them all, from Michael Browder, my first doctoral student, to Brett Wilson, my last, but the one who has done me a singular service is Ali Altaf Mian. Ali entered the Ph.D. program in Islamic studies at the very end of my career at Duke. I had the pleasure of knowing him in several classes, though I was not on his Ph.D. committee. Ali Mian did me the extraordinary favor of registering all my writings in a list that he produced for me toward the end of his course work at Duke. Like most academics, I have a curriculum vitae, one that I updated annually, sometimes semi-annually, in order to demonstrate my level of scholarly production. Ali's list went beyond a seriatim record, however. He also thought of categories into which different essays, articles, and book chapters might be slotted, and that produced a thematic template of my scholarship, one that I had never conceived or had even imagined as possible.

What you have before you is the outcome of Ali Mian's diligent labor, from the sketch of an overview to the arrangement of selections within parts, each with an introduction that makes all the chapters register as a coherent whole. Moreover, he has made sense of my scholarship in the broadest possible forum. Above all, I have striven to produce, as he writes in the introduction, "scholarship that crosses territorial and disciplinary boundaries to account for Islam's difference and multiplicity. Such scholarship is relevant in today's world, for it bridges barriers between Muslim and non-Muslim communities, between local and global concerns, between popular and scholarly networks." Ali Mian's hope is also mine: "To stage an argument for the political purchase and analytical value of compassionate, engaged scholarship on Islam and Muslims." May the outcome of this volume be the success of this argument, not least among those who have yet to experience the full challenges of the twenty-first century. May it motivate today's students to become tomorrow's citizens, prisoners of hope striving for a global comity enhanced by Muslims, enriched by Islam!

ACKNOWLEDGMENTS

Bruce B. Lawrence

I could never have undertaken this project without the insight, generosity, and patience of Ali Mian. While a Duke graduate student, he grasped my ideas through several assignments, pursued other publications not assigned, and then at a point back in 2013, over seven years ago, proposed that he would like to assemble a Bruce Lawrence Reader. He excelled in everything, from big ideas to small tasks, monitoring the process as though it were his own first monograph. He enlisted numerous students at Seattle University to help him as typists, and we met both in Seattle and Durham on more than one occasion to review progress, and correct mistakes, together. Though I cannot repay it, I must acknowledge my deep gratitude to him.

In addition, Miriam Angress, also a former student, responded to the project with imagination and diligence in her role as a Duke University Press editor, and as we ploughed through several versions, Miriam also sought outside readers, all anonymous but all generous, who gave their time and perceptive feedback.

Also attuned to the project and reading it with the eye of a generalist who sees mistakes small and large was Dr. James Cross, father of yet another Duke student, Jonathan Cross. Finally, Professor Scott Kugle, who studied at Duke some two decades ago, helped trace sources and gave valuable suggestions. Another colleague, the late Professor Richard C. Martin, offered suggestions that helped shape the final version into a better book. My closest family members were also vigilant: my daughters, Rachel and Anna Lawrence, both read parts of the whole and offered their vision of what it could and should be. Further, my wife and soul mate, Professor miriam cooke, did what no one else could do: she urged me forward even when it seemed there were too many hurdles, and too big a challenge, to assemble all the parts of this book you are now about to read. I am in miriam's debt for many of the individual pieces, including the introduction to a book that we co-edited, but even more for the devotion and support that make a distant dream now a near reality. Finally, backstage but still invaluable are the publishers of all that appears in these pages: I thank numerous presses and journals for giving Ali Mian permission to reprint my work here.

To all these sundry and varied folks, I give deep and heartfelt thanks while also relieving them of any responsibility for errors or oversights or shortfalls in what has resulted; those failings belong to me and are solely mine to bear.

INTRODUCTION

Ali Altaf Mian

Connectivity, Compassion, and Critique

Motivating this volume is the belief that scholarship should bridge cultures even as it must elaborate their differences. The historian of religion Bruce B. Lawrence models such an approach in his scholarship on Islam and Muslims. I have learned many valuable lessons from Lawrence, who was my teacher at Duke University and with whom I have had the privilege of staying in close intellectual contact over the last decade. But what he has taught me most of all is that scholarship can and should play an important role in realizing intercultural connectivity even as scholars seek to elucidate and analyze cross-cultural differences. At face value, this statement might strike you as another platitude that aspiring pluralists throw around. Yet, consider the idea that connectivity is one of the cornerstones of imaginative scholarship. It takes empathetic imagination to study convergences but also divergences between subject and object, self and other, past and present, local and global, and other figurations of knowledge, subjectivity, temporality, and spatiality. To the imaginative humanist and social scientist belongs the restless task of finding commonalities and connections between seemingly disparate traditions and societies.[1] Lawrence's contributions to the field of religious studies, particularly his engagement with Islam and Muslims, model this productive mode of inquiry.

The scholarship collected in this volume crosses territorial and disciplinary boundaries to account for Islam's heterogeneity. Lawrence bridges divides between Muslim and non-Muslim communities, local and global concerns, and popular and scholarly networks. The dual tasks of identifying cross-cultural connections and then analyzing the ideas, actors, and institutions that forge such connections carry an invaluable ethical and political purchase. Historical inquiry, informed by both critique and compassion, enables us to "move beyond stereotypes—to interrogate their hard edges, to unravel their seamless classificatory logic, and to make all groups part of a common future that has a shared past as well as a contested present."[2] Lawrence's interpretive labor militates against the dividing and divisive forces of intercultural conflict, often linked to territorial nationalism.

Lawrence's approach is particularly relevant in our current political context, in which Muslims are dubbed an external threat to the prosperity of the so-called West and Euro-Christian culture. Lawrence's writings on Islam are instructive, for they elaborate Muslim diversity but also demonstrate the connectivity of global Islam and what Muslims share with others in terms of their civilizational ideals and religious aspirations. Lawrence places Islam in the frame of global history but also translates the diverse ways in which Muslims hear, speak, contemplate, and feel the idea of God.

For the student of religion, it is insistently important to analyze *when* notions of God or gods are deployed, by *whom* to *what* objectives, *where* such deployments go beyond historical precedent, and *how* they might participate in projects of justice but also those of injustice and violence. The critical yet compassionate style of inquiry that Lawrence models so nimbly gives a certain ethical-political inflection to the rigor and range of his textual, historical, and cultural studies. He draws on this approach to analyze the key global events that have shaped the image of Islam and Muslims in the West during the last five decades. Let me mention two key events: the Iranian Revolution of 1979 and the terrorist attacks of September 11, 2001. These were seismic events not just for Muslims in Western Europe and North America but also for Islamic thought and culture in Muslim-majority contexts. Lawrence's deft analyses of religious fundamentalism and violence as well as his sociohistorical analysis of Asian, especially Asian Muslim, immigrants to the United States document a scholarly response to public perceptions of Islam and Muslims after 1979. His writings on Sufism, Allah and the Qur'an, in addition to those on Muslim citizenship, have aimed to educate the general public both at home and abroad, in Europe, Africa, and Asia as well as in America, in the aftermath of 9/11.

What Is *The Bruce B. Lawrence Reader?*

The Bruce B. Lawrence Reader: Islam beyond Borders assembles twenty-four essays that I have organized into six thematic parts. Each piece should be seen as a reflection of Lawrence's emergent thinking at a particular time within the evolution of his scholarship. Lawrence and I have revised each piece to reflect the broader arc of his contribution to the study of religion, particularly Islam, and for clarity of argumentation, convenience of accessibility, and consistency of style. This reader also includes a 2018 interview that alludes to some key moments of Lawrence's career, especially his time spent at the Aligarh Muslim University in the company of the late Khaliq Ahmad Nizami. The interview also introduces readers to Lawrence's most recent monograph, *The Koran in English*, and highlights his appreciation for *American Qur'an*, a creative rendition of the Muslim scripture by the American artist Sandow Birk.[3] The interview is followed by a passionate afterword from Yasmin Saikia, a cosmopolitan scholar of Islam in her own right and one of Lawrence's close friends. Saikia identifies the significance of the South Asian Sufi tradition for Lawrence, especially the legacy of Shaykh Nizamuddin Awliya' (d. 1325), a Delhi saint whose key teachings Lawrence made available to English readers with the 1992 publication of *Morals for the Heart*.[4] One can find bibliographic information about Lawrence's books and articles on Indo-Muslim Sufism as well as the other recurrent themes of his scholarship in "Bruce B. Lawrence's Writings." He has also penned scores of insightful book reviews that I had to exclude from this list for the sake of brevity. In the notes, I have from time to time suggested further readings that might aid curious readers and diligent students.

Many of the essays revised for this volume treat singular problematics in the study of Islam and are thus a ready resource in the classroom setting. Some essays take up a broad view of Islamic history (such as those on Islam in world history and Muslim engagement with violence and injustice). Others pertain to specific personages and texts (such as those sampled in part II and those on the Qur'an). In this way, readers are able to observe the enduring features of Muslim thought and Islamicate civilization. One of Lawrence's key analytical tendencies is the use of historical and contemporary case studies that enable us to grasp a general ideal by studying a specific embodiment or experience. Here, Lawrence delicately balances the accent on enduring values and attention to local, lived realities. In his own words, "There may be an abstract canvas of Islam or Islamism vs. the West or modernity, but what matters, both practically and analytically, are the local, the immediate, and the contingent aspects of each polity and society that determine its modus vivendi within the current world order."[5] Above all, the excerpts collected here model the methodological necessity of tethering empathetic description to critical reflection.

Let me briefly address the volume's structure, with a side glance at Lawrence's educational background, before discussing a couple of key terms in his oeuvre and then presenting synopses of the book's six parts. The parts are organized neither chronologically nor in terms of the various regions of the so-called Muslim world. Rather, each part models a particular methodological approach to the study of religion. The volume invites readers to engage with Islam and Muslims while also reflecting on and then critically thinking about the analytical purchase of six methodologies: theorizing, revaluing, translating, deconstructing, networking, and reflecting. To read the book from cover to cover will yield readers several dividends, not the least of which is an enhanced understanding of the various interpretive tools that Lawrence has deployed and invites others to deploy.

The volume speaks to the concerns and commitments of three groups of readers. First, it seeks to meet the pedagogical needs of college instructors who might find its essays evocative for teaching undergraduate students about Islam and Muslims. Instructors will find the emphasis on critical methodologies, instead of historical chronology or geographic regions, to be catalytic for meta-analytical discussion and debate in the classroom. Second, the volume offers insights to aid journalists and observers of global affairs, since it collects Lawrence's writings on fundamentalism, religious violence and modern Islam, and the challenges and promises of cosmopolitanism and religious pluralism. Here again, I hope that the volume's emphasis on six critical methodologies will encourage readers to become attentive toward frames of representation while also avoiding outdated rubrics such as tradition versus modernity when talking about Islam and Muslims. Third, this volume aims to reach the general English-speaking readership. Above all, it seeks to make a positive contribution in realizing religious pluralism and cross-cultural dialogue. Lawrence is able to communicate his insights to multiple sets of readers because of his own broadscale training—at once researching Muslims and teaching about Islam—in diverse settings.

Lawrence was trained "to interpret religion through a historical, which is always also a comparative, lens."[6] He studied Arabic and Islamic philosophy at Princeton University (1958–1962) and the history of religions (with a concentration in Hinduism and Islam) at Yale University (1967–1972). Between 1962 and 1967, he undertook a two-year stateside stint in the U.S. Navy and completed a master's degree from the Episcopal Divinity School in Cambridge, Massachusetts. In Princeton, New Haven, and Cambridge, his key teachers included James Kritzeck (1930–1986), Franz Rosenthal (1914–2003), Willard G. Oxtoby (1933–2003), and Wilfred Cantwell Smith (1916–2000). He also credits Annemarie Schimmel (1922–2003) with stoking his interest in South Asian Sufism as well as miriam cooke for influencing his turn to art and aesthetics. While he neither met nor studied with the renowned American global historian Marshall G. S. Hodgson (1922–1968), Hodgson's approach to Islamic history most profoundly shapes Lawrence's.

Lawrence has been acutely aware of the demands of historical scholarship and source criticism as well as their provenance and the interpretative strategies required for reading critically across various genres. Yet like Hodgson, Lawrence has aspired to theorize historical data and to scan empirical details for big-picture lessons. These lessons underscore historical continuity and change but also offer insights into the sociocultural, political, economic, ethical, and metaphysical ideas and institutions that make lives livable or unlivable, cities prosper or decimate, and civilizations endure or wane. Lawrence has theorized Islam in both historical and metahistorical terms, seeing it as at once a civilizational and cosmopolitan force. At the outset, therefore, it is important to specify how he approaches "civilization" and "cosmopolitanism."

Civilization and Cosmopolitanism

Lawrence defines civilization as "the broadest, most capacious envelope of cultural traits related—directly or indirectly, explicitly or implicitly—to geographical location and temporal shifts. In a thumbnail definition, civilization equals culture writ large over space and time. Space predominates."[7] Lawrence's use of civilization corresponds neither to the idea that civilization implies the repression of our basic instincts for the sake of social order nor to the notion that the world is divided into neat cultural blocs. Lawrence uses this term in a historical-critical sense, building on the pioneering vision of Hodgson. The latter emphasized contingency and contestation and demanded self-reflexivity on the part of the inquirer when defining civilization. What mattered most in these definitions was that civilization "must not be hypostatized, as if it had a life independent of its human carriers."[8] Like Hodgson, Lawrence also accentuates Islam's human carriers, many of whom we shall meet in the course of the following pages. Both historians study metaphysical and moral as well as poetic and political ideas not in the abstract but rather situated in and tethered to human practices as well as social institutions.

Lawrence also approaches "cosmopolitanism" in a broad and creative arc. Cosmopolitanism, in his view, provides "a trans-territorial and trans-temporal ethos" with deep roots in the formation and reception of Islam as an ethical and aesthetic sensibility.[9] This sensibility is captured best by the Arabic word *adab*, which applies to both beautiful conduct and didactic literature. *Adab* (cultural and behavioral refinement) permeated the networks of "trade, language, Sufism, and scholarship" in which Muslims interacted with strangers at home and abroad.[10] *Adab* allowed Muslims to appreciate and to appropriate the major cultural traditions of the Mediterranean and the Nile-to-Oxus region. Muslim cosmopolitanism features a world-affirming attitude and engenders a social ideal that includes three elements: an affirmation of life, an appreciation of literature, and an openness to change. While it is first and foremost an ethico-aesthetic orientation, "cosmopolitanism, to survive, needs institutional structures, an expanded public space, without which local tastes, restrictive norms, and punitive codes can, and will, prevail."[11]

For Lawrence, cosmopolitanism is more than a modus vivendi; it is also a modus operandi. This creative use of cosmopolitanism as an analytical lens has allowed him to advance the study of Islam beyond both orientalism and social science. Lawrence lives and works on the cusp of major events that have led Islam, for better or worse, to be linked with *jihad*. Western popular media and mainstream Euro-American pundits have redefined scholarship on Islam, accenting the idea of violence as integral to the ideological and institutional, familial and political, manifestations of all religion, but especially Islam. The relationship between violence and Islam crisscrosses the modern academy: it has become an important object of critical inquiry in religious and historical studies as well as in other disciplines such as political science and sociology. Lawrence tackles the uncritical linkage of violence with Islam in *Shattering the Myth: Islam beyond Violence* (1998). The introduction to that monograph opens part I.

Part I: Theorizing Islam in World History

The broader stage on which Islam is a set of aspirations and Muslims a set of actors is world history. Yet neither Islam nor world history should be understood as self-contained concepts; they refer to complex, often contested, meanings that reflect both cultural heterogeneity and the location of the inquirer using these terms. To theorize Islam in world history thus entails a capacious working definition of both terms. It also depends on critical analysis, content knowledge, and compassionate imagination. As Lawrence reminds us, "The early, middle, and modern periods [of Islam] require separate skills and caveats for their successful analysis. The most difficult period to analyze is the one closest in time, the modern."[12] Perhaps the most popular image of modern Islam is one that is framed by violence. Lawrence observes that the violence perpetrated by Muslims in the name of Islam is ultimately connected to the violence of European colonialism and other global forces of modernity. Yet one must be critical of the term "violence" itself; too often, pundits and preachers reduce violence to force—an exertion of physical force that maims or destroys bodies and buildings, among other things. In *Shattering the Myth*, Lawrence draws attention to other forms of violence, such as structural violence (the foreclosure of opportunities in everyday life to people who reside at the margins of social privilege). Sometimes, scholarly representation reproduces structural violence. A case in point is when scholars consult only male sources or analyze only masculine perspectives. *Shattering the Myth* critiques the violence of representational exclusion by foregrounding the figure of the Muslim woman. Connecting several forms of violence, whether physical, structural, or representational, it also connects the hurt and injury caused by Muslim actors to the dispossession and displacement that Muslims themselves have experienced in global discourses as well as in modern political and socioeconomic processes. In the opening text of this volume, Lawrence probes the intricate embeddedness of political Islam in the global circuits of violence.

Shattering the Myth can also serve as an introductory text to Islam for undergraduate students, journalists, and general readers. The intensification of violence on multiple sides, Muslim and non-Muslim, especially after the tragic events of 9/11, has only increased the need for such texts. In my view, the key pedagogical purchase of using *Shattering the Myth* is its capacity to locate Islam in mainstream cultural and political frames and then to move through these frames in order to problematize popular but unproductive clichés about Muslims and their heterogeneous religious traditions. In effect, violence is provincialized within specific structural and political etiologies, and Islam itself emerges as a civilizational praxis.

In defining Islam, Lawrence explores the implications of two different, yet connected, ideas: Islam as "religion" and Islam as "ideology." In the twentieth century, the religious elements of Islam have been deployed to serve modern ideologies such as ethnonationalism and Western exceptionalism. While addressing his methodology in *Shattering the Myth*, Lawrence writes, "I seek patterns that interconnect numerous Muslim histories, whether local, national, or regional, and also link them collectively to global forces." Thus he connects the idea of Muslim violence not just to various "Islamic" histories but also to multiple global forces, such as nationalism, capitalism, and the rapid movement of ideas and opinions facilitated by the internet.

Why is it important for us to analyze these interconnections between global powers and local Muslim narratives and networks? We live in an increasingly connected world, especially since the advent of the internet and social media. Therefore, the tasks of description and analysis fall on the shoulders of both insiders and outsiders. In this regard, Lawrence passionately states, "I reject the judgment that none but the persons invoked can talk about themselves." In other words, Lawrence rejects the "delusionary escapism" and "cultural relativism" that have been attractive to so many contemporary intellectuals. For him, the arenas of discourse on a particular idea, ritual, institution, or network are open for critical observation. They require careful judgment from both insiders and outsiders, especially because of the "interlocking character of late capitalist culture and social movements."

Yet, what also matter profoundly are one's social location and one's speaking position.[13] Hodgson was prescient in emphasizing this dimly lit mirror:

> Not only the scholars' cultural environment at large but their explicit precommitments, which brought the greater of the scholars to their inquiry in the first place, have determined the categories with which they have undertaken their studies. Only by a conscious and well-examined understanding of the limits of these precommitments and of what is possible within and beyond them can we hope to take advantage of our immediate humanness to reach any direct appreciation of major cultural traditions we do not share—and perhaps even of traditions we do share.[14]

Lawrence acknowledges his location when he writes, "I approach this task [of studying Islam] conscious that I am limited as well as enabled by who I am. I am male. I am Anglo. I am upper middle class. European in ancestry, I was born in America. Raised non-Muslim, I remain non-Muslim." Realizing these "ascriptive limits," Lawrence also reflects on his own connectedness to Islam and Muslims: "Yet after studying both the Arabic language and Middle Eastern history from an early age, I remain deeply attracted to Islam as a life force: it animates many Muslims with whom I have lived and worked and whom I count among my closest friends." Here, we see connectivity working at two levels: Lawrence connects disparate traditions and histories in his scholarship but he also connects to Muslims themselves. Note the affective touch or affinity he attributes to the latter sense of connectivity. This affective attachment enhances and enriches his analytical endeavor, rendering it humanistic in the fullest sense. Lawrence thus declares in no uncertain terms, "I choose to be both an intellectual and an unabashed humanist. Despite the many assaults on the humanities from within and beyond the academy, I remain not only a humanist but also a late modern humanist." The mirror shines brightest when its light is directed inward.

To pursue the question of violence in Islam from Lawrence's humanist perspective gives it a certain depth that allows him to engage with various storytellers and their narratives, be they Muslim activists and intellectuals or non-Muslim media pundits or policy makers. His empathetic mode of inquiry enables him to make a strong case for the continued relevance of humanistic inquiry and intercultural modes of scholarly engagement. His authorial presence is thus marked by two profiles—that of a historian who uses critical methodologies to describe and analyze the association of Islam with violence, and that of a compassionate translator who acknowledges the civilizational aspirations of his Muslim interlocutors.

Let me reiterate that it is not one or the other but the dual combination of critique and compassion that time and again defines Lawrence's engagement with Islam, even more so with Muslims. He is therefore able to demonstrate how contemporary Muslims have inherited many ideas, practices, and social institutions that might serve as resources for bridging cultures and forging connections with others. This idea is explored most fruitfully in "Islam in Afro-Eurasia: A Bridge Civilization" (2010). Following Hodgson, Lawrence theorizes Islam as a cosmopolitan civilizational force that can draw on various local resources such as cultural and behavioral refinement (*adab*), respect for individual privacy, urban coexistence, and hospitality as well as trust. In other words, the underlying analytical ambition of part I involves the two-pronged methodology of empathetic imagination and critical scrutiny. Both analytical postures come together to historicize the violence associated with Islam and Muslims as well as to point constructively to the resources that persist among Muslims to cope with the forces of injustice and violence, whether global, local, or both (see especially "Muslim Cosmopolitanism" [2012]).

Part II: Revaluing Muslim Comparativists

Part II identifies critique and compassion as integral components of the scholarly efforts of past Muslim intellectuals. To that end, it revisits and revalues four Muslim comparativists who linked their discursive activity to multiple bodies of knowledge. As a methodological protocol, to revalue one's object of study implies not only a committed rediscovery but also a reorientation of recognition beyond mere texts or contexts. What Lawrence revalues and recognizes about

Biruni, Shahrastani, Ibn Khaldun, and Sayyid Ahmad Khan is their quest for lessons of metaphysical and moral import within the immanent structures and processes of their worlds. In one way or another, these four scholars themselves valued comparison and turned to non-Muslim others in order to better understand Muslim selves.

Lawrence conducts "metastudies" of Biruni, Shahrastani, Ibn Khaldun, and Sayyid Ahmad Khan by first situating them in their contexts and then appreciating what they might have to offer to the contemporary reader. These scholars crossed discursive and territorial borders, applying to their datasets the most rigorous forms of analytical tools available. By revisiting their legacies, Lawrence models for the modern-day student of history, especially the history of religions, lines of critical inquiry that are afforded by Muslim cosmopolitanism, evidenced across millennia but also in the scholarly legacies of some of its best exemplars.

In terms of fame, no medieval Muslim scholar surpasses Ibn Sina (also known as Avicenna), yet it is to Biruni's legacy that Lawrence turns first. Biruni, in his view, models for us a productive skepticism: "Biruni surpassed Ibn Sina both in the breadth and catholicity of his skeptical erudition in the fields of history and chronology, mathematics, astronomy, geography, pharmacology, mineralogy, history of religions, and Indology." Biruni challenged Aristotle's cosmology, whereas Ibn Sina accepted many Aristotelian assumptions as axiomatic. For Biruni, the student of the cosmos must "view the evidence with as much openness to observation as his instruments and his knowledge permit." Crucial for Lawrence, "It is not a matter of philosophical certainty but of experimental openness that is at stake." From Biruni we learn the importance of subjecting all that we take for granted to continuous scrutiny. The student of knowledge must cultivate the capacity for sustained observation, "relentless logic, and repeated experimentation," all qualities that find their consummate expression in Biruni's works.

Precision and probability, epistemological postures but also material properties, play an important role in discovering cures and antidotes for bodies marred by disease and disability. In this regard, Biruni's precise analysis and epistemological openness paid off. At once scientifically rigorous, lexically encompassing, and socially useful, his text on medicine and herbal treatments, *Kitab al-Saydanah*, yielded durative results. Biruni modeled analytical skills that not only serve the scientist as he or she interrogates the cosmos or classifies flora and fauna but that also are useful when the humanist catalogs cultural phenomena. Biruni demonstrated the utility of scientific methodology in the field of humanistic inquiry in his magisterial work, *India*. The work is a testimony to

Biruni's scholarly empathy for the religious other and also his ability to travel between disciplinary methodologies. At the outset, as an Indologist, Biruni teaches us that scholars must cultivate a certain "liking" for, but not necessarily an identification with, the subjects they study. The scholar might not "like" the doctrinal or ritualistic content preached or practiced by the religious other, but he nonetheless cultivates a "liking" because only genuine and compassionate encounters with others can lead someone to see things from another's perspective. This self-awareness requires acquiring the needed facility in languages and sustained exposure to those whose lives and traditions we study. Thus Biruni not only "communicated but also evaluated" Hindu doctrines and rituals. The other major medieval Muslim scholar to write extensively about Indic religion was Shahrastani. In chapter 6, Lawrence analyzes Shahrastani's views on the Hindu tradition, particularly on idol worship, in a broadly comparative and intensely philological study. This 1973 article signals what became his enduring commitment to critical inquiry at once comparative and cross-cultural. Interested readers are encouraged to consult Lawrence's 1976 monograph on Shahrastani.[15]

Lawrence then turns to another major comparativist, Ibn Khaldun, who is credited with bridging the gap between social science and the empirical-based study of Muhammad's discourse and Islamic jurisprudence. Excerpted here is Lawrence's probing introduction to Franz Rosenthal's translation of Ibn Khaldun's *Muqaddimah*. Rosenthal, who was a leading Orientalist and Lawrence's doctoral supervisor at Yale, visited Duke University for a conference on Ibn Khaldun organized by miriam cooke in May 1982. The proceedings of that conference were edited by Lawrence and published as *Ibn Khaldun and Islamic Ideology* (1984). What Lawrence appreciates most about Ibn Khaldun is his interstitial logic: "While there are others who contributed to both Islamicate civilization and Muslim cosmopolitanism, Ibn Khaldun stands out for his interstitial logic, his rigorous pursuit of in-between-ness, the messiness of flux and change, for dynastic, regional, and global history."[16]

The legacy of Ibn Khaldun highlights the importance of place: his Mediterranean location proved vital for the types of connections between social and moral processes that he was able to observe and theorize. As a scholar of Muslim jurisprudence with a penchant for history, Ibn Khaldun studied the effects of urbanity on individual and social life. He keenly observed the ideological and institutional practices that agglutinated peoples and cultures. Key among such practices was poetic composition. Tapping into the power of words, their multiple resonances and registers, poetry drives home, into the hearts of people, the values they come to call their own. As we know, poetry was one of the key features of Muhammad's tribal society, and in emphasizing poetry's capacity to forge connections between humans, Ibn Khaldun was hinting at the powers of group solidarity, or what he called ʿasabiyya.

Ibn Khaldun developed his concept of communal formation in the *Muqaddimah*, a thick tome that served as the "introduction" to the science of history for his historiographical text, *Kitab al-ʿibar* (Book of lessons, or, history). Lawrence's introduction to an abridgment of Franz Rosenthal's translation of the *Muqaddimah* identifies Ibn Khaldun's key interpretive principle—that he reads historical processes through a theoretical lens refined by jurisprudential theory and Hadith criticism, two sciences that were wedded to questions of language and reliability. Consider the implications of linguistic analysis for Ibn Khaldun. The jurist-historian from the Maghreb argued that ordinary language contains the traces of shared opinions and conventions but also the potential for creating further connections and resonances. His originality lies in a double-fold interpretive move. First, he connects the two secondary sources of Islamic legal norms—consensus and analogy—to the formation of ʿasabiyya. Second, he applies the distinction, itself borrowed from Hadith criticism, between *khabar* (event) and *hadith* (tradition) to his historical analysis. The first interpretive move allows Ibn Khaldun to trace the success of urban polities, particularly in the fields of culture and economy, to pre-urbanite tribal formations. The second interpretive move enables him to subject historical reports and sources (*akhbar*) to the standards used to verify the probity of prophetic traditions (*ahadith*). While this move bolsters the authority of Tradition (*hadith*), it also creates a place within religious thought for historical knowledge derived from Event (*khabar*). Lawrence also explores Ibn Khaldun's steeped position within his own Muslim worldview. He was neither a defender of reason against revelation nor aloof from the mystical dimensions of Islam, that is, Sufi feelings, ideas, practices, and institutions.

The mystical dimensions of Islam, however, cannot be reduced to heterodoxy or "popular religion." They are connected at the deepest levels to jurisprudence and theology. Too often it is presumed that the reformist visionaries of modern Islam, such as the late nineteenth-century Indian educationist and social reformer Sayyid Ahmad Khan, espoused rationality without feeling. In chapter 8, Lawrence paints a different picture of this modern Muslim luminary and restores mystical ideas and rituals to their proper place in Sayyid Ahmad's life and thought.

The essay on Sayyid Ahmad Khan moves beyond description of its subject; we encounter Khan as an illustration of the predicaments of Islam and

Muslims in colonial India, especially after the decisive transition from Mughal to British sovereignty in the late 1850s. Lawrence demonstrates three main trends in the formative intellectual career of this key Indo-Muslim figure. First, mystical ideas and practices are privatized. Khan's Sufism, therefore, resonates with that of the reformist theologians. Second, he participates in the linkage of "the West" to Christianity. The study of Christianity, many modern Muslims believe, is essential if one is to acquire a sense of how the West works. Third, Khan encouraged and aided his British interlocutors to deepen their understanding of Islam and Muslims. These three trends in turn indicate that colonial secularity had already achieved some of its desired results by the second half of the nineteenth century. Yet, Khan's legacy demonstrates the constructive role played by dialogue and scholarship in navigating the imbalances of power between the colonized and the colonizer.

Lastly, Sayyid Ahmad Khan's sympathetic engagement with Sufi ideas and practices shows us the importance of Sufism even for reformist scholars (who sometimes claimed that Sufism is largely to blame for the "decline" of Islamic civilization). A large segment of Lawrence's work over the last forty years has analyzed Sufism, specifically in a conceptual idiom accessible to his readers, a topic he addresses in part III by analyzing the craft as well as the politics of translation.

Part III: Translating Institutional Sufism

In chapter 9, the first essay of this part, Lawrence draws attention to the intricacies of craft and concept involved in translating Indo-Persian Sufi poetics into American English. Translation connects the receptor and the host languages, and in this capacity the translator becomes a conduit of connections between linguistic idioms and regimes of intelligibility. Moreover, "the temporal symmetry of the languages must inform the translator's labor." The translator listens to the echoes of semantic difference through an inner ear and renders a poem from one language to another by means of "authorial imagination." Translation simultaneously honors differences of expression and connects them to similarities of meaning between languages.

Once readers have a good sense of the thematic and formal aspects of Indo-Muslim poetry and the translational dimensions structuring the study of the relevant sources, they are better equipped to appreciate the textual and social universe of the Chishtis, South Asia's largest Sufi network. Lawrence's pioneering scholarship on the Chishtis dates back to the mid-1970s. It is his dedication to their legacy that marks chapter 10, which is the introduction to *Sufi Martyrs of Love: The Chishti Order in South Asia and Beyond* (coauthored with Carl W. Ernst in 2002). Who are the Chishtis? The most obvious answer is a Sufi order or fellowship rooted in South Asia but now present in diasporic sites from London to Kuala Lumpur. However, the very idea of the Sufi order needs to be problematized, especially because its formalized definition in the academy is marred by judgments about authenticity and the decline of Islam. The question Lawrence and Ernst address most directly is the following: how might we describe and analyze the Chishti order so as to throw light on the general character of Sufi orders without erasing the particular features of the Chishtis or reifying a "universalist" picture of Sufi orders? A part of the answer to this question lies in tweaking our methodological approach to Sufism itself, as Lawrence and Ernst state: "We need to enlarge the concept of Sufism to include wider social and institutional contexts. Unlike the individualistic notion of originality found in romantic modernism, Sufism is a vast cumulative tradition. It rests upon multiple contributions to a common resource both contested and deployed over generations." This methodological move is key, for it encourages readers to defamiliarize themselves with what they know about religious authority and authorship, mystical experience and "oceanic feelings," and instead to explore the relationship between politics, social constructionism, and spiritual ideas, rituals, and spaces.

Instead of relying on worn-out temporal categories, such as ancient, medieval, and modern, Lawrence and Ernst propose an alternative, five-part diachronic development of Chishti saintly culture (inclusive of masters and disciples, Sufi lodges and spiritual exercises, manuscripts and manuals, and networks of patronage and transmission). Their temporal schema is important because it is derived from critical engagement with the relevant historical sources. This five-part diachronic framework enables the authors to expose the Chishti order's internal dynamism, allowing readers to appreciate the various ways in which Sufi personages and institutions are products of their political and sociocultural contexts even as they attempt to exceed these contexts.

The introduction to *Sufi Martyrs of Love* further examines colonial Chishtis, postcolonial formations, and recent developments in the South Asian diaspora, and it also analyzes reformist as well as progressive trends among modern Chishtis. As a microhistory of institutional Sufism, it anticipates the next selection,

"Sufism and Neo-Sufism," which presents a macro-history across time and space. Written for *The New Cambridge History of Islam* (2010), this essay surveys the development of modern (colonial and postcolonial) Sufi thought and practice in three contexts: Africa, Asia, and America. We learn of the persistence of major Sufi commitments, such as belief in the living presence of the Prophet Muhammad and the availability of his intercession—his mediating function in procuring divine favor—to all believers but especially to Sufi saints and masters. At the same time, Lawrence situates modern Sufis within "the material context of Euro-American modernity," with its forms of thought and patterns of practice that privilege secular disenchantment. Also integral to modernity are the oppositional forces that railed against the modern. A case in point is the Wahhabi movement: it reacts against the modern world but also retains something of modernity in its literalism and surface superficiality.

"Sufism and Neo-Sufism" is broadly diachronic: it furnishes readers with an overview of its subject matter that spans three different centuries and continents. The reader encounters the anticolonial profile of Sufi institutions in nineteenth-century Africa, surveys how Sufi actors overcame challenges of fundamentalist critique and official scrutiny from postcolonial states in twentieth-century Asia, and then discovers the new forms of music and meditation introduced into institutional Sufism (hence, neo-Sufism) in twenty-first-century America. The trajectory of Sufism in these diverse contexts reveals its lasting potential as both an individual and collective resource: to provide purpose and pleasure to aspiring spiritual seekers but also to embody symbol and spirit for emergent political movements.

Chapter 12, "Allah Remembered," is excerpted from Lawrence's *Who Is Allah?* This essay surveys the affective landscape of what is perhaps the most characteristic ritual of Sufi devotion: *dhikr/zikr* or "remembrance of God." As Lawrence explains, remembrance "requires an intense, dedicated practice of introspection." To chant God's most familiar name, Allah, or one or more of God's 99 Epithets (such as *al-Rahman* and *al-Rahim*), involves invocation and projection. Sufis pursue *zikr* with the acknowledgment that Who they are trying to access, the object of their contemplative longing and constant yearning, is not the essence but rather the idea of the Divine. Allah remains the elusive Beloved, the One always to be sought but never attained or contained by the seeker.

Toward the end of *Who Is Allah?* Lawrence studies another appropriation of the Divine, that espoused by Islamist extremists, including some who perpetrate violence in the name of Allah. Lawrence first examined the question of religious extremism and fundamentalism in his early monograph, *Defenders of God: The Fundamentalist Revolt against the Modern Age*, which is discussed in part IV.

Part IV: Deconstructing Religious Modernity

To use the term "religious modernity" is already an act of deconstruction. Not long ago modernity was seen as ushering in the end of religion—and the demise of enchanted subjectivity—and the beginning of secularity and the birth of disenchantment. Lawrence refuses this binarized view of tradition and modernity when he writes, "The major problem is dyadic logic: reasoning bracketed by, and limited to, sets of two that are not complementary but competitive, not providing an exit from, but a burrowing into, perpetual conflict."[17] Lawrence is thus able to analyze terms such as fundamentalism without reinforcing binaries such as tradition vs. modernity. This section's first selection, the introduction to *Defenders of God*, follows the lead of Hodgson, to whom the book is dedicated. It locates Islam within larger trajectories of world history. It deconstructs fundamentalism, not just in its Islamic face but as it appears across religious traditions in the modern world, through multiple interpretive strategies (an assemblage that might be seen as akin to deconstruction). First, Lawrence lays bare how fundamentalists deploy the discourse of the minority and majority to their advantage. Second, he exposes how the fundamentalist mode of engaging the other is neither constructive nor dialogical but contrarian and monological, suppressing rather than engaging differences. Third, fundamentalists appeal to ideas of religious purity and an exclusive right to govern states by a mixture of scriptural literalism and cultic charisma. Both a message and a messenger are required to deliver slippery shibboleths. Fourth, fundamentalists use many conventional religious terms but invest them with narrow meanings (a case in point would be the meaning of "creation" in Bible Belt Christianity in post-1945 United States). Finally, he argues that "fundamentalism has historical antecedents, but no ideological precursors." Here, Lawrence draws on another historian, Marc Bloch, who distinguished between ancestry and explanation; while earlier movements internal to religious traditions might have participated in the above tactics of interpretation and communal organization, they did not do so to propagate an antimodern ideology. The history of fundamentalism is incomplete without reference to its ideology, and so in the conclusion of this essay, Lawrence gives the reader an opportunity to observe "fundamentalism" from a different perspective: he discusses the threefold connective tissue of twentieth-century fundamentalism, consisting of (1) the hegemony of modernization, (2) the grip of authoritarian secularity, and (3) the regime of positivism.

The problems that fundamentalist interpretations impose on personal law are especially visible in postcolonial Muslim-majority contexts and in those national contexts where the sizable Muslim minority retains a modicum of legal sovereignty, such as in India. "The Shah Bano Case," excerpted here from *On Violence: A Reader* (coedited with Aisha Karim in 2007), argues two points: (1) "women bear an uneven burden" of representation, for they carry the weight of cultural norms that perpetually implicate them in uneven relations with men, and (2) in the field of personal law, modern judicial institutions further enact communalist divisions along gender lines even as they claim to redress violence. The implementation of classical Islamic law, therefore, does not always deliver justice, especially when nation-states place the interpretation of classical jurisprudence in the hands of traditionalists and Islamists.

Lawrence approaches Islamism, sometimes known as political Islam, as a subset of religious fundamentalism. No modern figure better captured the idealistic aspirations for world domination among a minority contingent of Muslims than Osama bin Laden, whom Lawrence often recalls through the acronym OBL. In 2005 Lawrence published a translation of OBL's texts that put on display the latter's scripturalist modes of reasoning. In the introduction to *Messages to the World*, Lawrence analyzes OBL's various profiles: the legendary freedom fighter, the eloquent rhetorician, and the international threat. Lawrence contextualizes OBL's "comprehensive case for individual *jihad* against the West." OBL's message reaches some Muslim ears as ultimate truth because of his deployment of "literary gifts," at once fiery polemics and fierce argumentation. Moreover, OBL shifted rhetorical registers, even if not the message, when speaking to various audiences. The two main sources of OBL's charismatic appeal among radical Islamists were his telegenic image as a hero in some Muslim circles and his "powerful lyricism," which *Messages to the World* documents. Lawrence provides a succinct summary of the implications of OBL's lyrical prowess:

> In place of the social, there is a hypertrophy of the sacrificial. Bin Laden's messages rarely hold out radiant visions of final triumph. His emphasis falls far more on the glories of martyrdom than the spoils of victory. Rewards belong essentially to the hereafter. This is a creed of great purity and intensity, capable of inspiring its followers with a degree of passion and principled conviction that no secular movement in the Arab world has ever matched. At the same time, it is obviously also a narrow and self-limiting one: it can

have little appeal for the great mass of believers, who need more than scriptural dictates, poetic transports, or binary prescription to chart their everyday lives, whether as individuals or as collective members of a community, local or national. Above all, there is no rush to restore a Caliphate today. Bin Laden seems at some level to recognize the futility of a quest for restitution. He sets no positive political horizon for his struggle. Instead, he vows that *jihad* will continue until "we meet God and get His blessing!"

From this statement, we might understand how OBL projected his message to the world and to multiple audiences. We can see points of convergence and divergence between this message and contemporary iterations of violent Islamism, such as the Taliban, al-Qaʿida, and ISIS.

Chapter 16, the final essay of this part, is an ideal pedagogical tool for this book's multiple groups of readers, since it offers a wide-ranging historical and critical assessment of *jihad*. In "Muslim Engagement with Injustice and Violence" (2013), Lawrence approaches Islam not as a bloodless text with rigid directives but as a living tradition in which the question of war and peace has evolved over the centuries; it continues to evolve today. The essay features a diachronic survey of when and why Muslims resorted to force, whether aggressive or defensive.

While this essay begins with Muhammad, it also underscores the constraints of seventh-century tribal Arabia, where Muhammad used *jihad* for the sake of survival and for defending his nascent community. It was only later that *jihad* evolved into broad-scale militancy for his successors and their constituents. In early Islam, *jihad* as defensive warfare quickly became a procedural protocol for the expansion of the burgeoning Islamic empire. The next phase of *jihad* involved its valorization as holy war; however, the very idea of "holy war" was common between Islamdom and Christendom. In the context of the Crusades, fidelity to faith and invocation of scripture largely supported violent xenophobia and justified the use of force to expunge the religious other. The wars between the Crusaders and their Muslim counterparts in the Middle Ages had a decisive effect on the denotation and deployment of *jihad*. The fourteenth century provides a crucial temporal marker in the history of *jihad*, for it was in the early decades of that century, as is clear from the writings of the Damascene jurist-theologian Ibn Taymiyya, when *jihad* was formally linked to notions of religious purity and protection.

In the following centuries, when power and prestige returned to Muslims in the form of the so-called gunpowder empires (the Ottomans, the Safavids, and the Mughals), violence became an exercise of state sovereignty. Violence was embedded in societal processes and bureaucratic structures, and in this context, as Lawrence notes, "there was never a question of eliminating violence but rather justifying its use for higher ends." Living as subjects in the gunpowder empires, Muslims largely participated in *jihad* movements against each other; *jihad*, in other words, became a legitimate, though always contested, means of transforming society and displacing sovereigns.

It is this evolved valence of *jihad* that defined its deployments throughout the long nineteenth century. Muslim militants invoked *jihad* to fight European colonizers in multiple contexts, from North India to western Africa. Yet, the level of violence unleashed by colonial powers against Muslims far exceeded the violence espoused by reactionary Islamic militants. At the structural level, colonial powers enacted violence in Muslim-majority contexts, fueling communalist tensions among Muslims and non-Muslims and at the same time igniting sectarian fires in intra-Muslim circles. Even contexts that were never fully colonized, such as Arabia and Iran, "still experienced the effects of colonial economic penetration into the eastern Mediterranean and Indian Ocean, and the structures that arose after independence reflect this influence, above all in the spheres of politics and law." Some noncolonized Muslims still wedded Islam to nationalism. That coupling later proved fatal for Muslim polities, as it fueled Islamists' rhetoric and violence against their own governments, the heads of which were, and continue to be, viewed as puppets controlled by Euro-America. Yet, if some Muslims have engaged with *jihad* as holy war once again in recent times, they remain a distinct minority; countless others call for reform and dialogical encounters with the other; they also advocate progressive social change and civic engagement, as well as deep renewal of traditional sources from within, and they do so as citizens of late twentieth-century and now twenty-first-century nation-states.

Part V: Networking Muslim Citizenship

This part's essays address precisely the question of Muslim citizenship and accentuate the idea and practice of agency. Here, too, Lawrence builds on Hodgson, analyzing how Muslims inhabit modernity. Modernity is "not limited to the West; it depends on the agency, the creative choices, and the equally creative responses of multiple players in different parts of the *oikumene* from the early sixteenth to the late twentieth century."[18] How Muslims experience and embody citizenship in Muslim-majority contexts differs markedly from their counterparts who do not enjoy majority status but instead live as minorities (in the Americas, Europe, East Asia, India, and also sub-Saharan Africa). In fact, the majority-minority binary restructures citizenship in the modern world: Muslim minorities, like other minority groups, face questions of representation and rights, integration and acculturation, as well as inclusion and exclusion. While Asia includes many subsets—west, east, central, south, and southeast—it is especially South Asians whom Lawrence considers in his analysis of the category of Asian American as a largely late-twentieth-century development in the history of American immigration and citizenship. Here he emphasizes Asian Americans' agency and their polyvalent identities: the experiences of Asian Americans are shaped by similar political realities but also diversified according to religion, class status, and mode of creative adaptation.

If South Asian Muslims embody polyvalent Islam, so too do other Muslims whose background and circumstances are local not global, indigenous not immigrant. The emphasis on polyvalence appears in chapter 18 in the form of an illustration from African American Islam. Lawrence shows how Imam W. D. Mohammed's ideas about racial justice and scriptural guidance are seen in America as an aspiration and a reality. Mohammed believed that blackness, Muslimness, and Americanness ought to be viewed not as contradictory but as complementary orientations of identification and belonging. Lawrence also connects scriptural commentary to Mohammed's reformist efforts. The latter transformed the Nation of Islam by broadening the idea and practice of communal formation "to create a new community." For this remarkable leader, "one must be liberated from one's instinctive identity and merged into another, networked identity." It is the centrality of a networked Islam that received its most extensive elaboration in *Muslim Networks from Hajj to Hip Hop*, a collection of essays that Lawrence coedited with miriam cooke in 2005.

Chapter 19 is the introduction from that collection. The essay explores the idea of "network" in multiple ways. To be "networked entails making a choice to be connected across recognized boundaries." Muslim networks span time and space, connecting people across territorial and cultural borders. A networked approach to Islam carries the methodological advantage of connecting social scientists to humanists in order to reveal the "radical heterogeneity of Muslim cultural, linguistic, and political exchanges." At the same time, with networks "one must see common issues that face all humankind; one must examine underlying economic patterns and shifting political priorities."[19] To understand the resourcefulness of networking as an analytical strategy, consider the example of the fourteenth-century Muslim scholar Ibn Battuta. He straddled intercontinental conceptual and commercial exchanges, connecting the Mediterranean to the Indian Ocean. To view Ibn Battuta from the vantage of "networking" implies identifying the extant circles of trade and ideas, shared gestures and modes of intelligibility, that made it possible for Ibn Battuta to forge his own intercultural connections. Yet even those Muslim authors and actors who spent their entire lives in a single locality invoke other networks. Much of traditional Islamic scholarship is a chain of transmissions and is organized according to intellectual genealogies. Moreover, rituals such as the annual pilgrimage (hajj) not only serve Muslims' spiritual needs but also feed into commercial and geopolitical networks. In this way, "network" remains a vital analytic to describe and theorize about Islam and Muslims.

No network of new media and nascent connectivity is more powerful than the internet. It paradoxically enacts connectedness and sharpens divisions among people located in diverse geographical and ideological locales. Chapter 20, the final essay of this part, discusses a positive use of the internet. Still another chapter from *The Qur'an: A Biography* (2006), it depicts how AIDS victims sought divine help online vis-à-vis a prayer website managed by an Indonesian Sufi healer. The essay introduces readers to the varied "inventory of Qur'anic invocations in use today throughout the Muslim world." This example illustrates how the internet connects people in times of afflictions and ordeals, bringing online matters of practical religion, spiritual mediation, and divine dispensation, often through the Qur'an. In the last fifteen years or so, Lawrence has made numerous contributions to Qur'anic studies and has begun to extensively study the meanings that Muslims and others attach to Allah.

Part VI: Reflecting the Divine Other in Words and Images

The last part demonstrates how Lawrence engages with artistic as well as discursive representations of the divine in a mode of analysis that is more reflective than descriptive. Chapter 21 is about "rhymed prose" (*saj'*), a literary feature that the Qur'an retains but adapts from pre-Qur'anic Arabic poetry. Where earlier we read about Lawrence's assessment of the challenges of translating Indo-Persian into American English, here we encounter a deep engagement with rendering the Arabo-Islamic scripture into ordinary English. The crucial lesson that Lawrence emphasizes is the inescapable importance of form: form determines content, and translation should reflect this mutual interaction of one with the other. In the context of the Qur'an, he encourages readers to appreciate the synchronicity between its formal features, such as rhymed prose, and the moral-metaphysical vision it expresses by deploying this form.

Chapter 22 is the epilogue to *The Qur'an: A Biography*. It covers in lyrical attention the Qur'an's continued appeal and resonance in Muslim life, and why the student of religion must approach this text not only as an object of critical study but also with compassionate appreciation. What makes the Qur'an a potent set of references and affects is its "openness to multiple, often contested, views of its meanings." This scriptural openness becomes all the more evident when the Qur'an travels beyond its immediate linguistic "home" and finds new expressions in other languages through translation.

Lawrence presses us not only to engage with written sources or the spoken word—discursive traditions and their performance in cultural and political contexts—but also to encounter and to analyze the visual word, the word displayed in works of art, ranging from architectural to figural forms. Elsewhere he investigates the Dome of the Rock and the Taj Mahal, two buildings that "embody" scriptural and spiritual themes (see *The Qur'an: A Biography*).

Chapter 23 is a sustained reading of the artworks of the famed Indian artist M. F. Husain. Crucial to Lawrence's methodology is the flexibility of movement between analytical description of and engagement with his sources, in their own worlds and in the pursuit of furthering their projects. This is certainly the case with Husain; his prolific and varied artworks reflect what Lawrence calls "metaphysical secularism." While this phrase might strike one as oxymoronic, Lawrence's analysis of Husain's oeuvre encourages the reader to cultivate a nuanced understanding of how art differs from what first meets the eye. For Lawrence, Husain masterfully plays with oppositions that appear but also disappear. Through art, Husain "critiques the state of the world in which he is at play; he does not shrink from noting betrayal, highlighting controversy, and using patronage as protection against enemies." If transcendental themes from the history of religious traditions, Christian and Hindu as well as Muslim traditions, find a place on Husain's canvases, so too do the themes of secularism, democracy, pluralism, and exile. Husain insists that we engage the aesthetics of Muslim cosmopolitanism. He embodied an Islam that crossed borders, urging Muslims to find connections with humanity writ large and not just with their coreligionists. For Husain, art, like religion, was a holistic instrument of expressing truth and realizing justice.

Chapter 24 is Lawrence's bracing conclusion to his 2015 manifesto, *Who Is Allah?* I find it apt to conclude my own selective survey of Lawrence's rich oeuvre with this piece because it emphasizes a methodological posture he also emphasizes time and again: epistemological humility in religious studies. While a significant part of religion centers on the idea of a transcendental reality that resists description and analysis, students of religion still need to analyze the meanings that religious actors and sources attribute to divine ineffability. Yet this analysis neither should stop us from being skeptical of the invocations of the Absolute One or the Transcendental Many nor should permit dismissing creative engagements with the ineffable. Above all, engagement with the divine—that unknown source of creative life and death—cannot be the business of the "chosen" few. Instead, it is, and will always be, an open field of play, where the One or the Many beyond human imagination must structure the affective scope and the epistemological depth of imagination itself. In this way, *Who Is Allah?* resists closure—either epistemic or literary, either creedal or performative—and Lawrence encourages us, his readers, to do the same.

Notes

1 For an exposition of the methodological usefulness of relationality and connectivity, see Walter D. Mignolo and Catherine E. Walsh, *On Decoloniality: Concepts, Analytics, Praxis* (Durham, NC: Duke University Press, 2018), 1–2. I thank Richard C. Martin (1938–2019), Bruce B. Lawrence, miriam cooke, and Cyrus Ali Zargar for their helpful comments on this introduction.
2 Bruce B. Lawrence, "Conjuring with Islam II," *Journal of American History* 89 (2002): 487.
3 Lawrence's *The Koran in English* was published as part of Princeton University Press's Lives of Great Religious Books series, which aims to make the reception history of key religious texts accessible to a general readership. See Bruce B. Lawrence, *The Koran in English: A Biography* (Princeton: Princeton University Press, 2017).
4 Bruce B. Lawrence, *Nizam ad-din Awliya: Morals for the Heart* (New York: Paulist Press, 1992).
5 Bruce B. Lawrence, "Afterword: Competing Genealogies of Muslim Cosmopolitanism," in *Rethinking Islamic Studies: From Orientalism to Cosmopolitanism* (Columbia: University of South Carolina Press, 2010), 306.
6 Lawrence, "Conjuring with Islam II," 486.
7 Bruce B. Lawrence, "Islam in Afro-Eurasia: A Bridge Civilization," in *Civilizations in World Politics: Plural and Pluralist Perspectives*, edited by Peter J. Katzenstein (London: Routledge, 2010), 157–75.

8 Marshall Hodgson, *The Venture of Islam: Conscience and History in a World Civilization* (Chicago: University of Chicago Press, 1974), 1:34. As Edmund Burke III and Robert J. Mankin explain, "Civilizations for Hodgson were not autonomous, culturally defined, and changeless spaces. Rather, they had had historically complex and often conflicting relationships internally as well as with their neighbors" (*Islam and World History: The Ventures of Marshall Hodgson*, ed. Edmund Burke III and Robert J. Mankin [Chicago: University of Chicago Press, 2018]), 2.
9 See "Muslim Cosmopolitanism" in this volume.
10 See introduction to *Muslim Networks* in this volume.
11 Lawrence, "Afterword," 319.
12 Lawrence, "Conjuring with Islam II," 491.
13 Lawrence has repeatedly emphasized "the location, the background, and the training of the interpreter" ("Conjuring with Islam II," 486) with reference to the meanings we attach to historical events and processes.
14 Hodgson, *Venture of Islam*, 1:28.
15 Bruce B. Lawrence, *Shahrastani on the Indian Religions*, foreword by Franz Rosenthal (The Hague: Mouton, 1976).
16 Bruce B. Lawrence, review of Syed Farid Alatas's *Ibn Khaldun* and *Applying Ibn Khaldun: The Recovery of a Lost Tradition in Sociology*, *Middle East Journal* 69, no. 2 (2015): 319.
17 Lawrence, "Afterword," 305.
18 Lawrence, "Conjuring with Islam II," 491.
19 Lawrence, "Conjuring with Islam II," 492.

PART I

Theorizing Islam in World History

"Islam" is contested territory in today's world. Is Islam prone to violence? Is Islam compatible with modern, liberal values? Does Islam need a Reformation? The "Islam" invoked in these questions is often assumed to be a theocratic ideology, imagined as a foreign country where Allah reigns supreme. The writings organized in part I caution us against reducing Islam to any single idea or image. The richness of religious traditions is mirrored in the complex lives and aspirations of religious folk, and their values cannot be reduced to simple binaries, such as violence and pacifism. Bruce Lawrence proposes, and pursues, a polysemic view of Islam in his monograph *Shattering the Myth: Islam beyond Violence* (1998); the introduction for that book is excerpted here as chapter 1. When viewed from the vantage point of civilizational discourse, argues Lawrence, Islam remains irreducible to religion or politics. While beliefs and rituals are integral elements in the everyday and historical experiences of Muslims, and while some contemporary Muslims do couch political loyalty in Islamic categories, Islam in its broadest arc points to a civilizational project with multiple, and sometimes competing, symbolic resources. Crucially, Islam's civilizational character is neither exclusivist nor parochial; the vision and the venture of Islam are at once pluralist and cosmopolitan. Along with historians of Islam such as Marshall Hodgson and Richard Bulliet, Lawrence encourages us to move back from the headlines and to view Islam within world history, including the recent history of European colonialism in Muslim-majority contexts. Like Hodgson and Bulliet, he advocates critical and constructive engagement with "civilization."

What is civilization? For Lawrence, as he asserts in the second selection, "Islam in Afro-Eurasia: A Bridge Civilization" (2010), civilization is "the broadest, most capacious envelope of cultural traits related—directly or indirectly, explicitly or implicitly—to geographical location and temporal shifts. In a thumbnail definition, civilization equals culture writ large over space and time. Space predominates." When viewed through the lens of civilization, what cultural traits are historically associated with Islam, and how have they persisted across epochs and oceans? The pieces gathered in part I throw light on the various cultural traits that have defined Islam since its inception, but especially during the last millennium. These cultural traits include hierarchy and deference, two overarching traits that structure how Muslims conceptualize and embody self, society, and the transcendental. The reader will notice Lawrence's sustained engagement with multiple bodies of scholarship in order to theorize Islam as a cosmopolitan, civilizational project involving many actors, each competing for symbolic resources that they redefine yet never exhaust. In these pieces, Lawrence attends to both popular representations of Islam and intellectual conversations within the humanities and the social sciences pertaining to not only "Islam," but also objects of inquiry such as civilization, politics, and modernity. Lawrence confirms Hodgson's bold vision, and also his revisionist terminology, but at the same time he brings Hodgson's understanding of the civilizational character of Islam into conversation with recent scholarship. More important, in order to place Islamicate civilization in broad historical and political frameworks, Lawrence draws on figures from the Islamic past (such as the premodern polymath Ibn Khaldun) and the Muslim present (such as the Iranian social critic Jalal Al-i Ahmad). These invocations illustrate that Muslims themselves have contemplated Islam as a civilizational force. Islam names the rich reservoir of symbols, discourses, and institutions available to Muslims for cultivating livable worlds, for themselves and with others, including non-Muslim others. If Islam figures as war and violence in some minds, it is because new ideologies, such as secularism, anticolonialism, and especially hypernationalism, have breached the civilizational vision of Islam, creating cognitive dissonance with the Hodgsonian vision of Islam as a *world-affirming* civilization at once urbane and cosmopolitan, its historical presence crossing without erasing geographical borders. In the penultimate essay of this part, "Muslim Cosmopolitanism" (2012), Lawrence deploys Istanbul as a place where history and contemporary conflicts meet. The legendary and contested capital of the Byzantine and Ottoman empires, Istanbul is at the crossroads for travelers, traders, crusaders, and scholars. Although Ankara has become the capital of the present-day Republic of Turkey, Istanbul remains the site for examining cosmopolitan as well as anticosmopolitan forces in the Mediterranean world and beyond. It provides context and insight for all the issues discussed in this part. This discussion of Istanbul is also a fitting prelude to the final essay in this part, "Genius Denied and Reclaimed: Hodgson's *The Venture of Islam*" (2014), a forty-year retrospective essay on Hodgson as a world historian who confirmed the broader arc of Islam, and underscored the persistent value of Islamicate influence, from premodern to modern times.

ONE

Introduction to *Shattering the Myth:*
Islam beyond Violence | 1998

My main argument is simple, yet it is at odds with most popular and academic understandings of Islam. I argue that Islam cannot be understood except as a major and complex religious system, shaped as much by its own metaphysical postulates and ethical demands as by the circumstances of Muslim polities in the modern world. The last two hundred years have witnessed challenge upon challenge, from colonial subjugation to sporadic revivalism to elitist reform movements to, most recently, pervasive struggles with fundamentalism or Islamism. During each phase, Muslims have had to address internal tensions as well as external threats. The success of anticolonial struggles was followed by the disappointment of indigenous neocolonialisms. More recently, postcolonial Muslims—some Arab, most non-Arab—have been playing ever greater roles in economic changes, both regional and global. As the impact of these changes has become evident on societies everywhere, they have propelled new actors into public view. The most remarkable new presence is that of Muslim women.

In what follows I argue that the experience of Muslim women, above all, calls for a more nuanced approach to Islam and global change. It is time to counter negative stereotypes about Muslim women with knowledge about their newly constituted roles.

Yet few books attempt to synthesize data from regionally separate and geographically discrete countries with a majority Muslim population. Where such an effort has been made, it is usually through multiauthored or edited volumes that belie the very coherence suggested by their titles. While I do offer an in-depth study of one pivotal judicial saga, from India, I have otherwise drawn together data provided by others in order to demonstrate (a) that Islam is not inherently violent and (b) that the longer view of Muslim societies offers hope, rather than despair, about the role of Islam in the next century.

I thus offer three convergent foci: the crystallization of Islamic sociopolitical movements, women as the key index of Muslim identity, and finally the staging of new global economic developments that bode an unexpected Muslim difference in world affairs.

The Muslim difference will remain hidden, its force unacknowledged, unless the dominant stereotype is exposed: Islam is not violence, nor are Muslims intrinsically prone to violence. The stereotype amounts to a slur, and it must be addressed at the outset if the emerging profile of postcolonial Muslims is to be understood.

Islam beyond Violence

Islam is ... Islam is ... Islam is ... Islam is many things. Just as there is no single America or Europe or the West, a seamless caption etching diverse groups and persons with the same values and meanings, so there is no single place or uniform culture called Islam. There is no monolithic Islam. There is a Muslim world spanning Africa and Asia. It is as pluralistic as the West, outstripping both Europe and America in the numerous regions, races, languages, and cultures that it encompasses. The Afro-Asian Muslim world is also internally pluralistic, containing multiple groups who might be said to represent Islamic norms in each Muslim country. And Muslims themselves are aware of how necessary, and how difficult, it is to specify differing notions of Islam. An Indonesian friend of mine once quipped: "There are three Islams: the popular Islam which anthropologists are fond of studying, mostly as curious spectators; the public Islam with which political scientists, journalists, and policy makers identify, mostly as adversaries; and the academic Islam in which Orientalists delight, whether as art historians, linguists, or religion scholars, each studying artifacts esteemed by their guild. In Indonesia we try to provide our visitors with all three."[1]

If Islam is so diverse and Muslims so accommodating, then why has Islam so often been viewed by non-Muslims as alien at best and violent at worst? I suggest that the principal reason for the negative view of Islam is the predominance in popular thinking of the second view: public Islam. In that view, Islam emanates from a hostile, "Arab" Middle East. Most journalists, and many policy makers, continue to discount any but Arab Islam, or what is conjured up as Arab Islam, in projecting the orthodox face of puritanism and militancy. In the 1990s most Euro-American journalists continued to echo the sentiments that drove European kings and their subjects to launch their crusades almost a millennium ago, crusades whose enemy was Arab Muslims. In the aftermath of the Cold War the enemy, once again, has become the one Islam, the militant, unyielding, violent face of "Arab" Islam. Whether one picks up a popular book claiming to represent "Western cultures and values" under attack from Islam, or lead articles of the *New York Times*, such as the recent "Seeing Green: The Red Menace Is Gone. But Here's Islam," the message is the same: Islam is one, and Islam is dangerous.[2]

The Muslim enemy is invariably male, whether a foreign warrior conjured from the past or a potential terrorist stalking modern America. The fierce Kurdish anti-Crusader Salah ad-din Ayyubi, known popularly as Saladin, seems to have multiple contemporary look-alikes. Whether it is Ayatollah Khomeini denouncing the United States as the Great Satan or the Egyptian Sheikh Omar Abdel Rahman plotting to bomb the World Trade Center and other New York public buildings, Muslim leaders continue to be newsworthy principally for their adversarial words and deeds.

Behind the hostile Muslim men, Americans imagine the faces of Muslim women, homebound creatures marked alike by seclusion from the outside world and apparent oppression by their tyrannical husbands. The reality of Muslim women's active participation in their societies is glossed, covered, as it were, by a veil that projects the violence of male "Arab" Muslims everywhere. They hate the West and abuse their women.

Both images depend on singularizing Islam and then describing it as both different and violent. That stereotype remains remote from Islam as lived experience. Popular Islam is more than just the remote village or exotic domain of anthropologists. It is also the shared notion of a worldview and a pattern of living that characterizes most Muslims in Asia and Africa. It provides enormous challenges and hopes and satisfactions for Muslim women and for Muslim men. Islam offers all Muslims no fewer possibilities than every major religious tradition offers the women and the men who identify with it.

Because gender imbalance pervades both popular understanding and Muslim historiography, I will call attention to the places where women have been excluded. I will also draw out the implications of their exclusion. How best to weave the multiple levels of women's history and their interests into a narrative that also takes account of macropolitical changes has not been an easy task. [For example,] the Shah Bano case is important for India but also for its Muslim majoritarian neighbors, Pakistan and Bangladesh. Since these three polities govern the largest number of Muslims in the world, I have tried to demonstrate how the Shah Bano case discloses the juridical structures that define, and also restrict, the public opportunities for Muslim women throughout the Asian subcontinent.[3]

I argue for the inclusion of a perspective on Muslim women that complicates the standard interpretation of Muslim norms and values, at the same time that it does not obscure the prevalence of violence as a condition that affects both Muslim men and Muslim women, in much of Asia and Africa but also in Europe and America.

Why do I begin with violence? Because violence is where most non-Muslims begin to think about Islam, especially if they live in a society where Muslim citizens are either silent or absent. In some cases, Muslims are too few to be properly viewed as multiple rather than singular in their outlook. Such is the case with America in the mid-1990s, where popular attention focuses on Louis Farrakhan and his message of hatred as if that messenger speaks for most Muslims as well as many African American males.[4]

Though there are episodes in which Muslims, like members of any contemporary religious community, do commit violence, and though there are other Farrakhans in the world outside the United States, violence remains an aberration rather than the norm. Violence is no more intrinsic to Islam than to Judaism, Christianity, Hinduism, Buddhism, or Sikhism. The distorted link of Islam to violence has to be brought into the full light of critical inquiry.

It is to restore balance to the popular Euro-American understanding of Islam and Muslims that I begin my foray into recent Muslim history by focusing on violence. Violence fully exposed can illumine how Islamic rhetoric and symbol function for Muslim leaders and institutions. If violence pervades Muslim public life throughout this century, it is because violence pervades the world order, old and new. It affects all Muslims indirectly, but it has a direct and immediate impact on those who are marked as Muslim political figures.

To disconnect the equation of Islam with violence, I will employ a double stratagem. The first stratagem will be definitional: I will explore how Islam is more than what is commonly presupposed as religion. In the deepest sense, Islam remains a religion, since those who profess belief in Allah and in Muhammad as His final prophet are marked with a distinctive set of rituals and laws. Yet Islam is also a modern ideology subordinated to the dominant ideology of this century, nationalism, and it is the relationship of Islam to nationalism that is at once pivotal and understudied.

It is fashionable in some circles to debunk nationalism, and to project either the "end of history" (in Francis Fukuyama's misguided slogan) or a "coming clash of civilizations" (in Samuel Huntington's vaporous restaging of postnational, global conflict).[5] A close look at day-to-day affairs, however, suggests both that nationalism is alive in the mid-1990s and that the nation-state is far from obsolete as an instrument of power. As one shrewd observer has lamented, the nation-state remains "the politics of the first person plural." It coalesces ideological forces precisely because "the sense of being 'we'... is the necessary foundation for any durable political system" and "only the nation-state possesses this necessary sense of identity." "The nation-state will last longer than most people had thought."[6] And because most Muslims exist within postcolonial Muslim nation-states, the ubiquitous character of nationalism has to be acknowledged in any discussion of contemporary Islam. At the same time, one must be alert to recall, as Bruce Kapferer has reminded us, that nationalism itself is far from a unitary movement; it reflects much more than European norms, First World values, or elitist experiences.[7]

If my first stratagem is to revisit and redefine basic categories, my second stratagem will be discursive: I will focus on how European colonial powers have used religion in the service of ideology to divide and control major segments of the world, from West Africa to Southeast Asia. The record does not permit blanket condemnation of all legacies from the colonial period, for the modern sector of Muslim societies has produced creative advocates and notable benefits. Yet fifty years after the founding of the United Nations and the near elimination of European control over much of Asia and Africa, one must remain wary of how postcolonial independence has been shaped by the immediate past. The British may have gone home, and the French mission to civilize (*la mission civilisatrice*) declared a failure, but British and French, as also Dutch and Russian, legacies persist in the Muslim world.

I approach this task conscious that I am limited as well as enabled by who I am. I am male. I am Anglo. I am upper middle class. European in ancestry, I was born in America. Raised non-Muslim, I remain non-Muslim. Yet after studying both the Arabic language and Middle Eastern history from an early age, I remain deeply attracted to Islam as a life force: it animates many Muslims with whom I have lived and worked and whom I count among my closest friends.

While these are ascriptive limits shaping my viewpoint, I am further limited by what I embrace: I choose to be both an intellectual and an unabashed humanist. Despite the many assaults on the humanities from within and beyond the academy, I remain not only a humanist but also a late modern humanist.

I am not a postmodernist humanist, however. I continue to scan metanarratives in the pursuit of local histories. I seek patterns that interconnect numerous Muslim histories, whether local, national, or regional, and also link them collectively to global forces. At the same time, I reject the judgment that none but the persons invoked can talk about themselves. In that case, only the words of informants count, and they must be cited as the trump authority, or if one does not cite their exact words, goes the argument, then at the least one must use terms that these same informants would be comfortable having others use.[8]

The Syrian philosopher Sadik al-Azm has exposed the foolhardiness of embracing rank nominalism as a benchmark of scholarship. Rhetorically, he asks: "Were I to take seriously the subjectivist advice of those who ask us never to 'apply words to describe people that they would not accept and apply to themselves,' would I ever be able to say that such and such a Middle Eastern ruler is 'a brutal military dictator,' considering that he never applies such words and descriptions either to himself or to his regime?"[9]

The evident answer is "NO!" But too often it is a muted or defensive "No!" It needs to be announced again and again as a "NO!" "NO" to relativism, "NO" to delusionary escapism from the interlocking character of late capitalist culture and social movements that relate to it even when they claim to be independent of its influence.

At the same time, I do not advocate the total neglect of other people's self-presentation. It does matter what people say about themselves, the categories they use, the arguments they construct, or the goals they advocate. It does matter what people say, yet as the American religious critic Robert Segal deftly put it, "there is a difference between starting with the actor's point of view and ending with it.... The actor may be right, but the assumption that the actor automatically is right is dogmatic."[10]

Beyond trying to make comparisons through explicit and interdisciplinary categories, I espouse cross-cultural inquiry as a genuine form of academic labor. It is not reducible to the new Orientalism that the feminist critic Gayatri Spivak claims it to be. In Spivak's view, cross-culturalism serves only to perpetuate banality in a postcolonial world, but it can do more: it can also become a pathway to exploratory dialogue that is both interdisciplinary and international.[11]

But cross-culturalism, if it is to generate useful dialogue, must first accept "open appraisal, the typical plausibility tests, the bargaining adjustments regnant in an open pluralist market of ideas." These criteria are set forth by the sociologist José Casanova.[12] I advocate the same criteria, and I advocate them as a humanist who is at the same time a perspectivist. In an open pluralist market of ideas, I set out self-consciously what beliefs, attitudes, and assumptions inform my approach to the social reality of the Muslim world.[13] And it is from the perspective of the humanities that I challenge both humanists and social scientists to rethink how their own prior convictions—religious, political, and social—have shaped their approach to contemporary Islam. What units of analysis are suitable to assessing Muslim thought and Muslim societies? What presumptions do some of the taken-for-granted categories carry? How do we account for the difference that they convey from a context that is predominantly Christian and secular to one that is Muslim and often nonsecular?

I begin with the category of religion.

Islam as Religion and also not Religion

> The history of the twentieth century has confirmed something well known to all the historians of the past, something our ideologies have stubbornly ignored: the strongest, fiercest, most enduring political passions are nationalism and religion.
> —OCTAVIO PAZ, *One Earth, Four or Five Worlds*

To unhinge the reflexive stereotyping that plagues too much scholarship on modern-day Muslims, I begin at a point of reference outside the Muslim world but within the so-called Third World. I take as my starting point Octavio Paz, the Mexican Nobel Laureate in Literature. Like many contemporary Euro-American intellectuals, Paz implies not only that religion and nationalism are equivalent passions but also that religion, like nationalism, is an undifferentiated whole that evokes deep-seated political passions. He concurs with the cultural historian Daniel Pick that nationalism is a form of mimetic religion, "involving a kind of faith, indeed something of the aura of 'religion' which it arguably both displaces and substitutes."[14] In that sense, religion can be both opposed to nationalism and allied with it. Yet religion is more than political and it is other than passion; it also entails language, values, and institutions. One cannot begin to compare religion and nationalism without recognizing at the outset that they are very different categories of individual expression and collective experience. While they have been engaged, each with the other, since at least the sixteenth century, Paz argues that it is in the present century that their interrelationship has become most explicit and most dangerous. Why? Because only in the twentieth century did historians for the first time recognize nationalism as evoking a passion equivalent to religion; only then did both become enduring passions—not just enduring, but "the strongest, fiercest, most enduring."

While religion can be and should be conjoined with nationalism, there remains a deeper, crucial question: is religion privileged or diluted by being paired with nationalism? The question cannot be avoided, and Paz does give an implicit answer: in the twentieth century religion has been superseded by nationalism. Its influence, defensive and residual, becomes felt to the extent that its advocates can couple their goals with nationalist aspirations, their structures with the administrative, political, and commercial apparatus of the state. In short, for Paz religion can succeed, but it can succeed only when it becomes part of the nationalist agenda.

Yet Paz's notion of religion, never stated, seems restricted to Christianity and at the same time divested of the early modern history of Christian missions. He ignores the role and influence of "colonialism" as the vanguard and often the partner of Christian missions.[15] His notion of religion needs to be expanded beyond its most immediate referent group, Euro-American Christian elites living in the postcolonial era. Few Muslim intellectuals, still facing the legacy of colonialism, juxtapose religion to nationalism as equivalent categories, for Islam still retains a symbolic force independent of nationalism, just as it projects a pragmatic function that can, and often does, challenge nationalist ideologies.

Islam—no less than Christianity or Judaism, Hinduism or Buddhism—is shaped by its world historical context, in which nationalism occupies center stage. However much religious symbols may be invoked or religious leaders co-opted, or religious buildings sprinkled on the landscape, nationalist fervor remains at heart a rival to the universalist claim of religious fervor. In the twentieth century nationalism and ethnic/regional markings have superseded religion as the hallmark of collective identity. Nationalism does for the modern era what religion did, or tried to do, in the premodern era: to direct the hopes of the majority toward its norms while also engaging their energies in its public life.

The displacement of religion by nationalism on these grounds needs to be closely examined if we are to understand the shifting valence of Islam in the high-tech era. Can religion become an adjunct of the state and still function as religion, or does co-optive nationalism amount to little more than a thinly disguised variant of the secularization hypothesis?

These questions are crucial to any reconsideration of postcolonial Muslim hopes, for behind all the arguments about Islam and politics remains the twinfold assumption that (a) Christianity defines "true" religion, and Islam as religion must, or should, resemble Christian models, and (b) all religion is premodern and antirational while the state is both modern and rational. Assumptions die hard, and the most closely held resist even sympathetic exposure. Underlying the critique of religion in general and Christianity in particular is an evolutionary bias. Religion, whether Christianity or Islam, could not stand the light of scientific truth. When the modern era fully dawned, the superstitious and backward nature of antecedent myths (scriptural dicta, creedal formulae, local magic) became evident, their hold on believers gradually eroded or disappeared. And in those instances where religion did not vanish, it was at least revalued and consigned to its proper domain, which is to say, private spaces of individual choice, far from the public realm of scientific progress and rational pursuits. To the extent that civil society was independent of political society and the state, it provided a haven for belief in, and pursuit of, prescientific myths.[16]

Such is the assumption of evolutionary "believers." Seldom exposed, their convictions permeate much so-called neutral or objective scholarship on religion. A corollary of evolutionism is also claimed with equal conviction, namely, that societies where religion lingers as something other than a gnostic symbiosis between self and other remain suspect.[17] In the new order heralded by all modernists (and not just liberals), public loyalty to religious precepts connotes what Laroui once called historical retardation. That is to say, religion comes to symbolize a willful resistance to the tidal wave of change that must move the premodern (religion) off center stage in order to propel the modern (nationalism) onto it.[18]

By this approach, there can be good and bad nationalisms but no religious nationalisms since the very phrase "religious nationalism" embodies a logical impossibility, an illusion, an oxymoron. Major First World nationalisms, according to one widely cited sociological study, can be deduced from the review of five nation-states, all of which have forged more or less adequate roads to modernity. All are roads to the modern, which is to say, the industrial, high-tech era. The dominant trope, the goal to which these and other nationalist polities aspires, is liberal democracy; no other candidate of social organization can be admitted. Religious structures, like religious actors, are omitted, or else defeated, in the great venture of nation-building.[19]

Just as nationalism is deemed to be the exclusive carrier of secular modernity, so is it further presumed that the reason only some countries succeeded in the high-tech era is that only some were able to modernize. Nationalism becomes but one more way of differentiating the modern West from all its precursors, which in the post–Cold War era have also now become its dreaded nemeses. Nationalism cannot be ascribed to any premodern point in the pre-industrial past.[20] With nationalism, as with industrialism, all those groups who have not already succeeded can succeed only by mimesis. Nationalism occurred in one place, among those groups prefiguring the high-tech era. They clustered as the nations of Western Europe and North America. All other nations came later. They were compelled by events beyond their control to imitate antecedent Euro-American models. In Richard Falk's haunting phrase, all the non-West was transformed into state-nations hoping to become nation-states, yet destined to flounder and fail.[21] Economic inequality led to despair and often violence, causing the have-nots to drift still farther to the margins of global exchange.

There have been some who question this view of nationalism, but they choose to make theirs a rearguard protest. They resist from the margins, as those who acknowledge their powerlessness even while voicing their opposition to the dominant view. The 1980s witnessed the emergence within critical theory of a new generation of Asian and African intellectuals. They challenged extant paradigms of nationalism. In particular, they "opposed much of the prevailing academic practice in historiography and the social sciences because it failed to acknowledge the subaltern (i.e., the indigenous non-elite) as the maker of his [or her] own destiny."[22] Despite excesses and shortcomings, a group of scholars linked to the Asian subcontinent, known as the Subaltern School, has made evident the problem of social scientific assertions about what nationalism means and how it can best be studied. To the centrist, top-down gaze of Ernest Gellner and Benedict Anderson, subaltern scholars counterpose views from the margins or from the bottom up. To complicate a public-sector, masculine view that excludes women actors or voices, they highlight a private domain where women, along with elders and minors, contribute to postcolonial developments.[23]

Yet even those who oppose a hegemonic, Eurocentric view of nationalism have not thought to restore religion to a place of distinction compatible with other ideological options. The ideal nationalism remains one that enshrines Profit, Progress, and Peace. (The other P's—Poverty, Population, Pollution, and Proliferation—are usually ignored, or else treated as problems that will be solved along the way.[24]) Where is religion in this forward gaze? Religion might relate to Peace: insofar as it either protects or threatens peace, it can be included in the nationalist project, but it is deemed out of bounds on the major subjects of Profit and Progress. Mark Juergensmeyer, for instance, not only has given new life to the term "religious nationalism," he has also argued that religious sensibilities should be conjoined to the nationalist project, where they would serve as a valuable counterweight or deterrent to violent outcomes.[25]

Religion in the national interest? That suggests a return to theocracy, and a nationalist theocracy would attempt to transform history, not merely recuperate and validate a golden past. As Juergensmeyer himself notes about the Iranian

Revolution, "it was not simply a revival of an earlier form of Muslim rule, but a new form of Islamic politics. In a curious way, it was the Shah's vision of an Iranian nationalism come true."[26]

Despite the clarity of Juergensmeyer's thesis, late twentieth-century theocracy frightens most analysts of religion and nationalism. It conjures up particular fear when applied to the case of Islam because ideal Islam, like the premodern Catholic Church, functions as the comprehensive defining code for public as well as private pursuit. While every religion, from a modernist viewpoint, is "bad," to be minimized or better excluded, there remain degrees of exclusion. Islam remains the worst religion, the spoiler for a nationalist utopia. It remains the worst because many scholars argue that no Muslim nation-state, including Turkey and Tunisia, has ever experienced social modernity. Social modernity is linked to the formation of an urban middle class. Turkey since the 1920s may have come close to generating an indigenous secular bourgeoisie, but even Turkey is said to have failed, just as Tunisia appears to have been stymied by an overgrown urban bureaucracy. Other newer Muslim nations, like Malaysia and Indonesia, are excluded because the general public and even many academics deem them too remote from the Middle East heartland to be considered "real" Muslims.[27]

Yet the historical "failure" of Turkey and Tunisia is minor compared to the ongoing "threat" of Iran. For among all those premodern nations that cling to Islam as arbiter of public norms, Iran stands out as the most glaring culprit. While official Turkey in the 1920s distanced itself from Islamic symbols in trying to emulate European/secular norms, the Iranian Revolution of the 1970s threatened to bring Islam from offstage to center stage in the realm of global politics. It posed a twin threat, making Islam central and the West villain. It was against this twin threat of the Iranian Revolution—its perceived impossibility, its geopolitical unacceptability—that the dread of Islam's antiquarian status as antimodern was rekindled. In its most distinctive religious guise, Islamic "fundamentalism" was seen to be inseparable from the undiluted opposition of Muslims to Christian or pluralist influence. From Iran a flood of literature suggested the opposite, to wit, that Islam can never become modern, not because Muslim countries lack a bourgeoisie, but because Muslims—in this case, Iranian Muslims—themselves invoke religion to perpetuate the continuing, unremitting primitiveness of Islam. The renowned Iranian essayist Jalal Al-i Ahmad speaks for numerous others when he lauds an "Islamic totality":

> India reminds one of Africa as a linguistic Tower of Babel and agglomeration of races and religions. Think of South America becoming Christianized with

one sweep of the Spanish sword or of Oceania, a collection of islands and thus ideal for stirring up dissensions. Thus only we in our Islamic totality, formal and real, obstructed the spread (through colonialism, effectively equivalent to Christianity) of European civilization, that is, the opening of new markets to the West's industries. The halt of Ottoman artillery before the gates of Vienna concluded a process that began in 732 C.E. in Andalusia. How are we to regard these twelve centuries of struggle of East against West if not as the struggle of Islam against Christianity?... In the present age, I, as an Asian, as a remnant of that Islamic totality, represent just what that African or that Australian represented as a remnant of primitiveness and savagery.... I, as an Asian or an African, am supposed to preserve my manners, culture, music, religion and so forth untouched, like an unearthed relic, so that the gentlemen can find and excavate them, so they can display them in a museum and say, "Yes, another example of primitive life."[28]

Al-i Ahmad cannot escape the contradiction embedded in his eloquent lament. Though he decries the reification of a Muslim mindset as unchanging, at once anti-Christian, anti-Western, and now antimodern, he perpetuates the mindset that he opposes. He offers no alternative to what he opposes and, by invoking an Islamic totality, confirms the stereotype of European observers, and now their American successors. Al-i Ahmad demonstrates that Islamic obscurantism is not solely the whimsical distortion of colonial administrators and political commentators; it also becomes the project of certain Muslim advocates insofar as they repeat, without modifying, the profile of a primitive and unchanging, a defiant and challenging Islam.

To offset the dialectic of self-other, progressive-primitive that pervades Muslim and anti-Muslim rhetoric alike, we must reveal its tenuous, recent origins; we must examine the many faces of Islam that, though less evident, are as real as its one face, the face of bloclike antagonism, whether to Christians, to the Christian West, or to the post-Christian modern world.

The Many Faces of Islam

While Islam is not "mere" religion, it is also more than "mere" religious politics. Islam can be as well a kind of symbolic resource or worldview that invites accommodation to other worldviews, not confrontation with them. Islam as religion, Islam as politics, Islam as worldview—all three, and not merely the first two, need to be explored.

Such categorization emerges out of critical reflections on the role of imagination in defining and projecting identity. Imagination is both collective and individual. Collectively imagination is nourished by the institutions of a society; individually it is shaped and reshaped by members of that society. In religious discourse, it is imagination—the ability to play with the material world and its limits, including the too evident limits of love and death—that sustains the conscious advocacy of a range of beliefs and practices deemed to be inseparable from the "real" force of life. Names abound for the Object/Subject of imagination: Yahweh, God, Allah, the Other. Let us call it the Other. The Other is always a transtemporal force; exceeding time, it also exceeds all other human limits. Yet the Other also must always be mediated in human discourse and through social institutions. In its most intellectual form it becomes theology, in its most pervasive expression popular religion, and in still another form ideology.

Numerous Muslim apologists who assert that Islam is, above all, religion mean that Islam as religion concerns itself with the practice of imagining the Other, also known as divine revelation. Whether systematic or pragmatic, theological, popular, or ideological, Islam, in their view, is always religion. Even when it assumes a political dimension, Islam expresses a religious impulse. It is the impulse to align the human imagination with the divine imagination, so that social norms and individual conduct are always directed toward a path already specified. While obstacles on the path may vary, the contours of the path, as also the requirements it imposes on those who would tread it, have not changed. This is the message, for instance, of Muhammad Qutb in his diatribe, *Islam: The Misunderstood Religion* (1977). Examining all the facets of modern science and European civilization, he summarizes them as embodiments of an age-old pattern of slavery. Islam rejects slavery, slavery of men and women, slavery of whole nations and classes. Since both capitalism and communism, the two ideologies of the modern West, continue age-old patterns of slavery, they must be opposed in the name of Islam. It is only Islam as the "third" way that can provide guidance on the path that will help humankind "get out of the darkness it has long since been plunged in."[29]

While Muhammad Qutb's writings do have a political message, the message is implicit rather than explicit: he does not advocate a specific political system nor a set of political reforms. Others do. More than a few modern-day Muslim writers see Islam as preeminently an ideology, that is, "an organized and polarized formulation" of a system that must be equally secular and sacred, encompassing the instrumentalities of politics as well as the pieties of mosque, court, and home. Among those who argue for political Islam is Muhammad Qutb's older brother, Sayyid Qutb. He is the oft-cited ideologue of Islamic extremism or fundamentalism. A founding figure of the Muslim Brethren in prerevolutionary Egypt, he opposed Nasser when the latter came to power. His opposition led to jail and eventually to the gallows: he was hanged, along with two other Brethren leaders, in August 1966.

But it was not just Nasser whom Sayyid Qutb opposed. Sayyid Qutb opposed Nasser as the advocate and embodiment of Arab nationalism. The true evil was nationalism—whether Arab, Iranian, Turkish, or Pakistani—nationalism as an ideology rivaling Islam. Qutb's numerous writings gradually came to stress a Manichaean divide. On one side was justice, rule according to the precepts of the Qur'an and Islam, that was the sign of *hakimiyya*, or divine lordship. On the other side was *jahiliyya* or opposition to *hakimiyya*, the willful persistence in ignorance, perversity, and error. It consisted of glorifying any -ism, whether communism or capitalism, scientism or humanism, instead of God. Nationalism became one more Godlessism. Loyalty to it, like loyalty to any other -ism, was false. It was a sign of *jahiliyya*. The difference between *hakimiyya* and *jahiliyya* was epitomized by Sayyid Qutb in a famous set of slogans that subverts the nationalist agenda. In true Islam, when *hakimiyya* prevails, according to Qutb, "nationalism will be recognized as belief, homeland as Dar al-Islam, the ruler as God, and the constitution as the Qur'an."[30]

Yet those who advocate Islam either as an oppositional religion (Muhammad Qutb) or as religious politics (Sayyid Qutb) reduce Islam to a single platform of protest against the dominant forces of the modern world system. Despite the urgent, impassioned, and often impatient tone of their writings, they do not advance arguments that integrate Islam either with its own past history or with the issues that commonly confront humankind. They too easily elide human imagination with the divine imagination read as divine will. As one shrewd observer of Islamic movements wrote, their advocates make political philosophy shoulder the role of metaphysics: "God's relevance can only be seen in a political context."[31]

"Divine" politics is a meaningless concept unless related to history. Raimundo Panikkar, a seasoned cultural critic, was only half-right when he declared that in the modern period "religion without politics becomes uninteresting, just as politics without religion turns irrelevant."[32] The crucial factor remains historical location, and for contemporary Muslims the most significant dimension of their history is marked by European colonial expansion and consequent anticolonial nationalist movements. One cannot talk about modern Islam without paying attention to the world-transforming activity of the eighteenth, nineteenth, and early twentieth centuries. It was only in the colonial period that nationalist movements involving Muslims first emerged, and the subsequent history of Islam is inseparable from nationalisms both European and indigenous. There are specific turning points in this history that merit recapitulation, if we are to understand why Islam is more often the victim than the agent of violence.

1   Colonial rule gave birth to national movements organized in *secular* terms with mythical appeals, structural features, and institutional mechanisms that reflected, even when they did not imitate or replicate, the same instruments characteristic of the colonizers' country of origin. Ethnic nationalism became the primary organizing principle or symbolic engine to liberation from overseas rule. This was so even when religious symbols were invoked, or religious movements, such as Pan-Islamism, drew sizable numbers of followers. It is crucial not to accept at face value the assertions of Muslim revivalist leaders. For instance, one scholar, after charting the Pan-Islam movement in massive detail from primary sources, concluded that in the 1990s "Pan-Islamists (along with other consociational groups) may well turn a 120-years' old dream from what seemed a utopia into a political reality."[33] Yet another scholar, taking a functional view of this same movement, chose to look not at what Pan-Islamists say, but rather at the impact their movement had on subsequent nationalist endeavors. In so doing, he reached a conclusion opposite to the first scholar: not only is there no future to Pan-Islamism, but "the rise of Pan-Islamic sentiments helped to establish the credentials of particularized nationalisms."[34] Why? Because Pan-Islamic ideologues posed, albeit indirectly, the question of permeable boundaries and drew attention to both ethnic nationalism (*qawmiyya*) and region-specific nationalism (*wataniyya*) as alternative polities—alternative not only to European rule but also, more importantly, to the universal Muslim community (*umma*). Pan-Islamism may conjure the "fear of Islam" yet it itself proved to be a restricted, short-lived movement. The antidote to fear is to look beyond slogans and examine the historical development of a protest movement. Pan-Islamism relies more on ideological accents than on pragmatic strategies. Throughout the twentieth century links among Muslims of different races, regions, and languages remain

more rhetorical than pragmatic, signaling a loose affinity of faith, not an actual alliance of forces, whether military or political or both.

2. Islam as a pragmatic referent in organizing social or economic life was denied autonomy under colonial rule, even when certain farsighted elites attempted to forge a link between Muslim and national identity, as did Muhammad Abduh, for instance, in British Egypt. "What had begun as an attempt to protect Islam by reinterpreting it tended to end as a discussion of the possibility of creating a secular society with nationalism as its animating principle, and with Islam as its inherited culture rather than a guide to social action."[35] The subordination of Islamic ideals and values to political pragmatism continued in postcolonial polities. As a result, Islam remained a reservoir of symbolic dissent, often couched in violent terms, available to marginalized, aggrieved groups.

During the postcolonial period, as political independence was achieved by more and more newly formed Muslim polities, appeals to Islam were slow to garner attention. Whether hidden from European eyes or ignored by indigenous elites, it was not until the late 1960s and early 1970s that Islamic rhetoric and Islamic loyalty were brought to the forefront of domestic, regional, and international issues. Nationalism did not provide the panacea for a host of ills and inequities, and Muslim spokespersons began to contend not only with external non-Muslims but also, just as often, with internal, "impure" Muslim others.

Again, there is no uniform view of the "Islamic difference." Even within the ranks of social science, the lack of consensus is evident. Two social scientists concerned with Egypt disagree on how Egyptian elites viewed the ideal postcolonial polity. One German-based political theorist argues that nationalism, like modernization, rules out religion. He cites as proof of this maxim the stance of the nineteenth-century Egyptian Rifaʿa al-Tahtawi, for whom "the social was more important than the religious." Al-Tahtawi's neologism *hubb al-watan*, "love of country," was thoroughly secular, since it conveyed the sense of *wataniyya*, the Arab(ic) equivalent of patriotism, a concept divorced from religion.[36] But in the view of an American political scientist, it is not al-Tahtawi but another twentieth-century Egyptian theorist, Tariq al-Bishri, who augurs the future stance for his country: neither a secularist nor a fundamentalist but a liberal (of sorts), al-Bishri argues that Arab nationalism cannot omit Islam, while at the same time admitting that Islam cannot be made the sole basis for Arab/Egyptian nationalism. What should be the modus operandi then for Muslims and the state? Islam, according to al-Bishri, should play an instrumental role in fostering what are the primary goals, namely, "independence, cultural authenticity, and political integration."[37] While al-Bishri does not offer his own prescription for an ideal Muslim state, his engagement with Islam is a far cry from al-Tahtawi's vision of a secular state.

3. It is the presence of colonialism that linked all Muslim collectivities, throughout the Afro-Eurasian *oikumene*, especially in that heavily populated cosmopolitan area south and east of the Mediterranean. There has been an attempt from time to time to isolate Saudi Arabia, as though what happened on the peninsula was immune from events around it. But it was not, for as the American historian Marilyn Waldman has pointed out, "though not all Muslim territories were colonized, nearly all experienced some kind of dependency, be it psychological, political, technological, cultural, or economic.... Even in Saudi Arabia oil exploration, begun in the 1930s, brought European (and then American) interference."[38]

If the colonial experience has a crucial mediating role in the development of the present-day Muslim world, it is a role that commands attention in order to avoid a double myopia. One is the myopia of indigenous elites who claim to be exponents of "true" Islam. To the extent that they ignore the colonial period, except as a reminder of the "defeated" enemy, such elites tend to project their own polities as homogeneous associations, at once natural and voluntary. The other myopia is that of dissidents who claim, on behalf of Pan-Islamic ideology, that there has always been a borderless Muslim nation, that all nation-states are fictive, postcolonial inventions, their leaders impeding the reemergence of the pristine Muslim collectivity, the *umma*.

The misfortune of recent scholarship is to perpetuate, rather than correct, these reinforcing myopic readings of the Muslim past. There are two dominant social scientific approaches to Islam and nationalism. One offers a straightforward narration of Muslim polities, linking them to each other and not to neighboring or similar non-Muslim polities, as if the mere label "Islam" were sufficient to merit their clustering as a discrete group separate from all other groups.[39] The other approach traces how Muslim polities took on relevance only with reference to an invasive colonial administration, whether Dutch or Russian, French or British. This blindness is much more serious than the first, because it erases the Islamic "difference" and freezes all Muslims into the role of defensive opponents of an emergent global order. Its proponents claim that Muslim elites, in competing with one another under the same non-Muslim aegis, became redefined: they came to differ as much from their precolonial Muslim ancestors as they did from their contemporary non-Muslim compatriots. The cultural marking of Islam, if not irrelevant, was at best residual, while the temporal marking of modernity became all-important. From the premise that the European/Christian West as colonial overlord provided the crucial dimension is drawn the conclusion that only attention to the colonizing process will generate analytical insights into the relationship of Muslim polities to nationalism.[40]

While the first approach oversimplifies the emergence of Muslim polities from a common colonial past, the second overloads the significance of the colonial experience. Its advocates deny the agency of their Muslim subjects, dismissing urban intellectuals, for instance, as little more than hapless purveyors of an ossified or retarded civilizational legacy.

The truth is more complex. If Europe transformed the Muslim world, it did not itself remain immune from change. The direction of influence between Europe and the Muslim world was never unilinear; it was always interactive. Those European colonial powers that extended their influence, whether by direct or by indirect rule, were themselves reshaped by the experience of their colonial subjects.[41] But they seldom acknowledged their own reshaping as a direct experience of the other. Instead, colonial history, when not luxuriating in the romance and mystique of the Orient, masked its own change as economic gain, commercial profit, overseas investment, or civilizational uplift. Implicit in the exercise of massive military and political power was the denial of agency anywhere in Africa or Asia, including countries with major Muslim populations.

Yet not all Europeans acted with the same motivation or the same set of interests: in the early phase of British colonial rule in India, for instance, not only administrators but also often linguists identified with their subjects, as Richard Fox has shown in his critique of the Orientalism thesis.[42] And when the imperialists did succeed the colonialists, as happened in most cases after the 1870s, there was a heightened degree of intra-European rivalry—from French-British in the Sudan to British-Dutch in the Asian archipelago—that shaped the regional outcome of colonial projects.[43]

Often wrapped into social scientific analysis of Islam is a variant of the economic determinist argument: capitalist forces are placed in the foreground and credited with changing the colonial and postcolonial Muslim world. Particular emphasis is placed on the dismemberment of the central premodern Muslim polity, the Ottoman Empire.[44] Modern-day Turkey becomes the chief negative case representing all Muslim polities stumbling into the twentieth century: its leaders could neither reverse outdated modes of production nor generate a viable middle class.[45] Absent in the Turkish case as elsewhere, we are told, were mechanisms of exchange. Without either accountability or obligation, how could one produce either a viable democracy or a modified authoritarianism? One could not, according to these theorists, and so most African/Asian polities were doomed to be undemocratic; oil merely worsened their economic malaise in the late twentieth century.[46]

Perhaps the most negative assessment of oil production/export and its impact on Arab/Muslim state formation has been set forth by the Lebanese political commentator Georges Corm. Corm offers an intensely detailed, closely argued variation of Delacroix's thesis about the evils of a distributive economy and rentier state. Corm is especially bitter about the petromania unleashed since the early 1970s. "In the deserts of the Arabian Peninsula... the oil-exporting countries of the Gulf barely had sufficient manpower, managerial staff, technicians, employees and teachers to meet the needs and projects this new oil wealth gave rise to. Other Arab countries (and also Pakistan and Bangladesh) were suddenly drained of the most dynamic among their active populations, which further undermined their already eroding social structures."[47] In the case of Pahlavi Iran, petromania did not cause an influx of Muslim outsiders, but it did create a too rapid immigration of rural Iranians to Tehran, leading to structural asymmetries that have persisted in post-Pahlavi Iran.[48]

To place the colonial period and the determinist interpretations of Islam in a broader perspective, one must move beyond both politics and religion to the contingencies of history. The best place to begin is with the boldly revisionist thesis of the world historian and American Islamicist Marshall Hodgson. As Hodgson explained, Islamic loyalties relate above all to a larger, complex process that he labels the Great Western Transmutation. The Great Western Transmutation was "great" because it was global: European norms of political rule and social and economic exchange were introduced throughout Asia and Africa. It remained "Western" not only because it was European in origin but also because it reflected changes going on in the New World, especially North America. But finally it remained a transmutation because it depended on a variety of factors rather than a single, predictable response to European events and actors; it was not inevitable to one region or one culture or one time; it was not even a transformation but rather, following biological models, a transmutation.

The Great Western Transmutation was local as well as global, since the process it spurred was framed within indigenous contexts and limited by indigenous responses, in our case Muslim responses to European norms. To the extent that we can depict a composite Muslim profile, it emerged only after World War I and did not achieve widespread prominence till after World War II.[49] What it revealed was a world turned inside out.[50] Neither Muslim collectivities nor individual Afro-Asian Muslims could any longer operate from a position of parity in the world-system.[51] All Muslim elites—whether by choice or compulsion, whether explicitly adjusting or implicitly demurring—were reshaped by European norms and expectations.[52] Precisely because their lives were under constant stress, their identities remained in flux, and Islam became a symbolic resource both shared and debated. Colonial and postcolonial reverberations were most evident in urban metropolitan centers, yet their impact also extended to rural or peripheral groups, even when these groups seem not to be affected or represented by the momentous events occurring at the center.[53]

To understand the difficulty of this circumstance, but also to locate the kernel of hope within it, one must revisit the colonial period and attempt to analyze its internal shifts, or successive phases, reflecting the views of Muslim "others" as well as European overlords. One must recognize that not all colonizers had the same agenda nor did all periods yield the same record of brutal conquest and systematic negation of Africans and Asians who happened to be Muslim. Instead, one must look at three major periods that overlap but still need to be distinguished each from the other: revivalist, reformist, and fundamentalist.[54]

Notes

Bruce B. Lawrence, "Introduction: Islam across Time and Cultures," in *Shattering the Myth: Islam beyond Violence* (Princeton, NJ: Princeton University Press, 1998), 3–29. Copyright © 1998 by Princeton University Press. Reprinted by permission.

1. A paraphrase from Dr. Tawfik Abdullah, dinner conversation in Jakarta, Indonesia, May 12, 1983.
2. See Robert Morey, *The Islamic Invasion: Confronting the World's Fastest Growing Religion* (Eugene, OR: Harvest House, 1992); and Elaine Sciolino, "Seeing Green: The Red Menace Is Gone. But Here's Islam," *New York Times Week in Review*, January 21, 1996.
3. *Editor's Note: See "The Shah Bano Case" in part VI.*
4. Again the book by Morey is representative of a spate of books that reduce Islam in America to "the Black Muslim Movement" as if it were monolithic and antiestablishment. Louis Farrakhan is cited (172–73), while W. D. Muhammad, a "moderate" Muslim, is ignored.

5 Francis Fukuyama, *The End of History and the Last Man* (New York: Free Press, 1992); and Samuel P. Huntington, "The Clash of Civilizations?," *Foreign Affairs* 72, no. 3 (Summer 1993): 22–49.
6 Anonymous, "The Shape of the World: The Nation-State Is Dead, Long Live the Nation-State," *Economist* (December 23, 1995–January 5, 1996): 17–18.
7 See Bruce Kapferer, "Nationalist Ideology and a Comparative Anthropology," *Ethnos* 54, nos. 3–4 (1991): 161–99.
8 I have exposed the limits to this kind of thinking elsewhere, in *Defenders of God: The Fundamentalist Revolt against the Modern Age* (San Francisco: Harper and Row, 1989), 91–95.
9 Sadik al-Azm, "Islamic Fundamentalism Reconsidered," *South Asia Bulletin* 13, nos. 1–2 (1993): 95.
10 Robert Segal, "Joachim Wach and the History of Religions," *Religious Studies Review* 20, no. 3 (July 1994): 200.
11 Gayatri Spivak, "Postcoloniality and Its Implications for Cultural Studies," plenary speech delivered at the 1988 convention of the Modern Language Association in San Francisco.
12 José Casanova, *Public Religions in the Modern World* (Chicago: University of Chicago Press, 1994), 166.
13 I take the term "perspectivist" from Steven Lukes, "Relativism in Its Place," in *Rationality and Relativism*, ed. Martin Hollis and Steven Lukes (Cambridge, MA: MIT Press, 1982), 298–305, though I disagree with Lukes that perspectivism can have only a weak form (deferring to actors' perspectives) or a strong form (acknowledging the interpreter's perspective). My perspectivism announces that freedom and tolerance, understood as cultural pluralism and religious multicreedalism, are decisive. One may say either that they finally do matter (weak form) or that they, and they alone, count as universal desiderata (strong form).
14 Daniel Pick, *War Machine: The Rationalisation of Slaughter in the Modern Age* (New Haven, CT: Yale University Press, 1993), 158.
15 On the overlapping relationship of missions and missionaries within the larger colonial project of reorienting colonized subjects, see especially the evocative case study by Johannes Fabian, *Language and Colonial Power: The Appropriation of Swahili in the Former Belgian Congo 1880–1938* (New York: Cambridge University Press, 1986).
16 It is a mark of how thoroughly secular the debate about civil society has become that religion enters not as an independent variable but rather as a substratum of trust, justice, benevolence. From Kant to Strauss to Habermas, one can trace the effort to invoke a transcendent morality without positing the need for a Transcendent Being, and the chief debate becomes why nationalism produced one kind of civil society in Western Europe and a very different kind in eastern Europe. While there is much of value to pursuing this debate on its own terms, it ignores the larger shift from metaphysical to instrumental notions of truth; see Adam B. Seligman, *The Idea of a Civil Society* (Princeton, NJ: Princeton University Press, 1992), esp. 156–66.

17. Harold Bloom, *The American Religion: The Emergence of a Post-Christian Nation* (New York: Simon and Schuster, 1992), 16–17.
18. Abdallah Laroui, *The Crisis of the Arab Intellectual: Traditionalism or Historicism?* (Berkeley: University of California Press, 1976), 174.
19. Liah Greenfeld, *Nationalism: Five Roads to Modernity* (Cambridge, MA: Harvard University Press, 1993).
20. Among several exponents of this view, three stand out: Ernest Gellner, *Nations and Nationalism* (Ithaca, NY: Cornell University Press, 1983) and *Conditions of Liberty: Civil Society and Its Rivals* (New York: Allen Lane / Penguin Press, 1994); Eric Hobsbawm, *Nations and Nationalism since 1870* (London: Canto Press, 1991); and Fukuyama, *End of History and the Last Man*.
21. Richard Falk, *The Endangered Planet* (New York: Vintage Random House, 1971), 227. See, for example, Basil Davidson, *The Black Man's Burden: Africa and the Curse of the Nation-State* (New York: Times Books / Random House, 1992), for a particularly strong critique of the postcolonial legacy in sub-Saharan Africa.
22. Ranajit Guha, *Subaltern Studies 4* (Delhi: Oxford University Press, 1985), vii.
23. All the volumes of *Subaltern Studies* articulate this viewpoint, as do the following two: Gayatri Spivak, *In Other Worlds: Essays in Cultural Politics* (New York: Methuen, 1987); and Robert Young, *White Mythologies: Writing History and the West* (London: Routledge, 1990).
24. The political theorist Kenneth Waltz, for instance, treats the four P's as but four flash points in an argument for the danger posed by interdependence in a convergent world system; see Kenneth N. Waltz, *Theory of International Politics* (New York: McGraw-Hill, 1979), 139.
25. See Mark Juergensmeyer, *The New Cold War? Religious Nationalism Confronts the Secular State* (Berkeley: University of California Press, 1993), 193–202.
26. Juergensmeyer, *New Cold War?*, 50.
27. For the clearest exposition of this theory, see Bryan Turner, *Marx and the End of Orientalism* (London: George Allen Unwin, 1983), 67–68. But equally damning of the absence of social change among Muslim nation-states, using the Universal Declaration of Human Rights as a yardstick, or rather a bully club, is Martin Kramer, "Islam versus Democracy," *Commentary* 95, no. 1 (January 1993): 35–42. Overlooking the differentiation within and between Muslim societies is not only short-sighted, it also reinforces the cultural stereotypes invoked by such glibly ahistorical commentators as Fukuyama and Huntington in order to stoke the prospect of a "new Cold War."
28. Jalal Al-i Ahmad, *Occidentosis: A Plague from the West* (Berkeley, CA: Mizan, 1984), 33–34.
29. Muhammad Qutb, *Islam: The Misunderstood Religion* (Damascus: Holy Koran Publishing House, 1977), 52.
30. Sayyid Qutb, *Ma'alim fi't-Tariq* [Milestones on the path] (Cairo: Dar ash-Shuruq, 1964), 146. One of Sayyid Qutb's most popular tracts, it has often been translated

into English, and the above quotation can be found also in Sayyid Qutb, *Milestones* (Cedar Rapids, IA: Unity Publishing, n.d.), 126. On the rhetoric of *hakimiyya*, there now exists the unprecedented and invaluable two-part study of Islamic fundamentalism in a comparative context by Sadik al-Azm (see "Islamic Fundamentalism Reconsidered").

31 Ahmad Moussalli, *Radical Islamic Fundamentalism: The Ideological and Political Discourse of Sayyid Qutb* (Beirut: American University of Beirut, 1992), 241.

32 Raimundo Panikkar, "Religion or Politics: The Western Dilemma," in *Religion and Politics in the Modern World*, ed. Ninian Smart and Peter Merkl (New York: New York University Press, 1983), 46.

33 Jacob Landau, *The Politics of Pan-Islam: Ideology and Organization* (Oxford: Oxford University Press, 1990), 311.

34 James Piscatori, *Islam in a World of Nation-States* (Cambridge: Cambridge University Press, 1986), 77. Not only on this point but in his general approach, Piscatori highlights the need for constant vigilance in separating rhetoric from outcome, polemics from pragmatic action. His book confirms a hopeful, long-range view of Muslim polities that is at variance with most media assessments even as it is consonant with the arguments here advanced. For a useful update of his approach, see the analysis forged with Dale Eickelman in *Muslim Politics* (Princeton, NJ: Princeton University Press, 1996).

35 Albert Hourani, *Islam in European Thought* (Cambridge: Cambridge University Press, 1991), 73.

36 Bassam Tibi, *Arab Nationalism: A Critical Enquiry* (1981; New York: St. Martin's Press, 1990), 87.

37 Leonard Binder, *Islamic Liberalism* (Chicago: University of Chicago Press, 1988), 280.

38 Marilyn Waldman, "The Islamic World," *Encyclopaedia Britannica* (Chicago: Britannica Publishing, 1987), 130.

39 The most egregious examples of this approach are James Bill and Carl Leiden, *Politics in the Middle East* (Boston: Little, Brown, 1979); and Edward Mortimer, *Faith and Power: The Politics of Islam* (New York: Random House, 1982). More nuanced, balancing Islam as worldview with attention to numerous, often competing Muslim ideologies, especially in the introduction and conclusion, is James Piscatori, ed., *Islam in the Political Process* (Cambridge: Cambridge University Press, 1983).

40 The most subtle example of this approach is Clifford Geertz, *Islam Observed: Religious Development in Morocco and Indonesia* (Chicago: University of Chicago Press, 1968), though one must quickly add in defense of Geertz's approach that he tries to retrieve a cultural boundedness for *all* social existence that earlier analysts of Muslim history largely ignored. Other scholars, less sensitive than Geertz to the colonial optic, include Christopher Harrison, *France and Islam in West Africa, 1860–1960* (New York: Cambridge University Press, 1988); and Ian Talbot, *The Punjab and the Raj, 1849–1947* (Riverdale, MD: Riverdale Company, 1988).

41 David Laitin, *Hegemony and Culture: Politics and Religious Change among the Yoruba* (Chicago: University of Chicago Press, 1986), 164–69, has detailed the similarities and differences in a West African context.

42 Richard Fox, "East of Said," in *Nationalist Ideologies and the Production of National Cultures*, ed. Richard Fox (Washington DC: American Anthropological Association, 1990).

43 For a broad global view of this protracted rivalry, see Geoffrey Barraclough, ed., *The Times Atlas of World History* (Maplewood, NJ: Hammond, 1982), 207–95. For a region-specific view that takes account of all of Asia, see Rhoads Murphey, *A History of Asia* (New York: HarperCollins, 1992).

44 Huri Islamoglu-Inan, ed., *The Ottoman Empire and the World Economy* (Cambridge: Cambridge University Press, 1987); Resat Kasaba, *The Ottoman Empire and the World Economy: The Nineteenth Century* (Albany: State University of New York Press, 1988).

45 Turner, *Marx and the End of Orientalism*, highlights this argument, especially in chapter 4.

46 Delacroix's thesis is restated in Lisa Anderson, "Obligation and Accountability: Islamic Politics in North Africa," *Daedalus* 120, no. 3 (1991): 93–121.

47 Georges Corm, *Fragmentation of the Middle East: The Last Thirty Years* (London: Hutchinson, 1988), 137.

48 For a thorough, often critical review of these trends, one can do no better than Hooshang Amirahmadi, *Revolution and Economic Transition: The Iranian Experience* (Albany: State University of New York Press, 1990).

49 Marshall Hodgson, *The Venture of Islam: Conscience and History in a World Civilization* (Chicago: University of Chicago Press, 1974), 3:176–222.

50 Michael Gilsenan, *Recognizing Islam: Religion and Society in the Modern Arab World* (New York: Pantheon, 1982), 215.

51 Charles Barone, *Marxist Thought on Imperialism: Survey and Critique* (Armonk, NY: Sharpe, 1985), 115–16, provides a keen exposition and broad-scale critique of Marxist theory on this point.

52 The degree of influence can be overstated, however, as is the case with the unidirectional and triumphalist thesis of Theodore Van Laue, *The World Revolution of Westernization* (New York: Oxford University Press, 1987).

53 For the Iranian case, there is much evidence of global patterns impinging on local contexts, often with unanticipated consequences. See especially Paul Vieille and Farhad Khosrokhavar, *Le discours populaire de la revolution iranienne*, 2 vols. (Paris: Contemporaneite, 1990). See also Erika Friedl, *Women of Deh Koh: Women's Lives in an Iranian Village* (Washington, DC: Smithsonian, 1989), the companion study to Reinhold Loeffler, *Islam and Practice: Religious Lives in a Persian Village* (Albany: State University of New York Press, 1988).

54 I agree with James Piscatori that we cannot absolutize successive stages of Muslim protest, implying that the rhythm of history explains *all* social change and potential

development; see Piscatori's critique of Hamid Enayat in *Islam in a World of Nation-States,* 36. Yet it still seems valuable to differentiate the sequence of public responses to British, French, and Dutch colonial empires. The unexpected has happened and will continue to happen, but sketching patterns of possibility can help understand a long-term process, even when the next turn in the road remains invisible, and the road itself very bumpy.

TWO

Islam in Afro-Eurasia: A Bridge Civilization | 2010

Why Civilization?

In the most extensive effort yet mounted to trace civilization as a category of critical inquiry, the Dutch sociologist Johann Arnason invokes the pithy dictum of A. N. Whitehead: "Without metaphysical presupposition there can be no civilization."[1] But which metaphysics, tracing which analytical trajectories, produce a consensus about the sources and patterns, the projects and ideologies that cluster as "civilization"?

The major distinction that characterizes Arnason's approach is to differentiate civilization as a unitary concept from civilizations as multiple units, none of which can be understood except through sustained, comparative analysis with their counterparts. He further distinguishes cultural from noncultural approaches, citing well-known sociologists such as Weber, Durkheim, and Eisenstadt, or famed historians, such as Toynbee, Spengler, and Braudel, but also lesser luminaries, such as Borkenau, Patocka, and Krejci. Deftly he tries to move from civilizational discourse to subsequent debates about modernization, globalization, and postcolonialism. The comparative analysis of civilization, in his view, both anticipates and continues to permeate all macro-level reflection on human society, world history, and political theory.

The core issue remains culture, and it informs the provisional definition of civilization for my own essay. I define civilization as the broadest, most capacious envelope of cultural traits related—directly or indirectly, explicitly or implicitly—to geographical location and temporal shifts. In a thumbnail definition, civilization equals culture writ large over space and time. Space predominates. The geographical lens of premodern civilization focuses on the ecumene, or the Afro-Eurasian *oikumene*.[2] Civilization presupposes cities, commerce, travel and trade, warfare and alliances. The *oikumene* is the known world connected through urban nodes, at once locally rooted and regionally, as also transregionally, linked to other nodes. Time becomes crucial in trying to chart change in modes of production and patterns of influence that characterize civilization from premodern to modern phases of world history.

The axial era looms large as the major temporal marking for all civilizational analysis. The "Axial Age," first coined by the philosopher Karl Jaspers, was developed extensively by Eisenstadt and Hodgson, among others. Cities preceded it, from 3000 to 800 BCE, but then in the middle of the Agrarian Age, from 800 to 200 BCE, "great bursts of creative and many-sided cultural innovation… resulted in an enduring geographical and cultural articulation of the citied zone of the Oikoumene into regions."[3] The Post-Axial Age persisted for two millennia, from 200 BCE to 1800 CE, when it was replaced by the Technical Age. The last major hinge of history is also the most complex. It is an age marked not only by the emergence of Occidental or Western dominance but also by a breakdown of the parity that had previously made possible the diffusion and adjustment to technical changes among Afro-Eurasian citied societies.[4]

In what Braudel terms *la longue durée*, or the broad expanse of historical time, there was no single civilization but multiple civilizations, and it is important to wrestle with the cultural envelope which each provides. The present essay will focus on the distinctive cultural traits of Islamic, or Islamicate, civilization, but it will also try to make sense of its relationship to civilizations that both preceded it and were contemporaneous with it. It must also reckon with the dominance of Western civilization in the Technical Age.

Since material culture pervades in any reckoning of hierarchy between civilizations, scientific breakthroughs had to combine with technological mastery to create the Technical Age. These provided the necessary, albeit not the sufficient, cause for the global hegemony of Western Europe, generally, and the rise of British and French empires, in particular. The sufficient cause was the ideology of empire. It relied on civilizational discourse. It presupposed the superiority of urban elites, within as well as beyond their national boundaries. "The civilizing mission," explains Michael Adas, "was more than just an ideology of colonization beyond Europe. It was the product of a radically new way of looking at the world and organizing human societies."[5] It prized time, work, and discipline.

It believed that the entire world could be converted through commerce and bureaucracy, as practiced by Western science and management. It pervaded the nineteenth and early twentieth centuries, only to face challenges from abroad, as well as dissents from within, after World War I. The "Great War" undermined the civilizational superiority of Western Europe, whether etched in Duhamel's polemical *Civilization 1914–1917* or Orwell's satirical *Burmese Days*, at the same time that other popular writers were drawn to Asian civilizations in their search for a more long-term, metaphysical cure of the human condition.[6]

Religion early and often became linked to culture as a crucial civilization marker. Weber charted the breakthrough of Western modernity as itself part of a complex historical dynamic that also had to account for India and China, and later the Islamic world.[7] For Braudel, too, religion is the civilizational phenomenon par excellence.[8] The dominant civilizations were reckoned to be Indian/Hindu, Chinese/Confucian, Irano-Arabic/Islamic, and Western/Judaeo-Christian. Yet this listing conceals as much as it reveals. Neither India nor China was marked exclusively by one religion or by a unitary cultural impulse. Islam included many racial, linguistic, and cultural trajectories that exceeded the Middle East, while the modern West included elements of metaphysical dread and its opposite, Protestant triumphalism, both of which preclude a symbiosis of Jewish with Christian norms and values.

Perhaps the most bewildering of all cartographic elements to fit into the Islamicate or any civilizational mold is Southeast Asia. It contains the largest number of Muslims in a single country: 227 million, or 87 percent of the population, in Indonesia. Though ignored in most theoretical studies on civilization, it is prized by geographers, along with Central Asia, as one of the major interstitial zones within a world regional framework.[9] For K. N. Chaudhuri, the foremost historian of premodern Asia, the case of Southeast Asia belies the connective tissue, and disposition to generalize, that civilizational discourse requires: "The technique of filtering the identity of a civilization by fixing the outer and inner limits in the conceptual image of the social structure, adopted for Islam and India, which is also relevant for China, breaks down in the case of South East Asia. There is no single dominating ideology here that creates through a dialectical process of acceptance and sanctions a single unified civilization."[10] To paraphrase from our earlier thumbnail definition of civilization, there is no "culture writ large over space and time" that can be projected as an ideology inclusive of the myriad islands, the spatial, temporal, linguistic, and material elements of what Friend calls "the Phil-Indo Archipelago."[11]

Yet civilization is more than a shibboleth for religious claims or cultural irredentism; it is also an inescapable part of the effort to forge a ranking of cultures, and even to claim the superiority of one over rival others. In this sense, civilization rests on a taxonomic contrast that pits dyadic opposites against one another. Even before the civilizing mission of British and French (and, more recently, American) missionaries in Africa and Asia, there was a distinction between civilized folk and barbarian "others," just as there was also the ternary division of time into corresponding social units. Desert tribes or agrarian communities were deemed to be "primitive," and major premodern empires "classical," while "modern" was reserved for democratic, capitalist-based nation-states.[12] In political theory, "modern" means that "the achievement of a liberal state (is seen as) a precondition for the creation of a modern civilization."[13] So inextricably was "modern" linked to capitalism, that "a certain relation between unrestricted commercial activity and the jurisdiction of a limited state was central to this new, higher stage of civilization." What characterized the superiority of modern (read: Euro-American plus Japanese) civilization from earlier stages of social development was "a society of civility, in the sense of social order, pacification, and restraint. It was a society of civility in the sense of gentle manners, opposed not merely to the wildness and violence of primitive or warlike peoples, but also to the great volatility caused by the passions of military aristocrats or conquering rulers."[14]

In effect, the new turn to civil society, like the prior invocation of "the civilizing mission," becomes yet another transformation of civilizational discourse into a metaphysical truth. In this case, there is a mysterious, unsubstantiated link between the bourgeois middle class as agents of commercial prosperity and advocates of political openness. While A. N. Whitehead would be pleased, a more robust analysis of civilizational discourse requires not just a look at the present but a review of the past: one must explore routes not taken, meanings not explored, and also pioneers not acknowledged, especially in the realm of Islam and Muslim subjects.

Ibn Khaldun: The First Proponent of Civilization

In order to relate Islam to civilizational discourse, one must revisit the foundational moment for the concept of civilization. It was Islam or, rather, a major Muslim intellectual who founded civilizational discourse. ʿAbd ar-Rahman ibn

Muhammad ibn Khaldun (d. 1406 CE) wrote an introduction to history or *Muqaddimah* which Arnold Toynbee called "undoubtedly the greatest work of its kind that has ever yet been created by any mind in any time or place."[15] Not only does the *Muqaddimah* chart "the emergence of the Islamic world system 1000–1500," it was also the first major work to deal with Civilization as an analytical category.[16] Beyond assessing in brilliant strokes the peculiarities of Islamic history, Ibn Khaldun inaugurates an entirely new discipline, one he terms the science of civilization or human society (ʿilm al-ʿumran). The very nature of his argument belies the effort to see West and East as irreducible opposites, with Islam as some persistent enemy or restive outlier to the dominant ethos of Western civilization. The historian of Eurasia Stephen Dale sees in Ibn Khaldun not only a judge, a litterateur, and a sometime poet but also a rationalist, a social theorist, and, above all, a rigorous linguist searching for universal principles.[17]

Ibn Khaldun focused on the meaning of Political Events. The full title of the larger book, *Kitab al-ʿibar*, to which the *Muqaddimah* serves as an introduction was *Kitab al-ʿibar wa-diwan al-mubtadaʾ wa-l-khabar fi ayyam al-ʿArab wal-ʿAjam wal-Barbar wa-man ʿasarahum min dhawi as-sultan al-akbar*. In translation the title becomes *The Book of Lessons and Archive of Origins, Dealing with Political Events Concerning Arabs, Non-Arabs and Berbers, and with Their Contemporary Major Rulers*. While Ibn Khaldun hopes to offer ʿibar (instructions or lessons), their content revolves around understanding Political Events. Political Events are the bookends of history, the beginning and the end, with *khabar* having a multilayered meaning. Each Political Event may be cause or outcome. Ibn Khaldun used linguistics in the service of a science of society or civilization. Its subject becomes the early conditions, or first instances, of social organization, namely, *badawa* or desert civilization. The very first civilization is not the city but the desert, and it is the desert that sets the stage for what follows, namely, the emergence of world civilization (ʿumran) through sedentary or urban civilization (*hadara*). *Badawa* and *hadara* contrast, and even compete, with one another, but their dyadic tension becomes the basis for ʿumran, the inhabited world connecting the parts of Islamdom but also relating them to places and perspectives beyond an Islamicate circumference.

And so if we are to think of civilizational politics in the twenty-first century, we cannot conjure a genealogy that is traceable to the northern Mediterranean or to the Enlightenment or to European empire building from the sixteenth century on. Instead, we must go back to a North African Arab jurist who understood Aristotle and used Aristotelian logic to construct a new science, the science of world civilization. Civilizational discourse is neither an invention of nor a social construct limited to the West. It is a product of cosmopolitan, juridical Islam in the shadow of classical Greek philosophy, and its key term is Event. Because Ibn Khaldun was a jurist before he became a world historian, Event retains a juridically weighted meaning. Event is integral to Tradition scholarship—that is, trying to discern whether statements attributed to the Prophet Muhammad were in fact authentic or, as too often happened, spurious. Events were accounts from persons whose integrity was being reviewed in order to verify or disqualify what they reported as Tradition. But, for Ibn Khaldun, the grammatical and juridical meanings of Event expand into something more vital and visionary: the surplus of labor, but also of thought, that produces a model of civilization across time and space. The linchpin to transforming Event into this new conceptual domain was *mutabaqa* or conformity. Even while eschewing the notion that all forms are external, Ibn Khaldun did believe in conformity—namely, that what one remembered as Event could, or should, conform to historical reports of what others witnessed as Event.

If this sounds familiar it is because already, in the early fifteenth century, Ibn Khaldun was pondering what later became in Western social science the distinction between categories of practice (what was remembered through oral reports) and categories of analysis (what could be confirmed through actual witnesses). Like every other Muslim jurist, he was faced with the daunting task of winnowing out true from false Traditions. By the third century after the *hijra* (exodus), the tracing of *isnad* or chains of transmission had become a fixed part of Islamic legal training.[18] One book even catalogs all the various categories of malfeasants who make up Traditions. They range from atheists and heretics to outright falsifiers of Traditions, including those who would invent Traditions in order to embellish religious stories they told in mosques and hence collect larger donations from gullible believers![19]

In order to establish his new science, Ibn Khaldun the jurist had to affirm his own practice of Tradition criticism, but through it go beyond its parameters in order to open up another way to approach human social organization, itself the basis of global or world civilization (*ʿumran al-ʿalam*). In effect, his forensic skill as a litterateur allowed him to cite Event, itself an ancillary part of Tradition scholarship, as an independent term conveying the surplus of meaning that he wanted to impart to the study of human social organization or the history of world civilization. Distinguishing Tradition from Event, while affirming both, became the pathway to his new science.

At the same time, Ibn Khaldun needed to fashion a new language, whether by using existing terms in novel ways or by inventing new words—that is, neologisms—to convey the added complexity he saw in human social relations. *'Asabiyya*, or "group feeling," is the major neologism permeating all of Ibn Khaldun's work. It is a variable pinned between religion (*din*) and the state (*dawla*), both of which demand loyalty, but of variant, even incommensurate kinds. Explains a leading Maghribi historian: "At one and the same time, *'asabiyya* is the cohesive force of the group, the consciousness that it has of its own specificity and collective aspirations, and the tension that animates it and impels it ineluctably to seek power through conquest."[20] This last element—the drive to power through conquest—seems to fall outside the juridical realm, unless one realizes that the law is also an instrument of power, whether through persuasion or domination. It is this fluid itinerancy in Ibn Khaldun's linguistic usage that needs to be underscored: *'asabiyya*, in effect, becomes "a concept of relation by sameness, opposed both to the state (*dawla*) based on relations of difference or complementarity, and to religion (*din*), which alone supersedes it."[21]

Reliance on metaphor allows Ibn Khaldun to demonstrate how the same word, like the same event or person, can be viewed differently over time, and also from different places in the same time frame. In other words, he demonstrates from within an Islamicate worldview how civilization projects "culture writ large over space and time." Perhaps the most crucial argument that Ibn Khaldun makes on behalf of history as an Islamic science is that historians alone among Muslim scientists can explain how Islam arose out of a context of orality and nomadism/primitivism (*badawa*) to become a proponent of both writing and urban civilization (*hadara*). What had been speech and a habit became writing and a craft.[22] Yet the very lifeline of Islam depended on maintaining the connection between literacy and orality, between writing and speech, as also between civilized and nomad. In short, analogy, while it had its most immediate application in law, could, and did, apply to the understanding of the laws of history—above all, the history of Islamicate civilization.

Yet analogy conceals what is the most basic aspect of Ibn Khaldun's methodology that links him to all future proponents of civilizational discourse: the propensity to rely on dyads for explaining the force of intellectual inquiry and the utility of analytical judgments. Ibn Khaldun never ceases to frame all issues in terms of competing or complementary sets of two. The most basic for history is the *badawa/hadara* dialectic, framed within the overarching concept of *'umran*. But also evident and recurrent are his references to *'arab* and *'ajam* as two linguistic resources, with *'arab* the superior but *'ajam* the more creative. Additionally, there is the accent on oral and written as two expressions of language, with oral expressing the greater claim to *'asabiyya* or intrinsic solidarity, while written is the more necessary for bureaucratic activities essential to urban society, sedentary culture, and statecraft.

Finally, of course, there is the dyad of ʿaql and naql, or reason and tradition. They are as much complementary as competitive, both belonging to a larger conception of ʿilm. This is evident in the syllabus formation of Ghubrini, Ibn Khaldun's Maghrebi predecessor and author of a seminal work in which he distinguishes between two types of knowledge: ʿilm al-diraya and ʿilm al-riwaya. One is the subject of discussion and debate, the other of memorization and transmission, yet in actual syllabi some topics fall within both diraya and riwaya, ʿaql and naql.²³ Among them are fiqh (jurisprudence) and din (religion), undercutting the too-neat oppositions that often mark the dichotomous, post-Enlightenment reading of Ibn Khaldun as the advocate of reason over religion, logic over belief. All dyads need to be collapsed into a spectrum of possibilities, not into a neat either/or classificatory judgment.

The showcase for Islamicate civilization was its ability to self-replicate across the ecumene or the Afro-Eurasian oikumene. According to a recent Turkish researcher, there was a clearly identifiable Islamicate civilization with its epistemic communities interlinked across the "court societies" of Istanbul, Isfahan, Herat, Delhi, and Cairo, among others, manifested along the three related domains of cities, empires, and religion. Islamic empires depended on Islamic cities, which grew out of, even as they in turn reinforced, Islam as a religion and worldview (Weltanschauung). Arabic was the universal medium of religious discourse, Persian often the language of high culture, and there was a commonly shared set of canonical readings, including nonreligious literary masterpieces such as the poems of Omar Khayyam as well as famous interpretations of the Qurʾan. Architects made careers building palaces and tombs, fountains and bridges, from Agra in India to Sarajevo in Bosnia.²⁴

One of the most famous witnesses of a clearly identifiable Islamicate civilization was Ibn Battuta (d. 1368), a Maghrebi jurist and contemporary of Ibn Khaldun. Ibn Battuta was able to travel from Timbuktu in Mali to the Middle Volga, from northern India to Muslim Spain. Everywhere he went he could, and often did, speak about a range of topics in Arabic with the learned men in these regions. Today we know about Ibn Battuta not only because of his travels but because of the royal attention and support they attracted. The Moroccan Sultan Abu ʿInan was so impressed with the peripatetic jurist that he commissioned a belle lettrist, Ibn Juzayy, to record and embellish his countryman's twenty-nine years on the road and at sea, from 1325 to 1354.²⁵ The resulting Rihla tells the legendary travels of a Moroccan religious scholar who journeyed throughout the Afro-Eurasian *oikumene*.[26] Patronage was not so easily obtained in every instance and, as Cornell has shown in an astute essay on Ibn Battuta, not even his generous royal patron could be fully trusted.[27] Yet for many centuries throughout Islamdom, there was a fierce competition between the palaces in Istanbul (Ottoman), Isfahan (Safavid), and Herat (Timurid) over the most talented poets, architects, and musicians, each dynast offering a competitive package of benefits to the artists and intellectuals in his court or within his reach.

Two Successors to Ibn Khaldun in Civilizational Discourse

Whether Islamicate civilization stands by itself or in conjunction with other civilizations, it remains a focal point for exploring larger fields of inquiry. Is the largest field of inquiry world history or world systems? Both have a well-established provenance in social science literature, but which is to be preferred in thinking about Islam, Muslim nation-states, and Muslim actors, whether in macro or micro terms? Put bluntly, is Islam best understood as a singular civilizational construct within world history, or is it instead a mere subset of some larger world system?

I will argue below that *both* genealogies are possible, though the choice is fraught with consequences for evaluating Islamicate evidence. Islam does stand apart from other civilizations, especially in its notions of hierarchy and kingship. Yet neither of these concepts is intrinsic to Islam as religion, and so Islam in civilizational discourse must be viewed as a cultural variable, linked to but exceeding religious connotations. Just as the noun Islamdom encompasses the Muslim-majority regions of Africa and Asia, so the adjective Islamicate best describes those features of cross-regional filiation that link discrete parts of Africa and Asia and form the Islamicate subset of the Afro-Eurasian *oikumene*. In other words, Islamicate civilization evokes a larger geocultural grid than would be defined solely by loyalty to Islam as creed, liturgy, and law. While Islamicate civilization cannot, and should not, be viewed as part of some inherent or deterministic world system, it also cannot be understood apart from the other civilizations with which it interacted, both shaping and being shaped by them, in its long historical trajectory. Functionally speaking, Islamicate civilization is the bridge from ancient to modern social systems, though the work of Western scholars and Muslim apologists alike has obscured that crucial link function of Islamicate norms and values, actors and processes.[28]

In making this argument, and in using this vocabulary, I am following the lead of Marshall G. S. Hodgson, the premier Islamicist of his generation. Because Hodgson has been consistently ignored by most major theoreticians—even Edward Said did not deign to give him a footnote in *Orientalism*—it is crucial to revisit his labor and to extrapolate his unique, compelling perspective on Islamicate civilization.[29] The value of Hodgson's labor becomes clearer when his oeuvre is compared, and contrasted, with that of Immanuel Wallerstein, the author of world systems. Unlike Hodgson, Wallerstein has enjoyed widespread recognition for his rethinking of the relationship between material and cultural elements that define large-scale social units. Indeed, Wallerstein stands out among contemporary social scientists for his adroit combination of developmental theory with historical sociology, though he stumbles onto Islamic data and remains a minor figure in civilizational discourse.

Wallerstein

The major unit in Wallerstein's scheme, the cornerstone of his theory, is the capitalist world economy.[30] More than the sum total of capitalist nation-states, the capitalist world economy amounts to a world system because it functions as "an economic entity spanning continents and polities, [making it] a unique and encompassing social system." In effect, the world according to Wallerstein is run by economics, not by politics, with nation-states being interlinked through a dynamic socioeconomic system in which they participate but over which they have no ultimate control. Ironically, the Marxist redux becomes a capitalist promoter, at least in theory, since the absence of centralized political control means that "economic actors have greater freedom of movement, which enhances their opportunities to amass wealth and promote accumulation on a global scale."[31]

Having foregrounded the world system or the capitalist world economy, Wallerstein does not ignore other units. He also compares nation-states, regions, and cities to the modern world system, but their chief value is instrumental: to demonstrate the role they play in making the world system as a whole continue to work.

The evidence for Wallerstein's theoretical corpus comes not from his own fieldwork but from the *Annales* school. He uses the work of the *Annalistes* for a bluntly political agenda, to wit, "not only to understand the history of the capitalist world system, but also to attempt to prepare the intellectual ground for the coming of a world socialist system."[32] It is more than mere coincidence that the center which he has overseen and which has been the engine for his academic production is called the Fernand Braudel Center or, in its fuller title, the Fernand Braudel Center for the Study of Economies, Historical Systems, and Civilizations.

Often criticized as reductive, Wallerstein's millenarian socialism omits two crucial features that are important for the Muslim world and especially relevant to the viability of Islamicate civilization as an analytical category: (1) sustained attention to the semi-peripheries and (2) recurrent emphasis on cultural production as a decisive element both for collective identity and for ultimate survival.

The semi-periphery remains one of the most original and ingenious of Wallerstein's units of analysis. While his crucial frame of reference is center-periphery, a familiar dyad, the semi-periphery, by straddling the center and the periphery, highlights regions/nation-states that are neither driving nor driven by the world system yet function as bridge players, aligned in some features with the center, in others with the periphery. Major examples for Wallerstein are Venice and Spain in the late sixteenth century, Sweden in the seventeenth, Prussia in the eighteenth, Russia in the nineteenth and twentieth, Japan in the late nineteenth and early twentieth, and, today, Brazil and South Africa.

What is noticeable for its absence from the above list, and from Wallerstein's work in general, is attention to the major Muslim nations of the Asian subcontinent and the archipelago. It is almost as if the canopy of colonialism, cast over this vast region principally through the second wave of modernity represented by the British and the Dutch, has occluded from Wallerstein's systemic, model-building vision all the elements of middle Asia. He remains riveted to the westernmost region of Asia, now known as Europe, along with its island neighbor, Britain, and alternatively to the easternmost region of Asia, China and its neighbors, but the Muslim middle is largely missing. Because of this almost reflexive oversight, Wallerstein fails to elaborate the central function of Islam as a bridge civilization, an extended semi-periphery with resilience that affirms, even as it modifies, his originary conceptual vision.

There is one Islamic polity that does figure in Wallerstein's model building. Repeatedly he draws attention to the Ottoman Empire; perhaps because of all the premodern Muslim polities, it is the Ottoman Empire which seems to conform to Wallerstein's own a priori judgments. It is closest to Europe. It is part of a larger European trajectory into world history and contemporary geopolitics, so much so that in 1998 the eighth biennial Conference of the Fernand Braudel Center for the Study of Economies, Historical Systems, and Civilizations highlighted the Ottoman Empire and the world economy, with special attention to issues of law and legitimation. Omitted from consideration were the myriad aspects of cultural production in the most major and long-lasting Muslim empire of the premodern period.[33]

Crucially absent from Wallerstein's project is any deep reading of culture as intrinsic to civilization. If civilization is culture writ large over space and time, as has been argued repeatedly above, then it does not fit the Wallersteinian template of civilization as a precursor to the dawn of a world socialist system. When Wallerstein does invoke the plural "civilizations," it is largely as a polemic: only because of the supposed superiority of the West—a world-dominant civilization equated with progress, enlightenment, and universalism—are other civilizations adduced, their counter-values "limited" to identity, autonomy, and diversity.[34]

Hodgson

The central question facing Wallerstein was the same as that facing all major social scientific theorists, namely, "Why the West?" The answer he gave was the distinctive interaction of politics and economics, with almost no attention either to technical inventiveness or to cultural motives. In retelling the familiar story of the emergence of modernity, he mines the deep memory of but one strand of world history.

There is another answer given by others, Max Weber principal among them. It is to stress the interaction between cultural norms and economic or market forces. As Eisenstadt lamented, most of the opponents of Orientalism have not escaped what the Iranian critic Jalal Al-i Ahmad lamented as "Westoxification." "They have tended to see Weber as a Eurocentric author," noted Eisenstadt, "preoccupied with the analysis of the origin of modern capitalism, demonstrating the superiority of the West but neglecting the other side of his argument that emphasized the continual internal dynamics of different civilizations."[35]

Hodgson provides the necessary corrective to crude Weberianism. He intended to slight neither the social achievements nor the cultural norms of non-Western societies; he wanted to reclaim and to underscore what they had deemed to be both creative and productive. And so in his major essay on the ambiguous character of modernity, published over fifty years ago (1967), Hodgson drew attention not to Euro-American global dominance but to the downside of this dominance for the dominated or the marginalized.

In accenting the underside of the emergent capitalist world economy, Hodgson prefigures the tone of Wallerstein's own analysis, yet he sees the road to recuperation in utterly opposite terms. Hodgson argued:

> It was part of the transmutational character of the new Transformation that it broke down the very historical presuppositions in terms of which gradual diffusions had maintained parity among Afro-Eurasian citied societies. In the new pace of historical change, when decades sufficed to produce what centuries had produced before, a lag of four of five centuries was no longer safe. The old gradual diffusion or adjustment was no longer possible.... Those untransmutated agrarianate-level societies that did not share Western cultural presuppositions had perforce to continue developing in their own traditions at their own pace, adopting from alien traditions only what could be assimilated on that basis. Hence the Western Transmutation, once it got well under way, could neither be paralleled independently nor be borrowed wholesale. Yet it could not, in most cases, be escaped. The millennial parity of social power broke down, with results that were disastrous almost everywhere.[36]

From this point of parallel with Wallerstein's project, Hodgson then diverges. For him, as for Antonio Gramsci, the dominance—and also hegemony—of Western Europe/North America was closely allied to imperialism and colonialism. Since cultural capital as much as economic capital is involved in propagating and resisting the myth of Western superiority, one cannot escape an analysis of religion. Religion is deeply implicated in the debate about the origin and scope of Euro-American global influence. Insofar as resistance to that influence can be theorized and traced in multiple cultural contexts, they represent voices from the Martinican psychiatrist Frantz Fanon to the American political theorist James Scott. While Fanon advocated the benefit of violence against colonial impositions in Algeria and elsewhere, James Scott demonstrated how sophisticated are resistance strategies, or hidden transcripts, against postcolonial state structures in Southeast Asia but also in the American South.

In this reading, transformation becomes the rhetorical capstone of victors "inasmuch as the major historical forms of domination have presented themselves in the form of a metaphysics, a religion, a world view," yet to oppose domination others have also resorted to religion as a symbolic capital, so that the discourse of the victors has "provoked the development of more or less equally elaborate replies in the hidden transcript [of those oppressed or marginalized]."[37]

In the spirit of Hodgson, one must render problematic wholesale, unwieldy abstractions such as the West and the Third World, center/periphery, and metropolitan/local. Janet Abu-Lughod, for instance, argues that one must take seriously the local differentiation of culture and the multiple referents of the world system in each region and in each axial period of history. If one does, she goes on to assert, then it is necessary above all to look at the distinct character of regions as nodes of culture and, above all, of religious loyalty and practice, values, and norms. While each religion, including Islam, has a universal scope encompassing all races, languages, and cultures, it is still the case that each cosmopolitan/metropolitan setting frames the character and tone of religious life according to its own rhythm and resources.[38] For the Indian Ocean region, the centerpiece of Islamicate civilization, the major goal, as Sugata Bose intimated, is "to keep in play an Indian Ocean inter-regional arena of economic and cultural interaction as an analytical unit while avoiding the pitfalls of assuming any uncomplicated and unsustainable thesis about continuity."[39]

I would argue, following Bose but also Chaudhuri cited earlier, that it is the Indian Ocean region, rather than MENA—the Middle East and North Africa—that has given Islam its particular civilizational shape, making Islamicate civilization a vital, pivotal category for historical and contemporary analysis. Through its presence in the Indian Ocean, Islam became a pan-Asian cultural agent. It influenced—and continues to influence—the beliefs and practices of millions of Asians, from Central to South to Southeast Asia. While there are other pan-Asian religions—Hinduism to the far south, Buddhism to the Far East—none spans the southern rim of the Asian continent to the extent that Islam does.[40]

Premodern Kingship

Civilization invokes religion and also exceeds it. Civilization requires attention to the social as well as cognitive markers for those patterned by Islamic loyalty. Warriors and traders were crucial agents of change in both South and Southeast Asia. It was Muslim invaders from the northeast who brought with them, or developed after arrival, traits that have since characterized the Islamic experience in South Asia for much of its known history. Centuries later, it was Muslim traders, coming from Arabia as well as India, who began to settle in significant numbers in the archipelago known today as Southeast Asia. They too professed and pursued Islamic loyalty, but in different circumstances, with disparate outcomes.

Much more important for their ultimate destiny, however, was the shaping of Asian Muslim polities by a model of governance known as kingship. It derives from patterns of social mobility and civic organization that typify South Asia from the pre-Axial Age (c. 1000 BCE on):

- a militarized society, with a standing army which requires regular use, often to invade and conquer adjacent regions;
- autocratic rule by a military leader invested with instrumental power but often claiming divine authority and patronizing scholars to further that claim;
- monuments commemorating religious heroes as well as rulers of the past, built by the military leaders to strike awe in the living.

In this sense, the prehistory of Islamic South Asia is not to be located in the life of Muslim societies further to the west but rather in the reigns, or imagined reigns and legacies, of the most illustrious kings of previous dynasties. Two stand out from the Axial Age: Alexander the Great (356–323 BCE) and Asoka the Munificent (r. 272–236 BCE). Together they project Greek and Buddhist legacies into South Asia. Alexander was a brilliant soldier who wanted to be remembered as a wise king. Among the scholars he patronized was Aristotle. He represented the Achaemenid style of governance linked to the Persian emperors Cyrus and Darius. Asoka founded the Mauryan dynasty. He had no courtier to rival Aristotle but, through the monumental building inspired by his dramatic conversion to Buddhism, he continued the style of royal patronage familiar from his Persian-Greek predecessors. Even though no literary texts survived, Asoka's monuments did persist, and they were used and reused by successive dynasties, including the later Muslim monarchs of Central Asia whom we examine below.

Persian is the crucial element. While one can identify Arabic and Turkish elements in South Asia, they matter less than the Persian. Despite the fact that Islam is often identified with Arabic language and Arab norms, they provided merely the patina for Muslim expansion into the subcontinent. While Turks comprised the main resource for Muslim armies, neither the Turkish language nor Turkish cultural forms characterized the outlook of these newcomers to Hindustan. Beyond the Arabic patina, as also the Turkish frame, was the central image of this newly emerging social formation. The picture had its own design, and it was Persianate.

Persianate is a new term, first coined by Marshall Hodgson to offer a different explanation of Islam in the world system than that extrapolated from Wallerstein. While Persianate depicts a cultural force that is linked to the Persian language and to self-identifying Persians, Persianate is more than either a language or a people; it highlights elements that Persians share with Indo-Aryan rulers who preceded Muslims to the subcontinent. Two elements are paramount:

- *hierarchy*, which consists of top-down status markings that link all groups to each other but in a clear order of rank that pervades all major social interactions;
- *deference*, which requires rules of comportment toward those at the top of the status scale, especially the reigning monarch or emperor.

The office of emperor depended, first of all, on military prowess, with defense of the realm, provision of public works, cultivation of land, collection of taxes, and dispensation of justice among his major administrative tasks. But equivalent to these functional aspects of his office were the adornments of that office: magnificent palaces, expansive gardens, a lofty throne, and garments of unimagined splendor. In short, the emperor was the focal point of a court culture that included a whole set of specialists: architects and artists, craftsmen, musicians, poets, and scholars. Ibn Battuta, as noted above, had his equivalents in the courts of Istanbul, Isfahan, and Herat.

If the above profile describes the totalitarian ideal of a hermetically sealed hieratic system of governance, it omits several crucial elements that came to describe the kind of imperial rule exercised by the new Aryan elites—the Persianate Turks who came to dominate North Indian life from the tenth century on. Chief among these, as Robert Canfield has noted, were the use of the Persian language itself in a wide range of functions, administrative as well as literary, and then the development of an expanding cultural elite that saw itself expressing Persianate values, even when they were not fully allied with Islamic norms.[41]

One might call this expansion and rearticulation of Indo-Aryan social values either Persianate, if one wants to stress the importance of Persian as a linguistic component, or Islamicate, if one wants to acknowledge the way in which Islam itself is invoked even when the connection between cultural observance and religious loyalty is very slim. Sometimes the two terms are so close that they can be used interchangeably. Crucial in each case is their expansion of connotative meaning to include more than linguistic usage (Persian) or religious commitment (Islamic).[42] By either reading, culture cannot be reduced to "mere" economics or regional patterns of socioeconomic dominance.

Decisive for civilizational analysis, in the Muslim world generally but especially in South and Southeast Asia, is the polyvalence of Islam. The paramount need is to examine Islam as more powerful symbolically than either its exponents or detractors project it to be. Civilizations draw on the imaginary as well as institutional power of *all* available religions yet they do not exhaust the availability of any one religion to oppositional groups. Time and again, we find groups who resist a Muslim ruler in the name of the same God, the same Prophet, and the same community of believers as their opponents. The contest is over political authority even when it is framed as a contest over religious truth, and, as Sanjay Subrahmanyam has argued with telling force, future historians need to pay still more careful attention to social groups—their composition, their tensions, their outcomes—rather than simply to invoke the charismatic individual as an explanatory model.[43] The lesson from both South and Southeast Asia is to recognize Islamic norms and values as transferable and persistent in multiple contexts, whoever the rulers and whatever the stake in local or regional contests for power. It is a lesson that Hodgson would applaud; it is one that Wallerstein and his disciples have yet to apply to the juggernaut of macro-economics, with scenarios that exclude culture and so occlude the actual dynamics of historical struggle and human contingency in shaping civilizational politics.

Modern Correctives

In the mold of Hodgson, but with an eye to cadences of contemporary media, the historian Richard W. Bulliet has tried to expand the analytical power of civilization and to twin Islam and Christianity as cooperative members of the same civilization rather than oppositional members of competitive civilizations. In a monograph provocatively titled *The Case for Islamo-Christian Civilization*, Bulliet advances Islamo-Christian civilization as a neologism suited for the present, post-9/11 moment in world history.[44] While many Muslims reduce the whole of the West to the United States, and while most Americans tend to see the Islamic world only in the template of Arab/Muslim terrorists, the truth is more complex. Against Samuel Huntington's prediction of a clash of civilizations (between the West and the rest, especially Islam), and against Bernard Lewis's rhetorical query "What went wrong?" (everything, it turns out, linked to the name of Islam), Bulliet espies a future beyond the screeds of American Islamophobes but also against the hopes of Muslim extremists, whether they be religious fanatics or secular tyrants. "The past and future of the West cannot be fully comprehended without appreciation of the twinned relationship it has had with Islam over some fourteen centuries. The same is true of the Islamic world."[45] Each depends on the other. Neither makes sense without its sibling, which is also its rival.

Each must produce leaders who espouse, embody, and embolden inclusive ideals. A historian turned prophet, Bulliet concludes that "the next twenty to thirty years will see [Muslim] religious leaders of tolerant and peaceful conscience, in the mold of Gandhi, Martin Luther King [Jr.], and Nelson Mandela, eclipse in respect and popular following today's advocates of jihad, intolerance, and religious autocracy."[46]

Despite the hyperbole of this self-conscious manifesto, the case for reconsidering the future of humankind through the lens of civilizational analysis is secure. Dyads are never unqualified, and some of the most major cleavages rest on "small" differences that conceal larger elements of convergence and comity. The benefit of focusing on civilization, either singly, or better, in tandem, is to understand the cultural-religious framework within which identity and authority, hope and loyalty are shared, even more than they are contested.

In the context of Afro-Eurasian Islam, Islamicate civilization becomes a bridge civilization that decenters a narrowly Western-Islamic dialogue, and instead offers the full spectrum of contemporary West-East vignettes, whether it be Afro-Islam in Senegal and other parts of postcolonial Francophone North and West Africa, or the indirect British legacy in Saudi Arabia and Iran, reflecting and also reinforcing the larger Sunni/Shi'a divergence in the Middle East, or, further to the East, the British impact in Malaysia, the Dutch in Indonesia.[47] No category is mapless. Context matters, and the historical context generated by European expansion and colonial rule cannot be ignored in thinking about either Islamic identity or Muslim subjectivity, wherever one looks in the Afro-Asian *oikumene*. There is no Islam without Muslim subjects, and it is the latter who project the cosmopolitan legacy of Islamicate civilization into the twenty-first century.

Those who follow a political rather than a historical model of civilization, and civilizational patterning, may demur. The favorite dyad in political scientific discourse about the Muslim world is religion versus politics. The too-familiar canard is that "they" are not like "us"; Muslims, unlike post-Enlightened West European liberal democratic capitalists, do not separate religion from politics. Talal Asad has questioned this facile reflex in several of his writings, and Abdullahi an-Na'im has now published a major study arguing that religion not only can but should be, and historically has been, separate from state machinations in the Muslim world.[48]

Among political scientists there are also significant efforts to rethink, and so complicate, the nature of the religious and the political in Islam. Two efforts merit special consideration. Peter Mandaville, following the lead of Asad, has argued that defining what is religious and political depends on prior notions of the secular. While religious and secular law were never clearly distinguished in most of the Muslim world until recently, the advent of colonial rule produced dual legal systems, separating common law (regarding civil and criminal matters) from religious law (defining personal status, as in marriage, divorce, and inheritance), with the result that the religious law, or *shariʿa*, came to imply the benchmark of Islamic loyalty or authenticity. Mandaville concludes that despite Muslim protests against secularism as a godless, "material" ideology, there is a de facto institutional secularism that pervades and shapes most Muslim-majority polities.[49]

Another political scientist, Olivier Roy, goes still further in blurring the line between secular and religious identities, both individual and collective. For Roy, modern communications, combined with diasporic displacements, whether voluntary or (more often) involuntary, have produced a wholesale shift in contemporary Muslim identity:

> Muslims are at once deracinated and deterritorialized as never before. Civilisation is itself simply part of the outdated vocabulary that no longer reflects the ground level reality of Muslim self-expression and group desire. Change not continuity is the harbinger for the future. At a time when the territorial borders between the great civilizations are fading away, mental borders are being reinvented to give a second life to the ghost of lost civilizations.... *These new ethnic and religious borders do not correspond to any geographical territory or area.* They work in minds, attitudes and discourses. They are more vocal than territorial, but all the more eagerly endorsed and defended because they have to be invented, and because they remain fragile and transitory. Deterritorialisation of Islam leads to a quest for definition, because Islam is no longer embedded in territorial cultures.[50]

Roy has been quoted at length because his views repeatedly surface in discussions about Islam, especially among nonexperts.[51] The difficulty is that most Muslims, like most non-Muslims, carry passports. That is to say, the globalized citizen is still the member of some territory. She or he is marked by that territorial, political location, as distinct from others who are denied the privilege, as also the burden, of a particular nation-state identity. While politics is not limited to the state, and while civil society ensures, or should ensure, the plurality of group identities apart from the surveillant gaze of the state and its guardians, it is still majority Muslim nation-states that embrace the notion of a collective, homogeneous identity. It is they who advance themselves as the carriers of a distinctive Islamic(ate) civilization. We do not have to share, or approve, their commitment to its content, yet we cannot dismiss boundaries and censuses, flags and armies, as merely "secular" symbols of a modern nation-state. They also convey a Muslim identity that, while it has many parts and disparate interpretations and divergent outcomes, has been projected over space and time through a single, continuous vehicle: Islamicate civilization.

Notes

Bruce B. Lawrence, "Islam in Afro-Eurasia: A Bridge Civilization," in *Civilizations in World Politics: Plural and Pluralist Perspectives*, edited by Peter J. Katzenstein (London: Routledge, 2010), 157–75. Used courtesy of Taylor & Francis.

1. J. P. Arnason, *Civilizations in Dispute: Historical Questions and Theoretical Traditions* (Leiden: Brill, 2003), v.
2. See Marshall G. S. Hodgson, *The Venture of Islam: Conscience and History in a World Civilization* (Chicago: University of Chicago Press, 1974), 1:109–10.
3. Hodgson, *Venture of Islam*, 1:112.
4. Hodgson, *Venture of Islam*, 3:200.
5. Michael Adas, *Machines as the Measure of Men: Science, Technology, and Ideologies of Western Dominance* (Ithaca, NY: Cornell University Press, 1989), 209–10.
6. Adas, *Machines as the Measure of Men*, 386–92.
7. See especially Bryan Turner, *Weber and Islam* (London: Routledge and Kegan Paul, 1974).
8. Fernand Braudel, *Civilisation and Capitalism, 15th–18th Century*, trans. Sian Reynolds, 3 vols. (New York: Harper and Row, 1979), 2:495.
9. Martin W. Lewis and Kären E. Wigen, *The Myth of Continents: A Critique of Metageography* (Berkeley: University of California Press, 1997).
10. K. N. Chaudhuri, *Asia before Europe: Economy and Civilisation of the Indian Ocean from the Rise of Islam to 1750* (Cambridge: Cambridge University Press, 1990), 59.
11. Theodore Friend, ed., *Religion and Religiosity in the Philippines and Indonesia* (Washington, DC: Brookings Institution, 2006), 10.
12. The ternary myth is exposed by Abdullah Laroui, *The History of the Maghrib*, trans. R. Manheim (Princeton, NJ: Princeton University Press, 1977), 11.
13. Sudipta Kaviraj and Sunil Khilnani, eds., *Civil Society—History and Possibilities* (Cambridge: Cambridge University Press, 2001), 292.
14. Kaviraj and Khilnani, *Civil Society*, 294.
15. Arnold J. Toynbee, *A Study of History* (New York: Oxford University Press, 1947–57), 3:322.

16. Robert Irwin, "The Emergence of the Islamic World System 1000–1500," in *The Cambridge Illustrated History of the Islamic World*, ed. Francis Robinson (Cambridge: Cambridge University Press, 1996), 35.
17. Stephen Dale, "Ibn Khaldun: The Last Greek and the First *Annaliste* Historian," *International Journal of Middle East Studies* 38 (2006): 431–51. For a critical reading of Dale's assessment of Ibn Khaldun as a rationalist, see Robert Irwin, *Ibn Khaldun: An Intellectual Biography* (Princeton, NJ: Princeton University Press, 2018), esp. 196–99.
18. *Hijra* is the exodus of the Prophet Muhammad from Mecca to Medina, due to the threats on his life, and those of his followers, from hostile Quraysh. It occurred in 622 CE and became the baseline for measuring years and centuries in the lunar or Islamic calendar. The relation of Ibn Khaldun to the technical sciences of Islamic scholarship has been further developed in my introduction to Franz Rosenthal's translation of Ibn Khaldun's *Muqaddimah*.
19. Farhat J. Ziadeh, "Integrity (*'Adalah*) in Classical Islamic Law," quoting al-Busti, *Kitab al-majruhin*, in *Islamic Law and Jurisprudence: Studies in Honor of Farhat J. Ziadeh*, ed. Nicholas Heer (Seattle: University of Washington Press, 1990), 89.
20. Mohamed Talbi, *Ibn Khaldun: Sa vie—son oeuvre* (Tunis: Université de Tunis, 1973), 4.
21. Jon Anderson, "Conjuring with Ibn Khaldun," in *Ibn Khaldun and Islamic Ideology*, ed. Bruce B. Lawrence (Leiden: Brill, 1984), 120.
22. It may be confusing to speak of writing as a craft when the sciences include the sciences linked to the Arabic language—grammar, lexicography, syntax, style and criticism as well as literature, but Ibn Khaldun's unwavering criterion is manual labor, so that both the art of writing and book production are listed as crafts (*Muqaddimah*, chapter 5, 29, 30), while not only medieval Arabic language but also Qur'anic Arabic (Mudar) and South Arabian Arabic (Himyarite) and Spanish Arabic—all are treated, along with poetry and the distinction between poetry and prose, in *Muqaddimah*, chapter 6, as instances of scientific production.
23. Aziz Al-Azmeh, *Ibn Khaldun in Modern Scholarship—A Study in Orientalism* (London: Third World Centre for Research and Publishing, 1981), 102.
24. Sener Akturk, "What Is a Civilization? From Huntington to Elias: Varying Uses of the Term 'Civilization,'" in *Global Orders and Civilizations: Perspectives from History, Philosophy and International Relations*, ed. Sadik Ünay and Muzaffer Senel (New York: Nova Science Publishers, 2009).
25. See the illustrative map in Bassam Musallam, "The Ordering of Muslim Societies," in Robinson, *Cambridge Illustrated History of the Islamic World*, 166–67.
26. Ross Dunn, *The Adventures of Ibn Battuta: A Muslim Traveler of the 14th Century* (Berkeley: University of California Press, 1989).
27. Vincent Cornell, "Ibn Battuta's Opportunism: The Networks and Loyalties of a Medieval Muslim Scholar," in *Muslim Networks from Hajj to Hip Hop*, ed. miriam cooke and Bruce B. Lawrence (Chapel Hill: University of North Carolina Press, 2005), 31–50.

28 Among the many analytical efforts to locate Islam/Islamicate civilization in the cluster of great, global, or world civilizations is Arnason's *Civilizations in Dispute*. After a review of the entire literature on the subject, Arnason concludes by advocating two kinds of civilization as important to the history of the West: those from the past, and those from the contemporary world (or better, contemporary phase in world history). He cites the Indian and Chinese cases as primary examples of otherness, and then depicts Islamicate, along with Byzantine, civilization as "intermediary cases between the two poles of otherness" (327). I demur from this analysis, because it constructs an implicit hierarchy of civilizations, one that Hodgson had lamented in the third volume of *The Venture of Islam*.... Conscious and unconscious invocations of hierarchy in civilizational analyses are inevitable, but they also need to be problematized. In my view, while hierarchy—both internal and external—is crucial to understanding formative elements in the emergence and development of civilizational profiles, the Islamicate evidence is far more complex than Arnason and like-minded macro-sociologists allow.

29 Bryan Turner, while critiquing Hodgson's notions of piety and conscience, still argues that he uniquely proposed an alternative to Orientalism, "a discourse of sameness which would emphasize the continuities between various cultures rather than their antagonism.... In the case of Islam, it is clear that we may regard Islamic cultures as part of a wider cultural complex which would embrace both Judaism and Christianity. We need therefore a new form of secular ecumenicalism," one that reflects "the historical and moral sensitivity (which) clearly underlined the work of Marshall G. S. Hodgson" (Bryan S. Turner, *Orientalism, Postmodernism, and Globalism* [London: Routledge and Kegan Paul, 1994], 53–66, 102). One of the major efforts to see Occidentalism as itself a reflex, a kind of mirror opposite, of Orientalism, is provided in Ian Buruma and Avishai Margalit, *Occidentalism—A Short History of Anti-Westernism* (London: Atlantic Books, 2004). Yet Islam is treated merely as a Middle Eastern cultural force. There is no mention of Islam or Islamicate civilization in South and Southeast Asia, apart from the Pakistani ideologue, Abu'l-Aʿla Maududi, and his high-minded opposite, the poet-philosopher Muhammad Iqbal (Buruma and Margalit, *Occidentalism*, 121–25).

30 Charles Ragin and Daniel Chirot, "The World System of Immanuel Wallerstein: Sociology and Politics as History," in *Vision and Method in Historical Sociology*, ed. Theda Skocpol (Cambridge: Cambridge University Press, 1984).

31 Immanuel Wallerstein, *The Modern World-System II: Mercantilism and the Consolidation of the European World-Economy 1600–1750* (New York: Academic Press, 1980), 287.

32 Wallerstein, *Modern World-System II*, 307.

33 For a partial corrective, see John M. Rogers, *Empire of the Sultans: Ottoman Art from the Khalili Collection* (London: Nour Foundation, 2000).

34 See the critique of Arnason, *Civilizations in Dispute*, 7–10.

35 Shmuel Eisenstadt, "Introduction: Paths to Early Modernities—A Comparative View," *Daedalus* 127, no. 3 (1998): 1–22, 6. Others besides Eisenstadt have noted the

benefit of a civilizational rather than world system episteme or paradigm for cross-cultural analysis. Among them is Yitzhak Sternberg, who argues that for both macro- and microanalysis "it seems to me that the concept 'historical civilization' is more appropriate than the concept 'historical system,' suggested by Wallerstein" (Yitzhak Sternberg, "Modernity, Civilization, and Globalization," in Eliezer Ben-Rafael with Yitzhak Sternberg, *Identity, Culture and Globalization* [Leiden: Brill, 2002], 90). Yet neither Sternberg nor any of the other contributors to the volume he coedited include reference to either Islamicate civilization or the contribution of Marshall Hodgson. Similarly, Arnason, cited above, critiques many of the narrowly Westocentric views of civilization, yet himself discusses Hodgson only briefly as a corrective to the crudest form of Weberianism, which projects Islam as "a regressive version of monotheism" (Arnason, *Civilizations in Dispute*, 245–46). Later, he does commend Hodgson for proposing "a distinction between Islamic religion and Islamicate civilization" (292), but does not elaborate on the implications of such a distinction.

36 Marshall Hodgson, *Rethinking World History: Essays on Europe, Islam and World History*, ed. with introduction and conclusion by Edmund Burke III (Cambridge: Cambridge University Press, 1993), 70–71.

37 James Scott, *Domination and the Arts of Resistance: Hidden Transcripts* (New Haven, CT: Yale University Press, 1990).

38 Janet Abu-Lughod, *Before European Hegemony: The World System A.D. 1250–1350* (Oxford: Oxford University Press, 1989), 24–38.

39 Sugata Bose, "Space and Time on the Indian Ocean Rim: Theory and History," in *Modernity and Culture: From the Mediterranean to the Indian Ocean*, ed. Leila Tarazi Fawaz and C. A. Bayly (New York: Columbia University Press, 2002), 365–88, 376.

40 See, for example, Edward Simpson and Kai Kresse, eds., *Struggling with History: Islam and Cosmopolitanism in the Western Indian Ocean* (New York: Columbia University Press, 2008).

41 Robert Canfield, ed., *Turko-Persia in Historical Perspective* (Cambridge: Cambridge University Press, 1991).

42 See Muzaffar Alam, "The Pursuit of Persian: Language in Mughal Politics," *Modern Asian Studies* 32, no. 2 (1998): 317–49; Richard M. Eaton, *The Rise of Islam and the Bengal Frontier 1204–1760* (Berkeley: University of California Press, 1993). In Alam's essay, both the contingent and ideological elements of Indo-Persianate culture are addressed, with principal attention to distinctive aspects of the Mughal period and its polity. The same point is picked up and elaborated, with documentary concision and analytical agility, in Eaton's monograph, regarding the Islamization of Bengal during the Mughal period. *Editor's Note: See also Muzaffar Alam, The Languages of Political Islam: India, 1200–1800 (Chicago: University of Chicago Press, 2004).*

43 Sanjay Subrahmanyam, "Hearing Voices: Vignettes of Early Modernity in South Asia, 1400–1750," *Daedalus* 127, no. 73 (1998): 90–112.

44 Richard Bulliet, *The Case for Islamo-Christian Civilization* (New York: Columbia University Press, 2004).

45 Bulliet, *Case for Islamo-Christian Civilization*, 45.
46 Bulliet, *Case for Islamo-Christian Civilization*, 161.
47 See Reinhard Schulze, *A Modern History of the Islamic World* (London: Tauris, 2002), 86–89.
48 Abdullahi an-Na'im, *Islam and the Secular State* (Cambridge, MA: Harvard University Press, 2008).
49 Peter Mandaville, *Global Political Islam* (London: Routledge, 2008), 10–15.
50 Olivier Roy, *Globalized Islam: The Search for a New Ummah* (New York: Columbia University Press, 2004), 20.
51 Appiah, for example, cites Roy as the paramount authority for his own argument regarding the ahistorical disposition of Muslim fundamentalists or, as Roy terms them, neo-fundamentalists. See Kwame Anthony Appiah, *Cosmopolitanism: Ethics in a World of Strangers* (New York: Norton, 2006), 138–39. *Editor's Note: On Appiah, see the special issue of New Literary History 49, no. 2 (Spring 2018), "On Kwame Anthony Appiah," especially the essays by Marie Ostby and Ranjana Khanna.*

THREE

Muslim Cosmopolitanism | 2012

The Larger Frame

To talk about Muslim and cosmopolitan one must go beyond standard nomenclature. Culture is not religion, yet the latter cannot and does not escape the impact of the former. The best neologism to square the circle is "Islamicate culture." It was the visionary world historian Marshall Hodgson who invented the neologism Islamicate culture to explore what he termed *The Venture of Islam*. Hodgson's vision needs to be invoked but also amplified. Islam is radically cosmopolitan. It goes back to Arabia but quickly expands beyond it. Islam, born in an Arabian niche, became a cultural and trade entrepôt linking the Mediterranean world to the Indian Ocean via the Red Sea.

As Islam spread in all directions of the compass, it brought a cosmopolitan sensibility to the cultures with which it interacted, even as early Muslims retained strong spiritual, aesthetic, and cultural ties to the desert environment out of which they emerged. Centuries after the founding of Islam, Mecca and Medina remained deeply tribal desert cities, filled with foreigners, but they were also connected with new centers of cosmopolitan activity under Muslim rule—Cairo, Damascus, Baghdad, Cordoba, Delhi, and Samarqand.

Nile-to-Oxus, as Hodgson announced, then demonstrated, is the core region that defined, and was itself redefined by, Islam. The Muslim presence became established through trade, cultural exchange, and political experiments. There were no Muslim empires, but rather a commonwealth of networks marked by caliphates, sultanates, and kingdoms, each reflecting an ethos of internal reciprocity as much as external competition with regional rivals. There was no equality—itself an Enlightenment concept—but there was parity, a long-standing feature of Islamicate norms, ethics, and practices.

Foreigners, far from being excluded, were welcomed to the major cities of Muslim empires, welcomed, above all, for the variety of skills they provided. Some were Muslim, some were not, but all shared in a world marked by cosmopolitan structures, activities, and values. Patronage was channeled into and through the major Muslim courts. Greek thought into Arabic science, but also Indian numerals, with Chinese designs—all evolved under the crescent of Islam. The astrolabe, for instance, though not invented by Muslims, became an instrument of shared scientific interest. As the eleventh-century Turkic scholar Ahmad al-Biruni noted, it did not matter that the Byzantines first used the astrolabe; it became Muslim when times of prayer were imposed on the Byzantine calendar. And to those purists who objected to his recycled use of a "Christian" instrument, claiming that it showed imitation (*tashabbuh*) of unbelievers, Biruni rejoined: "The Byzantines also eat food. Then do not imitate them in this!"

What made science or culture or political structures specifically Muslim was not their origin but their dedicated use. The crucial question about all objects or practices was: How did they begin to reflect a worldview that was Islamicate, encompassing both Muslims and non-Muslims and thus projecting a new ethos that was suffused with the spirit of Islam?

The Muslim Accent

Muslim cosmopolitanism is, above all, Muslim because it focuses on tribal/urban networks in comparative perspective for the first time in human history.

The defining elements of Muslim cosmopolitanism had been set in place from Spain to China by 1402, when Ibn Khaldun met Tamerlane in Damascus. Culture was inseparable from patronage, and both were channeled through civilization: Ibn Khaldun's *Muqaddimah* introduces the benchmark for reflecting on all human history. It is the inhabited world, the *oikumene*, mapped by the Nile-to-Oxus, but also including the Mediterranean and Indian Ocean. Of course, there was cosmopolitanism before Islam, but what made Muslim cosmopolitanism distinctive was its location on the bridge of the Afro-Eurasian *oikumene*, at the heart of what became the first cosmopolitan world system.

While cities are the crucial index of a Muslim difference, one cannot and should not forget the relationship of urban to rural or tribal norms and values, structures, and options. In reviewing Ibn Khaldun's *Muqaddimah* and Hodgson's

The Venture of Islam, especially volume 2, one finds a recurrent accent on *both* tribalism and urbanism. They are intertwined in a synergistic coil—not just as geographic markers but also as ethos or value systems, each having benefits that exceed their limits.

What is needed in 2011 is not an escape from history but a bold effort to revisit its shadows as well as its bright lights. Beyond the end of empires and the rise of the modern West, we must rethink comparative world systems through an Islamicate lens. Tribalism, for instance, is not just a fixed moment in history now surpassed by modern-day cities. Tribalism can be an urban as well as a rural ethos. The key term ʿ*asabiyya*, translated from Ibn Khaldun, means connectedness or boundedness. It projects tribalism as a metaphor that applies to all elites who are internally bound together by blood ties (or their functional equivalents), whether the Medicis in the sixteenth century, the oil/steel/railroad barons in late nineteenth-century America, or the Arab Gulf emirs in the twenty-first century. Small urban polities patronize and sustain a myriad of cosmopolitan projects—musical and literary as well as aesthetic and architectural. While religion may not be their main note, it is an inescapable index of their belonging to one space and time, matched with their longing to be part of a trans-territorial and trans-temporal ethos. Islam, like other religions, is also always and everywhere part and parcel of networked connections.

If there is a major distinctiveness to Muslim cosmopolitanism, it is the expansive arc of cities that serve as nodes of cosmopolitan networks throughout the Islamicate world. Tracing the influence for Muslim cosmopolitans would require attention to metacities that have been eclipsed as well as those just beginning to come into prominence: from Aden to Doha, from Samarkand to Kuala Lumpur, from Harar to Dakar. Other major urban locations that qualify as Muslim cosmopolitan metacities include Baghdad, Beirut, Cairo, Damascus, Delhi, Isfahan, Jerusalem, Lahore, Marrakesh, Muscat, Sarajevo, Xi'an, and, of course, Istanbul.

Istanbul as the Showcase

In 2010 Istanbul was feted as the Capital City of European Culture. It was a new high mark in the upward trajectory of that city's symbolic prestige within and beyond Turkey. The current article asks a related but more difficult question: Is Istanbul also the capital city of *Muslim* cosmopolitanism? To answer that question, one must address the prior question: Is Istanbul genuinely cosmopolitan?

Istanbul is the jewel of the East. It straddles Asia and Europe. It looks north to Russia, south to Greece. It borders three expanses of water: the Bosporus Straits that run to the Black Sea; the Marmara Sea, extending to the Mediterranean; and in between them the Golden Horn, along with nine islands, that dot its several horizons. From the shores of Africa to the isles of Indonesia, there are many maritime ports that have also become major metropolitan centers, but none combines the topographic complexity or scenic beauty, matched by strategic advantage and historical longevity, of Istanbul.

But is Istanbul cosmopolitan? If the stream of tourists who visit the city every year could vote, the answer would be a resounding YES, and they could use as confirmation of their choice the tagline from one of the many *Lonely Planet* promotions on Turkey: "Istanbul is the cosmopolitan heart of Turkey," writes *Lonely Planet* author Virginia Maxwell, and she goes on to provide "her insider tips on the city she fell in love with—from kooky cab drivers and awe-inspiring mosques to one of the world's most dangerous liquors: raki!"

The sights and sounds, from music festivals to upscale museums to outdoor theaters to rides on the Bosporus—all contribute to the notion that Istanbul is not just the best that Turkey can offer but also the best that pluralist pleasure seekers could hope to find, to explore, and to enjoy in the twenty-first century. In the parade of European cultural capitals, *Istanbul 2010* was marked by an explosion of entries in local, national, and international presses, including Facebook, which began with this upbeat glowing announcement from the Turkish government:

Istanbul: A Tale of Two Cities
It's a city of contrasts, brought together by east and west, Islam and Christianity. The people of Istanbul are tolerant by nature, which explains why the mostly Muslim city harbors a significant Jewish presence as well as Greek-Orthodoxy. It's a crossroads between north and south, east and west.

The accent on Istanbul as a model of social, geographic, and religious integration continues till the end of the Facebook entry where we are told not only that synagogues flourish but also that "Istanbul remains a place where such antiquated symbols of Judaism can survive alongside the 20th-century mosques, where an ever-increasing influx of peasants can bring a time-honored tradition to the most progressive of Muslim cities." Whether or not this amounts to confirmation of a cosmopolitan identity or mere hype for commercial gain by Turkish and Euro-American holiday vendors is another question. It has been thoughtfully explored, with a teeming set of entries on keywords, in a 2008 multiauthored publication, *Becoming Istanbul—An Encyclopaedia*. The answer is as elusive as the book's title. There is no fixed something called Istanbul. It is always in process, ever changing and becoming something else. And so to address the question of Istanbul as a cosmopolis, one faces the daunting entanglement of motives, agendas, and outcomes that shape and reshape the city. They are exposed by several contributors under diverse entries that include "Cinema," "Cleaning," and "Cultural Transformation," and then extend down the alphabet to encompass "Museum," "Ottoman Neighborhood," and "scaffolding." What one discovers is a repeated, detailed, and blistering critique of the consumerist practices that mark and too often mar the cosmopolitan image of early twenty-first-century Istanbul. From a ground-up view of Istanbul, it seems, one must exercise restraint about large-scale generalizations. Instead, one is compelled to conclude that the verdict about the cosmopolitan status of Istanbul is at best mixed, the outlook for future, upward adjustment opaquely contingent.

Perhaps the most thorough effort to recuperate contemporary Istanbul as cosmopolitan is provided by the Turkish anthropologist Öykü Potuoğlu-Cook. In her broad-gauged article "Beyond the Glitter: Belly Dance and Neoliberal Gentrification in Istanbul," she moves beyond categorical judgments.[1] Challenging both an abstract notion of cosmopolitanism and the holistic claims of cultural tourism, she looks at performance in general and belly dancing in particular. She highlights "the aesthetics of performance codes, venues, and processes that consequently restructure public intimacies and the broader cultural logic of neoliberalism." Among her everyday Muslim subjects is Zeynep, a veiled prospective university student and clerk who belongs at once to the *umma* (global Muslim community) and to the Turkish nation. Zeynep struggles with both daily class limitations and strict secular regulations against public Islam. Her lifestyle choices, from belly dance to veiling, generate and reflect "the embodied possibilities and constraints along the national-cosmopolitan spectrum, a spectrum defined by commodified Ottoman nostalgia."

By bracketing together belly dancing and veiling, the global *umma* and Turkish nationalism, European aspirations with Ottoman nostalgia, Potuoğlu-Cook raises the question central to this essay: can Istanbul be considered a *Muslim* cosmopolitan city, and if so, what does that mean both for the status of Istanbul and the content of Muslim cosmopolitanism? Rather than discard a cosmopolitan label, she redefines what it means to be poor and marginal as well as Muslim and cosmopolitan in contemporary Istanbul.

A parallel, equally interesting question is: Can Istanbul also be considered a *Jewish* cosmopolitan city? What does it mean to relate Istanbul or any city to a religiously coded projection of cosmopolitan longing, whether Muslim or Jewish? Until recently, the answer to the query regarding Istanbul as a site of Jewish cosmopolitanism would have been yes/no. Yes, because during its earliest period as a Muslim capital city (for the Ottoman Empire, from 1453 to 1924) it did provide refuge, opportunity, and quasi-citizenship for Jewish refugees from autocratic, discriminatory regimes, especially Spain after the Reconquista of 1492. No, because after the formation of the Republic of Turkey (1923), with an emphasis on Turkish ethnic over Ottoman pan-ethnic identity, life became increasingly difficult for Turkish Jews in general, and Stambouli Jews in particular.

That assessment now has to be revisited and revised. An American anthropologist, Marcy Brink-Danan, has argued that representational codes as much as diachronic narratives and constitutional norms shape the status of minorities.[2] She examines how Stambouli Jews deal with the issue of representation, and how this kind of knowledge is interpreted and mediated by different actors and audiences as well as through the prism of what these various participants think is expected of them. What they exhibit is not an ethical showcase of universal, timeless norms but instead "lived cosmopolitanism: an awareness of multiple audiences, some of whom might be antipathetic ones." Indeed, "cosmopolitanism among Turkish Jews involves a much more private, practical, and protectionist way of managing difference. Rethinking cosmopolitanism along these lines suggests not just a shift at the level of theorizing the phenomenon but also a shift in method, toward studying cosmopolitanism as knowledge performed, focusing on the dissonance between rhetorical cosmopolitanisms and lived ones rooted in local contexts." It is a shift away from choice and ethics, the presumptive Kantian approach, and toward a complicated knowledge of difference, the approach etched by Walter Mignolo and other border-thinking theorists. In tone it echoes and complements the same particularist, contextualized approach to Muslim cosmopolitanism etched by Potuoğlu-Cook. What both authors make possible is the use of cosmopolitan logic to depict minorities—ethnic such as Gypsy or religious such as Jews—and not just the dominant group.

Exemplary Icons from the Distant Past and the Near Present

The issue of whether or not Istanbul—however varied and disputed its historical/contemporary profile—can be viewed as an emerging model for Muslim cosmopolitanism depends on local actors, but it also draws on a set of contradictory indices that need to be marked and then explored. Part of what distinguishes a metacity from its parallel urban neighbors is its sense of celebration. There are always multiple public moments to celebrate, a calendar of performances or events that monopolize the everyday gaze and suggest the hinge importance of this one city as a perpetual resource of social capital. Celebration is also linked to restoration: buildings must be maintained but also renewed, just as heroes must be recalled, their memories expanded, in the public domain.

And so urban elites—whether governmental or private—must be adroit at both recuperating the past and reinforcing its present value. This process can be charted throughout Istanbul's 1,700-year history but especially since the 1990s, one can trace how Stambouli advocates have proven themselves skillful in asserting their ownership of four individuals who are crucial for all Turks. These national heroes sort out into two sets of actors. The first defines the public, political role of Islam. They are (1) Mehmet II, known as Fatih Sultan Mehmet, said to be the guiding figure in the initial Islamization of Istanbul, and (2) Ataturk, or Mustafa Kemal, Mehmet II's opposite and yet also his complement, the guiding figure for the secularization of post–World War I Turkey. These two military heroes embody not only contradictory ideologies but also competing roles as emblems from the Ottoman past and at the same time signposts for Republican Turkey as it approaches its centenary in 2023.

Political Icons: Mehmet II and Mustafa Kemal

Among the many ironies that link Mehmet II and Mustafa Kemal are their names. Both have names that can be traced to the Prophet Muhammad. Mehmet is a Turkish abbreviation of Muhammad, while Mustafa is one of the alternate titles he enjoyed. Mustafa means "the chosen" (one), and while it referred to Muhammad as the one sent by God in 610 to be the last prophet in an Abrahamic lineage stretching back to Adam, for Ataturk it signaled his choice to be the Turkish leader of a war against European and local enemies that secured the Republic of Turkey as a new nation-state with defensible borders in 1922. The span of 1,300 years connects them and binds them together.

The overlaps between Mehmet II and Mustafa Kemal extend further. Each is marked by a set of four traits: (1) military skill, including maritime prowess, to secure battlefield victories, often against great odds; (2) expansionary zeal, to not only conquer but to incorporate other domains within their own empire/

state; (3) administrative/bureaucratic finesse; and not least (4) the undefinable yet critical trait of charisma.

Mehmet II inherited a powerful Turkic warrior state that had claimed much of Anatolia and extended into southern Europe. But it had been denied the greatest urban prize, the capital city of the Byzantine Empire, which had rebuffed all efforts at Muslim conquest and only been breached once, by fellow Christians, in the Crusader invasion/occupation from 1204 to 1261. When Mehmet II went against the advice of senior officers and resolved to capture Constantinople, he had to make extraordinary preparations for a combined sea-land assault that have been described in vivid detail by a near contemporary source.

No less brave was Ataturk's decision to fight against the British-Australian soldiers who were determined to capture Istanbul from the then Ottoman Empire in 1915. It is a battle known by its place as Gallipoli, and the record of its impact is emblazoned in every Turkey guidebook as well as in numerous history books. In Turkey the battle became known after the port of Canakkale where the British Navy was repulsed in March 1915, but even more the story became part of a durable repertoire about the heroic story of the nation's revered founder, Mustafa Kemal. The victory at Canakkale did more than any other event or person in creating Turkish nationalism, with Mustafa Kemal later Ataturk as its beneficiary. Like Mehmet II, he went against the advice of his commanders, and also overcame huge enemy forces with an order to his troops that every Turkish school child can still repeat: "I am not ordering you to attack, I am ordering you to die. In the time it takes us to die, other troops and commanders will arrive to take our places." His regiment was wiped out, and later he himself was hit in the chest by a piece of shrapnel, but, as the story goes, his pocket watch prevented fatal injury. Despite the loss of more than half the Ottoman forces, he went on to become not only the hero of Gallipoli but also the general who carried Turkish fortunes beyond the war.

Following their initial successes, both Mehmet II and Ataturk had other military engagements, many of which they won, some of which they lost, but all of which expanded their domains, across Europe for the Ottoman Empire in the late fifteenth century, and across Anatolia, despite forswearing Europe, especially Greece, in post–World War I Turkey.

Also important for Mehmet II was the myth of completion, to wit, that his conquest of Constantinople marked a centuries-old ambition of previous Muslim warriors, dating back to the era of the Prophet Muhammad. It is for that reason that the huge flux of pilgrims to Eyub Sultan's grave and mosque projects the image of Mehmet II as the devout ghazi or warrior to present-day Stambouli Muslims. No less relevant, though much less noted, is Mehmet II's connection to the other popular saint's tomb, located not on the Golden Horn but on the Bosporus. Well beyond the urban center of Istanbul lies the modest mountainside tomb of Telli Baba. He is said to have watched over the Bosporus and safeguarded the movements of Mehmet II in his bold assault on the Byzantine Capital. Located near Saruyer district, the Telli Baba Turbe has become the frequent destination of Muslim pilgrims seeking to have prayers answered, whether for prosperity, safety, or marital success. An element of charisma pervades both the recollection of Mehmet II and even more Mustafa Kemal. There is the impressive Diorama 1453, which opened in 2009 in the Topkapı district of Istanbul. Bus drivers can, and do, download from its website onto their Blackberries videos of Fatih Sultan Mehmet's conquest, while Ataturk's picture is everywhere, even as tattoos on women's arms. Especially notable is the Ataturk museum in Istanbul and, of course, his monumental tomb, with the museum attached to it, in Ankara. Beyond all the impressive display of military memorabilia are two items that tell more about the man than his destroyed watch fob (which actually traveled to Berlin, then disappeared, after World War I). There is his rowing machine that he used to maintain a daily regimen of physical fitness, and then his extraordinary library—at once huge, diverse in topics, and multilingual in the books that it contained. We now know from recent scholarship that he even concerned himself with Turkish vernacular translations of the Koran.

Though this might seem like a slim connection to Turkey's religious past, it is not lost on devout Turks that even the "secular" Ataturk did concern himself with religious meaning as well as religious laws, structures, and institutions. To make the Republic of Turkey succeed, the core of Islamic faith had to be accessible to modern Turks. Unlike Bourgiba in modern-day Tunisia, Ataturk did not try to modify one of the pillars of Islam, but instead to convey its scriptural anchor, the Holy Qur'an, in a language that was at once authentic and modern.

There are limits to the Turkish experiment, however. It rests on a delicate, shifting consensus, the sense of engagement not only with internal others but also with immediate neighbors, such as Syria (a former ally and now a nemesis) and Iran (always an unpredictable player as friend or foe). The economy must also continue to grow, and the generals have to be content with military, not political, ambitions. At the same time, Turks abroad do continue to relate enthusiastically and supportively to their homeland. With all those elements in place, can we deduce that Istanbul will thrive as a cosmopolitan center blazing the path for other Muslim megacities of the twenty-first century? The answer is another yes/no. Yes, all can and should be drawn to understand both the continuities and transformations of Istanbul during the recent past, but at the same time, there is no Turkish model for Muslim cosmopolitanism. If there is a culturally specific Turkish Islam, as some have claimed, then it is, in its best light, an Islam marked by cosmopolitan traits: liberal, tolerant, pluralist, and democratic, but these variables are contested even within Turkey, and to the extent that they have shaped Turkish history, society, culture, and religion, they are not easily transferable. They have shaped—and one hopes, that they will continue to shape—the distinctive trajectory of Istanbul in the post-Soviet and now the post-2001 world. Other cities, other regions, and other networks will find their own path to a cosmopolitan future, but it will parallel rather than emulate the Turkish, Stambouli model.

Conclusion

What derives from looking, even cursorily, at the question of Muslim cosmopolitanism with an Istanbul-centered focus is the need to imagine Muslim/cosmopolitan as a permeable category, one with multiple local variants and contingent criteria that are never juxtaposed without also being simultaneously contested. Just as Zeynep, the devout Muslim belly dancer, projects a paradox, so do modern-day Turks: they embrace both the ghazi hero Fatih Sultan as the emblem of their faith and the anti-caliphate nationalist Ataturk as their exemplar patriot. Instead of reducing or eliminating the "Muslim" element of cosmopolitanism, Stambouli residents and Turkish citizens mark it as the ambiguous hope that it can, and should, be in all cultural contexts.

A Jewish or Christian—or Hindu or Buddhist—cosmopolitanism is as viable and as contingent as is its Muslim counterpart. Whether minority or majority, whether Asian or European, all cosmopolitan projects stretch the canopy of time and meaning across a spectrum of the cosmos or universe that is also marked as polis or city states. All have common interests as well as competing agendas.

Counter-cosmopolitan forces also exist in major parts of Muslim-majority and Muslim-minority pockets of the Afro-Eurasian *oikumene*. One cannot eradicate the forces of counter-cosmopolitanism, those who reject border or *barzakh* thinking in favor of abstract universalisms, including cosmopolitanism. At the same time, however, by projecting the persistent longing and belonging of multiple groups who embody and perform cosmopolitan traits, Stamboulis, the current residents of a great city and citizens of an evolved republic, demonstrate that true cosmopolitanism is always possible as long as it is denoted, that is, specified and complicated in multiple local contexts, more often with, than without, religious markings.

The major traits that mark Stambouli Muslim cosmopolitans are place specific. First, there can be no cosmopolitanism apart from cities, yet cities differ from one another even when they share common values. Those cities which dot the maritime expanse of the Mediterranean Sea and the Indian Ocean, moreover, share certain characteristics that include an accent on religious identity most often defined as Muslim. While Beirut or Alexandria or even Smyrna (pre–World War I) could be counted among the major Mediterranean maritime ports with a large or majority Muslim population, Istanbul remains exceptional, both in its long history and in its recent experience.

Istanbul provides a signpost not a template for Muslim cosmopolitanism. Part of what makes Istanbul remarkable is also what makes it exceptional: its intense diversity. One cannot understand Muslim cosmopolitanism in Istanbul without reference to antecedents and parallels, especially Jewish cosmopolitanism, but at the same time one must account for the complex admixture of social traits, defining moments, and symbolic heroes, all of which define the Muslim variant of global/Mediterranean cosmopolitanism distinctive to Istanbul.

The most significant, overriding conclusion concerns the grayness or piebald quality of all calculations that have as their subject cosmopolitanism. No cosmopolitan effervescence can be attributed to a secular rather than a religious identity, nor to a majority Turkish Muslim majority which does not also include other minorities both non-Muslim (Christian/Jewish) and non-Turkish (Armenian/Kurdish). Dissent and debate, or what Turam calls engagement in the public square, is essential to all evolved forms of cosmopolitanism. What makes cosmopolitanism both possible and visible in twenty-first-century Istanbul is a series of very public skirmishes between groups labeled as conservative or progressive, Islamist or secular, all of whom contend for the same mantle: to project Turkey as a majority Muslim, nonreligious state that dominates eastern Mediterranean–Central Asian networks of commerce, communication, and cultural and social exchange, with ambitions that exceed the region, even if they have so far not been acknowledged as globally pioneering by those outside the region. That goal is an advance for Muslims, for Turks, and for all cosmopolitans.

Notes

Bruce B. Lawrence, "Muslim Cosmopolitanism," *Critical Muslim* 2 (2012): 19–39. Used by permission.

1 Öykü Potuoğlu-Cook, "Beyond the Glitter: Belly Dance and Neoliberal Gentrification in Istanbul," *Cultural Anthropology* 21, no. 4 (November 2006): 633–60.
2 Marcy Brink-Danan, "Dangerous Cosmopolitanism: Erasing Difference in Istanbul," *Anthropological Quarterly* 84, no. 2 (2011): 439–74.

FOUR

Genius Denied and Reclaimed
Hodgson's *The Venture of Islam* | 2014

Marshall Hodgson was both a genius and a visionary. While he may have seemed to be just another university professor, at once restless, innovative, and genial, he was also an academic Übermensch with a global agenda. He wanted to change the world by changing the way we saw, understood, and engaged Islam within world history. Born in 1922, he was drafted but as a Quaker refused to fight in World War II. After serving five years in a detention camp, he returned to school, graduating from the University of Chicago with a Ph.D. in the early 1950s. He had been teaching from notes that became *The Venture of Islam* for over a decade before his demise in 1968. Forty-six years after his death, and forty years since the posthumous publication of his magnum opus, his legacy remains puzzling. Was he ahead of his time, or has he been overtaken by the Cold War and its aftermath, including the horror of 9/11, along with its own, persistent aftermath?

Hodgson was informed, above all, by a moral vision of world history. He thought that Islam mattered because it righted the intellectually wrong yet emotively triumphalist notions of Eurocentric domination in world history. Hodgson began by expanding the backdrop for Islam to include the emergence of all historically documented societies. He stressed the formative features of world civilization dating from three millennia before the Common Era. By 1500 BCE, there had emerged four core cultural areas: Mediterranean, Nile-to-Oxus, Indian, and Chinese. It was two rivers, the Nile to the south and Oxus to the north, which provided the map markers etching the core area of what became

Islamicate civilization. There was no Middle East or Near East, since in each case these qualifiers presumed an absent center: Middle to where? Near from where? East of where? Instead, it was these two major waterways, the Nile and the Oxus, which framed major developments characterizing the earliest three phases of Islamicate civilization. They are best viewed in alliterative or assonant pairs.

The first phase Hodgson called Formation and Orientation (500–634), which ends after the death of the Prophet Muhammad and his initial successor, Abu Bakr. The second is a phase of Conversion and Crystallization (634–870). Though Islamic rule comes to prevail, there are not yet Muslim majorities in all regions under Islamic rule. The third phase is Fragmentation and Florescence (970–1041), as Muslim polities splinter while Islam itself emerges as a major civilizational force for the first time.

What follows is no less important but not as easily summarized as those first centuries of Islamic expansion and rule. A fourth phase, Migration and Renewal (1041–1405), carries us through the early Mongol invasions and the aftermath of Tamerlane. It is followed by a fifth phase of Consolidation and Expansion (1405–1683); Hodgson ends this period with a glance at Indian Ocean Islam after reviewing three land-based empires, Ottoman, Safavid, and Mughal (or Indo-Timuri). Finally, there crystallizes the sixth phase of Reform, Dependency, and Recovery (1683–present); completed after Hodgson's death, it includes a postlude from World War II to the present, titled "Islam and Globalization: The Age of Mobility" (I borrow this wording from Marilyn Waldman, whose essay I discuss below).

Here *in nuce* is what Hodgson argued about the importance of seeing Islam over the time frame of 1,500 years but with an emplotment that was closer to 3,000 years. The interaction of the known world is crucial. The Nile-to-Oxus, the future core of Islamdom, was the least cohesive and most complicated of the four cultural core areas. Whereas each of the other regions developed a single language of high culture—Greek, Sanskrit, and Chinese, respectively— the Nile-to-Oxus region was a linguistic palimpsest of Irano-Semitic languages of several sorts: Aramaic, Syriac (eastern or Iranian Aramaic), and Middle Persian (the language of eastern Iran). The Nile-to-Oxus region, of course, became conjoined with the Arabian Peninsula through the expansion of early Muslim rule to neighboring regions, but the nature of the society, culture, and religion that evolved was bidirectional. Though the Arabs conquered, the people, the institutions, and the societies they conquered challenged and changed them. The crucial period is 800–200 BCE, known as the Axial Age because the world's first religions of salvation developed in each of the four core areas, and from these traditions—for example, Judaism, Mazdeism, Buddhism, and Confucianism—derived all later forms of high religion, including Christianity and Islam.

To begin to understand Hodgson the man or to appreciate his legacy, one must begin where he began: with a moral vision that accommodates civilizational continuity and change. At the World Congress for Middle East Studies in 2014, one of Hodgson's most distinguished students, Huricihan Islamoglu, epitomized that vision with four essential points: All of us are in this together, and there is a shared history more significant than the differences and conflicts that separate us; the individual matters in a pragmatic, economic context; all human action is historically contingent, subject to an ebb and flow that can only be understood retrospectively and with constant self-criticism; and finally, the individual counts not just as contingent subject but also as empowered agent of change.

Hodgson had precursors, including the fourteenth-century polymath Ibn Khaldun. Ibn Khaldun had argued that history was about social organization and civilizational patterns, and that religion mattered less for its heroes than for the patterns of social exchange they promoted. In a similar vein, Hodgson locates Islam not as an outsider but an insider to world history, with more than religion at stake. Islam was so broad, its influence so pervasive, it defies categorization as Muslim or Islamic, belonging only to Muslim actors and practices, creeds, rituals, or structures. Instead, for Hodgson, there is a vibrant, moving, resilient tradition that is best understood as Islamic*ate*. The *-ate* is much more than an added syllable: it is a stark challenge to rethink all that is meant by Muslim and Islam. It is the social and cultural palette that emerged from Islamic rule, encompassing and influencing non-Muslims as well as Muslims. Islamicate, with the *-ate* tacked on to the end, adds oddity and resonance to what becomes the heritage of Islam for world civilization.

Underlying this central argument is an even larger premise: there is only one world civilization and Islam is a part of it, not apart from it. Islamicate tradition encompasses but also projects all the elements of Islamic thought that came from pre-Islamic resources—Persian, Hebrew, Greek, Latin, by language; Magian, Jewish, and Christian, by religion; Byzantine, Sassanian, Mongol, by imperial domains. Islam—or, more accurately, Islamicate civilization—in turn, becomes part and parcel of the emergent West in developments that unfolded after 1800.

The Hodgsonian project did not end with his death. It is ongoing. In 2014 Islam and Muslims are still struggling to be part of world history on a global plane. The so-called clash of civilizations debate, linked to both Bernard Lewis and Samuel Huntington, as well as one of Huntington's former students, Francis Fukuyama, only highlights Euro-centrism and Western hegemony by other means, with old arguments recycled under new rubrics. Beyond the several critiques of civilizational theory one must locate an alternative path connecting premodern to modern history. To rethink the Afro-Asian *oikumene* (the known world before 1500 CE) as a cosmopolitan vision of polycentric nodes requires attention, above all, to metacities, and to networks that link disparate metropoles from Asia to America, from the Pacific and Indian Oceans to the Mediterranean and Atlantic.

Among all world historians of the twentieth and now twenty-first century, only Hodgson has accented Islamicate civilization as itself the locus of modern history: without developments in Islamdom (the counterpart to Christendom in historical reckoning), the so-called rise of the West would never have happened. *The Venture of Islam* corrects the fallacy that the defining arc of global civilization is centered in the West, with not just the Muslim world but also the so-called Third World and the larger Afro-Asian *oikumene* deemed to be parochial, traditional, and underdeveloped.

Hodgson uniquely underscored the pervasive notion of an inclusive, multicentered world order where Islamicate norms and values informed what have now become cosmopolitan longings and belongings. Constitutions were not just Western inventions but also adaptable, critical instruments, helping to shape an Islamicate cosmopolitanism during the twentieth and now twenty-first century. Legal pluralism predates the eighteenth century: Hodgson demonstrated how a hemispheric world history, paying equal attention to all parts as interactive nodes in a single system, requires us to see the multiple ways that Persianate, Turkic, and Indic cultures and societies redefine constitutionally mandated citizenship in accordance with Islamicate norms and values.

I consider Hodgson's contribution of pivotal importance to the ambiguous yet productive category "Islamicate cosmopolitanism." This category involves citizenship, cultural identity, class/gender perspectives, and, of course, network theory, across time and space but always relating to cities. It involves not just Muslims but all those who are engaged by Muslim others, whether in a majority or minority Muslim polity. Despite the screeds of terrorism and Islamophobia, Islamicate pluralism has emerged, and deserves analysis, as the unexpected yet evident consequence of Hodgson's moral, cosmopolitan vision.

I am an unabashed Hodgsonian, never having known him but having taught *The Venture of Islam* for over thirty-five years at several universities. Others have been charier of relating the Hodgsonian legacy to their own work. Consider the caveat of a sympathetic fellow academic, Anouar Majid. In his broad gauged manifesto, *Unveiling Traditions: Postcolonial Islam in a Polycentric World* (2000), Anouar Majid, a Moroccan literary critic teaching in the United States, noted Hodgson's focus on language: "Islamicate refers not only to the religion of Islam but also 'to the social and cultural complex historically associated with Islam and the Muslims, both among Muslims themselves and even when found among non-Muslims.' Although this eminent scholar made a compelling argument for the need to coin new terminology to deal with the history of 'Islamdom,' older prejudices continue to determine the questions asked by, and consequently the outcomes of, scholarship on Islam."

But just *how* do "older prejudices continue to determine the questions asked by, and consequently the outcomes of, scholarship on Islam"? One has to assess the reception of Hodgson in both the United Kingdom and the United States. Some ignore him, others read him selectively, still others have tried to refute him. The British historian Frances Robinson engages with Hodgson's ideas but not his terminology or frame of argument. He gives full credit to Hodgson for the inspiration and the goad to produce his own *Atlas of the Islamic World since 1500*.[1] A luxuriant coffee-table text, with more maps than Hodgson and also abundant, evocative pictures, it is dedicated to just the modern period, since 1500. While Robinson's *Atlas* sketches the major themes of political, economic, and religious history that define Islam in relation to the West, Islam remains outside the West, the "other" confronting yet also defining the West.

The American historian Ira Lapidus is similarly indebted to Hodgson. Not only does he reproduce maps from *The Venture of Islam* but he also echoes many of Hodgson's perspectives in his extensive work, *A History of Islamic Societies* (1988). Reducing the three-volume *Venture of Islam* (over 1,600 pages) to one volume (a "mere" 1,002 pages) is itself an advantage, yet Lapidus goes further. He also telescopes the history of Islam into three phases: Islamic emergence, or the emergence of what he calls Islamic mass societies; the long period of diffusion, including the growth of the major empires; and, most recently, the period of European dominance, relative economic decline, and also postcolonial nationalisms. Lapidus is not so much Hodgson-lite as an alternative way of understanding contemporary Islam, mainly as an urban-oriented cultural phenomenon with broad, often-unintended political and social consequences.

While both Robinson and Lapidus applaud without embracing Hodgson, some British scholars openly oppose Hodgson. Christopher Bayly of Cambridge, in his 2013 Humanitas lectures at Oxford now available as a podcast, critiqued Hodgson for his persistent Teutonic essentialism and his clandestine Third

Worldism.[2] Bayly argued that Hodgson tried to disguise his own marginal pursuits (he was a vegetarian as well as a pacifist) and to substitute Islam/Islamic world for Third World. Bayly alleged that Hodgson used Muslim persons and cases, along with Islam-specific arguments, in order to buttress his countercapitalist, quasi-socialist appeal as a world historian.

Bayly's view has been challenged, even within British academia. Faisal Devji of Oxford was invited to give the rejoinder to Bayly. Devji applauded Hodgson's effort to insinuate Islam between Europe and India, forging a new model of hemispheric history. In particular, he called attention to Hodgson as a moralist on the margins. Since Hodgson wrote but one short monograph, *The Secret Order of Assassins* (1955), speculated Devji, was not that work in some sense the weathervane for *The Venture of Islam*, itself a didactic project turned into a multivolume book? While Devji overstates the Persianate themes in volume 3, heavily edited after Hodgson's death, he still sees the big frame and the moral thrust of Hodgson's labor, a refreshing contrast to the narrow diatribes that mark Bayly's intervention.

What above all characterized Hodgson was openness about scholarly precommitments and the continuous, unending need to exercise self-criticism. To cite Huricihan Islamoglu once more, what distinguished Hodgson from his colleagues at the University of Chicago and elsewhere in American academia was his "unconstrained openness about himself, his ambivalences, and his strife. He was a man trying to discover or actualize himself as a man of Enlightenment (not *the* Enlightenment), a Westerner with all its contradictions. Not constrained by Quakerism or by narrowly defined leftism, he strove to re-cast himself as a universal man with a moral position. It is that quest that permeates Hodgson's life as also his work."

And now more than forty years after Hodgson, we are witnessing an uptick in the scholarly use of "Islamicate." Some recent publications have noted the robust resilience of Islamicate as a qualifier for premodern cultural/intellectual engagement across creedal, sectarian, or linguistic borders in Afro-Eurasia. From E. J. Brill in Leiden there is a new journal, *Intellectual History of the Islamicate World* (since 2013), while another academic collective with inclusive links to all periods and perspectives of world history has launched a website, Society for Contemporary Thought and the Islamicate World (since 2010), with both a book review and debate forum.

Hodgson's relevance to the twenty-first century can only be secured through the classroom, and it is over the value of his magnum opus as a teaching text that even the most rigorous and dedicated Islamic studies scholars remain divided. On the cusp of the new millennium Brannon Wheeler, another graduate of the University of Chicago, organized a conference to look at the process of what became the title for his edited book: *Teaching Islam* (2003). Asked to participate, I had to confess:

> I am the first to admit that communicating Persianate and Islamicate nuances to undergraduates is a challenge. One can duck it, but at the risk of oversimplification and reversion to stereotypes. One can take it up, but only with judicious use of sources that have appeared since Hodgson's *The Venture of Islam*. One might best begin by assigning the *Encyclopaedia Britannica (EB)* instead of the original text. It was an accomplished historian of premodern Afro-Asian Islam, Marilyn Waldman, who penned the *EB* entry "The Islamic World." Waldman builds on the work of her own teacher, who was none other than Marshall Hodgson. Like the inventor of Islamicate and Persianate accents, Waldman tries to make sense of the actual stages of shift within Islamicate civilization. Her prose not only mirrors Hodgson's but also simplifies and streamlines some of his major theses.

Over a decade later I still rely on Waldman. It was from her essay that I quoted at the beginning of this essay, and it is to her that belongs the credit for evoking the core themes, as also the salient neologisms, without reproducing all the arguments or ambiguities of the original three volumes published in 1974.

Waldman, like Hodgson, accounts for space, the known world at different moments in time. There are real junctures, defined by multiple forces and also compelling individuals, as well as novel structures. The major areas coalesce as the Afro-Asian *oikumene*, or in a nod to the ascent of Europe, the Afro-Eurasian *oikumene*. For the emergence of Islam, there are two crucial forces: the Iranian and Hebrew languages. Hence one needs the term Irano-Semitic, as also later Perso-Arabic. In effect, one cannot think of either Judaism or Islam without Iran. It is another vector, at once competing with and complementing its neighbors. Seamlessly yet effectively, Waldman weaves this distinction along with others into the artful narrative of her *Encyclopaedia Britannica* epitome of *The Venture of Islam*. Alas, however, because Waldman's essay, with the Zeghal codicil, is available only through *Encyclopaedia Britannica*, it has not received the broad attention it and Hodgson's vision merit.

The briefest and most poignant estimate of Hodgson's legacy must be his impact on the general public. Since 9/11, but arguably since the 1979 Iranian Revolution, we have endured the popular, media-stoked cry from the far right about the evil of Islam. While it has echoes in America, as in the recent flap about Bill

Maher's critique of Islam, it is from Europe that we find the strongest fires fanning the notion that Muslims don't fit in, and don't belong in, Western societies.

It was early summer 2014. I had visited Al-Jazeera's website for headline stories. One was entitled "On Anti-Semitism and Islamophobia in Europe." The story's author, a British sociologist with no political or ethnic axe to grind, starkly noted: "Though immigrants in general are singled out as a social and economic threat to European societies and workers, it is Muslims in particular who have come to epitomize the 'bad other.' This has been achieved not only through the xenophobic propaganda of the far right. Actually, conservatives and even liberal and left-wing parties have contributed to the fanfare."

Muslims as "the bad other"—it was Hodgson's nightmare, but it has become daily fare in twenty-first-century Euro-America. It does not matter whether Sara Harris, the author of the Al-Jazeera essay, is right or wrong in her assessment. From the deep perspective of the Axial Age, Muslims, like Jews, as also Christians and every other human community, will be vindicated by what they have done, not vilified by what has been done to them. Still, in the short term the headlines make it very difficult to turn from immediate crises that fuel the popular media to calmer assessments—at once more productive and more predictive—of historical change. That is why Hodgson is both so necessary and so perilous as a catalyst for our twenty-first-century engagement with Islam.

And so one must conclude that for the general public, we find a focus so obsessively honed on the perceived clash of civilizations and the ongoing war on terror that the subtleties of Hodgson are not just masked but also erased in shrill debates about Islamophobia/Islamophilia. Scholars are partly at fault for this flattening focus. Though unintentionally, Edward Said's *Orientalism* has impeded Hodgson's vision. Said's elegantly crafted 1978 manifesto reviewed and critiqued Orientalist scholars for their disguised political intent. He heaped scorn on Hodgson's dissertation director, Gustave von Grunebaum, an Austrian refugee of Nazi Germany, who taught at Chicago in the early 1950s before later moving to Los Angeles and founding the Near East Studies Center named after him at UCLA. Hodgson, however, is absent from the pages of *Orientalism*. He differed as much from von Grunebaum as he did from his Chicago colleagues. He was in a real sense a pre-Orientalist, post-Orientalist, but because he died before finishing his major book, the storm of protest, like the fawning praise, over *Orientalism* highlighted Said's approach rather than Hodgson's counter-approach. Even though he raised issues about scholarly pre-commitment long before Said's book appeared on the cusp of the Iranian Revolution, or self-doubt began to pervade American academia, Hodgson's contribution to a broader, more constructive view of Islam across time and space was occluded, first by the *Orientalism* debate in the 1980s and 1990s, and then by the war on terror from 2001 until now.

Generational change in tastes also cannot be ignored. To the extent that Hodgson's legacy has been reduced, it is not just because of his too-capacious historical vision or his choice of tongue-twisting key terms; it is also because the public at large can no longer see nuance within Islam, or Islam as nuanced within world history, to the degree that was possible for Hodgson back in the mid-1960s. Yes, those were terrible times for America: the Cold War, the Vietnam War, the grinding poverty of many, and the turmoil of the civil rights movement. But there was room for a moral vision, one that Hodgson provided and one that still beckons.

Notes

Bruce B. Lawrence, "Genius Denied and Reclaimed: Hodgson's *The Venture of Islam*," *Los Angeles Review of Books*, November 11, 2014, 4. Used by permission.

1   Francis Robinson, *Atlas of the Islamic World since 1500* (Oxford: Phaidon, 1982).
2   Christopher Bayly, Humanitas lectures, May 28, 2013, http://podcasts.ox.ac.uk/marshall-g-s-hodgson-islam-and-world-history. Bayly later revised his estimate of Hodgson's labor and legacy, producing a longer, more balanced assessment in Christopher A. Bayly, "Hodgson, Islam, and World History in the Modern Age" in *Islam and World History: The Ventures of Marshall Hodgson*, edited by Edmund Burke III and Robert J. Mankin (Chicago: University of Chicago Press, 2018), 38–52.

PART II

Revaluing Muslim Comparativists

In Islamicate civilization and thought, the urge to compare religious and social truths is driven by the desire to find instructive lessons. These lessons can be derived from rational thinking, critical observation, and historical inquiry, but at stake in every instance is the motivation and the goal of comparison. This section revisits Bruce Lawrence's wide-ranging essays on four major Muslim thinkers who were also comparativists: the Persian polymath Biruni, the Persian theologian Shahrastani, the North African jurist Ibn Khaldun, and the Indian archivist-turned-educator Sir Sayyid Ahmad Khan. The selections in part II furnish the reader with insights into how past Muslim thinkers pioneered the spirit of cross-cultural observation and analysis, shedding light on their use of comparative thinking to arrive at clearer understandings of self, society, and cosmos.

All four scholars straddled a cosmopolitan and multilingual world. Biruni and Shahrastani spoke Persian but made their major contributions in Arabic, Ibn Khaldun spoke and wrote in Arabic but extolled the scientific contributions of the Persians, while Sayyid Ahmad Khan brought to the Urdu language the intellectual riches of the Arabo-Persian knowledge base and Anglophone philosophical and historical traditions. Two of them—Biruni and Ibn Khaldun—are credited with having invented new disciplines: the former, "comparative religion"; the latter, "comparative sociology." Yet all these men excelled not in inventing new fields of study but in reorganizing extant disciplines by comparing knowledge across time and traditions. Ibn Khaldun and Sayyid Ahmad Khan, for instance, were particularly interested in observing and theorizing patterns of social action. Instead of evaluating the Other, they aimed to connect to and engage with other traditions, texts, and norms.

The first selection, "Al-Biruni: Against the Grain" (2014), is a popular essay written for the monthly thematic journal *Critical Muslim*, in a special issue dedicated to "dangerous free thinkers." We start with Biruni and not his more influential and renowned contemporary Ibn Sina, even though they shared common backgrounds: both men were Persian, both were supported by Muslim monarchs, and both expressed their dissent from regnant authorities even while remaining loyal and respectful to their patrons. Biruni's distinguishing mark is a capacity to seek the empirical basis for every form of knowledge. One arena in which he pursued this quest was comparing Muslims to Jews and Christians but also to Greeks and Romans. He was totally original in comparing Muslims to Hindus, but he went further, putting Indian elites on the same level as their Greek predecessors and Muslim contemporaries. Biruni was a scientist *and* a historian of science who pursued varied experimental work. He observed with a keen eye, cataloging and comparing both species of life and societies of human organization. He applied this nuanced method to the study of Indic traditions and Hindu beliefs.

A century later, Shahrastani returned to India, not with Biruni's observational eye but with the concerns of a theologian. As Lawrence notes in "Shahrastani on Indian Idol Worship" (1973), Shahrastani compared Muslim and Hindu beliefs from the vantage points of cosmology, ontology, and theology. He sympathized with the worshippers of Vishnu and Shiva; he respected all who identified with the Hindu tradition for their exploration of the Truth. Like Biruni, he was interested in the Greeks, but also in Manicheans and other pre-Islamic religionists, chief among them the Sabians. The latter people inhabited present-day Iraq. Mentioned in the Qur'an, the Sabians searched for the Truth on two planes: the planetary and the transcendental. They believed that prophets existed, related to yet distinct from angels. The Sabians posed a challenge for Shahrastani as a Muslim theologian: though he had to accept the legitimacy of their explorations, he also argued that the coming of Islam superseded them. Nowhere is Shahrastani's generosity of spirit more visible than in his approach to idolatry: while he acknowledges the practice of idol worship as derogatory, he praises those Indians who worship spiritual beings in material forms, distinguishing them from other Indians who are idolaters (*'abadat al-asnam*) because they limit spirit to its visual embodiment. Biruni inspired no school and no comparativist successor: few Muslims engaged Indic traditions at the level of careful inquiry modeled by either Biruni or Shahrastani until the ill-fated Mughal prince Dara Shikoh in the seventeenth century.

The third selection is Lawrence's introduction to Ibn Khaldun's *Muqaddimah* (2005/2015). Ibn Khaldun comes from the western rather than the eastern realm of Islamic civilization, but like his eastern precursors, he conceptually straddles many binaries: the premodern and the modern, the urban and the rural, the literary and the oral. Though Ibn Khaldun's training was in Islamic law, he expanded beyond jurisprudence to view the entire world through an empirical model of hierarchy. This wide view of human civilization upholds that no group in history can be described without recourse to their self-understanding. Ibn Khaldun compared multiple frames of reference to history, moving beyond the mere narration of events, scriptural rhetoric, or anecdotal reports. Tirelessly he searched to identify and examine societal processes, encapsulated in the dyads of urban/rural and written/oral. He linked the civilizing process to urban culture, crafts, and the written word, at the same time that he identified in rural and nomadic life the origins of group solidarity (ʿ*asabiyya*) and pointed to the conqueror Tamerlane as the embodiment of ʿ*asabiyya*.

What links Ibn Khaldun to our final comparativist, Sayyid Ahmad Khan, is their mutual focus on teaching and institutional life in its broadest arc. Both men were committed to shaping and reshaping powerful ideas by interacting with like-minded compatriots. Their insights, creatively framed and rigorously honed, in turn gave coherence and viability to urban institutions and their supporters.

Sayyid Ahmad Khan's context was continuous with his predecessors yet wholly original. As Lawrence demonstrates in his essay "Mystical and Rational Elements in the Early Religious Writings of Sir Sayyid Ahmad Khan" (1979), Khan was both modern and colonial in outlook. Trained as an archivist at the height of British rule, he became the most influential educator of Muslims in Hindustan (as precolonial India was popularly known). Instead of rejecting the British, he co-opted their methods and resources. He compared traditional (Eastern) and modern (Western) forms of knowledge, arguing that both approaches had things to learn from each other. Unlike his comparativist precursors, he pioneered social institutions and launched his own university to perpetuate his ideals: he founded in Aligarh the Mohammedan Anglo-Oriental College, the mere name of which speaks to his varied commitments to Islamic education, modern British learning within an Indic/Oriental environment. Aligarh, or AMU, as it was known, became the key site of Muslim education for late colonial India.

It promoted the previously unimagined, combining under one roof a school of Islamic theology with an initiative devoted to translating scientific works from English to Urdu. Neither a systematic thinker like Ibn Khaldun, nor an empirical scientist like Biruni, Sayyid Ahmad Khan was instead oriented to thinking about religious topics in a modern idiom albeit one firmly rooted in India. His Indic context demanded a serious consideration of Sufism or "Islamic mysticism." He addressed Sufism only in his early work, yet its influence permeated his entire life. The Sufis to whom he was attracted were pioneering reformers: while they saw the limits of institutional Sufism, they also saw its benefits. Those mystical exemplars with whom Sir Sayyid became most closely linked belonged to the Naqshbandi order, a Sufi fellowship rooted in Central Asia that became the lodestone for Muslim reform movements in the subcontinent during the late Mughal and early modern period of Indian history.

FIVE

Al-Biruni: Against the Grain | 2014

Abu Rayhan Muhammad ibn Ahmad Al-Biruni liked school. No, he loved school. The challenge to read and recite, to count and to calculate was fun, but the real sport was to contest the ideas of others, to engage their motives and call into question their goals. A Muslim, he was also a Persian. And the Persian gene—some would call it "genius"—was to argue, to debate, to advance through active exchange with the ideas of thoughtful others. Not everyone in his community was born thoughtful. Some never went to school. Some went to school and only memorized or repeated what others told them. He only did battle with equals, but he never ceased to find even his equals lacking.

Biruni was privileged to have a private tutor from a very early age. Born in 973, in the outskirts of Khwarizm (hence the name Al-Biruni, the outsider, or suburban), he may have lost one or both parents when he was very young. As a result, his academic tutor, Abu Nasr al-Mansur, also became his familial mentor. He made certain that Biruni learned all the basics of scientific inquiry in Arabic, and literary inquiry mostly in Persian. Abu Nasr also made it possible for his young protégé to undertake experiments on his own.

Biruni was impatient. A devout Muslim, he was also a skeptic about all received forms of knowledge. He was restless to know what the Author of the universe meant by the array of systems within the great system called the cosmos. He learned about distances, and loved geography. He excelled in mathematics, and delved into physics. He examined rocks and found their study, known as mineralogy, a constant fascination. He wondered about the nature of the earth and its component elements, their size, shapes, and subfields, anticipating geodesy. Thinking about medicine, he explored the use, or misuse, of plants and their extracts for cures; he excelled in pharmacology. But above all, he looked to the stars, to their relationships, their movements, their influences, and so he delved deeply into astronomy.

Biruni made his first independent astronomical observations when he was eighteen years of age, in 991. But he did not continue to work independently, or without interference. Though he had already developed strong views by the age of twenty, and even engaged in correspondence with an older Persian scholar, Ibn Sina, while still in his twenties, he had no job security. It was a politically turbulent period of Iranian history. He found himself compelled to leave his native home of Khwarizm. For a brief time, he secured patronage with the Samanids, then rulers of Bukhara, but after they were conquered, he settled in another Central Asian court for perhaps a decade before it too fell to hostile forces during 1000. It was the Turkish ruler Mahmud of Ghazna (971–1030) who captured the capital of Biruni's patron. His prize: to take hostage all the scholars of the defeated monarch and to employ them in his own expanded court.

Well, not quite all. There is a famous anecdote that depicts the defining moment of conquest and capture with a notable twist. Jealous of the splendor of his rival's court circle, Sultan Mahmud sent him an ultimatum demanding that all the leading scholars there be sent forthwith to Ghazna in order to adorn his own court. The story goes on to tell how the philosopher Ibn Sina escaped to the west, serving in the court of a western Persian monarch, the Kakuyid ʿAla al-Dawla Muhammad in Isfahan, till his death there in 1037. But Biruni, along with others, went to Ghazna and entered Mahmud's service. Biruni then spent the remainder of his life, what must have been well over three decades, on the borders of India in present-day Afghanistan, first with Mahmud, and then with his successors, notably Masʿud and Mawdud, till his own death in 1050.

None of these activities would have made Biruni a freethinker. He could have been, and was labeled, a great scientist. He was perhaps unique in his time in being a polymath. As one scholar noted, there were numerous notable Muslim scholars who were also exemplary scientists. In the eleventh century two stood out: Ibn Sina (980–1037) and Biruni. Yet Biruni surpassed Ibn Sina in both the breadth and catholicity of his skeptical erudition in the fields of history and chronology, mathematics, astronomy, geography, pharmacology, mineralogy, history of religions, and Indology.

It is Biruni the precocious student who let his curiosity and intelligence take him down many paths and whom we can justifiably describe as a freethinker. He challenged not just his scientific predecessors but also his foremost contemporary scientific colleague, Ibn Sina. Ibn Sina needs no introduction. He is, as Ahmad Dallal observed, "the greatest and most influential Aristotelian philosopher in Islamic history." But Biruni was his superior not just in the breadth of his knowledge but in the depth of his inquiry into the presuppositions of astronomy. Biruni challenges Aristotelian cosmology. The mathematical astronomer, in his view, is not bound to any prior system. He must view the evidence with as much openness to observation as his instruments and his knowledge permit. Because Ibn Sina had commented on the material nature of the universe, Biruni initiated a correspondence with him. He put forth a number of questions that critique the presuppositions of Aristotelian physics. Bluntly, but also politely, he asked Ibn Sina to respond to these questions, in effect, to justify his own predilection for, and reliance on, Aristotle.

Fascinated with the astrolabe, an instrument on which he relied and whose use he perfected, Biruni noted that one could pursue mathematical astronomy from either a geocentric or heliocentric perspective. It is not a matter of philosophical certainty but of experimental openness that is at stake. Like many scientists of his time, Biruni thought not only that the cosmos was shaped like a sphere and was made up of different regions but also that the earth was at the center of the solar system. Yet he was also aware of the probability—though not the absolute certainty—of a sun-centered system. Instead of arguing for either theory, he, unlike Ibn Sina, saw the scientific, psychological, and cultural importance of both models. Indeed, one cannot understate the radical nature of Biruni's challenge to Ibn Sina and so to Aristotle. Once it is possible to prove that some part of Aristotelian natural philosophy does not fit all the evidence, the entire system becomes suspect, its formulations unhinged. The stars and planets, that is, the heavenly bodies, are the subject on which Biruni begins his set of queries to Ibn Sina. Some may sound obscure or overly technical to a nonscientist. For example: How do you explore and explain weight in space? How do you determine whether or not heavenly spheres are heavy or light? But one issue is germane to all physical and metaphysical reflection: Are there other worlds than the cosmos as we know it from mathematical astronomy? For Aristotle, as for Ibn Sina, the answer was no. For Biruni, the answer was maybe. Though we cannot prove the existence of other worlds, neither can we disprove their existence, he argued.

As fascinating as the correspondence and the debate between Ibn Sina and Biruni—equivalent to the exchange between Einstein and Bergson on the theory of relativity or Einstein and Heisenberg on the uncertainty principle—are, they underscore how professional specialization was already an issue in the eleventh century. Ibn Sina, in trying to counter/refute the arguments of Biruni, often refers to his lack of knowledge in the mathematical sciences, where Biruni is expert, at the same time that he suggests Biruni does not have the credentials to venture into his field, which is natural philosophy. Biruni did not back down. As Dallal has acutely noted, "He refused to concede the intellectual authority of systems of knowledge outside his own system."

It would be hard to summarize his multiple accomplishments in the sciences. One writer has astutely observed that because he saw nature as a harmonious, self-regulating system, Biruni applied his philosophical observations of the world to his scientific studies of natural phenomena. But he did more than that. He used his powers of observation to describe the details of his environment, including birds, plants, minerals, and animals. While some of his theories about nature have been since disproved by modern biology, Biruni's studies of the natural world display his acute, unwavering reliance on empirical observations of natural phenomena.

Biruni was so successful in applying mathematics to his study of geography and the natural world that some consider him to be the founder of geodesy, the science of measuring the size and shape of the earth, mapping points on its surface, and studying its gravitational field. In *The Book on Astrolabe*, he considers how one can determine the circumference of the earth using geometry. His method involves climbing a mountain and using the horizon and the height of the mountain to create an equation. He attempted on different occasions to test this method, and used it successfully while traveling in India; his results do not differ significantly from those determined using modern methods.

As he did with his mountain experiment, Biruni sought to test many of his ideas with close observation, relentless logic, and repeated experimentation. In studying gems, for instance, Biruni used mathematics to arrive at the density of minerals. He began by using the weights of gold and the Oriental sapphire as a base for a variety of metals and gems. Through careful experimentation based on the displacement of water by the mineral substances, he was able to calculate the density of various minerals quite accurately.

A similar, radical empiricism characterized his study of geography. Biruni began with the ancient precept that the earth was divided into seven climatic zones. This idea was common to the Islamic world as well as in Greek, Zoroastrian, and ancient Babylonian beliefs, but Biruni was particularly concerned with understanding why certain portions of the earth were what he labeled "uninhabitable," while others were centers of civilization and agriculture. His study of the earth's surface reflects both his work in astrology and his belief that the world exists according to a harmonious design.

There are few areas of the geographical sciences that Biruni did not explore. In addition to human geography, he analyzed the weather, the climate, and landscape history. He took precise measurements of and mapped coordinates on the earth's surface. He also contributed knowledge about the effect of physical features such as rivers on the shaping of the landscape, and on the patterns of the monsoon in bringing rain to India. He developed an understanding of variations in the transference of the sun's energy to the earth at different times of the year. Among his most important contributions to the study of the earth's physical features are theories about erosion and landform creation, conclusions about the force of gravity, the argument that the speed of light is faster than that of sound, discussions of the movement of the sun and the earth, and botanical observations.

Biruni's understanding of the plants and animals inhabiting different parts of the earth later helped him to build knowledge of the pharmacological properties of certain species. One of his most well-known works on pharmacology is the *Kitab al-Saydanah*. It is a lengthy text, bringing together a variety of information relating to medicine. The book provides information on drugs and other forms of therapy, including lists of medicinal herbs and their names in a number of languages. Much of the book reflects Biruni's interest in language and how the names of each drug were derived.

Biruni used both mathematics and visual observations of the heavens to study the universe. Among his accomplishments in astronomy were the calculation of the sizes of the planets and their orbits. He arrived at these figures using a Ptolemaic principle concerning the ratios of planetary distances. He also tried to explain planetary motion, planetary and solar positions, and the phenomenon of the equinox.

As a mathematician, Biruni translated the Hindu methods of mathematical notation. His abilities in geometry led to the term "albirunic problems," used to refer to the most difficult geometry problems of his time. He was able to create an accurate method for measuring latitude and longitude, and knew the trigonometric function of the law of sines. Working from Ptolemy's theory of the sine table, Biruni discovered a more direct way to derive basic trigonometric formulas, and he succeeded in solving complex geometry problems, including the trisection of the angle. Much of his work in geometry and trigonometry involves theorems dealing with the chords in circles.

But Biruni's achievements in science only provide us with a limited understanding of his insatiable, free-ranging mind. What bedevils us in exploring, revisiting, and then reevaluating Biruni is the wreckage of time. Specifically, of the many, many books he wrote, only a very few have survived. We actually know how limited is our legacy of the preserved writings of Biruni from Biruni himself. In his autumn years, when he was perhaps sixty-two to sixty-three years of age, during 1035–36, Biruni catalogued both his own works and those of Razi. At the urging of a friend, he compiled an *Epistle* concerning a list of the books of Muhammad b. Zakariya al-Razi (d. 932). This consists of two parts. While the first is devoted to Razi and his works, the second provides Biruni's inventory of the books that he himself had authored up to that time. This sort of bibliographical treatment of an individual is modeled on those produced by Galen in antiquity and by the Syriac Christian scholar Hunayn ibn Ishaq in the ninth century. Razi was (in)famous in his own circle as a freethinker, so much that Ibn Sina, when struggling to refute Biruni in his correspondence, at one point opines that Biruni's objection to Aristotle must have been second hand, taken "either from John the Grammarian, who wanted to mislead Christians by pretending that he disagrees with Aristotle... or from Muhammad b. Zakariya al-Razi, whose pretensions in meddling with metaphysics made him overestimate his abilities, which were limited to dressing wounds and testing urine and feces."

The actual catalog of Razi's works, however, suggests that, pace Ibn Sina, he did more than toilet sampling. In Biruni's estimate, there are no less than 184 titles divided into eleven categories: medicine; natural science; logic; mathematics and astronomy; commentaries, synopses, and extracts; philosophy and assessment; metaphysics; theology; alchemy; heretical; and miscellaneous. After it, Biruni presents a chronological table of Greek physicians from Asclepius to Galen followed by brief notes on the history of medicine that relate it to the labor of his scientific predecessor, al-Razi.

In comparison, Biruni's catalog of his own literary production up to his sixty-third year, that is 1036, lists a mere 103 titles. They are divided into twelve categories: astronomy, mathematical geography, mathematics, astrological aspects and transits, astronomical instruments, chronology, comets, an untitled category, astrology, anecdotes, religion, and books of which he no longer possesses copies. After an account of the astrologers' predictions of the length of his life and of a dream he had a couple of years earlier, he adds ten more titles of his own works followed by twenty-five of those written in his name by other scholars. His own works, he says, he regards as his sons, and so also holds the same regard for those that were written in his name! We now know that Biruni composed at least 155 works. Some he wrote after he had finished his bibliography, others he simply forgot to include in it. But alas, perhaps five-sixths of the total number of 155 treatises are now irretrievably lost.

Of those that survived, two in particular demonstrate how radical a freethinker Biruni was, not only in his own epoch, but also across the ages, in all the annals of Islamic history extending to culture and religion as well as mathematics and astronomy. The first is *The Chronology of Ancient Nations*. The second is *Alberuni's India*.

The Chronology of Ancient Nations is interesting because it appeared so early in his career, when he was about twenty-seven years old, in 1000. It is peppered with charts, graphs, and tables, but also interlinear descriptions of major non-Muslim religious groups whom he had observed in his day. Biruni never hesitates to compare non-Muslims with their Muslim counterparts. For instance, in his account of the life of Zoroaster, he discusses at length the eschatological expectations that Zoroastrian and Muslim sects attached to the 1,500th anniversary of the appearance of the Iranian prophet. Particularly valuable is his detailed description of the Zoroastrian feasts, which contains much information on Zoroastrian beliefs, as well as on popular Persian superstitions of his day. And he shows deep respect for Mani, even while disagreeing with Manichaean dualism, not least for what he considers its lack of scientific verification. He even uses a Manichaean scripture to correct the chronology of the Arsacid kings, going out of his way to emphasize Mani's reliability: "Mani is one of those who teach that the telling of lies is forbidden; besides he had no need to falsify history." A fierce scavenger of primary sources, he found and used Arabic translations of the Old and New Testaments, but also other Jewish and Christian writings little known even within their own traditions. He devotes much space in *Chronology* to a description and critique of the Jewish calendar, concerning which his is apparently the oldest surviving source of any substance. Similarly, in his description of the celebrations of the Melkite (Greek Orthodox) Christians, he gives valuable bits of information about the Christians of eastern Iran, apparently supplied by Christian informants. When he cannot find informants, he apologizes for what he cannot say. Concerning the rites of Jacobite Christians, for instance, he is silent because "we have not succeeded in finding anyone who belonged to their sect or knew their principles."

As a scientific researcher and ethnographic observer, Biruni moves to a new level of sophistication when he undertakes to write about India. Had he followed Ibn Sina and gone to western Iran, or had his royal patron offered him less freedom than he had with the restless but hands-off Sultan Mahmud of Ghazna, he might never have explored India, learned Sanskrit, and delved into matters relating to the Indic/Hindu tradition. He first translated some major texts, with assistance from scribes/informants captured by Mahmud during his plunders of Gujarat and Rajasthan. They included Samkhya texts and the *Yogasutras* of Patañjali. Biruni was aware of both the novelty and the precariousness of this undertaking:

> Such is the state of things in India [he observes] that I found it very hard to work my way into the subject, although I have a great liking for it, in which respect I stand quite alone in my time, and although I do not spare either time or money in collecting Sanskrit books from places where I supposed they were likely to be found, and in procuring for myself, even from very remote places, Hindu scholars who understand them, and are able to teach me. What scholar, however, has the same favorable opportunities for studying this subject as I have? That would only be the case with one to whom the grace of God accords what it did not accord to me, a perfectly free disposal of his own doings and goings; for it has never fallen to my lot in my own doings and goings to be perfectly independent, nor to be invested with sufficient power to dispose and to order as I thought best. However, I thank God for that which he has bestowed upon me, and which must be considered as sufficient for the purpose.

It was sufficient to make Biruni not just the first but the unrivaled Muslim observer, commentator, and analyst of Hindu belief, thought, and practice. Composed around 1030, while Biruni was at the height of his analytical powers, the *India* represents both a distillation and an extension of what had been broached in his earlier translation of the Yogasutras of Patañjali, *Kitab Batanjal*: to classify and evaluate the major categories of Hindu philosophy and religion. Nearly two-thirds of the *India* (forty-eight of eighty chapters) reviews the achievement of Indian science in several fields. The *India* not only communicates but also evaluates the full range of Hindu thought and ritual. The initial twelve chapters provide a magisterial overview of Hindu notions of God, creation, metempsychosis (the passing of the soul at death into another body either human or animal), salvation, and idolatry. The Hindu approach to God, creation, and salvation is generously commended, bearing favorable comparison to reflections that emerged from ancient Greece and classical Islam. The same is not true for metempsychosis. While noting some parallels between it and the teachings of both Greek philosophers and Sufi masters, Biruni stresses the disjuncture between such notions and normative Muslim belief. He himself has memorialized the disjuncture by his oft-quoted remark: *al-tanasukh ʿilm al-nihla al-hindawiya* (metempsychosis is the password of Hindu belief). Nor is

Biruni sympathetic to idol worship. He portrays it as class-specific, being the indulgence of uneducated, superstitious masses, rather than the preference of those literate Brahmins with whom he himself was in frequent contact.

It is in chapter seven of the *India* that we find Biruni's longest and best-documented assessment of Hindu beliefs. If he is to be classed as a radical freethinker, it is perhaps at this moment of engaging the heart of Hindu metaphysical reflection with other traditions that he excels as a critical comparativist. He examines in detail the three paths to liberation, and in so doing, signals his preference for the teachings of Patañjali over the directives of other Indian scriptures, including the *Bhagavadgita*. The contest is framed by the discipline of devotion (*bhakti-yoga*) and the pursuit of knowledge (*jñana-yoga*). On the one hand, Biruni draws extensive attention to *bhakti-yoga*, especially in depicting ethical norms and drawing on parallel notions from the Sufi tradition. Many of the most extensive quotations illustrating the threefold path to liberation derive from the *Bhagavadgita*. On the other hand, however, the schematization of these paths and the topical sentences for each are directly quoted or paraphrased from *Kitāb Batanjal*. It is to *jñana-yoga* that Biruni draws attention time and again. Salvation in his view is inseparable from self-cognition; in its most direct form, "it is the return of the soul as a knowing being into its own nature," or as he states in the *India*, "the soul distinguishes between things by defining them and so grasps its own essence (*'aqalat dhataha*)."

If Biruni seems to be an inadvertent theologian in the early chapters of the *India*, in the later chapters he assumes the role of a premodern anthropologist. Ten of the last seventeen chapters in the *India* address ritual practices, principally initiation and funerary ceremonies but also obligatory sacrifices and dietary rules, together with fasting, pilgrimage, and festival observances. Textual evidence is constantly checked off against the declarations of personal informants, nowhere more tellingly than in chapter 71. Biruni begins by chronicling the mythical separation of scholars and warriors. The innate merit of the former failed because most Hindus, like most people elsewhere, were not philosophers, and so philosophers could not rule. Warriors filled the power vacuum. Becoming kings, they proved to be perverse purveyors of power: they exempted Brahmins from the death penalty but exempted themselves from the penalty of being blinded for theft. Hindu prisoners of war suffered the worst fate, however. According to canonical law (the *dharmashastras*), such prisoners could only achieve expiation by an elaborate rite requiring them to ingest *pancagavya*, the five products linked to the cow. While that requirement in itself seems extreme, even it is not adequate according to Biruni's Brahmin informants. In their view, no expiation is possible for Hindu prisoners of war who return to India: they are never allowed to resume their former status.

Throughout the final chapters of the *India*, Biruni continues to display his penchant for comparing and evaluating. While he tries to offer his readers a compendium of Hindu religious lore, as he read, heard about, and observed it, he also hopes to appropriate the "higher" truth of Indian philosophy, bracketing it with the Hellenistic corpus and integrating both into the worldview of educated Muslims. He cares little for the uneducated—whether Muslim or Hindu—and so the final chapters of the *India* that are devoted to Hindu rituals appear as a kind of ethnographic afterthought. They lend an air of completeness to his massive tome without, however, burnishing his own credentials as a scientific explorer or achieving his primary goal: to pursue the Truth. In the final analysis, Biruni is better classified as an anthropological philosopher than a philosophical anthropologist.

Yet Biruni, the maverick thinker and dogged scientist, stands at the apex of Islamic scholarship on non-Muslim religious traditions. After him no one followed his lead as a dispassionate inquirer into the subtleties of Hindu thought until the late medieval–early modern period of Indo-Muslim history. It remained for nineteenth-century European scholars to spark an interest in further study along the lines he had initiated, among both educated Muslims and also Western scholars of Islam.

Note

Bruce B. Lawrence, "Al-Biruni: Against the Grain," *Critical Muslim* 12 (2014): 61–71. Used by permission. *Editor's Note: On the larger trajectory of Biruni's historical reception, see George Malagaris, Biruni (Oxford: Oxford University Press, 2019).*

SIX

Shahrastani on Indian Idol Worship | 1973

Historically the presence of Islam in the Indian subcontinent is often viewed as an exemplification of political hegemony eliciting, if not requiring, religious conversion. In particular, Mahmud of Ghazna (fl. 997–1030 AD) qualifies as the prototype of the military conqueror cum administrator who destroys that which he does not understand (e.g., the idol at Somnath) and imposes his will on a reluctant populace.

Since Muslim rule in India began by force of arms and was extended as well as perpetuated for over seven hundred years principally by force of arms, it is not surprising that Muslim perceptions of Indians were initially and persistently shaped by the recognition of Muslim military superiority and political dominance.[1] Even the Sufi orders, often cited as a counterpoint to Mahmud's iconoclasm, had access to Bihar and Bengal through the passageway provided by Muslim victories on the battlefield.[2]

The imperialist tone of Muslim rule in India has impelled students of interreligious relations to look at the period prior to the Ghaznavids and Ghorids in searching for clues to the initial Muslim perceptions of Hinduism. Yet apart from the work of Biruni, to be discussed shortly, there is a dearth of substantive information about indigenous religious beliefs and practices in the earliest Muslim writings pertaining to India. Arab/Persian geographical works contain a trickle of data about Indian places of worship, while the ʿajāʾib literature dwells on the bizarre and magical element in Indian religion.[3] The normative character of the major sectarian movements, that is, Vaisnavism and Saivism, is neglected until the appearance of encyclopedic writings and topical catalogs. Gardizi's *Zayn al-akhbar*, Marvazi's *Taba'i al-hayawan*, Maqdisi's *Bad' wat-ta'rikh*, and Ibn an-Nadim's *Fihrist*—all contain isolated chapters, from eight (Ibn an-Nadim) to thirty-one (Gardizi), on Hindu sects, together with brief references to Buddhist practices.[4] Unfortunately, the tone of these compilations—with the exception of the *Fihrist*, which is too condensed to permit sober evaluation—is vituperative and often carping. Marvazi and Maqdisi, in particular, see little that is edifying in Hindu rites, the latter even suggesting them as a historical analogue to the pagan Arab idolatry which Muhammad initially opposed and successfully displaced.[5]

Around 1030 AD the remarkable Ghaznavid scholar Abu Rayhan Muhammad ibn Ahmad al-Biruni completed his study of Indian culture, commonly referred to as the *India*. Biruni's *India* is often viewed as a haven of truth to which the researcher may flee after having exhausted the fragmentary sketches on Indian religion found in the just-mentioned Muslim sources. Certainly the scope and intensity of Biruni's research into matters Indian are without parallel in medieval Muslim scholarship. His data on religious practices is especially helpful with respect to the Vaisnavas, whom he knew best.[6] Yet the erudite and sophisticated tone of the *India* cannot conceal the fact that Biruni shared the Muslim abhorrence of idol worship and condemned out of hand those Indians who put faith in monuments venerating the dead. "Only the common uneducated people" of North India worshipped idols, in Biruni's view, "for those who marched on the path to liberation, or those who studied philosophy and theology, and who desired abstract truth which they called *sara*, were entirely free from worshipping anything but God alone, and would never have dreamt of worshipping an image manufactured to represent him."[7]

To escape the twin pitfalls of political and intellectual imperialism, which entrapped even Biruni, the student examining Muslim perceptions of Hinduism would have to locate a medieval Muslim scholar who approached Indian traditions, including idol worship, as an interpreter rather than a conqueror. Curiously, the one Muslim theologian whose extant writings suggest that he adopted such an approach lived in eastern Iran during the period of the Ghorid ascendancy in North India. Apparently out of touch with contemporary events in the subcontinent, Abu'l-Fath Muhammad b. 'Abdul Karim al-Shahrastani (d. 1153 AD) obtained information on Indian religions which had been transmitted through a now-lost series of intermediaries and ultimately derived from an anonymous report compiled around 800 AD.[8] With some additions from classical sources and deletions of offensive details traceable to the original report,

Shahrastani reshaped his data on Indian religions and incorporated it as a chapter into his magnum opus, *Kitab al-milal wan-nihal*.[9] As the title suggests, the *Al-Milal wan-nihal* principally sets forth the sectarian divisions within Islam (*milal*) and elaborates the major Greek philosophical schools (*nihal*). Secondarily, Shahrastani describes non-Muslim religionists within the Semitic fold: Jews, Christians, Magians, Manichaeans, and pre-Muslim Arabs. The only non-Muslim, non-Semitic religious grouping treated in the *Al-Milal wan-nihal* are the Indians. For this reason, as well as the comparatively late date of the book and the second-hand nature of the author's information on India, most investigators into early Muslim-Hindu relations have overlooked or minimized the essay "*Ara' al-hind*" in Shahrastani's *Al-Milal wan-nihal*.[10]

Yet Shahrastani not only approaches Indian religion sympathetically; he also employs a unique analytical model (Sabianism) to portray Indian idol worship. It seems valuable, therefore, to examine "*Ara' al-hind*" for the insight it provides into one Muslim scholar's perception of Hindu traditions.

Though Shahrastani was the first Muslim theologian to describe the Hindus as Sabians, Sabianism itself had a long history as a quasi-historical, quasi-theological phenomenon stretching back to the origin of Islam. Sabians are mentioned three times in the Qur'an, probably with reference to a group of proto-Mandaeans.[11] There follows a hiatus of over two centuries in Muslim usage of the term Sabian, which is ended when theologians, including Shahrastani, begin to describe as Sabian numerous sects of ancient heathen.[12] Many of the sects are linked to the Hellenistic world, and so in the *Al-Milal wan-nihal* Shahrastani speaks of the first and ancient Sabians but also Greek Sabians (and finally, of course, Indian Sabians).

The theological ambiguity of the later Sabians (sometimes called pseudo-Sabians) focuses on the religionists of that name who inhabited the ancient Mesopotamian city of Harran. The syncretistic quality of Harranian thought is abundantly evident in Muslim sources, and recently its origin has been partially clarified by archaeological work linking Harran to the Greeks.[13] In *Al-Milal wan-nihal* the major tenets of Sabianism are exposited with reference to the Harranians, and the largest, most influential Harranian sect are called the *ashab al-ruhaniyat*, or proponents of spiritual beings.[14] In depicting their views, Shahrastani indicates the indebtedness of the Harranians to Athens at the same time that he points ahead to the importance of Hellenized categories for evaluating Indians as Sabians.

The *ruhaniyat* or spiritual beings whom Harranians worship are, according to Shahrastani, intermediaries providing access to the Wise and Productive

Author of the world. They are pure and sanctified indeed, substance and condition. In themselves they are lofty and delicate bodies of light, produced from nothing, unencumbered by matter, positive in nature and free in will.

Above all, it is their relationship to the planets which determines the celestial power of the *ruhaniyat*:

> It is through lofty abodes (i.e., the seven planets) that spiritual beings are particularized. Each spiritual being has an abode and each abode an orbit, and the relationship of the spiritual being to the abode in which it is particularized is the relationship of the spirit to the body. Moreover, the one is Lord, leader and guide of the other. At the same time, spiritual beings are not limited to planets. All elements—whether pure or compounded—result from the action of spiritual beings. Nothing in creation is void of their power or guidance if it is, by nature, receptive to such influence.[15]

The neo-Platonic character of the Harranian hierarchy becomes clear in Shahrastani's subsequent discussion of those "spiritual beings—not limited to planets." Though the stages of emanation from the spiritual to the physical realm are omitted, Shahrastani leaves no doubt that for the Harranians a pure person issues out of the combination of leaders (i.e., spiritual beings dissociated from the planets) with the untainted part of elements; indeed, God Himself is said to have appeared in the world in the form of such a person.[16]

If Hellenistic influences partially determined the Sabian definition of "a pure person," it was Muslim theological categories which controlled Shahrastani's estimate of this typological religious figure. To the author of *Al-Milal wan-nihal*, the pure person or spiritual being, as conceived by the Harranian Sabians, was both an angel and a prophet. He was an angel because spiritual beings are also, in origin, celestial beings. As an angel, therefore, he related to each stage of the creative process since angels, by nature, are linked not only to the species of rain but also to each individual drop of rain.[17] A spiritual being *qua* angel, in sum, enjoyed both a supervisory and a mediating capacity in creation.

A spiritual being *qua* prophet, on the other hand, could not be simply defined. To expand the concept of prophethood to include the Sabian *ruhaniyat* would have been tantamount to undermining the foundation of Muslim theology: the prophetic succession, beginning with Adam and culminating in Muhammad. While not denying that Sabian pure persons are prophets, Shahrastani attempts at the same time to preserve the sanctity of the Muslim line of succession, as the following passage from *Al-Milal wan-nihal* indicates:

Prophets are intermediaries in establishing the norm [*sunnah*] of law, just as angels are intermediaries in establishing the norm [*sunnah*] of creation, and since law is more exalted than the intermediaries of creation, prophets are superior to angels. And this is wondrous in the case where (a) spiritual beings who are associated with the law become intermediaries in creation and (b) persons associated with creation become intermediaries in the law, so that exaltation and completeness are attained through the combination of elements, not through [the existence of] simple elements. The determining factor [*yad*] pertains to the corporeal being, not the spiritual being.[18]

In effect, Shahrastani weights the argument of authority in favor of the corporal being, the intermediary in law and the prophet. As a Muslim scholar, he would have been open to the charge of heresy for any stand less affirmative of traditional prophecy.[19] Yet, as Chwolsohn noted long ago, Shahrastani treats the tenets of Sabianism "with the gentleness of an admiring foe"; for by his own reasoning a pure person or spiritual being, such as the Harranian and later the Indian Sabians worship, fits the requirements of category (b) in the above quotation: he is a person associated with creation who has become an intermediary in the law.[20] The neo-Platonic valuation of emanation is conventionally reversed, incarnation bringing not inevitable contamination but instead completion for spiritual beings. At the same time, however, the Muslim category of prophecy is modified. The spiritual being associated with the law is exalted and completed only when he becomes an intermediary in creation.

The role of a pure person or spiritual being for Harranians is critical to understanding Shahrastani's appraisal of Hindu sects. The material on the Harraniya, which comes at the beginning of part II of the *Al-Milal wan-Nihal*, is interpolated into the section on Indian Views at the end of part II. The typological figure who is at once angel and prophet, higher than the former yet lower than the latter, becomes identified with Indian as well as Harranian *ruhaniyat*. In "*Ara' al-hind*," the principal *ruhaniyat* are Visnu and Siva.[21] Both are prophets insofar as they came to the Indian people "with a commissioning as divine messengers in human form (though) without a written testimony." In their capacity as prophets, they "established laws and clarified norms" for their followers. At the same time, however, they are angels since they "abstained from temporal weakness and dispensed with food, drink, sexual intercourse and other things."[22] The theological implications of Shahrastani's brief description in "*Ara' al-hind*" may be summed up as follows: to the extent that Visnu and Siva are identified with angels, they are subordinate to prophets, but insofar as they combine the functions of angelhood and prophecy, acting as "persons associated with creation (who have) become intermediaries in the law," they attain "exaltation and completeness."[23]

The major point at which Visnu and Siva as "pure person" differ from the Muslim line of prophets, in Shahrastani's view, is their lack of a written testimony. For a Muslim scholar it is unthinkable that revelation could be fully transmitted without being finally reduced to a literary medium. The author of *Al-Milal wan-nihal* esteems Visnu and Siva as Indian *ruhaniyat*, even as he had acclaimed their Harranian predecessors, but he puts a firm stricture on their legitimacy from a Muslim perspective: they did not possess or deliver a document of revelation such as the People of the Book, and especially the Muslims, were given.

The exalted, if ambiguous, theological ranking which Visnu and Siva attain in *"Ara' al-hind"* is not shared by the other two groups which, like the *ashab al-ruhaniyat*, Shahrastani transposed from his earlier material on the Harranian Sabians. In chapter 3 of *"Ara' al-hind,"* Aditya and Chandra (the Sun and the Moon) are described as deities without any concomitant reference to them as mediators who provided laws and norms for their followers.[24] The introduction to the third chapter simply notes that the Adiyta- and Chandra-bhaktas venerate the Sun and Moon "without restricting worship to them." The creative and supportive functions ascribed to both Aditya and Chandra are laudatory in tone but not explicitly theological in purpose. Moreover, the unmitigated idol worshippers, whose views and activities are presented in chapter 4, are flatly condemned. Comparing such Indian idolaters to pagan Arabs, Shahrastani accuses them of having no deity beyond the wooden forms they themselves have chiseled; they have lost sight of the Lord of lords.[25] So severe is Shahrastani's treatment of Indian idolaters at the outset of chapter 4 that one scholar has concluded that the denunciations there apply to all sects cited in *"Ara' al-hind."*[26]

Yet the introduction to chapter 4 does not negate the positive assertions which the author had advanced in chapter 2 concerning the Indian *ruhaniyat*, viz., Visnu and Siva. The overall *Al-Milal wan-nihal* evaluation of the Sabians and the Indians as Sabians, though not removed from ambiguity, is overridingly hopeful in the functions as well as the origins it attributes to both Visnu and Siva.

The enduring contribution of Shahrastani's study is its sophisticated treatment of Indian attitudes toward idol worship. Though nearly all Indians are adjudged to be idol worshippers, only some are condemned as idolaters.[27] To enforce such a distinction, Shahrastani first posits Sabianism as a religious typology applicable to several historical groups. He then delineates the Sabian quality of the Harranians, dividing them into three categories—*Ashab ar-ruhaniyat*

(Proponents of Spiritual Beings), ʿ*Abadat al-kawakib* (Star-worshippers), and ʿ*Abadat al-asnam* (Idolaters). By applying the same categories to eleven of the fifteen Indian sects he cites in "*Araʾ al-hind*," Shahrastani accords the highest theological ranking to those Vaisnavas and Saivas who adhere to moral principles and law-giving structures derived from a spiritual intermediary (*malak ruhani*).[28] Though such Indians do not acknowledge or participate in the Muslim line of prophetic succession and also construct statues of their intermediaries, it is clear from the brief description of them in "*Araʾ al-hind*" and the lengthy treatment of their Harranian counterparts earlier in *Al-Milal wan-nihal* that the Indian *ashab al-ruhaniyat* are, for Shahrastani, good pagans; by his estimate, they are enlightened idol worshippers. Indian star worshippers, though they also distinguish the Lord of Lords from statues, are not similarly credited with the law-giving functions that characterize a community supported by revelation. Still others, the outright idolaters, are said to be hopelessly deluded by the forms of chiseled wood which they themselves created. In the end, therefore, Shahrastani does the expected: he condemns idolatry, and one could argue, with Minorsky, that his distinctions among idol worshippers in chapters 2–4 are specious, merely lending emphasis to his categorical dismissal of idolatry in chapter 4 of "*Araʾ al-hind*."[29] The evidence of both "*Araʾ al-hind*" and the section on the Harranian Sabians, however, suggests the alternative conclusion that Shahrastani's gradation of Indian idol worship permits a flexibility in interpreting the Hindu tradition, with the result that the *Al-Milal wan-nihal* profile of Visnu and Siva, together with their followers, can and does display an appreciation of their law-giving, almost prophetic character, a conclusion which is without precedent (and, unfortunately, without sequel) in Muslim theology.

The ingenious and sometimes opaque tone which pervades Shahrastani's analysis of Indian idol worship poses a problem for his interpreters. On superficial reading, it is not at all clear why he has transposed Sabian categories from the earlier section of *Al-Milal wan-nihal* on the Harraniya to the final section on Indian Views. The material within the essay, moreover, is arranged in such a way that one can easily overlook the high theological rating Shahrastani accords Indian spiritual beings. Many Muslim readers, predisposed to the normative condemnation of idolatry, would perceive the lengthy fourth chapter of "*Araʾ al-hind*" not only as the conclusive but also the dominant note in the author's interpretation of Indian idol worship. Further, the strangeness of the names of individual groups would be likely to cause most Muslim readers to gloss over the content of particular subchapters and read only the introductory prefaces, which again are unbalanced in favor of the condemnatory salvo of chapter 4.

It is not surprising, therefore, that Shahrastani suffered the same fate as Biruni in his exploratory interpretation of Indian religious practices and beliefs. Though he differed from Biruni in his information about the subcontinent (which was second- or third-hand), his interest in Indian religion (which was solely theological) and his influence on modern scholarship (which remains negligible for students of pre-Muslim India), Shahrastani, like Biruni, attracted no immediate successor to continue and expand the line of inquiry which he had initiated into the nature of Indian idol worship.

Instead, Muslim scholars who turned eastward in later centuries concerned themselves with the fate of Muslim communities in the subcontinent rather than the nature of Indian religionists with whom Muslims came in contact.[30] It is arguable that not till the Upanishadic translations prompted by Dara Shikoh in the late seventeenth century AD did there occur a serious revival of the interest in Indian religion which Biruni demonstrated as a historian and Shahrastani as a theologian.[31] Shahrastani's brief but sensitive account on Indian idol worship remains a unique specimen in the literature of medieval Islam. Though stifled by history, it continues to provide valuable attestation to the possibility of a Muslim-Hindu theological rapprochement on the critical topic of idol worship.

Notes

Bruce B. Lawrence, "Shahrastani on Indian Idol Worship," *Studia Islamica* 38 (1973): 61–73. Used by permission.

1. The reverse was equally true; the impact of the early Muslim invasions on Indian self-respect is still being analyzed. See R. C. Majumdar, "Hindu Reaction to Muslim Invasions," in *Potdar Commemoration Volume*, ed. S. N. Sen, D. V. Potdar, et al. (Poona, 1950), 341–51.
2. Aziz Ahmad, *Islamic Culture in the Indian Environment* (Oxford: Clarendon, 1964), 132: "The Sufi orders transplanted their hospices in India in the wake of the Ghurid conquest (late twelfth century A.D.)."
3. The most frequently cited shrine was the statue of Aditya at Multan. See, e.g., S. Razia Jafri, "Description of India (Hind and Sind) in the Works of al-Istakhri, Ibn Hauqal, and al-Maqdisi," *Bulletin of the Institute of Islamic Studies* 5 (1961): 10, 21. The shrine is also cited by Mas'udi (see chapter 7 of Abu'l-Husayn 'Ali al-Mas'udi, *Muruj al-dhahab wa-ma'adin al-jawhar*, ed. Yusuf As'ad Daghir [Beirut: Dar al-Andalus, 1965–66]) and by Biruni (see Muhammad ibn Ahmad Biruni, *Alberuni's India*, trans. Edward C. Sachau [New York: Norton, 1971], 1:116), among others. See, e.g., Buzurg

ibn Shahriyar, *Kitab ʿajaʾib al-hind barruhu wa-bahruhu wa-jazaʾiruh* = *Livre des Merveilles de l'Inde* (Leiden: Brill, 1883–86), the classic work of this literary genre.

4 V. Minorsky, "Gardizi on India," *Bulletin of the School of Oriental and African Studies* 12, no. 3 (1948): 625–40; V. Minorsky, *Sharaf al-Zaman Tahir Marvazi on China, the Turks, and India* (London: Royal Asiatic Society, 1942); Abu Zayd Ahmad ibn Sahl al-Balkhi, *Le livre de la création et de l'histoire*, trans. Cl. Huart (Paris: Leroux, 1912), 4:9–17; Muhammad ibn Ishaq ibn al-Nadim, *The Fihrist of al-Nadim: A Tenth-Century Survey of Muslim Culture*, ed. and trans. Bayard Dodge (New York: Columbia University Press, 1970), 2:826–36. Only Ibn an-Nadim provides a substantive description of both the person of the Buddha (Ibn al-Nadim, *Fihrist*, 2:831–32) and some of the teachings ascribed to him (2:824–25). The contribution is partially marred by a manuscript hiatus in the section on doctrine, but no other author except Shahrastani provides such rich detail on Buddhism.

5 See Huart, *Livre de la création*, 4:16: "And this is what the pagan Arabs say: 'we serve them (the idols) only that they may bring us closer to Allah' (Qurʾan 39.3)."

6 See A. Jeffrey, "Al-Biruni's Contribution to Comparative Religion," in *Al-Biruni Commemoration Volume* (Calcutta: Iran Society, 1951), 125–60.

7 Biruni, *Alberuni's India*, 1:113.

8 The informant was commissioned by the ʿAbbasid *wazir* Yahya b. Khalid al-Barmaki to travel to India for the purpose of collecting medical plants and describing the Indian religions; see Ibn an-Nadim, *Fihrist*, IX.2; Dodge, *Fihrist*, 2:826.

9 Principally chapter 1 (*Ashab al-tanasukh*) and chapter 5 (*Hukamaʾ al-hind*). Chapter 1 on the *Barahima* also reflects spurious material about Indian Brahmans which circulated in *kalam* circles; see P. Kraus, "Beiträge zur islamischen Ketzergeschichte: Das *Kitab az-Zumurrud* des Ibn ar-Rawandi," *Rivista degli Studi Orientali* 14, fasc. 2 (1933): 93–129. One such deletion, e.g., was the omission of the reference to Siva's phallus found in all the parallel Muslim accounts.

10 In *Islamic Culture in the Indian Environment*, Aziz Ahmad, for instance, mistakenly concludes that "the Hindus are not, in [Shahrastani's] view, likely to go beyond their idols to God" (85–86, 112). Minorsky, on the other hand, is bluntly critical of "*Araʾ al-hind*": "under Shahrastani's pen the data of the original [report] lose much of their liveliness and benefit little by being pushed into new pigeon-holes" (*Marvazi*, 130–31).

11 Qurʾan 2:59, 5:73, 22:17. See E. S. Drower, *The Mandaeans of Iraq and Iran; Their Cults, Customs, Magic, Legends, and Folklore* (Oxford: Clarendon, 1937).

12 The dated but still classic work on all aspects of Sabianism is D. A. Chwolsohn, *Die sabier und der sabismus*, 2 vols. (St. Petersburg: Imperial Academy, 1856); concerning the Muslim material on later Sabian sects, see esp. 1:169–70.

13 See J. B. Segal, "Pagan Syriac Monuments in the Vilayet of Urfa," *Anatolian Studies* 3 (1953): 97–119. Other recent studies that, in part, explore the Hellenistic affiliations of the Harranian Sabians are Y. Marquet, "Sabéens et Ihwan al-Safa," *Studia Islamica* 24 (1966): 35–80, and 25 (1966): 77–109; and F. Rosenthal, "The Prophecies of Baba the

Harranian," in *A Locust's Leg: Studies in Honour of S. H. Taqizadeh*, ed. W. B. Henning and E. Yarshater (London: Lund, Humphries, 1962), 220–32.

14 Much of the analysis in the pages that follow is based on the long section dealing with the *ashab ar-ruhaniyat* in *Al-Milal wan-nihal*, part II. See Muhammad ibn ʿAbd al-Karim Shahrastani, *Kitab al-milal wan-nihal*, ed. W. Cureton (London: Society for the Publication of Oriental Texts, 1842), 203–51; and T. Haarbrücker, *Religions-partheien und Philosophen-schulen*, part II (Halle: Schwetschke, 1851), 4–77. To minimize footnoting, only full-length quotations of the text will be cited.

15 Shahrastani, *Kitab*, 224, 204; Haarbrücker, *Religions-partheien*, 36, 6.

16 Shahrastani, *Kitab*, 250; Haarbrücker, *Religions-partheien*, 75–76.

17 Shahrastani, *Kitab*, 208; Haarbrücker, *Religions-partheien*, 11.

18 Shahrastani, *Kitab*, 226; Haarbrücker, *Religions-partheien*, 38–39.

19 As it is, Shahrastani's views were sufficiently controversial in his time to elicit the suspicion of heresy as well as undue fondness for the Shiʿas. Concerning the allegations in Ibn as-Samʿani's *Tahbir*, see A. Guillaume, trans., *The Summa Philosophiae of al-Shahrastani* (London: Oxford University Press, 1934), xi. On Shahrastani as a scholar particularly influenced by Ismaili metaphysics, see his *Musaraʿat al-Falasifa*, published in English as *Struggling with the Philosopher: A Refutation of Avicenna's Metaphysics*, ed. and trans. Wilfred Madelung and Toby Mayer (London: Tauris, 2001).

20 Chwolsohn, *Sabier*, 1:684.

21 In chapter 2, four spiritual beings are cited, together with their attributes and the activities of their followers. Siva is clearly the deity for the Mahadevakas (2B) and the Kapalikas (2C), while Visnu is the more common appellative for the deity of the Vasudevakas (2A). The identity of the fourth spiritual being, Bahadun (2D), remains a mystery.

22 Shahrastani, *Kitab*, 450; Haarbrücker, *Religions-partheien*, 363.

23 Shahrastani, *Kitab*, 226; Haarbrücker, *Religions-partheien*, 38–39.

24 Shahrastani, *Kitab*, 452; Haarbrücker, *Religions-partheien*, 366–67. Editor's Note: References to chapters are to Shahrastani's text.

25 Since "*Araʾ al-hind*" immediately follows a section entitled "*Araʾ al-ʿarab fiʾl-jahiliyya*," Razi (d. 1209 AD) concluded that in both portions of *Al-Milal wan-nihal* Shahrastani was simply copying Jahiz's now-lost work, *Kitab al-asnam*. (See P. Kraus, "The 'Controversies' of Fakhr al-Din Razi," *Islamic Culture* 12 [1938]: 146, fn. 2.) However, the fact that it is only at the beginning of chapter 4 in "*Araʾ al-hind*" that pagan Arabs and Hindus are explicitly compared and that the Sabian theological categories that pervade the entire essays are unique to Shahrastani would seem to blunt the force of Razi's long-standing accusation.

26 Minorsky, *Marvazi*, 131.

27 The exclusion of Brahmans (chapter 1) and Indian philosophers (chapter 5) is intentional: Neither group has Sabian markings, at least in the sources on which Shahrastani relied for his depiction of them.

28 The other four sects are included as subsects of the Brahmans, apparently because they, like the Brahmans, are incompatible with the Sabian categories Shahrastani has imported from the section on the Harraniya.
29 Minorsky, *Marvazi*, 131.
30 See Ahmad, *Islamic Culture in the Indian Environment*, 112–13.
31 For a detailed though unflattering summary of Dara Shikoh's thought, see Ahmad, *Islamic Culture in the Indian Environment*, 192–96. While Dara Shikoh's eclecticism is often penetrating, it still fails to perceive Hindu tenets from a Muslim posture that is at once sympathetic and independent. *Editor's Note: Readers can now consult Supriya Gandhi, The Emperor Who Never Was: Dara Shukoh in Mughal India (Cambridge, MA: Harvard University Press, 2020).*

SEVEN

Introduction to Ibn Khaldun's *Muqaddimah* | 2005/2015

This is the abridged version of the only complete English translation of the *Muqaddimah* (introduction), which was published in 1958 in three volumes for the Bollingen Foundation. The *Muqaddimah* is the most significant, and challenging, Islamic history of the premodern world. Its author was the fourteenth-century Mediterranean scholar Ibn Khaldun (1332–1406).

Ibn Khaldun was a man of his time, but he was not like others of his time. He was marked by travel, even before he was born. In the eighth century his ancestors emigrated from southern Arabia, or Yemen, to Andalusia, or southern Spain, then a part of the Muslim world. His full name attests to his Yemeni roots: ʿAbd al-Rahman Abu Zayd b. Muhammad b. Muhammad b. Khaldun al-Hadrami. Al-Hadrami links its bearer to Hadramut, a part of Yemen. Other privileged members of Andalusian society were also Arab immigrants, though many, including Ibn Khaldun's forbears, had intermarried with indigenous Berbers. What distinguished Ibn Khaldun was neither his Arab lineage nor his linkage to Berbers via marriage but his Mediterranean location. At the intersection of Jewish, Christian, and Muslim influences, heir to Greek science and Arabic poetry, and connected by trade and history to Asia, the Mediterranean Sea had become the nexus of Muslim cosmopolitanism by the fourteenth century. Social mobility as well as physical travel animated Mediterranean Muslims, especially those, like Ibn Khaldun, who rose to high posts in government, law, and education. Travel (*rihlah*) became the model for his autobiography, *At-Taʿrif bi-Ibn Khaldun wa-rihlatuhu gharban wa-sharqan*, or *Biography of Ibn Khaldun and His Travel in the West and in the East* (hereafter referred to as the *Autobiography*).[1] Though other Muslims wrote autobiographies prior to Ibn Khaldun's, his is unusual because he attempts to place his own life squarely at the intersection of East and West.[2] Begun in the last decade of his life and continuing up through his meeting with Tamerlane (in 1401), it situates him in the midst of the political activities of his time, but even more, it stresses how crucial is the awareness of geographical/historical factors in assessing political events and their consequences.

What made Ibn Khaldun different was not travel per se but rather his ability to travel in the imagination of his own world, to create another perspective that at once linked him to his contemporaries yet set him apart from them. Whether we call this disposition quirkiness or eccentricity, narcissism or genius, we must recognize it as the critical element of Ibn Khaldun that made it possible for him to conceive, then write the *Muqaddimah*, a study which the twentieth-century doyen of British historians, Arnold J. Toynbee, has called "undoubtedly the greatest work of its kind that has ever yet been created by any mind in any time or place."[3]

Marking himself as different was almost reflexive for Ibn Khaldun. He was different not just in his thought and speech but also in his dress. When he served as a judge in Cairo, he continued to wear Maghribi (or North African) robes instead of the lighter robes of Egyptian judges. Though he may have been uncomfortable, he was indicating pride in his Andalusian roots, without, however, suggesting that he was less than a faithful, observant Muslim or other than an obedient, subservient officer of the Egyptian state.[4]

In his writing Ibn Khaldun also expressed difference, but always within limits and often by inference. It must be remembered that he was not employed to be a historian. He was a juridical activist with a secondary interest in history. Particularly in the odd circumstances of his own life experience did he hope to find lessons (*'ibar*) that would be instructive for others. While his *Autobiography* ranges over many moments, none is more poignant, or more instructive, than his meetings with Tamerlane. The year was 1401. The place was Damascus. Tamerlane had just laid siege to the Mamluk city, which had not yet surrendered. During the previous twenty years Tamerlane had become the most feared and successful warrior from the East after the Mongol chieftain Chingiz Khan. Tamerlane was heir to Chingiz Khan in a double sense. Though Turkish and Muslim, he also had Mongol lineage, with shamanic loyalties, through his mother. Even more important, Tamerlane had inherited the Mongol ideal of universal sovereignty via military conquest. He had been systematic in his plundering and massacres, from Moscow in the north to Delhi in the south to Izmir in the west.

No one was spared: all those conquered, whether Muslim or not, were treated as prisoners. Some were tortured, many were slain, all were at risk.

When Ibn Khaldun was summoned by Tamerlane in January 1401, he met him outside Damascus, where the conqueror had camped while his army laid siege to the city. Ibn Khaldun feared for his life. Yet he also knew from reports that Tamerlane could be indulgent as well as cruel, and that he had befriended scholars and mystics on previous occasions.[5] Ibn Khaldun won Tamerlane's confidence, so much so that the account of their meetings justified his supplementary labor as a historian. Not only did Ibn Khaldun claim a role in gaining pardon for Mamluk prisoners of Tamerlane, but he also saw in the Central Asian world conqueror a Turco-Mongol vindication of his own thesis, to wit, that civilization is always and everywhere marked by the fundamental difference between urban and primitive, producing a tension that is also an interplay between nomad and merchant, desert and city, orality and literacy. Ibn Khaldun may have been projecting his own life's ambition in the subsequent portrait he provided of "Timur," or Tamerlane: "This king Timur is one of the greatest and mightiest of kings. Some attribute to him knowledge, others attribute to him heresy because they note his preference for 'members of the House [of ʿAli],' still others attribute to him the employment of magic and sorcery, but in all this there is nothing; it is simply that he is highly intelligent and perspicacious, addicted to debate and argumentation about what he knows and also about what he does not know."[6]

The final part of this description could have served as an epitaph for Ibn Khaldun, even without the legacy of his *Muqaddimah*: "he is highly intelligent and perspicacious, addicted to debate and argumentation about what he knows and also about what he does not know." It is his ability to test the limits of what is known and knowable that makes Ibn Khaldun an explorer of the mind and not a conventional intellectual in the terms of either his own time or later times in the history of Islamicate civilization.

The biggest difference between Ibn Khaldun and the cosmopolitan elites of his generation was his orientation to *adab*.[7] Though trained as a *faqih*, or jurist, and familiar with all the ancillary sciences of *fiqh* (jurisprudence), Ibn Khaldun was also an *adib*, or littérateur. A littérateur is attentive to words, to their expression in both speech and writing, but above all to their polyvalence. Words can mean many things in different times, places, and contexts. Though this may seem a truism today, it was far from accepted knowledge or the dominant outlook, even among the notables whom Ibn Khaldun knew and whom he engaged in discussion or debate.

As a littérateur Ibn Khaldun was especially concerned with poetry and prose. It is crucial to recognize, for instance, that he was engaged by the lyrical tones of verse, that he saw poetry as a register of local identity, and that he himself had poetic aspirations.[8] As a littérateur, he also moved beyond the range of what is usually thought to be literature. He engaged the full spectrum of sciences that were known in Arabic translations from Greek sources by the ninth century and which were then expanded through experiment and study by Muslim scientists during subsequent centuries. By the time of Ibn Khaldun, scientific activity had been professionalized—so much so that "most of the distinguished physicians and astronomers of twelfth- and thirteenth-century Syria and Cairo were employed as jurists, teachers in *madrasa*-like medical institutions, or timekeepers in the region's major mosques."[9] At first, it may seem odd that his treatment of the sciences would be delayed until the sixth and final chapter of the *Muqaddimah*. It is not because sciences are unimportant, or of second-order importance, to Muslim elites, but rather because sciences are not integral to urban life. Like other aspects of urban society, sciences are a luxury or convenience, neither natural nor necessary. Sciences are unlike crafts. Crafts are a necessity. They are linked to gainful occupations, and because they are, Ibn Khaldun introduces, then analyzes them in chapter 5 of the *Muqaddimah*, prior to his enumeration and assessment of the sciences.

Both the placement of science and the distinction between crafts and sciences reveal the organizational vision of Ibn Khaldun about his new science. It builds materially from manual, physical labor to refined, intellectual pursuits. It builds thematically from desert to sedentary civilization. It builds diachronically from notions of statecraft that relate to religious norms at different angles: peripheral in tribal dynasties, central in the caliphate, then asymmetric in the royal/military empires that followed the caliphate. The six chapters of the *Muqaddimah* sort out from the most general to the most specific:

1. On human civilization and the part of the earth that is civilized
2. On desert civilization, among tribes and savage nations
3. On dynasties, the caliphate, and royal authority
4. On sedentary civilization, countries, and cities
5. On crafts and ways of making a living
6. On sciences, their acquisition and study. (43)[10]

In assessing the *Muqaddimah* in general and its organizational structure in particular, one must remember that Ibn Khaldun was more than a jurist and a littérateur—he was also a teacher. Teachers repeat, not to be redundant but to communicate the same thought on different occasions and often to different audiences. A practicing jurist fond of *adab*, Ibn Khaldun wrote as he taught. He propounded novel ideas that he both documented and qualified. He repeated himself, often with different examples or sources, in order to make the same point in multiple contexts, and perhaps for multiple audiences.[11]

It is the principle of Ibn Khaldun's argumentation that remains the same. To appreciate that principle in its stark originality, however, we need to consider two crucial instances relating the bases of jurisprudence to the laws of evidence in depicting historical data. As a jurist he approaches his new science within the parameters of juridical reasoning, yet precisely because jurisprudence too is a science it is not till chapter 6 that Ibn Khaldun discusses the relationship between it and his own method. Jurisprudence is the crucial science for Ibn Khaldun. To understand his persistent, foundational use of juridical logic, one must first grasp what he says in chapter 6 about jurisprudence as a science and then return to chapter 1, where he introduces the decisive distinction between two terms that pervades his entire book but only makes sense from the perspective of juridical logic. The two terms are *khabar*, or Event, and *hadith*, or Tradition.[12]

For Ibn Khaldun jurisprudence is both a science and a pedagogical tool. Though its provenance is religious law, its practice also informs linguistics or rather lexicography. In chapter 6 the connection of these two scientific fields, *fiqh* and *lugha*, jurisprudence and lexicography, is made in compelling argumentation, at once novel and subtle. After establishing that *ijmaʿ*, or consensus, is a third kind of evidence (after the Qur'an and the Sunnah) for jurisprudence, Ibn Khaldun explains:

> Now many of the things that happened after the Prophet are not included in the established texts [the Qur'an and the Sunnah]. Therefore, they [religious scholars] compared and combined them with the established evidence that is found in the texts, (and drew their conclusions from analogy) according to certain rules that governed their combinations. This assured the soundness of their comparison of two similar (cases), so that it could be assumed that one and the same divine law covered both cases. This became (another kind of) legal evidence, because the (early Muslims) all agreed upon it [*bi-ijmaʿihim ʿalayhi*]. This is analogy [*qiyas*], the fourth kind of evidence. (347)[13]

The subtlety of this approach is its connection of analogy to consensus as part of a continuous process. Earlier, in the case for upholding the Sunnah, Ibn Khaldun had also argued that "the Sunnah, as it has been transmitted to us, is justified by the general consensus (to the effect) that Muslims must act in accordance with traditions that are sound."¹⁴ There are four elements without which law could not be law in an Islamic key: the Qur'an, the Sunnah, consensus, and analogy. Though the Qur'an would seem to be prior to consensus, it is in fact the consensus of the Community of Believers in Allah and His Last Prophet who confirm that the Book is the Revealed Word to Muhammad, just as the Sunnah becomes forceful because it too reflects this same consensus. Nor can analogy work, as the above quotation makes clear, except as a further application of the principle of consensus. Consensus, in short, is the glue, the cohesive element, that informs and fortifies every step of the judicial process that safeguards Islam as a divinely guided community.

To a person who has heard the lectures or read the book that became the *Muqaddimah*, it is evident that Ibn Khaldun is investing *ijmaʿ*, or consensus, with a special property, a collective will, an *ʿasabiyya*.

ʿAsabiyya is the major neologism permeating all of Ibn Khaldun's work. Franz Rosenthal translates it throughout as "group feeling." Some have criticized that standardized rendition of *ʿasabiyya*, considering it too static and natural an English equivalent of what remains for Ibn Khaldun a variable pinned between the state (*dawlah*) and religion (*din*). Mohamed Talbi, for instance, defines *ʿasabiyya* as "at one and the same time the cohesive force of the group, the conscience that it has of its own specificity and collective aspirations, and the tension that animates it and impels it ineluctably to seek power through conquest."¹⁵ The last element—the drive to power through conquest—seems to fall outside the juridical realm, unless one realizes that the law also is an instrument of power, whether through persuasion or domination. Jon Anderson comes closest to understanding the itinerancy of Ibn Khaldun's usage when he writes that "*ʿasabiyya* seems to be a concept of relation by sameness, opposed both to the state (*dawlah*) based on relations of difference or complementarity, and to religion (*din*), which alone supersedes it."¹⁶ Religion does supersede *ʿasabiyya*, but it does so by redefining it rather than denying it. The concept of consensus, valorized as the glue or binding element of Islamic law, functions with the force of *ʿasabiyya*, at least during the period of the early caliphate.

And so it is not ambiguous but ambivalent use of language that characterizes Ibn Khaldun. As a jurist who is also a littérateur, he does not employ a technical term out of context; rather he applies a concept to fit the argument at hand. As miriam cooke has observed, for Ibn Khaldun "a word used metaphorically may convey the meaning more clearly than a conventional word, because it conveys itself and also a 'possible consequence,' i.e., the double/multiple level of meaning prized by writers."¹⁷ The same may be said of his coining of new terms.

He coins new terms like *ʿasabiyya* or *ʿumran* or *badawah* with a specific range of meanings, one of which may be to amplify the notion of a known word, as *ʿasabiyya* deftly does with the juridical concept of consensus.

Reliance on metaphor also allows Ibn Khaldun to demonstrate how the same word, like the same event or person, can be viewed differently over time, and also from different places in the same time frame. Perhaps the most crucial argument that Ibn Khaldun makes on behalf of history as an Islamic science is that historians alone among Muslim scientists can explain how Islam arose out of a context of orality and nomadism/primitivism (*badawah*) to become a proponent of both writing and civilization (*hadarah*). What had been speech and a habit became writing and a craft.[18] Yet the very lifeline of Islam depended on maintaining the connection between literacy and orality, between writing and speech, as also between civilized and nomad. In short, analogy, while it had its most immediate application in law, could, and should, also be applied to the understanding of the laws of history—above all, the history of Muslim civilization.

> Now, when speech was a habit of those who used it [the pagan Arabs and early Muslims], these (linguistic matters) were neither sciences nor norms. At that time, jurists did not need them, because linguistic matters were familiar to them by natural habit. But when the habit of the Arabic language was lost, the experts who made it their specialty determined it once and for all with the help of a sound tradition and of sound rules of *analogy* they evolved. (Linguistic matters) thus became sciences the jurists had to master, in order to know the divine laws. (347–48; emphasis added)

Analogy applied to history is not the same as analogy applied to law, however. The strategy of one science is imported to the practice of another. It is crucial to understand how the connection emerged and developed in Ibn Khaldun's imagination, for the same term when used in divergent contexts also embraces new connotations.

Put differently, new connotations require new facts that analogy itself cannot provide. On this point Ibn Khaldun is clear, though his clarity as a historian has always to be qualified by his status as a jurist. As he writes in chapter 6,

> the meanings of words cannot be established by analogy, if their usage is not known, although, for jurists, their usage may be known by virtue of [the existence of] an inclusive [concept] that attests to the applicability of [a wider meaning] to the first [word].... [This is so] only because the use of analogy

[in this case] is attested by the religious law, which deduces the soundness of [the application of] analogy [in this case] from the [general norms] on which it is based. We do not have anything like it in lexicography. There, only the intellect can be used, which means [relying on] judgment.... It should not be thought that the establishment of word meanings falls under the category of word definitions. A definition indicates [the meaning of] a given idea by showing that the meaning of an unknown and obscure word is identical with the meaning of a clear and well-known word. Lexicography, on the other hand, affirms that such-and-such a word is used to express such-and-such an idea. The difference here is very clear.[19]

What Ibn Khaldun is explaining comes closest to what modern linguists call the distinction between stipulative and conventional definitions. Elsewhere, Ibn Khaldun notes that "knowledge of the conventional meanings in general is not sufficient for [jurisprudence]."[20] Lexical or conventional definitions link a specific word to a known idea, creating synonyms within a familiar realm of limited association, while stipulative or juridical definitions take an unknown and obscure word and link it to the meaning of a clear and well-known word, enlarging the connotative range of the latter while adding heuristic value to the former because of its novelty. While the difference is far from clear to most people, it is both clear and compelling to Ibn Khaldun: stipulative definitions become the hallmark of his new science.

The key strategy for students of Ibn Khaldun is always and everywhere to recall that he is at once a jurist and a littérateur. His move to the latter, as in the above excerpt, does not falsify his standing in the former. He is not trying to undercut the Islamic juridical tradition or to disparage the history of Islamicate civilization. He is trying to forge a new science that at once makes Islamic law more expansive and Islamicate civilization more resilient, at the same time that it foregrounds him as the interpreter who facilitates and protects both!

Having followed the linguistic turn in juridical logic outlined in chapter 6, we can now return to the beginning of the *Muqaddimah*. The major lexical term is *khabar*, or Event. Ibn Khaldun already highlights it in the full title for the larger book to which the *Muqaddimah* was intended as an introduction (though chapter 1 was later incorporated along with the introduction into what now appears as the *Muqaddimah*).[21] The crucial comparison is Event to Tradition. Trained as a jurist, Ibn Khaldun understood both the importance of Tradition and the danger of generalizing its usage. While it was impossible for him to write the history of Islam without attention to the religious sciences, he also deemed it impossible to do justice to the scope and depth of Muslim civilization if restricted to the religious sciences.

Ibn Khaldun strove to be different, to be a man of his times and more: to grasp a point of balance or measurement (*miʿyar*) between the norms of belief, religion, and law (*daʿwah*) and the demands of state, science, and practical reason (*dawlah*). In schematizing his view of history, he relied on observation and argumentation to offset a blind acceptance of stories, even those that could be confirmed by a "sound" chain of transmitters. He used the methodology of Tradition scholars but did not accept its claim to be universal in scope. To the claims of Tradition he counterposed Event, the sort of evidence that can be proven or disproven by independent inquiry.

The term Event, however, is itself open to qualification. In Arabic, the full title of *Kitab al-ʿibar* reads *Kitab al-ʿibar wa-diwan al-mubtadaʾ wa-l-khabar fi ayyam al-ʿArab wal-ʿAjam wal-Barbar wa-man ʿasarahum min dhawi as-sultan al-akbar*. In translation the title becomes *The Book of Lessons and Archive of Origins, Dealing with Political Events Concerning Arabs, Non-Arabs, and Berbers, and with Their Contemporary Major Rulers*. If Ibn Khaldun hopes to offer *ʿibar* (instructions or lessons), their content revolves around understanding Event. What is *diwan al-mubtadaʾ wal-khabar*? They are the bookends of history, the beginning and the end, with *khabar* having a multilayered meaning. It is both Event and outcome or sequel. Given Ibn Khaldun's disposition to use linguistics in the service of his new science, *al-mubtadaʾ wal-khabar* are framed as grammatical terms, specifically, the subject and the predicate, that is the beginning and the sequel or end, of a nominal sentence. The subject becomes the early conditions, or first instances, of social organization, namely, *badawah* or desert civilization, which sets the stage for what follows it, namely, the emergence of world civilization (*ʿumran*) through sedentary or urban civilization. From the very title of *Kitab al-ʿibar*, *khabar* becomes the key word, or signifier, the cipher, for what will be the showcase of his new science, namely, the interplay of oral and written, primitive and cosmopolitan, Arab and non-Arab, in the making of ecumenical or world civilization. *Khabar* is at once Event, sequel, outcome, civilization.

At the same time, however, Event retains another, more juridically weighted meaning. Event is integral to Tradition scholarship but as a subsidiary link: Events were the accounts of the persons whose integrity was being reviewed in order to verify or disqualify what they reported as Tradition. For Ibn Khaldun, the grammatical and juridical meanings of Event expand into something more vital and visionary: the surplus of labor, but also of thought, that produces a model of civilization across time and space. The linchpin to transforming Event into this new conceptual domain was *mutabaqa*, or conformity. Even while eschewing the idea that all forms are external, Ibn Khaldun did believe in conformity, namely, the correspondence between what one remembered as Event and historical reports of what others witnessed as Event. Methodologically, the passage linking Tradition to Event while also distinguishing between them is the most crucial one in the *Muqaddimah*. It occurs at the outset of chapter 1, where Ibn Khaldun sets forth the criteria of assessment for his own historical project. Here he pits knowledge of the nature of civilization against criticism of the personalities of transmitters. It is a double move: he is not saying that the appraisal or criticism of the personalities of transmitters is invalid or useless, but he is saying that its use should be limited to norms and values. While crucial to laying out a religious system, it cannot, and should not, guide historical inquiry.

Though Rosenthal's translation is apt, it is best comprehended within the larger argument about the rules of scholarly inquiry that separate law from history, Tradition from Event:

> Personality criticism is taken into consideration *only* in connection with the soundness (or lack of soundness) of Muslim religious information. [For Events, by contrast,] a requirement to consider is the conformity (or lack of conformity of the reported information with general conditions). [And so] the correct notion about something that *ought to be* [*insha'*] can [only] be derived from (personality criticism), while the correct notion about something that *was* [*khabar*] can [and should] be derived from (personality criticism) and external (evidence) by (checking) the conformity (of the historical report with general conditions).[22]

The difficulty of this passage is precisely its pithy understatement. At first glance, it seems to be just a matter of tenses, the shift between subjunctive (normative) and indicative (past/present/future). The Moroccan historian Abdallah Laroui has provided a straightforward translation that reflects this level of reading: "The normative draws its sense solely from itself, while the account, which is indicative, draws its sense both from itself and from an external fact which corresponds to it." Laroui is condensing the earlier, more complex analysis of another North African historian, the Tunisian Mohamed Talbi. Talbi, like Laroui, agrees that this passage is the decisive methodological statement in the entire *Muqaddimah*. Yet Talbi explains the intricacy of this phrase as turning on a linguistic usage, in this case not grammatical but rhetorical. "Arab rhetoricians," observes Talbi, "divide language into two categories: *insha'* and *khabar*. What is prescribed as a norm or Tradition (*insha'*) cannot be qualified with any other datum: it functions as a command or a query, while Event (*khabar*) is open to either confirmation, qualification, or refutation by other sources both internal and external to itself."[23]

For Talbi, the introduction of *insha'* as Tradition is yet another application of analogy by Ibn Khaldun. In other words, its rhetorical use is extended to a new field of inquiry, the demarcation of historical inquiry from juridical investigation. Since no scholar before Ibn Khaldun had summarized the process of Hadith verification as *insha'*, its use here stamps Ibn Khaldun as radically different; it demarcates his new science from the efforts of all his predecessors. But precisely because neither the dyad of Tradition/Event nor its importance will be transparent to nonspecialists reading the *Muqaddimah*, it seems necessary to frame the context in which this crucial use of analogy takes place.

The practice of law depends on the soundness of characters in the chain of transmitters. The core methodology for juridical scholars is the integrity or soundness of those who claim to have received the report of an esteemed person, in this case, the Prophet Muhammad, whose words and deeds become the Sunnah, or model for Islamic law, during all the successive generations of devout Muslims. To understand the centrality of Tradition studies, one need only consider the commendation of Tradition offered by Shah Waliullah Dihlawi, one of its most renowned and cosmopolitan advocates:

> There is no way for us to obtain knowledge of the divine laws . . . except through the report of the Prophet. . . . There is also no way for us to have knowledge of the sayings of the Prophet . . . except by receiving reports which go back to him by successive links and transmission, whether they are in his words; or they are interrupted Traditions whose transmission was verified by a group of the Companions and the Successors . . . and in our time there is no way to receive these reports except to follow the literature written in the science of Tradition.[24]

Even though the author of this passage lived in the eighteenth century, three hundred years after Ibn Khaldun, he was reflecting a comparable worldview. Observance of the law was the backbone of collective Muslim life. Jurists had to make decisions based on Islamic principles, and those revolved around a double axis: the Messenger and the Message, the Prophet and the Qur'an, each reinforcing the other, but with different textual domains. While the Qur'an exceeds 6,600 verses, most Muslim jurists and scholars agree that only some 500 verses have a legal content. Though these verses, often quite long, do provide elements for a coherent legal system, they need to be supplemented in a society based on divine law. And so the locus of attention became the vast legacy of attributions to the Prophet. Collecting, verifying, and systematizing Traditions occupied enormous scholarly labor in the aftermath of the rapid expansion, then consolidation of an Islamic polity.

Among the four schools of Sunni jurisprudence that evolved, the eponymous founder of one, Ahmad ibn Hanbal, was renowned for both his knowledge of Tradition and his skill in applying Tradition to the demands of jurisprudence. Once, we are told, Ahmad ibn Hanbal was asked how many Traditions a scholar needed to know in order to give a *fatwa*, or authoritative legal opinion. His response was three hundred thousand to five hundred thousand![25] Even if we were to accept the middle figure of four hundred thousand Traditions as the baseline of knowledge requisite for juridical scholars issuing *fatwas*, the dedication to Tradition dwarfs the attention to Qur'anic data, despite the towering importance of the latter.

Perhaps even more daunting than the task of mastering Tradition was the subsidiary task of winnowing out the true from the false. By the third century after the *hijrah* (exodus), the tracing of *isnad*, or chains of transmission, had become a fixed part of Islamic legal training.[26] One book catalogs all the various categories of malfeasants who make up Traditions. They range from atheists and heretics to outright falsifiers of Traditions, including those who would invent Traditions in order to embellish religious stories they told in mosques and hence collect larger donations from gullible believers![27]

In order to establish his new science, Ibn Khaldun the jurist had to both affirm his own practice of Tradition criticism while also allowing for another way to approach human social organization, which for him is the basis of global or world civilization (ʿumran al-ʿalam).[28] Hence it is crucial to understand how his forensic skill as a littérateur allowed him to cite Event, itself an ancillary part of Tradition scholarship, as an independent term conveying the surplus of meaning that he wanted to impart to the study of human social organization or the history of world civilization. Demarcating Tradition from Event, while affirming both, became the pathway to his new science.

As crucial as is the distinction between Tradition and Event, it is important not to overanalyze Ibn Khaldun's motives for invoking, then pursuing this distinction. Was he smuggling philosophical reason into the domain of law and history? Was he a secularist undermining transcendental absolutes with pragmatic alternatives? Was he a crypto-Sufi jurist offsetting external formalism with internal dynamism? Even while all these speculations have circulated about Ibn Khaldun, their confirmation, or disavowal, depends on a prior question: what difference did Ibn Khaldun project between himself and most of his predecessors as well as his contemporaries? Above all, he was a littérateur cast as a jurist. His novelty was linguistic: (a) to use old terms in new ways and (b) to introduce new terms that might reflect the deeper layers of actual experience. He remained engaged by dyads or binary expressions of major phenomena, even as he often invoked dyads in order to qualify or even invert them. The intricate relationship of crafts to sciences, earlier discussed, is but one major instance of dyadic logic pushed to new limits. Crafts are a crucial category, related to custom yet different from it. Crafts, like custom, may be practiced everyday, but the former are also marked as intrinsically useful. They are indispensable to science and the sciences, even when the latter seem to distance themselves from their material origins. In the same way, Ibn Khaldun seems to privilege writing over orality when, toward the end of chapter 5, he asserts that "writing is the most useful craft" (331). Writing allows for calculation and scientific inquiry. It permits one to move over the range of symbols. It makes possible "the habit of intellection" (332). Because writing emerges at the core of urban cosmopolitan life, it, rather than poetry or oral communication, would seem to be the centerpiece of world civilization. Yet poetry remains a desideratum at the heart of sedentary culture, and the final sections of the final chapter (6:51–59) of the *Muqaddimah* are devoted to extolling the benefits, and clarifying the challenge, of poetry for city dwellers, whether they be Arabs or non-Arabs.

No one will ever know the full set of conversations between Ibn Khaldun and Tamerlane.[29] Addicted, as both were, to debate and argumentation, they must have discussed the nature of dynastic power, the collective urge to control (*ʿasabiyya*), and also the relationship between primitive/nomadic life (*badawah*) and the demands of urban civilization (*hadarah*). Samarqand and the splendors of its courtly life remain the legacy of Tamerlane's cultural sophistication and organizational prowess; the *Muqaddimah* and, in its shadow, *Kitab al-ʿibar*, remain the legacy of Ibn Khaldun's juridically inspired and linguistically channeled genius.[30] If you cannot travel to Samarqand, you can read the *Muqaddimah*. In it you will discover the marvel of a civilizational vision that exceeds both time and space, precisely because it is so attentive to each.

Notes

Bruce B. Lawrence, introduction to *The Muqaddimah: An Introduction to History*, by Ibn Khaldun, translated by Franz Rosenthal, abridged and edited by N. J. Dawood (Princeton, NJ: Princeton University Press, 2005), vii–xxv. Copyright © 1958 and 1967 by Princeton University Press. Reprinted by permission.

1 The original Arabic version was edited by Muhammad Tawit at-Tanji and published in 1370 in Cairo. It was reprinted in 1951 and translated into French by Abdesselam Cheddadi as *Le voyage d'Occident et d'Orient* (Paris: Sindbad, 1980). Regrettably, as noted by the translator of the English edition, Franz Rosenthal, Cheddadi omitted almost all of the poetry that Ibn Khaldun quoted (Rosenthal, "Ibn Khaldun in His Time," in *Ibn Khaldun and Islamic Ideology*, ed. Bruce B. Lawrence [Leiden: Brill, 1984], 25n11).

2 See Walter J. Fischel, *Ibn Khaldun and Tamerlane* (Berkeley: University of California Press, 1952), 14–17. As Fischel makes clear, the *Autobiography* was initially conceived of as an addendum, integral to the larger work *Kitab al-ʿibar*. Only toward the end of his life did Ibn Khaldun make it into an independent work, though without a proper introduction and with the title itself an afterthought.

3 A study of Ibn Khaldun's relationship to Sufism, or Islamic mysticism, begins with the observation that his character reflected "many discrepancies between his ideas and his actions, the contrast between his attempts at social reform and his own transgressions of social codes, his public sense and his pronounced egotism, his scientific impartiality and his very obvious personal preferences, his wide comprehension and his personal vanity," yet the same author concludes that "most of these contradictions can be ascribed to the dualistic character of all genius" (M. Syrier, "Ibn Khaldun and Islamic Mysticism," *Islamic Culture* 21 [1947]: 264, as cited in Fischel, *Ibn Khaldun and Tamerlane*, 28n66). *Editor's Note: See now the English translation of Ibn Khaldun on Sufism: Remedy for the Questioner in Search of Answers: Shifa' al-Sa'il li-tahdhib al-masa'il, trans. Yumna Ozer (Cambridge: Islamic Texts Society, 2017).*

A. J. Toynbee, *A Study of History*, vol. 3, *The Growths of Civilizations*, 2nd ed. (Oxford: Oxford University Press, 1935), 322. Cited in Franz Rosenthal, translator's introduction to *The Muqaddimah: An Introduction to History* by Ibn Khaldun (New York: Pantheon, 1958), 1:cxv. While Toynbee's praise may seem excessive, it reflects the broad reception of the *Muqaddimah* and the deep engagement with Ibn Khaldun's thought, in both Arabic and European sources, among Muslims as well as non-Muslims. The major sources till the late 1950s have been noted in Walter J. Fischel, selected bibliography to *The Muqaddimah*, trans. Franz Rosenthal (New York: Pantheon, 1958), 3:485–512. An updated bibliography, which alas includes a gratuitous critique of Fischel's bibliography, is to be found in Aziz Al-Azmeh, *Ibn Khaldun in Modern Scholarship: A Study in Orientalism* (London: Third World Centre for Research and Publication, 1981), 231–318. Not all readers, of course, are convinced by Ibn Khaldun's novel and complex thesis. Even Toynbee qualified his commendation, observing that "a modern Western critic may feel that Ibn Khaldun's empirical foundation is rather too narrow to bear the weight or to justify the range of his masterly generalization" (*Study of History*, 3:475).

4   For more extensive annotation of Ibn Khaldun as self-consciously marked by his difference from contemporaries, see Fischel, *Ibn Khaldun and Tamerlane*, 70–71n54, and also Rosenthal, "Ibn Khaldun in His Time," 16–24.

5   Though Ibn Khaldun had heard of the torture of a prominent Damascene judge at the hands of Tamerlane prior to their meeting (Fischel, *Ibn Khaldun and Tamerlane*, 78–79n81), he also knew that the first successful approach for amnesty to Tamerlane had come from a group of Damascene notables, led by a Sufi master (30, 64–65n32). The subsequent plunder of Damascus, once the city fell to the Mongol siege, is recounted in sparse detail by Ibn Khaldun. He does condemn the outcome, though not without qualification: "This was an absolutely dastardly and abominable deed, but changes in affairs are in the hands of Allah—He does with His creatures as He wishes, and decides in His kingdom as He wills" (39).

6   Fischel, *Ibn Khaldun and Tamerlane*, 47.

7   For the first and fullest development of Ibn Khaldun as an *adib*, see miriam cooke, "Ibn Khaldun and Language: From Linguistic Habit to Philological Craft," in Lawrence, *Ibn Khaldun and Islamic Ideology*, 27–36. There is no single English equivalent of *adab*, and so I leave it untranslated, yet for stylistic ease I have taken the liberty of rendering *adîb*, one who practices and pursues *adab*, as "littérateur" throughout.

8   It is Ibn Khaldun's contemporary, Ibn al-Khatib, who remarks on "his promising bid for recognition as a poet," at the same time that Ibn al-Khatib praises Ibn Khaldun for the latter's partial commentary on a poem that he (Ibn al-Khatib) had composed on the principles of jurisprudence. See citations in Rosenthal, translator's introduction to *The Muqaddimah*, 1:xliv–xlv.

9   Ahmad Dallal, "Science, Medicine, and Technology: The Making of a Scientific Culture," in *The Oxford History of Islam*, ed. John L. Esposito (New York: Oxford University Press, 1999), 213.

10 This list has been modified slightly here for rhetorical effect. Hereafter, parenthetical citations of page numbers refer to the present edition of the *Muqaddimah*.

11 Muhsin Mahdi depicts this practice as an expedient strategy for Ibn Khaldun: "It was necessary for Ibn Khaldun to use a specific style of writing through which he could successfully impart to the intimate circle of the few the doctrines intended for it without allowing the many to suspect even the existence of such doctrines in the ʿIbar [the larger project to which the *Muqaddimah* is an introduction]" (Mahdi, *Ibn Khaldun's Philosophy of History* [London: Allen and Unwin, 1957], 117).

12 Because of their central role in Ibn Khaldun's method, these two words, Event (*khabar*) and Tradition (*hadith*), are capitalized throughout the remainder of this essay.

13 Words or phrases given in parentheses are the translator's, while those in brackets are mine.
14 Rosenthal, *Muqaddimah*, 3:25.
15 Mohamed Talbi, *Ibn Khaldoun: Sa vie—son oeuvre* (Tunis: Maison Tunisienne de l'Édition, 1973), 44.
16 Jon W. Anderson, "Conjuring with Ibn Khaldun," in Lawrence, *Ibn Khaldun and Islamic Ideology*, 120.
17 cooke, "Ibn Khaldun and Language," 36n27.
18 It may be confusing to speak of writing as a craft when the sciences include the sciences linked to the Arabic language—grammar, lexicography, syntax, style, and criticism as well as literature. But Ibn Khaldun's unwavering criterion is manual labor, so that both the art of writing and book production are listed as crafts (*Muqaddimah* chap. 5, 327–28), while not only medieval Arabic language but also Qur'anic Arabic (Mudar), South Arabian Arabic (Himyarite), and Spanish Arabic are treated, along with poetry and the distinction between poetry and prose, in *Muqaddimah* chapter 6 as instances of scientific production.
19 Rosenthal, *Muqaddimah*, 3:331–32 (emphasis added). The connection between ʿasabiyya (group feeling) and ijmāʿ (consensus) discussed earlier relies on just this distinction: Ijmāʿ is not identical with ʿasabiyya, yet ʿasabiyya in Ibn Khaldun's use of the word does convey the force of ijmāʿ.
20 Rosenthal, *Muqaddimah*, 3:26.
21 See Rosenthal, translator's introduction, *Muqaddimah*, 1:lxviii, for an explanation of how the original introduction and chapter 1 of the *Kitab al-ʿibar* became one book, known collectively as the *Muqaddimah*.
22 Rosenthal, *Muqaddimah*, 1:76–77 (emphasis added). "Personality criticism" is Rosenthal's choice to define the subdiscipline of Hadith scholarship known as ʿilm al-jarh wal-taʿdil. Ibn Khaldun provides perhaps his best explanation of this term in examining the appeal of the Mahdi among the Fatimids by surveying all the Hadith relating to the Mahdi. In introducing this long and often convoluted section (51) of chapter 3, he notes that "Hadith scholars acknowledge negative criticism [of the personalities of Hadith transmitters] to have precedence over positive criticism [ʿinda ahl al-Hadith anna al-jarh muqaddamun ʿala al-taʿdil]" (Rosenthal, *Muqaddimah*, 2:158). The one exception, of course, is the *Sahihayn*, the two *Sahihs* of al-Bukhari and Muslim, which, though still open to criticism, are considered to be at a different, higher order of soundness than other Sunni collections.
23 For Abdallah Laroui, see *Islam et l'histoire* (Paris: Flammarion, 1999), 144n11. Mohamed Talbi's *Ibn Khaldoun: Sa vie—son oeuvre* remains one of the outstanding introductory books on the distinctive terminology and the even more distinctive historical vision of Ibn Khaldun. The quotation here is taken from page 33, note 1.
24 Marcia K. Hermansen, trans., *The Conclusive Argument from God: Shah Wali Allah of Delhi's "Hujjat Allah al-Baligha"* (Leiden: Brill, 1995), 387.
25 Hermansen, *Conclusive Argument from God*, 445.

26 That is, the exodus of the Prophet Muhammad from Mecca to Medina, due to the threats on his life, and those of his followers, from hostile Quraysh. It occurred in 622 CE and became the baseline for measuring years and centuries in the lunar, or Islamic, calendar.

27 Farhat J. Ziadeh, "Integrity (ʿAdalah) in Classical Islamic Law," quoting al-Busti, *Kitab al-majruhin*, in *Islamic Law and Jurisprudence: Studies in Honor of Farhat J. Ziadeh*, ed. Nicholas Heer (Seattle: University of Washington Press, 1990), 89.

28 Hadith criticism is in effect the science of personality criticism (ʿilm al-jarh wal-taʿdil). Though introduced at the outset of Book One of *Kitab al-ʿibar* (see 35n1), it is not fully explained till much later, requiring the reader to make explicit the connection that is left implicit by Ibn Khaldun.

29 Fischel, *Ibn Khaldun and Tamerlane*, 29–48, provides an English translation of Ibn Khaldun's summary accounts of his meetings with Tamerlane, but they are clearly just that, summaries, at the same time that the larger report to which they allude was cast in the form of a letter to the Marinid ruler, Abu Saʿid, of Fez, and so are designed to please, or at least not alarm, the ruler of the region where Ibn Khaldun's closest personal and professional ties remained till the end of his life (Fischel, *Ibn Khaldun and Tamerlane*, 110–12nn199–201).

30 The modern Syrian playwright Saʿdallah Wannus imagines a parallel declaration from Ibn Khaldun, though his is penned as a retort by Ibn Khaldun to one of his students (Sharaf ad-din) who is critical of his collaboration with Tamerlane: "History will not remember except the science which I have created and the book which I have written" (Saʿdallah Wannus, "*Munamnamat taʾrikhiyah*" [Historical miniatures], in *Al-aʿmal al-kamilah* [Damascus: Ahali, 1996], 418).

EIGHT

Mystical and Rational Elements in the Early Religious Writings of Sir Sayyid Ahmad Khan | 1979

Of all the Indian Muslims who lived during the troubled nineteenth century, Sir Sayyid Ahmad Khan is deservedly among the most renowned. His energy was prodigious, his activities numerous, and his results remarkable by any canon of human judgment. He was also able to organize and inspire others to work for the same cause to which he dedicated his own life, namely, "to spread the light of learning among Indians and to remove the clouds of ignorance and darkness that enveloped them."[1] Whether by Indians Sir Sayyid meant only Indian Muslims or both Muslims and Hindus has been and will continue to be a subject of debate for those who examine the deeds and words of his long life. Yet there can be no doubt that he threw himself into the battle for advancing and disseminating a composite culture at once Indian and Western, traditional and modern. The prime target of his practical concerns was education. Even while in British government service (from 1833 on) he managed to find time to organize local *madrasas* (institutional extensions of traditional Muslim religious training), and later he undertook the foundation of the first secular university for Indian Muslims, at Aligarh in Uttar Pradesh.[2] Scarcely less important was Sir Sayyid's establishment of a society for translating Western scientific writings into Urdu: preceding the foundation of the Mohammedan Anglo-Oriental College (which later became Aligarh Muslim University), the Scientific Society actually created the emotional climate as well as the curricular base necessary for the future success of Sir Sayyid's university.[3]

In the midst of numerous projects and despite continuance in government service till 1876, Sir Sayyid managed to do research and writing on a wide range of subjects, the most significant of which were Urdu language, history, and religion. While his contribution to both his native tongue and his native heritage has earned him near unanimous applause, the final judgment on his religious thought is far from clear. Most scholarship to date has focused on his controversial approaches to the Islamic tradition, as set forth in *Tahdhib al-akhlaq*, the incomplete Qur'an commentary *Tafsir al-Qurʾan*, and some later speeches (most notably in Lahore in 1884). A series of monographs and a spate of articles, both in English and Urdu, have studied various dimensions of Sir Sayyid's religious thought.[4] Few of these, however, make adequate assessment of the man with respect to the context in which he lived; virtually all ignore the early period of his life (i.e., prior to 1870) or else treat it as trivial prelude to the "great" production of his later years.

Sir Sayyid's religious thought is an extension of his basic personality. In this matter, as in every subject to which he directed his nimble mind and facile pen, he was not a systematic but a probing, searching, didactic thinker. He drew on many sources from a library which, even after the disaster of 1857, appears to have been well stocked with works from every branch of traditional Islamic scholarship.[5] He utilized the information at his disposal to express his own views vis-à-vis the circumstance, time, and place where he found a need to clarify his own views or was asked by a friend to do so. Though one cannot lock Sir Sayyid into any single ideology, including rationalism, it is possible to locate the persistent, recurrent tendencies in his thought and to interpret them in a contextual framework.

Sir Sayyid's early religious writings relate to standard topics, including the Prophet's biography, moral treatises, and the translation of theological discourses; but two are speculative essays on mystical practices, part of another contains biographical sketches of contemporary mystics, and still another, perhaps the major religious writing of Sir Sayyid, apart from *Tafsir al-Qurʾan*, is a commentary on the Bible entitled *Tabyin al-kalam fi tafsir al-taurat wal-injil ʿala millat al-Islam*.[6] Not all these writings are original (at least one of them is, by Sir Sayyid's own later admission, a mild form of theological plagiarism). Yet they do indicate tendencies in his thought and throw light on the major question that must be asked about Sir Sayyid: Was his touted rationalism a clear break from his traditional past, or was it an evolution which, when linked to specific and often turbulent events in his life, becomes intelligible as the consistent product of a restless and inquisitive mind? The very phrasing of the question may reveal our inherent bias that the latter pattern more neatly describes what happened to Sir Sayyid than the former, at least up until 1870. To share with the reader the source of this bias, we will examine the mystical writings from the early period of Sir Sayyid's life.

Sir Sayyid's motivation to write on mystical subjects and the import of what he says on this topic directly relates to his early childhood and upbringing. He was attached to the Naqshbandi Sufi order through both his father and his mother, and he was first introduced to the awesome inner power of Sufi luminaries in the Delhi environment where he was born and spent most of his early years.

The Delhi background of Sir Sayyid is especially important. His initial and continuing attachment to the once-flourishing capital of Mughal India is evident throughout the pages of *Athar as-sanadid* (Traces of Great Events), his prodigious archaeological and historical recapitulation of Delhi life. Sir Sayyid's association with Delhi meant that his earliest memories were linked to the political, religious, and cultural activity of that city. His father was employed by the Mughal court; the son was also expected to work there. His father was attached to a renowned Sufi saint of the day, Shah Ghulam ʿAli (d. 1824); the son also became attached to him. Moreover, there were certain skills to which upper-class Muslims of nineteenth-century Delhi were introduced at an early age. One was the reading and writing of Persian as well as Arabic. Another was recitation of the Qurʾan, together with the classics of Persian poetry, especially the three collections often described as "the scriptures of Persian Sufis": the *Gulistan* and *Bustan* of Saʿdi and the *Diwan-i Hafiz*.[7] To learn Persian well enough to recite verses without hesitation or error was no minor task.[8] Frequently, a young Muslim boy of Delhi was tutored at home by his closest relatives or, in their absence, by a hired tutor. In Sir Sayyid's case, fluency in Persian required long, tedious, often frustrating hours of practice. Once it took hold, however, he became so wedded to the cultural idiom of Persian poetry that we find couplets from Saʿdi and Hafiz sprinkling his letters and essays right up to the final years of his life.[9]

Sir Sayyid's attachment to Delhi was early and continuous. Not only do his reflections in "Traces" and, via Altaf Husayn Hali, in *Hayat-i Jawid* (The Life of Jawid) indicate the fondness he harbored for his native city, but it is a simple fact that apart from a seven-year stint in government service at Agra and Fatehpur Sikri (1839–46), he resided in Delhi for the first thirty-four years of his life, not leaving there to go any distance (for a sustained period of time) till his reluctant assignment to Bijnor in 1855. One result of Sir Sayyid's long-term location at the center of Mughal India is a marked lack of interest in events and people, including notable Muslims, who flourished elsewhere. Both his historical and religious writings prior to 1870 reflect Sir Sayyid's preoccupation with the environment of Delhi. "Traces" evinces a knowledge and appreciation of all facets of life in the capital. *Jam-i Jam*, "The Essence of Kingship," his first published work (1840), charts the reigns of Delhi rulers. *Silsilat al-muluk*, "The Genealogy of Kings" (1852), gives similar dynastic information in an abbreviated form. Moreover, Sir Sayyid's three landmark editions of historiographical works form the medieval period—*Ain-i Akbari* (1855), *Tarikh-i Firoz Shahi* (1862), and *Tuzuk-i Jahangiri* (1864)—all reveal his interest in the background events that led to the concentration of political power in Delhi.

The saints who become the focus of spiritual loyalty for Sir Sayyid are naturally an integral part of Delhi life. They trace their roots back to the revival of Sufi activity during the eighteenth century, when four spiritual giants emerged in the Mughal capital:

1. Shaykh Kalimullah (d. 1729), who rejuvenated the Nizamiya branch of the Chishti order and has been described as "the greatest Chishti saint... to build up a central organization of the Sufi order (since) Shaykh Nasiruddin Chiragh-i Dihli (d.1356)"[10]
2. Khwaja Mir Dard (d. 1785), who, together with his father, Muhammad Nasir (d. 1748), fashioned a novel mystical/literary tradition within the Naqshbandi order[11]
3. Mazhar Jan-i Janan (d. 1781), a vigorous proponent of the teachings of Shaykh Ahmad Sirhindi (d. 1624), whose contributions to Urdu letters and broadminded perception of the Hindu spiritual heritage have been widely acclaimed[12]
4. Shah Waliullah (d. 1762), an innovative breed of scholar/saint, combining in his life and teachings an admixture of traditional, mystical, and even rational impulses, the collective effect of which was to reorient the normative outlook of educated North Indian Muslims. Shah Waliullah was also fortunate enough to have had four sons, one of whom, Shah 'Abdul 'Aziz, spearheaded the continuation of his father's teaching.[13] All four sons retained a sense of identity with their family home as well as their unique spiritual heritage. They, and their numerous offspring (spiritual as well as physical), were a major force in Delhi life throughout the last half of the eighteenth and the better part of the nineteenth century.

If we accept the generally held view that Shah Waliullah considered himself to be closer to the tradition of Sirhindi than to that of the other Sufi orders into which he was also initiated, the predominance of the recently arrived Naqshbandi order is obvious.[14] Yet the Naqshbandi bearers were not all of the same stripe. They represented different tangents of the common tradition that harks back to Shaykh Ahmad Sirhindi. These differences, which became important for understanding Sir Sayyid's early religious outlook, are traceable through the "Commemoration of the People of Delhi" section of "Traces."[15] In gauging Sir Sayyid's early religious views, one must look to the two subsections on major saints and notable religious scholars of his day, for the substantial biographies within each provide a valuable clue to his thinking. Among Sufi luminaries, Shah Ghulam ʿAli of Delhi and Sayyid Ahmad Shahid of Raebareli are more lengthily described than others; among scholars, Mawlana Shah ʿAbdul Aziz, Mufti Sadruddin Azurda, and Muhammad Ismaʿil Shahid are the major figures. Even more curious than the distinction between major and minor biographies, however, is the priority of subsections within "Commemoration" and the allocation of entries to particular subsections. Of first rank among Sir Sayyid's Delhi associates are the great Sufi luminaries linked to his family; *nearly all of them are Naqshbandis*. Not only are they Naqshbandis, but they are Mujaddidi Naqshbandis. Not only are they Mujaddidi Naqshbandis, but they are members of Shah Ghulam ʿAli's fellowship of disciples. The first four biographies of major saints describe the eighteenth-century descendants of Mazhar Jan-i Janan: Shah Ghulam ʿAli, Shah Abu Saʿid (d. 1860), and the following two contemporaries of Sir Sayyid: Shah Ahmad Saʿid and Shah ʿAbdul Ghani (d. 1876). Latter-day descendants of two other famous Delhi Naqshbandi families, Shah Muhammad Afaq and Muhammad Nasir, are mentioned in the same subsection, while the only Chishtis described are the Delhi initiates into the revitalized discipline of Shah Kalimullah. The remaining figures are minor, except for Ahmad Shahid.

In fact, the inclusion of Ahmad Shahid in the subsection on Sufi luminaries is puzzling. Admittedly, he was a Sufi and a political/religious figure whose influence was not lost on Sir Sayyid. Yet his citation as a Sufi luminary in "Commemoration" separates him from all the other Delhi religious figures with whom he was intimately associated, namely, the descendants of Shah Waliullah. This vast company of nineteenth-century divines and reformers are treated in the subsection on religious scholars. Sir Sayyid accords them the recognition which they richly deserve as the most learned and influential religious scholars (*ʿulamaʾ*) of their day. The subsection begins with a biographical sketch of Shah ʿAbdul ʿAziz, proceeds to a glowing notice on Mufti Sadruddin Arzuda, and then mentions the deeds and words but mostly the deeds of Mawlana Rashiduddin Khan, Shah Rafi'uddin, Mawlana Makhsusullah, Shah 'Abdul Qadir, 'Abdul Hayy, and Muhammad Isma'il, among others. Many of these figures, in particular Shah 'Abdul 'Aziz, 'Abdul-Hayy, and Muhammad Isma'il, were closely connected with Ahmad Shahid. Yet, except for 'Abdul Hayy, whose total biography covers less than half a page of printed text, the other two are described with only minimal reference to the connection between them and Ahmad Shahid.

The most favorable reading of this uneven distribution of attention is to suggest that Sir Sayyid recognized the superior spiritual attainments of Ahmad Shahid in the realm of mysticism and accordingly ranked him above the illustrious offspring of the house of Shah Waliullah. The other, less favorable reading is to deduce that Sir Sayyid saw the reformist efforts of both Shah 'Abdul 'Aziz and Muhammad Isma'il as their independent contribution to the life of Indian Islam in nineteenth-century Delhi. In this case, the organizational arrangement of "Commemoration" highlights their respective roles while minimizing their connection with Ahmad Shahid.

An overview of "Commemoration" in "Traces" reveals a double emphasis in Sir Sayyid's early religious outlook:

1. He defined as saints only those who were connected with his family line on his father's side, or others who resembled them in their practices. Most happened to be Mujaddidi Naqshbandis, and all fit into the traditional mode of the devout Sufi who is dedicated to the Qur'an, *hadith*, and meditation. Few are cited for their opposition to degenerate practices in Sufism, though it has been alleged that accommodation to magical and idolatrous practices from the Hindu tradition was widespread in nineteenth-century Muslim communities, whether in Qur'an exegsis (*tafsir*), *hadith*, jurisprudence (*fiqh*), or practical mysticism (*tasawwuf*) itself. Especially remarkable for what it does not say is the biography of Ahmad Shahid; his reforming efforts garner two sentences out of five pages and refer only to his travels beyond Delhi (specifically to Calcutta, where his presence was said to have deterred people from buying liquor and forced the local distillery to close down).

2. Sir Sayyid describes the descendants of Shah 'Abdul 'Aziz as primarily reformers rather than saints. They were, in his view, fierce opponents of separatist and traditional elements within Indian Islam; their constant endeavor was to reclaim the masses of Muslims for a pure Islam. Though pious ascriptions are directed to them (as they are to everyone in

"Commemoration"), they are not associated with specifically Sufi spiritual practices, such as "visualizing one's Sufi master" (*tasawwur-i shaykh*) and granting amulets (*taʿwidh*); yet sources other than "Commemoration" indicate that even the traditionist Shah ʿAbdul ʿAziz engaged in both activities.[16]

The separation of "religious scholars" from "Sufi luminaries" reflects something more than a spate of pages or a shift of titles. Personal detail is as absent from the "religious scholars" as it is present in the "Sufi luminaries." Several members of the house of Shah Waliullah were among Sir Sayyid's own teachers, but no suggestion of these ties appears in the biographical profiles of "Commemoration." It is known, for instance, that Makhsusullah was entrusted with the task of instructing Sir Sayyid in the Qurʾan, yet the brief biography of Makhsusullah in the "religious scholars" subsection of "Commemoration" omits mention of any relationship between Sir Sayyid and this esteemed grandson of Shah Waliullah.[17] Mamluk ʿAli, also acknowledged to have been one of Sir Sayyid's most influential teachers, is similarly accorded a cursory notice in "Commemoration."[18] No reference is made to the personal relationship that he enjoyed with Sir Sayyid.

When one considers the implicit as well as explicit data provided in "Commemoration," it seems fair to conclude that at the time Sir Sayyid wrote "Traces" (1846–47), he remained strongly attached to the spiritual legacy of his immediate family, especially on the paternal side. While he was intellectually the heir of the Mujaddidi Naqshbandi line as interpreted by Shah Waliullah and his many descendants, he still placed primary spiritual value on his affiliation with another Mujaddidi Naqshbandi line, that stemming from Mazhar Jan-i Janan through Shah Ghulam ʿAli to Abu Saʿid and Shah ʿAbdul Ghani.[19]

When Sir Sayyid's father died in 1838, he was buried by the side of his spiritual master, Shah Ghulam ʿAli, who had predeceased him by some fifteen years. It is not surprising, therefore, that in his later years, whenever Sir Sayyid returned to Delhi he used to visit the graves of both Shah Ghulam ʿAli and his father.[20] Though the spiritual descendants of Shah Ghulam ʿAli are alleged to have refused the gifts of Sir Sayyid after he joined the British civil service in 1839, the event does not seem to have diminished Sir Sayyid's affections for the successors to Shah Ghulam ʿAli.[21] Shah Abu Saʿid, Shah Ahmad Saʿid, and Shah ʿAbd ul-Ghani are described in "Commemoration" in scarcely less rapturous terms than their illustrious spiritual forefather.

It is the youngest son of Abu Saʿid, Shah ʿAbdul Ghani (1814–1879), who comes closest to being a contemporary of Sir Sayyid, and "Commemoration" repeatedly eulogizes his extraordinary devotion to ascetical practices. This detailed account of a comparatively obscure saint further underscores the deep, continuing attachment Sir Sayyid had for the spiritual progeny of Shah Ghulam ʿAli.²²

It is difficult to resist the conclusion that underlying Sir Sayyid's allegiance to this particular group of Mujaddidi Naqshbandi saints was the sense of an almost blood relationship. His father had been adopted by Shah Ghulam ʿAli as the latter's son; he himself regarded the saint as his grandfather. Since Ghulam ʿAli had no physical offspring, Sir Sayyid's family were his descendants, and hence brothers to those who inherited his spiritual mantle, namely, Shah Abu Saʿid and his successors. The accent on an almost blood relationship becomes reinforced in the actual blood relationship of Shah Abu Saʿid, who traced his physical descent back to no less a saint than Shaykh Ahmad Sirhindi through his two major successors—namely, his third son, Shaykh Muhammad Maʿsum, and the latter's grandson, the preceptor of Alamgir (Emperor Aurangzeb), Shaykh Sayfuddin.²³ One might play down the importance of such ties, except that it is Sir Sayyid himself who emphasizes their centrality both in what he says about Shah Abu Saʿid and what he does not say about contemporary Naqshbandi saints outside this Sufi lodge (*khanqah*): Shah Muhammad Nasir, the maternal grandson of Khwaja Mir Dard and a distant relative of Sir Sayyid via his mother's family, is mostly described with reference to his esteemed mother's forefathers; Sir Sayyid does not even mention the gatherings he frequently attended in his youth at the *khanqah* of Khwaja Muhammad Nasir.²⁴ As for the inheritors of Shah Waliullah via Shah ʿAbdul ʿAziz, they are, as we noted earlier, treated under an independent subsection of "Commemoration," with no mention of their allegiance to the Naqshbandiya or to any other Sufi order.

While Sir Sayyid was closely attached to his mother in many respects, it does not appear that the spiritual affiliations of her forefathers produced an enduring impact on him.²⁵ In the *Hayat-i Jawid*, Hali states that Sir Sayyid's mother admired Shah ʿAbdul ʿAziz yet offered her *bayʿa* (pledge of allegiance) to Shah Ghulam ʿAli.²⁶ The major Sufi group associated with Sir Sayyid's mother's family were the Rasul Shahis, a clan of *be-sharʿ majdhubis* (i.e., nonconformist ecstatics), who traced their lineage to the founder of the Suhrawardi Sufi order. In "Commemoration" Sir Sayyid devotes a separate subsection to the Rasul Shahis, and links them more closely to Muslim traditionalism than do other sources.²⁷ The account of his maternal great uncle, Shah Fida Husain (whom Sir Sayyid never mentions as his maternal great uncle), receives the most extensive treatment, including a citation of his several Persian verses on the theme of "unity of existence" (*wahdat al-wujud*).

Sir Sayyid's religious writings subsequent to "Commemoration" only dimly hint at the close ties he nurtured from the time of his childhood toward the followers of Shah Ghulam ʿAli. A series of minor epistles which span the period from 1849 to 1854 relate directly or inferentially to the *mujahidin* movement. Three of them seem to support the *mujahidin* without reservation. *Kalimat al-haqq* ("The Word of Truth"), written in 1849, criticizes the lack of firm guidelines for admitting *murids* or disciples into the various Sufi orders. No reference is made to specific instances of heretical practices (*bidʿat*) among Indian Muslims. Sir Sayyid, instead, focuses his attention largely on those passages from the Qur'an and *hadith* which he feels set forth the qualifications of a real Sufi master or *pir*. *Rah-i-sunnat dar radd-i bidʿat* (The Way of Correct Practice in Refuting Innovation), written in 1850, is a severe and lengthy critique of heretical practices among Indian Muslims. In a later preface, included in the collected editions of his writings, Sir Sayyid states that he was moved to write this polemical piece after an impassioned discussion with Mufti Sadruddin Azurda at a time when the so-called Wahhabi influence was pervasive in the Muslim community of Delhi. By his own admission, the major part of the treatise is derived from Shah Muhammad Ismaʿil Shahid's *Ihqaq al-haqq as-sarih fi ahwal al-mayyit wad-darih*.[28] Like *Rah-i-sunnat dar radd-i bidʿat*, the third epistle was inspired by a heated conversation, this time with Hajji Imdadullah, the most famous Sabiri Chishti of nineteenth-century India.[29] He had convinced Sir Sayyid that the moral corruption of young Muslims could only be reversed by supplying them with an indisputably authoritative moral alternative. Accordingly, Sir Sayyid had set out to translate the *Kimia-yi saʿadat* of Abu Hamid al-Ghazali (d. 1111), but only completed the introductory chapters before turning his hand to other tasks in 1854.

There was a fourth epistle produced in this period (1852): *Namiqa dar bayan-i masʾala-i tasawwur-i shaykh* (Epistle explaining the practice of visualizing the shaykh). Unlike the other epistles, it was written in Persian, and unlike them, it cannot be construed as supportive of the *mujahidin* movement. To understand why and how Sir Sayyid defended a traditional Sufi practice, we must first review his relationship to what has recently been termed the neo-Sufi movement.

The emergence of a new brand of Sufism within Indian Islam has been the subject of much recent scholarship on Muslim revivalist movements of the nineteenth century.[30] Specifically labeled as neo-Sufis are those Indian Muslims belonging to the Shah Waliullah school who rallied around the charismatic figure of Ahmad Shahid, participated in his extensive preaching campaigns and skirmishes with the Sikhs, and then either perished with him at the Battle of Balakot

(1831) or carried on his teaching in Patna, Jaunpur, or Calcutta following that military fiasco in which not only Sayyid Ahmad but his intellectual companion and close adviser, Muhammad Isma'il, together with many other Muslims, in the words of "Traces," "took the high road to heaven."[31]

The principal aim of these neo-Sufis or, more accurately, *mujahidin* was to pare down and revivify Islam by eliminating Hindu accretions to Muslim thought and practice while simultaneously exalting the *pir/imam* of the age, Ahmad Shahid. The link of this movement to incipient Islamic nationalism has been much exaggerated, both in defense and refutation of the thesis that Ahmad Shahid and his followers were conducting military *jihad* either against Sikhs or British or both and had a priori intended to establish a separate Islamic state on the subcontinent. The thesis has outlived its utility; it will not be embellished with still more attention in this essay.

Sir Sayyid's relationship to the principal figures in the *mujahidin* camp, namely, Sayyid Ahmad, Muhammad Isma'il, and 'Abdul Hayy, is usually gauged by excerpting encomia from the biographical accounts on them in "Traces," or by appealing to his post-1857 correspondence in their defense.[32] But the evidence of "Traces" suggests that Sir Sayyid is trying to work out his own solution to the problems posed by the *mujahidin*: if it is unavoidable to become a reformer, he at least wants to be a reformer on terms which are congenial to his own views of Muslim society and its fideistic infrastructure. And so when we examine closely accounts of the first *mujahidin* in "Commemoration," we find that Sir Sayyid's flattery of Ahmad Shahid is at best brief, at least in part superficial, and even on occasion sarcastic.[33] The portrait of Ahmad Shahid which emerges from the pages of "Traces" is one of a sincere mystic whose religious claims were slavishly accepted mostly by greedy and uncouth Afghans who themselves were manipulated by cunning Sikhs.[34] He seems to have made others the dupes of his own inner vision for martyrdom; his reformist efforts are tangential to his self-image as the *imam* and *pir* of the age. By contrast, Muhammad Isma'il is treated as a figure of immense personal and spiritual prowess. In Sir Sayyid's view, he was the real crusader against society's moral ills and heretical innovations. Though "Commemoration" also acknowledges the intensity of Muhammad Isma'il's relationship to Ahmad Shahid, only a small portion of the total biography of Muhammad Isma'il concerns their complementary activities in the *jihad* movement.

The evidence of "Traces" is mirrored and extended in writings from the next period in Sir Sayyid's life, the years from 1846 to 1854. Although he does author epistles in a reformist vein, it is Muhammad Isma'il, not Ahmad Shahid, whom he invokes authoritatively, even to the extent of reproducing a partial translation of one of his books without full acknowledgment. Yet his respect for Muhammad Isma'il stops short of accepting the latter's condemnation of certain aspects from the Islamic past which Sayyid Ahmad feels are fully defensible in the light of Qur'an and *hadith*. One issue of special importance in Sir Sayyid's life was the Naqshbandi practice of "visualizing the Sufi master" (*tasawwur-i shaykh*), which Ahmad Shahid had condemned as crypto-idol worship. Muhammad Isma'il had dutifully noted this critique in compiling the *malfuzat* (conversations) of his *pir*, which subsequently became the handbook of the *mujahidin* movement, *Sirat-i mustaqim*.[35]

The *Namiqa dar bayan-i mas'ala-i tasawwur-i shaykh* is Sir Sayyid's personal response to the charge of heresy leveled by the *mujahidin* against a time-honored spiritual practice of his forefathers. It reveals Sir Sayyid's independence from a movement which shaped his concerns but could not and did not govern his responses to those concerns. Its authorship in Persian at a time when most of Sir Sayyid's writings were essays in Urdu or translations of Persian works into Urdu indicates the special theological sanctity he accorded his thoughts on this subject.

The "Epistle" is, however, more than a polemical response to a delicate intra-Muslim issue. It also provides a clue to the change going on in Sir Sayyid's mind; for while publicly defending a traditional mystical practice, Sir Sayyid simultaneously advances arguments that suggest an incipient rationalism.

On both accounts—its critique of the *mujahidin* and its anticipation of the next phase in Sir Sayyid's religious thought—the text of "Epistle" warrants detailed consideration, not least in its affirmation of *tasawwur-i shaykh* or silent meditation as a legitimate, necessary practice, not the dubious *bid'a* or innovation depicted by its opponents. A relevant excerpt reads as follows:

> Now when you have understood these Prefatory Remarks, understand further that *our Naqshbandi saints* (*hazrat-i naqshbandiya-yi-ma*)—may the mercy of God be upon all of them—have ordered this same silent meditation (*muraqaba*), because the visualization of the Sufi master is necessary for the seeker (*murid*), both in the actual state of remembrance and otherwise. It is through sincere and continuous remembrance alone that love for the master wells up in the heart of the *murid*, till gradually the stage of annihilation in the master takes place. At that stage there develops a relationship between the perceptive faculty (*nafs-i natiqa*) of the master and the *murid* in which the benefit of the company and guidance of the master takes root

in the perceptive self of the *murid*. The base perceptive self is then purified and cleansed and brought to higher stages. In this station whatever I might say about the image of the master would be justified. If I say that the image of the master is a cushion (*anbub*) for receiving the mercy of God, I would have spoken the truth, and if I presume to say that without the image of the master I shall not find a way to God or the Prophet, then I would be right.

Now this love for the master is probably of two kinds: inherited (*wahbi*) and intentional (*kasbi*), the second coming by deliberate visualization and intentional remembrance. I call the first compulsory and the second voluntary, but *with respect to the result there is no difference between them*.

Nonetheless liars have concluded that these saints in the state of *muraqaba* presumed the master to be present and seeing and knowing and cognizant at every time and in every condition. And by *muraqaba* they mean the same thing, namely, that the master is present and looking at us without intermediary and is aware of the condition of the one who remembers him without any intermediary or without any physical cause.

God forbid that the pure skirt of these saints should be stained with such belief. To the contrary, as you know, the state of *muraqaba* is derived (*ma'khuz*) from the state and special devotions (*waridat*) of the companions of the companions and followers of the followers of the Prophet. The traditions of the Prophet are in support of this practice, and the religious scholars attach the same meaning to the invocation (*khitab*): Prayers and peace be upon you, O Prophet, together with the mercy of God and His blessing.

How then can this practice be an innovation (*bid'at*) and proscribed by the *shari'a*, especially since these saints regard *muraqaba* as an instrument and intermediary for higher purposes? As long as purification of the soul is achieved, together with annihilation in the Prophet—which I hope it may be the good fortune of all true believers to attain—I have no objection against anyone following this practice. What we have known is enough for us, though the ignorant may beat their heads against the rock.

And what Muhammad Isma'il has said in the *Sirat-i mustaqim* is also worth noting in this connection. To my knowledge he was a man of attainment (*banda-i kaifiyat*) and however much his writing was like this (i.e., condemning *muraqaba* and those who practiced it), he was in the service of those who regarded diligence in *muraqaba* as a binding duty day in and day out, and to his last breath he viewed those same Naqshbandi saints as his own pride and he never walked on the path of doubt toward them.

And may peace be upon those who are obedient to the guide.

Of the several interesting features of this passage, the rational intrusions and the critique of the *mujahidin* are especially relevant to evaluating Sir Sayyid's early religious thought.

To defend the practice of "visualizing the Sufi master" (*tasawwur-i shaykh*), Sir Sayyid used a form of deductive argumentation. He begins with the general proposition about the effect of company and from it proceeds to justify the specific practice of meditation on the image of the preceptor, and eventual annihilation in him. Sir Sayyid also imputes to reason the ability to perceive the intimacy of affection, even in connection with the pain of separation caused by death. ("What is meant by remembrance," he argues at one point, "can also be realized by the intellect.") It matters not that the argument may be logically weak; it is an early evidence of Sir Sayyid's constant search for a practical, commonsensical explanation of whatever problem he confronts.

Another equally significant rational element in the "Epistle" is Sir Sayyid's attempted reconciliation of two opposite viewpoints, the orthodox Muslim and the Sufi, by implying that both are describing a higher reality that is the same and, therefore, that the difference between them is merely nominal. At the outset of the Third Preface, he declares: "People have given different names to that which is implanted according to the nature of their admiration for the doer. Those whose souls have been burnt in the fire of passion call it love, while those who know the traditions of devotion call it faith." Similarly, with respect to the receptive capacity, he reasons: "Unless the receptive capacity—whether one calls it love or faith—has been created in you, love will not influence you." In one of the most puzzling passages of the "Epistle" cited previously, he applies the same conceptual approach to his depiction of love of the Shaykh: "Now this love of the Shaykh is probably of two kinds: inherited (*wahbi*) and intentional (*kasbi*), the second coming by deliberate visualization and intentional remembrance. I call the first compulsory, and the second voluntary, but with respect to the result there is no difference between them."

Sir Sayyid, of course, is not the first scholar to attempt to find the ultimate truth behind different labels. In the realm of Indo-Muslim mysticism Shah Waliullah broached the same exercise in his *Faysala-yi wahdat al-wujud wa'l-shuhud*. It is a mark of the synthesizing propensity common to rationalism and mysticism that they encourage efforts to bridge seemingly disparate realities by pointing to a higher reality inclusive of both. Implicit in such efforts, of course, is the assumption that the synthesizer has the ability as well as the authority to perceive a reality which is indisputably higher than that of either of the two opposing parties.[36]

The purpose of the rational arguments in the "Epistle" is to defend those whom Sir Sayyid describes as "our Naqshbandi saints." Whether these saints were only the followers of Shah Ghulam ʿAli or also the members of Shah ʿAbdul ʿAziz's school, who likewise practiced *tasawwur-i shaykh*, is unclear. The lack of references in "Commemoration" to the "religious scholars" as practicing Sufis suggests the restricted application of this argument to Shah Ghulam ʿAli's spiritual descendants, but the final paragraph of the "Epistle" contains a reference to those saints whom Muhammad Ismaʿil revered, i.e., members of the entourage of Shah ʿAbdul ʿAziz. What is more important, however, than identifying the saints whom Sir Sayyid had in mind at the time of writing the "Epistle" is his whole-hearted defense of them against the attacks of the Indian *mujahidin* or neo-Sufis, especially Ahmad Shahid. In a later review article on *Rah-i sunnat dar radd-i bidʿat*, Sir Sayyid repeats the allegation that the so-called Wahhabis often reckoned as *bidʿat* what was actually traceable to the *sunna* of the Prophet and his companions.[37]

On the basis of evidence from both "Traces" and the early religious epistles, especially the "Epistle," it is now possible to state that Sir Sayyid's views of the *mujahidin* shifted after 1857. Prior to that time, he viewed them as reactionaries as well as revivalists; he felt that they seemed so intent on purifying Islam that they were willing and eager to eliminate any practice that did not conform to their own interpretation of the Islamic past. After 1857, however, Sir Sayyid wished to stress the commonality of Indian Muslims as well as their loyalty to the British government. He therefore overlooks his own past differences with the *mujahidin*, and ignoring their Sufi origins (which distinguished them from the Arab Wahhabis) and their political intentions (which linked them to their Arab namesakes), he defines *all* Wahhabis as exemplar Muslims. In a letter to the *London Times* in 1871, he declares: "A Wahhabi is the faithful observer of the injunctions of the Koran and the precepts of the Prophet, and his religious opinions are anything but irrational. I cannot help believing that patient inquiry would show that more than half of the Mohamedan population of India belong to that sect, and yet they are as loyal subjects as it is possible for a foreigner to be."[38]

For our purposes, the major point to be noted in Sir Sayyid's own intellectual development is not his later views on the neo-Sufis or the so-called Wahhabis but his early and defiant departure from the platform of the *mujahidin*. While their presence and activities may have moved him to consider the necessity of reform for Indian Muslims, the nature and direction of that reform, as he conceived it, had to proceed on different lines from those promulgated by the *mujahidin*. After 1852, while remaining attached to the traditional sources of Islamic belief, especially the Qur'an and *hadith*, Sir Sayyid began to familiarize himself with the writings and conceptual apparatus of medieval Muslim rationalists. During the next decade he developed the fledgling attempt at rational justification which first appeared in the "Epistle" into a broad scheme for understanding all religious truth.

The incipient rationalism of Sir Sayyid might have remained limited to traditional Islamic topics except for the momentous catastrophe of 1857. He himself spelled out the nature of the so-called Sepoy Mutiny in a book which remains one of the classic sources on that event: *Asbab-i baghawat-i Hind*.[39] But what Sir Sayyid does not and could not describe in writing was the subsequent effect of the Mutiny on his entire life. It marked a precipitous shift. It is believed that Sir Sayyid's trip to England during 1869–70, which K. A. Nizami described as "the most significant event in his life," shifted his outlook perceptibly to a kind of exclusivizing rationalism that was as antithetical to medieval Islamic rationalism as it was to Sufism.[40] While his approach to the intellectual and practical dilemmas of the Islamic tradition was preponderantly rationalist after 1870, the larger arc of his influence was marked by his keen intelligence, boundless energies, and generous disposition. Collectively, these traits provided a worthy paradigm for his co-religionists and his fellow countrymen, one that endures till today.

Notes

Bruce B. Lawrence, "Mystical and Rational Elements in the Early Religious Writings of Sir Sayyid Ahmad Khan," in *The Rose and the Rock*, edited by Bruce Lawrence (Durham, NC: Duke University Programs in Comparative Studies on Southern Asia and Islamic and Arabian Development Studies, 1979).

1. The statement is adapted from a speech given at the foundation of the Ghazipur *madrasa* in 1864; it is quoted in K. A. Nizami, *Sayyid Ahmad Khan* (Delhi: Indian Ministry of Information and Broadcasting, 1966), 71.
2. The nature and shortcomings of *madrasa* education in the Asian subcontinent have been ably reviewed by S. Maqbul Ahmad, "Madrasa System of Education and Indian Muslim Society," in *India and Contemporary Islam*, ed. S. T. Lokhandwalla (Simla: Indian Institute of Advanced Study, 1971), 125–36. *Editor's Note: See also the excellent Ebrahim Moosa, What Is a Madrasa? (Chapel Hill: University of North Carolina Press, 2015).*
3. The original name of Aligarh Muslim University, still current among North Indian Muslims, was *madrasat al-ʿulum*. See Altaf Husayn Hali, *Hayat-i Jawid* (Delhi: Idara-yi

Adabiyyat, 1979), 19; H. K. Sherwani, *The Aligarh Movement* (Aligarh: Aligarh Muslim University, 1969), 26. *Editor's Note: See also David Lelyveld, Aligarh's First Generation (Princeton, NJ: Princeton University Press, 1978).*

4   The Lahore speech is quoted in several sources on the life of Sir Sayyid, e.g., in Sherwani, *Aligarh Movement*, 13–16. The standard three books on Sir Sayyid's religious thought are J. M. S. Baljon, *The Reforms and Religious Ideas of Sir Sayyid Ahmad Khan*, 3rd ed. (Lahore: Orientalia, 1967); B. A. Dar, *Religious Thought of Sayyid Ahmad Khan* (Lahore: Institute of Islamic Culture, 1957); Christian Troll, *Sayyid Ahmad Khan: A Reinterpretation of Muslim Theology* (New Delhi: Vikas, 1978). Among the notable articles on Sir Sayyid's interpretation of the Qur'an are H. K. Sherwani, "The Socioreligious Thought of Syed Ahmad Khan, with Special Reference to the Qur'an," in *India and Contemporary Society*, ed. S. T. Lokhandwalla (Simla: Indian Institute of Advanced Study, 1971): 53–59; and E. Hahn, "Sir Syed's 'The Controversy over Abrogation (in the Qur'an),'" *Muslim World* 64, no. 2 (April 1974): 124–33. *Editor's Note: See also Khurram Hussain, Islam as Critique: Sayyid Ahmad Khan and the Challenge of Modernity (New York: Bloomsbury, 2019); Yasmin Saikia and M. Raisur Rahman, eds., The Cambridge Companion to Sayyid Ahmad Khan (Cambridge: Cambridge University Press, 2019). For a comprehensive reevaluation of latent Sufi elements in Sir Sayyid's thought, see Jamal Malik, "Sufi Amnesia in Sayyid Ahmad Khan's Tahdhib al-Akhlaq," in Sufism East and West: Mystical Islam and Cross-Cultural Exchange in the Modern World, ed. Jamal Malik and Saeed Zarrabi-Zadeh (Leiden: Brill, 2019), 76–103.*

5   While no catalog of Sir Sayyid's personal library has been preserved, its size and worth may be inferred from the fact that when he needed funds for his 1869–70 trip to England, he not only mortgaged his house and borrowed money but also "disposed of his library" (Nizami, *Sayyid Ahmad Khan*, 54).

6   *Editor's Note: See Sayyid Ahmad Khan, The Gospel According to Sayyid Ahmad Khan (1817–1898), trans. and ed. Christian W. Troll, Charles M. Ramsey, and M. Basharat Mughal (Leiden: Brill, 2020). Bruce Lawrence has authored the foreword to this translation.*

7   Shihab ad-Din Suhrawardi, *'Awarif al-ma'arif*, trans. H. W. Clarke (New York: Weiser, 1970), 7.

8   An embarrassing incident about Sir Sayyid's early struggles with Persian is recounted in Nizami, *Sayyid Ahmad Khan*, 28n22, 35.

9   Examples abound in *Tabyin al-kalam*: see I:2; II:53, 97, 158, 164, 232.

10 K. A. Nizami, "Chishtiyya," *Encyclopaedia of Islam*, 2nd ed., 2:55. Aziz Ahmad (*Studies of Islamic Culture in the Indian Environment* [Oxford: Clarendon, 1964], 138) also speaks of the Shaykh's openness toward Hindus.

11 See A. Schimmel, "Khwaja Mir Dard, Poet and Mystic," *German Scholars on India* I (Varanasi: Chowkhamba Sanskrit Series Office, 1973), 279–93; and A. Schimmel, *Pain and Grace: A Study of Two Mystical Writers of 18th Century India* (Leiden: Brill, 1976), 31–147, on Mir Dard.

12 Consult, e.g., M. Mujeeb, *Indian Muslims* (London: Allen and Unwin, 1967), 386–88; Y. Husain, *Glimpses of Medieval Indian Culture* (Bombay: Asia Publishing House, 1973), 54–55; and Y. Friedmann, "Medieval Muslim Views of Indian Religions," *Journal of the American Oriental Society* 95, no. 2 (1975): 217–21. Editor's Note: See also SherAli Tareen, "Translating the 'Other': Early-Modern Muslim Understandings of Hinduism," *Journal of the Royal Asiatic Society* 27, no. 3 (2017): 435–60.

13 Little critical work has been done on the life and thought of Shah ʿAbdul ʿAziz; apart from constant reference to his *fatwa* against the British in 1804 (e.g., Aziz Ahmad, *Islamic Modernism in India and Pakistan* [New York: Oxford University Press, 1967], 19–21), slight attention has been paid to this major figure in eighteenth- and early nineteenth-century Indian Islam. Note, however, Azd ad-din Khan, "The Contribution of Shah Abdul Aziz to Islamic Theology and Mysticism," unpublished Ph.D. dissertation, Department of Islamic Studies, Aligarh Muslim University, Aligarh, 1974. Editor's Note: See Saiyid Athar Abbas Rizvi, *Shah ʿAbd al-ʿAziz: Puritanism, Sectarian Polemics, and Jihad* (New Delhi: Munshiram Monoharlal, 1982).

14 See especially the manuscript *Shawahid at-tajdid*, in which Shah Waliullah describes Sirhindi as the *mujaddid* of the eleventh century AH. A summary of the contents of this manuscript is set forth in Y. Friedmann, *Shaykh Ahmad Sirhindi* (Montreal: McGill University Press, 1970), 103–4.

15 Editor's Note: See Saiyid Ahmad Khan, *Asar-us-Sanadid*, trans. and ed. Rana Safvi (New Delhi: Tulika, 2018), 207–61.

16 On the practice of *muraqaba*, he was criticized by his fledgling disciple, Sayyid Ahmad Shahid, who urged him to give it up because it was simply an interiorized form of idol worship (see Muhammad Hedayetullah, *Sayyid Ahmad: A Study of the Religious Reform Movement of Sayyid Ahmad of Rae Bareli* [Lahore: Ashraf, 1970], 6). However, Shah ʿAbdul ʿAziz retained this practice, as did numerous other scholar mystics in British India (see, e.g., B. Metcalf, "The Compleat ʿAlim: Muslim Religious Leadership in the Late 19th Century," an occasional paper delivered at the University of Chicago, South Asia Committee, 1973, especially 33–36). With respect to *taʿwidh*, we have the curious account in *Hayat-i Jawid* (26), that Sir Sayyid's mother and her family, in spite of their dedication to Shah ʿAbdul ʿAziz, could not condone the often crude amulets he was in the habit of conferring on his disciples. In the same passage, however, it is stated that Sir Sayyid's own sons, Sayyid Hamid and Sayyid Mahmud, received from Shah ʿAbdul ʿAziz amulets on which letters were inscribed in chicken blood!

17 See, e.g., Sir Sayyid's own testimonial in *Tabyin al-kalam*, 58–59.

18 Ahmad, *Islamic Modernism*, 10.

19 Two religious pamphlets that Sir Sayyid penned prior to compiling *Athar as-sanadid* indicate his affinity with and reliance on the scholarship of the Shah Waliullah school. His own biography of the Prophet, *Jila ʾl-qulub ba dhikr al-mahbub*, echoes the title of Shaykh ʿAbdul-Haqq's famous travelogue, *Jadhb al-qulub*, while another work, *Tuhfa-yi Hasan*, gives a summary translation of chapters 10 and 13 from Shah

'Abdul 'Aziz's *Tuhfa-yi Ithna 'ashariyya*. Editor's Note: Shah 'Abdul Ghani is not to be confused with a son of Shah Waliullah with the same name.

20 Nizami, *Sayyid Ahmad Khan*, 26.
21 The incident is cited in K. A. Nizami, "Socio-religious Movements in Indian Islam," in Lokhandwalla, *India and Contemporary Islam*, 113. The truth of this assertion is open to question, however, since in *Hayat-i Jawid* (26) Hali states that members of the *khanqah* of Shah Ghulam 'Ali *always* refused gifts.
22 *Athar as-sanadid*, 473–74.
23 *Athar as-sanadid*, 469–70. On the alleged connection between Shaykh Sayf ud-din and Aurangzeb, see K. A. Nizami, "Naqshbandi Influence on Mughal Rulers and Politics," *Islamic Culture* 39 (1965): 49–50.
24 The exact relationship of Sir Sayyid to Khwaja Mir Dard was through his maternal grandfather, i.e., Khwaja Farid ud-din. See Nizami, *Sayyid Ahmad Khan*, 32.
25 Anecdotes depicting Sir Sayyid's affection for his mother abound in *Hayat-i Jawid*; see especially 24–25.
26 *Hayat-i Jawid*, 26.
27 *Athar as-sanadid*, 496–500; Nizami, *Sayyid Ahmad Khan*, 22, 35n18. Nizami follows Sir Sayyid in linking these saints to the Suhrawardi *silsilah*, but Aziz Ahmad (*An Intellectual History of Islam in India* [Edinburgh: Edinburgh University Press, 1969], 44) allies them with the Rifa'i subsect of the Junaydi *silsilah*.
28 Hedayetullah, *Sayyid Ahmad*, 152, gives an alternate title to the same work: *Idah al-haqq as-sarih fi ahkam al-mayyit wa'd-darih*. The original was written in Persian, and Sir Sayyid's essay is a translation into Urdu of select portions pertaining to *bid'a*.
29 It would be difficult to exaggerate the influence of Hajji Imdadullah on the formation of contemporary Indian attitudes toward Islam. Aziz Ahmad (*Islamic Modernism*, 104) links him to the school of Shah Waliullah, but he was first and foremost a Sabiri Chishti. "He attracted a very large number of externalist scholars to his mystic fold. Many of the outstanding Indo-Muslim *'ulama'* of the post-1857 period . . . may be counted amongst his spiritual descendants. Almost all the great *'ulama'* of Deoband are spiritually associated with the Chishtiya *silsilah* through him" (Nizami, "Chishtiyya," 2:54–55).
30 Among the most notable are Ahmad, *Studies of Islamic Culture*, 209–17; Hedayetullah, *Sayyid Ahmad*; and M. A. Bari, "A Nineteenth Century Muslim Reform Movement in India," in *Arabic and Islamic Studies in Honor of Hamilton A. R. Gibb*, ed. George Makdisi (Leiden: Brill, 1965), 84–102.
31 *Athar as-sanadid*, 495. On the events leading up to Balakot, the battle itself, and its immediate significance, see Bari, "Nineteenth Century," 99–100; and Nizami, "Socio-religious Movements," 105.
32 See, e.g., Bari, "Nineteenth Century," 87.
33 B. A. Dar (*Religious Thought*, 138) raises a false question about the exclusion of chapter 4 from the second edition of *Athar as-sanadid*, imputing to Sir Sayyid motives that are dubious and probably groundless. Christian Troll ("A Note on an Early

Topographical Work of Sayyid Ahmad Khan: *Asar al-Sanadid,*" *Journal of Royal Asiatic Society,* 3rd ser. [1972–73]: 143–44) indicates the nonpolitical nature of this omission, and also points out that the chapter in question was reprinted in full in the third edition of *Athar as-sanadid* during Sir Sayyid's lifetime and probably with his foreknowledge. The consecutive editions of *Athar as-sanadid* are Matba-i Nizami (Kanpur, 1904); Sayyid al-Akhbar (Delhi, 1947); Matbaʿ-i Ahmadiya (Delhi, 1954); Central Book Depot (Delhi, 1965); and Matbaʿ-i Newal Kishor (Lucknow, 1976).

34 See *Athar as-sanadid,* 494–95. Sayyid Ahmad Shahid's problems with the Afghans are aptly described by Nizami ("Socio-religious Movements," 105): "The tribal people were ready to die for the faith but they were not prepared to live according to it."

35 See Hedayetullah, *Sayyid Ahmad,* 2–9, for an English synopsis of its contents. On the actual method of *tasawwur-i shaykh* as practiced by the Naqshbandis, see J. G. Bennett, "Sufi Spiritual Techniques," *Systematics* 7 (1969): 250–51.

36 Yet it is obvious that no one promulgates a viewpoint to which he attaches ultimate meaning without believing that it is true not only for himself but also for others. Often, in the effort to overcome opposition between two conflicting groups, the synthesizer arouses still further hostility that is directed to himself. In the realm of mystical thought, the reaction of his fellow Naqshbandis to Shah Waliullah's *Faysala-yi wahdat al-wujud waʾl-shuhud* is a case in point: Mirza Mazhar Jan-i Janan, with whom he was otherwise on friendly terms, criticized him for this "reconciliation" and directed one of his own disciples, Ghulam Yahya, to write an essay refuting Shah Waliullah's position (Husain, *Glimpses of Medieval Indian Culture,* 54).

37 Sayyid Ahmad Khan, *Tasanif-i Ahmadiya* (Aligarh: Institute Press, 1883), 1:135–36. For a translation of the relevant text of Sir Sayyid's retraction, see M. Siddiqi, "Religious Thought of Sir Sayyid Ahmad Khan," *Islamic Studies* 6 (1967): 294.

38 Quoted in Bari, "Nineteenth Century," 87.

39 First published in Urdu in 1858, it was subsequently translated into English by two of Sir Sayyid's British friends. Hali (*Hayat-i Jawid,* 75–79) discusses the work in detail, referring to it as *Risala asbab-i baghawat-i Hindustan.*

40 Nizami, *Sayyid Ahmad Khan,* 71.

PART III

Translating Institutional Sufism

Sufis and Sufism serve as entry points into Islam for many Muslims and non-Muslims. Walk into American bookstores and you will find colorful volumes of Sufi poetry by Rumi or Hafiz. What is it about Sufism, or "the mystical dimensions of Islam," that propels it across temporal and spatial borders? In part, the appeal of mystical Muslims and Islamic spirituality derives from their rapt attention to universal human themes and feelings; yet, this view of Sufism is partial, and incomplete, without the material history of Sufi masters, their disciples, their oral and written performances, their lodges and shrines, as well as the broader, often transregional, contexts of their fellowships. Bruce Lawrence's writings on Sufism bring into view the institutional, political, and social aspects of Sufism; his scholarship complicates but also complements the preeminent themes of love, self-annihilation, ecstasy, and communion with the divine, as expressed in poetry, prose, and music. Lawrence's sustained engagement with Islamic mysticism spans the Sufis of medieval India and their contemporary counterparts: modern Sufi networks in the Information Age. Both serve as case studies for understanding Sufism in both its historical and transhistorical settings.

When Lawrence lived in India during the mid-1970s, he found himself engaged by research on Indo-Persian Sufi poetry and prose. The texts he read were alluring but also elusive, not least in translation. It is the challenge of translation that he addresses in the first essay, "Can Sufi Texts Be Translated? Can They Be Translated from Indo-Persian to American English?" (1990). "The task I face then as now," he observes, "is how to translate Sufi wisdom from the local idiom of Indo-Persian into another local idiom, American English." Inspired by the linguist Eugene Eoyang, Lawrence attempted to produce not just equivalent but coeval translations of texts. Some of these texts were in prose, but more often in prose and poetry. All embodied the wisdom of Indian Sufism. How to convey that wisdom in a "foreign" language, American English? Translation goes beyond mere equivalences (word-for-word or phrase-for-phrase). The elevated prose and style of the source language must be reflected in the host language. These challenges—to recognize, then produce affective translation—have been closely charted in the essay "Can Sufi Texts Be Translated?" The levels of Lawrence's own engagement with Indo-Persian are best displayed in his later translation entitled *Morals for the Heart*, a collection of conversations (*malfuzat*) from the leading Chishti master of medieval Delhi, Shaykh Nizamuddin Awliya' (d. 1325), compiled by his poet-disciple Amir Hasan Sijzi.

Every translation and translator is haunted by the specter of history. In the case of Sufism, the historical judgment is negative, so that renowned medieval Sufi masters and the loftiest poetry are often deemed elements of decline in a view that sees a classical "Golden Age," followed by a period of social and moral decline coinciding with the loss of the caliphate, and then finally the Age of Reform. This threefold view of Sufism prevails through the work of an Orientalist scholar, J. Spencer Trimingham, but it is also perpetuated by a Muslim apologist, Isma'il al-Faruqi. For both figures, Sufism suffered a decline that mirrored, and accelerated, a decline of Islam pervasive in the *umma*. The evidence of Sufism, as demonstrated in the second essay of this part, offers a counterargument, to wit, that every period has had, and will have, elements of brilliance, corruption, and self-criticism. There was a cycle in Indian Sufism but it had its own rhythm as charted in the book *Sufi Martyrs of Love*, which Lawrence coauthored with Carl W. Ernst. The introduction to this volume, excerpted here as chapter 10, demonstrates how the core of the Chishti order is lyrical. It connects to, and depends on, Sufi poetry. Indo-Persian couplets, quatrains, and *ghazals* reflect both an internal dynamic captured by the dialectic of "annihilation and permanence," *fana* and *baqa*, and an external dynamic, which is often labeled as Law and Truth, *shari'a* and *haqiqa*. A life of ecstasy is still a life lived in the material world, and while no Sufi order is exempt from internal criticism, along with external observance, the Chishtis succeeded as the major Sufi order of South Asia because they balanced *din* (the world beyond) and *dunya* (the here and now). The great masters eschewed excessive asceticism but still found the core of ecstasy in music (*sama'*). Theirs was a remarkable saga, traced through Shaykh

Nizamuddin and those known as the twenty-two masters of the Indian Chishti order.

But the Chishtis were not alone in experiencing change across time and place. In "Sufism and Neo-Sufism" (2010), Lawrence traces networks of spiritual affiliation from Asia to Africa but also to America. Further, in the contemporary Information Age, one needs to discuss cyber-Sufis, and to place Sufis alongside those whose mystical practice consists of devotions at tombs and shrines in Asia and Africa. The invocation of Allah is a deeply spiritual practice of the heart as well as the tongue, as explored in the final essay of this part, "Allah Remembered," a chapter from Lawrence's 2015 monograph, *Who Is Allah?*

The endless search for the divine in the human, the eternal in the transient, has been etched in poetry, and if one had to settle on one poet, one verse, and one image, who better than Rumi and what verse if not this single line on the image of love? "Go to a tavern where each morning the self is reminded, that a life without his love is but slow death." The issue of Sufism and the status of poetry have not been resolved in the Information Age. The endless quest for the Beloved cannot be fully or finally resolved in any age, but one can find traces of hope in its shade.

NINE

Can Sufi Texts Be Translated? Can They Be Translated from Indo-Persian to American English? | 1990

Translation is either an outrageous act of extraordinary hubris or an everyday transaction indispensable to human existence. According to linguistic theorists, it is both, though the quotidian quality of translation is more often stressed. The literary critic George Steiner once declared that "inside or between languages, human communication equals translation."[1] Yet speech and writing are not equivalent means of communication. While speech implies the preunderstanding of thought, writing requires the further refinement of speech into units of commonly held discourse. Translation, even literary translation, resembles speech more than writing: it offers metaphors of what we do every day, consciously but also unconsciously, in the privacy of our homes as well as in the full gaze of public attention.

While translation requires resources, the resource requirements vary from context to context. As difficult as it may be to forge and maintain a viable idiom within a single cultural field mapped by different languages, it is still more difficult to translate unrelated languages from disparate cultures, for example, Chinese to German, Arabic to French, Urdu to English. The most difficult chore of all, however, is to bridge disparate cultural traditions through a written translation that moves from one hybrid language to another.

Let me explain what I mean by "hybrid language." Americans speak a hybrid language. Though labeled English, it is actually American English, not only because Americans have a different vocabulary, but also because there is a different tonality to language on the western than the eastern side of the Atlantic Ocean. American English is derived from Britain but it is not a replica of the original. Nor is the language with which I have worked much of my professional life related, except as a simulacrum, to what Middle Easterners call Persian. There is a common body of literature, a parallel grammar, overlapping vocabulary, but a different pronunciation as also a divergent sensibility between Persian and Indo-Persian. The latter developed on the Indian subcontinent, from the thirteenth to the nineteenth centuries. Both Amir Khusraw and ʿAbdul Qadir Bedil were Indo-Persian poets, and yet they differed as much from one another as did Anne Bradstreet, a seventeenth-century American poetess, from Adrienne Rich, a twenty-first-century lyricist. The differences may seem slight to outsiders, that is, to those who are unfamiliar with either American or Indo-Persian poetry but for those who rhyme words or else listen to others who do so, the differences are at once apparent and striking.

How then can one bridge the linguistic space between Indo-Persian and American English? Or, once straddling that space, how can one try to bridge the still wider distance between the two cultures within which Indo-Persian and American English serve as vehicles of communication? Indo-Persian stands at an ambivalent mid-point in Islamic civilization. Beyond the classical but prior to the modern period, it is middle or medieval, but without a stable point of origin or canonical authority. It becomes an evolved linguistic/literary convention. It embodies Islamic loyalty, it projects Islamic piety, but it also reflects an Indic notion of fluid boundaries, the metaphysical correlate to a society that is at once highly structured on class lines yet tolerant of spiritual athleticism, the attainment of spiritual boons by the common as well as the elite. Indo-Persian literature could—and did—pose a challenge to all Muslims, whatever their social background or religious outlook.

From a Persian that is not quite Persian to an English that is less than its mother tongue, from a controlling religious culture to a culture beyond the control of religion, how does one translate? And if that task is not sufficiently daunting, how does one add a further variable, the variable of translating from poetry to poetry rather than from prose to prose?

Before sharing with you some of my own efforts at rendering Indo-Persian verse into American English, let me background my labor. At the request of the editor for a series called Classics of Western Spirituality (published by the Paulist Press), I began translating the foremost Indo-Persian Sufi conversations, *Fawaʾid al-Fuʾad* (hereafter referenced as *Morals for the Heart*), which is the recording of conversations with Shaykh Nizamuddin Awliya' (d. 1325), by his poet-disciple Amir Hasan Sijzi.[2] After five years, I had nearly completed the prose portions of *Morals for the Heart*. All that remained was some poetry. Since a contemporary Indian Muslim scholar, Ziya' al-Hasan Faruqi, had already begun an English translation, I felt confident that I could benefit from his renditions in shaping my own.[3]

I was attracted to the approach of the linguist Eugene Eoyang; he delineates three levels of translation: surrogate, contingent, and coeval.[4] At the first level, the work of translation stands at its own literary achievement, with no appreciable reference to any other work. It presupposes monolingual readers, readers knowing only the language into which the translation is being made. The translation becomes a replacement or surrogate for the original. By contrast, the second or contingent level of translation always privileges the original, appealing to a potentially bilingual audience. It is effective if it makes the translated text accessible to a student of that text. Finally, there is coeval translation. To quote Eoyang, "If a translation is to be considered a correlate to the original, to co-exist with it, neither as its replacement for those who do not read the original, but *as a possible rival* (and in the event of disappearance of the original, its replacement), then its audience is equivalently bilingual, its readers a more cosmopolitan polyglot tribunal. We may call these coeval translations."[5]

As attractive as the ideal of coeval translation appears to be, it would seem to be unattainable in the case of poetry. Not only are there semantic disparities between the translation and the original, not only are rhyme and meter elusive, but also there is what Valery once posited as the absolute criterion of excellence for poetry: "the prolonged hesitation between sound and meaning."[6] Few are the persons gifted as poets in their own right who can harness their art to the raw data of another artist from another culture. One such person is Naomi Lazard, a twentieth-century American poet who has rendered selections from Faiz for nearly a decade, in order "to bring his full-throated voice into English." She discovered in herself "an infinite patience for translations, the same patience I have for writing my own poems. I have learned that it doesn't matter how long it takes, how many transformations a poem must be brought through, until the English version works in the same way that a poem I have written myself works. It must be faithful to the meaning Faiz has given it. It must move in his own spirit, with the same feeling and tone. It must have the same music, the same direction, and, above all, *it must mean the same thing in English that it does in Urdu*" (emphasis added).[7]

I have stressed this last line because it sets such a high standard of cross-cultural communication that it would defy the ambitions of all but the most gifted and dedicated poet. If this was what coeval translation required, then I had to admit my own limitations: by myself I could not coax from Shaykh Nizamuddin's Indo-Persian verses anything like equivalents in American English. I had to resign myself to the more modest task of producing surrogate renditions of the original. I felt that such poems, though they did not prolong the distance between sound and meaning, would at least satisfy those monolinguist Americans who might read the Paulist Press series, just as Faruqi's contingent translations provided grist for English-reading South Asian Muslims who could comprehend the Persian original.

Yet I remained unhappy with the results. The English words cloyed the mind as well as the tongue. They seemed too flat and pedestrian. Uninspiring and insipid, they mimicked instead of memorializing the great Shaykh who once remarked that "while lying is a sin, a lie conveyed in verse is not a sin."[8] My dilemma persisted until I met Christopher Shackle of the School of Oriental and African Studies, London. We were both attending a conference in Germany. Shackle had read some of my earlier translations of the Shaykh's prose and poetry.[9] A skilled translator of Punjabi verse, he was convinced that beyond the surrogate or contingent renditions of poetry in the original text, coeval translations were possible. He read through all my prior efforts and then crafted a full forty pages of his own efforts. In some cases I agreed with him; in others I came up with further alternatives. Integral to our common labor was a constant wrestling with technical issues: what English meanings of Persian words best suit the text? Closely linked to such technical issues are hermeneutical questions: How does one communicate cross-culturally the pathos or the elan of verses that are not explicated but simply offered in the original text? How can one register for contemporary American readers the power of verses that in medieval North India had the potential to literally kill their listeners? For me the key move is to conjoin hermeneutical strategies with technical options, and to allow the former to guide the latter. In many of my later translations, it is interpretive hunches that inform technical choices, especially when the context suggests that an American accent might unlock and yet enfold the oddity of the Indo-Persian original. To illustrate the results of this protracted process, I have selected a few cases that thematically cohere on a single point: the beauty or cruelty of the Beloved.

Often, beauty and cruelty are Janus-like expressions of the same divine countenance. It is a mystery not easily wrestled into words, and so it is through verse rather than prose that one often finds the most sensitive registers of the seeming paradox that to be cruel is beautiful and vice versa. A necessary correlate is the exclusivity of love: before either beauty or cruelty can be experienced, there has to be the intention of seeking the Beloved, and when that intention does not dominate the seeker then to speak of love is mere hypocrisy. *Morals for the Heart* abounds with examples illustrating the pathos of the human engagement with transcendent Beauty. All rest on the conceit of being able to express through the ear that which cannot be experienced by the eye. Among Indo-Persian poets who have tried to encapsulate this theme, perhaps none has exceeded Qadi Hamiduddin Nagauri, a thirteenth-century Suhrawardi saint much esteemed by the Chishti standard-bearers.[10] One quatrain from Qadi Hamiduddin particularly transfixed Shaykh Nizamuddin (in this quatrain, and throughout the essay, I have used the following abbreviations: L1 = Lawrence, first try; S = Shackle; L2 = Lawrence, second try):

> An ʿaql kuja ki dar kamal-e to rasad
> Van ruh kuja ki dar jalal-e to rasad
> Giram ki to parda bar girifti zi jamal
> An dida kuja ki dar jamal-e to rasad
>
> L1:
> *Where is the intellect to perceive Your perfection?*
> *Where is the soul to attain Your majesty?*
> *I want you to remove the veil from the face of beauty?*
> *But where are the eyes to behold your beauty?*
>
> S:
> *What mind is the intellect to perceive Your perfection?*
> *What soul can truly feel your awesomeness?*
> *Your loveliness, I know, You have unveiled:*
> *What eye, though, can behold your loveliness?*
>
> L2:
> *Where's the mind to grasp Your sovereignty?*
> *Where's the soul to mirror Your majesty?*
> *Beauty's face, I know, You could unveil*
> *But where are the eyes to behold Your beauty?*

At first, I wanted to change the rhyme scheme to 2-3-4 but Shackle's effort convinced me to try again with the 1-2-4 rhyme scheme of the original poem. Either could fit but there is more of an edge to the *-ty* ending (as in "beauty") than the *-ness* ending (as in "loveliness") for a final rhyme in American English, or at least so it seems to my ear.

In both Persian and Indo-Persian Sufi poetry, a theme which complements the extraordinary, yet unattainable, beauty of the Divine Beloved is the affirmation of death. Death is affirmed but not as a natural process; rather it is affirmed as a necessary and welcome sequel to unqualified love. The primary exemplar of love to the point of physical death is Mansur al-Hallaj (d. 922 CE). A literal martyr to love, who lost his limbs before being beheaded, burned, and his ashes tossed on the Tigris, his memory is hallowed by all those Sufis who symbolically also commit themselves to losing selfhood on the path of love.

Beyond inflecting "death," Indo-Persian Sufis preferred the image of physical death through the sword to extinction on flames, and in the poetry they selected, as in the poetry they wrote, the dagger as well as the sword loom large. Consider the following verse, which comes from Persian rather than Indo-Persian, being credited to the little-known Khorasanian mystic Shaykh Ahmad-i Jam (d. 1141). The verse, like the name of Ahmad Jam, was celebrated in the subcontinent chiefly among the Chishti order:

Kushtagan-e khanjar-e taslim-ra
har zaman as ghaib jan-e digar ast
L1:
Those who are slain by the dagger of submission
Each moment from the Unseen receive a new life.
S:
On all the victims of submission's knife
Each moment the Unseen bestows new life.
L2:
All those by the knife of submission killed
Each moment from God with new life are filled.

The verse requires familiarity with the Sufi antonyms of *fana* (annihilation) and *baqa* (permanence). Within that referential field, *fana* is tantamount of loss of self, surrender to the Beloved, who is the Transcendent Creator (God). Total surrender equals self-effacement or death; hence those who submit are slain by the dagger of submission. But they do not die, for in each moment that they die, beyond death they experience *baqa* (persistence). It is a permanence vouchsafed by the same one who demands death and it is a permanence continuously renewed. *Each* moment from the Beyond or the Unseen or God, the slain receives a new soul, which is to say, new life in Him. The pivotal image that empowers this verse is the dagger or knife of submission. It is pivotal because its agent is ambiguous: is it God, or is it the submission to Him, that produces death? To the extent that the act of submission induces a response it is unimportant who or what the agent of death is, but the beauty of the couplet is its ability to play on the ambiguity as also the dyad of *fana–baqa* and thereby inspire would-be Sufi adepts.

Apart from juggling cross-cultural meanings in vastly different contexts, how does one render such a line into American English? It is in order to sharpen the focus of the original for an American audience that I have followed Shackle in providing rhyme where there was no rhyme. Indeed, I have exceeded Shackle's initiative by doubling the rhyme, rhyming not only two verbs at the end but also two nouns in the middle of this highly charged couplet. In two other aspects Shackle's approach has improved my own earlier efforts : (1) the linking of the first to the second line and (2) the generalizing of *baqa* from "a life" to "life."

Even more graphic, at once more poignant and more lyrical, than the couplet of Shaykh Ahmad-i Jam on death is the following anonymous verse, extant, as far as I know, only through its citation by Shaykh Nizamuddin in *Morals for the Heart*:

dari sar-e ma vagarna dur as bar-e ma
ma dost kushim o to nadari sar-e ma.
L1:
Take heed of me,
Else begone from me.
Though I kill my friends,
Still you heed me not.
S:
Take heed of me, or else Begone I say.
My friends I kill, but no heed you will pay.
L2:
Take heed of me, or else Begone I say.
Though my friends I kill, still no heed you'll pay.

Numerous are the critics who have commented on the fondness of Persian poets for word or phoneme repetitions, but in this verse it is carried to extremes: *dar-sar-gar-bar* in line one are followed by *dar-sar* in line two. The message is all the more powerful because the voice speaking from Beyond is understood to be the Divine Beloved. Rather than the passive voice of the submissive lover, which dominated Persian poetry, here we have the active voice of the jealous lover. It echoes the evocation of love's mystery provided by Shaykh Ahmad al-Ghazali in his *Sawanih*: "Jealousy (*ghayrat*), when it shines, is a ruthless sword. This is because jealousy belongs to the supreme domain of love's justice (*'adl*), and love's justice does not want equality, and the state of a rival or a peer. It wants nothing but commingling with love and attachment to it—even at the expense of doing injustice to the lover."[11]

How then can one recapture the power of this unusual imagery? Moreover, *ma* is accented twice in each line, each time in a stress position. Initially, I rendered *ma* as me (rather than us/we), with a nod to *be* (in begone), while Shackle expanded the rhyme to include the terminal say/pay rhyme. In L2, I retained his suggestion and added a further kill/still, in order to stress the thematic point of this intricate rhyme: the Friend/God kills His friends, yet they remain unaware that He requires death or *fana* (as the prelude to larger life or *baqa*). Without a sense of the cultural idiom being invoked, the reader might misread this verse as an instance of divine sadism. For those in the Indo-Persian Sufi tradition, however, it becomes a further, exquisite reminder of the high demands that Love makes on the would-be lover.

It is perhaps fitting to end all this talk of killing and dying with a short couplet from *Morals for the Heart*, where not only did I differ from Shackle but I differed from myself, that is to say, I could not decide which of two translations best fits the sense of the original Indo-Persian:

o sukhan as kushtan-e man mikunad
man ba-hamin khush ki sukhan mikunad.
L1:
Though He speaks of killing me,
That He speaks is thrilling to me.
S:
When He Speaks, I know he says He'll kill me
That He speaks is still enough to thrill me.
L2:
When He speaks, He declares that He will kill me.
Yet that it is He who speaks cannot but thrill me.

Perhaps it is expected that after having pored over texts and contexts, meanings and interpretations for so long, I would at last find myself unable to choose between options. Most days I still prefer L1, though I encourage the reader to opt for either S or L2, or better still to construct a fourth option, such as I finally did:

L3:
Though He says He'll kill me,
That He says it thrills me.

Conclusion

This brief examination of lyrical passages from *Morals for the Heart* provided the pretext for looking at the larger problem of translation. Let me summarize some of the principal problems encountered and also suggest strategies for further research.

1. While there are no fixed criteria for making effective translations, the techniques employed must reflect the receptor language as well as the source language. When syntactic and grammatical features vary widely between the languages involved, the perils of translation increase, and they increase exponentially when the source and receptor audiences are further separated by culture and time. If a translator must cope with both cross-cultural and diachronic difference, the likelihood of coeval translation is markedly reduced.
2. From Indo-Persian to American English involves engagement with two hybrid languages at contrasting moments in their respective cultural histories. The development of American English is at most two hundred years old, while Indo-Persian flourished for almost six hundred years. Yet American English continues to function for an extant community while Indo-Persian, shunted into anterior texts, has become, like Latin, a dead language. The temporal symmetry of the languages must inform the translator's labor.
3. Poetic translations from Indo-Persian to American English are not easily sorted out into categories of surrogate, dependent, and coeval. Surrogate is preferable to dependent if one wants to convey the flavor of the original to American readers. Coeval, on the other hand, entails a series of decisions about meter and rhyme that vary from translator to translator.
4. Coeval translation of poetry, to succeed, requires nothing less than an inner ear that functions in two registers with comparable facility. It entails maximum labor with minimal visible result. Yet when coeval poems are inserted into prose tests and the translator manages to mesh the former with the latter, the poems work like a series of incandescent

mirrors, refracting in the receptor as well as in the source language that inner glow of authorial imagination which no other literary form can capture. At least that is the goal. The reader must linger over the language of each translated poem, judging the results one by one. When less than fiery flashes appear, he or she must experiment with his or her own imagination. Surrender to prose must be a tactic of last resort, for as Tolstoy once observed, "mysticism without poetry is superstition, while poetry without mysticism is prose"![12]

Notes

Bruce B. Lawrence, "Can Sufi Texts Be Translated? Can They Be Translated from Indo-Persian to American English?," *Islamic Culture* 64 (1990): 25–46.

1 George Steiner, *After Babel: Aspects of Language and Translation* (Oxford: Oxford University Press, 1975), 49. *Editor's Note: I have updated this reference.*
2 For another translation in this same series that relates to Indo-Muslim spirituality, see Paul Jackson, trans., *Sharafuddin Maneri: The Hundred Letters* (New York: Paulist Press, 1980), to which I wrote the foreword (xv–xix).
3 Ziya' al-Hasan Faruqi, trans., "*Fawa'id al-Fu'ad* of Khwajah Hasan Dehlawi," *Islam and the Modern Age* 11 (1980): 166–91; 12 (1981): 63–73; 13 (1982): 33–44, 126–41, 169–80, 210–28; 14 (1983): 195–213; 15 (1984): 25–26, 167–92; 16 (1985): 231–42.
4 Eugene Eoyang, "Translation as Excommunication: Notes toward an Intrawordly Poetics," Indiana University, May 30, 1983. Though Eoyang is dealing with obstacles that he faces in translating Chinese into English, they are obstacles common to all endeavors at translation that attempt to cross seemingly unbridgeable cultural and temporal divides. From Indo-Persian to American English qualifies as one such towering divide.
5 Eoyang, "Translation as Excommunication," 51. The added emphasis is mine.
6 Josue Harari, ed., *Textual Strategies: Perspectives in Post-Structuralist Criticism* (Ithaca, NY: Cornell University Press, 1979), 372, quoting Roman Jakobson, *Elements de linguistique generale* (Paris: Minuit, 1963), n233.
7 Naomi Lazard, trans., *The True Subject: Selected Poems of Faiz Ahmed Faiz* (Princeton, NJ: Princeton University Press, 1988), xii.
8 *Fawa'id al-Fu'ad*, Book V, Assembly 23, the end. In response to a question from Amir Hasan, Shaykh Nizamuddin quotes this remark from an anonymous book he had read. He quotes it approvingly and, one imagines, with a smile at the religious scholars who would be offended by such an impious suggestion.

9 See Bruce B. Lawrence, *Notes from a Distant Flute: The Extant Literature of Pre-Mughal Indian Sufism* (Tehran: Imperial Iranian Academy of Philosophy, 1978), 28–29.
10 On this extraordinary lyricist combining juridical skills with mystical sensibilities, see Bruce B. Lawrence, "The *Lawa'ih* of Qadi Hamid ad-din Nagauri," *Indo-Iranica* 20 (1975): 34–53.
11 Nasrollah Pourjavady, trans., *Ahmad Ghazzali's Sawanih* (London: Routledge and Kegan Paul, 1986), 17.
12 Leo Tolstoy, *Resurrection* (London: Penguin, 1966), chap. 27.

TEN

"What Is a Sufi Order? 'Golden Age' and 'Decline' in the Historiography of Sufism," from *Sufi Martyrs of Love: The Chishti Order in South Asia and Beyond* | 2002,

Coauthored with Carl W. Ernst

The first and major point to make about Sufi orders is simple but perplexing: we don't understand them, or at least we haven't figured out how to understand them, as historical developments. Despite the abundance of texts about Sufi orders, their place in the emergence of Islamic civilization remains unclear. Many sources remain unstudied or undervalued, none more so than the biographical compendia known as *tazkiras*. Despite this gap between sources and certainty, some scholars have not hesitated to describe a historical pattern that applies to all Sufi orders. The most ambitious historiographical project comes from J. Spencer Trimingham, a specialist in the history of Islam in Africa. In his book *The Sufi Orders in Islam,* Trimingham enunciates a threefold theory of the development of Sufism that has more than a passing resemblance to the tripartite schemes that litter the landscape of Western historiography (ancient-medieval-modern). The valuable information collected in his compendium is marred by a theory of classicism and decline. Trimingham calls the first period of Sufism, from the ninth century on, "a natural expression of personal religion ... over against institutionalized religion based on authority." During the next period, beginning around the twelfth century, *tariqas* (ways) began to emerge. They brought together groups based on chains of masters and disciples. Then around the fifteenth century there began to appear *ta'ifas* (organizations). They marked the full institutionalization of Sufism. It is this third, and final, period of Sufism that persists to the present day. It is marked, above all, by decline, for once orders became linked to saints' tombs and the latter became state-sponsored centers of devotion, pure mysticism surrendered to popular, mass religiosity. Originality was forfeited, and sterile repetition prevails. The hereditary succession of authority is both product and cause of a "deeper spiritual malaise," according to Trimingham, producing in Islam a discomforting parallel to the Christian church and its clergy.[1]

Trimingham's observations contain a modern and strongly Protestant attitude. He champions "personal religion" over "institutionalized religion." He sees decline as inevitable once mysticism ceases to be a personal and individual phenomenon. The notion of historical decline becomes a rhetorical strategy for projecting personal values and the norms that derive from them. History serves as the mirror reflecting what one considers to be of real value and what deviates from the real. Trimingham is certainly not the first writer to use history as a proxy for moral advocacy. Most theories of the rise and fall of civilizations (from Gibbon to Toynbee) are also very selective in their comparative time frames, and they too advocate a link between moral status and political success that is anything but verifiable. The "classicism and decline" model has also exercised a fascination over students of Islamic culture.[2]

It is especially odd that the "decline" of Islamic civilization has prevailed among groups that seem to have little else in common. Until recently most Orientalists, secular modernists, and fundamentalists have all found their own reasons for asserting the decline of Islam. How else to explain that much of the Muslim world has been colonized? How else to account for the loss of political power that Muslims have experienced? It must be that either history or God—or God acting through history—has made a moral judgment upon Islam and, whatever the agency, the outcome is the same: Islamic civilization has declined because it was inadequate, and Sufism was a major factor in its decay. The remarks of Isma'il al-Faruqi sum up this position:

> The horses of mysticism lapsed into their wild nature and became indomitable. The *umma* suffered an eclipse from which it has been trying painfully to recover in the last two centuries. Instead of continuing to discipline man to obey God and observe the *shari'a,* to deepen his commitment to Islam and purify and lift his soul on the path of righteous action, *tasawwuf* became

a disease causing or exacerbating [multiple] symptoms... that ruined the health of Muslim society during half a millennium from the fall of Baghdad to the Tatars in 655/1257 to the rise of the Wahhabiyyah, the first anti-Sufi reform movement, in 1159/1757. Under the Sufi spell, the Muslim had become apolitical, asocial, amilitary, unethical, and hence nonproductive, unconcerned for the *umma* (the world brotherhood under the moral law), an individualist, and, in the last resort, an egoist whose prime objective was to be saved himself, to be absorbed into the consuming majesty of the divine being. He was shaken neither by the misery, poverty, disease, and subjection of his own society nor by the lot of mankind in history.[3]

During the colonial period the notion of the decline of Muslim nations was especially attractive to the self-image of Europeans: it provided a noble justification for conquest and empire; it supported the "civilizing mission" of the West. But we reject all these agendas, and we therefore also question the basis for assuming that Islam in general and Sufism in particular rose, then fell—at once marked by a period of classicism and greatness, followed by another period of stagnation and decline.[4]

While Trimingham has linked the decline in Sufi orders to the failure of Muslims to become modern, another historian, Marshall Hodgson, has questioned the whole notion of decline. Hodgson argues that the notion of the rise of the West is itself suspect. The rise of the West, in his view, was not an unassisted triumph of one group over another, or one way of life over another, but rather a convergence of disparate historical circumstances. Hodgson's notion of the "Great Western Transmutation" takes as axiomatic that other civilizations in other periods and parts of the globe could also experience "greatness." At the very least, the so-called decline of Islam is not due to internal moral failure or to a flawed systemic view of the universe but rather to the relative standard of collective power and social formation augured by the Great Western Transmutation.

Similarly, when we look at a discrete Islamic institution, such as the Sufi order or fellowship, we cannot see it only through its great ones, the creative masters in whose name it is etched as a distinct form of spiritual life. Instead, we need to enlarge the concept of Sufism to include wider social and institutional contexts. Unlike the individualistic notion of originality found in romantic modernism, Sufism is a vast cumulative tradition. It rests upon multiple contributions to a common resource both contested and deployed over generations. When we come to the South Asian Chishtiyya, we have to link the stories of "the great ones" to the developments shaped around and beyond them by collectivities—of families, of networks, of institutions. The "golden age" syndrome so favored by Orientalists accords a handful of "the great ones," mostly from one early period, a kind of isolated hagiographical reverence bereft of other influences.

To be sure, this classical approach to Sufism itself mirrors a strong golden age historiography that is deeply etched in Muslim piety. It is based on the model of "a pristine Medina" that functioned under the leadership of the Prophet Muhammad. Seventh-century Arabia is seen as the perfect time and perfect place, which no other generation in any other part of the world could equal. Yet within Islamic tradition this backward-looking concept of history has always been balanced by a strong notion of renewal (*tajdid*), and typically renewal is embodied in at least one outstanding religious leader in each century (*mujaddid*). Hence we see an ongoing paradox: while even the earliest handbooks of Sufism proclaim that true Sufism no longer exists in their day, the ongoing reality of sainthood manifests a divine mercy that is still accessible, capable of producing extraordinary results.[5]

Chishtis themselves were aware of this paradox and the ironies it unfolds. It is related of the Chishti master Hasan Muhammad in the late sixteenth century (which some would consider falling within the period of decline) that a man of Lahore came to him and stated: "In this time there is no one worthy of listening to music (*samaʿ*)." He rejoined: "If there was no one worthy of listening to music, the world would be destroyed." The man said: "In times past, there were men like Shaykh Nasiruddin [Chiragh-i Dihli], the Emperor of the Shaykhs [Nizamuddin Awliyaʾ], and the revered [Fariduddin] Ganj-i Shakar. Now there is no one like them." Answered Hasan Muhammad: "In their time, men said the very same thing."[6]

Writing in the early nineteenth century, the biographer who transmitted this conversation was keenly aware of the constant need for the renewal of tradition. Repeatedly he observes of masters of the later period that they "gave life to the example of the Chishti masters."[7] We should be careful to distinguish this expression from the metaphor of bodily revival or human rebirth. Both these metaphors suggest a reanimation of something defunct, but to give life to tradition is to make tradition come alive, and that is a work that is needed in every generation. It is *not* subject to rise and decline; it persists and animates and directs all who stand within the same group oriented to a common past and seeking a common, but different, future.

Beyond criticizing other efforts at periodization, we must provide our own. We prefer to frame our own inquiry into the Chishti order with a comprehensive restaging of those major periods within which the patterns of piety and practice distinctive to them emerged. They are not defined in terms of greatness and decline but in terms of their faithfulness to Chishti values and norms. We propose five divisions in the history of the Chishti order, two early periods outside of South Asia followed by three cycles taking place in India:

1. The formative period (seventh–tenth centuries): Though to some extent a reconstruction from later literature, this is the clearly identifiable lineage from the Prophet Muhammad through Abu Ishaq Shami, the first Sufi master to reside at Chisht.
2. The foundational period at Chisht (tenth–twelfth centuries): It extends from Abu Ishaq Shami to ʿUsman Harwani. While it was almost entirely located at Chisht itself, it is known only from fragmentary testimonies in literature of the fourth and fifth periods, discussed below.
3. The first cycle of the Indian Chishti order (twelfth–fourteenth centuries): It begins when Muʿinuddin Chishti came to Rajasthan in the wake of the Ghurid conquest of northern India at the end of the twelfth century and culminates with the emergence of Nizamuddin Awliyaʾ as the foremost Indian saint of his generation, in the Tughluq capital of Delhi. Despite its critical significance, the primary literary sources are limited to oral traditions, whether actually recorded or later imagined.
4. The second cycle of the Indian Chishti order (fourteenth–eighteenth centuries): It marks the dispersal of the fellowship from Delhi to the far corners of the subcontinent, carried by the numerous disciples of Nizamuddin. Coinciding with the development of regional kingdoms, this period sees the profusion of sublineages that extends into the period of the Mughal empire. It also gives rise to an immense biographical literature that frames the narrative of the previous three periods.
5. The third cycle of the Indian Chishti order (eighteenth–twenty-first centuries): The decline of the Mughal hegemony, along with British ascendancy in India and Wahhabi control of Arabia, led to tensions over the internal reform of Sufism. The Chishtis debated internal reform at the same time that they redeployed their spiritual traditions both in combination with other orders and through new forms of expression, especially in the postcolonial period. The biographical literature of this period privileges the masters of the first cycle at the same time that it engages the legacy of multiple orders.[8]

Social Structures and Anti-Structure:
Sufis within and outside the Orders

The development of Sufi structures reflects the tension between inner transcendence and the need for outer forms: how could outer structures match inner longing? Nowhere is this tension better illustrated than in the emergence of the networks and lineages that we now call Sufi orders. Through the orders, from the twelfth century on, Sufism became much more widely known and practiced at multiple levels of society. Distinctive rituals of initiation and special practices were adopted among the many lineages that proliferated in Muslim lands. As Marshall Hodgson observed about the "unexpected" growth of medieval Sufi orders, "a tradition of intensive interiorization reexteriorized its results and was finally able to provide an important basis for social order."[9]

The experiential origin of Sufism as a set of social institutions rested on the master-disciple relationship. It is hard to overestimate the importance of this relationship. Manuals of practice and discipline contain extensive discussions of how the disciple is to behave with respect to the master. Obedience to a master was understood psychologically as renouncing the lower self and replacing it with a purified self, made possible because the master had annihilated his own ego. The master assumed an extraordinary role as the intermediary linked to the Prophet and to God. In the most extreme formulation, the disciple was expected to be to the master like a corpse in the hands of a corpse washer; nothing less than total compliance with the master's will was acceptable.

It is in this context that one realizes why the most common word for disciple was *murid,* the one who desires and seeks, while the master was called *murad,* the one desired and sought. Because of his pivotal importance, the master was also known as the elder: *shaykh* (Arabic) or *pir* (Persian), though the Sufi orders that originated in Central Asia and Khurasan, particularly the Chishtis and the Naqshbandis, often refer to their masters by the distinctive term for lord: *khwaja.*

It was during the twelfth and thirteenth centuries that the organizations of Sufi orders as teaching lineages crystallized. Most Sufi orders are eponymous; they are named after a famous figure who is viewed in effect as the founder. Hence the Suhrawardiyya is named after Abu Hafs al-Suhrawardi; the Shadhiliyya after Abu'l-Hasan al-Shadhili; the Kubrawiyya after Najmuddin Kubra. Each of the founders is usually a master who epitomized the distinctive teachings and practices of the order named after him. Most orders were also identified with particular regions, though a few, such as the Qadiriyya and the Naqshbandiyya, did achieve transregional stature, with networks throughout much of the Muslim world. Crucial to each order was its initiatic genealogy, also known as a *silsila*, or chain: each master's authority derived from that of his predecessor who, in turn, was linked to another predecessor, going back in a chain to the Prophet Muhammad. Within each order there were also frequently suborders, sometimes designated by composite names with two, three, or more elements to indicate each level of branching. One of the main branches within the Chishti order, for instance, is the Nizami-Chishti suborder.

Unlike other orders, the Chishti order is not named after a particular person but rather a place that symbolized an entire lineage. Chisht, not far from Herat, is one of the two ancient Sufi centers in eastern Khurasan (present-day Afghanistan), along with Jam, home to the famous master Ahmad-i Jam (d. 1141). Though the historical origins of the shrine at Chisht are shrouded in obscurity, it goes back at least as far as the early tenth century, when Abu Ishaq of Syria was directed by his Baghdadian master ʿUlu Dinawari to go to Chisht, then a remote outpost at the eastern edge of the Islamic world. While Abu Ishaq is reported to have returned to Acre to be buried, his disciple Abu Ahmad Abdal (d. 966) was buried at Chisht, thus inaugurating the first recognizable stage of the pre-Indian Chishti order.[10] It was not, however, until the thirteenth century, when Shaykh Muʿinuddin Chishti reached Hindustan, that the Chishti order emerged into the light of history and politics, linking piety to institutional support.

Institutional support for Sufism reflected how teaching circles were connected to centers of political power. Since the court was typically located in a major city, it was inevitable that any order that wanted to influence the tone of Muslim public life would become urban. From the time of Shaykh Muʿinuddin till now, the Chishti fellowship has remained an urban order, with consequential, but also ambivalent, links to the court and the state. The earliest Indian Chishti masters recommended avoiding formalities through endowment, yet they accepted donations in cash or kind with one stipulation: that they be quickly spent for appropriate purposes, such as food, modest clothes, and living quarters, as well as ritual necessities, including assemblies of music (*majalis-i samaʿ*). Typical was the instruction given to the major Deccan master, Shaykh Burhanuddin Gharib, when he was commissioned by Shaykh Nizamuddin as one of his successors. "Take worthy people as disciples," commended Shaykh Nizamuddin, "and on the subject of donations, 'no rejecting, no asking, no saving.' If anyone brings you something, do not reject it, but do not ask for anything, if they bring a little of something good, do not reject it (politely) in order to get it increased, nor should you specify everything (else that you need) in accepting it."[11]

Despite the desire to remain outside royal control, the significant resources at the disposal of medieval rulers created a constant pressure to accept patronage. When Shaykh Burhanuddin Gharib's lodge ceased to be controlled by a teaching master after the death of his successor, the trustees and attendant sought donations and eventually land endowments from the sultans of the Deccan. By the eighteenth century, the shrines of Shaykh Burhanuddin and his disciples had become extensions of the authority of the court, with royal music balconies being built into the shrines themselves for the performance of court ceremonies.

Already by the sixteenth century the Mughal emperors had established elaborate bureaucratic hierarchies that dispensed royal funds and land revenue to Sufi shrines, often appointing the trustees and regulating the internal affairs of the shrines. Shrines were exempted from ordinary taxes, on the condition that the attendant pray for the welfare of the ruling dynasty. Descendants of Sufis frequently had opportunities to enter the ranks of nobility or to serve as courtiers. If most royal support was directed at the shrines, it was because the rulers remained at heart pragmatists: they foresaw more benefits and fewer conflicts with dead saints than with living exemplars.

However, the established Sufi orders were not the only social option for mystics. A radical interpretation of dervish poverty unleashed a very different form of Sufism in the *qalandar* movements.[12] Scorning Sufi establishments as themselves part of the worldliness that Sufis were pledged to eschew, these self-conscious deviants embraced an itinerant lifestyle not unlike that of Hindu mendicants (*sadhus*). They challenged domestic life, public structures, and expected modes of behavior. They were dropouts who claimed to be the "only" ones tuned in with their own times, and also with eternity. Their modes of extreme ascetic rejection were so varied that they came to be known in different regions by different names: Haydaris, Qalandars, Malamatis, Torlaks, Babs, Abdals, Jamis, Madaris, Malangs, and Jalalis. They rejected all property. They begged. They wandered. They remained celibate. They often mutilated themselves. They flouted not only ritual prayer but also those who put stock in prayer and other Islamic rituals. They seldom bathed. They went about naked or near naked, wearing rough dark wool. Often they sported a bizarre assortment of hats and other paraphernalia, including iron chains. They were often popularly referred to as people who lived beyond the protocol of Islamic law.

These extreme male ascetics shaved not only their heads but also their facial hair. Again, in opposition to social expectations of comportment and appearance for proper adult Muslim males, many of these nonconformist mystical groups also engaged in the use of hallucinogens and intoxicants, prompting even more abusive behavior toward "normal" Muslims, including Sufi masters. Though some Chishti masters such as Baba Farid and Shaykh Nizamuddin tolerated, and even seemed to admire, the feistiness of the *qalandars,* they could be dangerous; one of their number, called Turab, attacked Shaykh Nasiruddin Chiragh-i Dihli with a knife.[13] Though seriously wounded, Shaykh Nasiruddin forgave his assailant, and so have subsequent hagiographers forgiven all the excess of the *qalandars,* remembering instead how necessary their challenges and provocations were. One early figure associated with the Qalandar movement, Bu ʿAli Shah Qalandar, is credited with some dazzling verse, and is reputed to have been a follower of the early Chishti masters.[14] The name Qalandar continues to be intoned in popular *qawwali* lyrics of the Punjab, and it has been appropriated by a mainstream Sufi group, the Indian Qalandari order centered at Kakori near Lucknow.

Lineages of the Chishti Order: Initiation and Rules of Conduct

Within the Sufi tradition, the formation of the orders did not immediately produce lineages of master and disciple. There are few examples before the eleventh century of complete lineages going back to the Prophet Muhammad. Yet the symbolic importance of these lineages was immense: they provided a channel to divine authority through master-disciple chains. It was through such mimetic chains that spiritual power and blessings were transmitted to devotees as well as disciples.

In another respect, the transhistorical character of Sufi initiation subverts the usual, expected sense of succession. The model subversive is Uways al-Qarni, a Yemeni contemporary of the Prophet Muhammad who never met him, yet was considered a follower, deeply devoted to the Prophet and his spiritual quest. The nonphysical binding of two like-minded Sufis is called the Uwaysi initiation, and it shows up with particular force in the Sabiri branch of the Chishti order. It is Shaykh ʿAbdul Quddus Gangohi (d. 1537) who declares himself to be the beneficiary of an Uwaysi initiation through the spirit of the deceased Shaykh ʿAbdul Haqq Rudawlavi (d. 1434).[15] Remarkably, this initiation preserves the historical form of the typical initiatic genealogy while also dispensing with the need for external physical contact. The initiated person creates for himself or herself the line of spiritual transmission and authority to validate his or her experience through the central figures of Sufism. It is, moreover, always a selective recall of seminal figures, and does not require attention to the whole panoply of spiritual forbearers going back to the generation of the Prophet Muhammad.

Yet some link to the Prophet himself was crucial, so crucial that all lineages are recited as prayers with a chain of masters in each lineage traced back to the Prophet Muhammad. In later times this practice was supplemented by writing out the names of the masters of the order; what resulted was a filial tree, or *shajara*. Knowing the names of the previous masters constituted a virtue comparable to the recitation of the 99 Beautiful Names of God. It was believed that the recitation or even the writing of the names of these lofty souls would confer on the reciter/scribe the spiritual benefits that they uniquely possessed. Even distance in time from the Prophet Muhammad was not a barrier to this lodestone of spiritual power: since the chains were attested by trustworthy masters, those with more links had greater merit, just as additional lamps provide more light to a room.

While the genealogical tree is probably the most elemental representation of a Sufi order, it is subject to varied, and intriguing, elaboration. Some *shajara* documents contain brief biographical notes, often showing circles of minor disciples emanating from the major masters. Not all are presented in book form: while a simple tree document may be only one page long and easily presented by itself or as part of another document, there are shrines in South Asia where genealogical scrolls extend to hundreds of feet. These more complicated diagrams require oral commentary to be understood. What is clear is that each document represents a principal line of transmission, one that eventually reaches the disciple whose name is inscribed at the bottom.

Each graphic representation suggests a simple statement of authority, yet at the same time it conceals significant differences of opinion about legitimate succession. As with the Shiʿi imams, Sufi masters did not always have a single successor, one whose authority was recognized by all devotees of that order. The result was branching off of sublineages. Each branching off is the acknowledgment of multiple authorities within a Sufi order. At the same time, each individual representation of the order considers itself and its *shajara* a single uncontested chain of mystery.

Consider the case of the South Asian Chishtis. Within it there is a longstanding formulation of "the twenty-two masters," forming a discrete but clear cycle of authority. Throughout northern India, many Chishtis begin with the name of the archangel Gabriel as the first in their spiritual genealogy and reckon as the final—the twenty-second master—the major successor of Shaykh Nizamuddin Awliyaʾ (d. 1325), that is, Shaykh Nasiruddin Mahmud Chiragh-i Dihli

(d. 1356). However, the branch of the Chishti order that predominates in the Deccan follows a different *shajara*. It starts with the Prophet Muhammad and counts Shaykh Nizamuddin's successor, Burhanuddin Gharib (d. 1337), as twenty-first and his major successor, Zaynuddin Shirazi (d. 1369), as the twenty-second master.[16] Hence, the same structure can, and does, support competitive identification of the standard-bearers of the Chishti order.

In the biographical dictionaries of saints (*tazkiras*), the *shajara* documents took on still more complicated dimensions. The early hagiographies broke down their subject into generations, and some Mughal *tazkira* authors, such as Shaykh ʿAbdul Haqq Dihlawi (d. 1642), who was himself a *hadith* scholar, followed that model. But other authors were inspired by the proliferation of orders to reconstruct the past following the lineage of their mystical order. Shaykh ʿAbdur Rahman Chishti, for example, went so far as to link all saints from separate regions of the Muslim world to his Chishti exemplars. A Sufi order thus became not merely remembered but reimagined through narrative and hagiographical texts. For an individual master the profiles could vary considerably, from the "simple" invocation of the saint by a biographer to the complex elaboration of his significance by a hagiographer.

One of the major ways that the Chishtis were reimagined was as part of a cluster of different orders. Some of the more inclusive—and often unwieldy—*tazkiras* took their cue from the eleventh-century theorist of Persian Sufism, Shaykh ʿAli Hujwiri (d. 1077). He classified the Sufi orders into twelve, linking each to a famous early Sufi master, despite the fact that there was seldom a correspondence between these early ascetics and the well-known Sufi orders of later times. Both Sultanate and Mughal *tazkira* writers increased the number of families by two, and most of the major Chishti and non-Chishti *tazkiras* categorized the Sufi orders as dispersed through "fourteen families," of which the Chishtiyya were prominent. Even here, however, there were major disagreements about how to depict "the fourteen families."

On one point all the biographical authors do agree: the major satisfaction, and basic requirement, of Muslim piety was to find a spiritual master. Without a master, one's life, one's work, one's hope, one's destiny was at risk. A master provided security, direction, and structure. He also provided a link back to the earliest days of Islam; he connected his disciple to the Prophet and to the Prophet's practice (*sunna*).

It was the Prophet Muhammad himself who blazed the Sufi path of initiation. He formalized the relationship he had with his companions through an oath of allegiance that they swore to him. They then became his emissaries to the rest of the expanding Muslim community (*umma*). The Prophet is alleged to have said: "My companions are like the stars: whichever of them you follow, they will guide you." The Sufi masters, including those of the Chishti order, saw themselves as transmitters of this same practice.

A more difficult question facing the master was to judge the worthiness of a would-be devotee to become an actual disciple. How did Sufi masters judge whether or not someone should be taken on as a disciple? Frequently it was said that a master would gaze upon the tablets of destiny to see if the disciple's oath had been decreed from preeternity; and not every seeker's name was found to be inscribed.

Initiation itself varied from order to order. The Chishti initiation has been well documented, at least from the fourteenth century. It went as follows. If someone wanted to be honored with initiation, he would fast that day, give alms, and perform ritual prayer. Then three further conditions had to be fulfilled: the master had to accept him with a handshake; the disciple's head had to be shaved; and he had to be invested with a cloak (or other emblematic garment). When the master actually accepted the prospective initiate, he would clasp the disciple's hand in his own, saying:

> You have sworn an oath (*'ahd*) with this broken one, and with the master of this broken one, with the masters of Chisht, with the followers of the followers, with the followers [of the Prophet], with the Messenger of the Lord of Creation, with the bearers of the Divine Canopy, and with God Himself. Guard your eye, guard your tongue. Do not speak evil of anyone nor think evil of anyone. Do not bring harm to anyone, and do not approach forbidden things. Remain on the path of sacred law (*shar'*). You have sworn an oath to all of this, so observe these conditions.

The disciple would then say: "I have sworn an oath to all of this." After this he would be shaved. They take hair from the right side of the head and cut it with scissors, and do the same for the left. They put a hat on his head. The master invokes the name of God, announcing (in Arabic) that this is the clothing of piety, the clothing of well-being. The disciple then replies (in Arabic): "I intend to perform two cycles of supererogatory prayer; rejecting all that is other than God, I turn my face to the noble Ka'ba. God is Most Great." After performing the prayer, he then prostrates himself before the master, touching his head on the master's feet. Rising, he presents some gift to the master and joins other companions of the assembly. Later the master determines his capacity and gives him appropriate instruction.[17]

There were women disciples also admitted to the Chishti fold. For their initiation the master used special procedures, again based on the usage of the Prophet Muhammad. The crucial step was for the woman to place her hand into a cup of water, in this way avoiding inappropriate physical contact. The master, following the example of the Prophet, would then put his own hand in the water and proceed to administer the oath of initiation given above.[18]

For Chishtis, as for other Sufis, correct behavior (*adab*) was crucial at all times and in all places. Rules detailing the norms that were to be upheld, and the procedures to be followed, were elaborate. Even before the orders came into existence, there were manuals specifying social relations, as between master and disciple, or with fellow disciples, and also moral exercises, especially those that aim to control the lower self. With the emergence of the first Sufi lodges in eastern Iran, a list of rules came into popular usage. Linked to the master, Shaykh Abu Saʿid ibn Abiʾl-Khayr, they numbered ten. They stressed four ideals of good conduct: purity, constant prayer, meditation, and hospitality.

Later rules became more elaborate. They included many dispensations or relaxations of stricter rules, suggesting a wider circle of adherents with variant degrees of commitment to the strict life of the lodges. Especially important were rules on behavior during the performance of music or the recitation of poetry. How, for instance, was one to distribute pieces of Sufi cloaks that had been torn in ecstasy and were therefore prized by all in attendance? Manuals gave directives for those in need of an authority to ratify what otherwise would be seen as an arbitrary dispensation of spiritual benefits. Mostly, however, the manuals dealt with more routine matters, such as how to approach the master, how to behave while traveling, how to respond to offers of food when fasting, or how to deal with pride in one's literary accomplishments. Disciples were also warned to refrain from bad company. In this regard bad company was especially linked to the company of "mad *qalandars*," wine drinkers, and disreputable Sufis.

So frequent are the reminders about certain points that one suspects the infractions they are intended to correct were frequent and widespread. The sheer volume of the many *adab* manuals generated by Sufi authors testifies to the normative appeal of the lodges to convergent circles of teaching in diverse locations: Muslims in general shared the Sufi preoccupation with regulating one's behavior with God, with holy men, and with fellow Muslims. In this sense, one should acknowledge the Sufi orders, including the Chishti order, as bellwethers for society as a whole. They projected not merely mystical insights for like-minded mystics, but also practical points of responsible behavior, with an ethical appeal to Muslims from numerous classes and professions in urban sites throughout the Afro-Eurasian *oikumene*.

Notes

Bruce B. Lawrence, "What Is a Sufi Order? 'Golden Age' and 'Decline' in the Historiography of Sufism," in Carl W. Ernst and Bruce B. Lawrence, *Sufi Martyrs of Love: The Chishti Order in South Asia and Beyond* (New York: Palgrave Macmillan, 2002), 11–26. Reproduced with permission of Palgrave Macmillan.

1. J. Spencer Trimingham, *The Sufi Orders in Islam* (Oxford: Clarendon, 1971), 70–71. Surprisingly, this study has been reprinted (Oxford University Press, 1998) in unaltered form, with a new preface by John Voll that lauds the book as still providing the standard account of Sufi orders. It is our contention that the main historiographical thesis of the book needs to be rejected.
2. Gustave E. von Grunebaum and Willy Hartner, eds., *Klassizismus and Kulturverfall* (Frankfurt: Klostermann, 1969).
3. Isma'il R. al-Faruqi and Lois Lamya' al-Faruqi, *The Cultural Atlas of Islam* (New York: Macmillan, 1986), 303–4.
4. Trimingham explicitly states that "the decline in the orders is symptomatic of the failure of Muslims to adapt their traditional interpretation of Islam for life in a new dimension" (*Sufi Orders in Islam*, 256–57), i.e., the failure of Muslims to become totally Westernized. One of the most powerful critiques of the simplistic notion of the "decline" of Islamic civilization was provided by Marshall Hodgson in *The Venture of Islam: Conscience and History in a World Civilization* (Chicago: University of Chicago Press, 1974), vol. 3, *The Gunpowder Empires and Modern Times*, esp. 165–248.
5. Yohanan Friedmann, *Prophecy Continuous: Aspects of Ahmadi Religious Thought and Its Medieval Background* (Berkeley: University of California Press, 1989), 94–101.
6. Gul Muhammad Ahmadpuri, *Takmila-i siyar al-awliya'* (MS K. A. Nizami), fols. 43b–44a.
7. Ahmadpuri, *Takmila-i siyar al-awliya'*, fols. 19a (Kamal al-Din 'Allama, d. 1355), 24a ('Alam ibn Siraj, d. 1406), 42a (Hasan Muhammad, d. 1575). The phrase used is *ihya'-i sunnat*.
8. *Editor's Note: To emphasize the structures of Sufism, a theoretical reflection entitled "The Dialectic of Love and Knowledge" has been omitted from this selection.*
9. Hodgson, *Venture of Islam*, 2:218.
10. Mutiul Imam, "Abu Eshaq Sami," in *Encyclopaedia Iranica* (Costa Mesa, CA: Mazda Press, 1989), 1:280; Mutiul Imam, "Abdal Cesti, Abu Ahmad," in *Encyclopaedia Iranica*, 1:175.

11 Burhanuddin Gharib, *Ahsan al-aqwal*, comp. Hammaduddin Kashani (Khuldabad ms.), 82–83.
12 For a detailed analysis of this highly diverse nonconformist movement, see Ahmed T. Karamustafa, *God's Unruly Friends: Dervish Groups in the Islamic Later Middle Period, 1200–1550* (Salt Lake City: University of Utah Press, 1994).
13 K. A. Nizami, *The Life and Times of Shaikh Nasir-u'd-din Chiragh-i Dehli* (Delhi: Idara-yi Adabiyyat-i Dihli, 1991), 63–64.
14 See Bruce B. Lawrence, *Notes from a Distant Flute* (Tehran: Imperial Iranian Academy of Philosophy, 1978), 79–82, for a review of the skepticism about his Chishti affiliations, and also the translation of an excerpt from the famed *Masnavi* attributed to him. It compares *dunya* to a deceitful hag and also invokes the still more famous verse from Mawlana Rumi: "If your desire is both for God and the mundane / This is illusory, impossible, insane."
15 Bruce B. Lawrence, "Abd al-Quddus Gangohi," in *Encyclopaedia Iranica*, 1:1388–40; Bruce B. Lawrence, "Ahmad Rodowlavi," in *Encyclopaedia Iranica*, 1:653–54.
16 For an elaboration of these differences, see Carl W. Ernst, *Eternal Garden: Mysticism, History, and Politics at a South Asian Sufi Center* (Albany: State University of New York Press, 1992), 118–23.
17 Burhanuddin Gharib, *Ahsan al-aqwal*, 46–47.
18 Ruknuddin ibn ʿImaduddin Dabir Kashani Khuldabadi, *Shamaʾil al-atqiyaʾ*, ed. Sayyid ʿAtaʾ Husayn, Silsila-i Ishaʿat al-ʿUlum, no. 85 (Hyderabad: Matbuʿa Ashraf Press, 1347/1928–29), 48–49.

ELEVEN

Sufism and Neo-Sufism | 2010

Overview on Wahhabism, Colonialism, and Sufi Networks

Institutional Sufism from the nineteenth century to today can be assessed under three discrete but related rubrics: Sufi Africa, Sufi Asia (including the Middle East), and Sufi America. If this accent is locative, it is also temporal, marking the nineteenth, twentieth, and now twenty-first centuries by Sufi developments in particular parts of the globe. Overarching and connecting these subsets is a common theme: Sufism/neo-Sufism intensifies Islamic loyalty, while also distinguishing Sufi from non-Sufi Muslims, by underscoring the unique status of the Prophet Muhammad.

A single question demarcates Sufi from non-Sufi Muslims: is the Prophet Muhammad alive or dead? For non-Sufi Muslims, the question is itself a mark of heretical intent. Of course, the Prophet is dead, and with his death in seventh-century Arabia there ceased to be any human mediator between the living and the dead. What the Prophet bequeathed to his followers was the Qur'an and *hadith*, sayings that later became codified as *sunna*, his own model of exemplary conduct. *Sunna* complemented, even as it amplified, the Qur'an. Together the Qur'an and the *sunna* have been interpreted by the *'ulama'*. There is no authority in Islam apart from the books and the learned custodians of the books. To the extent that the Prophet lives, it is through his legacy in books, preserved and mediated by the *'ulama'*.

But for Sufis, the Prophet continues to live as an active agent in every historical epoch. He intercedes for the faithful in heaven, but he also appears to his most devout followers, that is, to saints or Sufi masters, in dreams and even occasionally in wakeful moments. He lives also through the institutional trajectories, or *tariqas*, that is, the fellowships, that Sufi masters or shaykhs direct. He is as available to the ordinary believer as he is to the advanced saint.

Sufis of all generations have held this view of the living Prophet, yet the nineteenth century witnessed a more explicit, and more openly public, awareness of the Prophet as the crucial link between God and humankind. It has been etched in the phrase *al-tariqa al-Muhammadiyya*. *Al-tariqa al-Muhammadiyya* was identified both with the North African movement of Muhammad ibn ʿAli al-Sanusi and with the north Indian movement of Sayyid Ahmad Shahid of Raebareli. What underlies *al-tariqa al-Muhammadiyya* in both cases is not just loyalty to the Prophet but connection to his reality (*al-haqiqa al-Muhammadiyya*) and to his light (*al-nur al-Muhammadi*). There is no denial of the mystery and meaning of Prophetic mediation, such as Wahhabi teaching would require, but there is also no substitution of the Prophet for God, which would entail blatant *kufr*, or unbelief.[1]

At the same time that the overt stance of Sufi or neo-Sufi advocates becomes more pronounced in the nineteenth century, it becomes more pronounced in the context of a world transformation known as European, and then Euro-American, modernity. Neither Sufism nor neo-Sufism can be understood as social movements apart from the material context of Euro-American modernity. Euro-America is crucial for understanding Sufism/neo-Sufism, just as it is for analyzing all institutional expressions of Islamic loyalty during the past two centuries. The accent is double: the weight of colonial conquest and the wealth of Muslim networks. Each defines and qualifies the other. Together they become the basis for Sufi, and also neo-Sufi, self-expression as social movements.

The nineteenth century provided elements of continuity, and also incentives for change, in institutional Sufism. The impact of Wahhabism has been exaggerated. To the extent that Sufi-derived movements, such as the *jihad* of Sayyid Ahmad Shahid in the Punjab and the Faraʾidis in Bengal, are labeled Wahhabi, their actual nature is occluded: the former was an early protest against British influence, but also Sikh ascendancy, in northern India, while the latter was at once a class movement against Hindu landlords and a reassertion of Sufi (specifically Qadiri) norms and values.[2]

More importantly, beyond India, from West Africa to Southeast Asia, from the late eighteenth century until now, the Muslim world witnessed a vigilant effort to redefine and internalize the boundaries of Islamic loyalty. The Wahhabis were not so much an inspiration as they were a product of the wholesale changes afoot. Muhammad ibn ʿAbd al-Wahhab (d. 1792) offered what amounts to a carping, narrow notion of unbelief. The eponymous founder of the Wahhabi movement acknowledged three kinds of *tawhid* as integral to the intellectual defense of Islamic belief: *tawhid al-rububiyya, tawhid al-uluhiyya*, and *tawhid al-sifat*. He scarcely mentions the last, however, since it focuses on the oneness of God as projected through the beautiful names ascribed to Him in the Qur'an, and these same beautiful names were the linchpin of Sufi reflection and practice. Ibn ʿAbd al-Wahhab bracketed them from his outlook, focusing instead on the distinction between the first two kinds of *tawhid: tawhid al-rububiyya* and *tawhid al-uluhiyya*. The first acknowledges God as creator and lord of the universe. Arabs from "the age of ignorance," prior to the advent of Islam, were acknowledged as monotheists in this sense: they worshipped God as One, but they associated others with Him, or sought other lofty figures—whether angels or prophets—to mediate with Him on their behalf. They were guilty of *shirk*, that is, idolatry, and so they could not and did not worship God in His transcendent solitude. Professing *tawhid al-uluhiyya*, true believers had to dissociate themselves from the quasi-monotheists, even as they ignored the ultra-monotheist Sufis. Not only did true believers have to dissociate themselves from all other believers but they also had to repudiate their fellow monotheists, exposing the error of their words and the damage of their deeds.[3]

The project of purifying Islam was internal as well as external in its focus. While *shirk* was evidenced in the material forms of graves or amulets, *kufr* (disbelief) was a disease of the heart. Nourished in secret, it had to be constantly confronted: it required not just individual but collective vigilance of the most intense nature. *Kufr* could be subdued only by persistent attack on all those who did not self-identify with Ibn ʿAbd al-Wahhab and his teaching. That included not just Sufi masters and their followers but also all devout ʿ*ulama*' and *fuqaha*' (scholars as well as jurists), who derived their authority and projected its value within the traditional schools (*madhhabs*).

In other words, most observant Muslims became the enemies of Wahhabi ideology. For all Sufi-oriented elites, as also most ordinary believers, the touchstone of devotion remained the Prophet, but not the Prophet solely as a human messenger sent by Allah to seventh-century Arab pagans. The Prophet, from the Sufi perspective, was also a majestic, omniscient, metahistorical presence, alive from Pre-existence (*abad*) to Post-existence (*azal*). Exemplary persons, also known as saints (*awliya*'), especially the loftiest of saints (*aqtab*), were thought to share in this same timeless omniscience. Hence intercession with the Prophet, as also with the saints, was deemed to be part of Divine Grace.[4]

One could trace the origin and development of such Sufi beliefs to the great proponents of sainthood, themselves deemed to be saints from the storied past, whether Ibn ʿArabi, Jalaluddin al-Suyuti, or Shah Waliullah. What distinguishes neo-Sufism is not so much abrupt doctrinal shifts from their illustrious predecessors, whether independent or in response to Wahhabi influence, but rather a gradual accommodation—at once complex and local—to the multiple challenges of a colonial order. It included new transregional mobility, new local institutions, new multilingual forms of education, and also new print networks. Colonialism, not Wahhabism, became the midwife of neo-Sufism, or "the third wave of institutional Sufism."[5]

Colonial rule paradoxically served to strengthen as well as weaken Muslim networks. While the French in West Africa undermined networks by breaking down connections between specific local Muslim groups (Berbers and Arabs), they ironically fostered the revival of these groups in resistance to European domination. Indeed, the same networks that opposed European rule also linked Muslims to the metropolitan capitals of France and England. Education, both secular and religious, was crucial in expanding Muslim networks, including but not solely those promoting Sufi loyalty, throughout Africa and Asia. Education included more than curricular content; it also inscribed usage of European languages in new contexts. During the nineteenth century, French and English became regional *linguae francae* for Muslim communities, sometimes displacing local Muslim languages, whether Urdu, Persian, Pashto, or Bengali. Owing to its liturgical prestige, Arabic was the major Muslim language to retain its prestige during the colonial period, and one could argue that its prestige, along with the prestige accorded Persian and Urdu, was enhanced, especially for Sufi-minded Muslims, through the print revolution.

The Nineteenth Century: Sufi Africa

"The nineteenth century was Muslim Africa's Sufi century," wrote R. S. O'Fahey.[6] Is this provocative statement, from the most prominent historian of East African Sufism, true? And if it is true, what are its implications for Sufi orders and their response to the twin challenge of colonialism and Wahhabi/Salafi opposition?

Especially in nineteenth-century Africa, colonial rivalries as well as competition between the *tariqas* were crucial to understanding the role of institutional Sufism. The French, like their British rivals, were uncertain how to engage the fellowships. Mauritania provides a case instance of their unending dilemma. The attitude of the French to Islam in Mauritania fluctuated between a general sympathy and a limited backing for certain marabouts among the alleged "Berber" *zawiyas* (lodges). They were obsessed with the threat of a pan-Germanic and pan-Islamic alliance; in it they deemed Sayyid Maʾ al-ʿAynayn (d. 1905) to be playing a particularly important role. Colonial authorities banned the circulation of Arabic newspapers from abroad and closely observed the *zawiyas*. Mail was sometimes censured. Arabic higher education also suffered. Differences between the Qadiriyya and the Tijanniyya Sufi orders were exploited wherever possible. In French West Africa, up until the First World War, Islam (or the Islamic Peril) became close to an obsession of French foreign policy. Where the French allowed and at times encouraged religious schools (*madrasas*) to be built, it was principally to facilitate tribal control and to intensify their surveillance of local tribes. They also encouraged certain marabouts to visit their flocks in adjacent Black Africa to impress a far-wider Muslim public.[7] Yet some Tijani leaders, such as Shaykh Hamallah, rejected the French. Repeatedly deported or under surveillance, he died in obscure circumstances in January 1943 and a number of his followers, as well as two of his sons, were executed.[8]

The legacy of Maʾ al-ʿAynayn also projected his anticolonial stance. When Maʾ al-ʿAynayn died, his principal *zawiya* was desecrated but his sons did not retire from the struggle. Descendants of Maʾ al-ʿAynayn, especially his son, Murabbih Rabbuh (d. 1942), became master planners and part-executors of attacks on French posts.[9] They were not alone. Even while the French were building new *madrasas* in Mauritania, beyond Mauritania in other parts of West Africa, dissident marabouts were able to maintain and expand their networks of resistance to colonial rule.

Indeed, it is possible to argue that the greatest expansion of Islam in sub-Saharan Africa took place in the colonial period, particularly under the British in Nigeria and the Sudan as well as the French in Central and Western Africa. Ironically colonial administrators did not cooperate in every instance with their missionary counterparts. Often they strained to develop institutions and practices that enabled their Muslim subjects to be peaceful participants in the colonial project. They co-opted portions of the Islamic legal and educational systems. They tried to control the mechanisms, and also the participants, in the annual pilgrimage. They hoped to create colonial forms of Islam. The best known attempt was *islam noir*, the Black Islam, that the French held up as characteristic of French West Africa. The French tried to outdo the British in India, and also the Dutch in Indonesia, in projecting themselves as a Muslim power advocating the interests of their Muslim subjects against those of their colonial rivals.[10]

The dominant narrative for the nineteenth century places the Hijaz, especially Mecca and Medina, within the Wahhabi camp from the late eighteenth century, yet a number of Sufis and Sufi-minded *'ulama'* populated the Holy Cities and formed study circles there that were well attended by pilgrims and others, from Asia and Africa as well as the Mediterranean basin. Moreover, the Wahhabi sack of the Haramayn, destructive though it was, was followed by over a hundred years of re-occupation by Egyptian/Ottoman forces at odds with Wahhabi, and later Salafi, ideology. Early nineteenth-century Mecca remained a cosmopolitan site, the nodal point attracting multiple networks of Muslim saints and jurists, merchants and travelers. Among the North African saints who found themselves in Mecca on the cusp of the nineteenth century was Ahmad ibn Idris al-Fasi (d. 1837). His influence pervades several of the new orders that drew inspiration from him and later became clustered as standard bearers for neo-Sufism, primary among them the Mirghani and the Sanusi Sufi orders.[11]

The profusion of neo-Sufi orders should not conceal a key element that links them to all preceding orders: their founders competed with one another for the mantle of spiritual excellence. Nominally, they followed the same supreme master and accepted the same initiatic lineage, yet in fact, they were spiritual rivals for the hearts and minds of their contemporaries.

The Mirghaniyya or Khatmiyya is named after an eighteenth-century Sharif, or descendant of the Prophet Muhammad, whose family came from Central Asia. As a youth, Muhammad 'Uthman al-Mirghani was initiated by Ahmad ibn Idris al-Fasi but sparred with his other chief disciples, Muhammad ibn 'Ali al-Sanusi and Ibrahim al-Rashid. Which of them was best suited to succeed Ahmad ibn Idris al-Fasi? The question took on urgency when Ibn Idris died in 1837: faithful to the *sunna*, or exemplary behavior of the Prophet Muhammad, Ibn Idris had died without naming a successor. His legacy therefore was contested, and because of his Sharifian credentials, al-Mirghani was supported by many Meccan notables.

Al-Mirghani, in common with al-Sanusi, followed the example of Shah Waliullah from Delhi and Ahmad al-Tijani from Fez (and Cairo). Like these earlier saints, he claimed that his order included all the orders but also superseded them. The Naqshbandiyya, the Shadhiliyya, and, of course, the Qadiriyya, one of the oldest and most prestigious Sufi orders, were deemed to be of value but their value was reduced next to the spiritual power of the Mirghaniyya.

Nor did inter-*tariqa* rivalry end with al-Mirghani's success in the Hijaz over his Idrisi contemporaries. He also opposed Muhammad Ahmad ibn 'Abd Allah when he declared himself as Mahdi in the Sudan. After the British destroyed the Mahdist state in 1898, al-Mirghani's descendants were able to reap the advantages of his "loyal" advocacy of true Islam against the upstart, and rebellious, Mahdi. The tale of the Mahdi's own dalliance with Sufism, and then his later sublimation of its principal tenets, anticipates the odyssey of Ustadh Mahmud Taha (d. 1985) a century later, also in the Sudan.[12]

Ahmad ibn Idris al-Fasi's other main successor was Muhammad ibn ʿAli al-Sanusi. Sanusi had the advantage of having been taught by Ibn Idris in Mecca and also in Yemen. He had been initiated into several orders—the Shadhiliyya, the Darqawiyya, and the Tijanniyya—before he met Ibn Idris in Mecca in 1826. A spiritual vision from the Prophet confirmed Sanusi's resolve to become Ibn Idris's disciple. In the authority Ibn Idris conferred on his prize disciple, he included proficiency in Prophetic traditions, Qur'an commentaries, and jurisprudence along with Sufism. Among the several Sufi orders to which Sanusi was initiated was *al-tariqa al-Muhammadiyya*. Sanusi then became the eponymous founder of his own Sufi order, the Sanusiyya. The order provided a rallying point against both Ottoman influence and European inroads. When Sanusi died in 1859 his successor, Sayyid Muhammad al-Mahdi, took over the leadership of 146 Sanusi *zawiyas*. The struggle against the Italians continued under Mahdi and his son, who became King Idris of Libya. Later, the Sanusi played a critical role in precipitating an early Italian withdrawal from Tripoli, during the Second World War.[13]

Competing with Idrisis and other orders, especially in West Africa, were the Tijanis. The Tijaniyya trace their origins to a Moroccan master, Shaykh Ahmad al-Tijani (d. 1815). Though a relatively late order, the Tijaniyya challenged what had been till then the dominant order in West Africa: the Qadiriyya.

The Tijaniyya exemplify what is novel about neo-Sufism. It was less doctrinal innovations than creative repackaging of elements from previous generations, especially those linked to Ibn ʿArabi. Just as the Prophet had been in direct contact with Ibn ʿArabi, inspiring, for instance, one of his seminal works, *Fusus al-hikam*, in a single night's dream, so Shaykh Ahmad al-Tijani saw himself inspired by the Prophet, not just in dreams but also in a waking state. In one of his many Prophetic visions, Shaykh Ahmad saw himself confirmed for a role that Ibn ʿArabi had earlier claimed: he was designated as the seal of the saints, just as Muhammad had been designated the seal, or final capstone, of all preceding prophets. Shaykh Ahmad went further in paralleling his experience to that of the Prophet. He pronounced his order as unique and superior to its antecedents, just as Islam had fulfilled and surpassed all previous monotheistic religions. These were huge claims. They amounted to a mandate for proselytization, among other

Muslims as well as among non-Muslims. Not surprisingly, they elicited confrontation with rival *tariqas*, whose leaders saw themselves as better conduits of Divine Favor than Shaykh Ahmad.[14]

In their rivalry with the Qadiriyya and the Idrisiyya, the Tijaniyya benefited from French colonial rule. Intent to impose peace in western Africa, French officials needed the Sufi masters or marabouts as their intermediaries. They supported the marabouts as long as both the marabouts and their disciples paid taxes, respected colonial laws, and pursued farming as their major source of income.

The Tijanis illustrate the force of colonialism as well as the emergent profile of neo-Sufism. Based in West Africa, they reflected the French presence at many levels. Their resistance was fortified through increased participation in the pilgrimage, itself fostered by new patterns of communication that facilitated rather than reduced networks of travel and patronage to the Haramayn. They met the challenge of French education, aggressively pursued by the colonial authorities, through alternative forms of Islamic social organization and higher education in a broad range of religious and nonreligious topics. The new colonial situation spurred the adoption of Western teaching methods as well as curricula in the *madrasa*: while the language of instruction could be, and often was, Arabic, the range of topics expanded to meet the demands of French West African society that Tijani leaders faced.[15]

Yet not all the Tijanis were co-opted by the French as al-Mirghani and his followers had been co-opted by the British. Some, like ʿAbdul Qadir al-Jazaʾiri (d. 1883), were co-opted by the French, even serving as their surrogates, but then later broke off relations and actively opposed them. Among African Sufi leaders who opposed the French was al-Hajj ʿUmar al-Futi, or al-Hajj ʿUmar Taal. He became a Tijani in the 1820s when, en route to the Pilgrimage, he met another Tijani master, Muhammad al-Ghali. He studied with al-Ghali till he obtained a license (*ijaza*) from him. Returning to West Africa, he preached among the Hausa. He followed the early precedent of another western African opponent of the French, ʿUsman dan Fodio, also a Sufi activist, and made Sokoto his base, but by the time he undertook the *jihad* in 1855, he had made many Muslim enemies. Betrayal by fellow Muslims not only weakened but defeated him: al-Hajj ʿUmar Taal was killed in 1864 by rival Muslims. Nor did his offspring share his antipathy to the French: his son and successor, Ahmadu Taal, and even more his grandson, Saydu Nuru Taal, became proponents of the French "civilizing mission" (*la mission civilisatrice*).[16]

The Nineteenth Century: Revivalist Sufi Movements Outside of Africa

Whether measuring successful resistance or failure to resist colonial forces, one cannot concede the nineteenth century entirely to Sufi Africa, or to African Sufis. There were revivalist movements in other parts of *dar al-Islam*. Like those in Africa, they had indigenous roots and issues as well as foreign, colonial provocations. The two most often linked to Sufism are the *jihad* movements of Sayyid Ahmad Shahid in northern India (Rae Bareli) and the Fara'idis. Ahmad Shahid had begun as a local soldier frustrated by British inroads into his native region. Giving up military service, he moved to Delhi and began studying with Shah 'Abdul 'Aziz of Delhi, son of the major north Indian reformer Sufi, Shah Waliullah. Ahmad Shahid became a Sufi initiate, with powers to initiate others. Among his followers were members of Shah 'Abdul 'Aziz's own family and close supporters. He moved toward an agenda of armed conflict with Sikhs in the Punjab, but first decided to make a pilgrimage to Mecca. Announcing his intent before he went to the Hijaz, he attracted numerous followers, especially in eastern India. He met with Wahhabis in Mecca, strengthening his resolve to conduct *jihad*. On his return, in 1826, he undertook the *jihad*. He enjoyed initial success, occupying the major Afghan city of Peshawar, but internal disputes as well as external confrontation weakened his movement. He had to withdraw from Peshawar in 1830 and then was killed in armed conflict with Sikhs the following year (in Balakot).

The other major north Indian Sufi-related reform movement was the Fara'idis, under Hajji Shari'atullah (d. 1840). Again inspired by an 1821 pilgrimage to Mecca, its leader was a Bengali religious scholar who was also a Qadiri adept. Hajji Shari'atullah railed against the *bid'a* (or innovation) of his coreligionists, and urged his followers to center their faith on the basic duties (*fara'id*) and to discard all else, yet he also encouraged the practice of *dhikr* (remembering God), and it seemed that his intent was to resist the economic exploitation of Muslims by Hindu landowners more than it was to create a new Islamic order or to expel the British.[17]

Nor was Central Asia lacking for Sufi-derived movements in the nineteenth century. An entirely new era in the history of the Naqshbandiyya in Anatolia and in Central Asia began with the rise of the Khalidi branch in the first quarter of the nineteenth century. Before the Khalidiyya, the Naqshbandis had been prominent and respected, both in Istanbul and elsewhere, but they never came close to enjoying the near-monopoly on Sufi activity that they had exercised in Central Asia. The Khalidis, however, made the Naqshbandiyya the paramount order in Turkey, a position it retained even after the official dissolution of the orders by Kemal Ataturk.

Illustrative of the power of Sufi networks, Mawlana Khalid Baghdadi (d. 1827) was a Kurd who obtained initiation into the Naqshbandiyya Mujaddidiyya in Delhi at the hands of Shah Ghulam ʿAli (d. 1824). Though he supported Ottoman rule in Kurdistan, Ottoman bureaucrats regarded the new movement with suspicion. One of his successors, ʿAbdul Wahhab al-Susi, did succeed in making inroads among the Ottoman elite. Like other key figures in the history of the Ottoman Naqshbandiyya, he recruited numerous religious scholars as well as bureaucrats and men of letters. Successors to Mawlana Khalid allied themselves with the Ottoman state. Even though their emphasis on sacred law provided a point of stability during the reign of Sultan Abdulhamid II (r. 1876–1909), it was never possible for the Naqshbandis to preempt the favor shown to competing orders by royal as well as administrative members of the Ottoman hierarchy.

It was beyond the Ottoman state that the Khalidi branch of the Naqshbandiyya attracted followers from all parts of Anatolia, so much so that they could boast an influence equal to, or even greater than, their Mevlevi rivals in Konya. Elsewhere, in the Middle East the Khalidiyya supplanted almost entirely all other branches of the Naqshbandiyya, while in Kurdistan it wrested supremacy from the Qadiriyya to become the chief order of that region.

But the most powerful and enduring legacy of the Khalidi Naqshbandiyya may have been in the northern Caucasus. Nineteenth-century Czarist Russia was determined to root out the resistance of Imam Shamil and the rugged mountaineers who were his devout supporters. Already in the late eighteenth century they had pursued *jihad* against superior Czarist forces, and then in the early nineteenth century a regional branch of the Khalidi Naqshbandiyya became the lodestone of Muslim loyalty in Chechnya and Daghestan. Naqshbandi warrior shaykhs led by the legendary Imam Shamil fought a protracted war of attrition against Russian forces. The Muridist Insurrection, named after his followers, lasted from 1824 to 1855. After its defeat in 1859, many of the Naqshbandi leaders were exiled, or forced to emigrate, yet unrest in Chechnya continued. It provided a venue for the Qadiriyya: though hardly a new order, they made new inroads into Chechnya and Ingushetia. In some cases, Qadiri masters converted marginal Muslims to a revitalized Islamic observance channeled through Sufi practice. In other cases, they reclaimed and mobilized those who previously had followed Imam Shamil and the Khalidi Naqshbandiyya. Again, Russian authorities imprisoned or exiled their leaders, yet they could not prevent a joint Naqshbandi-Qadiri uprising against the state in 1877–78. The Sufi rebels lost the battle but the war continued, and, even more importantly, local support for the fellowships and their leaders grew. It was a pattern that continued well into the twentieth century, giving the northern Caucasus a claim that, at least in political terms, it was they who marked the end of the nineteenth century as a Central Asian Sufi century.[18]

The Nineteenth Century: A Note on Southeast Asian Sufi Orders

Southeast Asia too was notable for the activities of its Sufi networks during the nineteenth century. In a broad sense, networks that linked Sufi masters across the Mediterranean world had expanded with the opening of the Suez Canal in 1869, but the colonial world that produced British and Dutch competition in Southeast Asia also increased the number of Malay Muslims making the Pilgrimage. As Islamic learning in Arabic deepened, so did the reflex to impose a Wahhabi-type orthodoxy on urban circles of Sufism in Java and Sumatra. The most notable movement is the Padri Reform movement that took place in West Sumatra between 1784 and 1837. Like the Fara'idi movement in Bengal, it combined Sufi and Wahhabi impulses; in this case, affiliation with the Shattari Sufi order spurred a *jihad* movement against both internal and external enemies. Also parallel to the Fara'idi movement there were internal enemies: feudal nobility caused economic hardship among agricultural classes, at the same time that Dutch and English colonial powers represented a political as well as an economic challenge to Sumatran Muslims.

Also like other regions of the Muslim world, Southeast Asia in the latter half of the nineteenth century saw open competition between Sufi orders, notably between the Shattaris and the Qadari-Naqshbandi subgroup. The latter came to Sumatra in increasing numbers through a network based in Mecca under the leadership of an Indonesian master, Ahmad Khatib Sambas. In the interim period between the recapture of Mecca/Medina from the Wahhabis in 1813 and its surrender to the Saudis in 1916, many *fiqh*-minded, or juridically oriented, Sufi masters thrived in the Haramayn. Among them was Ahmad Khatib Sambas, together with his rival, 'Abdus Samad Palembang of the Sammani order.[19]

The Twentieth Century: Sufi Asia

Despite the intense activity of fellowships in Central, South, and Southeast Asia during the nineteenth century, the weight of scholarship upholds the claim that the nineteenth century was indeed Muslim Africa's Sufi century. The twentieth century, however, produced a series of new developments that moved beyond Africa and its many Sufi orders. While O'Fahey's apt provocation offers a thumbnail summary of Sufism in the nineteenth century, it invites a retort for the twentieth century: "To the extent that the nineteenth century was Muslim Africa's Sufi century, then the twentieth century became Muslim Asia's quasi-Sufi century."

In brief, what characterized the twentieth century was the presence and influence of Sufi orders, despite the absence of governmental support for Sufism and also the appearance of groups that often opposed Sufism while adopting Sufi principles. The twentieth century filtered the experience of Sufi orders, often diluting the Sufi project of interiorization and transcendence while at the same time repackaging some of the instrumental features that accounted for the fellowships' success.

Arguably, five major events defined Islam in the public square of global politics in the twentieth century: the Young Turk revolt of 1908, the Bolshevik revolution of 1917, the Muslim Brotherhood of Hasan al-Banna launched in 1928, the Iranian Revolution of 1978–79, and the al-Qaʿida bombings of the 1990s. Yet none of these five events, or the forces they unleashed, involved Sufism. Instead, they projected the opposite of Sufism, either an avuncular secularism, as with Young Turks and communists, or a tide of Salafi/ʿAlid nostalgia, with the Brethren, the terrorists, and the mullahs directing their ire against morally tainted Western targets. Beneath the surface, and often outside the gaze of the media, much was happening, however, that suggested lingering Sufi influence. It either emanated from Asia or took place in Asia.

The Twentieth Century: Sufism in South Asia

If the twentieth century is deemed to be Muslim Asia's Sufi century, then a major aspect of that recuperated Sufi identity is due to the influences from the Asian subcontinent, what had been India under colonial rule, and then after Partition in 1947 became first two competitive nation-states: India and Pakistan, and after 1971 three rival states: India, Pakistan, and Bangladesh. Among the layers of Sufi identity in twentieth-century Muslim South Asia were residual traces, coded revaluations, and explicit retrieval of the legacy from the major Sufi orders, but especially the Chishti Sufi fellowship.

Residual traces came from a surprising source: Sayyid Abu'l A'la Maududi, founder and leader of the revivalist organization Jama'at-i Islami. Not only did Maududi admire the Chishti giants of the past, even while deploring contemporary saint worship, but he also benefited from the central notion of *tajdid* (revival), projecting himself as the *mujaddid* (renewer) of the current age. Perhaps most surprising were the poems found among his personal effects after his death in 1979; they included some highly allegorical Sufi verse.

The coded revaluation of Sufi categories came through a group often viewed as anti-Sufi or "fundamentalist": Tablighi Jama'at, founded by Mawlana Muhammad Ilyas (d. 1944).[20] The Mawlana came from a family of religious scholars and Sufis in northern India. Trained as a jurist-theologian, he went on his second Pilgrimage in 1925, then remained in the Haramayn for another five months. He returned to Delhi and to the mosque founded by his father in proximity to the most famous Sufi shrine in Delhi: Hazrat Nizamuddin. The principal custodian at Nizamuddin, Khwaja Hasan Nizami, had begun his own Tablighi Mission among the untouchables, but Mawlana Ilyas directed his project to a group of rural Muslims: the Mewatis, an illiterate and half-converted tribe living in the eastern regions of Delhi. By the 1930s he had expanded his mission to include the merchant classes of Delhi, and during ensuing decades it became an all-India, then a global movement. While its membership is difficult to estimate, it convenes annual meetings in Pakistan and Bangladesh that number over two million persons in each, with lesser but still sizable attendance at other meetings in India, England, and North America.

It is best understood as a quasi-Sufi movement, despite its overt hostility to traditional Sufism and especially to the lively cult activities at Hazrat Nizamuddin in Delhi. The purpose of the Tablighi movement is at once apolitical and individualist. Unlike the Jama'at-i Islami of Abu'l A'la Maududi, the Tablighi Jama'at eschews engagement in political issues or advocacy of political parties. It fosters reform of the individual by attention to six points. The first two points are simply the profession of faith (*kalima*) and the five daily prayers (*salat*), but the intent is to make the *kalima* part of one's inner being, not a mere verbal formula, and the next four points reinforce that intensity of faith (*iman*). They stress remembrance of God (*dhikr*), reciting praise of the Prophet, invocation of God, and supplication of forgiveness at least a hundred times each day, in addition to *salat* or the ritually prescribed five prayers. That practice of continuous remembrance then makes possible the last three points: to respect other Muslims, to make one's intent pure and sincere, and finally to dedicate time to work with other like-minded Muslims in propagating the true faith.

Despite the rejection of institutional Sufism, and in particular their opposition to neo-Sufi groups such as the Barelwis, the Tablighi six-point program redirects the Sufi ethos into a popular movement. Mawlana Ilyas, both by training and temperament, was at home with the male isolation of *khanqah* life as well as the intellectual rigor of *madrasa* teaching. He had called his movement "a *khanqah* on the move," advocating moral development for the masses and not just for intellectual elites. He communicated with his followers through letters (*maktubat*) but also through moral dialogues (*malfuzat*), a distinctly Sufi literary genre. Among the six points, the double accent on *dhikr* and sincere intent (*ikhlas-i niyya*) echoes the Chishti worldview, just as the periods of withdrawal from ordinary life include a *chilla* (a forty-day retreat), incumbent on advanced Tablighis, as it once was on Chishti virtuosi, to perform once a year.

The Tablighis eschew the hierarchy of a master-disciple relationship that characterizes Sufi orders, and they have also projected their networks of male emissaries on a transnational scale that facilitates movement while minimizing administrative duties. Yet modern communications, from print to cell phone, from airports to email, define their activity as much as it does non-Tablighi Muslims.

A further tangent of South Asian Sufism in the twentieth century explicitly embraced the Sufi legacy of the past. It also embraced politics, including nationalism, in the name of a higher principle: devotion to God and the Prophet. Sabiri Chishti masters in Pakistan embodied this approach. Deviating from the precedent of their premodern predecessors, who largely avoided urban spaces and networks of royal patronage in favor of a life of spiritual quietism and withdrawal in rural locales, three Sabiri Chishti masters—Muhammad Zawqi Shah, Shahidullah Faridi, and Wahid Bakhsh Rabbani—entered the contested public sphere to stake their own claims to Islamic authority and authenticity. Though it is clear that their principal loyalties and commitments were directed to their duties as teaching shaykhs, they also recognized the need to defend the Sabiri Chishti tradition in public forums. Zawqi Shah is the most prominent of the three. Evoking the model of political engagement established by his nineteenth-century predecessor Hajji Imdadullah Muhajir Makki (d. 1899) and Rashid Ahmad Gangohi (d. 1905), both linked to the Deoband movement, Zawqi Shah drew on his expertise as a journalist to inscribe a new version of Chishti Sabiri identity through a diverse range of publications. The Shaykh went even further in his political activism. Attending the first meeting of the Muslim League in Karachi in 1907, he formally joined the organization in 1940 and became a confidant of Muhammad ʿAli Jinnah from 1937 to 1947. Zawqi Shah wrote a series of letters to Pakistan's future leader, in which he sacralized the Indo-Muslim past. "Hindustan is the inheritance of the Chishtis," he reminded the secular Jinnah. Even those who were neither Chishtis nor Sufis understood the appeal of this spiritual lineage. It was as though a single principle had guided and preserved the Indo-Muslim community from the eleventh to the twentieth centuries: dedication to the saintly mediation of Chishti masters.[21]

Neither the Chishtis nor any Sufi order dominated the transregional, multilinguistic subcommunities of South Asian Islam. Yet legacies from the Sufi past do provide traces of memory and nodes of loyalty that persist beyond the contemporary media's headline concerns with political Islam and extremist ideologies. Sufism is a less visible light but it casts a long shadow over Muslim identity and public activities.

The Twentieth Century: Sufism in Turkey and Central Asia

Amplifying the claim that the twentieth century was marked by Asian Sufis was the residual impact of the Naqshbandiyya in Turkey and beyond Turkey, in Central Asia. A Khalidi Naqshbandi shaykh had already distinguished himself by fighting, together with his followers, in the Russo-Ottoman war of 1877. This example of military engagement was followed by several other Naqshbandi shaykhs who fought on various fronts during the First World War and the Turkish War of Independence. Nonetheless, the Naqshbandis found themselves denied legitimacy under the Turkish Republic: all the Sufi orders were proscribed in September 1925.

Even after the Republic reforms Khalidi shaykhs continued to be active in Turkey. Despite surveillance and often detention by state officers, Naqshbandi devotees became actively involved in national politics, first through the National Salvation Party (Milli Selamet Partisi) and then its successor, the Welfare Party (Refah Partisi). Yet the continuing importance of the Turkish Naqshbandiyya derives, above all, from their spiritual practices conforming to Mawlana Khalid and his successors.[22] In this respect they are both rivals and allies of the much newer Nurculuk movement.

Nurcus are followers of Badiʿuzzaman Saʿid Nursi (d. 1960). Like Khalid Naqshbandi, he was a Kurd born in eastern Turkey. Said Nursi did not even begin to speak Turkish till his late teens. He was initiated into the Naqshbandis, but instead of pursing the role of a traditional shaykh, he redirected his spiritual energy toward education. He believed that modern education was not incompatible with Islamic principles. He supported the constitutional movement, and also Ataturk in the Turkish War of Independence that followed the First World War (1919–22). Yet he was continually portrayed as a covert ally of political enemies of the Kemalist state, and forced into exile, he committed himself to writing the lengthy *Risale-i Nur*. At once a vast commentary on the Qur'an and an application of the Sufi principle of outer/inner to the natural world, it became the basis for what is known as the Nurculuk movement. It recenters public and private life on the pillar of Islamic ethics, addressing contemporary problems with a plea for social and economic justice.[23]

The Nur movement tried to remain aloof from national politics, but it did become embroiled in the National Salvation Party (1973–81) and then in the 1980s it inspired the Fethullahcilar movement, named after its founder, Fethullah Gulen. His project, like Said Nursi's, tried to reconcile religious and secular elements under the umbrella of an Islamic version of scientific positivism. It was an educational experiment that extended beyond Turkey into Central Asia and also the Balkans, again following the Sufi networks of the revitalized Naqshbandi order. Its strongly religious tone brought it into conflict with the military establishment, as also with civilian advocates of a secular ethos, but it remains a core part of what some have described as the creeping Islamization of Turkish public life.

The impact of Sufism beyond Turkey did not recede with the advance of communism. The Naqshbandis were only one of several orders to have subgroups within those parts of Russia that became Soviet Central Asia after the Bolshevik revolution in 1917. Other orders included the Qadiris, the Yasavis, and the Kubravis. All these orders, along with other non-Sufi Muslim organizations, were proscribed under communist rule. In their place was set a statist religion, even if in some individual cases they were devout Muslims as well as members of the Communist Party. Yet the orders did not disappear. While Azerbaijan remained Shi'i dominant, other majority Muslim regions in Central Asia, the Middle Volga, and northern Caucasus were Sunni in outlook and often Sufi in practice. Most of the leaders of these fellowships went underground, functioning as a parallel Islam, openly condemned by the Soviet-appointed official Islamic establishment but still attractive to practicing believers in Central Asia and adjacent regions. The very survival of Islamic loyalty in the former Soviet Union indicates that the antireligious propaganda disseminated by specialists of the Kremlin could neither exterminate nor redirect Sufi dissidents. Visitation to saints' shrines was proscribed, Qur'anic instruction by living masters was curtailed, and Muslims, whether Sufi or non-Sufi, when drafted into the Soviet army, were forced to eat pork and also to drink vodka as a rite of survival.

One question persists: to what extent did the vital force of institutional Sufism remain after more than eighty years of proscription, persecution, and counter-education in the USSR? The answer varies, and it varies according to region. In places with a strong tomb cult history, such as Turkmenistan and Kirghizstan, Sufism regained a role in private devotion and also public life after 1989. In other regions, such as Tajikistan, Uzbekistan, and Kazakhstan, Sufi practice of *dhikr*, along with public observance of *salat*, was less evident.[24]

The one place where Sufi-Muslim identity remained vital as a core of resistance to Czarist, Soviet, now Russian rule was Chechen-Ingush territory. Following the Bolshevik revolution, it was Soviets rather than Czarists who became the occupying enemy in the northern Caucasus. From 1918 to 1923 the rebels tried to create an independent Muslim state in Daghestan. Though they failed, and their movement was repressed from 1923 to 1926, the resistance continued until the Second World War when Stalin made a momentous decision: deport the entire Chechen and Ingush populations to Siberia and Kazakhstan. Some, however, escaped to the mountains, where they have continued their "terrorist" reorganization and resistance until now.

The actual number of *murids* in the fellowships is almost impossible to ascertain, but at least one Soviet source allowed that despite the 1944 mass deportation of Chechens to Siberia, for every ten thousand present-day Chechens who would subscribe to officially sanctioned atheism there would be two hundred thousand to two hundred and fifty thousand Sufi *murids*.[25] Whatever the outcome of their political struggle it is impossible to deny that Islam in the northern Caucasus has survived due to the tenacity and organizational skill of Sufi leaders. Not just in the northern Caucasus but throughout Central Asia it has been the orders which have not only saved Islam as belief and as way of life but also projected it as a nationalist culture, to be defended against every Russian adversary. From the Khalidi Naqshbandiyya in the nineteenth century to the Chechen-Daghestan network of the twenty-first century, Sufi resistance in Central Asia has marked Russia as well as Islam.

The Twentieth Century: Southeast Asian Sufi Orders

Finally, the twentieth century witnessed a continuation of patterns begun in the nineteenth century, with the Hijaz-based network of reform-minded teachers influencing the nature of Sufi activity in the archipelago. Relying on the new print culture, credentialed Islamic scholars from Indonesia who often resided in the Haramayn, or returned home after long stays there, attacked the authority of institutional shaykhs. The Naqshbandis, whose influence had expanded in the last half of the nineteenth century, were challenged for their authenticity, and they in turn critiqued the bona fides of their challengers.

At the same time as these debates and exchanges were taking place between traditional scholars, a new wing of Islamic reform organization emerged in Yogyakarta. The Muhammadiyah was founded as a benevolent organization in 1912, but it gained adherents throughout Java and also Sumatra in succeeding decades to become one of the major Muslim movements in contemporary Indonesia. Though Muhammadiyah members criticized certain Sufi practices, their leaders refrained from a wholesale condemnation of institutional Sufism, and in West Sumatra, at least one major Naqshbandi master also promoted Muhammadiyah principles and belonged to its local chapter.[26]

Indeed, the sharp ideological edges that may be detected elsewhere become softened, even invisible, in Indonesia. Most of the twentieth-century conflicts involving Sufi orders were within rival *tariqas*, not between Sufi masters and their reformist opponents. The popular Muhammadiyah leader, Hamka, subscribed to "modern *tasawwuf*," that is, a Sufi ethos and worldview divorced from the tomb cult and ritual practices of the orders. Many upscale urban Indonesians, whether students or mobile and highly literate young professionals, found in the traditional orders a resource for their own religious formation as modern-day Muslims.

The Twentieth Century: Sufi Africa

On the ledger of institutional Sufism the activities and influence of African Sufis that marked the nineteenth century did not disappear in the twentieth. Two orders in particular—the Tijaniyya and the Muridiyya—continued the legacy that had made the nineteenth century Sufi Africa's peak century, even as they combatted Wahhabism within Islam and colonialist strictures from without.

Indeed, an uneasy trust between local Tijaniyya and the French authorities worked to the programmatic benefit of some Tijani, such as the Niassene Tijaniyya of Senegambia/Senegal. Far from promoting French colonial interests, the Niassene Tijaniyya used French support to Islamize the Senegalese hinterland, to spread their order at the expense of others, and to outflank colonial authorities whenever and wherever possible.

Peanuts provided the common commodity, and peanut farming the common industry, that benefited both parties and made the alliance work. The French administrators encouraged the cultivation of peanuts by constructing a railway that linked the hinterland to the sea. Tijani disciples would travel to distant parts to cultivate peanuts but also, in their "spare time," to give religious instruction to would-be converts.

The Tijaniyyya increased in number and influence under French rule. They also expanded to Nigeria. It was during a pilgrimage to Mecca in 1937 that Ibrahim Niasse (d. 1975) met the emir of Kano from northern Nigeria. He persuaded the emir that he was the pole of saints, the top of the spiritual hierarchy in a Sufi worldview. He also relied on the distinctively Tijani view of *fayd* (Divine Grace), linking it hieratically to the Muhammadan Truth, channeled from God to the Prophet Muhammad, and then through him to Shaykh Ahmad al-Tijani and to his successors. This link, and it alone, is the most direct route to Divine Grace.

The triumphalist brand of Tijani Sufism enabled the Niasse sub-branch to spread from Kano through the rest of Black Africa, especially after the Second World War. It was not only charisma and teaching, however, but also location and networking that helped. Kano in Nigeria, like Kaolack in Senegal, was a key commercial center. Kano remains till today one of the largest industrial and commercial axes in western Africa, and so the Tijanis, like other Sufi orders, benefited from layering their spiritual network with material, specifically commercial, interests. It was an intensely reciprocal relationship: Tijani missionaries were involved in trade. Their location at the apex of northern Nigerian political economy helped reinforce their spiritual credentials and influence. They maximized both profit and the Prophet in their networking.[27]

The networks of Tijani influence also expanded across the Atlantic. Just as local celebrations reinforce intraregional solidarity and link Tijanis from major Arab states to their West African coreligionists, so there are relationships with American *zawiyas* (local nodes), all of whom connect to an immigrant spiritual leader, the grandson of the founder, Shaykh Hassan Cisse. While a student at Northwestern in the 1970s, he related to the needs of African Americas. From the early 1980s, he developed a following in New York, Chicago, and Atlanta, establishing further *zawiyas* in each city.[28]

Still another example of a networked West African *tariqa* is the Muridiyya.[29] Mamadou Diouf has analyzed the Senegalese Murid trade diaspora as a vivid example of Sunni Sufi networking in his essay on vernacular cosmopolitanism. Tracing the history of a West African Sufi order from its foundation in the nineteenth century to the present, Diouf claims that the network grew "by offering a new religious form, a new memory and new images to peasant communities that had been disrupted and severely disturbed by colonial military campaigns [and] epidemics connected with the Atlantic slave trade."[30] Concurrently engaged in exclusivist mystical practices and an international peanut business prized by the French, they were able to reconcile Islam with colonial modernity. Theirs was what Diouf calls "a unique cosmopolitanism consisting in participation but not assimilation, thus organizing the local not only to strengthen its position but also to establish the rules governing dialogue with the universal."[31] A major phase in the spread of the Murid network came in the 1970s when drought drove peasants into the Senegalese cities and later overseas. They wove an immense global network linked to their spiritual capital of Touba, with economic and distribution centers in Sandaga and Dakar. Wherever they went they established a firm discipline and an unbreakable trust.

What took place in the Senegalese trade and spiritual network provides a model case of the integration of Muslims qua Muslims into the contemporary global economy. Muslims were able to turn to their advantage oppressive structures that colonial powers had put in place. Networks provided the means and also set the limits for Sufi fellowships: only those groups with resources and mobility could project abroad, remaining religious agents on a global scale in the twenty-first century.

The Twenty-First Century: Sufi America

And precisely due to the expanded influence of transnational networks the twenty-first century might yet become the century of Sufi America. If the nineteenth century was Sufi Africa (despite Sufi developments elsewhere) and if the twentieth century was Sufi Asia (secular and Islamist appearances notwithstanding), then how can the twenty-first century belong to Sufi America? A new spiritual imperium has been emerging in the shadow of the American empire at once militaristic and political. The ascendant West may be peaking in this century, but its twilight comes in the Information Age. The Information Age magnifies and projects networks from the prior two centuries, but it does not accord equal weight to all nodes on the information superhighway. The sequel to Muslim Africa's Sufi century, and Muslim Asia's quasi-Sufi century, may be Euro-America's Sufi millennium, ushered in on the internet by Mevlevi and Akbarian devotees from the New World.

To the extent that traces of Islam and Sufism will pervade the twenty-first century, they may follow the path of the print revolution. So pervasive was the print revolution, in fact, that one could argue it redefined what is most distinctive about Sufism, and also neo-Sufism. Perhaps the most remarkable aspect of the emergence of Sufism as a topic in the nineteenth and twentieth centuries has been the publicizing of a previously esoteric system of teaching through modern communications media. Today, Sufi orders and shrines in Muslim countries produce a stream of publications aimed at a variety of followers from the ordinary devotee to the scholar. Just as the recording industry democratized the private rituals of *sama'* (listening to music) for a mass audience, so the introduction of print and lithography technology made possible the distribution of Sufi teaching on a scale far beyond what manuscript production could attain. Ibn 'Arabi's Arabic works, when they emerged into print early in the nineteenth century, transformed a work that had existed in at most a hundred manuscripts from around the world to one that was now easily available at a corner bookstore through print runs of up to a thousand copies.[32]

The publicizing of Sufism through print (and, more recently, electronic media) has brought about a remarkable shift in Sufi protocol. Advocates of Sufism have defended their heritage by publishing refutations of fundamentalist or modernist attacks. In this sense the media permit Sufism to be contested and defended in the public sphere as one ideology alongside others. The numerous publications of the South Asian Barelwis, for instance, defend the devotional practices of Sufism against scripturalist attacks from the rigorous Deoband school. Likewise, leaders of Egyptian Sufi groups have responded directly to reformist criticisms posed to them by newspaper editors; countering that Sufism is at the core of Islam, they defend Sufi rituals as well as the master-disciple relationship. Through modern public media, Sufism has ceased to be an esoteric community constructed largely through direct contact, ritual interaction, and oral instruction.

At the same time, however, the dissemination of Sufism through mass printing has exacerbated the tension between local and transnational networks of Muslim loyalty. There is an inescapably local element to any Sufi tradition or order. It is expressed by devotion to particular shaykhs, ritual at certain shrines, and writing in vernacular languages. This very concreteness of local networks exists in tension with universal notions of community. As Sufis attempt to trump the systematic ideologies of reformist critics, they stake a claim to the key symbolic capital of the Qur'an and the Prophet Muhammad through polemical and academic publications, yet actual Sufi lineages continue to depend on face-to-face contact and real communities that are of necessity more limited.

Sufi Music and Popular Culture

In the twenty-first century, both in North America and Western Europe, Sufism as expressed in music and film, on DVDs and the World Wide Web, seems destined to remain a niche industry, capturing the hearts of new audiences who gravitate to spaces of meditation, where the spirit is revived, the self reinvented.

The wedding of spiritualism and commercialism is not unique to Sufism but it has affected the latest phase of mystical Islam. Music is a case in point. It is integral to Sufi practice, except for the most austere orders. Yet contemporary Sufi musical production does not emanate from the traditional Sufi orders. It is, instead, a reconfiguration of cultural products for resale on the mass distribution market; it is a dimension of pop culture.

In recent years, Sufi music has been the subject of a new appropriation that may be called "remix." In world music albums, international festivals, and fusion performances, Sufi music has been performed in contexts never before envisioned. To take but one example, the *qawwali* music of Pakistani singer Nusrat Fateh ʿAli Khan ("Dam Mast Qalandar") was remixed by the British hip hop group Massive Attack in 1990 to become an international dance hit with a strongly reggae flavor. At the same time, performers who were once low-status service professionals catering to the spiritual experience of elite listeners have made the shift to become box office superstars who are regarded as spiritual personalities in their own right. A glance at the top twenty-five recordings listed under Sufi music on Amazon.com indicates the remarkable variety and profusion available to the world of consumers today. But this is best described as a cultural and commercial appropriation of Sufism rather than as the dissemination of Sufi teaching and authority.

Yet neither commercialism nor online presence completely displaces earlier forms of communication and technology. The history of technology indicates that older cultural forms persist alongside newly introduced forms of communication. Well after the introduction of writing, and even after the invention of printing, oral forms of culture have persisted up to the present day. The vast majority of participants in the Sufi tradition in Muslim countries still come from social strata that have very little access to the most modern forms of electronic communication, and many are indeed illiterate. Lower-class devotees who attend the festivals of Sufi saints in Egypt and Pakistan are not represented on the Web. Authors of Sufi websites tend to be members of cosmopolitan and globalizing classes: either immigrant Sufi leaders establishing new bases in America and Europe, immigrant technocrats who happen to be connected to Sufi lineages, or Euro-American converts to Sufism in one form or other. Outside of America and Europe, the chief locations for hosting Sufi websites are predictably in high-tech areas like Australia, South Africa, and Malaysia.

The spread of new communications media has had unforeseen effects in allowing popular culture to displace ideology. South Asian Muslims who came to the United States after the Immigration and Naturalization Act of 1965 have tended to be middle-class technical and medical specialists who gravitated toward reformist and fundamentalist forms of Islam. Their college-age children have been unexpectedly enchanted by the world music phenomenon; large numbers of them are discovering Sufism through the powerful music of Nusrat Fateh ʿAli Khan and others. In view of the overwhelming anti-Muslim media bias, the stunning popularity of the Sufi poetry of Rumi is another surprising embrace of a manifestation of Islamic culture—although, to be sure, Rumi's Muslim identity is frequently underplayed or elided in favor of a universalist spirituality. Remarkably, in the face of Saudi-financed forms of anti-Sufi traditionalism, there are increasing signs of engagement with Sufi devotionalism in American Muslim communities.

Sufism beyond Islam?

In addition, Sufism is no longer just for Muslims. One such Sufi group that has succeeded in modern America is the Sufi Order International. This fellowship projects the oldest presence of institutional Sufism in Europe and America, dating from the early years of the twentieth century. It was begun by the Indian master Pir Inayat Khan (d. 1927) and continued by his son and successor, Pir Vilayat Khan (d. 2004), and then by his son and successor, Pir Zia Inayat Khan (b. 1971). Pir Inayat Khan was trained as a Chishti master but then reformulated Sufism as a universal religion detached from normative Islam. To his followers, he represented a new kind of missionary, attempting neither to proselytize nor to convert, asking no one to change his or her religious beliefs. Though he did transmit a repackaged version of traditional Sufi wisdom, he also pointed out its compatibility with all of the world's religions. His teachings have been elaborated and expanded by Pir Vilayat Khan and now Zia Inayat Khan, but they have also been channeled through other American devotees, notably Rabiʿa Martin and Samuel Lewis.[33] The Sufi Order International defies the predictions of anti-Sufism fundamentalists that Sufism will erode Islamic loyalty. Moreover, their edgy universalism is balanced by groups whose leaders insist on Sufism as the true essence of Islam. They include the Shadhili, Qadiri, Tijani, Naqshbandi, Jarrahi, Chishti, and Niʿmatullahi orders, all of which have a virtual presence as well as local branches in the United States. Sufism has arrived—indeed, it flourishes—as a battleground of competing identities, announced, proliferated, and performed through all the new forms of communication available in the Information Age.

Notes

Bruce B. Lawrence, "Sufism and Neo-Sufism," in *The New Cambridge History of Islam*, vol. 6, *Muslims and Modernity: Culture and Society since 1800*, edited by Robert W. Hefner (Cambridge: Cambridge University Press, 2010), 355–84. Copyright © by the Cambridge University Press. Reprinted with permission.

1. Uri Rubin, "Pre-existence and Light: Aspects of the Concept of Nur Muhammad," *Israel Oriental Studies*, 5 (1975): 62–119; Vincent J. Cornell, *Realm of the Saint: Power and Authority in Moroccan Sufism* (Austin: University of Texas Press, 1998), 218–29.
2. The *locus classicus* for examining both movements is William R. Roff, "Islamic Movements: One or Many?," in *Islam and the Political Economy of Meaning: Comparative Studies of Muslim Discourse*, ed. William R. Roff (Berkeley: University of California Press, 1987), 31–52. Editor's Note: For Sayyid Ahmad Shahid, see Sana Haroon, "Reformism and Orthodox Practice in Early Nineteenth-Century Muslim North India: Sayyid Ahmad Shahid Reconsidered," *Journal of the Royal Asiatic Society* 21, no. 2 (2011): 177–98.
3. Esther Peskes, "The Wahhabiyya and Sufism in the Eighteenth Century," in *Islamic Mysticism Contested: Thirteen Centuries of Controversies and Polemics*, ed. Frederick de Jong and Berndt Radtke (Leiden: Brill, 1999), 145–61.
4. Primary sources are provided by Jamil M. Abun-Nasr, *The Tijaniyya: A Sufi Order in the Modern World* (Oxford: Oxford University Press, 1965), 27–57.
5. On arguments for and against the term "neo-Sufism," see R. S. O'Fahey, "Neo-Sufism: Reconsidered," *Der Islam* 70 (1993): 52–87. For an alternative to neo-Sufism, one can use, but again within quotation marks, "the third wave of institutional Sufism."
6. R. S. O'Fahey, *Enigmatic Saint: Ahmad ibn Idris and the Idrisi Tradition* (Evanston, IL: Northwestern University Press, 1990), 6.

7 David Robinson, "Africa, Islam," in *Encyclopedia of Islam and the Muslim World*, ed. Richard C. Martin (New York: Macmillan, 2004), 17–18.
8 For Shaykh Hamallah, see Louis Brenner, *West African Sufi: The Religious Heritage and Spiritual Search of Cerno Bokar Saalif Taal* (Berkeley: University of California Press, 1984), 45–59. Editor's Note: See also Benjamin Soares, *Islam and the Prayer Economy: History and Authority in a Malian Town* (Ann Arbor: University of Michigan Press, 2005).
9 On Ma' al-'Aynayn, the most extensive account appears in Bradford G. Martin, *Muslim Brotherhoods in Nineteenth-Century Africa* (Cambridge: Cambridge University Press, 1976), 125–51.
10 Robinson, "Africa, Islam," 18.
11 O'Fahey, *Enigmatic Saint*, 130–52, analyzes the relationship between Ahmad ibn Idris and his two principal disciples.
12 On the complex relationship between the Mahdi and several Sufi orders, including the Mirghaniyya, see R. S. O'Fahey, "Sufism in Suspense: The Sudanese Mahdi and the Sufis," in de Jong and Radtke, *Islamic Mysticism Contested*, 267–82. On the Marxist as well as Sufi influences on Mahmud Taha, see Mohamed A. Mahmoud, *Quest for Divinity: A Critical Examination of the Thought of Mahmud Muhammad Taha* (Syracuse, NY: Syracuse University Press, 2006).
13 A full list of secondary sources on the Sanusiyya is provided by Nicole Grandin, "Libye: Elements bibliographiques," in *Les orders mystiques dans l'Islam: Cheminements et situation actuelle*, ed. Alexandre Popović and Gilles Veinstein (Paris: École des Hautes Études en Sciences Sociales, 1986), 268–69.
14 On the Tijaniyya, the shortest account is provided by Mervyn Hiskett, *The Development of Islam in West Africa* (New York: Longman, 1984), 250–56, but it should be supplemented by Rüdiger Seesemann, *The Divine Flood: Ibrahim Niasse and the Roots of a Twentieth-Century Sufi Revival* (Oxford: Oxford University Press, 2011).
15 On how colonial co-optation actually worked in one phase of the Tijaniyya, consult David Robinson, "Malik Sy: Teacher in the New Colonial Order," in *La Tijaniyya: Une confrérie musulmane à la conquête de l'Afrique*, ed. Jean-Louis Triaud and David Robinson (Paris: Karthala, 2000), 201–18.
16 For Al-Hajj 'Umar Taal, the exhaustive study is David Robinson, *The Holy War of Umar Tal: The Western Sudan in the Mid-Nineteenth Century* (Oxford: Oxford University Press, 1985); also see Hiskett, *Development of Islam in West Africa*, 227–32.
17 In addition to Roff, *Islam and the Political Economy of Meaning* (40–41), Ushya Sanyal, *Devotional Islam and Politics in British India: Ahmad Riza Khan Barelwi and His Movement, 1970–1920* (Delhi: Oxford University Press, 1996), 32–33, tries to place both groups within religious debates and movements for renewal in nineteenth-century Muslim India. Also noteworthy is Marc Gaborieau, "Criticizing the Sufis: The Debate in Early Nineteenth-Century India," in de Jong and Radtke, eds. *Islamic Mysticism Contested*, 452–67.

18. For a detailed, well-documented treatment of the Khalidi Naqshbandiyya, see Hamid Algar and K. A. Nizami, "Nakshbandiyya," in *Encyclopaedia of Islam*, 2nd. ed., ed. P. Bearman, T. Bianquis, C. E. Bosworth, E. van Donzel, and W. P. Heinrichs, accessed May 18, 2020. http://dx.doi.org/10.1163/1573-3912_islam_COM_0843.
19. Two sources for the role of fellowships in nineteenth-century Indonesia are Denys Lombard, "Les tarekat en Insulinde," in Popović and Veinstein, *Les orders mystiques dans l'Islam*, 139–63; and Martin van Bruinessen, "Les orders dans l'espace: L'asie du Sud-Est," in *Les voies d'Allah: Les orders mystiques dans l'Islam des origins á aujourd'hui*, ed. Alexandre Popović et Gilles Veinstein (Paris: Fayard, 1996), 274–84.
20. On the Tablighis, two brief and insightful sources are Christian Troll, ed., *Islam in India: Studies and Commentaries*, vol. 2: *Religion and Religious Education* (New Delhi: Vikas, 1985), 138–76; and Barbara D. Metcalf, "'Remaking Ourselves': Islamic Self-Fashioning in a Global Movement of Spiritual Renewal," in *Accounting for Fundamentalisms*, ed. Martin E. Marty and R. Scott Appleby (Chicago: University of Chicago Press, 1995), 706–29. Also of value is Muhammad Khalid Masud, ed., *Travellers in Faith: Studies of the Tablighi Jamaat as a Transnational Islamic Movement for Faith Renewal* (Leiden: Brill, 2000).
21. Robert Rozehnal, *Islamic Sufism Unbound: Politics and Piety in Twenty-First Century Pakistan* (New York: Palgrave Macmillan, 2009).
22. See Algar, "Nakshbandiyya," and on the role of Naqshbandis (Tur. Naksibendis) in Turkish politics, as also the parallel profile on the Nurculuk movement, consult Heinz Kramer, *A Changing Turkey: The Challenge to Europe and the United States* (Washington, DC: Brookings Institute, 2000), 57–69.
23. For Badi'uzzaman Sa'id Nursi and the Nurculuk movement, consult Serif Mardin, *Religion and Social Change in Modern Turkey: The Case of Bediuzzaman Said Nursi* (Albany: State University of New York Press, 1989). But for English translations of excerpts from *Risale-i Nur*, see *Fruits from the Tree of Light*, trans. Hamid Algar (El Cerrito, CA: Risala-i Nur Institute of America, 1975).
24. Alexandre Bennigsen and S. Enders Wimbush, *Mystics and Commissars: Sufism in the Soviet Union* (Berkeley: University of California Press, 1985), 150–56. The notion of "parallel Islam" is problematic, leading the authors to evoke a Soviet version of the "Islamic Peril," yet their broad geopolitical range of evidence provides rare insight into the regional distribution of Sufi fellowships in nineteenth-century Russia and twentieth-century Soviet Union.
25. See Bennigsen and Wimbush, *Mystics and Commissars*, 49–67, for the proportionate estimate of atheists to believers but also for an expanded analysis on the notorious difficulty of calculating how many practicing Sufis there are in the Chechen–Ingush region.
26. Martin van Bruinessen, "Controversies and Polemics Involving the Sufi Orders in Twentieth-Century Indonesia," in de Jong and Radtke, *Islamic Mysticism Contested*, 717n23.

27 Muhammad S. Umar, "The Tijaniyya and British Colonial Authorities in Northern Nigeria," in Triaud and Robinson, *La Tijaniyya*, 327–55.
28 The creation of a transatlantic Tijani network, linking Senegal to the United States, is explored in Ousmane Kane, "Muslim Missionaries and African States," in *Transnational Religion and Fading States*, ed. S. H. Rudolph and J. Piscatori (Boulder, CO: Westview Press, 1997), 47–62.
29 On the twentieth-century emergence of the Muridiyya, the classic treatment is Donald B. Cruise O'Brien, *The Mourides of Senegal: The Political and Economic Organization of an Islamic Brotherhood* (Oxford: Oxford University Press, 1971). On the development of Touba as its center, see Eric Ross, "Touba: A Spiritual Metropolis in the Modern World," *Canadian Journal of African Studies* 29, no. 2 (1995): 222–59.
30 Mamadou Diouf, "The Senegalese Murid Trade Diaspora and the Making of a Vernacular Cosmopolitanism," *Public Culture* 12, no. 3 (2000): 682.
31 Diouf, "Senegalese Murid Trade Diaspora," 686.
32 In much of what follows, I am indebted to the insights and data provided by Carl W. Ernst in his pioneering essay, "Ideological and Technological Transformations of Contemporary Sufism," in *Muslim Networks from Hajj to Hip Hop*, ed. miriam cooke and Bruce Lawrence (Chapel Hill: University of North Carolina Press, 2005), 191–207.
33 Many valuable insights into the Sufi Order International can be found in Pirzade Zia Inayat Khan, ed., *A Pearl in Wine: Essays on the Life, Music and Sufism of Hazrat Inayat Khan* (New Lebanon, NY: Omega, 2001). *Editor's Note: For more on the Inayati Order and New Age Sufism in twentieth-century America, see Robert Rozehnal, Cyber Sufis: Virtual Expressions of the American Muslim Experience (London: Oneworld, 2019).*

TWELVE

"Allah Remembered: Practice of the Heart," from *Who Is Allah?* | 2015

Beyond invoking or defining Allah lies the task of remembering Allah. At first glance, one might ask: what distinguishes invoking Allah from remembering Allah? The two seem very close. Both are practices dedicated to Allah, yet there is a discernible line separating them.

Invoking Allah is a performative activity; it becomes part of the inventory of activities expected of a devout Muslim. While it might be reflective, it can be, and often is, simply instinctual or habitual. Remembering Allah, however, requires an intense, dedicated practice of introspection. It begins with a specific intent to focus only on that name, that mood, that presence of Allah. Allah is not just Lofty and Exalted but also Present, immediately and vividly Present to the one remembering Allah, by whatever Name He is remembered.

In the starkest language, all remembering of Allah presupposes invoking Allah. Allah cannot be remembered without being invoked. But Allah can be, and often is, invoked without being remembered. Alternatively, one might think of the invocation as utterance, and remembrance as self-conscious meditation on the utterance. The real goal, in either case, is not just invoking or uttering the name Allah; it is to project the Thing, the Absolute, the One as the *sole focus* of attention in the act of immersive remembering.[1]

The Meditation of a Sufi Master

Sufis delight in the complex array of ways to approach the remembrance of Allah. To remember Allah through observation is the preliminary step. Yet the Qur'an itself makes clear that human beings can never perceive or connect to Allah's essence; they only have access to His traits or attributes, that is, the qualities that attach to His Name, making of the one Name many Names. Even though in this world it is impossible to see Allah with ordinary human eyes, each person can and should try to perceive and comprehend the qualities of Allah. These are the 99 Names, "the part of Him nearest to us," in Montaigne's haunting phrase. The 99 Names are windows into the invisible. One might think of them as portals of light onto a blinding flash, or handholds guiding us through a fathomless depth, or in terms of contemporary science, the range of frequencies that transmit energy in the electromagnetic spectrum. In the words of a notable Sufi master, they can be "like patterns on a great rug called 'the carpet of intimate conversation (*munajat*).' Once it is spread wide for you, its patterns become endless. At times, Allah seats you on the expanse of poverty and you call out to Allah, *Ya Ghani*! O self-sufficient One! At times, Allah seats you on the expanse of humility and you call out, *Ya ʿAziz*! O mighty One! At times, you are seated on the expanse of weakness and you call out, *Ya Qawi*! O powerful One! There are other patterns on this widespread carpet, each corresponding to one among the Divine Names (*asmaʾ*)."[2]

But why are there only 99 Names? Why do we have only ninety-nine portals, lights, or patterns of the Divine? And why are these ninety-nine so vital to human well-being in this world and the next? These questions will concern us below, but it is important to first note the utter weakness of humans to grasp the enormous challenge of Allah. In effect, we are all bounded by the limits of what is known or knowable. Tibetan Buddhists tell the story of an old frog. He had lived all his life in a well. One day a frog from the sea got lost and came to his well. The sea frog told the well frog how much deeper and more expansive was the great ocean from which he came. The well frog followed the sea frog back to the ocean, but "when the frog from the well saw the ocean, it was such a shock that his head just exploded into pieces."[3]

And so, in the Muslim tradition of practicing restraint, many wise, well-traveled souls urge patience. Instead of venturing to the edge of an expanse that is mind shattering, Sufi masters commend the incremental approach:

> *O you who believe,*
> *remember Allah the Lofty*
> *with repeated remembrance. (Q 33:41)*

Recollection or remembrance becomes like an impregnable fortress, making it possible for Sufi adepts to surround their hearts with walls of light, each brick bearing the name Allah![4] The metaphor of the body as a house, and Allah as its (invisible) bricks and mortar, is extended to Allah as the very blood that flows through the veins of the devout Muslim in the act of remembrance. But remembrance requires persistence, along with patience, a keen appetite for discovering the true self that resides in each of us. This true self, the divine self within, is an echo of Allah.

The Practice of *Basmala*

For Sufis this task of discovering Allah by discovering the self comes through immersive remembrance—conscious, continuous, systematic, and disciplined remembrance—of the Names given by the One who is beyond Names. These ciphers of the Divine Other are derived from the Holy Qur'an, not just a book of law or worship but also the pathway to inner peace. The overall message of the 114 chapters of the Qur'an is summed up in the words of the *basmala* that opens the first chapter, and every other chapter but one: "*Bismi(A)llah ar-rahman ar-rahim*" ("O Allah Full of Compassion, Ever Compassionate"). Its opposite would be "*Bismi(A)llah al-mudhill al-mumit*" ("O Allah the Despiser, the Instrument of Death"). Many might be surprised to see these two sets of names side by side, yet both are clustered in the circle of names linked to Allah the Lofty, both in the Qur'an and in everyday usage. The play on pairs or doubles recurs, as in the wisdom of Seth, from Ibn ʿArabi's classic study, *Rings of Wisdom* (*Fusus al-hikam*).

It is said that Seth, the third son of Adam and Eve (after Cain and Abel), was the conduit for two gifts, gifts from the Divine Names and gifts from the Divine Essence. And it is the Divine Giver who tailors each gift to the recipient. They might be gifts given through specific requests (the Names projected and perfected through remembrance) or gifts bestowed without request (an outpouring from the Thing, the Absolute, the One).[5] In other words, Allah can give out of His own largesse, not solely and simply in response to human petitions, however sincere and persistent may be the petitioner.

Qur'anic Passages on the Beautiful Names

The Divine Names unfold in numerous Qur'anic passages. The fullest citation comes at the end of Q 59, "The Mustering (on the Day of Judgment)":

> *He is Allah*
> *Other than He there is no Allah*
> *The Knower of the Hidden and the Manifest*
> *He is Full of Compassion, ever Compassionate*
> *He is Allah,*
> *Other than He there is no Allah*
> *The Sovereign*
> *The Holy One*
> *The Source of Peace*
> *The Faithful*
> *The Preserver of Safety*
> *The Exalted in Might*
> *The Irresistible*
> *The Supreme*
> *Glory be to Allah above the partners they ascribe to Him.*
> *He is Allah*
> *The Creator*
> *The Evolver*
> *The Bestower of forms*
> *To Him belong the Most Beautiful Names;*
> *All that is in the heavens and the earth praises Him,*
> *And He is Exalted in Might, the Wise. (Q 59:22–24)*[6]

Most Sufis focus on the qualities of these Beautiful Names. According to a contemporary Sufi master, not all the names have the same value, just as the 99 Names are not always the same. And the seeker—even the most avid seeker—wants to find some order that reduces or redirects their multiplicity into a pattern, one that can be evoked, remembered, and also recited. Many admire, and seek to follow, the strategy of Shaykh al-Akbar, Muhyiddin Ibn ʿArabi, deemed by some to be the foremost Sufi exponent of the Path (*tariqa*). Let us call this strategy *One plus Three*.

Here is the *One*. In keeping with many others, Ibn ʿArabi gives the honor of first place to Allah. Why Allah apart from and above all others? Because we can only name Him by what He names Himself. While all the Names connote His Presence, the name Allah *is* the Presence (*hadratu[A]llah*) that comprehends all Presences. "Allah, Allah, Allah—His signs (*ayat*) have passed judgment that He is Allah. Glory be to Him! (*subhanahu*)—there is no Allah but He. He alone possesses a Name not shared by another."[7]

At the same time, there are clusters of *Three*. Because they reflect Allah in different forms, Shaykh al-Akbar allocates all the other Beautiful Names, those beyond Allah but always linked to Him, into three distinct yet overlapping categories:

1. Affirmative attributes of the essence: knowing, powerful, willing, hearing, seeing, living, responder, thankful.
2. Relational or correlated descriptions: first and last, opener and closer, manifest and hidden, rich and enricher, guide and light.
3. Names that disclose acts: creator, provider, author, shaper, destroyer, abaser, and death-giver.

In this way every possible quality or trait of Allah can be classified. All the Divine Names can be acknowledged as one of these kinds. Every one of them also denotes the Essence, so that this Presence (Allah) contains all the Presences, and He who knows Allah knows all things.[8]

Even those Sufi authors, adepts, and masters who find the metaphysical turns of Shaykh al-Akbar too intellectually tortuous still seek to pursue the pairing of the Beautiful Names that he has foreshadowed. Special focus is often directed to the Qur'anic passage that depicts Allah as "having two hands," that is, a constant, reinforcing polarity.

The "two hands" embody benevolence and anger, fear and hope, intimacy and awe, but also knowability and unknowability, so that what might seem like apparent contradictions are not contraries but instead dyads—mysterious to humans yet part of *faydAllah*, the expansive surplus of the Lofty the Exalted. The metaphor is bodily, specific to the human form, but its significance is metaphysical, beyond what wo/man can know or imagine. There are many ways to grasp this notion of two proximate yet distinct qualities, but the best is *barzakh*, the space of connection/separation that permeates this life and the next, both the world beyond and every day in the present world.

Two examples of this approach reflect the medieval and the modern phases of Sufi practice. The noted fourteenth-century master Ibn 'Ata' Allah reckoned the two hands of Allah as His two decisive modes: the left hand symbolizes His majesty and power, the right hand His Beauty and Compassion.[9] In a similar vein, the contemporary South African master Shaykh Fadhlalla Haeri sees left-right as the gender complementarities of male (majesty: *jalal*) and female (beauty: *jamal*).[10]

Ibn 'Arabi was clear that not all contrasts were complementary. Two polar opposites in approaching the Other were to be avoided: (1) *tanzih*, transcendence or thinking of Allah as so lofty that he could not be related to humankind, reducing him to abstraction; and (2) *tashbih*, immanence, or making Allah almost human, that is, anthropomorphizing his traits to the point of absurdity. Even though both poles were to be avoided, Shaykh al-Akbar favored the Sufis who did embrace both, like the early master, Qushayri, or the common folk who only see Allah as *tashbih*. He disdained the scholars—theologians (*mutakallimun*) as well as philosophers (*falasifa*)—who were prone to see only the Lofty and Exalted One, that is, the abstract Other, devoid of human connection except through the instruments of logic and metaphor.[11]

Allah Embodied as Light

In the end, we are left with many nodes of connection, from the human to the divine, from the many to the One. While all function as part of the spectrum of immersive remembrance, a few attributes stand out, not least because of their close association with the material world, and also with the human form. Might this practice be construed as anthropomorphizing Allah? Could one say that under the guise of the Many Names, seemingly devout Muslims are actually reverting to a form of idolatry, eschewing outer forms but still forming deep, inner attachments that divert them from the Thing, the Absolute, the One? The answer is: yes and no. Yes, for the literal minded, this practice could lead to heresy, but not for those pure in intent. Patient and persistent believers seek to connect themselves to Allah by any means possible. For them, not only the universe of letters but also the parts of the human body become the most immediate, the most palpable instruments for that vertical connection to the Other. It is *An-Nur*, the Radiant, Unending Light that pervades, Allah as Light, the Light of heavens but also the Light radiant throughout the human body; our entire body is, as the *hadith* reminds us, "formed in the image of Allah." And so we can, or should, radiate Light with many, and splendid, colors. Consider how Ibn ʿArabi explains the Divine Light as it becomes an outpouring or effulgence that at once captures and transforms the devotee:

> When the servant comes to know Allah in Himself, he knows that he is not created according to the form of the world, but only according to the form of Allah (*al-Haqq*). Allah makes him journey through His names, in order "to make him see His signs" (Q 17:1) within him. Thus the servant comes to know that He is what is designated by every divine Name—whether or not that

Name is one of those described as "beautiful." It is through these Names that Allah appears in His servants, and it is through Them that the servant takes on different "colorings" of his states; for they are Names in Allah but "colorings" in us.... For there is no Name that Allah has applied to Himself that He has not also applied to us: through His Names we undergo the transformations in our states, and with them we are transformed by Allah.[12]

Who could imagine that the One beyond knowing would make His deepest Self known to mere mortals through colors? For Sufis, the different facets of Allah, as expressed by His many Names, are like a prismatic refraction of white light into the multitude of colors; these colors reflect aspects of what to us can only be thought of as beauty, subtle forms of beauty, staggered and staged to match who we are before we recognize them as part of our own deepest self.

From the Divine Other to the Divine Beloved

Many Sufis beyond Ibn ʿArabi appeal to the sensorium, the full array of senses. Their intention also is immersive remembrance, or *dhikrAllah*, remembrance of Allah at every moment in every action in every thought. Their preferred medium is verse, abundant verse, most often imagined, spoken and written as love poetry. In these lyrical volumes, known as *divans*, or collections of poems from a single author, the Divine Other becomes the Divine Beloved, while the human is cast as the seeker, at once the devout slave and the crazed lover of the Other.

The bard's task is to discover or recover Him. Recovery here is an especially potent process. It requires retrieval through remembrance, and it involves the entire sensorium.[13] The mirror is more than mere seeing; the body may be finite in existence but it becomes infinite in its response to divine stimuli. Verse, whether inspired by love or induced by pain, or both, opens the whole range of human bodily connections to the material world—not just seeing or reading, hearing or speaking, but also smelling, touching, and tasting.

Allah: The Poison of Separation

The restless lovers never cease to complain about the physical cruelty of the Divine Beloved. Even as they remember Allah with their entire being, they complain to Him about the intensity of their unrequited love. Among these mystically aroused complainants were the Mawlana Jalaluddin Rumi (d. 1273) and his contemporary Muslihuddin Saʿdi (d. 1292). Addressing Allah as the Beloved, Saʿdi laments:

> *Come! Out of the pain of love for You*
> *I am bewildered without You.*
> *Come! See in this pain how unhappy I am without you.*
> *O Beloved, not for one moment have You given me*
> *the drink of Your union;*
> *It is the bitter poison of separation that I taste forever.*
> *I have given the message, and I have said:*
> *"Come! Make me happy!" You have answered*
> *and said: "I am happy without you!"*[14]

The physicality of Saʿdi's poem privileges sight, followed by pain (reflecting touch), and then the taste of poison, "the bitter poison of separation." And in the same vein Saʿdi occasionally invokes smell as an echo of separation:

> *I live for your aroma, wherever you are.*
> *I long for the sight of you; where are you?*[15]

But even more tangibly olfactory, evoking the very scent of the Beloved's hair, is the verse of Jahan Malek Khatun (d. ca. 1382). It is rare to find a woman's voice in this galaxy of supplicants for Divine favor. Why? Because "women were considered to be private citizens who had no business in public affairs," notes a famed critic, here speaking about premodern Persian poetry, but also commenting about Muslim mores in general. Fortunately, Jahan Khatun, a fourteenth-century contemporary of the famed Hafez Shirazi, did write extensively, if in private, and when her complete poems were discovered and published twenty years ago, they included this verse:

> *Sweet breeze return to me, you bear*
> *The scent of my beloved's hair.*
> *I suffered while you were away;*
> *You'll bring the balm for my despair.*
> *My doctors are so sick of all*
> *My sicknesses: but I know where*
> *The medicine lies—it's in the scent*
> *You'll bring to me from his sweet hair.*[16]

Allah: The Tavern of Love

For Mawlana Jalaluddin Rumi, however, the entire lyrical landscape becomes more than sightings or sickness, beyond cure or perfume. Love turns the heart upside down, inside out. It becomes a brawling tavern. Here is his most sensuous, if also paradoxical, verse. Through the raw physicality of wine and blood, he weaves a narrative that brings heaven to earth, rather than raising the dreamer into a divine embrace or the seeker into a connection with the Other. Divine intoxication pervades the tavern of love:

> *Who has ever seen such a mess?*
> *The tavern of love filled with drunkards.*
> *We drink the wine of our own blood, aged*
> *in the barrels of our own souls*
> *We would give our lives for a sip of that nectar,*
> *our heads in exchange for one drop.*
> *Another morning! Pour the wine!*
> *A life without His love is nothing but slow death.*
> *It's up to you—accept the cry of the silent rubaab*
> *Or endure this burning heart filled with grief.*
> *O eyes, look only in His direction.*
> *O soul, hang your clothes on the wheel of life and death.*
> *O tongue, let the lover sing.*
> *O ears, become drunk with His song.*[17]

"A life without His love is nothing but slow death." Hearing, drinking, singing, burning—all of these become a Sufi reflex, evocative of the twist toward sensory religion in the endless quest for Allah, witnessed by the parade of Persian poets. All acclaim feeling as the deepest source of the Divine, the pain of separation as the only path to true love, itself the path to true religion. Allah never ceases to move up and down the ladder of His names, but here He is marked as the transcendent/immanent Beloved of Persian verse. Thus He is ever sought but never caught. He is seen as Light but only in the mirror of our deepest self. He remains the object of endless sighing, the throb of ecstatic singing, beguiling yet eluding the besotted, burning lover.

Conclusion

If the ordinary believer asks for guidance through prayer and invoking Allah's name, the devout Sufi seeks to access the One beyond and before all that is, or ever will be, through remembrance. Remembrance is an intense pursuit of the deepest interior connection with Allah. Sufi masters have traveled the perilous Path (*tariqa*)—through poetry and prose, music and dance, with dieting and fasting—to find the Beloved. The pain of separation is palpable as well as visible, always beckoning, never ending, satisfying only the patient and persistent, the ceaselessly remembering seeker.

Notes

Bruce B. Lawrence, "Allah Remembered," in *Who Is Allah?* (Chapel Hill: University of North Carolina Press, 2015), 84–117. Copyright © 2015 by the University of North Carolina Press. Used by permission of the publisher.

1. I am indebted to Leela Prasad for this and other insights into the arguments of this chapter.
2. Ibn ʿAtaʾ Allah al-Iskandari, *The Book of Illuminations*, trans. Scott A. Kugle (Louisville, KY: Fons Vitae, 2005), 210–11.
3. Sogyal Rinpoche, *The Tibetan Book of Living and Dying* (San Francisco: HarperSanFrancisco, 1999), 41.
4. Scott Kugle, *Sufis and Saints' Bodies* (Chapel Hill: University of North Carolina Press, 2007), 142.
5. Ibn ʿArabi, *Bezels of Wisdom*, trans. R. W. J. Austin (New York: Paulist Press, 1980), 62.
6. From Muhammad Asad, as quoted, with modifications, in Safi, *Memories of Muhammad* (San Francisco: HarperOne, 2009), 93–94.
7. William Chittick, "Divine Names and Theophanies," in Muhyi al-din Ibn al-ʿArabi, *The Meccan Illuminations: Selected Texts*, trans. William C. Chittick, Michel Chodkiewicz, Denis Gril, and James W. Morris (Paris: Sindbad, 1989), 75–116, 111.
8. Chittick, "Divine Names and Theophanies," 113.
9. al-Iskandari, *Book of Illuminations*, 19–20.
10. Fadhlalla Haeri, *Calling Allah by His Most Beautiful Names* (Centurion, SA: Zahra Trust, 2002), 37. "According to Islamic cosmology, all existence is based upon a harmonious polarity of the active or male (*jalal*) and the receptive or female (*jamal*) attributes."
11. Michael Sells, *Mystical Languages of Unsaying* (Chicago: University of Chicago Press, 1994), chaps. 3 and 4. An illumination of Qurʾanic citations for sixty-six of the 99

Divine Names can be found in the original chapter from *Who Is Allah?* Here, we have omitted that section for purposes of coherence and accessibility.

12 James W. Morris, "Ibn al-ʿArabi's Spiritual Ascension," in Ibn al-ʿArabi, *Meccan Illuminations*, 351–81, 363.

13 This deepened sense of recovery is yet another insight that I have gleaned from Leela Prasad, in her attentive, and creative, reading of an earlier draft of this manuscript.

14 From the *Divan* of Saʿdi, not as famous as his *Gulistan* or *Bustan* but cited here from a contemporary Iranian edition: Muslihuddin Saʿdi, *Kulliyat-e Saʿdi*, ed. Zaka al-Mulk Furughi (Tehran, 1975), 832.

15 Muslihuddin Saʿdi, *Kulliyat-e Saʿdi*, 790.

16 Hafez Shirazi, *Faces of Love: Hafez and the Poets of Shiraz*, trans. Dick Davis (New York: Penguin, 2013), 148. See Davis's introduction to Jahan Malek Khatun in Hafez, *Faces of Love*, xlii–lviii, 148, and 161.

17 Jalaluddin Rumi, *A Garden beyond Paradise: The Mystical Poetry of Rumi*, trans. Jonathan Star and Shahram Shiva (New York: Bantam, 1992), 44–45.

PART IV

Deconstructing Religious Modernity

The preceding parts presented various faces of Islam—accenting its historical, comparative, and mystical dimensions. This part turns to a different picture of Islam, one that portrays the religion and its adherents as violent. The trope of the Muslim as terrorist pervades both mainstream news and entertainment media. The essays presented here furnish the reader with a historical view of the modern world in which Islamic fundamentalism exists but not as an exceptional expression of one religion. Muslim fundamentalists share common views and resources with contemporary fundamentalists of other religious traditions. The first essay deals with the emergence of global fundamentalism as a paradox. It relates to what Hodgson has called "the Great Western Transmutation, or GWT," and it analyzes the response to GWT by Jewish, Christian, and Muslim fundamentalists. Lawrence defines religious fundamentalism as an ideology opposed to modernism and evaluates how fundamentalists appropriate the resources and also the objectives of the modern world. Just as the modern state is different from its premodern predecessor, so too do fundamentalists differ from the reformers and revivalists who preceded them. The modern media plays an ambivalent role in monitoring fundamentalist activities: on the one hand, it calls attention to the threat of fundamentalism, and on the other hand, it promotes interest in fundamentalism for its consumers. Nowhere is this ambivalence more center stage than in gender inequities perpetuated by political Islam's implementation of *shariʿa* at the level of the body and the ascent of

Osama bin Laden as both the leader of al-Qaʿida and the inspirational force behind 9/11.

The second essay, "The Shah Bano Case," here excerpted from *On Violence: A Reader* (2007), takes as its focus the case of a single woman whose minoritized status provides a portal into the intersection of secularity and legal theocracy. Lawrence analyzes the debates over Shah Bano's case to comment on the broader plight of Muslim women in both Muslim-majority contexts and so-called secular places such as India. The case of Shah Bano illustrates how female subjectivity cannot be reclaimed without recourse to courts and also collective action on behalf of individual women.

The third essay featured here introduces a translation of Bin Laden's major speeches. In his introduction to *Messages to the World* (2005), Lawrence seeks to understand the motivations behind Bin Laden's message but also his appeal within the broader Muslim populace and his legacy for contemporary Islamism. Bin Laden's skillful use of Qur'anic quotations and Arabic poetry links him to Islam, but his advocacy of *jihad* links him to other revolutionaries such as the Russians after 1917 and the Cubans after 1959. Absent from his apocalyptic appeal is a moral vision for the Muslim community (*umma*). Though this essay was written before Bin Laden's death, it predicts that his posthumous fame, like that of Che Guevara, will linger. Yet Islam and violence have a much longer history than Bin Laden, and it is necessary to trace the rise of Islam against the background of violence often perpetrated against Muslims.

The fourth essay, "Muslim Engagement with Injustice and Violence" (2013), expands the usual time frame for interfacing Islam and violence. It shifts our analytic gaze from 9/11 to 611, the year after the Prophet Muhammad was first called on to be God's Messenger. His was a radical message of social reform cloaked in theological garb. Many Qur'anic passages allow us to trace the Prophet's opposition to societal violence. He resisted the use of force: neither he nor his followers engaged in war until after he was forced to flee his home and become a refugee in Medina (622). The several battles that he fought were defensive and his constant struggle was to avoid war, to make peace with his rivals rather than to attack and eliminate them. Crucial to understanding Muhammad's message and the formation of Islam is the term *jihad*. This essay charts the four major transformations of the idea of *jihad* in Islamic history. Its historical variations notwithstanding, *jihad* always combines means with outcomes—warfare is never an end but an instrument. In the beginning, *jihad* was invoked not as usual warfare but as a struggle for higher good. But it became a military doctrine during the Crusades, when Muslims deployed the idea of "holy war" to fight Crusaders.

Jihad was transformed yet again during the great empires that emerged after the thirteenth-century Mongol invasions. In the Muslim empires of the Ottomans, the Safavids, and the Mughals we can see how *jihad* became an instrument of the bureaucratic machinery of the imperial state. In the nineteenth century we witness yet another, the fourth transformation of *jihad*; it occurs with the advent of European colonialism and expansionism. In response to the perceived threat of Western cultural and political encroachment, some Muslims justified anticolonial resistance through recourse to *jihad*. Among them is the eighteenth-century Arabian reformer Ibn'Abd al-Wahhab. He saw *jihad* as the answer to foreign incursion and internal decay represented by Sufism and Shi'ism. It is this invocation of *jihad* that circulates in modern times, often linked to Abu'l A'la Maududi from Pakistan and Sayyid Qutb from Egypt, though it takes on different meanings for Islamists. Some deploy militancy but most pursue the democratic process. It is this variety of Islamisms but also Muslim alternatives to Islamism that are treated in the final essay of this part.

THIRTEEN

"Fundamentalism as a Religious Ideology in Multiple Contexts" and Conclusion, from *Defenders of God: The Fundamentalist Revolt against the Modern Age* | 1989

Fundamentalism as a Religious Ideology in Multiple Contexts

Fundamentalism is a multifocal phenomenon precisely because the modernist hegemony, though originating in some parts of the West, was not limited to Protestant Christianity. Through the Enlightenment it affected significant numbers of Jews, and due to the colonization of much of Africa and Asia in the nineteenth and early twentieth centuries, it touched the lives and destinies of many Muslims. The modernist hegemony did not end with World War II or with the attainment of political independence by the so-called Third World countries.[1]

Preexisting commercial and military dependencies were rarely forfeited by the former colonizers. Moreover, the mindset of modernist bias (quantity over quality, change over continuity, commercial efficiency over human sympathy) was often perpetuated by indigenous elites who took control in the first stage of national independence. The accelerating structural shift into a global economy put a premium on accommodation. At the same time, it penalized isolation or lag-time repose to new conditions.

To the extent that indigenous codes of behavior acted as a countervailing force to the homogenizing influence of commercial networks and communications accessibility, it is still valuable to think of Western and non-Western cultural spheres. One must recognize two features of this new phase: first, the modernist mindset was linked to the West by both sides, Euro-Americans who thought they were privileged by history or destined by God to control as well as indigenous elites who admired or resented Euro-American power; and second, the part of the modernizing West that was excluded from power included not only Christians and Jews but also Muslims. Those who see the new hegemony in parochial terms, equating modern with Western and European, dismiss Islam as peripheral. Yet if we examine the reduced public role of all three monotheistic traditions, fundamentalism emerges as a potential development within each, its potential expanded by the peculiarly Western outlook that they hold in common, from the use of language to the formation of institutions to the projection of universal patterns of expectation (utopian) and disappointment (tragic).

Fundamentalism per se is neither a causal force nor a mere epiphenomenon of more basic, underlying forces, whether demographic, economic, or political. Rather, in our view, fundamentalism is a novel ideology congruent with the interests of specific groups responding to social tensions generated by the contemporary world. It is, moreover, a *religious* ideology since the beliefs of its adherents, their practices, their challenges, and aspirations, all are framed in discourses that authorize action through scriptural, creedal, and moral referents.

But why must we speak of fundamentalism as an ideology first and a religious disposition second? During the late twentieth century, modes of scholarly discourse, like writing instruments, are changing. (Could one imagine authoring a book on a personal computer before 1980? Could one imagine being grateful for the absence of a computer virus before 1988?!) We must be faithful to the markings of the present phase of global history. In the Agrarianate Age, religion, despite its detractors, was the parent and superior of ideology. In the Technical Age (nineteenth century and first half of the twentieth century), religion and ideology were in latent conflict, operating in separate spheres: ideology referred to the public arena of politics and economics, religion to the private sphere of individual conscience and creedal profession. They seldom conflicted or overlapped, except in the minds of a few prescient scholars, such as Owen Chadwick and Eric Hobsbawm. But now in the High-Tech Era (since 1950), ideology, despite its critics, supersedes and subsumes religion.

We are still adjusting to that shift of authoritative categories. It is central to understanding both the emergence of modernism and the fundamentalist reaction to its emergence. Most of the authorizing thinkers are European, whether one looks to the Germans from Kant and Nietzsche to Gadamer and Habermas, or to the French, most recently, Ricoeur, Bourdieu, Foucault, and Derrida. An occasional American, such as Dewey or Peirce, surfaces. The British have contributed Coleridge and Collingwood. But the names are initially less important than the sum total of what they collectively suggest as modernists or late modernists. Meaning is to be separated from truth, function from metaphysics, human from god. What Nietzsche proposes as a theory of art, Kant requires as an axiom of morality. The end result is the same: ideology comes to supersede religion, just as theology is displaced by sociology.

Two quotations will help to illustrate the analytical force of the momentous shift from the Agrarianate Age to the Technical Age in Western thought. Both quotations also underscore the social limitations of Enlightenment exponents, despite their rhetorical nimbleness. Partisan to his subject, a leading historian of the philosophy of the Enlightenment declares, without a trace of hyperbole,

> In the 18th century the intellectual center of gravity changes its position. The various fields of knowledge—natural sciences, history, law, politics, art—gradually withdrew from the domination of traditional metaphysics and theology. They no longer look to the concept of God for their justification and legitimation; the various sciences themselves now determine the concept on the basis of their specific form. The relations between the concept of God and the concepts of truth, morality, law are by no means abandoned. But their direction changes. *An exchange of index symbols takes place.* That which formerly had established other concepts now moves into the position of that to be established and that which hitherto had justified other concepts, now finds itself in the position of a concept that requires justification.[2]

The "exchange of index symbols" is emphasized because it summarizes the message of the entire passage. God becomes an index symbol, exchanged for truth, morality, law. It is a dramatic shift, yet Ernst Cassirer gives no hint about the size or composition of the group who accepted it as authoritative. He deems it to have been a momentous step for the influential *few*.

In the next century that step produced an epistemological about-face, again for the few. In the words of the literary critic Gerald Bruns,

> since the beginning of the 19th century the interpretation of texts or statements has come to rely increasingly upon the separation of meaning and

truth as an authorizing principle. "By Bentham," J. Stuart Mill once wrote, "men have been led to ask themselves, in regard to any ancient or received opinion, Is it true? And by Coleridge, what is the meaning of it?"... This distinction, which... became the first principle of historicism, was a death blow to the ontological seriousness—one might say the eminence—of the human sciences (not only literature and history but also philosophy and theology).[3]

Obviously, most people reading this statement choose to focus on its *force*. It reverses the traditional way of looking at the world. Yet it is equally important to take into account the *scope* of this statement. Who, if anyone, outside the academy welcomed this rigorous cleavage between meaning and truth, deemed to be authoritative by Coleridge as also by the budding cadre of historicists? Once adopted, it led to a widening spectrum of questions about religion, and even to a redefinition of religion in terms of the meaning that it held for its adherents rather than the truth that it claimed to reveal to all humankind. But the loss of influence was not universal; it was limited to those groups within or aligned to Enlightenment circles. Even within the academy, religion was not "dead."

Though theology may have lost its preeminence as an academic pursuit, religion did not cease to be less engaging for those historicists who tried to uncover the multiple mechanisms of human societies. Whether welcoming or fearing the criterion of value neutrality, sociologists and, later, anthropologists became spiritual mutes. They systematically disengaged from any but the rationally defensible aspects of their subject. For them and for their successors, "religion should be treated as a datum [the meaning of which is] to be *explained*." They removed themselves from "the religious man [who] sees religion as a human experience [the truth of] which needs to be *understood* in its own terms."[4]

In relating to fundamentalist discourse without accepting its premises or conclusions, we depend on ideology as a medial category. Ideology reflects the modernist mindset to which religion is the corrosive inertia of the past. While most political ideologues have been concerned with meaning rather than truth, a religious ideology conjoins truth with meaning. For this reason alone, fundamentalism would be better understood as a religious ideology than as any other form of cognitive, moral, or social patterning.

But there are further reasons why it is useful to identify fundamentalism as a religious ideology. It conforms to a cluster of traits; what Wittgenstein might have called family resemblances. All of them separate fundamentalists both from their modernist opponents and also from their contemporary coreligionists. Five are especially important:

1. Fundamentalists are advocates of a pure minority viewpoint against a sullied majority or dominant group. They are the righteous remnant turned vanguard, and even when the remnant/vanguard seizes political power and seems to become a majority, as happened in Iran in 1979, they continue to perceive and project themselves as a minority.
2. Fundamentalists are oppositional. They do not merely disagree with their enemies, they confront them. While the evil other is an abstract sense of *anomie* or uprootedness, it is located in particular groups who perpetuate the prevailing "secular" ethos. Fundamentalists confront those secular people who exercise political or judicial power. Often they also confront "wayward" religious professionals.
3. Fundamentalists are secondary-level male elites. They claim to derive authority from a direct, unmediated appeal to scripture, yet because interpretive principles are often vague, they must be clarified by charismatic leaders who are invariably male. Notions of a just social order in Iran, or a halakhic polity in Israel, or a Christian civilization in America require continuous, repeated reinterpretation. In each instance what seems to an outsider to be arbitrary retrieval of only some elements from a common past is to fundamentalists the necessary restoration of an eternally valid divine mandate. And it is a mandate mediated through exclusively male interpreters.
4. Fundamentalists generate their own technical vocabulary. Reflecting the polysemy of language, they use special terms that bind insiders to one another, just as they preempt interference from outsiders.[5] *Halakha* for Jews, *shariʿa* for Muslims, and "creation" for Christians represent three terms, each of which would be open to several interpretations but which fundamentalists invest with a particular meaning that exceptionalizes, even as it appears to validate, their ideological stance.
5. Fundamentalism has historical antecedents, but no ideological precursors. As Marc Bloch warned, one should never confuse ancestry with explanation. Though the events and figures invoked by fundamentalists are varied and distant—the Maccabean revolt for Jews, the Protestant Reformation for Christians, the Wahhabi revolt for Sunni Muslims, the martyrdom of Husain for Shiʿis—fundamentalism as a religious ideology is very recent. It did not emerge in Protestant America until the end of the last century. It has only become apparent within Judaism during the last fifty years, and since it represents a delayed reaction to the psychological hegemony of European colonial rule, it could only occur

in majoritarian Muslim countries after they had become independent nation-states, that is, in most instances, after World War II.

The last trait is the sine qua non for our approach to fundamentalism. While other sectarian or separatist movements can be characterized by the initial four traits, about no other religious protest groups could it be said that they originated in direct response to that global pattern of change known as the Great Western Transmutation (GWT) or modernization, and what has now emerged as multiple instances of religious extremism—apparent in Buddhism and Hinduism as well as the so-called Abrahamic religions—are in effect countertexts marking the fundamentalist revolt. The five traits I cited above cluster in the countertexts that provoked multiple fundamentalist revolts in several cultural settings: modern day quasi-Hasidim and *haredim* in Israel, Protestant Christians in America, Sunni Muslims in Malaysia, Egypt, and Pakistan, as well as Shi'i Muslims in Iran and southern Lebanon.

Conclusion

The historian Fernand Braudel once remarked: "There is no problem which does not become increasingly complex when actively investigated, growing in scope and depth, endlessly opening up new vistas of work to be done."[6] Comparative research on fundamentalism, already complex, will open up still further vistas as more become convinced of its importance and engaged by its opportunities. When those engaged are Euro-American scholars, they will be impelled to look beyond their own cultural legacy. In examining the multiple religious responses to modernism, one cannot remain confined to a single tradition, not even the supposedly foundational tradition of Progressive Patriotic Protestantism. Only an inter-creedal, cross-cultural investigation reveals the true nature of fundamentalism, that all expressions of fundamentalist fervor are shaped by the redefining and restructuring of religion that takes place in the modern world, and it is modernism, emerging as the dominant ideological strand of modernity, that has decisively shaped the latest chapter, the High-Tech Era, of global history.

Nowhere is the triumph of modernist ideology more firmly enshrined than in the nation-state. The social theorist Anthony Giddens examines the process of nation-state formation about as well as anyone. Without amplifying his distinction between core, periphery, and semiperiphery structures, we can concur with his general thesis that what characterizes the High-Tech Era, above all, is "the diffusion of the means of waging industrialized war."[7] The effectiveness of this diffusion has made the nation-state system the inescapable political norm for all humankind. Fundamentalists, whether in the First or Third World, have to elicit followers and mobilize movements within a reflexively monitored, hierarchically structured polity that neutralizes all moral absolutes under the rubric of its own unassailable sovereignty. Nationalist ideology preempts other invocations of transcendence; fundamentalists must perform on a stage that they did not construct and cannot destroy.

The instrumental strength of the modernist hegemony shields without erasing its cognitive limits. Apart from the intrinsic bias against religion, one must note other limits. Based on technicalism, it has a single monolithic view of reason. It is adept at enumeration; inventories proliferate in the High-Tech Era. Yet it is weak in analysis, substituting origins for beginnings and often neglecting causal relationships of a basic nature.[8]

Nor are modernists prone to take account of limits. Given the pervasiveness of cognitive and emotive codes within the Western tradition, one might have expected a tradition of skepticism, if not self-criticism, to emerge among more philosophically minded scientists. Yet novelty itself has been so enshrined in the modernist canon of sciences and technology that only the literary disciplines or human sciences are criticized as premodern, traditional, irrational.

The modernist hegemony, by its very emphasis on change, has disguised the extent to which it itself embodies continuity and opposes change. An innovative mathematical theorist illustrates the problem of how the intrinsic appeal to referentiality becomes cloaked beneath the patina of scientific discourse. In the introduction to *Metamagical Themas*, Douglas Hofstadter explains why he is drawn to the study of mathematics. He is trying to discover the relationship between the mind, creativity, and music. Mathematics, in his view, "more than any other discipline, studies the fundamental, pervasive patterns of the universe,... [and] the deepest and most mysterious of all patterns is music, a product of the mind that the mind has not come to fathoming *yet*." Hofstadter sets for himself the task of unlocking *now* the mystery of musical creativity: "In some sense, all my research is aimed at finding patterns that will help us to understand the mysteries of musical and visual beauty, [and] even though I find the prospect [of reducing music to mathematical formulas] repugnant, I am greatly attracted by the effort to do as much as possible in that direction [especially since] in computers [we have] the ultimate tool for exploring the essence of creativity and beauty."[9]

Hofstadter, in effect, is divinizing his research program. On the one hand, he eschews the endeavor to render musical creativity formulaic, but at the same time, he dedicates himself to that endeavor because he now has an efficient tool, in fact, "the *ultimate* tool for exploring the essence of creativity and beauty" (my emphasis). Yet his audacity presupposes that his readers continue to associate ultimacy with *Truth*. And to any reader who has the faintest memory about theological claims that the source of creativity and beauty is *divine*, it is Hofstadter who seems blasphemous, his quest not unlike that of Pascal: "to make God a mathematician whose secrets they could discover, and so come perilously near to identifying one's human power as a mathematician with *ultimate Truth*."[10]

It is only against the background of the modernist apostasy, launched long before Hofstadter and embraced by others than him, that we can consider ideologies alternative to the dominant ethos in Asia and the Middle East as well as in Euro-America. Among those ideologues who advocate a scriptural idiom and claim the public sphere as sacred space are the secondary male elites labeled "fundamentalist." The sociologist John Wilson located the crucial relationship when he declared that "the strident reassertion of a presumed tradition in a condensed, purified, or even reductionist form" is itself "a response to modernity, [for] fundamentalisms ... are no less than modernisms determined by the modern culture that they so stridently reject."[11]

The indispensable starting point is to locate fundamentalism in contemporary discourse. Though it has religious labels, fundamentalism functions as an ideology. Fundamentalist leaders are self-proclaimed churchmen or observant Jews or faithful Muslims, but they are in reality ideologues because they must operate within the modernist hegemony even while challenging not only its original premises but also its pervasive authority. They intuit as much as they verbalize the discrepancy between their worldview and the dominant worldview. They act boldly on behalf of their values.

In this study we have attempted to specify which subgroups within Christianity, Judaism, and Islam are fundamentalist, namely, one branch of Protestant Christians in America, scattered groups of quasi-Hasidic and *haredi* Jews in Israel, and certain cadres of Muslims—Sunnis in Egypt, Pakistan, and Malaysia; Shiʿis in Iran and southern Lebanon. We have also addressed the nature of the issues that fundamentalists seize upon, stressing that despite their religious labels, each is identified with a particular ideology of opposition to the Technical Age, or more recently, the High-Tech Era. The common object of their revulsion is the modernist hegemony. For Muslims, it is a Third World ideology of protest; its defining characteristics relate as much to the Third World socioeconomic condition of the majority of Muslims as it does to universal Islamic creedal appeals, for either Shiʿis or Sunnis. For Protestant Christians, on the other hand, fundamentalism is a First World, overtly capitalist ideology of reform. Progressive Patriotic Protestants are but narrowly separated from their politically conservative but often agnostic fellow citizens, those whom Henry May has labeled Progressive Protestant Patriots. Only for quasi-Hasidic and *haredi* Jews is it an ideology seeking to transpose premodern religious values into a modern nation-state. Neither First World not Third World but between worlds, Jewish fundamentalism comes close to being an ideology of recuperation.

The label "fundamentalism" helps us to see what these groups have in common. Too many of the arguments used to refute fundamentalists, or even to deny that they are fundamentalists, rely on etymological sleights of hand that miss the major point: something did happen on the way to the twenty-first century. The seismic divide separating the High-Tech Era from antecedent eras needs to be recognized by advocates of modernization as well as by their opponents.

The deepest level of power derives from economics, and it would be foolhardy to discuss the GWT or its consequence, both in the First and the Third Worlds, without recognizing the commercial edge of technicalization. Yet the most immediate level of authenticity depends on religion, for no projection of power can escape the cultural constraints of religious observance. Most studies fail to examine one or the other. Understanding fundamentalism requires attention to both economics and religion, especially their interaction at several levels—global, national, and local.

Fundamentalism is a concerted movement of disparate, mutually antipathetic groups. American Protestant fundamentalists provide the first explicit test case of the modernist/fundamentalist struggle. The movement, like the word "fundamentalism," initially emerged among Presbyterians and Baptists in the early decades of the twentieth century. Its checkered history only partially conforms to the criteria for fundamentalism set out above. While they were openly confrontational to representatives of liberal Christian doctrine, Progressive Patriotic Protestants did not oppose the American political system. They tried to work within it to change its direction. Their viewpoint always remained that of the unsullied minority. They remained a minority even when they joined with others to press for legislation that banned alcohol and later tried to introduce creation science into the curriculum of public schools. Secondary male elites provided their leadership, extolling women as mothers and custodians of family values but never recognizing an individual woman as authoritative teacher. Their technical language, communicated through their own literary media and eventually through television and the internet, demarcated Protestant American fundamentalists from other Christians, though evangelicals rivaled them for the mantel of gospel purity and also staked out competing claims to their symbolic space.

Jewish fundamentalism did not surface till after the establishment of a Zionist state in the late 1940s. Fundamentalism within Judaism nonetheless has roots that predate all others. The social origins of Jewish fundamentalists are traceable to the ghettoization of European Jewry (the Ashkenazim) in the eighteenth and nineteenth centuries. Alienated by culture from the mainstream of the European Enlightenment, many provincial Jews, especially in Poland and Hungary, did not benefit from the commercial successes of renascent Europe. There were exceptions to the rule: individual Jews who succeeded by becoming part of the dominant culture not as Jews but as modernists, and to the extent that they modernized or Westernized, they were regarded by other Jews, especially those from East European ghettos, as renegades to the ancestral legacy. Unfaithful to the embodiment of Jewish values, namely, the Torah, "enlightened" Jews appeared to their quasi-Hasidic and *haredi* counterparts as non-Jews. The tension between these opposite views of tradition, though never resolved, did not explode into the public domain till the formation of Israel in 1948. Hence Jewish fundamentalism seems more recent than Protestant American fundamentalism, despite the fact that its origins are, in fact, older.

The case is different with Islam. We can only begin to understand the varied sources for Islamic fundamentalism when we accept the extreme complexity of Islam itself. The question has often been posed, Are Muslims too varied an aggregate to be discussed under a single rubric such as "the Muslim world"? Yet the same question could be posed of Jews and Christians. To talk of scripture, for example, Qur'an, Torah, Bible, is one thing, but to speak of communities that relate to that scripture, with any honest recognition of their ethnic, linguistic, geographical diversity, is to admit the persistence of de facto pluralism, whatever the monotheistic creed or unifying mandate of scripture. Yet if we conceptualize Jews and Christians as worldwide communities, we must also admit that Muslims belong to a single *umma*. The *kehilla*, the church, the *umma*—each does exist. Each has points of cross-cultural identification and transnational loyalty. One must assert them while at the same time *not* claiming them as authoritative guides in any particular instance without also acknowledging the persistent force of local counterclaims.

It is especially important to note Islamic fundamentalists as a group apart from other Muslims. First cited by the British Orientalist H. A. R. Gibb in the 1940s, fundamentalism did not become a widely recognized Islamic phenomenon until the success of the clerically led Iranian Revolution in 1978–79. Prior to 1979, Egyptian and Pakistani oppositional groups were more often called extremist or militant than fundamentalist. They only became "fundamentalist" after the Iranian Revolution, by association with and comparison to Iran. Bluntly stated, without the Iranian Revolution, Islamic fundamentalism does not exist as an inclusive designation for antimodernist Muslim activists. In its stead, you have dissident radicals, a descriptive epithet that some scholars still prefer but one with pejorative political connotations.

The cauldron of religious ideology in which Islamic, as also Jewish and Christian, fundamentalism has been brewing needs to be carefully examined. Its practitioners offer a unique cure for the ills of the High-Tech Era: they rely on modern instrumentalities while rejecting the goals of modernism.

Though most observers tend to discuss fundamentalism as a reaction against the modern world, I prefer to emphasize not only the fundamentalist reaction but also the threat against which fundamentalists are reacting. While the dominance of strategies and values labeled "modernist" characterize the Technical Age and now the High-Tech Era, there are reactions against modernism other than fundamentalism. There are motives for fundamentalist groups other than antimodernism. But the core content is between two incommensurate ways of viewing the world, one which locates values in timeless scriptures, inviolate laws, and unchanging mores, the other which sees in the expansion of scientific knowledge a technological transformation of society that pluralizes options both for learning and for living.

The seriousness of the modernist challenge to religious values, symbols, and worldviews is concealed by the shield of material ease that privileges major segments of Euro-American society. It is difficult to challenge that which seems basic to everyday life, from digital clocks to compact disc players to hard-disk personal computers. The technological achievements of the High-Tech Era do not, however, produce a single set of ideological projections. The challenges we have reviewed above relate to specific modernisms: the nation-state as obedience-context for Jews and Muslims, the ubiquity of civil religion in American society, the claims of sociobiology for scientific investigators of every continent. Although the forms of fundamentalist protest may be questionable and even offensive to nonfundamentalists, there is ample evidence to support the fundamentalists' contention that religious symbols and claims have been devalued in the public discourse of many societies. The nation-state has defined and then usurped the space of symbolic purity.

Yet few modernists recognize the conflict with fundamentalism as anything but a rearguard mop-up operation. The *real* issue in their view is to delineate the nature of a postmodern (or postliberal or postneoorthodox) world. Once emergent, that world, it is presumed, will render moot claims to scriptural authenticity and institutional autonomy, both advocated by fundamentalists on behalf of "true religion."

While speculations that promote a nontheistic worldview inclusive of the present epoch in global history are the grist of Marxist philosophy, the most resounding death knell to God-talk comes from a contemporary German philosopher. The philosopher is Hans Blumenberg. His major work, *The Legitimacy of the Modern Age*, has been hailed as "a great sweeping history of the course of European thought." It is, in fact, the most extensive effort yet mounted to disassociate modern science from *any* religious antecedents. By implication, the modern age also should be severed from all preceding epochs of world history. The title itself poses a rhetorical question: Is the modern age legitimate? Can it claim authoritative points of identity that assure its independence? Is it self-referential rather than linked to legacies of the past or prospects for the future? The answer to all these questions, for Blumenberg, is a resounding "yes." He targets religious categories as the bête noire—to be isolated, defined, attacked, and demolished. Their persistence, despite Enlightenment critiques and competitive ideologies, is most evident in the attempts of other philosophers to explain the modern age as a *continuation* of premodern notions in new verbal guise. Even Nietzsche is suspect since he once commented that "how science could become what it now is can only be made intelligible from the development of religion."[12] Instead of legitimizing modern discourse with reference to its prior religious impulses, Blumenberg wants to sever the Gordian knot and proclaim the *de novo* character of both human self-assertion and theoretical curiosity in the modern age. For him, worldliness is a self-referential category. Worldliness does not have to be claimed as the result of secularizations. Like the modern age, it stands on its own.

Blumenberg's arguments may or may not capture the imagination of Euro-American intellectuals. They do, however, offer a plumb line by which we can measure the efforts to assess fundamentalism within the academy. Most of the debates thus far mounted have been polemical quibbles or rhetorical asides. Consider the attempt to differentiate fundamentalists from evangelicals in the Euro-American context of Protestant Christianity. Evangelical modernists like James Barr have tried to distance themselves from Protestant fundamentalists, at the same time that fundamentalist preachers like Jerry Falwell have come forward to depict themselves as the *true* evangelicals, inviting others to join them.[13] This jousting over sectarian identity misses the larger point: in neither camp is there a sustained *intellectual* counterchallenge to the issues posed by the Technical Age, issues tantamount to scientific positivism. It is science shorn of religion and history that threatens the metaphysical basis of human thought and the search for ethical guidelines in human conduct. The threat is recognized by fundamentalists yet the response mounted to it, for instance in the creationist controversy, seems overly defensive and rhetorically freighted.

Another debate has been waged within Judaism: to try to establish what are the defining characteristics of the Jewish collectivity and to maintain them against all secular assaults. The divergent responses from Neturei Karta and Gush Emunim have puzzled those who want to exalt nationalist identity, specifically loyalty to the state of Israel, as the highest allegiance of the Jewish collectivity. It is a battle that at first seems remote from Blumenberg's appeal for a confirmation of the independent, nonreligious authenticity of the modern age. Yet the process of Israel's formation as a nation-state in the High-Tech Era lends partial support to Blumenberg's thesis. The majority of Israel's political leaders have come from segments of European society caught up with Enlightenment fever. They migrated to Palestine and worked to create a new polity that promoted technical skills, ensured the autonomy of its citizens, and strove for progress. If one could strip Israeli society of its minority dissidents, that is, the National Religious Party and the contemporary zealots who belong to Neturei Karta and Gush Emunim, the Zionist state might come closer than any other modern state to fulfilling Blumenberg's model of a legitimate nonreligious polity. Even the Talmudic ritual antecedents that color Israel's civil religion might fade in a couple of generations. But that secularist utopia will not appear in Israel precisely because a religiously vocal minority does intrude into the public sphere. Politicized as religious ideologues, they insist on the historical continuity between the pre- and post-Enlightenment Jewish collectivity. They cannot be silenced or ignored, and so their aspirations for an uncompromisingly Jewish identity in the modern nation-state guarantee at the least a creative tension between them and their less observant Jewish compatriots. Too often, tension between religious and secular Jews erupts into physical confrontations within Israel that preempt compromise, preclude peace, and ensure protracted stalemates in Israel's external relations.

So radical is Blumenberg's reappropriation of modernity that the force of his arguments trivializes the search for some label other than "fundamentalist" to describe the numerous religiously motivated protests in the Islamic world. "Revivalism," "radicalism," "extremism," "activism," "militancy"—each has been touted by certain observers as a less culturally charged, more descriptively neutral substitute for the term "fundamentalism" in examining the religious protest common to Israel and its Muslim neighbors. Some go so far as to suggest that English vocabulary must be abandoned altogether and that one must resort to the French equivalent for fundamentalism, *intégrisme*. Still another move is to reclaim George Steiner's model of bifurcated linguistic-cultural spheres: upholding the specificity of any group's language and history as incommunicable, we must accept "the failure of Western secularized languages and Western historical parallels to provide *perfect* analogies for realities within the Muslim [or non-Western] world."[14]

By their nature, no analogies can be perfect. But the problem with monadist, atomistic logic, is the blindness of its advocates to the universality of certain themes and problems. While Muslims are not to be lumped together with Christians and Jews, they do have common concerns that are often best drawn out in a comparative frame of reference. Comparison must not be jettisoned. It is tough work that can yield results once technical terms are justified and analytical categories established. Aggregation and referentiality are inescapable, yet prejudice can be minimized, positivism blunted.

The measure of how well our analysis of fundamentalism succeeds depends on the adequacy of five criteria.... Are fundamentalists best described as (1) minority advocates of scriptural idealism who are (2) oppositional to the dominant ethos? Do their leaders and followers tend to be (3) secondary-level male elites who are bound to one another by (4) a religious ideology that relies on insider, technical language? Despite their own claims to distant and near antecedents, are fundamentalists (5) only to be found in the Technical Age as tenacious opponents of modernist ideologies that challenge their scriptural ideals and spiritual loyalties?

Each case needs to be reviewed with reference to these questions and the criteria they set forth. While Progressive Patriotic Protestants are not vocally opposed to the nation-state system of the United States of America, they conform in other respects to the normative outlook and behavioral pattern that characterize Israeli Jewish and Egyptian-Pakistani Islamic fundamentalists. All reject the dominant ethos of the society in which they live. All are marginalized male elites, co-opting women by claiming to protect them as custodians of domestic space. All use a technical vocabulary that reinforces minority group identity, even as they try to reclaim the public sphere as a space of symbolic purity, whether it be for the observance of *mitzvoth* in Israel or enforcement of *shariʿa* precepts in Islamic countries or furtherance of the ideals of Christian civilization in America. And none can be understood outside the parameters of religious ideology. The pattern of their emergence as self-conscious groups depends on the variant force of the GWT, as it first surfaced in Protestant America at the turn of the century, in Israel after the achievement of statehood (1948), and in Muslim nations most fully since the 1970s.

The overlap of fundamentalists in their defining characteristics allows comparison, but it does not overcome the profound distinctions between them. The major distinction is historical. It is, therefore, also socioeconomic. Fundamentalists have not equally appropriated the Technical Age. The clearest divide is between Christian and Muslim fundamentalists. Their competitive creedal assertions are exacerbated by divergent historical experiences. The Technical Age, and now the High-Tech Era, has produced a cultural gradient that reinforces the other differences between First and Third World societies.[15] Those who have been excluded from the front rank of technicalizing societies suffer structural inequities within their own societies of a different order than First World societies. To compare Christian and Muslim fundamentalists without acknowledging the disparate horizons of opportunity that their respective societies allow is fruitless. The obvious handicaps that most Muslims experience as Third World citizens needs to be reiterated: political limitations, reflected by the prevalence of military dictatorships or clan rulership permitting limited popular participation; economic inequities, situating a few landed or mercantile rich above masses of urban poor with minimal possibilities for the emergence of a middle class; educational restrictions, reflected in the existence of few universities and almost no high-tech training institutions, compelling the children of elites to study abroad; and gender asymmetry, using tradition as an excuse to exclude women from the public sphere even though it is the prevalence of competitive, unemployed men that reinforces the need to curtail women's professional horizons.

The situation in each Third World Muslim country will get worse, not better, for the remainder of this century and well into the next. Objective realities will not allow an economic miracle to rescue oil-poor Egypt or oil-rich Iran. Even the Islamic revolution in Iran has not reduced the massive economic disparities of an aridisolatic society, a society in which patterns of aridity and irrigation still determine vocational opportunities and class structures.[16]

Inequitable distribution of resources may fuel popular discontent and heighten the appeal of fundamentalist Islam in the short run, yet it does not brighten the prospects for an ultimate fundamentalist success, either in Iran or elsewhere. State obedience will always win out, even after a revolution. Fouad Ajami's shrewd assessment of Egypt after Sadat's assassination remains true. Echoing David Apter's analysis, Ajami depicts the examination of terrorism, in itself a "growth industry" flourishing under the jurisdiction of the modern nation-state: "What begins as a challenge to the state ends up confirming its rationality, its monopoly steering a reasonable course in a world that either is mad or is capable of becoming so at any moment. The state is said to be (by its custodians, by its many, many spokesmen) the only dike against great upheaval and disorder. This is a game that all states play; this also happens to be a game at which the Egyptian state is particularly skilled."[17]

The prospect for Jewish and Christian fundamentalists is similarly limited by the nature of the modern-day nation-state system, increasingly conservative during the High-Tech Era. Technology acquisition and scientific advances depend on the availability of large sums of capital. Only nation-states, and Euro-American large corporations, can provide that level of expenditure, and their custodians will always ensure that they also control the ends to which their investments are directed. As long as the marriage of statehood to modern instrumentalities remains viable, displacement by foes, whether representing fundamentalist aspirations or other marginalized interest groups, will not succeed. Self-interest will compel dominant groups to co-opt or suppress all foes.

What fundamentalists have done or tried to do, on the one hand, and what their several activities represent to the rest of humankind, on the other, are two separate issues. We have spent most of our study addressing the first. We also need to examine the second. The crucial question may be framed as follows: how do we understand the valence of religious values as autonomous from the modernist construction of the material world? Is the Algerian-born French Islamicist Mohammed Arkoun correct when he asserts about the Muslim world that "the so-called religious revivalism is a powerful secular movement disguised by religious discourse, rites, and collective behaviors"?[18] The same query could be made of Christian and Jewish fundamentalist movements. But the word that needs to be stressed is "disguised," for the dominance of technology is such that if by secularization Arkoun means "the domination of nature to increase the powers of man," then there is no escape from the secular, even though proponents as well as opponents of revivalism-fundamentalism may not recognize the secular residue of their thoughts and actions.

Yet secularization, as we have seen earlier, is a term admitting of several definitions. Arkoun himself provides two other definitions for secularization that could apply in an Islamic setting: first, a decaying of the prior capacity for receiving divine inspiration and guidance and second, a cultural and political program of emancipation from theological thinking and ecclesiastical dominance.[19] Neither of these definitions, however, applies to Islamic fundamentalists. They feel certain that divine guidance is still available and that they alone are guided to do God's will. They also are convinced that emancipation from either the *shariʿa* or *shariʿa*-mindedness is impossible for Muslims and that an Islamic society and state can emerge only with the full implementation of the divine law. The sole definition of secularization that fits, therefore, is the one that links secularization directly to its technological preamble: the domination of nature to increase the powers of the human. And so we come full circle back to our original premise. Islamic fundamentalists, whether consciously or more often unconsciously, must be secular insofar as the instrumentalities they rely on to project their views are technical in origin, prized for their proficiency rather than their purity.

Yet fundamentalists continue to be distinguished from other moderns by their persistent identity as a minority religious subculture opposing scientific triumphalism. In fact, human societies do not work as macrocosmic extensions of scientific research paradigms. In contemporary Euro-America there is no consensus about what comprises the common good and how one ought to proceed in order to assure its perpetuation for future generations. The benefit of pluralism is also its liability: there are several competing subcultures whose adherents all believe that they can wrest the mantle of the future from others if only their views can be projected through the most efficient medium to the widest possible audience. By the scientific reasoning of modernization theorists, fundamentalism should have been expelled once liberalism became sufficiently integrated into the scriptural studies, theological outlook, and social practice of mainline Protestant churches. Instead, the threat that the Enlightenment posed to religion in its liberal-modernist guise became accentuated. Rather than reducing, it heightened the fundamentalist appeal, especially to secondary male elites.

The protagonists were different, yet the process of fundamentalist coalescence in quasi-Hasidic and *haredi* Judaism as well as Sunni Islam was similar to its first emergence in Protestant American Christianity. The modern state relentlessly improved its capacity to function as the court of ultimate reference, the context of inclusive, enforceable obedience. For Judaism, the premodern period had allowed the development of many responses to an Enlightenment to occur in Europe. It was only when refugees from the Enlightenment clashed with emissaries of the Enlightenment in Palestine that the religious issues at the core of their struggle became hardened and the state had to serve as the enforcer of its own quasi-religious ideology. For Sunni Muslims, it was the period of colonialism that masked the full extent to which the *shariʿa*-minded were isolated from their coreligionists who deemed some accommodation to the dominant European powers as inevitable. Gaining nominal independence, Muslim elites continued to rely on Euro-American instruments of social exchange (newspapers, radios, and, in time, TV) as well as on institutions of military-political control (professional armed forces, constitutions, and national holidays). Reliance on them ensured that the modern nation-state would remain the forum of ultimate power.

The period of the great Muslim empires (Ottoman, Safavid-Qajar, and Mughal) lasted from the sixteenth till the end of the nineteenth century. During that period, there was always an ambiguous relationship between religious dissent and political treason. The two merged with the advent of the nation-state. To profess a variant interpretation of Islam was treason, and vice versa: if one wanted to make a statement against the government in power, religion became the most visible and evocative vehicle of protest. Although there was enormous variation in the way that modern Muslim nation-states handled the explosive issue of religious conformity, nearly all reduced rather than increased the scope for creedal dissent, linking it to political disloyalty. Sunni fundamentalists reacted by claiming that both the rulers in power and the official religious classes were corrupt. The Shi'i opposition to the shah claimed that he had not preserved the right of the clergy to speak on behalf of the faith, and so had forfeited his own right to rule. In both instances, opposition to the state increased when it drew on religious resources, but by the same token, religious specialists could only succeed by controlling and directing the modern nation-state apparatus to their own ends. In Iran, the Shi'i 'ulama', after coming to power in 1979, had to be both fundamentalist and modernist. It was, and remains, a challenge redolent with contradictions, contradictions that will continue to test the staying power of the Islamic Republic of Iran.

In the long run, fundamentalists will not be able to control the tone of discourse or activity in the public sphere of any major nation-state. By the end of the twentieth century, the post-Khomeini era of Iranian history will have demonstrated the near impossibility of juggling theocratic and technocratic goals in a premillennial Shi'i polity. In Israel, the likelihood of a continued ascent for Gush Emunim depends on their willingness to compromise with the pervasive statist ideology of the major political parties; Neturei Karta will remain spoilers, not principal actors. And the Moral Majority, or their future equivalent in the United States, have perhaps the least chance to succeed in dominating pluralist America. In the past, their predecessors met with occasional success, as in the fundamentalist-inspired prohibition movement, but the gains proved temporary. Since fundamentalists themselves felt uneasy with continuous involvement in the political realm, the pendulum swung back toward the majority will of an American electorate rededicated to pluralism after rejecting the excesses of puritan denial.

If failure in the political realm is inevitable, how can fundamentalists succeed? They must recognize the intellectual impulse behind the present symbol production. In the High-Tech Era, they must mount a counterchallenge to modernism that makes sense of the spiritual mandate they claim as eternal. They must confront issues of First and Third World economic disparities without postponing them to millennial solutions. Above all, fundamentalists need to redefine issues that have been too narrowly the province of scientific specialists.

Even if they fail to rise to this challenge, fundamentalists of some stripe will survive for a long time to come. In the foreseeable future they will probably appeal to a variety of marginalized male elites. On the other hand, scientists of all stripes will continue to be the most powerful brokers of modern culture. Even though they may lament that their respective fields are in an epistemological quandary, they remain hermeneutical foragers engaged in a common quest once summarized by the philosopher Richard Rorty as the attempt to free humankind from Nietzsche's longest lie, "the notion that outside the haphazard and perilous experiments we perform there lies something (God, Science, Knowledge, Rationality, or Truth) which will, if only we perform the correct rituals, step in to save us."[20]

For Rorty, as for most scientists, there is nothing out there *pragmatically*. One can believe what one will, but belief has no acknowledged place in scientific method. There remains an unbridgeable chasm between the head and the heart, despite the fact that both science and belief are projections of the human spirit. Reprieve from the modernist hegemony will not be easily won. The battle joined by modernists and fundamentalists must engage others if there is to be a postmodernist future that offers unity instead of division, hope rather than despair, God beyond human echoes.

Fundamentalism, to be understood, requires the microstudy of communities on a scale at once comparative and global. That task, barely begun, ought to engage social scientists as well as humanists. Both must pursue a degree of methodological self-examination, scanning their academic disciplines as well as their personal backgrounds, to recognize the limits of Enlightenment presuppositions concerning the origins of the Technical Age.

Even if fundamentalist ideology does no more than elicit discussion of religious issues in the mainstream of American public discourse, it will have served a useful end. Of course, it will try to do more, not only in America but also in Israel and in the Muslim world. It will agitate for the imposition of a religious lifestyle in all sectors of society. Though its adherents are unlikely to prevail, their brief moments of public notoriety will cause others to rethink the quandaries posed by the Technical Age, and in the High-Tech Era we may yet dare to hope for the emergence of a universalist vision that admits the legitimacy of the goads to fundamentalists without surrendering to their apocalyptic remedies.

In the meantime, we must guard against the innate human urge to mesh our own end as finite, physical beings with the end of all recognizable time. Pervasive concern with the end of "ordinary" time preoccupies both modernists and fundamentalists. Intrinsic to the Judeo-Hellenic circumference is the search for a moment beyond time. However much one expands (or, like Rorty and Blumenberg, denies) the "greekjew" synthesis at the heart of Western culture, the quest for catharsis it launches seldom finds resolution. It is a quest that races to the future yet lingers, fearful of its own presentness. Only the deepest level of self-reflection, yielding equal draughts of ambivalence and certitude, can permit us to look at the destiny of humankind beyond the cognitive as well as biological limits that constrain our own most powerful endeavors to exert control. The final word, as Ayatollah Morteza Motahhari once noted, must belong to the poet or seer rather than to the philosopher or scientist. It is the poet Wallace Stevens who perhaps best evokes the conundrum, which is also the hope, we share as moderns: to discover that "we believe without belief, beyond belief."[21]

Notes

Bruce B. Lawrence, "Fundamentalism as a Religious Ideology in Multiple Contexts" and conclusion, in *Defenders of God: The Fundamentalist Revolt against the Modern Age* (San Francisco: Harper and Row, 1989), 96–101, 227–45. Copyright © Bruce B. Lawrence. Used by permission of the author.

1 A rare effort to explain the persistent diffusion of modernism in sociological terms is offered by Roland Robertson, "The Sacred and the World System," in *The Sacred in a Secular Age: Toward Revision in the Scientific Study of Religion*, ed. Phillip E. Hammond (Berkeley: University of California Press, 1985), 347–58.

2 Ernst Cassirer, *The Philosophy of the Enlightenment* (Princeton, NJ: Princeton University Press, 1951), 159 (emphasis mine).

3   Bruns's reply to Gadamer's article "The Eminent Text and Its Truth" is set forth in *The Horizon of Literature*, ed. Paul Hernadi (Lincoln: University of Nebraska Press, 1982), 217.
4   Keith Dixon, *The Sociology of Belief: Fallacy and Foundation* (London: Routledge and Kegan Paul, 1980), 105.
5   George Steiner, *After Babel: Aspects of Language and Translation* (Oxford: Oxford University Press, 1975), 34.
6   Fernand Braudel, *On History*, trans. Sarah Mathews (Chicago: University of Chicago Press, 1980), 15.
7   Anthony Giddens, *The Nation-State and Violence* (Berkeley: University of California Press, 1987), 254.
8   For instance, on the continuing mystery of that basic function called human speech, see Steiner, *After Babel*, 293–94.
9   Douglas R. Hofstadter, *Metamagical Themas: Questing for the Essence of Mind and Pattern* (New York: Basic Books, 1985), xxv, with minor adaptations to clarify the relatedness of the passage to our argument.
10 John U. Nef, *The Conquest of the Material World* (Chicago: University of Chicago Press, 1958), 312 (emphasis mine).
11 John Wilson, "Modernity," in *The Encyclopedia of Religion*, ed. Mircea Eliade (New York: Macmillan, 1987), 10:21.
12 Hans Blumenberg, *The Legitimacy of the Modern Age*, trans. Robert M. Wallace (Cambridge, MA: MIT Press, 1983), 15.
13 See James Barr, *Beyond Fundamentalism* (Philadelphia: Westminster Press, 1984), 156; and Jerry Falwell, ed., *The Fundamentalist Phenomenon: The Resurgence of Conservative Christianity* (New York: Doubleday, 1981), 221–23.
14 See Umar F. Abdallah, *The Islamic Struggle in Syria* (Berkeley, CA: Mizan Press, 1983), 26 (emphasis mine).
15 The landmark article remains Carl E. Pletsch, "The Three Worlds, or the Division of Social Scientific Labor, circa 1950–1975," *Comparative Studies in Society and History* 23 (October 1981): 565–90.
16 The peculiar constellation of economic forces in Iran is exposed in the insightful but complex article of Homa Katouzian, "The Aridisolatic Society: A Model of Long-Term Social and Economic Development in Iran," *International Journal of Middle East Studies* 15 (May 1983): 259–81. For the comparative data from before and after the 1979 revolution, consult Shahrough Akhavi, "Elite Factionalism in the Islamic Republic of Iran," *Middle East Journal* 41 (Spring 1987): 199, and with reference to continuing gender asymmetry in the public sphere, see Val Moghadam, "Women, Work, and Ideology in the Islamic Republic [of Iran]," *International Journal of Middle East Studies* 20 (Fall 1988): 221–43.
17 Fouad Ajami, "In the Pharaoh's Shadow: Religion and Authority in Egypt," in *Islam in the Political Process*, ed. James S. Piscatori (New York: Cambridge University Press, 1983), 34.

18 Mohammed Arkoun, *Rethinking Islam Today*, Occasional Papers Series, Center for Contemporary Arab Studies (Washington, DC: Georgetown University, 1987), 23.
19 Arkoun, *Rethinking Islam Today*, 19.
20 Richard Rorty, *Consequences of Pragmatism (Essays: 1972–1980)* (Minneapolis: University of Minnesota Press, 1982), 208.
21 Wallace Stevens, "Flyer's Fall," cited from *The Mentor Book of Major American Poets*, ed. Oscar Williams and Edwin Honig (New York: New American Library, 1962), 286.

FOURTEEN

"The Shah Bano Case," from *On Violence: A Reader* | 2007

Nowhere have the contradictions posed by an Islamist solution become more evident than in the case of a South Asian Muslim divorcee who sought support from her husband through the court system. To examine the case of Shah Bano is to call attention to the pivotal yet problematic role of one mode of governance, the judiciary, as it functions in the three major Muslim states of South Asia: India, Pakistan, and Bangladesh. I will argue two points that emerge when one looks at women as an independent category and the judiciary as a crucial dimension of governance. The first is that women bear an uneven burden to represent the cultural norms shared by both men and women. The second is that court cases involving women's legal rights not only reflect boundary markings between Muslim and other communities, but also heighten tensions about their maintenance, even as they complicate notions of what it is to be both Asian and Muslim in the late twentieth century.

Shah Bano was the daughter of a police constable. At an early age she was married to her first cousin, Muhammad Ahmad Khan. During more than forty years of marriage she had borne him five children. Then one day in 1975, according to her account, he evicted her from their home. At first he paid her a maintenance sum, as required by Islamic law, but he ceased payment after some two and a half years. When she applied to the district court for redress, he divorced her. Uttering the formula disapproved by the Prophet but authorized (yet still discouraged) by the Hanafi school of law, he declared, "I divorce you, I divorce you, I divorce you."

At that point they were divorced, but, complying with a further provision of Islamic law, Muhammad Ahmad Khan paid Shah Bano the dower of about three hundred dollars that he had set aside at the time of their marriage. Legally he had fulfilled all his responsibilities to her.

Shah Bano, however, was left impoverished. She had no means to support herself, having worked as a housewife for over forty years in the home from which she was now debarred. She sued her former husband by going to the magistrate of a provincial court. The magistrate ruled that Muhammad Ahmad Khan, having violated the intent of Muslim Personal Law, was obliged to continue paying Shah Bano her maintenance. The court awarded her the sum of roughly two dollars a month. She appealed, and two years later, in 1980, the High Court of her state (Madhya Pradesh) awarded Shah Bano approximately twenty-three dollars a month.

It was at that point that Muhammad Ahmad Khan appealed the High Court's decision. A lawyer himself, he took the case to the Indian Supreme Court, arguing that he had fulfilled all the provisions of Muslim Personal Law and hence had no more financial obligations to his former spouse.

The Shah Bano case dragged on for another five years. Without the financial support of "fairly well-off male family members (Shah Bano's sons)," she could not have pursued her appeal. Finally, in 1985, seven years after she had begun litigation in the lower courts, Shah Bano was vindicated. The Indian Supreme Court upheld the Madhya Pradesh High Court judgment, and her former husband had to comply with its verdict. The Supreme Court justices in dismissing Muhammad Ahmad Khan's appeal cited the section of the Criminal Procedure Code of 1973 that refers to "the maintenance of wives, children and parents."

None of the above narratives makes Shah Bano exceptional. Neither her plight nor the length of her legal battles lacks precedents. Numerous studies of South Asian women underscore the discrimination they experience even after the International Women's Decade (1975–85). It is no small irony that Shah Bano's legal vindication came just as the International Women's Decade was ending, but the favorable outcome of her case had more to do with a legislative act than with public advocacy of women's rights. It was a change in the Code of Criminal Procedure, enacted in 1973, that made possible the reconsideration of provisions for divorced Muslim women. Under this code, two Muslim women had been awarded maintenance in 1979 and 1980. Their cases provided the precedent with reference to which the Supreme Court opted to rule in favor of Shah Bano.

The legal drama and its political consequences are dense. Often the case seems to remain only a watershed for identity politics in the continuing struggle for inclusive norms within postcolonial India. What needs to be stressed, however, is the nature of the legal system that made all three cases possible. These women resided neither in Bangladesh nor in Pakistan, the two majoritarian Muslim nations of the subcontinent, but in the Republic of India. As Indian citizens, they lived under an ad hoc system evolved since British colonial rule. Throughout the nineteenth and early twentieth centuries there was no uniform manner of applying Muslim family law within the lower courts. The number of rules regulating marriage and inheritance were restricted, and they were enforced through a strict hierarchical structure where appeals moved haltingly from a subordinate district judge to a state high court to the London Privy Council, replaced after 1947 by the Indian Supreme Court.

Due to the omissions and excesses of this system, it is not surprising that customary law, unfavorable to women, was often applied instead of the more favorable terms of Islamic law. Muslim women in the western and northern regions of India were especially vulnerable to facing the denial of property inheritance and dowry settlements, both provided to them under Islamic law. Finally, in 1937, under pressure from Muslim elites, the Shariat Law was passed. It required all Indian Muslims to be governed solely by Islamic juridical norms in family matters, including marriage, divorce, maintenance, adoption, and inheritance. But at independence ten years later, Parliament passed an All India Criminal Procedure Code that applied, as its title suggests, to all Indian citizens, whatever their religious affiliations. One of its provisions stipulated "the maintenance of wife, children, and parents." It was that provision which the Supreme Court justices cited in 1985 when they ruled in favor of Shah Bano and against Muhammad Ahmad Khan.

Personal law, in effect, acquired a double tracking: one pertaining to the Muslim community, the other to the collective Indian citizenship. While that double tracking created tension between secular and religious authorities after independence, such tension was nonetheless successfully negotiated prior to 1985. Were the issue itself a sufficient provocation, then both the 1979 and the 1980 cases should have set off a nationwide row. In fact, they did not.

The case of Shah Bano became decisive for one reason: its timing. It did not occur in the mid-1970s, when Mrs. Gandhi's declaration of a state of emergency had muzzled the court system, nor will it occur again in the mid-1990s, for reasons that will be made clear below. It was the changed climate of religious identity in the mid-1980s that set the stage for the Shah Bano debacle. There were several necessary conditions, but the one sufficient condition was Muslim Personal Law, that is, law that applied to the personal status of each Muslim within the family domain. Personal law became the litmus test of Indian Muslim collective identity, its fragility underscored by the creation in 1972 of an All India Muslim Personal Law Board to maintain and defend its application.

Even so, personal law by itself would not have created the Shah Bano debacle. The case came to public attention in the aftermath of Indira Gandhi's assassination at the hands of Sikh extremists. Riots in Delhi and elsewhere had shredded the myth of communal harmony. Everyone worried about their Hindu, Muslim, Sikh, or tribal identities. Although Sikhs had been the primary targets of the Delhi riots, Muslims still felt vulnerable.

It was in this charged atmosphere that demagogues sought pretexts to "prove" that the ruling party was but a front for furthering Hindu hegemony, at the expense of all minorities but especially the largest, which was the Muslim, minority. The Shah Bano case provided Muslim ideologues, abetted by the All India Muslim Personal Law Board, with "clear" evidence that there was a juridical slide toward uniform civil codes, codes that would enforce majoritarian Hindu values on all Indians. Rajiv Gandhi's Congress-I was then the ruling party. When Congress-I supported the Supreme Court decision, an incensed Muslim politician ran against the Congress-I candidate (who was also Muslim). The demagogue won, lambasting the anti-Muslim impact of the Shah Bano judgment. How could Muslims preserve their separate identity, he argued, if even their personal laws were subject to arbitration in the higher, "secular" courts of India? The All India Muslim Personal Law Board, having won a victory at the regional level, ratcheted its claims to the next level. Its members pressed on the national front, appealing to legislators, ministers, and, of course, journalists. They were abetted by Muhammad Ahmad Khan, a barrister arguing his own case! Together the aggrieved former spouse and representatives of the Muslim Personal Law Board carried the banner of Muslim juridical autonomy to several members of Parliament, their every move broadcast by the press.

The role of the press in dramatizing the Shah Bano case has been considerable. In volume of print and decibels of emotion it exceeds all other spectacles, even the storming of the Sikh golden temple in Amritsar, even the assassination of Mrs. Gandhi and later her son, Rajiv. It exceeds even the Rushdie affair, with which it has sometimes been linked. The Shah Bano case exceeds all these because it concerns a process that has tapped into communal fears, and drawn out appeals to communal loyalty, not witnessed since independence. Its only competitor for sustained media attention is the Ayodhya mandir/Babri masjid dispute. That dispute erupted in 1986 as a politically motivated effort to reclaim all of India as "Hindu" by pinpointing, with scant historical evidence, one pilgrimage site as the birthplace of the god Ram and then alleging that sixteenth-century Mughal invaders built a mosque on this same site in order to affirm their superiority over Hinduism.

Important though the Ayodhya dispute is, in a real sense it occupies an adjacent and not a preferred space on the same spectrum of communally marked confrontation as Shah Bano. Ayodhya becomes the sequel to Shah Bano since it was the latter that pushed Muslim-Hindu antagonism to new levels. Unlike the local protagonists of previous communal riots, the India-wide Hindu protagonists of Ayodhya's sacral purity were used in the media to stage a grievance identical to that of the Shah Bano case, namely, that Muslim and Hindu worldviews were finally incommensurate and that the Republic of India could not grant both equal representation.

In such an inflamed atmosphere the value of religious identity is heightened, and appeals to creedal shibboleths abound. The ideological weapon wielded on both sides quickly became identified as fundamentalism. It was fundamentalism Indian-style, but it was still the bugbear of fundamentalism. The challenge was thrown down by the demagogue who used Shah Bano as the rallying cry for his own election to Parliament in 1985. Syed Shahabuddin decried the Supreme Court decision as "clear" evidence of Hindu contempt for Muslim law. He opposed it not only for himself and for his Muslim constituents but also for all believing Muslims who, like himself, were fundamentalists. Fundamentalists? Yes, fundamentalists, because to be a true Muslim, in his view, was to bind oneself to the literal revelation of the Qur'an. "Historically," declared Syed Shahabuddin, "the Qur'an was revealed to the Prophet 1400 years ago but it is the final message of God to mankind. Not one syllable is subject to change. . . . It is in this sense that the Muslim is by definition a fundamentalist."

There are, of course, enormous contradictions in this assertion, since the Qur'an itself is subject to variant interpretations *within* the Muslim community. Despite the consensus shared by all Muslims that the Qur'an is the final message of God's final messenger, its rare legal passages engender multiple interpretations, arising as they do in a myriad of human circumstances. When Syed Shahabuddin and his followers appealed to Qur'anic finality, they were really staking out a claim for themselves as the sole valid interpreters of what they took to be a singular meaning mandated by Qur'anic verses. Yet equally devout Muslims can, and do, challenge those claims, offering in their stead equally valid alternative readings of both the Qur'an and Islamic history.

In a time of crisis, a dispassionate view of the Qur'an may be less plausible than the unequivocal reading claimed by Syed Shahabuddin and other fundamentalists. The mid-1980s were such a time of crisis for many Indians. India's Muslim fundamentalists challenged the Shah Bano ruling at a moment when the center seemed to be unraveling. Their appeal to Parliament to reverse the Shah Bano decree seemed implausible, and the uproar about Shah Bano would have quickly subsided had their appeal failed. But for a variety of political considerations both the Congress-I and Prime Minister Rajiv Gandhi perceived themselves as vulnerable to "the Muslim vote." Out of expediency, the Indian Parliament in 1986 passed a bill often referred to as the Muslim Women's Bill. That bill withdrew the right of Muslim women to appeal for maintenance under the Criminal Procedure Code. In other words, after 1986 Shah Bano could have no successors. The Muslim Women (Protection of Rights on Divorce) Bill, in fact, discriminated against Muslim women: it removed the right of any Muslim woman to juridical appeal for redress of the award made to her under Muslim Personal Law.

Damaging though the outcome may be to the invisible seam of multiculturalism without which Indian democracy cannot function, its most dire consequences may yet be muted by the logic of its initial success. Rather than closing debate on the Shah Bano case, the legislative reversal of the Supreme Court ruling raised new questions about who has the right to speak on behalf of the Muslim community. The Supreme Court judge who read the majority decision made his own claim to best understand Muslim interests when, in concluding his argument for the court's ruling, he justified it as "more in keeping with the Qur'an than the traditional interpretation by Muslims of the Shariat." His move to separate the purity of Qur'anic principles from the obfuscation of Muslim jurists was followed by others, including a score of journalists. In an exchange that enlivened the *Illustrated Weekly of India* during early March 1986, a Hindu journalist, Arun Shouri, argued that "while there was much oppression of women under Islamic law, the Qur'an, rightly interpreted, would make possible the removal of the injustices they suffered." But, according to his respondent, the Islamic scholar Rafiq Zakaria, Shouri only appeared to be concerned about true Islam; his stated concern actually masked a contempt for Muslims and a not-so-subtle attempt to undermine Muslim religious identity. Nor did the debate disappear once the Muslim Women Bill became law. Women's groups opposed the bill, and leading Muslims spoke out on *both* sides of the issue. Seldom before had religious identity and gender parity been so publicly framed in antithetical, competing terms. No wonder that Shah Bano subsequently rejected the court verdict in her favor and occasioned still another round of debate about the meaning of her subjectivity as a Muslim woman.

Note

Bruce B. Lawrence, "The Shah Bano Case," in *On Violence: A Reader*, ed. Aisha Karim and Bruce B. Lawrence (Durham, NC: Duke University Press, 2007), 262–67.

FIFTEEN

Introduction to *Messages to the World: The Statements of Osama bin Laden* | 2005

Although Osama bin Laden has become a legendary figure in the West, not to speak of the Arab world, the body of his statements has till now never been available to the public. Occasional fragments are cited, and—much more rarely—a few speeches have been reproduced here and there in the press. Yet official pressures have ensured that, for the most part, his voice has been tacitly censored, as if to hear it clearly and without cuts or interruption would be too dangerous. This does not mean that Bin Laden's messages have reached no audience. But they have done so by flying below the radar screen of official—government and media—discourse about the war on terror, and entering an alternative sphere that is largely confined to Arabic speakers. Although his addresses are typically scriptural in mode, his rise to prominence mirrors the latest phase in the Information Age, the techniques of which he has in his own way mastered. In a period of ten years that coincide with the emergence of a virtual universe, moving from print to internet, from wired to wireless communication around the globe, Bin Laden and his associates have crafted a series of carefully staged statements designed for the new media. These include interviews with Western and Arab journalists, handwritten letters scanned onto discs, faxes, and audiotapes, and above all video recordings distributed via the first independent Arabic-language news outlet, the Qatari satellite television network Al-Jazeera. *Messages to the World: The Statements of Osama bin Laden* makes possible, for the first time, informed critical discussion of Bin Laden's outlook; his statements are no longer limited to the scrutiny of secretive government agencies and counterterrorism experts.

To understand his textual performances, it is necessary to know something about the biography of their author. Osama bin Muhammad bin Laden was born in 1957 in Saudi Arabia. His father was an illiterate Yemeni laborer from the Hadhramaut whose business acumen enabled him to secure building contracts for the Holy Sanctuaries, and to become a trusted confidant of the al-Saud family. When he died suddenly in 1968, Muhammad bin Laden left a fortune of $11 billion to his fifty-four children, by twenty or more different women. Bin Laden's mother, who was Syrian, quickly divorced his father, and remarried another Yemeni. His father died when he was ten. The young Bin Laden attended the Management and Economics School at King Abd al-Aziz University in Jeddah. Though he was an indifferent business student, he took courses in Islamic studies taught by ʿAbdullah ʿAzzam and Muhammad Qutb that seem to have influenced him deeply. ʿAzzam (1941–89) was a Muslim Brother from Palestine. He studied at al-Azhar University in Cairo in the early 1970s, before moving to Jeddah in 1978. Muhammad Qutb was the younger brother of Sayyid Qutb, the Egyptian thinker who became one of the most powerful voices of radical Islamic protest against both Arab nationalism and Western hegemony in the time of Nasser, and who was executed in 1966. Bin Laden dates his own political awakening from 1973, when an American airlift ensured Israeli victory over Egypt and Syria in the Yom Kippur War, and King Faisal of Saudi Arabia imposed a temporary oil embargo on the West.

After leaving university without having completed his degree, Bin Laden entered his father's construction empire. He proved himself a successful manager of several of its businesses, and seems to have accumulated a sizable personal fortune, though not as much as is often attributed to him. While still a very young man, he seems to have either volunteered or been picked by Riyadh to help organize the flow of Saudi funds and equipment to the *mujahidin* who had taken up arms against the Russian-backed regime in Afghanistan. He first arrived in Peshawar, on the border between Afghanistan and Pakistan, in 1980 when he was only twenty-three. There he worked with ʿAzzam, contributing to his free circular *al-Jihad,* while also setting up his own operation in Peshawar, a guesthouse for Arab recruits to *jihad* against the Soviet Union. Called Sijil al-Qaʿida (Register of the Base), it was later known simply as al-Qaʿida (the Base). At this time, he cooperated closely with the Pakistani secret service of ISI (Inter-Service Intelligence Agency), and the CIA, the two other external patrons of the *mujahidin*. He may have been uneasy about his connection with the CIA—he later denied it altogether—but there is no contemporary evidence of his moral dilemma. With American and Saudi funds, and his own construction experience, he helped build mountain bases, including at the cave complex called Tora Bora, and training camps in the border regions. Later he seems to have fought courageously in the battle around Jalalabad, as one of the many thousands of Arab volunteers in the war against the Soviet occupation of Afghanistan.

When Russian troops pulled out of Afghanistan in 1989, US funds were abruptly withdrawn. The battle-hardened Arab Afghans, largely split into national groups, were left to war amongst each other in Peshawar. Only the training camps remained, used throughout the next decade by the ISI for Afghan and Kashmiri *jihad*. In 1990 Bin Laden returned to Saudi Arabia. There, when Saddam Hussein invaded Kuwait some months later, he offered to organize a fighting force of Arab Afghan veterans to defend the Kingdom against the threat from Iraq. The Saudi royal family not only rejected his proposal, but also invited half a million American and other foreign troops into the country to protect the ruling dynasty in Kuwait. It was these "infidel" forces that launched Operation Desert Storm against Iraq. Their presence in the Land of the Two Holy Sanctuaries was blessed by the leading Saudi *'ulama'*, including Sheikh 'Abdul 'Aziz bin Baz, Grand Mufti of the Kingdom, as well as the Sheikh of al-Azhar in Cairo. Religious scholars and others who protested were harassed or jailed by the Saudi authorities. Bin Laden was among them. Under brief house arrest, he was able to leave the country for Sudan in 1991. He was still only thirty-four.

For the next five years, Bin Laden settled in a large, well-guarded compound outside Khartoum, under the protection of a Sudanese military regime which at that time was linked to the radical Islamist leader Hassan al-Turabi. Other Arab Afghans, including the Egyptian who was henceforward to be his most important associate, Ayman al-Zawahiri, joined Bin Laden there. Although remaining active as a businessman in Sudan, Bin Laden seems to have organized the arrival in Somalia of Arab Afghan veterans. He would later claim that they were the "true" *mujahidin*, who had delivered decisive blows against US forces that had arrived there under UN auspices in 1993, but were soon withdrawn after suffering humiliating setbacks. It is virtually certain that Bin Laden was also attempting to organize underground opposition to the regime in Riyadh. The Saudi authorities tried to assassinate him several times, without success. In 1994 they stripped him of his citizenship. At the end of the year he responded with his first major public statement: an attack on the Grand Mufti bin Baz's blessing of the Oslo Accords, released in London by the newly established Advice and

Reform Committee, an expression of the indignation felt by the radical Muslims at the "apostasy" of Arab rulers who were cooperating with the West.

Six months later, the Egyptian president Hosni Mubarak, on a state visit to Addis Ababa, narrowly escaped death in an ambush. When the organizers were traced to Sudan, Washington and Cairo added to the pressure already on Khartoum from Riyadh to expel Bin Laden from the country. In May 1996, he and his entourage returned to Afghanistan, taking refuge in the Tora Bora mountains, north of Jalalabad. By September, the Taliban had captured Kabul and over the next two years imposed, with Pakistani support, the most unified rule the country had known since the fall of Afghan Communism. Enjoying mutually respectful, if not always warm relations, with the Taliban regime, Bin Laden set about organizing the resources, finance, training, and safe havens needed in which to reassemble young fighters for "defense of Islam." At the same time, he sought to project his aims to a wider audience, conceding interviews and proclaiming the creation of a World Islamic Front in conjunction with al-Zawahiri and two leading Pakistani Islamists in early 1990. Six months later, simultaneous bombings of American embassies in Kenya and Tanzania left more than two hundred dead and many more injured. This was the first major terrorist action indisputably traceable to Bin Laden. Yet the Clinton administration dismissed proposals to have him extradited from Afghanistan and instead launched a cruise missile attack on one of his bases in Khost in August 1998, seeking but failing to kill him. He was now world-famous. Three years later, al-Qaʻida activists hijacked four planes in the United States and in suicide missions destroyed the World Trade Center and severely damaged the Pentagon, killing three thousand people, most of them Americans.

It was not until 2004 that Bin Laden publicly acknowledged his role in planning and organizing the attacks of 9/11, but from the start few doubted that he was the author of this epochal act of terrorism. The Bush administration's response was swift. In early October, Operation Enduring Freedom unleashed the heaviest bombing assault on any country since World War II, flattening Taliban resistance and facilitating the conquest of Afghanistan by US proxies. Bin Laden, the prime target of the campaign, escaped capture, as did the Taliban leader Mullah Omar. In places of deep hiding somewhere along the Pakistani-Afghan border, he has continued to defy all attempts to find him, despite a $50 million bounty on his head and massive sweeps by Pakistani and US forces. The capacity of the loose network of affiliates emanating from al-Qaʻida to act outside the Arab world may have been greatly weakened, but it has not been extinguished, as the bombings in Madrid of February 2004 and in London of July 2005 have shown. Within the Middle East, on the other hand, the Anglo-American invasion of Iraq has created a fertile recruitment ground for Bin Laden's conception of *jihad* against the West. Though physically cut off from the battlefields of Mesopotamia, his voice resounds across them through audiocassettes and satellite TV, inspiring many of the most ferocious attacks on the occupiers and their local allies. He released a series of messages to the people of Iraq, the nations of Europe, and the citizens of the United States. Collectively these textual performances underscore that Osama bin Laden remains a force to be reckoned with.

But what kind of force? We have only glimpses of Bin Laden's personality, and much remains mysterious about the man. Few of his early associates saw him as a potential leader. The newly appointed Saudi ambassador to Washington recalls him as "a very shy person, very self-effacing, extremely sparse in his words and generally a do-gooder."[1] But is it possible that something of the spirit of his father moved him from the start? Muhammad bin Laden had risen from nothing to untold wealth in the shadow of the newly petro-rich Saudis, in a career that must have involved many a gamble. Bin Laden would prove himself as much a risk-taker as his father, but in another way. Coming out of the shadow of docile Muslim leaders, within a world order dominated by the West, he rallied fellow believers in the pursuit not of fortune but of *jihad*, beyond all the allures of prosperity, professionalism, or familial comfort. He also must have inherited some of his father's practical gifts. Already in his twenties he seems to have been a capable manager, at the head of a large construction complex, applying natural organizational skills he would later use to channel Saudi money and material to Afghanistan. The creation of an international network of sacrificial activists and the complex logistical planning of 9/11, in conjunction with his small group of associates, can be regarded as the culminating achievements of this side of Bin Laden.

Yet these organizational gifts alone, magnified as they were by the ample financial resources at his disposal, would never have given him the position he enjoyed in the Muslim world. That is due to no human qualities. Bin Laden is not an original thinker. Most of his ideas stem from writings by early mentors, in particular ʿAbdullah ʿAzzam's *Defending the Land of the Muslims Is Each Man's Most Important Duty*, which, published in Peshawar in 1985, laid down a comprehensive case for individual *jihad* against the West. Nor is Bin Laden an outstanding Qur'anic scholar: he lacks the command of textual subtleties that mark Wahhabi exegetes in Arabia, or their Azhari counterparts in Cairo. Yet he is well versed in the classical scriptures of Islam, and uses them to great advantage. He moves easily in the Qur'an as a book of day-to-day guidance, a source from which even the illiterate can draw strength both as pious Muslims and as advocates of radical change within the world they uneasily inhabit with other, less zealous believers. This level of learning, real if not exceptional, provides the basis of religious authority for his pronouncements. What gives these their unique force, however, are his literary gifts. Bin Laden has earned many labels by now—fanatic, nihilist, fundamentalist, terrorist—but what actually distinguishes him, among a host of those described in these ways, is that he is first and foremost a *polemicist*. The many different statements collected in this book are nearly all constructed as arguments with real or imagined opponents and interlocutors.

In each case, there is an adjustment of the polemical register to the particular audience for whom the message is intended. Common to all these messages is the literary skill with which they are composed. Not everything in them has necessarily been written by Bin Laden himself: there is reason to believe that in some cases other hands may have contributed to the final text. But what is crystal-clear is that these messages are not ghostwritten tracts of the kind supplied by professional speechwriters to politicians in the West, whether American presidents, European prime ministers, or their Middle Eastern counterparts. They speak in the authentic, compelling voice of a visionary, with what can only be called a powerful lyricism. Bernard Lewis, no friend of radical Islam, described a typical message published below as "a magnificent piece of eloquent, at times even poetic, Arabic prose."[2] Bin Laden's standing in the Muslim world is inseparable from these literary gifts.

Beyond the organizer and the polemicist lies, finally, the hero. To Westerners for whom Bin Laden is the incarnation of evil, this may seem the last word in perversity. But for millions of Muslims around the world, including many who have no sympathy with terrorism, Bin Laden is a heroic figure. His worldwide charisma is based not just on his success in so far eluding Americans and their allies, exhilarating as that may be for many ordinary Muslims. It is because Bin Laden has demonstrated that he can forgo the temptations of wealth, that he dares to strike powerful wrongdoers, and that he refuses to bend before superior might. "Bin Laden is seen by millions of his co-religionists—because of his defense of Islam, personal piety, physical bravery, integrity and generosity—as an Islamic hero, as that faith's ideal type, and almost as a modern-day Saladin," reports Michael Scheuer, head of the CIA unit charged with hunting Bin Laden. "For nearly a decade now," observes Scheuer, "bin Laden has demonstrated patience, brilliant planning, managerial expertise, sound strategic and tactical sense, admirable character traits, eloquence, and focused, limited war aims. He has never, to my knowledge, behaved or spoken in a way that could be described as 'irrational in the extreme.'" Indeed, for all the terror sown by Bin Laden's actions, Scheuer concludes that "there is no reason, based on the information at hand, to believe bin Laden is anything other than what he appears: a pious, charismatic, gentle, generous, talented, and personally courageous Muslim. As a historical figure, viewed from any angle, Osama bin Laden is a great man, one who smashed the expected unfolding of universal post–cold war peace."[3] These encomia express the admiration felt by a professional for a particularly skilled enemy. Yet even discounting their hyperbole, such tributes are striking; they provoke further reflection on the man behind the many personae.

How are such eulogies, from friend and foe alike, to be reconciled with the actions for which Bin Laden has been responsible? Is the West wrong to call him a terrorist? His messages make it clear that, by his own admission, the answer is no. Bin Laden freely concedes that he has practiced terror. What the messages invariably go on to say, however, is that this is a *reactive* terror—a response to what he perceives as the much greater terror exercised by the West over an incomparably longer period of time. In this sense, Bin Laden's is a counterterrorist form of terror; his principal innovation has been to organize terrorist actions thousands of miles away from the territories he is seeking to liberate. And this, he insists, is itself only retaliation for the innumerable prior acts of Western aggression in the Muslim world, thousands of miles away from Christian homelands. For two hundred years now, the *umma* (the global community of Muslims) has been under attack, from the first French invasion of Egypt in the last years of the eighteenth century and the seizure of the Maghreb in the nineteenth century, the British grab for Egypt and the Italian for Libya, the carve-up of the Middle East by Britain and France at the end of World War I, the support for Jewish colonization of Palestine, the suborning of normally independent rulers in the Arabian peninsula, down to contemporary American dominance in the entire region.

Is this an exaggerated description of the unbalanced relationship between the West and the Muslim world? All the lines of intrusion and violence historically do run in one direction. Yet such aggression does not condone Bin Laden's acts of terror; they are abhorrent not only to Westerners, but also to many Arabs and Muslims. Yet in the Middle East, few can forget the much heavier loss of life caused by centuries of Western domination. Bin Laden's victims number perhaps five thousand—about half as many as the number of civilians said to have died under American bombs in Afghanistan. As he never ceases to point out, the West has killed far larger numbers in the region within living memory. The crushing of the Palestinian uprising of the 1930s, then France's colonial war in Algeria in the 1950s and 1960s, have been followed now by deaths through malnutrition and disease inflicted on the children of Iraq in the 1990s, due to UN sanctions. Bin Laden, ever alert to the principle of reciprocity, dwells insistently on the enormous extent of Iraq's suffering. He exaggerates its size: starting with six hundred thousand victims, he ends with 1.5 million; the real figure is probably nearer three hundred thousand. Yet he is correct about the staggering disproportion in the numbers of those killed on both sides. "Because you have killed," he warns Westerners, "we must kill. Your innocents are not less innocent that ours." Even though nothing can ever justify Bin Laden's own retaliatory killing of innocent people, the indifference of Western leaders to the atrocities committed against Muslims helps explain why, despite widespread revulsion at his use of terror, he continues to be admired and even trusted by some ordinary people in the Middle East.[4] Should Bin Laden then be described as a contemporary anti-imperialist fighter adaptive to the Information Age? This is the view of the prominent sociologist Michael Mann. He writes: "Despite the religious rhetoric and bloody means, bin Laden is a rational man. There is a simple *reason* why he attacked the US: American imperialism. As long as America seeks to control the Middle East, he and people like him will be its enemy."[5] Objectively speaking, Bin Laden is waging a war against what many—admirers as well as critics—now call the American empire. But it is crucial to note that he himself never uses the word "empire." He defines the enemy differently. For him, *jihad* is aimed not at an imperium but at "global unbelief." Again and again, his texts return to this fundamental dichotomy. The war is a religious war. It subsumes a political war, which he can wage with terms appropriate to it, as he demonstrates in his addresses to the peoples of Europe or of America. Yet the battle in the end is one of faith.

Does this matter, or is it just a question of vocabulary? For some, Bin Laden's use of Qur'anic authority for his struggle is little more than a convenient mask, disguising the reality that al-Qaʿida is actually an Arab version of the Red Brigades or the ultra-left groups that practiced terrorism in Europe in the 1970s—their lineal successor, so to speak. But this view is not convincing. Of the intensity of Bin Laden's piety there can be no doubt. What is more controversial is his purported orthodoxy. His critics have from the beginning charged him with selective use of the Qur'an and Traditions, for purposes incompatible with the intention of God's Word or the teachings of His Prophet. Certainly, it is difficult to find in his writing any echo of the traditional Islamic views of generosity, hospitality, and tolerance. Yet it is also true that everything he has written falls within the framework of a reaction against aggression, for which he has strong scriptural support. Islamic jurisprudence distinguishes between offensive war (*harb*), a campaign of conquest launched under official leadership against the land of the impious, and defensive struggle (*jihad*), to be waged as a matter of individual obligation by all Muslims when the *umma* has come under attack. In the latter case it is the *dicta* of the fourteenth-century Syrian jurist Ibn Taymiyya, who rallied the faithful against the terrifying scourge of the Mongol invasions, which provide the most authoritative guide for conduct. His *fatwa* reads: "the first obligation after the (profession of) Faith is to repel the enemy aggressors who assault both sanctity and security."

Taking this injunction seriously, Bin Laden points to passages in the Qur'an that he reads as authorizing a generalized *lex talionis*, one capable of covering even the killing of innocent infidels in revenge for the killing of innocent believers. In much the same way, he invokes a lethal directive against Jews, attributed to Muhammad, and less ferocious but still hostile passages in the Qur'an, when dealing with modern Israel. It would be wrong to dismiss these references as imaginary, but at the same time it would be wrong to take them as representative of contemporary Muslim opinion. From everything we know about the best Muslim political theorists, it is conceivable that some of them might also have called for a *jihad* to expel infidels from the Land of the Holy Places. Yet such a select reading of scriptural sources and extra-scriptural authority does not sit well with the great majority of contemporary Muslims: for all but a few, implacable warfare in the name of *jihad* is not the sole or the best measure of Islamic loyalty. There must be a search for social justice, at home and abroad. There is more to life than dying for a cause, however noble the cause.

What then are the prospects of this cause for which Bin Laden is prepared to lay down his own life? It is clear that what originally launched him on his hugely ambitious undertaking was the confidence instilled by the victory of the *mujahidin* over the Red Army in Afghanistan, followed by the withdrawal of American forces from Somalia in 1993. If one superpower could be defeated, and even ultimately destroyed, by warriors of the faith, why should not the other, which had proved much less resilient in Mogadishu? This dream was based on two great miscalculations. Like many revolutionaries—the Russians after 1917, the Cubans after 1959—Bin Laden and his associates ignored the special conditions that had given them victory in one society, imagining it could be reproduced with the same tactics in other societies. But Afghanistan was like no other country of the Middle East: it was economically and culturally much less developed, ethnically more divided, geographically much more inaccessible, with unique traditions of mountain warfare and resistance to the invader. Even so, it required massive amounts of US finance and weaponry, and the full backing of the Pakistani state, for the *mujahidin* to prevail. Bin Laden's reluctance to admit the scale of this assistance meant that he later overestimated the ability of the Taliban, isolated from any external support, to withstand the subsequent American assault. The Afghan experience could not be mechanically repeated elsewhere; it was more vulnerable in itself than he had imagined. As for Somalia, the inconsequential American landings there, more a public relations than a strategic operation, were no gauge of the powers of the Pentagon. The effect of both Afghanistan and Somalia seems to have been to lure him into illusions of US fickleness and weakness.

Connected to these miscalculations is the nature of his religious vision itself. One of its most striking features is the absence of any social dimension. Bin Laden was barred from the kind of analysis that would have allowed him to distinguish the different structural features of the various Muslim societies in which *jihad* was to be awakened, and made him hesitate in inflecting the notion of "One, Two, Three, Many Afghanistans." Morally, he does denounce a host of evils. Some of them—unemployment, inflation, and corruption—are social. But where is an alternative vision of the ideal society? There is an almost complete lack of any social program. This alone makes it clear how limited al-Qaʿida is as a phenomenon. The lack of any set of social proposals separates it not just from the Red Army Faction of the Red Brigades, with which it has sometimes mistakenly been compared, but—more significantly—from the earlier wave of radical Islamism, whose leading thinker was the great iconoclast Sayyid Qutb.

In place of the social, there is a hypertrophy of the sacrificial. Bin Laden's messages rarely hold out radiant visions of final triumph. His emphasis falls far more on the glories of martyrdom than the spoils of victory. Rewards belong essentially to the hereafter. This is a creed of great purity and intensity, capable of inspiring its followers with a degree of passion and principled conviction that no secular movement in the Arab world has ever matched. At the same time, it is also a narrow and self-limiting one: it can have little appeal for the great mass of believers, who need more than scriptural dictates, poetic transports, or binary prescription to chart their everyday lives, whether as individuals or as collective members of a community, local or national, regional or global. Above all, there is no rush to restore a caliphate today. Bin Laden seems at some level to recognize the futility of a quest for restitution. He sets no positive political horizon for his struggle. Instead, he vows that *jihad* will continue until "we meet God and get his blessing!"

Despite these crippling weaknesses, the force of Bin Laden's appeal is far from spent. The reason for that is clear. Not only has the West's long-term abuse of the Middle East, which gives his movement its moral power, not been in any way amended since he began his struggle. It has now been aggravated by the Anglo-American occupation of Iraq, visiting biblical humiliation, destruction, and chaos on the third most hallowed land of the *umma* (after Mecca/Medina and Jerusalem). If ordinary Muslims doubted the designs ascribed to the West by Bin Laden before the invasion of March 2003, and all that has followed, fewer are likely to do so today. In the infernal landscape created by the shattering of Iraq, dedicated fighters inspired by his summons proliferate to carry out deadly suicide missions, alongside a nationalist resistance which has learned to cooperate with them. The ranks of *jihadis* are being replenished with every week that American forces and their allies remain. Can the carnage cease until they are driven out or devise a face-saving way to retreat?

Bin Laden's own fate remains uncertain. Unless he dies a natural death in hiding, it seems inevitable that sooner or later his hunter will catch him. *[Editor's Note: This happened on May 2, 2011.]* If captured alive, he will doubtless be killed on the spot, as Che Guevara was forty years ago. He is not troubled by the predictability of this end:

So let me be a martyr,
dwelling in a high mountain pass
among a band of knights who,
united in devotion to God,
descend to face armies.

The poem, which concludes his Sermon for the Feast of the Sacrifice, could be Bin Laden's epitaph.

His posthumous legend will live on, like that of Guevara, to inspire other such knights, until such time as different, more humane heroes can attract the idealism of Muslim youth, and chart a better way not only to liberate their homelands but also to forge a brighter future for those liberated.

Notes

Bruce B. Lawrence, introduction to *Messages to the World: The Statements of Osama bin Laden*, edited and introduced by Bruce B. Lawrence, translated by James Howarth (London: Verso, 2005), xi–xxiii.

1 "Questions for Prince Turki al-Faisal," *New York Times Magazine,* August 28, 2005, 11.
2 Bernard Lewis, "License to Kill," *Foreign Affairs,* November-December 1998.
3 [Michael Scheuer], *Imperial Hubris: Why the West Is Losing the War on Terror* (Washington, DC: Brassey's, 2004), 104, 114, 168, 103.
4 The Pew Trust Global Attitudes survey released on June 23, 2005, found that while Muslims are worried about the consequences for themselves of the war on terror, a surprising number still have confidence in bin Laden's conduct in world affairs. The sixteen nations covered in the survey included neither Saudi Arabia nor Iraq, where the extent of support for him was likely to be much greater than in the countries surveyed.
5 Michael Mann, *Incoherent Empire* (New York: Verso, 2003), 169.

SIXTEEN

Muslim Engagement with Injustice and Violence | 2013

In thinking about Islam and violence, when do we begin to track the connection of the two? Do we begin with 9/11 or 611? 9/11 is all too familiar: it conjures the stealth attack of Arab/Muslim suicide bombers, co-opting two planes, on the twin towers of the World Trade Center, a third plane attack on the US Pentagon, and a fourth crashed plane in Pennsylvania. After 9/11 and as a result of the traumatic death of more than three thousand people, the US government declared war on two Muslim-majority nations, global airport security forever changed, and American Muslims, as well as Muslims coming to the United States, became potential terrorist suspects.

But if 9/11 redefines Islam and violence, does it not also distort the long historical view of Muslims and their multiple responses to violence? If one begins not with 9/11 but almost 1,400 years earlier with 611, the story of Islam and violence changes dramatically. There was no Islam in 611, just an Arab merchant who felt called to be a prophet. The previous year, 610, when Muhammad ibn ʿAbd Allah experienced revelation for the first time, only his wife and a few others accepted his claim. His claim to prophecy depended on intermittent revelations, delivered in the face of hostility from local tribesmen, merchants, and idolaters in his hometown of Mecca. When Muhammad began preaching publicly, as he did in 612, the public reaction was not only negative but violent. From 612 till 622, there was continual, punitive violence directed against Muhammad and his tiny band. It was expressed at many levels: disregard of his lineage, since he had been orphaned, then raised by an uncle; disdain for his relative poverty, since he was not among the wealthy elite of Mecca; and outright rejection of his claim to represent a superior divine channel, a single all-encompassing God called Allah, rather than a pantheon of competing deities with several names.

Violence in the Earliest Phase of Islamic History

THE TIME OF THE PROPHET: SOCIETAL VERSUS MILITARY VIOLENCE

If we begin in 611 rather than 9/11, the first expression of violence and Islam is not violence directed by or sanctified through Islam but rather violence against Muslims. Often that violence was a response to efforts by early Muslims to curtail pre-Islamic forms of violence. Throughout human history, societal violence has been as prevalent as military violence, and in early seventh-century Arabia one finds numerous forms of societal violence. These included, for instance, female infanticide, along with the abuse of orphans, the poor, and marginal. Against such forms of societal violence, the revelations mediated through Muhammad were clear, incontrovertible challenges to the social order of tribal Mecca. For instance, they prohibited the pre-Islamic Arabian practice of female infanticide as well as other bodily and social abuses through directives set down, transmitted, and encoded in the Qur'an. Consider the following:

> *And when the infant girl who was buried is asked*
> *For what offense she was killed*
> *[the person who killed her will have to answer*
> *for his sin on Judgment Day].*
> *(Qur'an [Q] 81:8–9)*[1]
> *Do not kill your children out of fear of poverty;*
> *We will provide for them, and for you.*
> *Indeed, killing them is a great sin. (Q 17:31)*

What these two passages reflect is that in pre-Islamic Arabia killing of female infants was very common; often the moment a female was born she was buried alive. Islam not only prohibits female infanticide, but it forbids all types of infanticide, irrespective of whether the infant is a male or female. Consider the following:

> *You should not kill your children on account of poverty—*
> *We provide for you and for them.*
> *And do not approach the property of the orphan,*

> *except with what is better till he comes of age.*
> *Take not life which God has made sacred. (Q 6:151–52)*

It is difficult to imagine how precarious life was in 611 and not just for children and women but also, and especially, for orphans. Consider the following directive, set forth in the chapter dedicated to women:

> *Give orphans their property,*
> *Without exchanging bad for good;*
> *—And if you fear you cannot*
> *Do justice by the orphans,*
> *Then marry women who please you,*
> *Two, three, or four;*
> *But if you fear you won't be equitable,*
> *Then one, or a legitimate bondmaid of yours,*
> *That way it is easier for you not to go wrong. (Q 4:2–3)*

The irony of the preceding passage is its misapplication during subsequent Muslim history. In the course of centuries, Muslim jurists overlooked both the context for this revelation—to care equitably for the orphan—and its qualification—if you cannot be equitable to two, three, or four women (who have been previously married and have children now orphaned without a father), then marry but one woman or cohabit with a legitimate bondmaid, as Abraham did with Hagar, producing Ishmael. Caring for orphans is the crucial rationale for plural marriage during the earliest period of Islamic history. It could even be argued that it is the sole rationale for plural marriage, and so the first signpost of violence in Islam is not the violence inherent in Qur'anic dicta but rather the greater violence of the preceding, non-Islamic period known as *jahiliyya*, or period of ignorance. And the revelation of the Qur'an, along with the formation of a Muslim community (*umma*), was intended to curtail rather than to expand or export violence.

THE QUR'AN AS A GUIDEPOST FOR EARLY MUSLIMS

It was difficult, however, to sustain the purity of thought and the dedication of purpose indicated in those early chapters (*surahs*). They were revealed to the Prophet intermittently over twelve years, from 610 to 622, and during that time Muslims were the nonviolent members of Arabian society in general, urban Mecca in particular. At one moment, it seemed that Muhammad's nonviolent responses to the provocations of his hostile countrymen would jeopardize the entire Muslim experiment. In 617 the Prophet sent some of his closest followers and relatives next door, across the Red Sea, to Abyssinia (Ethiopia). Their enemies followed them and demanded that the traitorous Muslims be handed over to them and returned to face justice, that is, certain death, in Mecca. When the Christian king asked the fearful Muslims to explain their faith, one of their band recited to him a revelation that had just come to the Prophet. It included the first forty verses of *Surat Maryam,* and so closely did these verses parallel Christian scripture, belief, and hope that the king granted them asylum. That first *hijra,* or exodus, was yet another instance when violence was prevented, rather than abetted, by the earliest Muslims, and the medium of their pursuit for justice, peace, and equality were those revelations that later became the Noble Book, the Holy Qur'an.

Later the bar of restraint moved higher and higher for Muhammad and his followers. By 622, life had become intolerable for the hardy cohort of Muslims. Consider the power of their enemies. All of them were connected to Mecca, either to Muhammad's close relatives or to tribesmen who had resolved to defeat him and, if possible, to kill him. The early followers faced curses and death threats from prominent Meccans, some of whom were relatives of the Prophet. Public spectacles were made of slaves who had converted to Islam, and they were targeted for verbal shame as well as physical harassment. In instance after instance, violence was directed at Muslims, not perpetrated by Muslims.

THE FIRST INSTANCES OF MUSLIM-INITIATED WAR

Once Muhammad established a community of followers in Medina, he had no choice but to fight his Meccan enemies who continued to pursue him. As the Qur'an represents it, God had declared: "Permission to fight is given to those on whom war is made" (Q 22:39).

But war was always and everywhere to be defensive. The war Muhammad waged against Mecca was not a struggle for prestige or wealth; it was, in his view, a war for survival, of both the community and the faith. His helpers from Medina joined the migrants from Mecca. They provided the migrants with food and with shelter from their own resources, but they were all stretched to the limit. They had to raid caravans. They raided only small caravans at first and never attacked during those times when fighting, especially blood feuds, was prohibited by Meccan custom. As someone who had guided many a successful caravan to its destiny, Muhammad knew the routes. He knew the seasons. He also knew the wells where Meccan traders would pass with their camels and their goods.

In December 623, more than a year after the beleaguered Muslims had fled to Medina, Muhammad ordered a small detachment to spy on a caravan to the south. It was proceeding along the route to Yemen, at the oasis of Nakhlah that links Mecca to Taif. Since it was a holy month, he had ordered his followers not to attack but they disobeyed. Killing some, they took others captive and brought the caravan back to Medina. Muhammad was appalled. Not only had his followers disobeyed him, but they had disobeyed the divine command to fight only in defense of one's own life and property. Their actions mirrored his leadership. He was responsible. The prophet who had pledged to be a divine mediator had betrayed his own prophecy. Riven with distress, he prayed to God. He needed guidance from above. And when it came, it was at once clear and compelling:

> *They ask you about war in the holy month.*
> *Tell them: "To fight in that month is a great sin.*
> *But a greater sin in the eyes of God is*
> *to hinder people from the way of God,*
> *and not to believe in Him,*
> *and to bar access to the Holy Mosque*
> *and to turn people out of its precincts.*
> *And oppression is worse than killing."*
> *They will always seek war against you till*
> *They turn you away from your faith, if they can.*
> *But those of you who turn back on their faith*
> *and die disbelieving will have wasted their deeds*
> *in this world and the next.*
> *They are inmates of Hell,*
> *and abide there forever. (Q 2:217)*

This revelation had replaced a rule of principle with one of practical moral value. Yes, killing is forbidden in the sacred month (Q 2:191), but worse than killing is oppression, hindering people from the way of God. Empowered by this divine dictum, Muhammad accepted and divided the spoils of war from his followers at Nakhlah.

More war would follow. Muhammad and his followers entered into an unending conflict with their Meccan kinsmen and opponents. From 623 to 632, Muhammad planned thirty-eight battles that were fought by his fellow believers. He led twenty-seven military campaigns. The nonviolent protestor had become a general, waging war again and again. The first full-scale military campaign came at the wells of Badr, in 624, less than four months after the skirmish at Nakhlah. Muslims chose to attack a caravan coming south from Palestine to Mecca. The Meccans learned of their attack, opposing them with a force that far outnumbered the Muslim band. Muhammad and his followers should have lost; they would have lost, except for the intervention of angels (Q 3:122–27).

While the Battle of Badr projected the small Muslim community onto a stage marked as cosmic, with divine intervention as the basis for military victory, its outcome provoked fear in the Meccans. It also made them resolve even more firmly to defeat the upstart Muslims. By 625 the mighty Meccan general Abu Sufyan had assembled a huge army of both foot soldiers and cavalry. He marched toward Medina. The Muslims countered by moving out of the city proper. They engaged their rivals on the slopes of a nearby mountain, Uhud. Despite the superior numbers of the Meccans, it went well for the Muslims till some of Muhammad's followers broke ranks too early, in anticipation of another victory such as Badr. The Meccans then counterattacked, and Khalid ibn al-Walid, one of the brilliant Meccan nobles, led his squadron to the unprotected rear of the Muslim formation and, catching them unawares, began a great slaughter. The Muslims were soundly defeated, with Muhammad wounded in the mayhem that day.

Yet the Prophet resolved to learn the deeper lesson behind this bitter defeat. He regarded the defeat of Uhud to be as important for Islam as the victory of Badr, for in defeat as in victory the Muslims had to acknowledge that their fate was not theirs but God's to decide. The aftermath of the Battle of Uhud also reinforced Muhammad's resolve to secure the loyalty of all his followers—both those who were Muslims and those who were non-Muslims yet bound to him by treaty. There followed some difficult, often bloody purges of tribes near Medina, and then the major Battle of the Trench in 627. A mighty Meccan army was led again by Abu Sufyan, the architect of Uhud. Abu Sufyan had tried to invade Medina, to defeat and destroy Muslims once and for all. Yet as understood by Muslims, God—and God alone—granted Muslims victory there. In the aftermath of this victory, fierce foes such as Abu Sufyan and the fiery Khalid ibn al-Walid ceased to oppose the Muslims and instead joined their ranks.

Beyond the battlefield, Muhammad never ceased trying to convert his Meccan opponents to the religion of Islam. Though he had forsaken nonviolence, he had not embraced violence as a way of life, only as an expedient to a higher end. He contacted the Meccans to propose a peaceful pilgrimage. He assured their leaders of his intention, yet they doubted him. It took until 629, seven years after he had left Mecca, before he and his followers were allowed to reenter their native city. At last all Muslims—those Meccans who initially had immigrated to Medina, those Medinans who had joined them, and other tribes who had become their allies then also submitted to God—were able to return to Mecca in a peaceful pilgrimage.

When they returned in January 630, Muhammad made a singular decision. Instead of vengeance, Muhammad forgave all but his bitterest enemies. Yet another military encounter quickly followed on the heels of the peaceful pilgrimage. It happened one month later, in February 630. It was a bigger battle than any Muslims had seen since Uhud, and it came not from Mecca but from beyond. Many Bedouin tribes who were opposed to Islam saw the reentry to Mecca as provocation for their own ferocious, full-scale assault on the Muslims. The Battle of Hunain was indeed fierce. Many of Muhammad's followers panicked. Once again, from the Muslim point of view, it was the Almighty and the angelic host—not Muslim numbers or their military prowess—that brought them victory. The Qur'an once again marked the event:

> *Indeed God has helped you on many occasions,*
> *Even during the battle of Hunain,*
> *When you were elated with joy at your numbers*
> *Which did not prove of the least avail,*
> *So that the earth and its expanse became too narrow for you,*
> *And you turned back and retreated.*
> *Then God sent down a sense of tranquility*
> *On His Apostle and the faithful;*
> *And sent down troops invisible*
> *To punish the infidels.*
> *This is the recompense of those who do not believe. (Q 9:24b)*

Muslims had scarcely absorbed the victory of Hunain when other challenges beyond their borders arose. They had to engage the Byzantines, they had to levy taxes among recalcitrant Bedouin tribes, and, above all, they had to purify their central rite, the pilgrimage or hajj, removing every vestige of pagan practice.

MUSLIM WARS AFTER MUHAMMAD: THE SPECIAL CASE OF RIDDA AND THE PROBLEM OF RETALIATION

After Muhammad's death in 632, his experiment, based so squarely on his personal authority, almost came unhinged. It was a delicate moment when a new leader, one of his trusted followers, Abu Bakr, was elected his successor, or *khalifa*. When several tribes tried to withdraw from the treaty that bound them to Muhammad, Abu Bakr fought them in what became known as the Ridda wars, the wars of apostasy or repudiation of Islam. For many scholars, this period initiates the practice of open warfare in the name of Islam. It is said to be the time when *jihad*, or war in defense of the faith, came to be associated with Islamic expansion. Yet according to the historian Fred Donner, the Ridda wars, while testing the new Muslim state's capacity to integrate and organize Arabia's tribesmen, did not meet the standard of *jihad*, and neither the Ridda wars nor the expansionary wars that continued through the next period of nascent Islamic history should be defined as *jihad*.

According to Donner, the following three interlocking concepts defined the nascent Muslim experiment: (1) the idea of a single, indivisible community united by faith, that is, "the universal community of believers, reflecting its character as the body of worshipers of the one and universal God"; (2) the concept of absolute authority mediated through a binding, divine law; and (3) the notion of a central human authority transferable from Muhammad to his successors.[2] The second concept—absolute authority mediated through divine law—was crucial since it curtailed, while not eliminating, the protocol of retaliation, requital, or *lex talionis*. Qur'anic passages support this shift:

> *Believers, requital is prescribed*
> *For you in cases of murder;*
> *The free for the free, the slave for the slave,*
> *And the female for the female.*
> *But if anyone is forgiven*
> *Anything by his brother,*
> *Let fairness be observed*
> *And goodly compensation. (Q 2:178)*
> *And do not take a life*
> *That God has made sacred,*
> *Except for just cause*
> *And if anyone is killed unjustly,*
> *We have given his next of kin*
> *A certain authority;*
> *But he should not be excessive in killing;*
> *For he has been given divine support*
> *(to be restrained). (Q 17:33)*

Especially crucial is the protocol for requital among believers, announced in the fourth chapter of the Qur'an. It is long but pivotal and consequential for Muslim attitudes toward interpersonal violence:

> *It is never right*
> *For a believer to kill a believer,*
> *Except by mistake;*
> *And one who kills a believer by mistake*
> *Is to free a believing slave,*
> *And compensation is to be handed over*
> *To the family of the deceased,*
> *Unless they forego it to charity.*
> *If the deceased was from a people*
> *Warring against yours,*
> *Yet was a believer,*
> *Then free a believing slave.*
> *But if the deceased was from a people*
> *With whom you have a treaty,*
> *Then compensation is to be paid*
> *To the family of the deceased,*
> *And a believing slave is to be freed.*
> *And if one has not the means,*
> *Then one is to fast*
> *For two consecutive months,*
> *As an act of contrition granted*
> *As a concession from God.*
> *And God is all-knowing, most judicious. (Q 4:92)*

All of these conditions—God as authority, the community as resource, the successor as leader—are crucial for defining both the Islamic polity and its impetus for expansion through war. *Jihad*, when it does occur, appears only as an ancillary, incidental concept. Of course, early Muslim warriors were motivated by the prospect of either booty (if they survived) or paradise (if they were slain), but *jihad* entered as "a product of the rise of Islam, not a cause of it—a product, to be exact, of the impact of the new concept of the *umma* on the old (tribal) idea that one fought, even to the death, for one's own community."[3] While there is a lot of fighting depicted in Islamic historical sources, such military encounters are known mostly as *maghazi* (raids) or *futuh* (conquests). Whenever *jihad* is invoked, it is a sidebar, not a central feature of the narrative depicting early Muslim warfare.

JIHAD INVOKED, REDEFINED, AND REAWAKENED

Over time what had been an incidental, qualified part of the Qur'anic message and the earliest Islamic worldview became an independent force on its own, so much so that some have declared *jihad* to be a sixth pillar of Islam (beyond the standard five—faith, ritual prayer, alms charity, fasting, and pilgrimage). The seminal text cited by all proponents of *jihad* as a collective duty incumbent on all Muslims is *Surat at-Tawbah* (Q 9). Here, Muslims are told that idolaters must be fought, polytheists leveled, and that the reward for those who struggle will be paradise:

> *(But) the messenger*
> *And those who believe with him*
> *Struggle with their possessions and their persons.*
> *So the good things are for them,*
> *And they are the successful ones.*
> *God has prepared gardens*
> *Under which rivers flow,*
> *Where they will abide.*
> *That is the great attainment. (Q 9:88–89)*

Yet neither this verse nor other Qur'anic pericopes motivated Muslims to engage in perpetual warfare against Byzantines, Sassanians, and other "people of the Book" after the death of Muhammad. In an analysis marked by consummate concern with detail and context, Carole Hillenbrand has shown how, by the early eighth century, Muslim navies had given up their century-long quest to conquer Constantinople. "It became the practice for both empires to engage in annual campaigns, described in the Islamic sources as *jihad* but these gradually became a ritual, important for the image of the caliph and the emperor, rather than being motivated by a vigorous desire to conquer new territories for their respective faiths."[4]

It was not until the eleventh century, with Saladin and the crusader conquest of Jerusalem, that *jihad* was revitalized. The crucial events were the fall of Jerusalem to the Crusaders in 1099; the recapture of Edessa from the crusaders by Saladin's father, Zengi, in 1144; and then, in 1187, Saladin's recapture of Jerusalem.

It was during the fateful twelfth century that the doctrine of *jihad* was revived and heralded as a paramount duty to preserve Muslim territorial, political, and symbolic integrity. "The process of the reawakening of *jihad*," notes Hillenbrand, "must have been slow and gradual, and in some part at least it must have come as a direct response to Crusader fanaticism, witnessed first-hand."[5]

One scholar has even gone so far as to argue that "the Crusades triggered the *jihad* mentality as we know it now." It was in response to the Crusades that Zengi and Saladin produced, for the first time in Islamic history, "a broad scale propaganda effort to praise *jihad* and *jihad*-warriors. Jerusalem became the center of *jihad* propaganda, and Saladin extended its sanctity to Syria, reminding everyone that Syria (too) is the Holy Land and that Muslims are responsible for defending and protecting it (against foreign assaults)."[6]

Later, the doctrine of *jihad* was amplified and applied anew in the thirteenth and fourteenth centuries after the Mongols plundered Baghdad, ravaged the Muslim world, and then themselves became Muslims. It was Ibn Taymiyya (d. 1328), one of the most influential jurists in Islamic history, who inveighed against the Mongols. His favorite tool for anathematizing them was *jihad*. "With Ibn Taymiyya," observes Hillenbrand, "*jihad* to [save] Jerusalem is replaced by an internal movement within the Dar al-Islam itself, both spiritual and physical.... Ibn Taymiyya sees the Muslim world assailed by external enemies of all kinds, and in his strong desire to purify Islam and Islamic territory from all intrusion and corruption, he advocates: "the only solution to fight [is] jihad so that 'the whole of religion may belong to God.'"[7]

Violence in the Gunpowder Empires

THE OTTOMAN CASE

Is violence waged by an Islamic empire or nation always an expression of *jihad*, or religious violence? One could argue that it is less *jihad* than other features of structural violence that came to characterize the major Muslim empires of the premodern era. Beginning in the fifteenth century and, in part, due to the violence unleashed by the Mongols, a simpler political map of the Nile-to-Indus region, or the core Islamic world, emerged. It was characterized by three regionally based empires: the Ottoman, Safavid, and Mughal. They represented the core population of the Muslim world by 1800, perhaps 70 percent of all Muslims, and much of what today is regarded as Muslim expressions of violence can be traced to the structural elements that characterized each of these empires.[8] For clarity of insight into violence—its causes, expressions, and outcomes—the focus will be on the Ottoman Empire. The Sunni Ottomans, based in Anatolia and southeastern Europe, absorbed nearly all of the Arabic-speaking lands with the exception of Morocco and parts of the Arabian Peninsula. Theirs became the dominant regional power, although Shiʿa Iran emerged as a formidable foe and bloody conflicts between the two countries erupted periodically. Mughal India, officially a foe of neither the Ottomans nor the Safavids, benefited from their mutual antagonism. Especially the persecution and expulsion of non-Shiʿa Muslims from Safavid Iran provided some of the human resources—artistic, intellectual, and religious—that made possible the splendor of the Great Mughals. Islam remained a central focus of identity as well as the ideological underpinning for a variety of social and political movements. The period saw the establishment of Shiʿism as the state religion of Iran, with the forced conversion of its largely Sunni population under Safavid pressure. New Sufi orders emerged throughout the region, one of them actually serving as the precursor to the state-sponsored Shiʿism of Safavid Iran. Often Sufi orders became vehicles of protest against the establishment, nowhere more evidently than the Naqshbandi-Mujaddidi movement of North India. Toward the end of this period in Arabia, the Muslim puritanical movement of the Wahhabis rose to challenge both Sufi practices and Ottoman authority.

Violence must also be traced through its implication in the political order, not least in the way that it was managed for the preservation of the empire so that the rulers of various Muslim empires, like their non-Muslim counterparts elsewhere, became the sole legitimate purveyors of violence. There was never a question of eliminating violence but rather justifying its use for higher ends.

One must instead ask again the question: is warfare, when declared by a Muslim ruler, always and everywhere a reflex of Islamic norms and values? That was the question that occupied Ibn Taymiyya, but its practical consequence was nil, since much of the violence that characterized premodern Islamic polities was intra-Islamic, that is, Muslims were fighting Muslims for imperial gain, better taxation, and public prestige. Consider the case of the Ottomans.

In its origins, the Ottoman Empire goes back to the thirteenth century and the Seljuks. The first of the newly converted Turkish nomads to expand beyond their Central Asian homeland, the Seljuks had overrun Buyid Iran in the eleventh century and conquered Baghdad by 1055. The Seljuks created a new empire in the name of Islam, but they also drew on Sasanian traditions still in place with their conquered subjects. They had a graduated taxation system that depended for its efficiency on *iqtas,* or land grants. Warriors were supported through *iqtas* in return for their service on behalf of the Seljuk rulers.

The Seljuks were also assisted and tested by Turcomans, nomadic frontiersmen with less interest in settled or city life than the Seljuks. The Turcomans helped the Seljuks by operating as *ghazis,* or warriors for the faith, on the frontiers with the Byzantine Empire. They readily invoked *jihad* in their cause. After the Battle of Manzikert, where the Seljuks defeated the Byzantines in 1071, the Turcomans helped to Islamize and Turkify the region of Anatolia, still culturally linked to Byzantium.

The Seljuks might have become the masters of Anatolia and survived much longer had they not become victims of the Mongols. The same Mongol invasion that led to the sack of Baghdad in 1258 had earlier led to a Seljuk defeat in 1243. The Seljuks survived as a reduced polity in Asia Minor but also as a vassal Mongol state; their last sultan died in 1306. In the meantime, between 1260 and 1320, the Turcomans, mobilized by their *ghazi* tribal chiefs, and in tandem with the Seljuks, waged *jihad* against Byzantine forces that still held parts of Anatolia. Their leader was Osman Ghazi, who held the frontier land in western Asia Minor that was farthest north and closest to the Byzantines. He gained immense prestige when he defeated an imperial Byzantine army in 1301 at the Battle of Baphaeon. Many other nomadic Turkish soldiers came to Konya, Osman's capital. They became known as *beys,* commanders of complements of fighters who were loyal to them, just as they, in turn, were loyal to Osman. At Osman's death, his son, Orhan, expanded the empire still further, capturing major strategic and commercial cities in Anatolia. Bursa became the new Osmanli capital after 1326 and remained so until 1402.

At the same time as they were expanding in the east, the Ottomans were also making inroads into the Balkans, and a measure of their success is that one of Orhan's successors, Murad, made Adrianople (also referred to as Edirne) his capital in order to consolidate Ottoman conquests in what was known as Rumeli. The success of the Ottomans invoked Islam and the doctrine of *jihad,* but it was banked on the logic and limits of conquest. They formed a pyramidal military state, with roots that went deep into local society, and allowed the Ottoman sultan at the apex to control the *beys,* who also represented geographical and economic interests crucial to the burgeoning state.

As ideal as the system sounds, it had limits inherent in the very strengths that made the system possible. Ottomans were heirs to the Byzantine as well as the Sasanian empires. Like their Umayyad predecessors, it was the Byzantine model, especially as reflected in Istanbul, which both fueled and restricted their imagination. They expanded by conquest, making the army responsible for two fronts: one in Asia and one in Europe. Yet the army could only fight when the sultan was on the battlefield to lead his troops in person. The competitive pull of two war zones produced a major donnybrook for the fledgling Ottoman state in 1387. Murad I had to confront an Anatolian resistance movement, the Karmanids, at the same time as the Serbs, joined by dissatisfied Bosnians and Bulgarians, were posing a challenge in the Balkans. Though the Ottomans won the Battle of Kosovo in 1389, Murad was killed in the fray, and in its aftermath his son and successor, Bayazid, executed the Serbian king, Lazar.

More threatening to the state than Anatolian or Balkan rivals, however, was the emergence in the east, in Rum, of a threat from Central Asia. It came from the Chagatai Turkish successor to the Mongols: Timur Leng, or Tamerlane. When Ottoman and Timurid forces clashed in Ankara in 1402, the Timurids were victorious. Bayazid, humiliated as well as defeated, died at his own hand a year later in 1403. The Ottoman experiment, like many of its *ghazi* emirate neighbors, might have vanished with Bayazid, but it survived for several reasons. First, it had attained legitimacy as a Muslim polity when Bayazid, anticipating the threat of Tamerlane, had invested himself with recognition as an official Muslim ruler: the Mamluk ruler of Cairo had become the caliph or nominal leader of all Muslims after the Mongol sack of Baghdad in 1256, and in 1394 he made Bayazid the sultan of Rum. Second, he had introduced a system of recruitment and administration that conjoined the *timar* land-grant system with the expansion of territory. Like his Seljuk predecessors, he recruited non-Muslim youth, then, after converting them to Islam, had them trained as slaves, or *ghulams*, for military and palace duty. In effect, Murad began what became known as the janissary system, a backbone of later Ottoman state policy.

The religious establishment was important as a third element of regime enhancement. Bayazid fostered it as he did the janissary or slave system, extending patronage to its recipients but at a price: preferential deferral or even outright acquiescence in the authority of the state. Muslim scholars and teachers, Sufi masters, and juridical experts came from neighboring Islamic polities to Anatolia and to the Ottoman court. They came because the emperor offered patronage: they were expected to assist him in his effort to be not just a conquering *ghazi* but also a Muslim sultan. In other words, Islam became an explicit ideology, and a building block of public prestige, for the newest Turkish Muslim empire.

The defining moment for the new Ottoman polity came in 1453 when Muhammad II, also known as Mehmed the Conqueror, achieved an ambition that had eluded all his Muslim predecessors: the conquest of Constantinople (Istanbul). It was a singular moment that saw not just the collapse of the truncated Byzantine Empire but also the dedication of Constantinople as a Muslim capital city.

Following the conquest of Istanbul, Syria, Egypt, and the Hijaz region of Arabia were conquered in the early sixteenth century. The conquest of Egypt conferred further Islamic legitimacy, as the caliphate devolved from the defeated Mamluks to the victorious Ottomans. With the possession of Jerusalem, Mecca, and Medina, they controlled the three holiest cities in Islam. Rumeli (the Balkans) remained no less important to the imperial ambitions of the sultans: by the sixteenth century, Belgrade and Hungary, Moldavia, and Wallachia and Transylvania had all become tributary principalities under nominal Christian rulers. But the Ottomans were limited by the need to maintain supply lines to their sources. On the European front, they could not go beyond Vienna, where the time frame for sieges was limited and so never succeeded. On the southern rim of the Mediterranean, they continued to expand beyond Egypt, annexing Algiers, Tripoli, and Tunis and establishing *beys* and *deys* as rulers or surrogates on behalf of the Ottoman sultan, who was now also the commander of the faithful. Thus, at its apogee under Suleiman I in the mid-sixteenth century, the Ottoman realm was the most powerful empire in the world.

Overshadowing his nearest European rival, Suleiman I enjoyed revenue twice that of Charles V. But the state had limits both theoretical and empirical. In theory, it sustained an Islamic empire, with the sultan the uncontested source of religious as well as secular authority. He combined in himself the apogee of *shariʿa* (religious) and *qanun* (civil) law. Suleiman was known as *Suleiman qanuni*. The notion of the state as a harmonious structure permeated the state military and civilian bureaucracies. It derived from the classic Perso-Turkish source, Nasiruddin Tusi (d. 1273). No theory or account of Islam and violence can be complete without reference to Tusi's circle of justice. The circle of justice became the basis for Ottoman consciousness. Since the Sasanian social ethic emphasized order, stability, legality, and harmony among the theoretical four estates of priests, soldiers, officials, and workers, Tusi recycled Sasanian principles within an Islamic program. Tusi projected a dual function: hierarchical duties mirroring a consensual reciprocity between different groups, each aware of its specific role in the hierarchy. While the loyalty structure is a pyramid, its function is projected as a circle, the circle of justice. There can be no royal authority without the military (*askeri*):

> There can be no military without wealth
> The reaya or agriculturalists produce the wealth
> The sultan keeps the loyalty of the reaya by ensuring justice
> Justice requires harmony in the world
> The world is a garden,
> its walls are the state
> The state's axis is the religious law
> There is no support for religious law without royal authority.[9]

The elegance of this formulation belies its inner tension. The accent is on justice rather than right religion as the basis for effective rule, not eliminating conflict or violence but redirecting its force to the benefit of the state. While the ruler and the ruled depend on each other, their relationship remains asymmetric, for the circle begins and ends with the state and its supreme subject, the ruler. Only the middle line suggests that harmony and justice are coterminous one with the other, yet justice is not justice between equals but rather justice as "just" rewards or allotted payments for participation in the system. It never approaches parity, much less equality. The religious classes, custodians of religious law, require state support, just as the state, in turn, requires the *askeri* or military classes as both custodians of security and forward line of conquest. One could either label this system as controlled violence or the harmonious balance of competing self-interests, but it projects a consistent stress on justice.

Enlightenment notions of nonreligious loyalty to a state marked by both equality and justice for all are confounded in the Sasanian, then Ottoman notion of justice as a circle with the ruler at its center and also its apex. The pyramidal nature of authority becomes clear when one traces the circle via the four classes or differentiated orders, also derived from Tusi. The men of the sword dominate, with the men of the pen as their closest allies, while all other groups, whether Muslim or non-Muslim, urban or rural, have a lesser stake in the system but cannot escape its influence.

A review of its empirical limits demonstrates the fault lines within the Ottoman Empire. The system could only work as long as the conquests continued. Suleiman's reign may have been the apogee of power, but it also cast a shadow on the subsequent period of Ottoman history. The last significant conquest in the Mediterranean theater was Cyprus in 1570 (soon after his reign), and no other conquest came till Crete in 1664 almost a century later. The battles to the east of Rum, specifically with the Iranian Safavids, did not produce any major territorial gains. Without conquests, the Ottoman state could not claim to be the major Muslim empire of its day. Lack of conquest undermined its own logic, signaling its reduction in status and eventual demise. The empire's ideology was two pronged. It was dominated by and oriented toward the bureaucracy and governing institutions, yet at the same time it was reinforced by the religious schools and courts. The focal point of the ideology was the emperor; the success of the system depended on his personal stature. The emperor was at the same time the supreme religious leader, the owner of all land, and the commander in chief of the armed forces.

So there were indices of autocratic violence—structural, societal, and political—that characterized not only the Ottoman Empire and also its rivals, the Safavids and Mughals, but also its regional subsets, later to become independent polities, from Morocco on the edge of the Atlantic to Egypt at the base of the Mediterranean.

Overshadowing these rivalries, however, was engagement with Europe, above all, a response, sometimes cooperative but more often oppositional, to European initiatives to control parts of Africa and Asia. Commercial trade became the Achilles heel for Ottomans as for other Muslim polities. Closely controlled by the state, trade was primarily in luxury items (Ottoman silk and Asian spices). It did not propel the economy out of its sense of self-sufficiency nor did it enable the state to control the number of competing centripetal forces within the empire that put Ottoman officialdom at risk in dealing with external polities, whether European or Muslim. Diplomatic relations with France revealed the strength as well as the weakness of the Ottoman system. A French-Ottoman alliance, forged in order to combat Charles V and the Holy Roman Empire, effectively delayed the Ottoman need to enter into permanent relations with other European powers until 1793, with the result that the Ottomans actually knew little about their future rivals, including the Russians. There were efforts to recuperate lost opportunities in the nineteenth century, but the great chase deprived not just the Ottomans but other Muslim polities from any sense of parity vis-à-vis their European rivals, then rulers.

COMPARATIVE PERSPECTIVES ON REGIONAL EMPIRES

Comparable political economic processes informed the Ottomans along with their neighbors and rivals, the Safavids and Mughals. The rise of each empire involved the imposition of a strong state with tribal origins on a predominantly agrarian economy and society. In all three cases, after a prosperous period of stable reproduction of social relations and expansion of wealth in the sixteenth century, a retreat or decline seems to have been registered in the seventeenth century in the form of agrarian crises with political economic causes and political outcomes.

Several major developments altered the political scene in the seventeenth and eighteenth centuries: the Ottoman Empire became decentralized as Istanbul's hold on the provinces weakened and autonomous authorities sprang up almost everywhere; the Safavid regime collapsed, giving way to several decades of internal fragmentation and turmoil; and Mughal India reached its apogee, only to be sacked by Nadir Shah, an Afghani adventurer, in the early eighteenth century.

Alongside the shifts in the internal power relations came changes in the region's position in regard to Europe. While Safavids, Ottomans, and Mughals remained largely untouched by European culture, they now fought and traded with Europeans on a more extensive basis than before and on increasingly unfavorable terms. Military conflict with European countries raged along a wide front extending from the Black Sea area and the Balkans to the western Mediterranean and the Indian Ocean. The region's armies were able to hold their own until the second half of the eighteenth century, when disastrous defeats by Russia and the easy fall of Egypt to Napoleon brought home to the Ottoman leaders the recognition that global power had shifted definitely in favor of Europe.

EUROPEAN COLONIAL PRESENCE AND VIOLENT MUSLIM RESPONSES

There is no generic category of religious protest that applies to the modern period of world history, from 1600 to the present.[10] Instead, there are three distinct phases of Islamically valorized protest. In each phase, certain Muslim groups revolted against the ascendant, which has become the dominant, world order linked to Western Europe. Only the first phase is properly speaking revivalist. It is succeeded by a second that can and should be termed reformist, and it is only after the revivalist and reformist phases and, in large part, due to their failures that what is now termed Islamic fundamentalism or Islamism emerged.

All three—revivalism, reformism, and fundamentalism—are historically specific socioreligious movements propelling marginalized male leaders into public view as they attempt to reclaim the space challenged and reduced, impoverished and redefined, by the expanding sea powers of Western Europe. From the eighteenth century to the present, all the major Muslim polities experienced financial crises, demographic disruption, and agricultural stagnation. If there is a case to be made for structural violence as the backdrop and often the catalyst for physical violence, then the European interlude must be considered when addressing the topic of Islam and violence. Some of the malaise in early modern Muslim polities resulted from indigenous challenges. Provincial Arabs chafed under Ottoman Turkish rule, Afghans protested Qajar control within Iran, and Marathas rebelled against Mughal hegemony in South Asia. In each instance, however, the situation of ruling elites was complicated and worsened by the external diversion of commodity trade from the Mediterranean and Indian Ocean routes to the Atlantic Ocean following the discovery and exploitation of the New World and the internal infiltration of European trade through a nexus of foreign merchants and local middlemen or compradors cooperating to establish new products, new markets, and new communication networks also as new sources of profit and reinvestment. Islam, in effect, became an idiom of protest against the gradual contraction of internal and external trade, brought about by the mercantile activities of European maritime nations, specifically, the Portuguese, Spanish, Dutch, British, and French.

What was contested in the name of Islam by Islamic revivalists was control over vital commodities—slaves, textiles, coffee, tea, and spices—as well as gold, all trafficked along the major trade routes from the Atlantic coast of West Africa to the Indonesian archipelago. The major Muslim revivalist movements were without exception preindustrial. Their leaders mobilized followers in response to the European redirection of global trade, even when they did not acknowledge the extent to which European advances were reshaping their lives.

One of the earliest instances of European influence concerns the upstart Wahhabis. In western Arabia, the Wahhabis aligned with a Najdi chief named Ibn Saʿud. That combination in time produced what is now regarded as a legitimate government, though it remains the only Muslim polity named after a tribal group: the present-day Kingdom of Saudi Arabia. Both Ibn Saʿud and his appointed ideologue, Muhammad Ibn ʿAbd al-Wahhab, benefited from the loss of revenues suffered by their chief rival, the *sharif* of Mecca, who in the eighteenth century reigned as the legitimate ruler of the Hijaz. Dependent as he was on the lucrative Indian trade, primarily in textiles, indigo, and spices, the *sharif* could not sustain its diversion away from the Arabian Peninsula by the British. Weakened economically, he also became vulnerable militarily. His Najdi rivals rallied to their side other groups who had been deprived by the British ascendancy in trade, and toward the end of the eighteenth century they were able to dislodge and replace the *sharif* of Mecca. Although the Wahhabis had other battles to wage, with the Turks and also with Muslim loyalists from rival tribes who did not accept their leadership, their initial success was a by-product of incipient European colonialism.

Unfortunately, the influence of Ibn ʿAbd al-Wahhab on both Muslim and non-Muslim scholarship of Islamic revivalism has led his movement to be overvalued beyond its actual historical achievement. It is often presumed that a literal, text-restricted reading of the Qurʾan prevailed from the origins of Islam. It did not, nor has it ever been the practice for most observant Muslims. Ibn ʿAbd al-Wahhab had a narrow reform agenda not shared with other eighteenth-century and later Muslim reforms. Even his notion of the boundaries of faith were limited to exploring and explaining the concepts of *tawhid* and *takfir*, *iman* and *kufr*, that is to say, how you make God exclusively one and declaim all other Muslims who fail to express the same level of creedal commitment. Ibn ʿAbd al-Wahhab never claimed to be a reinterpreter of the scholarly legacy of the past. He never concerned himself with the wider Muslim community and its integrity. He never addressed issues of tyranny and social justice.

Yet the Wahhabi paradigm created numerous analogues elsewhere on the seams of commercial activity that became increasingly under British rule. In northwestern India, Ahmad Shahid of Raebareli tried to wage war against indigenous groups, the Sikhs and Hindus, but the latter were better positioned than the north Indian *mujahidin* in regard to British commercial interests. The *mujahidin* were strategically isolated before being defeated on the battlefield by Sikhs. Elsewhere, in northeastern India, the Faraʾidis perceived the shift to a moneyed, international economy as advantageous to Hindu landlords while impoverishing Muslim peasant laborers. They mobilized resistance, at first in local protests, later in regionwide acts of defiance; neither succeeded in reversing the tides of change.

It was the same story, with different actors but a similar outcome, in Africa. The best-documented of the revivalist movements is the Fulani-Qadiris in Nigeria. It pitted Muslim herdsmen and traders against British markets and middlemen who were often being recruited from rival Muslim tribes. Though the revivalists enjoyed superb Islamic credentials, they were eventually defeated on the battlefield. There were temporary successes: the Sanusis prevailed in the Cyrenaica region near the Ottoman province of Libya, strengthening Islamic identity for more than fifty years until the Italian invasion of 1911. A Somali chieftain too was able to mobilize interior tribes against British, Italian, and French forces in the coastal areas near Mogadishu. He won several battles and continued to rule for more than twenty years, only to have the British bomb and machine-gun their way to victory in 1920. Finally, on the other side of the

Muslim world in Southeast Asia, a puritanical movement known as the Padris galvanized Sumatran Muslims dispossessed by the shift from gold and pepper trade to a new cash crop, coffee. During the course of the nineteenth century, the Padris were harassed and coerced, enduring defeat after defeat in bloody encounters before finally succumbing to the Dutch authorities.

All these revivalist movements were violent, yet they followed a pattern of responsive violence. It is not accidental that they all occurred at crucial seams in the expanding imperium of maritime Europe. All were Sunni Muslim movements. The single parallel within Shi'a Islam were the Baha'is, a group still despised by Twelver Shi'a clergy. The vilification masks a deeper fear: the first Baha'is embodied and projected the latent messianic impulse of Twelver Shi'ism. Yet the Baha'is became harbingers of ecumenical pluralism and so represent a graphic example of how Islam and violence cannot be neatly matched.

Apart from the Baha'is, Islamic revivalist groups were succeeded by Islamic reformers. Interposed between Islamic revivalism and Islamic fundamentalism, Islamic reformers are closely linked to nationalist movements, and in retrospect it can be seen that, despite their universalist rhetoric, almost all the Islamic reformers were shaped by the influences of the colonial period. Especially keen is the emphasis on science and technology in education, constitution and parliamentary democracy in politics, and the revised role of women in social life. If Muslim nationalism became mimetic, movements that claimed a loyalty to Islam were no less mimetic, picking up elements of the West that they hoped could be transformed into an Islamic system. Far from reacting with violence to European presence and control, they attempted to accommodate to an emergent, if asymmetric, world system. There is no independent Muslim movement after the colonial period; all are reacting to some force or series of forces that emanate from the Western world, which is to say northern Europe and the United States.

Muslim reformers recognized the power of the institutions that were propelling European maritime nations to a unique position of global prestige. The reformers came from those countries whose Muslim elites were most engaged by the specter of European commercial and military penetration—Egypt and India, Iran and Turkey before World War I, but then, following the war, also Tunisia, Algeria, and Morocco. The North African reformers coalesced into a movement known as Salafiyya, or Islamic scripturalism. Criticized for their unwitting promotion of anachronism, its leaders seemed to hark back to a golden age that never existed or at least could never be reconstructed, and so their passionate pleas merely drained energies away from the task at hand, to accommodate to the new reality of a European world order. Yet most of the reformers acted in good faith, as committed Muslims conflicted by the gap between Europe's pragmatic success and what seemed to be its spiritual vapidity. It was as though they were witnesses to a novel and "unholy" revelation. For them, "the arbiter of truth and knowledge suddenly ceased to be enclosed in the revealed word of God. Another text, with no specific author or format, had made a permanent intrusion. It was the West in its political systems, military presence and economic domination which now appeared in the background as an authoritative code of practice."[11]

But the authoritative code was not uniform. The intervening European powers quarreled with one another. Some Muslim polities, such as the Sharifian kingdom of Morocco, benefited from these quarrels, able to resist direct rule because no Mediterranean power wanted its rivals to control the seat of the Arab/Muslim West. But all polities were affected by the great wars, sometimes known as the Christian wars, which were waged by these self-same powers twice in the twentieth century. It was only due to the enormous expenditures and consequent destruction of these wars that protest movements among Muslims and others were able to mobilize into national liberation movements. Gradually, as the smoke cleared from the second of these horrific Christian wars, most Muslim ruling elites were able to grasp the laurel of independence. Even so, they were marked by divergent political systems.

Many countries that were not colonized directly, such as Saudi Arabia and Iran, still experienced the effects of colonial economic penetration into the eastern Mediterranean and Indian Ocean, and the structures that arose after independence reflect this influence, above all in the sphere of politics and law. It was because the nature of self-rule was shaped as much by European as by indigenous models that one must speak of "mimetic nationalism." Though Arab, as also non-Arab, Muslim leaders embraced nationalism to chart the path to independence, the models of governance were derived from the departing colonials. Whether one looks to constitutional charters or to the adoption of separate executive and legislative bodies, the impress of European precedents is evident. At the same time, the boundaries of new nations reflected a patchwork of compromise that was worked out by the European powers, not by their Muslim subjects. Saddam Hussein's invasion in the fall of 1990, justified by the prior manipulation of Iraq's borders with Kuwait, was at once justified and spurious. It was justified because the borders of all African and Asian countries were set in the colonial period or its immediate aftermath. It was spurious because many countries benefited as well as lost from such manipulation: without the addition of parts of Kurdistan, especially the oil-rich region around Mosul, Iraq, for instance, would not have had the geopolitical resources that make it potentially the economic giant among all Arab states.

The truth about the process by which postcolonial borders were decided may be simpler, though no prettier, than conspiracy theories allow: disparate communities of Asia and Africa had been welded together as parts of the British, French, or Dutch empires. They could not be dissolved and reconstituted in their precolonial form with independence. Often the conditions of self-rule had to be set by colonial authorities and imperial administration, because consent could not have been secured on any other basis. Yet the end result was to make the entire process of Arab/Muslim nationalism seem imitative or mimetic. It appealed only to a limited stratum of elites. The mechanisms to curb military control and to spur the emergence of a middle class were never set in place. Structural violence took on a new face, but it was still violent and its tensions, contradictions, and excesses continue to the present day.

While most Europeans and Americans have lived within "secure" national borders for several generations and see themselves as beneficiaries of the tradition of nation-state loyalty, many Third World citizens, and Afro-Asian Muslims, in particular, do not share either their experience or their trust. For most Muslims, it is hard to applaud the random, top-down process by which almost all their polities came to assume their present form. Not only the external boundaries of territory but also the internal boundaries of identity are open to challenge and reformulation. In thinking about Islamic protest, it is especially important to note how the clash at the core of all other clashes between nationalists and fundamentalists is the totalizing impulse guiding each. In the Muslim world, the state functions as an obedience context, and the rulers of the Muslim state demand total compliance with the state's vision of Islam. Tacitly it recognizes that the norms it imposes are not universally shared by all Muslims, yet publicly it arrogates to itself and to its custodians the right to decide which elements of Islamic belief and practice are to be supported. The memory of other Islams is too strong, however, to be erased. In each instance, Muslims have to decide how to preserve their symbolic identity within a public order that is antireligious at worst, as in the Union of Soviet Socialist Republics, China, Indonesia, and Turkey or pseudo-religious at best, as in most Arab states, Iran, Pakistan, and Bangladesh.

Twentieth- and now twenty-first-century nationalism produced for the entire Muslim world a cleavage of enormous magnitude. The most evident rift was between Muslims and the dominant culture of Western Europe. But an equally great divide developed among Muslims themselves, between those who were attracted to European achievements, seeking to appropriate their benefits, and those others who sought to oppose them.

While the legacy of colonialism reshaped the Muslim world into truncated territories and contested borders, capitalism left it with economies that could only function on the margins, benefiting the major powers of the high-tech era. These powers were the technologically advanced, professionally differentiated, and economically privileged societies of Western Europe, North America, and, now, East Asia. Even before the rubric of First, Second, and Third Worlds was invented in the 1950s, a Third World existed. It embraced all Muslim societies, even those benefiting from the petrodollar infusion that began in the 1950s and 1960s but did not accelerate until the 1970s and 1980s.

JIHAD IN MODERN TIMES

Among the ongoing effects of the postcolonial legacy in Muslim polities has been the overwhelming attention to Islam and violence. From medieval to modern to contemporary history, the trope of Islam as violence has focused on *jihad*, and so it is important to note how those who came to be labeled fundamentalists invoked the early experience of the Prophet Muhammad and the Medinan state on behalf of their own authority to proclaim *jihad*. None did so more stridently than Sayyid Qutb, the Muslim brother who opposed Nasser, the Egyptian president from 1954 to 1970. Executed on charges of sedition in 1966, Sayyid Qutb produced a series of writings, some from prison, that exposed modern-day nationalism as itself a form of *jahiliyya*. In effect, it was equated with the kind of tribal order that Muhammad had opposed and that he, together with his early followers, had to overcome in order to establish the *umma*, or single supra-tribal Muslim community. In one of his most memorable string of homologies, Qutb reappropriated nationalism for "true" Islam: "nationalism is belief, homeland is Dar al-Islam, the ruler is God, and the constitution is the Qur'an."[12]

Qutb's message and his resort to *jihad* as the just cause for Muslims under threat resonated through Egypt and the Arab world and with the Taliban and the attackers of 9/11. It is impossible to make this temporal transition from the seventh to the twenty-first century without noting how eschatological religion is instrumentalized through modern means, not least martyr operations. The connection has been nimbly charted by Hans Kippenberg:

> When they attacked the United States in September 2001, jihadists were interpreting the Middle East conflict in Islamic concepts, but they did so in

a radically different manner from the mainstream of the Muslim Brethren (following the lead of Sayyid Qutb rather than his predecessors). The power of the United States and Israel has made Islam so rotten and corrupt that no external institution is now able to represent it credibly; it is only the pure intentions of the last surviving upright believers that can form the core of a new community of the elect. And this is what they demonstrate by means of martyr operations (carried out by Al-Qaeda and in the name of Osama bin Laden).[13]

THE LEGACY OF OSAMA BIN LADEN: THE COSMIC WARRIOR MEDIATED

We now come full circle from 611, the beginning of a nonviolent protest movement led by an Arab merchant turned prophet, to 9/11, the day of infamy for twenty-first-century Americans. The source of that violence that brackets Islam with the worst forms of violence was Osama bin Laden, the Islamic apocalypticist as mediated through modern visual and satellite technologies. Now that Osama bin Laden has been killed by a US Navy Seal team in Abbottabad, Pakistan, in early May 2011, it is possible to reflect on his impact on Islamic notions of war and violence.[14]

There is probably no aspect of Bin Laden's profile that is more critical nor less understood than his use of the media, especially *Al-Quds Al-ʿArabi* and Al-Jazeera. One episode from late 2003 illustrates how intertwined the interests of the Saudi dissident and the major Arabic-language media were. On December 10, 2003, the London-based Arabic daily *Al-Quds Al-ʿArabi* reported that al-Qaʿida, headed by Osama bin Laden, "is gearing up for a big operation to coincide with Eid Al-Adha [February 2, 2004] ... a new videotape of bin Laden will be circulated shortly before the holiday ... it will surface in conjunction with 'a great event that will shake the region,' and it will be broadcast by Al-Jazeera television." The source explained that al-Qaʿida had an agreement with Al-Jazeera by which it was committed to broadcast any videotape that the Sahab Institute provides about al-Qaʿida. He pointed out that the institute would sever its relations with the station if it refused to broadcast a videotape, and reiterated that the station is obligated to broadcast any videotape sent to it.

In the several messages included in my edited collection of Bin Laden's writings, his reliance on Al-Jazeera becomes almost as important as his decision to wage *jihad*.[15] Prior to December 1998, when the United States and Britain launched an attack on Iraq, called Operation Desert Fox, Al-Jazeera had been a local satellite news service. Founded in February 1996 by the emir of Qatar, its goal was to promote freedom of information among Arabic-speaking citizens of the Gulf and its neighbors. In 1998, the Baghdad office got a big break when they filmed the missiles launched against Iraq from British and American airplanes. Bin Laden gave an interview that was broadcast on Al-Jazeera in December, and he became an instant international attraction. So significant was the impact of this interview that, nine days after September 11, 2001, it was rerun by Al-Jazeera. Accompanying the ninety-minute video were pictures of Bin Laden firing a gun. The message, in images as well as in words, was that the war is religious, the war is between aggressive crusaders and defensive believers, and Muslims have a stark choice, either to side with the infidel oppressors or to support the beleaguered but pure and resolute Muslim defenders.

The same message was articulated in all of Bin Laden's subsequent epistles that were broadcast via Al-Jazeera. Each was tailored to the audience he addressed. Jason Burke observed that "bin Laden seemed to show an incredible instinctive grasp of modern marketing techniques."[16] Flagg Miller goes further, explaining why the genre of epistles may be one of the best marketing techniques for his message:

> Epistles became a defining medium of eloquence in the 9th-century Abbasid court of Baghdad. In epistles colorful pleasantries, competitive verbal jousts, and political wrangling are all of a piece. Bin Laden deploys the genre with his own rhetorical flourishes. As pious public lecturer, militant jihadist, and now enfranchised literate scribe, Bin Laden excoriates ruling Saudi leaders for corruption, fiscal mismanagement, human rights abuses, and especially for their alliance with "American Crusader forces" since the Gulf War of 1990. Such accusations gain religious significance for Bin Laden as apostasy (*shirk*) insofar as Saudi leaders are represented as recurring to man-made state law instead of to true Islamic law (*shariʿa*), the latter of which remains confidently underspecified. Overall, the pious tenor of Bin Laden's epistle is consistently maintained as an act of remembrance (*dhikr*), so central to Islam's message that mankind is essentially forgetful, and is thus in need of constant reminding.[17]

The epistles functioned as sermons, delivered from on high and projected globally in ways that enhanced Bin Laden's charismatic stature.

His epistles to the Iraqis were elaborated with scriptural and historical citations and also with poetic verses, some from his own pen. His epistle to the Afghans flowed with cascades of Qur'anic citations as he reminded them of his struggle on their behalf against the Soviets. His letter to the Americans and

Europeans, by contrast, contained an unadorned accusation: they were blindly following leaders who were dooming them to an endless war of attrition. In every instance, he was an anti-imperial polemicist on behalf of global *jihad*, shaping the message to reach his audience.

In the sermon he delivered in 2003 on the holiest day in the Islamic calendar, ʿId al-Adha, he combines elements from all his letters and declarations to address Muslims around the world. He talks to individuals directly, commending each one's worthiness to participate in global *jihad* and accusing their leaders of criminal corruption. Like the first encounters that the seventh-century Arabs had with unbelieving Persians, the current *jihad* pits absolute good against absolute evil. Psychologically speaking, it is as though Bin Laden is charged with a paranoid certainty about the end time, the apocalyptic moment which only he and the guided warriors from al-Qaʿida understood fully. Numerous Qurʾanic citations and prophetic traditions are woven into his fervent appeal to believers to take up arms against the United States, Britain, Israel, and their collaborators in the Arab world. Like the Prophet Muhammad's followers, Bin Laden's Muslim armies will prevail. They have a recent history of victories over the superpowers. Who was it that defeated the Soviet Union in Afghanistan and the Russians in Chechnya if not the Afghan-Arab *mujahidin*? Was it not they who conquered the Americans in Lebanon, Somalia, Aden, Riyadh, Khobar, East Africa, at home, and, most recently, in Afghanistan? The myth of American democracy and freedom has been shattered, thanks be to God! And then, remarkably, he concludes with his own poem in which he vows to fight until he becomes:

> *a martyr,*
> *dwelling in a high mountain pass*
> *among a band of knights who,*
> *united in devotion to God,*
> *descend to face armies.*

Unfortunately, due to the dizzying shifts of technology in the Information Age, one loses all sense of just how dramatic Bin Laden's moves as a risk taker were. As one analyst explains:

> Bin Laden's bold comparisons between hallowed personages of early Islamic history and contemporary actors and events subject him to decided risks. Not only does he hazard alienating Muslim listeners by compromising the unique role that the Prophet played in Islam; he also risks becoming a poor historian, one whose antiquarian zeal fails to re-connect narrated events

with present concerns. It is precisely here that Bin Laden adopts an entirely new tactic, one that moves him from his role as pious public lecturer to the roles of tribesman, poet, and ultimately cosmic warrior. In the midst of this set of transformations, the temporal distinctions of "then" and "now" become entirely blurred, and listeners are invited, through the most sonorous and impassioned portions of the cassette, to mobilize as eternal holy combatants.[18]

The oracle who speaks has recast himself as a cosmic warrior, auguring both the end time and its "certain" outcome.

While Bin Laden not only mastered modern media and was also its primary beneficiary, no one should assume that Bin Laden benefited from his use of the media, in general, and Al-Jazeera, in particular, without some cost to his project. The channel of influence and of risk taking runs two ways. Bin Laden advocated the maximal response to imperialism. He constantly called on sacrifice, especially of youths through martyrdom for a greater cause, yet he gave no hint of a future frame beyond the shibboleth "Islamic state" or "rule of God on earth." The emptiness of his political vision was made clear in the Taysir Alluni interview in October 2001, when he declared that *jihad* will continue until "we meet God and get His blessing!" Yet earlier, in the Bin Ladenese epistle of August 1996, he had seemed to call for a deferral of apocalyptic rewards, insisting on the value of oil revenues for a near term Islamic state: "I would like here to alert my brothers, the Mujahidin, the sons of the nation, to protect this (oil) wealth and not to include it in the battle as it is a great Islamic wealth and a large economic power essential for the soon to be established Islamic state, by the grace and permission of God." Still later, in his second letter to the Iraqi people (February 11, 2003), he called again for establishing the rule of God on earth but only through incessant warfare against multiple enemies, with no agenda for structure or network that succeeds the current world system.

While there are many ways to connect Bin Laden to the early generation of Islam, perhaps the crucial move is to see how he contrasted the seeming perfection of early Islam with the broadscale desecration of the twenty-first century. In the same way that former president George W. Bush saw freedom and democracy as standards of global virtue, projecting both holistic soundness and indivisible oneness for "the axis of good," so Bin Laden saw sacrifice and war as the dual emblems of early Islam that persist until today as "the axis of hope" for all committed Muslims who recognize the seriousness of the moment. Yet his was a hope that could never be realized under the current world order because all its denizens were living in an end time of total crisis. There was no rush to restore the caliphate nor to remake the Ottoman Empire in the pre–World War I image of a pan-Islamic Muslim polity. Instead, the ultimate criterion was "meeting God and getting his blessing." That was a deferred hope: since it could not be achieved in this world during the lifetime of Muslim martyrs, it was deferred for all humankind to experience in the terrible reckoning that God Almighty has prepared.

THE MUSLIM LEGACY POST–OSAMA BIN LADEN

The great unaccounted for in the scenario of Osama bin Laden are those Muslims who still consider themselves custodians of the faith and followers of the Prophet yet do not see perpetual warfare in the name of *jihad* as the only measure of Islamic loyalty. Instead of opposing perfections, they try to see the will of God in this age through different instruments, affirming the current world order, at once trying to maximize its benefits while curbing its excesses. They need more than scriptural dictates, poetic balm, or binary shibboleths to chart their everyday life, whether as individuals or as collective members of local communities, nation-states, and the world at large. For them, Bin Laden's legacy, especially in the aftermath of his death and with seeds of hope sprouting from the Arab Spring (January–June 2011), is one of deviance and damage rather than persistence and profit in the cause of Islam. The world is not coming to an end, and other means have to be found to advance Islamic principles and the well-being of the Muslim community (*umma*).

For pragmatists, Muslim as well as non-Muslim, the real work is to prepare for an eventuality beyond the diatribes of apocalyptic doomsayers. It is not easy but it is the only way forward, and if God wills, it may yet augur the next chapter in Islam beyond violence, mirroring the first phase of the life of the Prophet Muhammad as also the consistent intent of the full panoply of divine directives mandated in the Holy Qur'an and pursued through the major epochs of Muslim history.

Notes

Bruce B. Lawrence, "Muslim Engagement with Injustice and Violence," in *The Oxford Handbook of Religion and Violence*, edited by Mark Juergensmeyer, Margo Kitts, and Michael Jerryson (New York: Oxford University Press, 2013), 126–52. Used by permission of Oxford University Press.

1. Unless otherwise noted, all the Qur'anic verses quoted here and subsequently derive from or are adapted from Thomas Cleary, *The Qur'an: A New Translation* (Burlington, VT: Starlatch, 2004).
2. Fred M. Donner, *The Early Islamic Conquests* (Princeton, NJ: Princeton University Press, 2011), 54–61.
3. Donner, *Early Islamic Conquests*, 295–96.
4. Carole Hillenbrand, *The Crusades—Islamic Perspectives* (Edinburgh: Edinburgh University Press, 1999), 93.
5. Hillenbrand, *Crusades*, 108.
6. Souleiman Mourad in an email dated September 23, 2003.
7. Hillenbrand, *Crusades*, 243.
8. In the analysis that follows, I have benefited from the seminal work of Marshall G. S. Hodgson, *The Venture of Islam: Conscience and History in a World Civilization* (Chicago: University of Chicago Press, 1973), vol. 3, *The Gunpowder Empires and Modern Times*.
9. See Cornell Fleischer, "Royal Authority, Dynastic Cyclism and 'Ibn Khaldunism,'" in *Ibn Khaldun and Islamic Ideology*, ed. Bruce B. Lawrence (Leiden: Brill, 1984), 48–51.
10. The issue of Muslim responses to European colonial presence in Afro-Eurasia has been explored in Bruce B. Lawrence, *Shattering the Myth: Islam beyond Violence* (Princeton, NJ: Princeton University Press, 1998), and in what follows, I have relied on the analysis provided in chapter 2, "Islamic Revivalism: Anti-Colonial Revolt," especially 41–52.
11. Youssef M. Choueiri, *Islamic Fundamentalism* (Boston: Twayne, 1990), 35. I am indebted to Choueiri for his clear exposition of Islamic fundamentalism, but I demur from his use of "radicalism" to refer to the last or most recent phase of Islamic protest. The term "radical," unlike "revivalism" and "reformism," has no positive referent. It presupposes some other norm, and in my view, that norm is a strict religious code or sense of inalterable, all-encompassing fundamentals. Thus, I use "fundamentalism" in preference to "radicalism" to denote the last and most significant phase of Islamic protest.
12. Quoted in Lawrence, *Shattering the Myth*, 68.
13. Hans G. Kippenberg, *Violence as Worship: Religious Wars in the Age of Globalisation* (Stanford, CA: Stanford University Press, 2011), 201.
14. See Bruce B. Lawrence, "Osama bin Laden: The Man and the Myth," in *The Leader: Psychohistorical Essays*, ed. Charles B. Strozier, 2nd ed. (New York: Springer, 2011), 119–34.
15. Editor's Note: See Bruce B. Lawrence, ed., *Messages to the World: The Statements of Osama bin Laden*, trans. James Howarth (London: Verso, 2005).
16. Jason Burke, *Al-Qaeda: The True Story of Radical Islam* (London: Penguin, 2004), 175.
17. Flagg Miller, "'On the Summit of the Hindu Kush': Osama bin Laden's Declaration of War Reconsidered," unpublished talk delivered at the University of Michigan,

March 2005; cited here by permission of the author. *Editor's Note: For the role of poetry and audiocassette culture in Bin Laden's ascetic imaginary, see Flagg Miller, The Audacious Ascetic: What the Bin Laden Tapes Reveal about al-Qaʿida (New York: Oxford University Press, 2015).*

18 Miller, "On the Summit of the Hindu Kush."

PART V

Networking Muslim Citizenship

A crucial element of religious modernity is citizenship. Citizenship brings up categories of majority/minority but also indigenous/immigrant. These categories were reimagined and thrust into the thicket of political and popular imagination with 9/11. Two years prior to this tragedy, Bruce Lawrence had been invited to deliver the ACLS Lectures in the History of Religions. In these lectures, he theorized the intersections of religion, immigration, and national belonging in the American context. Racism and racial identity and profiling existed before 9/11 but became standard after it. What we present here in chapter 17, from *New Faiths, Old Fears* (2002), are broader reflections on how Asian immigrants, especially Muslims, relate to long-standing patterns of immigrant rights and options and the challenges of 9/11. The novelty of the initial essay is underscored by analyzing not only the exclusions and stigmatizations but also the agency of ordinary immigrants. The opposite of prejudice in this essay is polyvalence, the self-conscious ability to speak both as Asian and American, as believer and citizen, and, above all, as men and women. This polyvalence allows us to see individual actors honor multiple religious loyalties and navigate diverse political circumstances. Bruce Lawrence argues for a kaleidoscopic approach that allows one to see different colors, creeds, and classes without establishing a single exclusive norm. Memories of 9/11 may not change America so much as challenge Americans to embrace the polyvalence of religion, class, and race.

While American Islam often features prominent figures like Muhammad Ali and dramatic speakers like Minister Louis Farrakhan, the most significant mainstream American Muslim leader of his generation was the soft-spoken and mild-mannered Imam W. D. Mohammed. His ambition was to expand Muslim identity through scriptural and American networks. He wanted to integrate African American Muslims into the larger American community but without surrendering the benefits of either black culture or Islamic identity. His laserlike approach to the Qur'an, seeking to explicate its idiomatic relevance for African American Muslims, is the topic of chapter 18, the second essay included here. It highlights his distinctive contribution to Islamic discourse derived from, and modeled on, the Qur'an, here excerpted from *The Qur'an: A Biography* (2006), itself an effort to retell the origins and influence of the core of Islamic devotion not from textual but from biographical resources.

Chapter 19, the third selection, like much of Lawrence's scholarship, reflects his preference for collective rather than solitary research and writing. It is the introduction to a volume of essays, *Muslim Networks from Hajj to Hip Hop* (2005), that he coedited with his spouse and colleague, miriam cooke. The introduction, like the book as a whole, moves beyond America to cross the span of Africa and Asia. It focuses on Muslim networks as not area-bound and static but flexible and mobile. The core Muslim network revolves around the annual pilgrimage to Mecca, known as the hajj. As travel, it characterizes other Muslim forms of travel and exploration. If the quest is for knowledge, then its basis is trust, reflected in the saga of the fourteenth-century North African jurist Ibn Battuta, who memorialized his travels in an account that still captures the Muslim imagination. Physical travel and intellectual exploration also involve artistic creativity, nowhere more so than in Muslim millennial hip hop that is still guided by Muslim norms and values, but with a diversity of worldviews and resources unimagined before the Information Age.

Chapter 20, the final essay, also excerpted from *The Qur'an: A Biography*, considers AIDS victims who rely on apotropaic texts to seek relief from pain and life-threatening illnesses. While their plight is still desperate, the internet is an instrument of hope, not merely information or insight, for these women and men who look to scripture for practical guidance as well as empowerment.

SEVENTEEN

Preface and Conclusion, from *New Faiths, Old Fears: Muslims and Other Asian Immigrants in American Religious Life* | 2002

Preface

What are the New Faiths of the third millennium? The New Faiths are identified with Asia. Dominant among them, in numbers and influence, are Islam, Hinduism, and Buddhism, with Sikhism a distant fourth.[1] Although all population estimates are provisional, Muslims worldwide are perhaps 1.2 billion; Hindus, 790 million; Buddhists, 365 million; and Sikh, 25 million. The numbers of Asian religions in the United States are far less than those of the second American religion, Judaism, except in the case of Islam. The number of American adherents to Asian religions is subject to conjecture: the total of American Muslims may number 5 million, with only 1.5 million being recent immigrants, while American Hindus may reach 1 million; Buddhists, 700,000; and Sikhs, perhaps 100,000. Despite their relatively small collective total (fewer than 3 million in a population of 260 million), almost all accounts of American religion in transition begin by noting that these new immigrant communities are growing faster than their Christian counterparts combined.[2]

All Americans, whatever their religion, became more acutely aware of Asian immigrants and their religious beliefs after September 11, 2001. In the early morning on that fateful day four commercial airliners were hijacked by Muslim militants allied with Osama bin Laden, a Saudi refugee living in Afghanistan. The four planes were then turned into weapons of mass destruction as they were guided to three destinations: two to the World Trade Center, the heart of New York City's commercial district, and a third to the Pentagon, the heart of the United States' operational planning as a military power. Only a cell phone call alerting those aboard a fourth plane about what had happened to the previous three gave some stunned passengers the courage to storm the cockpit and guide their own plane, passengers and hijackers together, to death in rural Pennsylvania, rather than to some other symbol of American power or prestige, with yet more lives lost, more buildings destroyed, and more innocents left to grieve.

Foreign and domestic policy pivoted to Asia where the US military initiated a war on unfriendly terrain, in the mountain reaches of Afghanistan, seeking the terrorist leader, hoping to destroy his network, trying to decapitate the brutal government that supported him. In place of the Taliban, with or without the death of Osama bin Laden, with or without the elimination of al-Qaʿida, the United States and its allies are hoping to forge a government friendly to American policy interests, even if not reflective of our own deepest social ideals. It is not a war the United States can win in the long term, since no foreign power has ever subdued and governed Afghanistan, and even "victory" there will not end the need for a continued military presence, as well as massive economic assistance to rebuild one of the poorest countries in Asia.

Simultaneously, another war has been waged within America. The war begun after September 11, 2001, on the domestic front, will not come to an easy or quick end. That war is directed against presumed enemies at home with alleged links to the Arab Muslim terrorists abroad who carried out the September attacks. Yet the links are not clear, the evidence merely circumstantial or inferential, and so a broad counterterrorist initiative has been launched by the attorney general to be implemented by the Federal Bureau of Investigation, in concert with the newly created Office of Homeland Security. Federal agents will detain and question thousands of young Arab Muslim Americans, some of them illegal immigrants but many legal citizens. As recently as mid-December 2001, it was reported that Justice Department officials were interrogating about five thousand Arab Muslim men in the Detroit area. What did they have in common? They were Arab, Muslim, and young (between the ages of eighteen and thirty-three). They also had temporary visas that allowed them to come to the United States during the past two years, and they all came from countries suspected of links to terrorism.

Combined with talk of military tribunals to try terrorist suspects, the dragnet operation in Michigan has had a chilling effect on American Muslims.

Nor will the spotlight of racial profiling be limited to Arabs or to Muslims. It will extend to other Asians, and North Africans, who look like Arabs, and others who may be identified as both "alien" and Muslim, even though they may be neither. The new faiths of Asian Americans will be refracted through one faith, Islam. Muslims will come to epitomize what Anglo-Americans most fear about an expanding immigrant community: they will have different values and alternative allegiances; they will not conform; they will obstruct social harmony and diminish the collective good. Despite the repeated efforts of public officials, from the president to the first lady to members of Congress, to declare that Islam is not the enemy, the very accent on Islam will only confirm what many flag-flying Americans have already decided: every citizen must be wary of all foreigners but especially those who look like Arabs, those who can be identified as Muslims.

Even before September 11, 2001, the new faiths had been stoking old fears of outside others and their impact on the dominant culture. But since September 11, and because all nineteen of the suicide hijackers have been identified as Arab Muslims, these fears cluster with increasing urgency around loss and disorder: loss of democracy, linguistic fragmentation, and cultural antagonism. It seems not to matter that most Asian newcomers are neither Arab nor Muslim. They may be Indians with Hindu or Sikh or even secular loyalties, yet all have been lumped together, feared because of how they look. Defined and perceived as alien, they threaten American space. They threaten, or seem to threaten, to make American space itself alien to "true" Americans.

Do these reflexes sound like caricatures? They are. Yet it is just these caricatures that inform much of what is debated as serious academic scholarship about Islam and other Asian traditions. Stereotypes and prejudices are no less real when crafted by academicians; if anything, they are more dangerous because they convey an aura of prestige and objectivity that justifies not just prejudice but also those who act out of prejudice.

During the years that have elapsed since I first gave these lectures, I have realized that the frame of reference is much larger, and infinitely more important, than was initially suggested by them. Back then, I had highlighted the notion of diaspora and, above all, the role of Asian Americans in weaving the religious as well as the social tapestry of late twentieth- and now early twenty-first-century America. I had tried to bridge several gaps—the gap between religion and culture, the gap between religion and politics (reconnecting church and state), the gap between religious loyalty and ethnic identity, the gap between religious practice and civil law, and, finally, the gap between the norms of religious texts and the images of religious experience.

But what I myself have experienced since then is an even larger gap, amounting to a double chasm, on both sides of this topic. The first comes from the side of theory. There is a crucial need to expand the conceptual center of Asian American studies, and to make all Asians equally important. The field is now weighted heavily toward East Asia. Pacific Rim immigrants or East Asian Americans are located in major urban centers, as well as within renowned universities. They have given a prominence to Asian American and especially East Asian American studies. So ingrained is East Asia in the academic study of Asian Americans that neither Koreans nor Japanese nor Chinese are marked as *East* Asian. They are simply Asian, while others, whether they be South or Southeast Asians, are marked as South Asian or Southeast Asian. In other words, they stand out from and apart from the dominant Asian minority, which is East Asian.

But what are we to make of those non-East Asian Americans who belong to the new Asian American profile of the twenty-first century? In what follows I try to remedy the dominant emphasis on East Asian Americans by providing South Asian accents, along with West Asian or Middle Eastern accents.[3] Of special interest to me is the bridge role that Iranians play. According to current interest in colonial and neocolonial categories, Iranians are thought to be Middle Eastern, as though Middle Eastern stands apart from both Europe and Asia. In fact, the Middle East, like the Far East, is a British colonial invention. It is more accurately labeled as West Asia, a geographically neutral referent. Iran, in particular, has played an enormous role in the history of both West and South Asia. Iranians are as much Asian as are Chinese or Japanese, and so I argue that Iranians be included in contemporary Asian American studies, hoping that future students of immigrant Muslim life will examine the Iranian difference within the spectrum of Asian American religious practices.

Yet the theory gap requires more than merely adding a national group. Beyond renewed attention to South Asian immigrants and their West Asian counterparts, I look at other American minorities who are not Asian yet share with Asian Americans some of the same experiences of dislocation and marginality. Non–Asian Americans often resist their redefinition as hyphenated or hybrid Americans. They see themselves as fully American. In the pursuit of life and liberty, along with happiness, they seek not just economic and political rights but also cultural citizenship within a polyvalent American ethos. Their fear, a long-standing one, is that, having been defined as alien, they cannot relate to one another as equals, much less achieve equality within the dominant Anglo culture.

Who are these non–Asian Americans and non-Anglo-Americans? They are first of all Native Americans. Though numerically few, Native Americans provide a crucial index as to how Anglo-American culture projects a frontier where Indians are still the Other. Indians are locked in an uneven relationship with the dominant culture: even as they run casinos patronized by Anglos, they seek restoration of property, especially burial grounds, long denied them in US courts.[4]

Alongside Native American voices are those of African Americans. Victims of court injustice and denial of rights even with the official end of slavery more than a century ago, they embody the racism that has marked US history since long before the first waves of Asian immigrants arrived at the turn of the twentieth century, and more recently, since 1965. All Americans, not just African Americans, "are imprisoned by the history of racial subordination in America," writes legal scholar Derrick Bell. While the way out of prison is to delegitimate racism, "we can only delegitimate it," argues Bell, "if we can accurately pinpoint it. And racism lies at the center, not the periphery; in the permanent, not in the fleeting; in the real lives of black and white [and red and brown and yellow and mixed] people, not in the caverns of the mind."[5]

The most evident face of racism, in my view, is a taken-for-granted system of hierarchical values imposed in the name of civil uniformity or cultural/religious assimilation; it denies dignity and overrides difference in the pursuit of "a higher good." Joining African Americans and Native Americans in the protest against hierarchical, conformist values are Latino/a Americans.[6] Their situation has its own internal complexity, not the least of which is the historical claim that they were part of the original America: far from crossing the border to go north, it was United States expansionism that pushed the US border south and so enveloped them. This issue of defining space as one's own is crucial. A young Chicano poet put it bluntly when she said: "No cruce la frontera, la frontera me cruzó a mi" (I did not cross the border, the border crossed me), referring to the US appropriation of Mexican territory after the War of 1848. Not just because of their large and expanding numbers, but also because of their complex implication in the rewriting of American history, Latino/a Americans require comparison to Asian Americans.[7]

In what follows I will try to cross and recross several borders, theoretical borders challenging the assumed center of Asianness in America, but also geographical borders re-inscribing the epicenter of American identity as piebald and plural. Over all discussion and analysis of Asian America hovers the specter of racism. In the United States racial prejudice becomes Anglo-English-Protestant prejudice against those deemed alien because they are neither Anglo in race nor English in speech nor Protestant in outlook. It includes a further class component because nearly all of those disadvantaged have a lower economic and class status than those judging them. Without sustained attention to racialized class prejudice, I argue, one can comprehend neither culture nor religion, neither the views of the dominant class toward immigrants and other marginal groups nor the hopes and fears that Asian immigrants share with other disadvantaged folk in twenty-first-century America.[8]

Conclusion

Grateful Here
After a sit-in at the Pentagon,
the arresting marshall misspelt my name.
Actually, though, I know I should feel grateful here.
In fact, just last week on the radio, I heard
that the Red Guards had broken the wrists
of a most promising young pianist. Among other things,
he had journeyed to the West to play Beethoven and Brahms.
—WING TEK LUM

On Being Asian American—For My Children
Of course, not everyone
Can be an Asian American.
Distinctions are earned,
and deserve dedication.

....

You are at the head
of succeeding generations,
as the rest of the world
comes forward to greet you.
—LAWSON FUSAO INADA

The first epigraph speaks to public life in the 1970s. It was then that there were protests, by Asian Americans along with other Americans, against the war in

Vietnam. The protest presents a double assault. Not just arrested but having one's name misspelled! Yet at the same time the Asian American dissident recalls another rhythm of public protest in 1970s Mainland China, where the offense was seemingly less confrontational yet the punishment more severe. The poet evokes the tension: to protest against US militarism while still recognizing and protesting Communist Chinese authoritarian practices. To choose to exercise one's conscience is a cultural act, yet within Confucian norms and values it is also a religious act; it is as religious as going to temple or taking part in a prescribed ritual. And so the protest poem counts as authentic Asian American experience, at heart a moral evocation but one with both religious and cultural value.

More than a quarter of a century later, the same issue of protesting both countries—one's homeland and one's new location—is still alive for Asian and African Americans. Following the September 11 attacks, the FBI in tandem with the Immigration and Naturalization Service arrested more than 1,200 immigrants to the United States, many of them Muslims from Mauritania (in West Africa) to Malaysia (in Southeast Asia). The poem of Wing Tek Lum could have been recited by one of the Mauritanians from Kentucky who was among those arrested. Though it was later confirmed that Mr. Ould Belal of Louisville was not a terrorist—he had nothing to do with the World Trade Center bombings or with the terrorist network that planned and carried them out—the experience of being interrogated for forty days on an immigration violation left him unnerved. Some Mauritanians protested his treatment, yet others noted that in his homeland he would have been treated far more harshly, as would all "foreigners" who looked like the terrorists. "If an attack like this happened in other countries," observed a leader of the Mauritanian community in Louisville, "they [the government security forces] would be out there killing people to find out what happened."[9] Arrests with a misspelled name versus incarceration with broken wrists, arrest with forty days' imprisonment versus murder as a revenge—the scales of response seem disproportionate, the actions of the US government, though heavy-handed, still better compared to some regimes of Africa and Asia.

And, if one is speaking to the next generation, as Lawson Inada does in the second epigraph, then it is the pride of American identity that would seem to triumph over the pain of social exclusion or intermittent injustice. Asian Americans, in Inada's view, will coalesce as a symbolic group in the future, projecting a force that will be felt not just in the United States but by "the rest of the world." Is this a matter of pride or fear or both? Pride that the rest of the world will take note may be the hope, but it is a hope laced with fear, fear that the distinction

"Asian American" may not be evident unless and until it is earned; indeed, it will only deserve recognition, both at home and abroad, once it is earned.

We are then left with two contrasting messages for the future. On the one hand, there is ambivalence about identifying too closely with any political agenda, especially one that advocated war abroad against one's coreligionists or former countrymen, and on the other hand, there is the utopian call for Asian American global preeminence, a distinctiveness earned at home combined with recognition generated from abroad as "the rest of the world comes forward to greet you."

How do we hold in tandem these very different scenarios for the future of Asian Americans? Will Asian Americans stand with, or stand apart from, other non-Asian immigrants? Do they coalesce as Asian Americans, or will each be linked to the part of Asia from which they have become American? At the very least, the lyrical quandary conjures questions that go beyond the notion of a dialogue among equals. There is neither a common ground nor a single table. There is instead a kaleidoscope of cultures, or better a kaleidoculture, where each culturally empowered group brings its own valence to the checkered future that it will help shape in contemporary America.

These questions underscore how unresolvable yet productive is the constant tug-of-war between religion and culture broached throughout *New Faiths, Old Fears*. The core issue may be summarized in a double aphorism: religion is about more than religion; Asian Americans are about more than Asia. Initially, religion must be linked to culture, for the very structures of religious communities are affected by the cultural markings of their members. African American Muslims do not share the same outlook as Arab or Iranian American Muslims. At the same time, Asian Americans are not the first immigrants or the only minorities in the United States. Asian Americans were preceded by African American involuntary immigrants, the largest racial minority in contemporary America. American Indians can claim to be the most aggrieved minority, having been the First Citizens of America five hundred years ago and now reduced to the tiniest of minorities, made even tinier by the strategies of the Bureau of the Census. Conjoined with both Amerindian and African Americans as another ethno-racial minority are Latino/as. In reality, large and rapidly growing, the Latinx community is internally disparate, neither homogenous nor reducible to a single label. It is as diverse as any other group despite the fact that in the Anglo-dominant view of America, for Progressive Protestant Patriots and their allies, members of the Latinx community remain defined as "yet another" racial minority.

Both the culture of religion and the plurality of minorities make Asian immigration a topic of explanatory value beyond the dyadic discourse about in-group integrity (cultural citizenship) versus top-down assimilation (national cohesion). An analytic lever to the larger problems posed by Asian immigration comes through capital. Economic capital shaped the turn-of-the-twentieth-century European immigration and is now shaping the turn-of-the-twenty-first-century Asian/Latino immigration. Then the United States needed more unskilled workers in industry and agriculture; now the top needs have been for skilled workers in the high-tech, medical, or commercial sectors of the workforce. The temptation is to turn away or to reduce the poor and uneducated migrants, a move which is hard to justify in humanitarian terms and ignores the deep history of immigration patterns to the United States.

Moreover, the mechanisms of global capital explain only the surface of change. While the regime of transnational corporatism produces a flow of "voluntary" immigrants that shows no signs of abating, bringing more and more Asians and other skilled immigrants, along with their less skilled countrymen, to the United States, that aspect of capital does not account for some of the most significant dimensions of Asian immigration. These come not through economic but through social or symbolic capital. Symbolic capital mirrors yet also refracts the logic of economic capital. It involves the perception and reception of persons who are defined as other by the prevalent norm. In the United States that norm, despite disclaimers to the contrary, remains the Anglo-Saxon Protestant norm. It now includes Catholics and Jews, but it does not yet include Muslims or Buddhists or Hindus, though anecdotal evidence may be mustered to highlight exceptions.

Jews, especially, provide one of the most interesting test cases for how difference and sameness are commingled in the self-perception of a notable minority, American Jewry. Many are the mechanisms by which American Jewish groups have bridged the social and religious side of their American identity.[10] Theoretically what the case of American Jews demonstrates, however, is the fungible, productive value of civil society as an analytical rubric. On the one hand, it could be argued that civil society is a flattening force that extends the power of Anglo-Protestant elites in cultural guise; yet there is also the contrary argument, to wit, that civil society is a genuine third track, mediating between the state and the market in ways that are less predictable than either the market or the state would suggest. Civil society can pose a challenge both to the dominant paradigm and to its own former profile: it offers not a blueprint but a blurry map to the future of America as a polyvalent kaleidoculture.

And everywhere civil society depends on the self-perception and agency of individuals. Self-perception may translate as accommodation, but its goal is prestige—to find not just acceptance but validation and success in the host culture. The other side of symbolic capital is equally important, though less pleasant. It is the side that reflects isolation or resistance from the immigrant group, but also from elements in the host society. This translates as prejudice, and it means that in terms of the Asian immigrants to the United States, there is a double side to prejudice: it is, in the first instance, the prejudice of extant norms and those who both enforce and perpetuate those norms, but it is also the internalization of those same norms by immigrants seeking success in the host country even while retaining loyalty to their country of origin. It is this double effect of prejudice that works so persistently against African Americans in general and African American Muslims in particular. Though they are a major, not a minor, component of whatever is defined as American Islam, they do not enjoy equivalent social status either with other non–African American Muslims or with other non-Muslim Americans.

A major analytical strategy that emerges from our study is to underscore and expand the doubling: double location, double consciousness, double speaking position. The key is not to stop at the doubling, but to realize that the multiplying effect of doubling continues at levels beyond the familiar frames. The doubling extends to gender, to location, to jobs, and to religion. Religion is not less significant for being part of the doubling process that pervades immigrant experience, yet its true significance cannot be gauged apart from this doubling. It is in fact the multiplying of doubling strategies that produces what I deem to be a particular advantage of the immigrant experience, polyvalence. Polyvalence is not mere diversity increased or difference deepened. Polyvalence is engagement with others and otherness; it becomes the constructive component of one's own changing but hopeful outlook. Polyvalence is the metastrategy for survival in a culture where one norm lurks beneath many structures, from the census to the courts to the schools to the media, and where to challenge that norm, Asian American immigrants need to construct a new norm, built on imaginative engagement with others. I call that new norm polyvalence.

While difficult and subject to backlash, it is possible to predict the seeding of polyvalence for Asian immigrants to twenty-first-century America. Academia is not the only testing ground, but examples abound in the journal produced by the Association for Asian American Studies. Though it remains tilted toward Asian Pacific perspectives and interests, with only one South Asian scholar on its thirteen-person editorial board, it nonetheless produced a thorough and evocative review of Asian American pedagogy in its first issue of the new millennium. It has also included reviews of new monographs on immigrants and the law, essays on post-1965 legislative and bureaucratic shifts on the race question, and attention to the popular media and their impact on perceptions of Asian immigrants.[11]

What I have not answered is the philosophical quandary: can cultural differences survive the move from multiple Asian settings to the setting of twenty-first-century North America and the challenges of cultural citizenship? This philosophical issue has been argued in the abstract. It has fueled a debate between Thomas McCarthy and Charles Taylor. Taylor has set forth in bold form the argument that while the normative view of modernity is said to be acultural, it, in fact, conceals a hegemonic, flattening cultural agenda: conformity to dominant norms falsely marked as universally evident and inevitable. A key example for Taylor is the slippage between "progressive" and "religious" as attributes: to progress or modernize is to become more rational is to become more secular is to become less religious. Yet Taylor challenges this set of equivalencies, showing how other cultural contexts can be both modern and religious without being schizophrenic. McCarthy disagrees. He believes that there has been not just a regional but a global pattern of rapid change during the last two centuries. Initiated by the West and labeled modernity, it promotes cultural convergence, or what others call assimilation. Instead of signaling loss, McCarthy argues that such cultural convergence is not only inevitable but also beneficial: it can fulfill the project of Immanuel Kant—namely, to reconcile nationalism with cosmopolitanism, for as more multicultural nation-states move toward greater agreement on principles (e.g., human rights, democratic structures, open markets), the entire world will move toward mutual understanding and peace. In other words, a certain type of conformity is a political good, the more widely shared and prevalent it becomes, the more beneficial.[12]

While this battle may seem like an abstract battle between utopian idealists, it should be clear that the evidence and argument of *New Faiths, Old Fears*, is weighted toward Taylor rather than McCarthy. Progressive Protestant Patriots try to place both religion and modernity in a single container: the Anglo-dominant brand of cultural fundamentalism that produces not just slogans like "In God We Trust" and "One Nation Under God" but also census forms, media stereotypes, and policy manuals that reinforce the inner and outer alien as the African/Asian/Latino/a other. Polyvalent kaleidoculture, on the other hand, argues that citizenship can be cultural as well as political, that it can express many forms of location and loyalty, all of which expand rather than inhibit an impulse to Americanness. Michael Lind may have been right that "the white overclass in the United States since the 1960s has specialized in ruling by fraud," but he is not correct when he says that the two biggest frauds are racial preference and multiculturalism.[13] While the multiculturalist project has been critiqued by both neoconservatives and neoliberals, there remains a trajectory of hope within cultural citizenship. Cultural citizenship can be polyvalent; it can function at many levels for the same individual and for different sets of individuals. It is not culture refracted but culture multiplied in piebald forms, some religious, some nonreligious. Together they indicate a culture in the making, a polyvalent kaleidoculture dimly imagined yet vitally necessary.

This approach will annoy many folk. It does not put religion center stage as an isolate from other features of American history or global exchange. Nor does it privilege Asia as a site for immigration different from, and ranked above, that of other countries/regions economically disadvantaged in the current global system. Nor does it make of race a card that can be played on behalf of one group against others. Rather it makes race a historical process, or series of intersecting processes, endemic to the United States. While racialized class prejudice is so laced into American economic and political, social, and religious life that it can never be fully eliminated, it can be recognized. Once recognized, it can be combated, and in time reduced through individual and collective strategies that extend beyond Asian Americans and include other minority groups.

Sustained attention to these issues will hardly affect the lives of all Asian immigrants, but they will become a part of the expanded worldview for being Asian American that Lawson Inada wants for his children. When outsiders look to Asian Americans, the former may be unable to see the latter, except as Americans, not because they are part of a single homogeneous culture but because America itself will have been redefined as a polyvalent kaleidoculture, a resilient, expansive culture where each part makes the whole more vivid, more colorful, more capacious without exhausting the limits for contest and for experiment, for challenge and for change. Is this a stable future? No. Is it predictable? No, But is it viable? Yes. Is it inevitable? Perhaps.

Yet it will not be a "common" future. Despite its other flaws, David Hollinger's analysis of postethnic America underscores why "common" is itself a problematic qualifier. "Americans have become too afraid of each other," he observes, "and too unwilling to take up the task of building a common future. Part of the problem is with the notion of 'common,' which when coupled with 'ground' is often taken rather preciously to imply a uniform opinion on whatever questions are at issue."[14] Stated more directly, the interpretive difficulty with a common ground is that for many it appears not as a level ground but as the leveled ground where all are made to seem like the dominant or Anglo-Protestant group.

Kaleidoscope in flux serves as the better metaphor for multiethnic and multireligious America than a common ground. And the kaleidoscope can work only if it is also seen as combining traits without collapsing them into a single profile. To build such a kaleidoscope, one must challenge both the Enlightenment bias against religion and the religious exclusion of culture. While religion and culture hardly elide, they can be related through expanding the connotation of both. Only then can one link religious studies to cultural studies. Scarcely charted, this elision is fiercely resisted both by divisions of academic labor and by public queasiness, yet it can, and will, provide analytical as well as practical benefits that accrue to Anglos and Asians, indigenes and immigrants.

New Faiths do much more than elicit Old Fears. If one sees only each religion and each culture as a stand-alone entity, the image of a chess match seems most apt. Each side has a limited number of players. Each move is fraught with peril. Each side must work out its own strategy and remain wary of its opponent. It is an endgame where finally one group will checkmate the other. There can be only one winner.

Yet the reality of twenty-first-century America is far more complex than a board game, even one as sophisticated as chess. We can only begin to understand that the complexity of American civil society if we acknowledge the underlying persistence of race-class prejudice that mocks alike the ennobling beliefs/rituals of religion and the hopeful ideals of equality and justice in democratic politics. Religion and culture elide between the public and private spheres. Civil society is a negotiated space where various groups compete with each other but also complement the potentials of family, state, and market to define the common good as well as the ultimate value of human existence. To come to terms with civil society one must first understand religion as plural and culture also as plural: one must prize the plurality and polyvalence of viewpoints within each religious tradition, as also their counterparts within the sociocultural spectrum of twenty-first-century America. Everyone has to have the chance to be a winner.

Can there be winners in mixed marriages? Can such marriages produce a genuine kaleidoscope, or will they remain just another telescope? I bristle to think that Robert Park's dictum, voiced in the binary, overtly racist period of 1920s America, still projects the worldview of most Americans. "A social equal, as ordinarily defined in America," he says, "is one that you will be willing to have your daughter marry."[15] And in a similar vein Arthur Schlesinger intones, "Sex—and love—between people of different creeds and colors can probably be counted on to arrest the disuniting of America."¹⁶ But is the only goal uniformity through intermarriage? Must the route to liberation always require obliteration of difference through biracial or interracial marriage?

The answer comes not from Booker T. Washington but from another major black intellectual in early twentieth-century America, W. E. B. Du Bois. Just as Du Bois understood the importance of educated blacks and the black public intellectual to African American solidarity, so he resisted not only Negro assimilation into Anglo culture but also racial admixture through interracial marriage, or what he called "amalgamation." A chief benefit of the polyvalent kaleidoculture is to oppose and move beyond amalgamative solutions to social inequity, itself a mask for racialized class prejudice. In Du Bois's view, not everyone needs to intermarry to produce a viable twenty-first-century America; instead, one needs to grasp how un-liberating are social "liberals" from Park to Schlesinger when they advocate "amalgamation" as the ultimate solution to the endemic American problems of racialized thinking and socioeconomic inequities.

How then does one evaluate America's kaleidoculture and prize polyvalence as a gain and the equivalence of all groups—racial, economic, and religious—as a near-term ideal? At the very least, one must go beyond the Pollyanna of multiculturalism or the dystopia of its opponents. In the third millennium one necessary platform is cyberspace, increasingly a value and not just an instrument of the High-Tech era. Arjun Appadurai argues that electronic media and immigration are interconnected diacritical markers of modern subjectivity. Together they create diasporic public spheres that transcend subjectivity at the same time that they transcend the boundaries of nation as well as ethnicity narrowly defined.

And so one ends not with answers but with more questions:

- How does internet-generated, or -accelerated, globalism affect the formation of immigrant subjectivity?
- Have recollection and reconnection become so instantaneous that immigrant subjectivity is now no longer a physical, technical reflex but rather a mental, social one, linked to inhabiting a particular node in the global network?
- Have loss, rootlessness, and nostalgia been replaced by a new brand of consumerism, a circuit of commodities that interpellate and re-inscribe immigrant desire into the discrete transactions of an affective economy?

For cultural theorists, these remain central questions, but they need to be expanded. The list should include questions about the internal variation that persists in the United States and elsewhere:

- How does one reduce huge disparities within the economic/social status of immigrant communities, for instance, between Bangalore/Silicon Valley immigrants, most high-tech mavens, and Afghani refugees driving taxicabs in New York City?
- How does one account for intergenerational difference, for instance, between older Asians who built Hindu and Buddhist temples in California and New Jersey, and younger Asians who create communities via the internet?
- And how does one connect with pro-immigrant interest groups in cyberspace while also opposing those who resent not only immigrant desire but also the immigrant presence in the United States?

Whatever the answer to these questions, two senses of religion/market will persist. One is self-limited, Religion One or religion as singular, each religious community siloed from others and internally consistent. Religions—defined institutionally and marked by creedal, ritual accents—will continue to be seen as both producers and vendors of the God product, whether they are Hare Krishna airport hawkers, Salvation Army volunteers, or website managers. But there is another, deeper sense of religion, Religion Two or religion as disparate and polyphonous. It too will persist. It will be shaped but not contained by global capital forces. It will reflect racialized class prejudice but as an enemy rather than an ally. Its practitioners will make choices that reflect other norms, other values, and other visions. The choices will not be the same for those who fill the skilled, elite labor-market demands at the top end, as they are for those who are unskilled mass laborers, at the lower end of the US economy. Both groups will be part of immigrant culture/religion in the twenty-first century, and the benefit for Asian studies will be to grapple with the contradictions and the irreducible differences, not just of Asians from Anglos, new elites from old elites, but of illegal from legal immigrants, lower-class from middle-class workers, heterodox from orthodox believers. The turmoil will not abate, it will increase. It may make global civil society less civil, and certainly less tidy, yet it will finally be the third way that cannot, and should not, be denied.

And it will be the way that proves increasingly necessary for more Americans to pursue in the aftermath of September 11, all the more so since profiling, far from being questioned, has now become a legal policy aligned with the international war on terrorism declared by President Bush. It is a war to be fought on domestic as well as foreign soil, and at home it means that security officers, from the FBI to National Guard to airport screeners, look more closely at those who look like the nineteen men who committed the crimes of September 11. Those nineteen men were Arab nationals from Muslim countries. Arab-Muslim-male cluster as a set of traits that places one minority group of Americans apart from others, and no matter how persistent is the claim, that no one can be targeted for how they look, the olive-complexioned, dark-haired Other, especially if his name is Muhammad or Ali, becomes subject to a long, furtive gaze in public space, and nowhere more so than on public transportation and at airports.

Can one take steps to separate all Asians—not just Arabs but Arab look-alikes, Asians from Pakistan and India as well as Bangladesh and Afghanistan, and not just Muslims but also Sikhs and Hindus—from the terror of unwarranted scrutiny that follows the war on terrorism, perpetuating its harm on innocent Others?

That is the challenge for American courts and schools and government agencies, but it is equally the challenge for ordinary American citizens. The answer is to affirm polyvalence not as a problem but as a prospect. Let us admit that difference is healthy and at the same time work for a kaleidoculture with every building block in the future American society given its worth and its place in the land of the free that is also the home of the brave. Who are the free? Who will dare to be brave? Every American, not just those with the privilege and power and history to claim America as *their* homeland. Equally American are Asian Americans and Latino/as, many of them recent immigrants, who share, with African Americans and Amerindians, a dream that America's future is greater than its past. For that future to be greater than its past, Progressive Protestant Patriots have to share the dream of a collective progress with other Americans, those no less patriotic or progressive though neither Protestant nor Anglo. Polyvalence will succeed because it must.

Notes

Bruce B. Lawrence, preface and conclusion, to *New Faiths, Old Fears: Muslims and Other Asian Immigrants in American Religious Life* (New York: Columbia University Press, 2002), ix–xvi, 133–44. Copyright © Columbia University Press. Used with permission of the publisher.

Epigraphs to conclusion: Wing Tek Lum, "Grateful Here," and Lawson Fusao Inada, "On Being Asian American—For Our Children," in *The Big Aiiieeeee! An Anthology of Chinese American and Japanese American Literature*, edited by Jeffrey Paul Chan, Frank Chin, Lawson Fusao Inada, and Shawn Wong (New York: Meridian, 1991), 596, 619.

1 There are, of course, numerous other Asian religions: Confucianism and Taoism from East Asia, Jainism and Zoroastrianism or Parseeism from South Asia, as well as Bahaism from West Asia. All these would warrant mention, and detailed analysis, in a comprehensive study of Asian religions in contemporary America, but the purpose of the current work is to prove and expose, then interpret and explain the contours of racialized class prejudice as it affects all Asian immigrants, but especially Muslims and Hindus. There are, of course, also Asian Christians, notably Protestants from South Korea and Roman Catholics from the Philippines. They will be considered, though not emphasized, since a study of them would stress the East Asian dimension of Asian religious immigrants, whereas the current study highlights the understudied and often-neglected South Asian immigrant communities.

2 A noted authority on American religion, Martin Marty, has observed that "while Christianity [in the United States] is growing by only 0.8 percent annually and Judaism not at all, Buddhism and Hinduism enjoy annual growth rates of 2.75 percent and 3.38 percent, respectively, and Islam outpaces them all [yet starts from a much smaller base]." At the same time, Marty does not see the preeminence of either Christianity or Judaism under threat in the near term ("New Faces of God: The Third Millennium," *Religion and Ethics Newsweekly* [1999]: 2–3). The figures for Marty's projections come from David B. Barrett and Todd M. Johnson, "Annual Statistical Table on Global Mission," *International Bulletin of Mission Research* 23, no. 1 (1999): 24–25. While these figures may exaggerate some numbers, especially those for Christians, given as two billion in 2000, and understate others, including those for Jews, given as fourteen million, they still provide benchmark approximations that help explain why, in addition to Judaism and Christianity, the major religious communities to consider in twenty-first-century America are Islam, Hinduism, and Buddhism, with Sikhism a lesser but still notable fourth Asian religion. Neither Shintoism nor Confucianism is included in these tallies, and their exclusion would seem justified in terms of both global populations and their representation in the United States.

3 The gap remains, despite some valiant interventions by South Asianists to engage the question of Asian American location from an integrated perspective that is inclusive of South as well as East Asian Americans. Among the advocacy publications by South Asian scholars, see especially the anthology edited by Lavina D. Shankar and Rajini Srikanth, *A Part, Yet Apart: South Asians in Asian America* (Philadelphia: Temple University Press, 1998). The introductory essay, "Closing the Gap? South Asians Challenge Asian American Studies," 1–22, summarizes several issues, elsewhere addressed by both South Asian and occasionally non–South Asian issues, elsewhere addressed by both South Asian and occasionally non–South Asian scholars. For a full list of references as of February 2000, see Shilpa Dave et al., "DePrivileging Positions: Indian Americans, South Asian Americans, and the Politics of Asian American Studies," *Journal of Asian American Studies* 3, no. 1 (February 2001): 67–100. Many East Asian scholars either omit reference to South Asian immigrants or give them limited space, as does Ronald Takaki in *Strangers from a Different Shore*

(New York: Penguin 1989), in which Asian Indians are the major subject of but one short chapter (chapter 8) and hardly visible elsewhere. David Palumbo-Liu also excludes South Asians and South Asian evidence from his wide-ranging analysis of Asian immigrants, *Asian/American: Historical Crossings of a Racial Frontier* (Stanford, CA: Stanford University Press, 1999). He is concerned with "how the discourse on the modernizing of America has been deeply linked to East Asia and how the development of the global economy has focused on the specific expansion of East Asia and Southeast Asian regions" (8). He defers until the conclusion of his book "the deconstruction of this Asia Pacific paradigm," which he deems to be "a crucial task for Asian American studies, one that might be facilitated by *an analysis of alternative modernities in South Asia*" (8), yet the actual conclusion gives little hint about what might be the actual shape of an inclusive pan-Asian paradigm.

4 See Jack Forbes, "Undercounting Native Americans: The 1980 Census and the Manipulation of Racial Identity in the United States," *Wicazo Sa Review* 6, no. 1 (1990): 2–26. Forbes highlights how the actual number of First Nation tribes and tribal members was systematically discounted by the 1980 census takers.

5 Derrick Bell, *Faces at the Bottom of the Well: The Permanence of Racism* (New York: Basic Books, 1992), 197–98, as quoted in William Ayers, "To the Bone: Reflections in Black and White," itself a response to Tahar Ben Jelloun, *Racism Explained to My Daughter* (New York: New Press, 2000), 170–71, provided as an epilogue to his book.

6 I am, of course, not claiming that all Latino/as, or African Americans, or Native Americans act with one motive or claim on strategy or speak with one voice. On the contrary, what several studies have shown, perhaps none more compellingly than Michael Omi and Howard Winant, in *Racial Formation in the United States: From the 1960s to the 1980s* (New York: Routledge, 1986) and *Racial Formation in the United States: From the 1960s to the 1990s*, 2nd ed. (New York: Routledge, 1994), is that shifts in both the structural and the subjective dimensions of race formation in the United States, especially since 1965, have eliminated the possibility of intragroup consensus: Neoconservatives, but also neoliberals, have co-opted minority perspectives, splintering the discourse of minorities and assuring the continuity of structural inequities. See Omi and Winant, *Racial Formation in the United States*, especially 128–54. With respect to African and Native Americans, however, there remains a refreshing clarity to bell hooks's argument that pre-Columbian Africans and Native Americans shared a hospitality code that persists despite "white supremacist constructions of history [that] have effectively erased from public collective cultural memory the recognition of solidarity and communion among Native Americans, Africans and African Americans" (bell hooks, *Black Looks: Race and Representation* [Boston: South End Press, 1992], 181–82).

7 I am especially indebted to the lucid essay by Renato Rosaldo, "Cultural Citizenship, Inequality, and Multiculturalism" (in *Latino Cultural Citizenship: Claiming Identity, Space, and Rights*, ed. William V. Flores and Rina Benmayor [Boston: Beacon, 1997], 27–38), not just for the citation from an anonymous Chicana poet but also

for framing the issue of *respeto*, or respect, as crucial to the cultural citizenship that Latino/as seek in twenty-first-century America.
8   While the United States does not account for all of North America, I consistently use the term *America* as synonymous with the United States of America. In a fuller study of the issues raised here, one would like to expand the geographical coverage to include Canada, especially the urban areas of Vancouver and Toronto, two of the largest magnets for South Asian as well as East Asian immigrants during the last half of the twentieth century. Lack of experience and time has imposed on me the more circumscribed reference to the United States of (North) America.
9   The incident concerning Mauritanian immigrants in Kentucky is reported in David Firestone, "Federal Sweep Shifts Attitude of Immigrants about the U.S.," *New York Times*, December 5, 2001, B-1. The civil problem is much greater than Mauritanians or Muslims, whether from Africa or Asia. It evokes the insidious danger of profiling, that any group, simply because of the way its members look, can be identified with similar-looking enemies, or terrorists. The line from Japanese Americans imprisoned during World War II to Asian Americans arrested after September 11 is too clear to be ignored, and it remains one of the public ironies of the post–September 11 world that the Bush administration's transportation secretary, Norman Mineta, is a Japanese American who was incarcerated during the 1940s.
10 See Rabbi Irving Greenberg, "Jewish Denominationalism Meets the Open Society," in *One Nation Under God? Religion and American Culture*, ed. Marjorie Garber and Rebecca L. Walkowitz (New York: Routledge, 1999), 32–59.
11 Five essays, including a bibliographic review essay on the experiences of Asian Pacific Americans in higher education, are provided in *Journal of Asian American Studies* 3, no. 1 (February 2000): 1–109.

For reviews of new monographs on immigrants and the law, see especially Angelo N. Ancheta, *Race, Rights, and the Asian American Experience* (New Brunswick, NJ: Rutgers University Press, 1998), which offers a careful synthesis on the relation between Asian Americans and specific areas of civil rights and immigration law. The line between others' perception and self-perception remains slippery, as A. S. Chen makes evident in his comprehensive review of the book in *Journal of Asian American Studies* 1, no. 3 (October 1998): 293–97.

For essays on post-1965 legislative and bureaucratic shifts on the race question, a notable example is Rebecca Chiyoko King, "Racialization, Recognition, and Rights: Lumping and Splitting Multiracial Asian Americans in the 2000 Census," *Journal of Asian American Studies* 1, no. 3 (October 1998): 293–97.

Many examples of works on popular media and their impact on perceptions of Asian immigrants could be provided, but see especially the third in a trilogy of dedicated issues from *Journal of Asian American Studies* at the outset of a new millennium. The February 2000 issue was dedicated to pedagogy, and the June 2000 issue to race while the third and final issue offered essays on cultural performance from Asian American perspectives. The tilt to East Asia is evident, as three of the four articles focused on Asian Pacific Americans, and only one, a fascinating exploration of Indo-chic and its elision with Afro-Am chic, highlighted South Asian Americans. See Sunaina Maira, "Henna and Hip Hop: The Politics of Cultural Production and the Work of Cultural Studies," *Journal of Asian American Studies* 3, no. 3 (October 2000): 329–69.

12 Charles Taylor, "Two Theories of Modernity," and Thomas McCarthy, "On Reconciling Cosmopolitan Unity and National Diversity," in *Alternative Modernities*, ed. Dilip Parameshwar Gaonkar (Durham, NC: Duke University Press, 2001), 172–96 and 197–236, respectively.

13 Michael Lind, *The Next American Nation: The New Nationalism and the Fourth American Revolution* (New York: Free Press, 1995), 139.

14 David A. Hollinger, *Postethnic America: Beyond Multiculturalism* (New York: Basic Books, 1995), 157.

15 Robert Park, *Race and Culture* (Glencoe, IL: Free Press, 1950), 366.

16 Arthur Schlesinger Jr., "Has Democracy a Future?," *Foreign Affairs* 76, no. 5 (1997), cited in Palumbo-Liu, *Asian/American*, 384–85.

EIGHTEEN

"W. D. Mohammed: Qur'an as Guide to Racial Equality," from *The Qur'an: A Biography* | 2006

1978 CE

To be black and Muslim in the United States of America has always been a challenge. It is a particular challenge for Imam W. D. Mohammed, the foremost spokesperson for more than two million African American Muslims. Since 1932, his father Elijah Muhammad had led the Nation of Islam. During the forty years that followed, the Nation of Islam had become known not only for its embrace of Islam but also for its racial separatism. W. D. Mohammed reformed that attitude. In 1976 he became the leader and changed the group's name to the World-Community of al-Islam in the West, then to the Muslim American Society, and most recently to The Mosque Cares. In each phase W. D. Mohammed has championed Islam as an authentic American religion, and he has consistently opposed racism in all its expressions, especially among Muslims.

Soon after W. D. Mohammed succeeded his father, his authority was rejected by rivals, chief among them Minister Louis Farrakhan. In 1978 Minister Farrakhan revived the Nation of Islam with the same racial separatist message as Elijah Muhammad. Quietly W. D. Mohammed has persisted in distancing himself from both his father and Farrakhan. To distinguish true Islam from what he deems to be false versions of Islam, he often refers to Islam as al-Islam, that is, *the* Islam—the real Islam—not its disguised distortion in the old and new forms of the Nation of Islam.

In a 1978 speech entitled "America: The Beautiful and the Beast," he demonstrated how thoroughly his view of Islam was grounded in a distinctive reading of the Qur'an. Imam W. D. Mohammed eschews racism. In its stead, he offers hope that Qur'anic precedents can inform the thinking of Caucasians as well as African Americans, non-Muslims along with Muslims, in order to make America the beautiful and not the beast.

> God is a merciful God. All praises are due to Allah.
>
> Dear beloved people, the Holy Quran tells us to look at color. Not only that, the Holy Quran says that in the heavens and in the earth, and the workings between heaven and earth, as well as in yourselves too, that you will find instructing signs from God. God teaches us through His creation, He designed His creation to speak wisdom to the mind of the thinking man.
>
> How do you think that the Caucasian has come to the high position that he has in science and in other fields of human endeavors and achievements? It's because he got the message from the Quran and was able to see the problem in the Bible, separate his intelligence from the Bible and give his intelligence to the great kinds of influences—the nourishing and productive influences of Quranic teachings.
>
> The Constitution of America is influenced by Quranic teachings. Even the capitalist concept of business is influenced by Quranic teachings. The idea of human dignity that the Constitution expresses is more in accord with the concept of man in the Quran than it is with the concept of man in the Bible. And many wonder why the Chief Imam [W. D. Mohammed] now wants to save America. I want to save America because I see two lives in America. The lifeblood of truth and the lifeblood of lies. And I think that all we have to do is just separate ourselves from that lifeblood of lies and we will have a beautiful America, indeed.
>
> Stop listening to tales about Arabs as slave traders. Wake up. The day of your great victory is here. Don't sleep. Do you think that an intelligent man—even if he knows for certain that some Arabs were in the slave trade business—would separate himself from the great past, from his great history and dignity in Al-Islam, simply because some Arabs had a part in the slave trade? No intelligent man would do that kind of foolish thing. Did anybody ever try to make you believe that a man, simply because he accepts Al-Islam becomes pure and spotless, safe from doing anything wrong? No. Allah says

in the Quran that the righteous people are not to be identified by skin or by their religious labels.

Allah says, in the Quran, that righteousness isn't turning your face East or West. Righteousness is in being God-fearing, in obedience to God. Righteousness is in carrying out the wishes of God. Righteousness is in believing in God, His books, His prophets, His angels, His promises to His people or to the faithful—that righteousness is in kind, charitable treatment of the next of kin, to the near relative. And also to the widows, to the orphans, and to the person in the road who has no place to stay tonight. All of that comes from the definition of righteousness in the Quran. It didn't say righteousness is the Muslim. The Muslim should be righteous if he is in accord with his Muslim nature and with the guidance given. But if he wants to rebel, he is free. God says, in the Quran, that if He had wanted to make people one community, He could have done so. He is the God, the Creator, and has power over everything. If He wanted to, He could make us all one in the same community. We would all be making Salat (Prayer) and facing the Kaʿba and we all would be practising universal brotherhood. We would have no racism. We would have the true Al-Islamic concept. God said, if He wanted to bring it about, He could have done so.

And again God says in the Quran that I have made you tribes and families so that you would recognize each other and not despise each other. The Quran plainly tells us that the superiority or righteousness, or piety is not to be looked for under skin color or under a religious label. It's a content that God makes. It should be the Muslim conscience. But sometimes Muslims are not in agreement with their conscience.

So, if history shows me that an Arab or some Arabs or hundreds of thousands of Arabs were involved in the slave traffic, that would not change my faith. That would not make me walk any slower toward my Arab brother who is a Muslim. I will keep the same love and appreciation for my Muslim Arab brother. I will keep my same devotion to Allah. I will keep my eyes and my whole self turned toward the Kaʿba at Mecca—I don't care what the Arabs did or what they do.

No Arab could ever do those things and come out with the Holy Quran in his arms. But also question those who told you that the Arabs did those things. Question their history and see the evil things that they did with the Bible in their arms. I'm not trying to say that the Christian is bad, but I'm saying you shouldn't throw stones if you live in glass houses. And I've just pulled out a little bit of the trash that's under your rug.[1]

Evident in this speech, as in all the writings of Imam W. D. Mohammed, is engagement with the Qur'an as a Book of Signs that cuts across racial, linguistic, and cultural divides. Invoking the Noble Qur'an without need to quote chapter and verse is part of his strategy to naturalize the message. He folds it into the texture of everyday life. He insinuates it into the vocabulary of Muslims and non-Muslims.

Elsewhere he is very specific about what the meaning of the Qur'an is, or should be, for Muslims. He offers a novel of interpretation of the Opening Chapter. While the initial verse has been variously rendered as:

Praise to God, the Lord of all Creation

or

Praise is due to God, Lord of the Universe

or

Praise be to God, Lord of all Worlds,

Imam W. D. Mohammed ponders the deeper meaning of the word "worlds." He wonders why the root word for "world" in Arabic is also the same root for "knowledge." He ingeniously chooses to combine the two, offering a unique rendition of the inaugural command of the Opening Chapter of the Qur'an:

Praise be to Allah, Lord of All Systems of Knowledge

"Worlds" are no longer spheres of outer space or the realms of life beyond death. Instead, "worlds" become "systems of knowledge." The stress is not just on knowledge, but *systems* of knowledge, and redoubled is the accent on *all* systems of knowledge: no matter what their origin or who claims them or who uses them, all derive from God. Great wisdom, whether from Caucasian writers of the US Constitution or from Arab scientists of the caliphate era, has a Divine source.

Did not these same groups sometimes function as antagonists to African Americans? Yes, but the achievements of Caucasians and Arabs are no less God-derived for their racial exclusion. Their wisdom belongs to Allah, since *all* systems of knowledge belong to Him. In effect, Imam W. D. Mohammed is warning African American Muslims to avoid the impulse to reject everything about whites or Arabs just because the latter have hurt African Americans. His listeners can, and should, claim the knowledge that whites and Arabs have produced. Why? Because ultimately that knowledge and its application belong to God; they are vehicles to edify, not stratify, God's servants.

The obligation for African American Muslims is clear and broad. When they praise Allah as Lord of *all* systems of knowledge, they make knowledge the core Muslim value. All systems of knowledge include etiquette, or personal behavior. They include global history, from the rise of Islam to modern world systems. They also include science. Religious knowledge and scientific inquiry become parts of a single package. Both are integral to Islam, since the One who is "Lord of All Systems of Knowledge" is omniscient as well as omnipotent. Divine omniscience extends from the Day of Creation to the Day of Judgment. Just as there is nothing that God did not know before the first atom was formed, so the revelation of the Qur'an anticipated all knowledge that came after the time of the Prophet. That includes modern science. The Qur'an is the Book of Science as well as a Book of Signs. Sayyid Ahmad Khan and Muhammad Iqbal, two other notable Muslim educators, would agree.

"Lord of All Systems of Knowledge" is more than an apologetic response to scientific prestige. In practice, the followers of Imam W. D. Mohammed make "Lord of All Systems of Knowledge" a pedagogical tool, from junior school to university. Its purpose is to encourage young Muslims to recognize that the Meta-Book is also the Book of Nature, and part of their own history.

When Jibril [Gabriel] told Muhammad, "Read," explains a teacher in one of The Mosque Cares Sunday schools, "he didn't have a book to read, so what did he read? What was the angel telling him to read? Read Allah's creation! Read the sunrise, read the world! Jibril is not talking about a physical book; he's talking about the creation. When we start kids in school, they don't know how to read, so we start them off with picture books. There were slaves that couldn't read, but they could read the North Star, to keep the star in front of them as they walked to freedom!"

And so both the natural world and everyday life are to be understood by careful observation and by deep empathy, in all times and in all places. Even slaves, observing the cycle of sunrise and sunset, could read them as Signs for creation and liberation. Like the Prophet Muhammad, African American slaves could not read books, yet illiteracy was no more a handicap for them than for him: the key goal was, and still is, to read the Signs and submit to their message.

"Submit!" *is* the insistent message of the heavens, of the Qur'an, and of Islam. The very word "al-Islam" becomes the leitmotif for the holistic worldview of the African American Muslim. In the words of this same Sunday school teacher, "When Allah says, 'Submit,' you've got to submit *everything*. You have to become a *scientist* when you become a Muslim. You have to have a *whole curriculum*. Give up your Afrocentric way of thinking, give up your whole way of life, and *submit*."

The challenges are double: to create a new community, one must be liberated from one's instinctive identity and merged into another, networked identity, but at the same time, society as a whole has to accept the presence of an indigenous Islam. Muslim holidays have to become part of the seasonal calendar, with Eid festivals celebrated next to Christmas and Hanukkah, and mosques have to be as natural and as welcome in the American landscape as churches and synagogues. It will not happen soon. Imam W. D. Mohammed and the Muslim American community face a long journey. Even as they remold their own community to move beyond the barrier of Afrocentrism, so they must educate the larger community to free itself from the stain of white racism. Their sheet anchor in this project is a Book of Signs that crosses every barrier of time and place, culture and race. As those who submit to the One who is "Lord of All Systems of Knowledge," they can dare to envisage a future where inclusive rather than exclusive virtues prevail, beginning in the United States.[2]

Notes

Bruce B. Lawrence, "W. D. Mohammed: Qur'an as Guide to Racial Equality," in *The Qur'an: A Biography* (New York: Atlantic Monthly Press, 2006), 163–71. Used by permission.

1   Warith Deen Muhammad, *As The Light Shineth from the East* (Chicago: WDM, 1980).
2   *Editor's Note: For more on W. D. Mohammed, see Edward E. Curtis IV, Islam in Black America: Identity, Liberation, and Difference in African-American Islamic Thought (Albany: State University of New York Press, 2002), esp. 107–27; Muhammad Fraser-Rahim, "Imam W. D. Mohammed, the Patron Saint of American Islam: Personality, Intellectual Teachings and Reformation," Journal of Muslim Minority Affairs 38, no. 4 (2018): 503–20. For W. D. Mohammed's views on Qur'anic commentary, see Timur Yuskaev, Speaking Qur'an: An American Scripture (Columbia: University of South Carolina Press, 2017).*

NINETEEN

Introduction to *Muslim Networks from Hajj to Hip Hop* | 2005,

coauthored with miriam cooke

From Mecca to Medina, from Arabia to Senegal to Indonesia and always back to Arabia and to Mecca, this has been the spatial rhythm, the mobile trajectory of Islam over the past fifteen centuries. Mecca is the birthplace of the Prophet Muhammad. It is the capital city of Islam. And more. The foundational focus of Islamic ritual and imagination, Mecca has become the defining node for a worldwide community of believers who are linked to the Prophet Muhammad and to Mecca and to one another through networks of faith and family, trade and travel. To be Muslim is to be connected to coreligionists who each day turn toward Mecca five times. Each year, Mecca attracts millions of Muslims from all over the world who perform the great pilgrimage, or hajj, one of the basic requirements of Islam. Daily and annually across time and space, the history of Islam flows from Mecca and back to Mecca. It flows through myriad networks. They connect individuals and institutions, at once affirming and transforming them.

"Muslim networks" is a key term with two parts. "Networks" refers to phenomena that are similar to institutionalized social relations, such as tribal affiliations and political dynasties, but also distinct from them, since to be networked entails making a choice to be connected across recognized boundaries. "Muslim" refers to a faith orientation, but also to a social world in which Muslims are not always dominant. Both the networked nature of Islam and the impact of Muslim networks on world history are pivotal. Yet neither has received its due from scholars. A correction is needed. This volume intends to provide it. The authors of essays in this volume are humanists and social scientists, insiders and outsiders, Muslims and non-Muslims. In examining aspects of Islamic civilization, they highlight transnational interactions, they foreground exchanges, and they explore connections from Dakar in Senegal to Jakarta in Indonesia, from the seventh century to the twenty-first.

Muslim Networks as Medium and Method

Precisely because Islam is not homogeneous, it is only through the prism of Muslim networks—whether they be academic or aesthetic, historical or commercial—that one can gain a perspective on how diverse groups of Muslims contest and rearticulate what it means to be Muslim. Humanists and social scientists focus on different elements of the diversity intrinsic to Islam. Some concentrate on individual Muslims who live and work in far-flung parts of the globe yet are frequently in touch with one another. Others examine the multiple expressions of Muslim piety all over the world. Humanists tend to accent language and subjectivity; their goal is to understand and interpret the lives of individuals and communities and the specific histories and texts that shape identities. Social scientists, on the other hand, generally emphasize collective actors—Muslims versus non-Muslims. Their intent is to clarify, and, if possible, predict, social, cultural, political, and economic conflict and change. Only a networked approach puts humanists and social scientists into conversation with each other. What it reveals is the radical heterogeneity of Muslim cultural, linguistic, and political exchanges.

One key word frames the medium for constructing Muslim networks, even as it suggests a method for their analysis. That word is *umma*, commonly translated as "global Muslim community." *Umma* is flexible rather than static; it signifies all Islam, but does so within the broadest boundaries defining Muslim collective identity. Its history has no single trunk narrative, but its many strands stretch back to the seventh century. Mecca is their common node, and Arabia their focus. The first Muslim networks overlay the trading networks of pagan Arabia that linked a merchant named Muhammad to the metropolitan world of Mesopotamia and beyond. Networks of negotiations made possible the exchange of material goods, ideas, and people; they defined cultural practices in the earliest phases of Islamic civilization. Today, advances in microelectronics have produced new networks in cyberspace, and hip hop has become one of its Muslim idioms. While these new networks link formerly marginal or disenfranchised Muslims with one another, they also provide forums for new groups, whether in Arabia or in America, to assert their understanding of Islam as normative.

Until the twentieth century, Muslim networks privileged men. Whether they were networks of travel, pilgrimage, or proselytizing, they were mainly networks of men on the move. The only network in which women's participation was traditionally acknowledged was the annual hajj. It brought Muslims from Africa and Asia to the Red Sea and to the Hijaz region in western Arabia. Clad in the *ihram*, the plain cloth worn around their bodies, both male and female pilgrims worshipped together. The hajj is limited to one month, yet pilgrimage routes function throughout the year. The hajj routes overlay the multiple networks of traders, travelers, and seekers of knowledge that connect Muslims to each other. Other pilgrimages may take Muslims to places like Tanta, Ajmer, Touba, and Karbala, but each models itself on the hajj network.

The most durable feature of the hajj is travel. Through literature, we learn about the networked nature of Muslim mobility that accents the hajj but also extends beyond it to privilege travel of all kinds to many places. Between the tenth and the fifteenth centuries, *adab al-rihla*, a genre of travel literature, emerged. Professional writers were commissioned to write *rihlas* (travelogues). These became so popular that some of the later *rihlas* seem to have relied on earlier versions to fill in descriptions of places that their authors had not visited. Such *rihlas* were not so much fictions as recycled accounts. By the fourteenth century, the genre was so well established that the armchair travel writer could obtain narratives from far-flung corners of the Muslim world and then adapt them to his purposes.

The travel writer often required a patron. For instance, the Moroccan sultan Abu 'Inan Faris (d. 1358) was so impressed with the peripatetic career of his countryman, the famous traveler Ibn Battuta (d. 1368), that he wanted to preserve the memory of his career. The sultan commissioned the belle-lettrist Ibn Juzayy to record and embellish Ibn Battuta's adventures. The resulting *Rihlat Ibn Battuta* tells of the legendary travels of a Moroccan religious scholar who journeyed throughout the fourteenth-century Muslim world. It was a Muslim world scarcely recognizable today. Ibn Battuta's journeys included a lengthy stay in Al-Andalus, as Muslim Spain was known from the eighth century on. His journeys also included an extended stopover in West Africa long before the Atlantic slave trade emerged and devastated that part of the sub-Saharan African *umma*.

Among Ibn Battuta's contemporaries and coreligionists was the celebrated North African historian Ibn Khaldun (d. 1406). Jurist, philosopher, litterateur, and historian, Ibn Khaldun circulated in the same regional network as Ibn Battuta, drawing on centuries-old connections that were moral as well as material. His major work, *Muqaddimah*, demonstrates how Arabic had become the *lingua franca*, with Mecca and Medina the geographic nodes, of a vast premodern Muslim network. The network was at once political and apolitical. In Albert Hourani's words, Islamic civilization rested on "a body of knowledge transmitted over the centuries by a known chain of teachers that preserved a moral community even when rulers changed."[1] The moral community persisted beyond physical dislocation, when individuals were uprooted from their countries of origin; the sense of shared experience animated, indeed sustained, those like Leo Africanus who were compelled to leave their land of birth. An exile from Spain at the outset of the sixteenth century, the historical geographer Leo trod the paths of Ibn Battuta and Ibn Khaldun, traveling from southern Spain to northern Africa to Arabia, even enduring a "conversion" to Christianity while captive in the Vatican.

Leo's case is instructive. An involuntary Muslim traveler who was not a trained jurist, Leo Africanus began his journeys when he was forced to leave Granada by the *Reconquista* of Spain's King Ferdinand and Queen Isabella. A reluctant migrant, Leo was the victim of a turbulent history.[2] Ibn Battuta, by contrast, reveled in the opportunities that travel facilitated. Wherever he went, he found himself integrated more and more into *dar al-Islam* (the domain of Islam). To be Muslim and to be a Muslim judge opened up for him the full benefits offered by "a networked civilization."

Through Ibn Battuta's account, we are given a template for understanding Muslim networks. His *rihla* demonstrates how a religiously defined network can become a mirror reflecting premodern Muslim cosmopolitanism. The itinerant scholar revealed a world identified as Muslim that spanned continents and oceans. *Dar al-Islam* included both non-Muslims and Muslims within its borders. It was an urban-based, cosmopolitan world, at once diverse and plural. It was connected from West Africa to the East Indies through waterways, port cities, and centers of political and religious power. Berbers, Arabs, Indians, and Sudanese could travel to the outer limits of *dar al-Islam*. Whatever obstacles they faced, they could rely on the hospitality of their coreligionists: everywhere, they found food and lodging simply because they were Muslims. From the caravanserais to the Sufi *zawiyas*, or lodges, to the generosity of local rulers, the traveler versed in Islamic sciences expected to find a welcome wherever he went. Often it was travel itself that conferred prestige and wealth. During his twenty-four years on the road and at sea, Ibn Battuta was honored with more than a maintenance allowance: as he moved further and further away from his North African roots, he found himself materially rewarded and also encumbered. En route to India, he was surrounded by a large retinue of slaves, companions, and richly laden beasts of burden that he had acquired from his latest patron.

But how did this fourteenth-century network become so ubiquitous and so effective? There are several factors that distinguish the Muslim world, making its networks at once more interconnected and interactive than those of other contemporary communities. They include trade, language, Sufism, and scholarship, but above all they include common moral ideals and social codes.

Prior to the rise of Islam, trade networks had been widespread, extending across the Mediterranean to the Indian Ocean and the South China Sea. Muslim traders built on these networks but also gave them added value. In China, for instance, there were trading links with the Arab world that could be traced back to the second century BCE. This commercial connection comprised overland networks cutting across the northern territories, also known as the Silk Road, and a southern sea route. Not long after Muhammad's death in 632 CE, Muslim envoys crossed the Asian continent, using these established networks of trade and cultural exchange to carry the message of Islam. Well-armed and militarily trained, Muslim soldiers helped the emperors to quell local rebellions while strengthening existing commercial and cultural ties. They basked in imperial favor. Their experience anticipated that of later Muslim traders who made the perilous sea journey to the southern ports of China. These traders settled in major Chinese cities and, like their coreligionists in the north, benefited from the patronage of a state that recognized in them effective and loyal allies. The trust was transferable: the Mongols were enemies of Chinese royalty, yet during the thirteenth and fourteenth centuries they singled out local Muslims for their commercial experience and expertise. Mongol leaders appointed Muslim traders to administrative office. They consolidated Muslim networks throughout imperial China while also helping to incorporate them into an expanded, transregional system of Muslim networks. So prestigious were these trading networks that some people converted to Islam merely to benefit from the commercial security promised by their religious affiliation, though many were also sincere converts.

Communication was facilitated by the fact that Arabic and Persian were linguae francae used by most elites. Some command of one or both helped individuals to integrate easily and quickly into a local Muslim trading network. The linchpin for Muslim networks was not language per se but a double emphasis on reciprocity and hierarchy. Reciprocity, or *taskhir*, implied a mutual exploitation of the ruler and the ruled, the patron and the scholar, the divine and the human. Hierarchy was indispensable to reciprocity. In its most schematic form, Muslim society of the fourteenth century had four categories—men of the pen, men of the sword, men of negotiation, and men of husbandry—ranked from the highest, men of the pen, to the lowest, men of husbandry. While justice itself was the paramount virtue, it was justice seen not as equality but rather as equity through the balance of reciprocal obligations. The ruler may have been privileged, but he was not exempt from the rules of society as a whole, being dependent on each of these four categories of men, just as they were on him. Nor did the ruled automatically support the ruler. Ibn Battuta, for instance, was expedient rather than subservient, linked to those like himself, men of the pen, rather than attached to those who were unlike him, men of the sword, or rulers.

Though the cohesiveness created by shared values was not limited to men of the pen, or ʿulamaʾ, they were its primary exemplars. Traveling throughout transnational networks, the ʿulamaʾ disseminated Islamic knowledge; they also added value to the networks they inherited and developed. The cosmopolitan, scholarly language of Islamic religious discourse cuts across multiple frontiers, constructing a universe of reciprocal benefit to those who master it. This religious discourse is at once flexible and transferable across time and space. Not only did it span the known world of the fourteenth century, but it also persisted across the vicissitudes of political and economic change that separated the premodern from the modern world system. From the Indian scholars Shibli Nuʿmani (d. 1914) and Abuʾl-Hasan ʿAli Nadwi (d. 1999) to Yusuf al-Qaradawi, an Egyptian jurist currently preaching and issuing legal opinions out of Qatar, twentieth-century Islamic scholars were bound to their predecessors by a shared commitment evidenced in a shared practice. Today's ʿulamaʾ, like their predecessors, participate in a historically articulated interpretive tradition that legitimizes and gives meaning to authoritative interpretations of foundational texts. They form interpretive communities that may be mobilized against outside forces, whether twelfth-century crusaders or twenty-first-century neocolonialists. Yet this mobile and enduring juridical authority comes at a price. While their shared discourse has always allowed ʿulamaʾ to communicate easily with each other wherever they happened to be, it has sometimes blocked their ability to communicate with other Muslims not in their social class. The majority of premodern Muslims were villagers or rural agriculturalists; they did not concern themselves with juridical values or the custodians of those values, the ʿulamaʾ. Premodern networks were expansive, but they prioritized and therefore privileged the elite.

During the fourteenth century, institutional Sufism was beginning to take hold. Sufis obeyed the same rules of reciprocity and hierarchical value that characterized other men of the pen. Sufi fellowships supplemented and competed with juridical forms of Islamic loyalty. Sufi adepts traveled from one Sufi master to another, acquiring esoteric knowledge and certificates of competency (*ijazas*) as evidence of their growing erudition. The masters (shaykhs) generally presided over *zawiyas* that offered accommodation and set no limit to how long visitors might stay. They facilitated a form of horizontal, or social, trust between believers that presupposed the existence of a vertical, or spiritual, trust between the individual believer and the transcendent other. At the core of this trust was the value of hospitality to "the son of the road" (*ibn al-sabil*). Hospitality was more than a cultural mandate; it was also an act of piety.

While pursuit of spiritual knowledge motivated mobility, travel in itself could be—and often was—considered a religious act. A famous tradition of the Prophet Muhammad exhorts Muslims to seek knowledge even if it required traveling as far as China. In most places, Muslim travelers could find lodging in a *madrasa* (religious school) or a *zawiya* or a more secular form of hostel. In Anatolia, for instance, *fityan* associations, or brotherhoods of young idealists, prided themselves on their generosity to learned strangers. Like the *madrasas* and *zawiyas*, they operated on an unspoken but resilient notion of trust.

Trust was perhaps the most important factor in Muslim travel because it was at its core the key trait of Islamic spirituality. The basic meaning of Islam is submission to the One who is the Creator, Guide, and Arbiter of all human existence. Even when travelers were not in the vicinity of a *zawiya*, *madrasa*, or *fityan* association, they could rely on a pervasive code of hospitality.

Trust translated into hospitality that was religiously underwritten by *zakat*, or almsgiving, one of the five pillars of Islam. Trust in others, hospitality, and charity were measures of one's trust in God; they were vital elements of the pervasive social code of Muslim travel. So important was the practice of *zakat* that rulers competed with each other to show foreigners expansive generosity. Wherever Ibn Battuta traveled, according to Ross Dunn, he found hospitable people "who shared not merely his doctrinal beliefs and religious rituals, but his moral values, his social ideals, his everyday manners ... his tastes and sensibilities."[3]

Ibn Battuta's experience was unexceptional for a man of his class and education.[4] By his own admission, he was not especially learned, yet he was able to find patronage wherever he went because he had been trained in Maliki jurisprudence. Even basic instruction in one of the four schools of Sunni jurisprudence qualified adventurers for employment. The farther they went beyond their points of origin, the more appreciated were their talents. *'Ulama'* traveled widely, especially to frontier kingdoms that needed jurists. Since the ʿulamaʾ were deemed to be official guardians of Islamic law, practice, and morality, there was mutual benefit to be gained from peripatetic scholarship. Foreign ʿulamaʾ mediated between newly Islamized rulers and their people. As imported scholars, they gave prestige to rulers, whose appreciation of the scholars' learning proved their own credentials. Thus empowered, nascent Muslim rulers could link themselves to the heartlands of Islam. The scholars, for their part, gained prestige and also remuneration from generous patrons.

So it was with Ibn Battuta. When he left Tangiers in 1325, he was twenty-one years old. With the exception of a short stint as *qadi* of the Tunis hajj caravan, Ibn Battuta was constantly on the move. He went wherever he could market his juridical skills. He benefited from the largesse of his fellow Muslims until he arrived eight years later in the court of the Delhi sultan Muhammad ibn Tughluq, who immediately appointed him *qadi*. By 1334, Ibn Battuta had acquired a profile for which his education alone would not have sufficed. His travels had included several extended visits to Mecca. He became a *mujawir*, that is, someone honored for having lived for long periods in the precincts of the Kaʿba. More than the ordinary pilgrim who came to Mecca for the annual pilgrimage, the *mujawir* was "credited with exemplary devotion to God and to His House." Ross Dunn explains, "In a more practical light, a season or more in Mecca gave him the chance to make friends . . . , associations on which he might draw for hospitality over the ensuing two decades."[5] These titles were proofs of personal piety that added weight to his professional formation and allowed Ibn Battuta to move easily and comfortably throughout *dar al-Islam*.

Travel demonstrates how Muslim networks function as a medium; approaching Islamic civilization from a slightly different angle, it also underscores their function as a method of knowing. Though networking through travel is not uniquely Muslim, it compels attention to key elements in a Muslim worldview that are otherwise ignored. Travel accents both mobility and place. It gives place, or location, an important role in the production of knowledge within a networked civilization.

Courtly patronage throughout the region facilitated the travel and residence of writers and artists in many nodes of the transregional network that defined and sustained premodern Islamic civilization. In other words, royal courts served as more or less secular loci for the articulation of the larger Muslim network of scholarship and creative production. And so in the tenth century we can follow the peregrinations of the poet al-Mutanabbi through sources of livelihood—now in Cairo praising his patron, now in Baghdad satirizing him—to reimagine the *umma* in his day. Through examining the urban-based networks of writers and artists, we can begin to understand the world they inhabited, and to grasp how that world was filtered through their writing and painting.

Intellectual history reflects both movement and place. Medieval history acquires a new life when we put dates, people, and places into conversation with each other. Ibn Battuta becomes the product as well as the subject of his far-flung travels. When we think about the materiality of the places he inhabited as also their cultural and political climates, we can detect how his travel influenced him; the places he visited shaped his understanding of Islamic norms. We can ask: How did his interaction with patrons and also with Asian scholars affirm, then extend the legal knowledge he had brought from Africa? How did he transform bits of information from his urban hosts into his own body of knowledge?

Ibn Battuta's *rihla*, like all premodern Muslim accounts, needs to be reread in such a way that the place of enunciation is highlighted rather than ignored or minimized. History will provide a series of signposts, each pointing to the zigzag process of connection and transition, each providing cultural translations, however fragmentary and provisional. If orthodoxy remains a reflex of power, as Talal Asad has argued, then moments of exchange and conflict complicate a monolithic narrative of Islamic orthodoxy precisely to the extent that they specify and localize knowledge production.[6] Individual actors and narrators need to be read in terms of an open-ended process that is always fluid. It is an exchange affecting actor and narrator as much as audience, revealing unpredictable outcomes linked to multiple strands of Muslim memory and imagination. Networked exchanges may reinforce established norms and orthodoxies at the same time as they submit them to constant scrutiny and challenge. One of the aspects of this premodern itinerary that still challenges our imagination is the sequence of pilgrimages that the restless Ibn Battuta undertook after his twenty-year sojourn in the East. Not content to stay at home in Morocco, he undertook first of all a journey to Granada in southern Spain, where he enjoyed the hospitality of the last Muslim kingdom of al-Andalus. While there, he remarked upon the presence of Sufi dervishes: they seemed much the same as those he had seen in Persia and India. What he did not remark upon was the naturalized presence of a Muslim culture as part of Europe, something that has been denied vehemently by the official conservators of Spanish nationalist culture. Ibn Battuta observed the continuity of life between Islamicate Spain and the regions of the East where he had spent much of his life. The current opposition between Islam and a Euro-American "West" would have been incomprehensible to this restless voyager. After Granada, Ibn Battuta took another trip, this time to West

Africa, a rich arena for the exploitation of both gold and slaves. Here Ibn Battuta observed the region that within a century would become the chief harvesting ground for the slave trade of North America, where Muslims would constitute one-sixth of the population of enslaved Africans. Again, its sequel as the center of slave trade in the West would have never occurred to him. In other words, he was a "silent" witness to both the millennial presence of Islam in Europe and the prospective participation of Muslims in America.

In many exchanges, there are elements that do not translate well, yet they still provide opportunities for reflection. Breaks in communication reveal gaps in the seamless logic of the narrative. These silences or gaps in the historical record undermine the taken-for-granted. They inspire new questions that interrogate the dynamics of intellectual exchange. It is in the situated dialogue between scholars of very different backgrounds that we begin to detect how it is that networks allow for the ongoing adaptation and rearticulation of Islamic norms. How did Ibn Battuta's Moroccan-based knowledge impact the production of local knowledge in India or China? We do not know directly, yet we can infer that adapting knowledge produced in one place to the exigencies of another will always involve compromises, reversals, and sacrifices, even as it also opens up exciting new ways of viewing the world.

Conclusion

Over the past fourteen hundred years, Muslim societies have been constantly networked. Networks are not new. What is new is the proliferation of Muslim networks through communications technology. Knowing that they are potentially in touch all the time provides Muslim cybernauts—and also their non-Muslim counterparts—with a new way of knowing and of being in the world, a new way of connecting across time and space. Nowhere is this more evident than in the global phenomenon of hip hop. Hip hop has networked Muslims in many national and linguistic subcultures. If hip hoppers are the most recent Muslim cybernauts, they share a common challenge with all Muslim cybernauts: how to be hip and Muslim, how to be part of a transformative moment while retaining the anchor of one's own identity. The information revolution emerges out of current technological developments and organizational patterns that are global, yet to understand Muslim networks as a part of that revolution, one must explore both their historical antecedents and their adaptation to novel elements of the Information Age that have emerged since the mid-1990s.

The boundaries of digital Islam reflect the scriptural, creedal, and historical boundaries of Islamic thinking. There can be no Islam without limits or guideposts. You cannot have a straight path unless you know what is beyond or outside or against that straight path. Cyberspace, like social space, must be monitored to be effectively Muslim. As Gary Bunt has noted, "Much is done by Muslims in the name of Islam that is dismissed as inappropriate, or worse, by other Muslims."[7] The horizontal, open-ended nature of the internet makes the boundaries of digital Islam at once more porous and more subject to change than those of its predecessors. There are still the same guideposts: the scripture (the Noble Qurʾan), the person (the Last Prophet), and the law (the *shariʿa*, or broad path, with the *ʿulamaʾ*, or religious specialists, as its custodians and monitors). Each term—the book, the prophet, the law, the monitor—has to be defined historically and then redefined in cyberspace in order to reflect the diversity of resources and worldviews within the *umma*.

Muslim networks provide a unique theoretical approach to Muslims and to Islam, highlighting transnational connections that are spatial yet not space bound. A networked epistemology pluralizes individuals. It allows them multiple contexts where no one identity predominates and none can be reified. Such an epistemology undermines all homogenized categories; it reveals beneath the apparently seamless whole the multiple strands that braid it together. Muslim networks mirror the relationship of Islam to world history and to other Muslim futures. Muslim networks mark a series of creative responses to global systems, past, present and future. They sustain and contest the systems of which they are a part. The work of Muslim netizens reveals the hope, but also the limits of hope, available to the twenty-first-century *umma*. The *umma* will persist as a universal community bound by faith and ritual practices. Yet, because Muslim networks will continue to define and sustain a multifaceted *umma*, they can and will offer rival nodes of authority, showcasing the resilient diversity of both Islam and Islamic civilization.

Notes

miriam cooke and Bruce B. Lawrence, introduction to *Muslim Networks from Hajj to Hip Hop*, edited by miriam cooke and Bruce B. Lawrence (Chapel Hill: University of North Carolina Press, 2005), 1–25. Copyright © 2005 by the University of North Carolina Press. Used by permission of the publisher.

1 Albert Hourani, *A History of the Arab Peoples* (Cambridge, MA: Belknap Press of Harvard University Press, 1991), 4.
2 Amin Maalouf captures Leo's alienation in these words: "I come from no country, no city, no tribe. I am the son of the road, my country is the caravan, my life the most unexpected of voyages" (*Leo Africanus* [New York: New Amsterdam Books, 1994], 1).
3 Ross Dunn, *The Adventures of Ibn Battuta: A Muslim Traveler of the Fourteenth Century* (Berkeley: University of California Press, 1986/1989), 7.
4 Ross Dunn describes Ibn Battuta as belonging to a "large class of lettered but not accomplished men who, for want of serious career possibilities in the central cities, gravitated out to the expanding Islamic frontiers, where a Muslim name, a reasonable education, and a large ambition could see a man to a respectable job, even to riches and power" (*Adventures of Ibn Battuta*, 312).
5 Dunn, *Adventures of Ibn Battuta*, 109.
6 Talal Asad, *The Idea of an Anthropology of Islam* (Washington, DC: Center for Contemporary Arab Studies, 1986), 15. Editor's Note: See Talal Asad, "The Idea of an Anthropology of Islam," *Qui Parle* 17, no. 2 (2009): 1–30; Basit Kareem Iqbal, "Thinking about Method: A Conversation with Talal Asad," *Qui Parle* 26, no. 1 (2017): 195–218.
7 Gary Bunt, *Virtually Islamic: Computer-Mediated Communication and Cyber-Islamic Environments* (Cardiff: University of Wales Press, 2000), 141.

TWENTY

"AIDS Victims and Sick Women: Qur'an as Prescription for Mercy," from *The Qur'an: A Biography* | 2006

People get sick. Some consult doctors. Others seek alternative healers. Among Muslims who become sick, some are illiterate or semiliterate. Yet they are no less devout, no less resourceful, because they are denied the written word. Many turn to the Qur'an for a cure.

How do devout folk who are not literate use the Qur'an? They explore a profusion of formulae linked to a single Arabic word: *taʿwidh*. *Taʿwidh* is derived from the first word in the last two chapters of the Qur'an (chapters 113–14): "I take refuge." *Taʿwidh* is the act of taking refuge, taking refuge with God from all the evils and illnesses in this world. *Taʿwidh* is best thought of as a prescription for mercy, imploring the Lord ("the Lord of all systems of knowledge") to listen, to respond, and to heal.

Many Muslims, illiterate and literate, call on Him through *taʿwidh,* above all for protection from ambient spirits or jinns. The Qur'an makes frequent reference to jinns. Jinns are spirits that inhabit the world between Heaven and Earth, between God and humans. Because they are deemed to be closer to Heaven than Earth, they are called jinn, deriving their name from the word in Arabic for Heaven: *jannah*. Jinns can work good or ill, but they are always at work. One cannot live without the interference of the jinn. To understand and control them is to prosper. To ignore or try to avoid them is to invite defeat, loss of health, and even death.

An entire Qur'anic chapter (chapter 72) is dedicated to jinn, lauding their belief in the Lord of Muhammad and humankind. There is also reference to jinn in the Chapter of Scattering Winds: "I have not created men and jinn except to worship me" (Q 51:56).

Ordinary believers, whether illiterate, semiliterate, or highly literate, are not capable of approaching jinn, much less directing them. It is a power given to certain persons. They too are mentioned in the Qur'an (for instance, in chapter 43:48–49, affirming Moses's power to heal). God never speaks to the believer except by inspiration or from behind a veil. Or else He sends a mediator (*wali*) to whom He reveals what He wishes. According to the Maghribi historian Ibn Khaldun, *walis* are saints to whom God has granted knowledge and Divine wisdom. They address different levels of intervention by spirits. They aid impotence, cure sickness, and promote well-being, almost always through the use of *ta'widh*.

Perhaps the most graphic use of *ta'widh* by a saint comes from Indonesia. There a Sufi master has devised a protective prayer formula that can be accessed via the internet. Its intended audience is not just literate but cybersavvy. Its express purpose is to assist and relieve those who suffer from HIV/AIDS. It coordinates times of recitation with different locations around the globe. On the website http://all-natural.com/sufi/, the first announcement is:

Sufi Healing
HIV/AIDS Treatment
With the Sufi Healing Method

The service is offered free through the Barzakh Foundation, and the site's webmaster is also a Sufi master. Muhammad Zuhri is someone who has practiced the Sufi healing method for more than twenty years. He claims to have cured many people afflicted with cancer, mental illness, leukemia, impotency, and paralysis, and he does it within Islam by using the Qur'an.

The very name of this group, the Barzakh Foundation, derives from a Qur'anic verse that confronts the fear of death:

When death finally comes to one of them,
He cries: "My Lord, send me back,
That I may do right by what I neglected."
There is no way; for that is just talk.
And before them is a gap (barzakh)
Until the Day they will be resurrected. (Q 24:99–100)

Barzakh is a word that Andalusian mystic Ibn ʿArabi (d. 1240) used repeatedly. For the Greatest Master, it became a key term connoting the passage from this physical world to the world beyond death that is spiritual, and also the space that each individual occupies after death and before the Day of Resurrection. Through their keen insight, Sufi masters like Ibn ʿArabi and Muhammad Zuhri are able to see the passage awaiting each person as they leave the material realm and before they experience the blinding light of eternity. This practice relies not only on ritual prayer, or *salat*, but also on voluntary meditation, or *zikr*. *Zikr* may be simply translated as "Divine remembrance," but it is much more than isolated or random remembrance. It is a rigorous daily practice, common to all Sufi groups, but here it is also practiced as a method to cure mental or physical illness. It requires repeating verses from the Qurʾan or God's Beautiful Names, including the pronoun *hu* or "He," under the supervision of Muhammad Zuhri, whether in person or by internet connection.

As a Sufi master, who mediated the Divine will and understood the *barzakh* awaiting each patient/petitioner, Muhammad Zuhri combines the uses of God's names and Qurʾanic verses with prayer in a specific and complex method. He intercedes with the jinn through formulations that may be written on paper, bone, or leather. Those things are then put in a glass of water to be taken by the patient, or buried in the ground, or carried around. The formulations can also be spoken aloud or kept silent in the heart.

Is this magic or religion, heresy or orthodoxy? Many have debated the question, and they will continue to debate it, but for the person affected, it is a matter of practical religion: what works should be used, and what works depends on trust—not just in the saint but also in the agency of the Qurʾan—for what is a Book of Signs to the believer if not also a book of secrets, its words portals that open to some larger, unseen, pervasive truth?

And in the case of Muhammad Zuhri and the Barzakh Foundation, *taʿwidh* is a pervasive and powerful application of the Qurʾan. While intended mainly for a Muslim audience, it also offers hope to all who come to this therapy with sincerity and trust, whatever their religious background. Muhammad Zuhri's pledge is "to cure the already infected patients using every way which is acceptable by human laws and morality or religion." For those who suffer AIDS yet exit this world on a path that parallels the Straight Path without intersecting it, that is, they are non-Muslim, this is perhaps the most radiant light from a Book of Signs. It is a prescription for Mercy from the One Full of Compassion, Ever Compassionate, toward all humankind.

Often it is devout women who use prescriptions for mercy as prescribed to them by *walis* or saints. A Muslim woman might be concerned about an illness, either one from which she suffers, or more likely, one that has befallen a family member. She might approach a professional healer and ask him to write certain passages from the Qur'an on the inner surface of a bowl. She will then pour water into the bowl, stir it until the writing has vanished, and then drink the blessed water on behalf of the afflicted person. The healer may also recite these words, as she consumes that water: "And He [God] will heal the breasts of people who believe" (Q 9:14).

Or it could be this verse: "O humankind! Good advice has come to you from your Lord, and a remedy for what is in your breasts" (Q 10:57). Or a similar verse that coincides with the preceding one: "And we sent down from the Qur'an what is a healing and a mercy for those who believe" (Q 17:82).

From Morocco to India to Indonesia, the professional healer might actually be a diviner or a saint. While he might use the Qur'an as a purifying substance, he might also use the words to mark a course of action. He might resort to the intimate channel of the Unseen: the Prophet Moses. Just as Moses was given the Book (Q 25:35) and blessed with miracles, such as the burning bush and the white hand, as Signs to confront Pharaoh (Q 27:7–12), so Moses's words in the Qur'an can be used to separate the wheat from the chaff, the good from the bad.

A woman client will tell the diviner/saint what she wants. Then the diviner will consult a blank book where each chapter is marked with one of two colored strings. One string has on it: "Whoever does even one iota of good will see it" (Q 99:7a). The other string: "Whoever does even one iota of evil will see it" (Q 99:7b). The diviner then thumbs through the book at random until his hand stops on one of the blank chapters. He looks at the color of the string, and then indicates to the client whether the action she contemplated will result in good or evil. He either commends or discourages her, and if she submits with faith, sincerity, and trust in the verdict from a Book of Signs, she will leave satisfied.

Numerology can also play a crucial role in the *ta'widh* or prescription for mercy that diviners/saints make to dispel the evil one. Every letter in the Arabic alphabet carries a value. Those numbers when added up can give you a total that symbolically represents the holy phrase. No phrase is deemed to be more important than the Opening Chapter. These seven verses, declared a Sufi practitioner, "provide the key to acquiring riches, success and strength. They act as a medicine and a cure, dispelling sadness, depression, anguish and fear." And the power of the Opening Chapter, for him and for others, is contained in its first words: "In the Name of God, Full of Compassion, Ever Compassionate." This phrase is known as the *basmala,* and since it represents 786, those numbers can convey its power if properly used. The number 786 may be written on a piece of paper or voiced as silent prayer. It may be spoken aloud as though it were a prayer or written on glass and the ink washed off, then drunk as medicine. It may be affixed to some part of the body or, in the case of a corpse, it may be buried with the deceased in the ground.

Often 786 is written at the top of a paper or material conveying the *basmala,* but then applied to specific words that are written out in Arabic scripts, in order to make the prescription for mercy effective. Still other formulae cover a variety of distresses, from nosebleeds to labor pains, from toothache to abscesses. Huge and varied is the inventory of Qur'anic invocations in use today throughout the Muslim world. Men may be the religious functionaries dispensing them, but many, if not most, of their clients, are Muslim women. Whether literate or illiterate, privileged or poor, they place their trust in the Noble Qur'an as the medical mediation for whatever afflicts them or those closest to them. A prescription for mercy from the Fount of Mercy, the Giver of life, is deemed to be the best cure, both for this world and for the next.

Note

Bruce B. Lawrence, "AIDS Victims and Sick Women: Qur'an as Prescription for Mercy," in *The Qur'an: A Biography* (New York: Atlantic Monthly Press, 2006), 184–92. Used by permission.

PART VI

Reflecting the Divine Other in Words and Images

Many of the preceding sections have engaged texts as well as contexts but not drawn attention to the aesthetic dimension that informs the cultural canvas and self-fashioning modes of Islamicate civilization. How do we combine yet keep discrete the multiple aesthetic registers that characterize both Muslim piety and the social-historical trajectory of Islamicate civilization? Any effort to approach beauty should begin with the Qur'an and with its own subtle evocation of both prose and poetry in what is known as "rhymed prose" (*sajʿ*). While the topic of rhymed prose is much discussed in Islamicate sources, it is only recently that scholars have recognized its importance for translations of the Qur'an, also known as the Noble Book. The first essay is titled "Approximating *Sajʿ* in English Renditions of the Qur'an: A Close Reading of Sura 93 (*al-Ḍuḥā*) and the *Basmala*" (2005), and it reviews the contested histories of *sajʿ* before affirming its necessity. Lawrence then assesses its value by deploying one Qur'anic chapter (*sura*), namely *Surat al-Ḍuḥā* (chapter 93), as a case study to test its options and limits in English translation.

Readers interested in Bruce Lawrence's broader engagement with the Qur'an, as both a historical-textual document and a site of diverse Muslim spiritual but also political performances, should consult both *The Qur'an: A Biography* (2005) and the more recent *The Koran in English* (2017). The second selection here, chapter 22, is the epilogue to the 2005 book. It underscores how crucial for

Lawrence, as for others, is the lyrical appeal of the Qur'an. He acknowledges the central role of Ibrahim Abu Nab in his approach and analysis. Though Abu Nab is little known in contemporary scholarship on the Qur'an or in public engagement with Islam, he remains a model not just for Lawrence but for all who seek layers of potential meaning within holy writ, Biblical, Talmudic, or Qur'anic.

Yet even Abu Nab would have been challenged by the imagination of the nonagenarian Indian-Qatari artist M. F. Husain. For Husain the sky is his canvas, and history unfolds as holy writ. Husain's *Last Supper in Red Desert* is described in the third selection, "A Metaphysical Secularist? Decoding M. F. Husain as a Muslim Painter in Exile" (2011). It evokes the defining liturgical moment of Jesus's life as a template of intense reflection for all seekers, whether Christian or Muslim or secular, Indian or Arab or American. Too often gender differences are excised in representations of Muslim exemplars, whether in literature, art, or history, but both men and women figure prominently in *Last Supper in Red Desert*.

The fourth selection, the final chapter from *Who Is Allah?* (2015), also seeks to redress, at least partially, the gender imbalance by looking to women subjects from Asia. The excerpt analyzes how the Southeast Asian performance artist Arahmaiani challenges normative views about Allah. It then moves to analyze how in West Asia, popularly known as the Middle East, two notable women, an artist and a novelist, strike high notes of feminist insight. The Iranian Shirin Neshat memorializes women as part of the Iran-Iraq war, while the Egyptian Nawal El Saadawi signals the oddity that though Allah is a male name, Allat, the female counterpart, would be equally valid for those who imagine God as multigender or, better, transgender. The ineffable eludes both words and images, yet the essays excerpted here provide fresh insights from many Muslim seekers of the Other—at once the Thing, the Absolute, and, above all, the One—beyond knowing yet ever sought, beyond depiction yet still imagined.

TWENTY-ONE

Approximating *Saj'* in English Renditions of the Qur'an: A Close Reading of *Sura* 93 (*al- Ḍuḥā*) and the *Basmala* | 2005

The challenge of *saj'*, or rhymed prose, continues to vex English translators of the Qur'an. Despite the axiomatic directive that the Prophet Muhammad neither knew how to read nor intended to recite in the manner of poets, the cadence of Qur'anic Arabic is one of its most endearing and elusive qualities. It is endearing because it assists the memory and pleases the ear, yet it remains elusive because it defies even more than do other parts of the Qur'an a satisfactory gloss of its sound pattern into another language. The full meaning of the Qur'an, of course, remains inchoate except in Arabic.

There exists an enormous literature about *saj'* within both traditional Islamic scholarship and critical Orientalist studies of Qur'anic language. Probably the most expansive view of this literature is set forth by Issa J. Boullata.[1] From the ranks of Islamic scholars Boullata looks at modern as well as medieval approaches to the aesthetic appeal of the Qur'an: he credits Sayyid Qutb (1906–66) for his exposition of *taswir*, the principle that underlies the distinctive style of the Qur'an, fusing together meaning and wording with such power that "it offers an effective image to the eyes, the ears, the senses as well as the imagination, the heart and the mind."[2] Boullata also lauds another Cairene scholar, ʿAʾisha ʿAbd al-Rahman (1913–1998). Her fresh approach, with its lexical and syntactic rigor, supports the conclusion earlier voiced by Taha Husayn (1889–1973), to wit, that "Arabic compositions should be divided into three categories, prose, verse and Qu'ran, *saj'* forming a part of prose but the Qur'an being a category of its own."³

What Boullata finds partially addressed in Islamic scholarship he finds largely ignored in Western or Orientalist scholarship, that is, the dimension of the Qur'an that exceeds the bounds of conventional composition, whether prose or poetry. Those passages from the Qur'an that approach *saj'* still elude all procrustean efforts to reduce them to an alternate form of *saj'*. The theological category of *i'jaz* encompasses this meta-rhetorical dimension of the Qur'an, but how to give it practical expressions in actual translations of the Qur'an? Of the major translators of the Qur'an into English, A. J. Arberry (1905–69) stands out for his sensitivity to the elliptical but crucial element of what Marmaduke Pickthall termed "that inimitable symphony."⁴ Some European scholars, such as Angelika Neuwirth and Pierre Crapon de Crapona, have tried to follow Arberry's injunction to grasp each *sura* as a self-contained unity, with its own intricate pattern of rhythm, rhyme, and assonance, yet few scholars have tried to improve on Arberry's monumental effort by applying his approach to new and still more rigorous renditions of the Qur'an into English. Even though all such efforts, like Arberry's, will remain but a "poor echo... of the glorious original," the echo might still be heard, with appreciation, by those for whom Arabic is inaccessible and English their primary, or sole, language of reference.⁵

In what follows I want to explore how that challenge of translating *saj'* into English can be met in a limited instance. Nowhere does the challenge of translating *saj'* seem more acute than in the Meccan *suras*, and so I will look at several, competing efforts to approximate in English the sound patterns, themselves both fluid and synergistic, of one of the earliest and shortest Qur'anic *suras*: Surat al-Ḍuḥā. Almost all commentators concur on its importance. It was one of the early Meccan *suras* that reassured the Prophet of his continuing mission, a reassurance especially welcome since it came after a long time had elapsed between his prior revelations and the revelation that became *Surat al-Ḍuḥā*.

Surat al-Ḍuḥā is a favorite Qur'anic *sura* in both scholarship on the Qur'an and popular usage. Two instances will indicate how differently used it is by equally devout Muslims who draw on its treasure house of sound and meaning. The first comes from a Saudi authorized rendition. Titled *Translations of the Meanings of the Noble Qur'an in the English Language*, it is the joint labor of two professors at the Islamic University in Medina: Dr. Muhammad Muhsin Khan and Dr. Muhammad Taqi al-Din al-Hilali. Their translation is to be found in many offices or hotel rooms or airport waiting rooms throughout the Arab world. It can also be consulted through one of the many digital versions of the Qur'an now in circulation, for example, *al-Muhaffiz*, cited here:

Surat al-Ḍuḥā
(The Forenoon "After Sunrise") XCII
In the Name of Allah,
The Most Gracious, the Most Merciful
[1] By the forenoon (after sunrise)
[2] By the night when it darkens (and stands still)
[3] Your Lord (O Muhammad, salla Allahu ʿalayhi wa sallam) has neither forsaken nor hates you.
[4] And indeed the Hereafter is better for you than the present (life of this world)
[5] And verily, your Lord will give you (all good) so that you shall be well-pleased.
[6] Did He not find you (O Muhammad, salla Allahu ʿalayhi wa sallam) an orphan and gave you a refuge?
[7] And He found you unaware (of the Qur'an, its laws, and Prophethood) and guided you?
[8] And He found you poor and made you rich (self-sufficient with self-contentment)?
[9] Therefore, treat not the orphan with oppression
[10] And repulse not the beggar
[11] And proclaim the Grace of your Lord (i.e., the Prophethood and all other Graces).

While this version makes no effort to reproduce the original Arabic rhyme in equivalent English, such is not the case with another popular invocation of *Surat al-Ḍuḥā*. It is to be found in Monica Ali's stunning novel *Brick Lane,* shortlisted for the 2003 Man Booker Prize. The heroine, Nazneen, is a Bangladeshi immigrant to London in a tedious marriage and an even more tedious daily routine. Once, on the streets of her neighborhood, she finds herself gliding God-like into others' lives and re-creating their personae. Distressed at this "un-Islamic" reflex, she cries, bumps into a stranger, and then, to calm herself, recites in her head her favorite *sura* (not otherwise identified):[6]

By the light of the day, and by the dark of night, your Lord
has not forsaken you, nor does He abhor you.
The life to come holds a richer prize for you than this
present life. You shall be gratified with what your Lord will give you.

Did He not find you an orphan and give you shelter?
Did He not find you in error and guide you?
Did He not find you poor and enrich you?

In what language did Nazneen recite the verses, in Arabic or in English? We do not know, though earlier in the novel on a similar occasion when she "had let her mind drift and become uncentered again, she began to recite in her head from the Holy Qur'an one of the *suras* she had learned in school. She did not know what the words meant but the rhythm of them soothed her."[7] The need to re-create the Arabic rhythm in English led the author, Monica Ali, to use one of the English renditions that does try to approximate *saj'*, in this case, *The Koran* as translated by N. J. Dawood.

The distance between the Khan/al-Hilali rendition of *Surat al-Ḍuḥā* and the N. J. Dawood version cited by Monica Ali suggests that strategies of translation are crucial in making sense of all *saj'* texts. Because *Surat al-Ḍuḥā* is but a mere eleven verses, the stark contrast of variant approaches reveals patterns that apply to the entire text of the Holy Qur'an. I have chosen to review nine efforts, beginning with the Victorian cadences of A. J. Arberry and ending with the chiseled phrases of Muhammad Abdel Haleem. Insofar as the page formatting chosen by the translator may influence the inflection in English, I have tried to reproduce the physical appearance of the text where the translation is provided. I have also chosen to divide the selected versions between non-Muslim and Muslim translators, for reasons that will become clear below.

First, from Arberry's *The Koran Interpreted*:

The Forenoon
In the Name of God, the Merciful, the Compassionate
By the white forenoon
and the brooding night!
Thy Lord has neither forsaken thee nor hates thee
and the Last shall be better for thee than the First.
Thy Lord shall give thee, and thou shalt be satisfied.
Did He not find thee an orphan, and shelter thee?
Did He not find thee erring, and guide thee?
Did He not find thee needy, and suffice thee?
As for the orphan, do not oppress him,
and as for the beggar, scold him not;
and as for thy Lord's blessing, declare it.[8]

Second, the attempt by Richard Bell:

The Morning Brightness
In the Name of God the Merciful, the Beneficent
By the morning brightness,
By the night when it is still
Thy Lord has not taken leave of thee, nor despised thee.
The last is better for thee than the first,
Assuredly in the end thy Lord will give thee to thy satisfaction
Did He not find thee an orphan and give thee shelter?
Did He not find thee erring and guide thee?
Did He not find thee poor and enrich thee?
So as for the orphan, be not overbearing
And as for the beggar, scold not,
And as for the goodness of Thy Lord, discourse of it.[9]

Two further efforts come from the same translator, the modern American poet Thomas Cleary. The first appeared in an abbreviated selection entitled *The Essential Koran*. It reads:

The Forenoon
IN THE NAME OF GOD, THE COMPASSIONATE, THE MERCIFUL (1–11)

By the forenoon, bright
And the night
When dark and quiet,
Your Lord has not abandoned you
And does not despise you.
Surely hereafter is better for you
Than what was before.
And your Lord will surely give to you,
And you will be pleased.
Did God not find you orphaned,
And provide you refuge?
And find you wandering,
And guide you?
And find you needy,
And enrich you?
So do not oppress the orphan,

or refuse the one who seeks,
And tell of the bounty of your Lord.[10]

The second effort by Cleary appears in a subsequent full version of the Qur'an in English: *The Qur'an: A New Translation*. In both appearance and content, it differs markedly from the prior rendition cited above:

93. The Morning
In the name of God, the Benevolent, the Merciful

1. By the morning, bright,
2. and the night when it is calm
3. your Lord has not left you,
and is not incensed:
4. hereafter will be better for you
than what was before;
5. your Lord will surely give to you,
and you will be content.
6. Did God not find you orphaned
and give you shelter?
7. And God found you wandering
and gave guidance.
8. And God found you needy
And gave sufficiency.
9. So don't oppress the orphan,
10. and don't rebuff the seeker.
11. And tell of the kindness of your Lord.[11]

The fifth and final effort from a non-Muslim scholar is provided by another American linguist, but one who is also an Islamicist: Michael Sells. Sells has attempted to impart a different kind of rhythmic rendition for *Sura* 93, beginning with the *basmala*:

The Morning Hours
In the Name of God the Compassionate the Caring

By the morning hours
By the night when it is still
Your lord has not abandoned you
and does not hate you
What is after will be better

than what came before
To you the lord will be giving (5)
You will be content
Did he not find you orphaned
and give you shelter
Find you lost
and guide you
Find you in hunger
and provide for you
As for the orphan— (10)
do not oppress him
And one who asks—
do not turn him away
And the grace of your lord—
proclaim.[12]

None of these efforts represents the labor of Muslim translators. Working on the same text through the eyes of faith, have Muslim scholars been able to evoke a sense of the Arabic text in English that differs appreciably from the preceding four, all by non-Muslim scholars dedicated to the task of bridging bilingual hurdles? To answer this query let us examine four Muslim renditions, beginning with one of the earliest as well as best known, and then concluding with one of the latest.

The first comes from the widely used translation by Mohammed Marmaduke Pickthall:

The Morning Hours
In the name of Allah, the Beneficent, the Merciful.

1. *By the morning hours*
2. *And by the night when it is stillest,*
3. *Thy Lord hath not forsaken thee nor doth He hate thee,*
4. *And verily the latter portion will be better for thee than the former,*
5. *And verily thy Lord will give unto thee so that thou wilt be content.*
6. *Did He not find thee an orphan and protect (thee)?*
7. *Did He not find thee wandering and direct (thee)?*
8. *Did He not find thee destitute and enrich (thee)?*
9. *Therefor the orphan oppress not,*
10. *Therefor the beggar drive not away,*
11. *Therefor of the bounty of thy Lord be thy discourse.*[13]

A second Muslim translator is Muhammad Asad. He prefers to give an interpretive translation, one that adds some explanation to the background and possible meaning of the text, but at the expense of a direct correspondence between the English rendition and the Arabic original. In a sense, Muhammad Asad's rendition is a precursor to the Khan/Hilali translation cited above, though with even more effort to explain how the *sura* should be correctly and fully understood.

The Ninety-Third *Sura*
Ad-Ḍuḥā (The Bright Morning Hours)

IN THE NAME OF GOD, THE MOST GRACIOUS, THE DISPENSER OF GRACE:
(1) CONSIDER the bright morning hours, (2) and the night when it grows still and dark. *

[* The expression "bright morning hours" apparently symbolizes the few and widely-spaced periods of happiness in human life, as contrasted with the much greater length of "the night when it grows still and dark," i.e., the extended periods of sorrow or suffering that, as a rule, overshadow man's existence in this world (cf. 90:4). The further implication is that, as sure as morning follows night, God's mercy is bound to lighten every suffering, either in this world or in the life to come—for God has "willed upon Himself the law of grace and mercy" (6:12 and 54).]

(3) Thy Sustainer has not forsaken thee, nor does He scorn thee:*

[*Sc., "as the thoughtless might conclude in view of the suffering that He has willed thee to bear."]

(4) for, indeed, the life to come will be better for thee than this earlier part [of thy life]!

(5) And, indeed, in time will thy Sustainer grant thee [what thy heart desires], and thou shalt be well-pleased.

(6) Has He not found thee an orphan, and given thee shelter?*

[*Possibly an allusion to the fact that Muhammad was born a few months after his father's death, and that his mother died when he was only six years old. Apart from this, however, every human being is an "orphan" in one sense or another, inasmuch as everyone is "created in a lonely state" (cf. 6:94), and "will appear before Him on Resurrection Day in a lonely state" (19:95).]

(7) And found thee lost on thy way, and guided thee?
(8) And found thee in want, and given thee sufficiency?
(9) Therefore, the orphan shalt thou never wrong,
(10) and him that seeks [thy] help shalt thou never chide,*

[*The term *sa'il* denotes, literally, "one who asks," which signifies not only a "beggar" but anyone who asks for help in a difficult situation, whether physical or moral, or even for enlightenment.]

(11) and of thy Sustainer's blessings shalt thou [ever] speak.*

[*Sc., "rather than of thy suffering."]¹⁴

In contrast to Muhammad Asad, Majid Fakhry, a third Muslim translator, provides a bilingual edition of the Qur'an, simply offering the English text, without comment or commentary, on the opposite side from the Arabic text. His English rendition reads:

Surat al-Ḍuḥā
(The Forenoon) 93
In the Name of Allah,
the Compassionate, the Merciful

1. *By the forenoon;*
2. *And the night when it falls calmly;*
3. *Your Lord did not forsake you or scorn you.*
4. *Surely, the last Day is better for you than the First.*
5. *Your Lord will surely give you [of His Bounty]; and so you shall be well-pleased.*
6. *Did he not find you an orphan, and then gave you refuge?*
7. *And found you in error, and then guided you?*
8. *And found you in need, and then enriched you?*
9. *As for the orphan, you shall not oppress him;*
10. *And as for the beggar, you shall not drive him away;*
11. *And as for your Lord's Favour, you shall proclaim it.*¹⁵

A fourth, and final, Muslim translation comes from Muhammad Abdel Haleem. Together with Cleary's second effort, it is also the most recent:

93. The Morning Brightness
In the Name of God, the Lord of Mercy, the Giver of Mercy

¹*By the morning brightness* ²*and by the night when it grows still,* ³*your Lord has not forsaken you [Prophet], nor does He hate you,* ⁴*and the future will be better for you than the past;* ⁵*your Lord is sure to give you so much that you will be well satisfied.* ⁶*Did He not find you an orphan and shelter you?* ⁷*Did He not find you lost and guide*

*you? ⁸Did He not find you in need and make you self-sufficient? ⁹So do not be harsh with the orphan ¹⁰and do not chide the one who asks for help; ¹¹talk about the blessings of your Lord.*¹⁶

What all these varied renditions illustrate is how very elusive must be every effort to approximate the Arabic words of the Qur'anic text, with even a vague semblance of their original evocative power, in the host language, English. The issue of whether Muslim translators have a better sense of the actual meaning and therefore can offer a more compelling English rendition than their non-Muslim counterparts seems moot. The major "Muslim" preference is to retain the use of Allah for the major divine name in the *basmala*, though Abdel Haleem breaks ranks in using the name of God, and also making both the qualifying names independent nominatives: the Lord of Mercy, the Giver of Mercy.

We will return to the question of translating the *basmala* below, but first let us make some initial observations about efforts to translate *sajʿ*, as reflected in this *sura*. Indispensable at the first stage is the commentary provided by Neuwirth, , to wit, that one must understand the liturgical practices of pre-Islamic Meccans in order to grasp the temporal context of this *sura*. *Ḍuḥā* or early morning is when thanksgiving prayers were performed. The night has not been kind, or at best has left doubts about divine intent. In this case, night can also be metaphoric, referring to the long period when the Prophet Muhammad had not received revelation prior to the disclosure of this *sura*, although Asad prefers to think of it as a much broader commentary on the sparseness of moments of happiness, in contrast to sadness, which is the common, prevalent human fate. (His commentary therefore provides a poignant reaffirmation for the use of "her favorite sura" by Nazneen, the emotionally challenged heroine of Ali's novel *Brick Lane*.) In the case of *Surat al-Ḍuḥā*, the morning brings with it not just a further revelation but also a strong evocation of hope, hope registered as satisfaction with the prophetic mission thrust upon Muhammad, and extended as a reservoir of hope for those after the Prophet who, like him, recite this *sura* in moments of distress.

Within this framework of expectation and response, the last six lines provide the rhetorical reiteration of the deepest element of fear: denial of parental protection, withholding of divine direction, as also persistence of physical distress or poverty. Each of these fears is then addressed, but indirectly and elusively rather than serially or conclusively. Though the Prophet was an orphan, it is not just to his condition that the answers speak but also to orphans in general; they are not to be oppressed. As for those who are poor and beg, they too are not to be suppressed. Yet the middle sentence, the most crucial of all, asks: how does one respond to the withholding of divine direction? The answer is given twice: first that God found Muhammad erring (or at a loss) and guided him, and then resoundingly the revelatory oracle compels him to respond by telling others that they too now have an unequivocal offer of guidance: *fa-haddith* "tell," "proclaim," "make known." The final verse comes almost like a jolt. Its disjunctive force is underscored by breaking the rhyme scheme and also the rhythm: "As for the goodness or bounty of your Lord, tell it, proclaim it, make it known." One should note that this effect is heightened in Arabic by the absence of any use of an aspirant from the initial invocation till the final word. After the *basmala*, and the familiar harmony of *al-rahman al-rahim*, there is not an occurrence of the aspirated *ha* till the final *fa-haddith*!

Neuwirth's insightful commentary stresses how much the weight of the entire message revolves around this final verse: "The closing verse with its encouragement to act according to the treatment experienced (verse 7: "did he not find you erring and guided you?") shows the way to transmit divine guidance to other men, namely through recitation [*fa-haddith*]."[17] And she suggests that the burden of that command is circular: it directs the Prophet (and by extension all Muslims) to recite through prayer, whether night vigils or early morning prayer, but always with prayerful search for guidance.

The liturgical thrust of this *sura* makes it even more imperative that any translation reflect the cadence of the Arabic, not just the rhyme scheme but the rhythm and the additive quality of the closely cropped rhetorical queries and the punctuated responses that follow them.

It is here that Arberry provides a guidepost that few of his successors have followed. He offers an arresting cadence, one that is nearly as rhythmic in English as it is in Arabic. It is for this reason that Boullata and others have commended his work; he demonstrates equal attention to the aesthetic and the rhetorical features of the Qur'an.[18] The dialogic antiphony that results in English is at once subtle and overpowering, especially in verses six through eleven:

> *Did he not find thee an orphan, and shelter thee?*
> *Did He not find thee erring, and guide thee?*
> *Did He not find thee needy, and suffice thee?*
> *As for the orphan, do not oppress him,*
> *and as for the beggar, scold him not;*
> *and as for thy Lord's blessing, declare it.*

Bell and Cleary fail to provide the interlaced cadence of the Arabic in their English equivalents, especially in their renditions of the punchlike responses to the rhetorical queries, though Cleary comes closer to the mark in his first rendition than in the second. Even Sells, who recognizes the challenges he faces and tries to meet it with sensitivity to the Qur'anic message, sounds less lyrical and certainly less rhapsodic than Arberry. Yet Sells and Arberry, in common with Cleary's first rendition, do capture the sense of the original Arabic far more directly and accurately than does Arthur Jeffrey, another major non-Muslim scholar who, in attempting to translate *Sura* 93, elected to substitute rhyme for meaning with the following result:

The Splendour of the Light
In the Name of God, the Beneficent, the Merciful

I swear by the splendour of the light
And by the silence of the night
That the Lord shall never forsake you,
Nor in his hatred take you.
Truly for you shall be winning
Better than all the beginning.
Soon shall the Lord console you, grief no longer overwhelm you,
And fear no longer cajole you.
You were an orphan boy, yet the Lord found room for your head.
Did he not find you poor, yet riches around you spread?
Then on the orphan boy, let your proud foot never tread,
And never turn away the beggar who asks for bread,
But of your Lord's bounty, ever let praises be sung and said.

What Jeffrey illustrates, in his excess attention to the requirements of English rhyme as the response to *sajʿ*, is the need to balance rather than overload the sound of the English version of this haunting yet elliptical *sura*. Exaggerating the rhyme of the original Arabic can be as much a handicap as ignoring rhyme altogether. A middle way, or modus vivendi, between the need for meaning and the desire for rhythmic equivalence has to be found. While each person, whether Muslim or non-Muslim, Arab or non-Arab, will find a different balance for themselves, I have been struck by the sensitivity and satisfaction of one particular effort to translate *Surat al-Ḍuḥā*. It comes from Shawkat Toorawa.[19]

Toorawa's is the daring rendition of a superb linguist with a musical ear. Toorawa also comes to the text as a devout Muslim. While he has not as yet rendered the entire Qur'an into English, he has attempted several imaginative renditions of major *suras* into English.[20] With respect to *Surat al-Ḍuḥā*, Toorawa has perhaps gone further than all others in wedding meaning to sound and therefore in trying, at least in part, to unlock some of the mystery of this Qur'anic *sura* in English.

Morning Light
In the Name of God, Full of Compassion, Ever Compassionate

By the morning light
And by the darkening night
Your Lord has not forsaken you—
There is no slight.
The hereafter is far better for you
Than this (first) life.
Your Lord will lavish (bounties) upon you,
And you will know delight.
Did he not find you an orphan,
Then give you respite?
Find you unaware,
Then guide you aright?
Find you wanting,
And then provide?
So as for the orphan, do not oppress
So as for the supplicant, do not suppress
And as for the bounty of your Lord, proclaim it abroad.

Of course, even Toorawa fails to match fully the tense and explosive rhyme scheme of the Arabic text. "Life" has a long *i* but does not rhyme with its preceding end-word equivalents: "light," "night," "slight" in the last verse of the prolepsis, or frame section of this *sura*. Similarly, "provide" has the weight but not the rhyme of its antecedents, "delight," "respite," and "aright," in the dialogic centerpiece of this condensed "oath cluster" (to use Neuwirth's happy phrase). Yet one could argue that precisely because they are close but not matching rhymes with other end words, the two "out of sync" words in Toorawa's rendition draw special attention to their meaning. Does not the accent on "life" and "provide" anticipate the final explosive nonrhyme, present in the Arabic [*fa-haddith*], and best rendered in English translation as "proclaim," or "proclaim it abroad"?

One must pause at the eschatological twist of Toorawa's translation. He seems to follow the initiative of both Asad and Fakhry, though not all Muslim translators (see Pickthall and Abdel Haleem). What may have been just a reference to the gap between revelations is here transposed into a foretaste of the world beyond ("the hereafter is better for you than this [first] life"). Also, the connection of bounties from the fifth verse to the eleventh verse may seem eschatologically weighted: "your Lord will lavish bounties upon you," and "as for the bounty of your Lord" links this world to the next in a seamless flow of divine outpouring. Yet since every translation is in the final analysis also an interpretation, the very boldness of the connections that Toorawa adduces makes his translation more resilient in English and more reflective of the divine intent, concealed as well as revealed in the Arabic original.

The point of this brief exploration of *saj'* is not to choose one from the other of the several renditions made of *Surat al-Duḥā*. Clearly I have my own preferences, which I have tried to justify above, but the larger point, beyond opting for one or another rendition, is to question how the very absence of any connection between the aesthetic and rhetorical features of the Qur'an makes some translations seem less satisfactory than others. Whatever the final judgment on the worth of Toorawa's effort, one must note that he has paid attention to the demands of *saj'* even in his rendition of the *basmala*. Many scholars glide through the *basmala* attentive to its meaning but not to its rhyme. Once again it is the mystery of *saj'* that begs to be addressed. Toorawa's nimble rendition can be seen in its sharp contrast to Sells's rendition: "In the Name of God the Compassionate, the Caring." The latter has the advantage of breaking the usual cadence of "Compassionate, Merciful" or "Compassionate, Beneficent," but "Caring" is too jarringly colloquial in English to recuperate and transmit the dignity of the Arabic doublet, "*al-Rahman al-Rahim*."

Even native Arabic speakers familiar with English cannot easily translate "*al-Rahman al-Rahim*." The two words share a common root: *r-h-m*. Both are also derived nouns or qualifying adjectives for Allah, which, of course, means God in Arabic. Yet *al-Rahman* and *al-Rahim* are consistently mistranslated. People falter, trying to make one vary from the other: "Oh, it's the beneficent, then the merciful, or, it's the merciful, then the compassionate." Both strategies fail, however, because unless the two words somehow rhyme with each other in English translation as they do in the original Arabic, they don't convey the sense of the Qur'anic phrase "*al-Rahman al-Rahim*." The point is as crucial as it is neglected. Whether treated as derived nouns or adjectives, both qualify the most important word in Arabic, certainly the most important word in Arabic or Muslims:

Allah. (The name Allah occurs no fewer than 2,696 times in the Qur'an.) And so the terms *al-Rahman al-Rahim* should be the major names of God, which every scholar tries to get right when translating them. Yet most get them wrong. Not because they don't care about it, not because they don't know both Arabic and English, but because they don't have the sense of the rhythm and the interaction of those two terms in Arabic, "*al-Rahman al-Rahim*." Language is important for religion, but it is also very, very tricky.

One of the major efforts to challenge the familiar practice of translating the same Arabic words with two different words in English comes from Muhammad Abdel Haleem. In his new translation of the Qur'an, Abdel Haleem, who had earlier rendered *al-Rahman al-Rahim* as the Most Beneficent, the Most Merciful, now shifts to "the Lord of Mercy, the Giver of Mercy."[21] In effect, Abdel Haleem is opting to make both phrases into freestanding derived nouns rather than dependent qualifiers. The result is to retain the sense of commonality of *r-h-m* in Arabic, but at the cost of relating both terms adjectivally to Allah. It is a choice not explained in his otherwise helpful introduction to a translation that fulfills his intent of "going further than previous works in accuracy, clarity, flow, and currency of language."[22]

In tackling the vexed problem of rendering "*al-Rahman al-Rahim*" into English, I would agree with Shawkat Toorawa: the preferred way to translate "*al-Rahman al-Rahim*" is to make both terms into dependent qualifiers that resonate one with the other. In this endeavor he is following the lead of Muhammad Asad who consistently rendered the *basmala*, as noted above, as "In the Name of God, the Most Gracious, the Dispenser of Grace." But Asad only translated the first attribute as an adjective. The second, like Abdel Haleem's recent rendition, makes of *r-h-m*, a nominal phrase: Asad's "the Dispenser of Grace" has become Abdel Haleem's "the Giver of Mercy." Yet it seems preferable from the viewpoint of sound and meaning, aesthetics and interpretation, to be consistent: one should make both attributes either freestanding derived nouns, as does Abdel Haleem, or dependent qualifiers, as does Toorawa.

The option of the dependent qualifiers seems closer to the Qur'anic tone. The first derived noun qualifying Allah, or God, is (the One) full of compassion. It defines what God is, namely, a reservoir of compassion; God is "full of compassion." And the second derived noun acknowledges that the One full of compassion is marked by a consistent, unending reflex of projecting compassion to (human) others. The same God who is "full of compassion" is also "ever compassionate." Even though al-Tabari (d. 310/923) is dealing with connotations in Arabic and not renditions into another language, many of the points that he raises about the relatedness of *al-Rahman* to *al-Rahim*, and also the distinction between them in meaning, approximate the principle of emphasis advocated here. In particular, al-Tabari notes that God as *al-Rahman* projects a general mercy that is all encompassing and unconditional, while *al-Rahim* directs His specific mercy to some of His creatures whether in every state or just particular states, either in the present world or in the world to come or both.[23] The best rendition of the *basmala* in English would therefore seem to be "In the Name of God, Full of Compassion, Ever Compassionate."

Not all would agree on the choice of "compassion" for *r-h-m*. Some may prefer mercy. That also works: "In the name of God, full of mercy, ever merciful." If you prefer beneficence, then opt for beneficence: "In the name of God, full of beneficence, ever beneficent." I'm less sure about grace, though you could also try to rhyme the two adjectives with grace as their common element: "In the name of God, full of grace, ever gracious." But whatever you do, you must be consistent, or else you lose all sense of the evocative power, at once rhetorical and aesthetic, connoting pleasure as well as praise, in the Qur'anic phrase. Without the same qualifier in both derived nouns, you miss the most elementary aspect of the *basmala*: each trait reinforces the other in sound as in meaning, and the one cannot be sacrificed to the other without a loss of the Qur'anic intent to link both to Allah as the first, and most enduring, expressions of divine character.

Next to this intervention about translating the *basmala*, all other aspects of translating *saj'* into English may be deemed trivial, though in fact, the entire Qur'an deserves attention to its layered meaning. Adepts, whether Muslim or non-Muslim, Arabic or English speakers, must constantly be alert to nuance, and all scholars, no matter the array of their skills or the depth of their faith, must remain, as was Arberry, at once humble and self-critical.

Notes

Bruce B. Lawrence, "Approximating *Saj'* in English Renditions of the Qur'an: A Close Reading of *Sura 93 (al-Ḍuḥā)* and the *Basmala*," *Journal of Qur'anic Studies* 7 (2005): 64–80. Used by permission.

1. Issa Boullata, "The Rhetorical Interpretation of the Qur'an: *I'jaz* and Related Topics," in *Approaches to the History of the Interpretation of the Qur'an*, ed. Andrew Rippin (New York: Oxford University Press, 1988), 139–57.
2. Boullata, "Rhetorical Interpretation of the Qur'an," 151.

3. Abdulla El Tayib, "Pre-Islamic Poetry," in A. F. L. Beeston et al., *Arabic Literature to the End of the Umayyad Period* (Cambridge: Cambridge University Press, 1983), 34.
4. M. M. Pickthall, *The Meaning of the Glorious Koran* (New York: Knopf, 1930), vii.
5. A. J. Arberry, *The Koran*, Oxford World's Classics (1955; New York: Oxford University Press, 1988), xiii.
6. Monica Ali, *Brick Lane—A Novel* (New York: Scribner, 2003), 40.
7. Ali, *Brick Lane*, 9.
8. A. J. Arberry, *The Koran Interpreted* (1955; New York: Touchstone, 1970).
9. Richard Bell, *The Qur'an, Translated, with a Critical Rearrangement of the Surahs* (Edinburgh: Clark and Clark, 1939).
10. Thomas Cleary, *The Essential Koran: The Heart of Islam* (San Francisco: Harper, 1993).
11. Thomas Cleary, *The Qur'an: A New Translation* (Burlington, VT: Starlatch, 2004).
12. Michael Sells, *Approaching the Qur'an: The Early Revelations* (Ashland, OR: White Cloud, 1999).
13. Mohammed Marmaduke Pickthall, *The Meaning of the Glorious Koran* (New York: Knopf, 1930).
14. Muhammad Asad, *The Message of the Qur'an* (Gibraltar: Dar al-Andalus, 1980).
15. Majid Fakhry, *An Interpretation of the Qur'an: English Translation of the Meanings: A Bilingual Edition* (New York: New York University Press, 2002).
16. Muhammad Abdel Haleem, *The Qur'an: A New Translation* (Oxford: Oxford University Press, 2004).
17. Angelika Neuwirth, "Images and Metaphors in the Introductory Sections of the Makkan Surahs," in *Approaches to the Qur'an*, ed. G. R. Hawting and Abdul-Kader A. Shareef (London: Routledge, 1993), 20–21.
18. Boullata, "Rhetorical Interpretation of the Qur'an," 156.
19. Shawkat M. Toorawa, "'The Inimitable Rose,' Being Qur'anic *Saj'* from *Surat al-Ḍuḥā* to *Surat al-Nas* (Q93–114) in English Rhyming Prose," *Journal of Qur'anic Studies* 8, no. 2 (2006): 143–56. All following citations from Toorawa are from this article.
20. For a previous example of this labor, see Shawkat Toorawa, "Seeking Refuge from Evil: The Power and Portent of the Closing Chapters of the Qur'an," *Journal of Qur'anic Studies* 4, no. 2 (2002): 54–60.
21. On Surat al-Fatiha, see Muhammad Abdel Haleem, *Understanding the Qur'an: Themes and Style* (1999; London: Tauris, 2001), 15.
22. Abdel Haleem, *Qur'an—A New Translation*, xxix.
23. See Tabari, *The Commentary on the* Qur'an, trans. J. Cooper (Oxford: Oxford University Press, 1987), 55–59, but especially 56.

TWENTY-TWO

Epilogue to *The Qur'an: A Biography* | 2006

If it is impossible to imagine Islam without the Qur'an, it is also impossible to exhaust the multiple meanings of a Book of Signs for both Muslims and non-Muslims. The Qur'an itself refers to the levels within levels of its self-expression:

> *Say, even if the ocean were ink*
> *For (writing) the words of my Lord,*
> *The ocean would be exhausted*
> *Before the words of my Lord were exhausted,*
> *Even if We were to add another ocean to it. (Q 18:109)*

The receding horizons of truth that encompass "the words of my Lord" daunt any human interpreter, yet they make it possible to gain some perspective on the debates about the Qur'an that have taken place over time.

The first concerns the authenticity of Muhammad as a prophet. In his own lifetime the skeptics—whether polite doubters like Abu Talib, or outright opponents like Abu Jahl—were not convinced that he was other than a merchant from the Quraysh with grandiose ideas. Yet the events of his life, especially the forging of a new, resilient community in Medina, underscored both the man and his message. One could continue to doubt Muhammad as God's messenger, yet the message of guidance, hope, and healing within the revelation given to him reinforced his authority as an exemplar, even as the reports about him reinforced the vitality of the Qur'anic text. The Book and the Prophet became a double authority for all devout Muslims, even when they differed about the exact application of both to the *umma,* or Muslim community.

Was Muhammad also the seal of all prophecy, and therefore the Final Prophet? The question continues to be debated. One branch of Sunni Islam, the Ahmadiyya, staked their own existence on the claim that Muhammad was the last legal Prophet, while their own founding figure was the last "spiritual" Prophet. Others, such as the Alevis of modern-day Turkey and Syria, have made of ʿAli a figure superior to Muhammad, and so branched off from the mainstream outlook of most Muslims. Yet neither the Ahmadis nor the Alevis undercut the distinctive role of Muhammad: he was a divinely inspired Prophet, and he was the Last Prophet in the Abrahamic roll call that began with Adam and ended with him.

The second issue concerns not the Prophet but the text of the Qurʾan itself. Is the normative version—the one finalized since the time of ʿUthman, the third Caliph or successor to Muhammad—still valid today, over fourteen hundred years later? Again, one can find instances of a challenge to the received text. Many Shiʿis believe that ʿAli possessed an independent text, one that also made explicit reference to him, which has since been repressed. Euro-American scholars have also suggested that there were other copies of the ʿUthmanic text that have not been destroyed, and that they contain "significant" variants from that text. In neither case, however, does the divergence sustain an argument for invalidating the received text. Just as Muhammad is the Prophet of Islam, so the Qurʾan, as it now exists, remains the cornerstone of Islamic belief, ritual, and everyday practice.

Recent headline events have tried to undercut both the status of Muhammad and the validity of the Qurʾan. In 1989 the Rushdie affair captivated England, then the world. Salman Rushdie, an Asian Muslim by birth but an atheist by conviction, wrote a novel, *The Satanic Verses,* which cast doubt on the consistency of Muhammad's response to a divine agent. Sections of the novel implied that Muhammad "fabricated" a verse or two, then later changed his mind. Added to the novel's sensationalism was its implication that the Prophet's wives led less than honorable lives in seventh-century Arabia. Rushdie would have been ignored had the Ayatollah Khomeini not taken offense at the novel and then issued a juridical decree, or *fatwa,* condemning Rushdie as an apostate and calling for his death. Khomeini died in 1989, within six months of issuing the *fatwa* against Rushdie, while Rushdie himself still lives, albeit with constant bodyguards.

The sensitivity to public uses and abuses of the Qurʾan remains. In spring 2005 a Dutch playwright was condemned to death for his denigration of certain Qurʾanic verses about women, and later he was killed. Then in summer 2005 the journal *Newsweek* published a brief article about the abuse of the Qurʾan by

American soldiers interrogating terrorist suspects held in the Guantanamo Bay prison camp. All the prisoners were Muslim, all their interrogators non-Muslim, and even though the story was later revoked by *Newsweek,* its publication created an outpouring of protest demonstrations in South Asia; scores of people were injured, while many died honoring the Qur'an and demanding retribution against those who had defiled it.

There will be more headline stories about the Qur'an. Though they will likely concern its abuse rather than its use, it is its use that will finally matters most in the decades and centuries ahead. Scholars will continue to debate its style and content, its medieval and modern interpretations, but also its application in law and politics as well as interfaith dialogue. Muslim intellectuals will strive to understand it within the range of their own experience and reflection, whether as traditionalists or feminists, Islamists or modernists, trained scholars or scriptural autodidacts. None has crafted an approach to the text that is beyond criticism, but what they all share needs to be restated: Muhammad was the Prophet of God, he was the last Abrahamic Prophet, and the Qur'an as now received, recited, and read remains the Word of God for all time. Beyond those common assumptions they have enormous differences. The feminist amina wadud challenges patriarchal notions of polygamy, divorce, and women's worth in her reading of the Qur'an. The linguistic philosopher Muhammad Arkoun argues for a religious anthropology that exposes multiple and changing contexts for interpreting the Qur'an. The engineer turned exegete Muhammad Shahrour calls for a process of defamiliarization, approaching the Qur'an as if the Prophet had just died, leaving this book as a guidance for his followers.

Central to the vitality of a Book of Signs is its openness to multiple, often contested views of its meaning. Nowhere is this more evident than in the act of translation. Dr. Ibrahim Abu Nab of Amman pursued what he liked to call in-context translation: "when translation becomes not a translation but a way of seeking the Truth of God, then it becomes different every day (Q 55:29), for it is impossible to put a limit on the limitless and say this is the exact meaning of any word, verse or chapter."

In approaching each word, verse, or chapter of the Qur'an, one must observe the caution, which is also the hope, of Ibrahim Abu Nab. He offered his translation of the *basmala* only after exhausting all other possibilities. "In the name of Allah the Compassion the Compassionate" seemed more apt to him than "In the name of Allah the Mercy the Merciful." On this most basic of all phrases we discussed at length questions about the Name: Was it better to have Allah or God in English? Was it possible to use a noun, then an adjective in English when the two dependent qualifiers of "God/Allah" in Arabic were both adjectives? In the end, we came out in different places. I preferred to render the Arabic phrase found at the beginning of all but one Qur'anic chapter as "In the name of God Full of Compassion, Ever Compassionate." To my ear the use of two dependent qualifiers seems closer to the Qur'anic tone than using a noun and an adjective from the same verbal root, or using two adjectives with similar meanings but different verbal roots. I follow the practice of the early Qur'an commentator, al-Tabari. The first derived noun qualifying Allah, or God, is the One Full of Compassion. It defines what God is, namely, a reservoir of compassion: God is "Full of Compassion." And the second derived noun acknowledges that the One Full of Compassion is also marked by a consistent, unending reflex of projecting compassion to human others. The One God who is "Full of Compassion" is at the same time "Ever Compassionate."

And it is the same message of compassionate compassion that persists throughout the Qur'an, including the eloquent summation of the Prophet's role in the chapter titled "Prophets":

The day We roll up the sky like a scroll
as We created original nature, we will restore it,
as a binding promise,
for We are the author of creation.
And we recorded in the Psalms,
as We did in prior Scripture:
"My righteous servants will inherit the earth."
there is indeed in this a message
for the servants of God.

We have not sent you (Muhammad)
except as a compassion for all humankind. (Q 21:104–7)

The message endures, as do its critics and its carriers. The ocean will not be exhausted; its waves will sustain generation after generation. A Book of Signs continues to challenge and to change both worlds.

Note

Bruce B. Lawrence, epilogue to *The Qur'an: A Biography* (New York: Atlantic Monthly Press, 2006), 193–99. Used by permission.

TWENTY-THREE

A Metaphysical Secularist? Decoding M. F. Husain as a Muslim Painter in Exile | 2011

The first sentence of commentary on this remarkable painting must circle back to a conversation between Maqbool Fida Husain and his Qatari patron, Her Royal Highness Sheikha Mozah: "'The Last Supper?' asked M. F. Husain in response to a query as to why he returned to this theme. 'I did it twenty years back, and I wanted again to look at betrayal. I wanted to express that in the context of this project. I said to [Her Highness] Sheikha Mozah that I thought it might create controversy. She said, Don't worry; we'll take care of it. This isn't India.'"[1]

Betrayal, controversy, patronage—all three of these themes resonate through the work of one of India's greatest painter, Maqbool Fida Husain, but to understand them one must first look at his life in relation to his labor. What is the best key to unlocking the secret of his art? Is it historical—where is he from? Or artistic—what spurred his creative expression? Or cinematic—the allure of Mumbai and its movie industry? It may be any or all of these, but it can also be metaphysical. M. F. Husain is often depicted not only as a spiritual person but also as a voyager, one who travels to diverse places in his mind and, above all, enjoys playing with opposites. In what follows, I want to suggest that in the last phase of his life, as an artist in exile from his native India, it was playing with opposites, or *coincidentia oppositorum*, that shaped both M. F. Husain and his work, above all, the 99 series in Doha, which includes his painting *Last Supper*

FIGURE 23.1 · M. F. Husain, *Last Supper in Red Desert*, 2007. Photographer: Khalid Valiyakath Abdulrahim; courtesy Mathaf: Arab Museum of Modern Art, Doha. Qatar Foundation Collection. Used courtesy of Qatar Foundation.

in Red Desert [abbreviated here as *LSRD*; figure 23.1]. Playing with opposites is not the same as the disappearance of opposition; it is not tantamount to the fusion of colors, but rather their juxtaposition. The outcome is to conjoin disparities in a new pattern without losing their distinctive, singular features.

The first set of opposites converges and elides in the person of M. F. Husain. Even in his nineties he remained childlike. A silver-haired leprechaun, he seemed to embody the truth of mystical Islam, for about old age, the epigone of Persian poets, the Maulana Jalaluddin Rumi, once observed: "Some say: Is there play after 80? I say: Is there play *before* 80?" And then Rumi adds, "God of His grace bestows on the aged a youthfulness the young cannot know. Such youthfulness refreshes, causes one to leap and laugh, and gives a desire to play." Rumi then concludes, "An older person who sees the world as new and is not weary of the world desires to play, leaps and bounds, and grows robust."[2] No contemporary observer could have better described M. F. Husain—a prolific artist even before he turned eighty, but one who since eighty, and until his death at age ninety-five in 2011, continued "to see the world as new." Far from being weary of the world, M. F. Husain "desired to play ... and to grow robust." And yet he also critiqued the state of the world in which he was at play; he did not shrink from noting betrayal, highlighting controversy, and using patronage as protection against his enemies.

To understand better the anomaly of a nonagenarian wunderkind, a childlike artist beset with contestation, one must troll through the statements of Husain and interpolate them with his latest works—in this case, the commission undertaken in Doha during 2007. Though his feelings about his role as artist/performer/activist have been disclosed in numerous interviews, two conversations seem especially relevant to the interlocking themes of this essay: betrayal, controversy, patronage. One provides the sources for the initial citation above. It comes from a March 2009 interview conducted by Deena Chalabi. Another, earlier interview was conducted by John Ridding for the *Financial Times* in January 2006. It took place in the now-scarred Taj Mahal Hotel in Mumbai. At the time Husain was a mere, spritely ninety years old. One of his paintings had just sold in London for two million dollars. As he contemplated new projects, he paused to reflect on 2003. With about thirty thousand pieces already in his portfolio, he marked 2003, the year of his eighty-eighth birthday, by producing eighty-eight oils across four Indian cities. "After open-heart surgery they said: 'take it easy, and only paint miniatures,'" he scoffed, referring to an operation he had had in 1988.

Though his wife subsequently died, and he was forced into exile from India, M. F. Husain still viewed himself as privileged—able, in his own words, to "enjoy a smooth existence." "Giacometti," he recalled in that 2006 interview, "needed crises for his works, but I need only muses. I have two or three simultaneously. It is all very open."[3]

Part of Husain's inspiration comes from India. "I see such dynamism in India," Husain observed. "For the past three or four years we have been growing by leaps and bounds." And it is not just the young or the suddenly rich but also the seasoned warriors of Indian cultural politics who bode well for the future. "We need to look to the elderly," he noted, with his characteristic broad grin. "The wisdom is there."

And so to find out what is the wisdom *there*, to grasp how it brackets seemingly contradictory opposites, I arranged to have Deena Chalabi of Mathaf: Arab Museum of Modern Art conduct an interview with M. F. Husain in Doha. It was patterned on questions I provided her to ask the painter in March 2009. Mathaf requires a brief explanation. It is one of several recent museums that has opened in Doha. Since Mathaf is still in the early stages of its articulation, it could not and did not house the initial exhibition of M. F. Husain's Doha project. That occurred in November 2008 not at Mathaf but rather at Doha's Museum of Islamic Art (MIA).

A further word of explanation is required about the MIA. If M. F. Husain is a remarkable nonagenarian, he competes with another in the field of cultural gymnastics. That other nonagenarian is I. M. Pei. Pei is famous for numerous innovations, including the Cube at the Louvre Pavilion in Paris. In early 2000, he was commissioned to do a world-class museum of Islamic art for Doha. Though he was reticent, the Amir of Qatar convinced him to explore multiple settings in the urban spaces of the Mediterranean Muslim world. Pei found the inspiration he sought in a ninth-century Cairene mosque—the asymmetrical mosque of Ibn Tulun. Transposing the major elements of that historic monument, he designed a massive structure that seems to float above water on its island perch just off the busy thoroughfare of downtown Doha. In November 2008, the I. M. Pei–designed Museum of Islamic Art was opened to great fanfare. Its patron was Her Excellency Sheikha Al Mayassa, daughter of the Amir and Sheikha Mozah and now director of the Qatar Museums.

It was an extraordinary opening, for the architect, for the painter, and for the woman who has patronized both—Her Royal Highness Sheikha Mozah. It would be impossible to exaggerate the importance of the relationship that Husain has with the then leading lady of modern-day Qatar. He himself describes their relationship forthrightly in the March 2009 interview:

> I came here in May 2007 and met [Her Highness] Sheikha Mozah—such a great opportunity she offered. I just jumped. I'll devote myself, I thought. My idea of the 99 paintings and the 99 names.... I'm not painting based on those names, just taking the figure, the idea of the number, to make a series on Islamic civilization. [Her Highness] Sheikha Mozah's idea was not just to do something about Islamic culture and civilization, but that it should be Arab and Islamic culture. I wanted to show the relationship between Christianity and Islam, for example, ... and included [Her Highness] Sheikha Mozah herself.... The power of the woman again. That was a key painting [on cross-culture dialogue (figure 23.2)].

In sum, the bargain M. F. Husain struck with Her Royal Highness Sheikha Mozah was structured yet open-ended. There were to be ninety-nine paintings, symbolic of the *asma Allah al-husna* (the 99 Beautiful Names of God), renowned but also contested in Islamic piety.[4] M. F. Husain was to do ninety-nine such paintings, reflecting on Arab/Islamic culture but specifically on the relationship between Islam and Christianity. It would be easy to dwell on the multiple contradictions here: an Indian Muslim artist patronized by a Gulf Arab royal, a minority Shiʿi, "secular" Muslim more familiar with Hinduism than Christianity

FIGURE 23.2 · M. F. Husain, *Cross-Cultural Dialogue*, 2008. Acrylic on canvas. 199 × 310 cm. Photographer: Khalid Valiyakath Abdulrahim; courtesy Mathaf: Arab Museum of Modern Art, Doha. Qatar Foundation Collection. Used courtesy of Qatar Foundation.

emblematizing both Islam and Christianity in their broadest profile to myriad insiders/outsiders visiting Doha and the Museum of Islamic Art. Yet even this partnership reveals the larger truth of M. F. Husain's life journey: the bringing together of seeming opposites in order to produce yet another epic project.

It is important to note M. F. Husain's enduring attraction to epic projects. He has done numerous series of paintings. In addition to the eighty-eight oils he did to celebrate his eighty-eighth birthday in 2003, he also did another series in London in 2005. That series is of direct relevance to the 99 series projected for Doha. Titled the Lost Continent, it consisted of twenty-one canvases that, according to K. Bikram Singh, "have a strong narrative element." But what is the wisdom there? What does it say to the viewer, who is also the seeker of meaning? Singh focuses on one painting, *Untitled*, though elsewhere it is listed as what it clearly is, *Empty Bowl at the Last Supper*.[5] Singh observes how the images and the colors mesh in a tapestry of mystery:

> Redolent of the biblical Last Supper as also his own *Last Supper in Red*, an empty food bowl rests on the table that is held in place by two goblins. Just like the *Last Supper in Red*, the presiding figure in ancient robes is faceless: there is only a mysterious dark grey symbol in place of the head. But now,

instead of a candle and a book before it, there is just a large book with blank pages in front of the figure. Has "the Book" lost its meaning in our time? Has it become indecipherable? Another figure in priestly robes seems to be a question to the faceless figure in the centre whose gesture shows that he has no answer. The lemon yellow of the figures makes a strong contrast against the red background. The balance in these contrasting colors is created by the selective use of black and white.[6]

The speculations of Singh are not informed by any clue from the artist. He does not provide a storyboard for this, or the other paintings in the Lost Continent series, and we will return to the significance of all these elements—the dominant table, the goblins, the empty bowl, the presiding figure, and the blank book—below, but first it is crucial to understand the distinctive narrative of the Doha series. Though projected to become ninety-nine canvases, only nineteen have been completed to date (summer 2009).[7] It is a series that highlights the raw energy, the vertiginous innovation, and the present-day complexity of Arab/Islamic civilization. Some of the paintings seem so small as to be inconsequential: three men talking to one another, a fisherman and falcon, red camel against black sky, a tea stall. Still others seem didactic: to highlight the achievements of Arab science, there is a tableau tribute to Jabir ibn Hayyan and the Brethren of Purity (Ikhwan as-Safa), as also to Arab astronomy. Still others evoke M. F. Husain's own ancestral country, Yemen (to which he is linked spiritually through the Sulaimani subsect of the Bohras), with a tribute to the Queen of Sheba and also to a modern street scene from Sanaʿa. There are but three that seem to embody the theme announced in the March 2009 interview: to show the relationship between Islam and Christianity. What all three have in common is to confirm how opposites elide rather than collide, and not through attention to religious doctrine but to the common elements of everyday existence that they share. It has often been said that to look only at religion is to miss the point of Islam. One must look beyond religion qua religion in order to explain the myriad features of Islamic/Arab civilization. To see only "religion" is to ignore the traces of a civilizational force that includes Islam but also exceeds it. The paintings that represent Islam in M. F. Husain's 99 series—at least in the first nineteen—always frame religious themes or actors in contexts that divert the viewer's gaze from a creedal or theistic message and toward an encompassing aspiration for all humankind.

While we may never know why the Doha series was commissioned by Her Highness Sheikha Mozah on the theme of Arab/Islamic civilization, one does know that she, like her husband, His Royal Highness Shaykh Hamad ibn Khalifa

Al Thani, is concerned to open the Arab world in general and the Gulf area in particular to outside forces of cosmopolitan change. The cultural politics within the Gulf are intense: Dubai and Abu Dhabi claim branches of some of the leading auction houses (Sotheby's and Christie's), while Bahrain boasts the foremost Qur'anic museum in the Arab/Muslim world. Against this background the selection of M. F. Husain to have the first showing of his Doha project in the MIA was a masterstroke. His newly commissioned and most recent paintings seem to have been intended to occupy a separate gallery within the MIA, but now they will be shown as part of the even newer Mathaf: Arab Museum of Modern Art. The fact that they were included in a temporary gallery for the November 2008 opening of the MIA, also in Doha, meant that the painting which is the object of this essay, *LSRD*, was on public display for the first time as part of a series on Christian-Muslim dialogue.

Does it matter that M. F. Husain is a particular kind of Muslim painter? Or might one even ask preliminarily: *Can Husain be called a Muslim painter simply because he self-identifies as "a believer"?* Ananya Jahanara Kabir argues that Husain has always had to do his work from the subject-position of a minoritized Muslim in post-partition (i.e., post-1947) India.[8] Tapati Guha-Thakurta also makes the point that, since 1996, Husain has been pushed further and further into the subject-position of representing the Indian Muslim minority.[9] But let me ask a different question: How can his Islamically valorized worldview be discerned from the three paintings that allude to Muslim-Christian dialogue in the Doha series? Though they present but a fraction of his larger oeuvre of thirty thousand–plus paintings, they have elements that both replicate familiar themes (such as *LSRD*) and suggest new horizons for the artist, above all, in the subtlety, and the irony, of his play with *coincidentia oppositorum*.

All three were done within the first weeks of December 2008, again echoing what M. F. Husain said about his work: "I made a lot of research, sketches, and then execution doesn't take much time.... [T]o create the vision takes time.... [M]y method of working is almost instantaneous and very very extempo."[10] Though all three were produced as part of a series, they need to be considered separately before being analyzed in relation to each other and to the total Doha series that marks Husain as a Muslim painter in exile.

The first of the three is the one to which M. F. Husain himself made reference when he said: "I wanted to show the relationship between Christianity and Islam, for example,... and included [Her Highness] Sheikha Mozah herself.... The power of the woman again. That was a key painting [on cross-culture dialogue]."[11]

This work is the inaugural canvas. It is an enormous acrylic painting that depicts a rabbi reminiscent of the Jesus figure in LSRD. In size it is even larger than LSRD, and it appeared at the entrance to the gallery at the MIA opening in November 2008 with the title in English and Arabic: *Debate (al-jadal) / Comprehension (at-tafahum)*. It portrays three central figures, along with one anonymous bystander. It is not the first painting on the theme of *trimurti* or a triumvirate, since he had earlier done watercolor evocations of three major Hindustani poets—Ghalib, Iqbal, and Faiz.[12] *Debate/Comprehension*, like that earlier *trimurti*, projects a distinctly Muslim optic. First it points to the importance of the book. Unlike the book as an open, blank page object in the *Untitled* work from the Lost Continent series of 2005, the book here is marked explicitly in the middle, elliptically in the far left, and canonically in the far right.[13] According to the Qur'an 3:7, there is a vast celestial scroll (*umm al-kitab*) that encompasses all human destiny as also every divine mandate. *Umm al-kitab* is literally the prototype or mother of all books; on its pages are written the fate of all humans but also the content of every divine writ or scripture. As scripture, it is transmitted to human beings through prophecy, specific to each group, each language, and each time in the unfolding of history.

In the Abrahamic tradition those prophecies include the Torah, the Prophets, the Psalms, the Gospel, and, of course, the final prophecy to humankind, the Qur'an. In M. F. Husain's opening canvas for the Doha series, the three central figures each have a book marking who they are. The bishop to the right has a closed book; one may suppose that is the Gospel, though it might include the Torah, Prophets, and Psalms as well. Its custodian, the bishop, not only has a cloak and miter but also a wheel symbolizing his secular authority.

The figure on the left can either be an anonymous rabbi or perhaps an anticipation of the Jesus figure in LSRD, and the book he holds, though marked in an indecipherable language, could allude to Hebrew. By contrast, the figure in the middle with a scarf and turban holds a book that is not only open but marked with five Arabic letters: *Hā-mīm-ʿain-sīn-qāf*. As I discuss below, this summary reference to *Hā-mīm-ʿain-sīn-qāf* is a metonymic invocation of the forty-second chapter of the Qur'an. Titled *al-Shura*, or "consultation," it is arguably Husain's "favorite" Qur'anic chapter, since he quotes it twice in the three paintings that address the theme of Christian-Muslim dialogue in the Doha series.

The juxtaposition or conjuncture of opposites is also made clear in the hand gestures of the "bishop" and the "imam." The bishop confirms with the thumb, forefinger, and middle finger of his right hand, "three," for the Trinity, while the imam holds up his index finger, also on the right hand, indicating one or oneness, *tawhid*, the central doctrine of Islamic belief. Similarly, the colors confirm the differences on a continuum of assent, represented by the folded back page, orange and yellow on the front indicating spiritual aspiration, with red and white on the back indicating passion and purity. Each of the three figures also projects what they embody through their colors: the bishop in gray is austere and remote; the imam in green is reflective, even philosophical; while the rabbi in Nilotic blue symbolizes attachment to nature and primal elements, further accented by his minimal garb, a mere waistcloth, compared to the full body cloaks of the imam and bishop.[14]

As alluring as is the complexity of the three characters, of equal, compelling interest are the five other prominent elements in this opening evocation of Muslim-Christian dialogue: the camel, the horse, the tree, the woman, the building. The camel evokes the desert of Arabia but also more generally, the animal world in which man and cities make space but do not, and cannot, replace. The camel seems puzzled by the gestures of the three religious potentates, or he may be simply staring not at them but at the tree, which represents the heavenly *sidra* tree, the emblem of Qatar. The horse and the woman belong together: they are identified through the story book that accompanies this, as also the LSRD. It reads:

> *From behind the golden*
> *pages of Arab civilization,*
> *emerges*
> *the "Queen of Qatar"*
> *forging ahead riding a red horse.*

This is a grand—and deserved—gesture toward his patron, Her Royal Highness Sheikha Mozah, and unlike the camel, the red horse is not simply an idle onlooker. It represents the passion for culture and celebration of the Arab past that motivate her to engage M. F. Husain in the Doha series.

That leaves the building in the background to be deciphered. It is not representative of any structure in Doha or elsewhere, but it could refer to the MIA, where the "Queen of Qatar" has designated the first section of the M. F. Husain Doha series to be displayed in public. Her gesture is redoubled: on the one hand, she is leaning into the folio of history that embodies all three religions—Judaism, Islam, and Christianity—but on the other hand, she is gesturing toward the modern evocation of that past through a new building, whether the I. M. Pei Museum of Islamic Art or perhaps the future home of M. F. Husain's entire portfolio of 99 (namely, Mathaf: Arab Museum of Modern Art).

Between *Debate/Comprehension* is another painting that up till now has largely been ignored in commentary on M. F. Husain in the Doha phase of his exile as a Muslim painter. It does not have a storyboard. Its title replicates the Arabic letters writ large across the top: *Hā-mīm-ʿain-sīn-qāf* (2007, figure 23.3).

In size it is smaller than the other two, and it seems to have a very compressed tableau. Two *kaffiyeh*-clad men are talking and gesturing to each other. They frame the main element. Overarching them is the Arabic anagram *Hā-mīm-ʿain-sīn-qāf*, and below them is another *kaffiyeh* man gazing at a lamb, which is looking away from him.

The colors in this small acrylic scene are muted: shadowy brown at the top, with dark red as the major background and orange as the color for three border parts to the right, to the left, and the bottom as well as for the third *kaffiyeh*-clad man and the left hand of one of the two main protagonists. Orange is the color of the cover to the Torah held by the orange bearded rabbi in the *Debate/Comprehension* painting. It has also been used as a color signifying the desert in a 2004 acrylic, *Islam beyond Desert*, and it is a color that M. F. Husain often used to depict Hanuman in earlier watercolors on the Ramayana.[15] In sum, it expresses desert or land for inanimate subjects, while for human subjects, it evokes loyalty and cheerfulness, lending a light mood to the darker colors of the background, as do the light brown colors that mark the face, and apparel, of the three human figures and also, especially, the lamb.

Though the lamb is not found in many of Husain's paintings, it is prominent in two previous paintings that project Islamic themes. One is a stark 1981 watercolor titled *Ibrahim*, and here the lamb standing erect looks at a figure floating above a mountain precipice, his outstretched hands grasping—or releasing?—his name: Ibrahim! Here the lamb is clearly the sacrificial lamb of Biblical and Qur'anic provenance, but the other, from the same year, 1981, is labeled "Ya Rahman, Ya Raheem" "O You, Full of Compassion, O You, Ever Compassionate," and the lamb is curled up beneath it as the recipient of this divine invocation.[16] The lamb of the 2008 acrylic, in fact, could have been taken from a study of the lamb in the 1981 watercolor: except for the position of the front legs, they are nearly identical.

But that visual detective work does not unpack the meaning of the tableau. It condenses the initial large-scale acrylic without revealing any qualities or beliefs peculiar to Abrahamic religion, whether Muslim, Christian, or Jewish. In this setting the conversation seems to be territorial. The two main *kaffiyeh*-clad protagonists are in fact representative of West and East. The one on the left represents Europe, the orange escarpment to his right, while the one on the right

FIGURE 23.3 · M. F. Husain, *Ha-Meem-Ain-Seen-Qaf*, 2007. Photographer: Khalid Valiyakath Abdulrahim; courtesy Mathaf: Arab Museum of Modern Art, Doha. Qatar Foundation Collection. Used courtesy of Qatar Foundation.

represents Asia, the other orange escarpment located to his left. The two figures below them seem to parse out as Arabia, marked by the orange *kaffiyeh*-clad man gazing at the lamb, representing Africa, which looks away from him, and indeed from the whole scene.

If these interpretations are close to accurate, then the larger message is that Europe and Asia must stay in dialogue, but they must not presume that either Arabs or Africans pay attention to their declarations. Africa may in fact have to look elsewhere for a word of hope (beyond the Atlantic Ocean, perhaps to America?).

It is this awareness of Husain's own place on a larger-than-India geographic plane that may be the major lesson from both *Debate/Comprehension* and *Hāmīm-ʿain-sīn-qāf*. It is a sense that he, as a Muslim painter forced into exile, is also compelled to look into the universal values at the heart of his own identity. They are found in family, religion, and art. Honored through patronage, they are sustained beyond controversy, yet they are continuously, inevitably marked by the possibility of betrayal.

The accent on betrayal goes to the heart of LSRD, which, like all Husain's art, does not readily reveal its multiple messages. It contains the strong line and bright colors suggestive of much of his painting. Above all, it is iconic rather than didactic. As Karin Zitzewitz observed, "For Husain the divine icon is not a singular image but a form evocative of multiplicities."[17] The divine icon here is the Last Supper. It is not the first, but merely the most recent, Last Supper depiction from M. F. Husain. Two earlier depictions of the Last Supper—one in red, the other in blue (done in 1991), and also *Untitled* from 2005—convey a different set of messages, yet these paintings are linked to the 2007 LSRD through a free-floating horizontal band, which, according to one critic, "provides the *raison d'être* for the assembly and (the) encounter between metaphor and history."[18]

Without dwelling on the symbolism in these earlier Last Suppers, one can, and should, deduce that Husain is not just old but mature. That is, he has made an inner calculation about what to stress in his own restatement of artistic meaning at the zenith of his productive life. "On the notion of maturity," writes Zitzewitz, "the artist, once having attained it, can be, and is prone to be recursive, returning to earlier themes, images, icons but recasting them in a fresh optic."[19]

LSRD is the fresh optic of the mature Husain in his early 1990s. Against a bright red background it displays a suspended table, supported by four angels, one heraldic, one demonic, and two others blithely playful. Behind the table stand four figures, with only one—bearded and naked from the waist up, gesturing to his left—clearly identifiable as the central figure. A camel looks on, as three bowls perch atop the table. An open book grazes the arm of the central figure.

Interpretive options abound as to what this scene might convey to multiple audiences. "In his best paintings," writes Geeta Kapur, "Husain's symbols perform actively, change meanings, relate unexpectedly to each other and establish new relationships within a fully integrated formal structure. Husain is able to create personal myths that are provocative, intimate incursions into the unconscious."[20] Intimate incursions into the unconscious radiate from LSRD. The new personal myth in LSRD is amplified through its storyboard, reminiscent of M. F. Husain's movie takes. This storyboard was inscribed on the wall of the gallery where the painting was first mounted in Doha. Husain's commentary, scribbled in bold gold letters, reads:

> *In Lenardo [sic] Da Vinci's*
> *"LAST SUPPER" Europe may*
> *may be heavily CODED, yet*
> *Arabia in my "Last Supper*
> *of the Desert in Red"*
> *remains UNCODED.*

But is the Last Supper *uncoded*, or instead *re-coded*, in Husain's stunning re-articulation of the central sacrament of Christian ritual devotion?

One way to read it is to place not just this LSRD but also all Last Suppers in the genealogy of Indian painters, especially those linked to the Progressive Artists Group, who are riveted by this same theme. Yasodhara Dalmia has provided an arresting commentary on this group, seeing it as a self-conscious link back to Da Vinci's masterpiece, in terms of not only technique but also the message suggested. Above all, there's the effort to confront the moment of betrayal. It is no longer reduced to a single act by one person—Judas carrying out his horrific assignment—but rather a dispersed inquiry where none of those present can escape the possibility that they too betrayed, or might betray, the Lord of the Supper. In Husain's earlier *Last Supper in Red*, all the figures seem to be complicitous, with the central Christ-like figure being marked by what goes on around him as much as by what he does, or tries to do. In Dalmia's reading, the proscenium table becomes "both assembly and encounter and for Husain it becomes a virtual study of the twentieth century.... There is Buster Keaton (the comic actor and filmmaker) on one end and Fra Bartolommeo (the 16th century Renaissance painter) on the other, while the central figure is headless with an outstretched hand flanked by a fallen angel and Damocles' sword, which divides the table into two. The central axis is the long wooden table, upheld by the devil from below. This well-structured painting, against a flaming red background, is nothing short of a theatrical performance much in the manner of Leonardo's masterpiece."[21]

By contrast, LSRD is far more compressed in its imagery than its predecessors, whether from Husain's hand or from other Indian artists. It is also less theatrically expressive. It does not announce a didactic, singular message. Instead it probes into the unconscious, broaching multiple possibilities that are at once more metaphysically robust, and less easily stamped, than those evoked in his earlier works. In what follows I will suggest multiple ways that LSRD can be read as *either uncoded or re-coded*, with my own preference being the latter way of interpreting this extraordinary work.

At the descriptive level, it projects an arresting composition, with contrasting colors: red for passion; light brown, dark gray, and white for lineages that are both conjoined and contrasted, sometimes within the same figure. The central cherub, holding up the table, is not dark as in *Last Supper in Red*, but white, as is the fellow cherub, holding up the table at the far left. But another cherub is light brown, while a fourth is both brown (in its feet) and white (in its hands, as also in its trumpet). Above all, these figures—identified by Singh as goblins—are at once formulaic and playful: their characters as human, subhuman, and angelic, or at least cherubic, merge with the solitary animal, who, while looking on, seems ready to move beyond center stage.[22]

What one sees here is common to all Husain's painting: economy of expression, the central, horizontal line drawing us to all the activities and the possibilities that extend from it yet are not bound by it. The impression is processual: we are moved to process across time and space, at both physical and metaphysical registers, through both horizontal and vertical lines. In ordinary time, this is just another meal, perhaps more a sipping party than a Last Supper, since there's no food but just three bowls. The camel looks on, just as in many of Husain's works, there is a bystander or onlooker, who is at once an outside observer, but also a marking presence. It is a presence linked to the natural rather than the cosmic world, in this case, the natural world of the Arabian desert, making this an Arab not a European remembrance and evocation of the Last Supper. [The camel is also the sole creature to have an "eye" cast on the entire scene!][23]

Uncoded, LSRD can also be re-coded. It is *not* the Last Supper of Leonardo or any Christian artist, including the fellow Indian Progressive painter Frances

Newton Souza, whose Last Supper preceded Husain's and who may have suggested to Husain at least one element, the strangely distortive double head, and perhaps also the outsized hair cropping of the dark figure on the far left. These figures decouple LSRD from the Christian Last Supper, since there are only four (not twelve) figures above and behind the table, along with four others under it, upholding it or beckoning others to take note of it, as the cherub with a bugle. Then there is the offstage wheel or compass that becomes an icon for life outside the rest of the scene, a reminder, as it were, that life itself moves on, that what the viewer is seeing center stage is but a snapshot or a movie frame in the larger tableau of human/creaturely existence.

Even more directly a Muslim re-reading, or re-coding, of LSRD could be two identifications of figures behind the table. I had taken pictures of the original and then shown LSRD to many individuals. Almost all were engrossed. Nearly everyone had their own interpretation. "Wow, this is an amazing painting" was a frequent first response, and then followed the announcement "Oh, by the way, this is what it means!"

Several Muslims told me, with deadpan certainty, that the figure behind Jesus is the Prophet Muhammad, while the one on the far right is the first African Muslim, Bilal! And it is in this reading that the gaze, evident in all the figures, even and especially the faceless or veiled figure to the right of the central figure, becomes crucial. Just as the light gray camel to the far left is an onlooker who hovers at the edge of the drama, so the dark brown figure with dreadlocks at the far right is turning away from the table and from the central figure, as is the other two-headed figure next to him. The person with his or her back to the Lord of the supper may be Mary or Muhammad, and if the latter, then would not the dreadlocked figure be a stand-in for Bilal?

What makes this reading plausible are two other elements not readily decoded in LSRD. First is the bowls. M. F. Husain, when interviewed about *Last Supper in Red*, was asked about the social commentary of this painting. Its focal point for him was the empty white bowl at the foot of the central figure beneath the table. "The empty bowl," he observed, "signifies betrayal."[24] From one bowl of betrayal in 1991 we have three bowls of betrayal in 2008. In case there is any doubt about the artist's intent, when Deena Chalabi asked Husain about his return to the Last Supper theme, he quipped: "The Last Supper? I did it 20 years back, and I wanted again to look at betrayal. I wanted to express that in the context of this project. I said to [Her Highness] Sheikha Mozah that I thought it might create controversy. She said, 'Don't worry; we'll take care of it. This isn't India.'"

We began our essay with this quote and return to it here since the abstract notion of betrayal is now specified not through one but through three bowls of betrayal. They are at different angles and with variant colors. The one to the far right is light brown and sits in front of the two-faced figure, who could either be doubting Thomas or Judas. Its contents are ignored or contested. The central white bowl that seems upright could be the cup of life offered by Jesus to those who read the Book, opened toward them, not him, and yet with the possibility that they might misread its message and therefore betray him as its messenger. Finally the bowl at the far left end of the table seems to be tipped up to suggest that it is empty. Placed in front of the onlooking, semidetached yet engaged camel, it could signify that the water of nature, without which no life can survive, is also betrayed by the central figures, who do not recognize from their angle of vision that the table itself is dark at either end and only light in the middle. It is an ambiguous, if not fateful, moment or memory being marked and now etched in canvas.

Complementing this notion of betrayal are the sheets that fold into and around the thick horizontal bar, that is, the table. The color coding may be crucial to understanding its symbolic coding. The sheet at the right is gray; its message is "divine," like the central book also in gray. The other folding sheets, however, have a light color to the front, while the gray underside is mostly hidden. Is not the message around doubting Thomas or Judas hidden from us as from him, both above and below the table? By contrast, the cloth or sheet on the far left of the table is not at all revealed. It conceals the lower part of the figure that could be Mary or Muhammad, though the upper part in gray is already revealed as a "divine" code.

However one reads the identity of the characters behind the table, their multiple gestures project a desire to communicate, even as the energy of the urchins or cherubs or goblins beneath the table suggests that the meaning of their existence relates to the activity which they try to sustain above, if not beyond, them.

And reinforcing the connection to Islam and Islamic motifs is the signature on the bottom right. While on display at the Museum of Islamic Art in Doha, there was no signature on the painting itself, apart from the spoked circle at the left corner, which all took to be the wheel of dharma, an Indian icon that also connected the picture to M. F. Husain as its Indian creator. But its most recent addition contains M. F. Husain's own signature. The word "Husain" was written on the bottom but above it were the three letters: *qaf meem ha*. Two are self-evident: the *ha* is Husain, the *meem* is Maqbool, but why the *qaf* instead of the *fa*, which would have indicated his middle name Fida? The trickster motif suggests that it is just M. F. Husain playing around again, making his own signature into a quasi-human face, with the two "dots" as eyes. That reading would be reinforced by K. Bikram Singh. Visiting M. F. Husain at his Dubai home in 2007, he noted the *qaf meem ha* painted on the front door.[25] A deeper, metaphysical reading would suggest an anagram, that *qaf meem ha* can stand not just for parts of the artist's name but also for three of the five letters that recur in this series of paintings as his "favorite" Qur'anic *sura*, chapter 42 (*Surat al-Shura*), which accents consultation, conversation, engagement with others. It is used twice in the nineteen paintings that have appeared so far in the 99 series that will one day grace Doha's Mathaf: Arab Museum of Modern Art, and it is also the central theme, along with betrayal, for LSRD.

Yet none of these invocations of Arabic and/or Qur'anic letters precludes a pervasive secular reading of LSRD. Cannot an individual, like a collective, be both religious and secular? Is this not the ultimate expression of *coincidentia oppositorum*, the inner reflex of all M. F. Husain's oeuvre? If so, what kind of secular identity is it that best fits M. F. Husain? Tapati Guha-Thakurta makes the case that modern art has claimed a privileged status for itself as "secular," yet since the 1990s it has increasingly been held accountable to religious interpretations. While I applaud her attempts to link the ongoing crisis of modernist art to the ongoing crisis of the secular, I want to turn the lens of the secular on to M. F. Husain. He has been depicted as a last-gasp secularist, that is, one whose secularism privileges faith and religious practice but also emphasizes syncretism. He seemed to say as much in the same interview with Deena Chalabi when he observed:

> My disposition now is not dogmatic at all. I am not a fundamentalist. [Laughter] There are different faiths. The personal faith is within you here [he points to his chest], but you have to respect everyone's faith. You're not a preacher, or a reformer, or a teacher or a thinker. As a painter you just work with the visual, which becomes universal. Islam is universal.

Is Husain's "secularism" then last-gasp, or does it instead depend on which secularism is invoked? There has been, and will continue to be, many commentaries on the particular nature of secularism in India. Especially instructive is a coedited volume by Anuradha Dingwaney Needham and Rajeswari Sunder Rajan that explores both the contradictions of secularism and the limits of dialogue within the secular state.[26]

I would argue, however, that Husain's secularism is not the vulgar or journalistic secularism of, say, Arun Shourie. By Shourie's reading all secularist discourses are contrived and deceitful, whether driven by political propaganda or by communal intrigue or by both. This *is* secularism on its last legs, with only the end of time as its resolution. But there is also philosophical secularism—whether articulated by Partha Chatterjee, Tiki Madan, Ashis Nandy, Amartya Sen, or Akeel Bilgrami. Perhaps the most hopeful tangent of philosophical secularism, as applied to art, comes from Nandy. "Indian-style secularism," observed Nandy in 1990, "must have space for a continuous dialogue among religious traditions but *also between the religious and the secular,* so that in the ultimate analysis, each of the major faiths (at least for Indians) includes within it an in-house version of the other faiths both as internal criticisms and as a reminder of the diversity of the themes of transcendence."[27]

In theoretical terms, this is the ontological outcome of M. F. Husain's art in general and the series on Arab/Islamic civilization in particular. Those paintings capture the spirit of the eclectic, resilient, inclusive spirit of Islamic civilization. It is not just for Arabs only, or for Muslims alone. It is not just about the past but also beckons the future; in Husain's own words, here we find "echoes of time past and early beginnings of the future" (from a penned commentary on one of his sketches about Yemen in the same MIA temporary installation). *LSRD* etches the future of many actors, agents, agendas of hope, and promises of comity as well as comedy.

Husain, as a painter forced into exile, as a Muslim shaped by Hindu cosmopolitan themes, and as an activist convinced that art will not just sell but transform its viewers, practiced a form of religion. When Deena Chalabi asked him in March 2009 about his current religious disposition, Husain replied:

> When I was young, five, six, seven, my family wanted me to become an imam [aka a Muslim priest]. I learned so much that I could lead prayer. But at one stage it became meaningless to me. I studied the cosmos, spiritual reality, and when I was 23 or 25 I met a very learned man who used to teach me. I was already painting in between, and he told me, you should devote your life to this. The religious life is not your path.
>
> So instead of an imam I became a painter. In my own small way, I'm still leading. That fire was there, right from the beginning. I have worked very hard, and I am still on my toes. I have all this energy. For the first twenty years, after I moved from a small town to Mumbai, when I was sleeping on

footpaths, I never regretted what I was doing. My concentration and focus never failed. That is the test.

Husain's art and inspiration survive. His other canvases, like the three we have examined above, promise to reveal still more about the core elements of our world, not least the benefit of dialogic civility among all its citizens, non-Abrahamic as well as Abrahamic, the full spectrum of humankind.

Notes

Bruce B. Lawrence, "A Metaphysical Secularist? Decoding M. F. Husain as a Muslim Painter in Exile," in *Barefoot across the Nation: Maqbool Fida Husain and the Idea of India*, edited by Sumathi Ramaswamy (New York: Routledge, 2011), 253–73. Used courtesy of Taylor & Francis.

1. Deena Chalabi, March 2009 interview. For the full interview, please consult Bruce B. Lawrence, "A Metaphysical Secularist? Decoding M. F. Husain as a Muslim Painter in Exile," in *Barefoot across the Nation: Maqbool Fida Husain and the Idea of India*, ed. Sumathi Ramaswamy (London: Routledge, 2011), 271–73.
2. Jalaluddin Rumi, *Signs of the Unseen (Fihi ma fihi)*, translated from Persian by W. M. Thackston Jr. (Putney, VT: Threshold Books, 1994), 140.
3. On Husain's "three" muses, whom he regards as three distinct women in his life: mother, wife, and the actress Madhurai Dixit, see Patricia Uberoi, "The Bliss of Madhuri: Husain and His Muses," in Ramaswamy, *Barefoot across the Nation*, 213–34. In his comprehensive survey of M. F. Husain's work, Singh separates the female form, linking it to his youthful passion for a Czech woman, from his engagement with heroic women—Mother Theresa and Indira Gandhi, but in terms of *coincidentia oppositorum*, they are part of the same sensitive mindscape, one that sees women in multiple moments, always spurring creativity while retaining a sense of mystery. K. Bikram Singh, *Maqbool Fida Husain* (New Delhi: Rahul and Art, 2008), 370.
4. Consult, for example, Imam Abu Hamid al-Ghazali's introduction to the debates of the late eleventh century regarding their significance, in his own magisterial book, *Al-Maqasid al-Asna fi Sharh Asma' Allah al-Husna*, translated as *Al-Ghazali on the Ninety-Nine Beautiful Names of God*, from Arabic by David Burrell and Nazih Daher (Louisville, KY: Fons Vitae, 1995).
5. Hwee Koon in a 2005 review refers to it as one "among the 21 paintings featured in this [the Lost Continent] exhibition; 'Empty Bowl at the Last Supper' has broken the sales record for contemporary Indian art at USD 2 million." The exhibition traveled from London to Singapore, where Hwee Koon reviewed it on December 9, 2005. See http://www.studio-international.co.uk/painting/lost_continent.asp.

6 Singh, *Maqbool Fida Husain*, 370.
7 One can surmise from the March 2009 interview, however, that the subject of a twentieth-century painting will be the first muezzin of Islam, Bilal al-Habshi. See below for further commentary, and the total number may be 33 (according to Qatari sources contacted in 2019).
8 Ananya Jahanara Kabir, "Secret Histories of Indian Modernism: M. F. Husain as Indian Muslim Artist," in Ramaswamy, *Barefoot across the Nation*, 100–115.
9 Tapati Guha-Thakurta, "Fault-lines in a Nationalist Edifice: On the Rights and Offences of Contemporary Indian Art," in Ramaswamy, *Barefoot across the Nation*, 192–97.
10 Susan S. Bean, *Epic India: M. F. Husain's Mahabharata Project* (Salem, MA: Peabody-Essex Museum, 2007), 32.
11 Chalabi, March 2009 interview.
12 See Singh, *Maqbool*, 278–81, and further discussed below.
13 For this reference, as to several others, I am indebted to Sumathi Ramaswamy for her close reading of my essay. The actual painting is set forth in the chapter "The Stretch of My Canvas" in Singh, *Maqbool*, 371.
14 One could find a further analysis of color choice, and their symbolic resonance, in Singh, *Maqbool*, 279–81. It is the same passage where he discusses three Hindustani poets—Ghalib, Iqbal, and Faiz—whom M. F. Husain painted and repainted, as he did the Last Supper, though in these 1980s paintings he adds poems in the second version, giving a firmer clue as to his intention in casting them as he did. Singh is quick to add that there can be no single ascription of meaning to color selection by Husain (or by any artist), but the range of possibilities also fit the depiction above of the three exemplars from Judaism, Christianity, and Islam. Blue is not discussed but "red can signify revolution, violence, and celebration. Golden can symbolize spiritual attainment and prosperity. Similarly, green can symbolize Islamic identity as also fecundity of nature" (Singh, *Maqbool*, 280).
15 Singh, *Maqbool*, 137–38, 140.
16 Singh, *Maqbool*, 160, 158.
17 Karin Zitzewitz, "The Aesthetics of Secularism: Modernist Art and Visual Culture in India" (unpublished Ph.D. dissertation, Columbia University, 2006), 353.
18 Yasodhara Dalmia, *The Making of Modern India Art: The Progressives* (New Delhi: Oxford University Press, 2001), 124.
19 Zitzewitz, "Aesthetics of Secularism."
20 Quoted in Zitzewitz, "Aesthetics of Secularism," 91.
21 Quoted in Zitzewitz, "Aesthetics of Secularism," 209.
22 Singh, *Maqbool*, 370.
23 It would seem logical to connect this commentary with Singh, *Maqbool*, 375–78, where the Al-Arabia Series was launched in 2006. It is not clear, however, what was included in this series, and at least one of its major paintings, noted as fig. 353, p. 376, in Singh is an exact replica of what becomes the Battle of Badr, number 14 in the

Doha series. Also quoting from a Qur'anic verse (48:1) that first appeared in a 1928 calligraphy by Husain (Singh, *Maqbool*, 27), this verse is linked to the first Islamic painting according to Husain himself in the March 2009 Chalabi interview: "The first pure Islamic painting to me is the Battle of Badr. I showed through the horses a black road behind, because the prophet always wore black."

24 *Times of India*, October 5, 2005, http://timesofindia.indiatimes.com/articleshow/1253808.cms.

25 Singh, *Maqbool*, 267.

26 Anuradha Dingwaney Needham and Rajeswari Sunder Rajan, eds., *The Crisis of Secularism in India* (Durham, NC: Duke University Press, 2007).

27 Ashis Nandy, "The Politics of Secularism and the Recovery of Religion," in *Mirrors of Violence—Communities, Riots, and Survivors in South Asia*, ed. Veena Das (New Delhi: Oxford University Press, 1990), 74.

TWENTY-FOUR

Conclusion, from *Who Is Allah?* | 2015

How to think the Unthought or imagine the Unimaginable?[1] It is at once a project and a challenge—to the mind, to the heart, and even to the notion of self for all those attached to the Name, the Thing, the Absolute, the One: Allah. It has occupied wordsmiths, intellectuals, scholars, mystics, and mainstream practitioners—from the seventh century to the twenty-first century. It has also occupied artists whose language is channeled through the hand and directed to the eyes, the ears, and also the heart. Artists ask: how can art redefine, and reconfigure, what is meant by Allah? Convention and orthodoxy resist both innovation and stimuli for creativity. Though artists often find space at the margin of social acceptability, sometimes in their attempt to bring others into a higher state of awareness, they go beyond what others accept and expect as normal. It is notable how often women have been the pioneers for renewed artistic attention to Allah in recent decades.

There is no single group, of either men or women, who can be labeled Muslim artists, and so the conclusion would miss the point of exploring Allah if it only looked at Muslim performers or painters, as though they represented "true" Islam, or took an alternate perspective, and looked at Muslim videogames and their entrepreneurs as though *they* were the custodians of Allah and His Word. Both these groups do project a view of Islamic creativity in the public domain. While we will examine representatives from several regions of the Muslim world, we will end by emphasizing an embodied approach to Allah that circles back to those spiritual warriors known as Sufi masters.

In the Name of Allah: Figural Death

To highlight the importance of performance art, we begin the conclusion without an epigraph and instead draw attention to an Indonesian woman artist's engagement with Allah, written on a perishing plate in Arabic. This artist writes the divine name on plates before shattering them in the course of a unique, interactive performance.

More than just another creative project, the Allah plate is intended to raise a crucial, oft-ignored perspective: there is no normative ethics for works of Muslim art with respect to their disclosures or affective aims. Arahmaiani is a contemporary Javanese performance artist, committed to Islam (her father's religion) but also engaged by Hindu Buddhist beliefs (her mother's persuasion). Whether or not she recognizes Om to have a similar power to Allah in evoking the Eternal Absolute, she aims to shock the sensibilities of Muslim viewers and participants regarding Allah. In her performance of *Breaking Words*, she wrote *Allah* on white ceramic plates in Arabic. She invited audience members to write on them as well, and then smashed them against the wall.

This iconoclastic gesture took advantage of the bundled material properties of ceramics and inks, but it also suggested the symbolic power of Arabic orthography. Its intent was to shake participants loose from attachments that, in Arahmaiani's view, border on the obsessive and compulsive, not just to know Allah and to obey Allah but to presume to act as Allah's sole custodian. For at least several viewers, the smashing of the plates was a hurtful, even hateful blow to Allah and to their affective attachments to Allah through material form. Complaints were lodged with the police at the opening performance and also in subsequent forums where the artist appeared.

What can we say about the moral status of this artist and her performance? "If some artists aim at ethical pleasure through their work," noted a prominent scholar of Indonesian culture, "perhaps we may say that Arahmaiani's strives for ethical hurt (not harm) or, better ethical unease. Arahmaiani is an artist of conscience, yet different people are made happy by different things [and so] object choices are not equivalent." Arahmaiani seeks to raise the serious but tangled question: in what context, and with what memories, does one appeal to the sacred as an unequivocal source of happiness? In shattering the Allah plates, she hopes to trigger others' awareness of the history of injustice occluded in the aura of happiness. Her ultimate aim, one might say, is to expose unhappy effects, to reimagine what else may count as the good life, but in order to find alternative models of the good, one must first "touch" the ultimate source of good and bad, hope and despair: Allah. Arahmaiani is even prepared to kill some forms of joy that her viewers take for granted when they see the name Allah. She also recognizes her own risk from having to live with the consequences of her provocation.[2]

Part of the outcry against Arahmaiani, of course, was not just her "harm" or "offense" to Allah, but also her resort to visual art, and to performance, as a means of communicating her message. Using Arabic as a pictorial rather than verbal sign is itself an Indonesian reflex that has other parallels, notably in the work of Abdul Djalil Pirous, not least of which is his acrylic representations of the Chapter of Sincerity (Q 112: *Surat al-Ikhlas*) and the Chapter of Noon (Q 93: *Surat al-Ḍuḥā*).[3]

But it also resonates with Iranian women artists, among them the University of California at Berkeley–educated Shirin Neshat. Neshat has mounted several exhibits of her photography, including the series *Women of Allah*, shown during the 1990s at major museums across the United States. Its centerpiece is a self-portrait of the artist holding a gun in front of her veiled countenance with Persian writing scrolling across her face. In explaining the layered elements of this photograph, Neshat notes its three components: the body, the veil, and the text, with an accent on the last. And it is this text that counters the visual veil, as though "through literature, one can show how Islamic women have historically 'unveiled' their feminist views, in order to transform their societies."[4] It dramatizes the little-known aspect of life under the Islamic Republic of Iran between 1980 and 1989, when women as well as men served in the horrific war with Iraq, many of them injured, maimed, or killed. But before Neshat's art most of these women were not recognized as warriors or soldiers. To recuperate "lost" Iranian women fighters may be a utopian project, on the edge of Muslim self-expression, but it is still within the scope of a quest to engage, and so be faithful to, Allah.

In the Name of Allah: Censorship, Prison, and Physical Death

Among those prepared to kill when offended by what they perceive to be an abuse of the name Allah are those who monitor public space in Egypt today. In 2011 the Egyptian short-story writer Karam Saber published a set of his short stories with the provocative title *Where Is Allah?* In these stories the writer, also a social activist, questions how an omniscient, omnipresent Other could be divinely monitoring what is happening in the world of the twenty-first century. Writing in the aftermath of the Tahrir Revolution (January 2011), Karam Saber was monitored by foreign media tracking Egypt. When he was brought to trial for insulting religion, the court found him guilty and he was sentenced to five years in prison. The author's arrest attracted the attention of international media, including NPR, which broadcast his story in early summer 2013.[5]

Yet Karam Saber was luckier than other Egyptian writer activists who have sought to shine light on injustice, and to rally others to enact justice, through invoking the name of Allah. In the 1990s, the Egyptian novelist Nawal El Saadawi had to leave Cairo after the assassination of a fellow writer/activist, Farag Foda. On June 8, 1992, Foda was murdered while leaving his home, his murder justified by a *fatwa* declaring him an apostate. While in exile, Nawal El Saadawi wrote and published a new book in the form of a play, entitled *Allah Resigns at the Summit Meeting*. In it she too boldly suggested a divine absence instead of omniscient presence, a rejection of hope, not an acclamation of belief, when facing the spectrum of (in)justice that defines our contemporary world, not least in the Middle East. In satirical terms, she suggested that if/when Allah looks at all that is happening in today's world, much of it in His Name, He resigns. He is offended by the hypocrisy of those who invoke His Name but do not follow His Command, above all, the Command for equity and justice for all. Nawal's play was intended to draw attention to the deficit in the contemporary world, not to offend any belief or practice linked to religion, yet the play was banned in 2006. Al-Azhar took her to court in 2007, accusing her of apostasy and heresy. She was not acquitted until 2008. In the meantime, her publisher received so many warnings that he withdrew the book from print publication, though it persists in cyberspace and remains available online in a Kindle edition.[6]

Provoking without Offending: The Case of M. F. Husain

Women have pioneered new—even audacious—ways of reimagining Allah. There are also some bold male artists intent on pursuing the same project. One of the greatest challenges is to create powerful images that evoke the Thing, the Absolute, the One with dignity but also with provocation. One is the Ka'ba Cube as reimagined by the Egyptian painter Dr. Ahmed Moustafa, but there is also the extraordinary evocation of "God is Great" (*Allahu Akbar*) in its foundational seventh-century context that is also linked to the twenty-first century. It comes from the Indian-Qatari artist M. F. Husain.

In his nineties and living in exile in Doha, Husain created a painting that depicts the Prophet's Companion, Bilal ibn Rabah, yet also alludes to Barack

Obama. The image is simultaneously political and cultural, connecting as it does, though obliquely, Bilal, the first African Muslim and first Muslim prayer caller (*muezzin*), with President Obama. Integral to Husain's imagination was bringing together past and present. He conjoined incongruous moments and actors in ways that seem far-fetched yet real, at once implausible and celebratory. The Bilal-Obama connection was inspired by the 2008 presidential election. Husain had stayed up late to listen to the results in Doha. He was so elated by the outcome that he could not sleep (at age ninety-three), and so he devoted himself to a painting of Bilal, one of the first converts to Islam, who also happened to be Ethiopian (*Habshi*).

The phrase *Allahu Akbar* is forever identified with Bilal because he was the first *muezzin* in the new Islamic faith, and so the words mark his identity. In the painting, the phrase *Allahu Akbar* looms large at the bottom, with the name Bilal written across the middle of the figure with upraised arms. One has to know the story of Husain's inspiration to conclude that Barack Obama is projected as the modern-day equivalent of Bilal al-Habshi. "It took America two-hundred years to do what Islam did in less than ten years," Husain quipped to me, when I asked him about his painting: "make a black man its major icon to the outside world." Bilal was, of course, not Muhammad; he was only the voice of ritual prayer in Medina, not leader of the entire Muslim community. Yet the comparison reflects the long reach of *Allahu Akbar* beyond its everyday evocation in Muslim public space, or its signature use by terrorists or suicide bombers in their final moments. It projects the artist's—in this case, M. F. Husain's—ability to mingle religion with politics, enriching one by contact with the other, while also denying either ultimate authority over the individual.[7]

The Allah Brand Name: Yusuf ʿAli Usurped

And so we must continuously ask: who is Allah in the twenty-first century of the common era? For Muslims Allah is still divine, but for many non-Muslims Allah is now the divide—between East and West, between the United States and the Middle East, but also among many Muslims, between the "true" literalist believers in God's Word (the Qur'an) and others who seek to see God manifest in His creation and also in His creatures. Is Allah no longer a monitor for humankind, but instead a moniker for one brand of sectarian rage, substituting a community united by faith to a maelstrom of competing ideologies? The current public outcry in Malaysia over the Christian use of Allah provides yet another instance of Islam politicized, with Allah center stage in a media war to claim ownership of the One beyond Naming, or Owning, or Outlawing.[8] One must ask: Where is the balance, the middle point, the broad way or *al-sirat al-mustaqim* that is announced as the Muslim path in the first chapter (Al-Fatiha) of the Noble Book?

To move beyond such dyadic choices, we must return to where we began: can or should Allah be translated as God? William Chittick, a major scholar of Islam with a strong Sufi bent, says, "Yes." But his emphatic affirmative gets converted to "No" by the leading propagators of Islamic orthodoxy, the Saudi establishment located in the two holiest cities of Islam in western Saudi Arabia. There we find not only Mecca, the hometown of the Prophet and pilgrimage center for Muslims, but also Medina, the city to which Muhammad migrated and where he died and was buried. The Saudi religious authorities have resolved the question of choice between Allah and God: they always substitute Allah for God, even when the text that they used to publish as an English translation of the Qur'an comes from a translator who elected to use God instead of Allah.[9]

Abdullah Yusuf ʿAli was perhaps the most successful, and certainly the most famous, translator of the Holy Qur'an into English. An Indo-Pakistani civil servant from colonial India, he first published his Qur'an translation in Lahore in the mid-1930s. Its odyssey has been bizarre. It would be the stuff of fiction were it not the staggering byline of actual history, amply marked at several stages. Yusuf ʿAli began his translation in the 1920s, after he had retired from the Civil Service and settled in the United Kingdom. First published in 1934, his original translation was already in its third edition at the time of his death in 1952.

But then in 1980, the Saudi religious establishment felt the need for a reliable English translation and exegesis of the Qur'an; they wanted to make an official Saudi-approved translation available for the increasing English-language readership across the globe. After surveying the various translations in print at the time, four high-level committees under the General Presidency of the Department of Islamic Research chose Abdullah Yusuf ʿAli's translation and commentary as the best available. No reason was ever given why Marmaduke Pickthall (an English convert, whose translation is also well known) or some other translator was not selected, but significant revisions were made to the Yusuf ʿAli translation in 1985 before it was printed with royal consent by the King Fahd Holy Qur'an Printing Complex.

In 1989, Amana Publications, which in 1977 had first introduced the Yusuf ʿAli translation to an enthusiastic American audience, published a "new" fourth edition. It featured revision of the translation and commentary undertaken with the help of the Saudi-funded International Institute of Islamic Thought. The new, revised Amana print reached its eleventh edition on May 2004. Among the several departures from the original of Yusuf ʿAli is the shift from God to Allah. Why? The awkward shift has been described by one Muslim writer as "the decision to 'detranslate' the word 'God' back into the Arabic."[10]

Though there is no commentary on the reasons for the change, it is implied that Allah has so thoroughly replaced God (for Muslims) that Allah, and only Allah, can be linked with the Abdullah Yusuf ʿAli Qur'an translation. Surf the internet in search of the original translation, and you will find nothing. It is a sad irony that some websites blandish the altered translation, substituting Allah for God, even while retaining Yusuf ʿAli's preface where he makes clear that it is Allah as God who for him shines through the pages of the Holy Qur'an.[11]

Despite the flaws in the original rendition, and also the manipulations of the successive versions printed from Amana (including the detranslation of God to Allah), the appeal of the Yusuf ʿAli original translation endures. Its checkered history cannot be traced on the internet. Despite the dizzying plurality of sites on Islam, Allah, and the Qur'an, there is none that details the saga just depicted.

As it happened, the modified Yusuf ʿAli Qur'an translation served as the officially sanctioned English translation in Saudi Arabia for slightly more than a decade before it in turn was replaced in 1998 by the still-more-distorted translation by Taqi al-Din al-Hilali and Muhsin Khan. In the words of a leading Muslim scholar, this translation "turns the Qur'an into a blueprint for replicating the xenophobic and misogynist Saudi society in every detail."[12] Others have also criticized the severe biases that make this not only an awkward, stilted, dry, and literalist rendition of the Noble Book but also one that is aggressively puritanical, authoritarian, misogynous, anti-Jewish, anti-Christian, and anti-pluralist.

Perhaps none of this would matter, except that the al-Hilali/Khan English translation has been distributed largely free through mosques, seminaries, religious organizations, and Muslim bookshops throughout Africa, Asia, Europe, and the United States. Often, on my own trips to the Kingdom of Saudi Arabia, it is the al-Hilali/Khan version that I find in my hotel room, tucked away in a drawer of the bedside table. All the words from Allah, and all the descriptions of Allah, in the Qur'an must be literally true; all the prescriptions attributed to the Thing, the Absolute, the One must be slavishly, unquestionably followed. And, above all, Islam must be sealed off, kept free of contamination from other Abrahamic religions. But the more one seeks to distance Islam from its Semitic neighbors, the more one reinforces negative stereotypes that much of the world already has of Islam.

A Final Quest to Invoke and Embody Allah

Should you then succumb to despair and doomsday predictions? Granted that negative images of Allah will persist, is it reasonable to assume that they will dominate the imagination of this generation and future generations? Will Muslims and non-Muslims alike accept these images, while ignoring other devout Muslims who also claim to project the Thing, the Absolute, the One, the Lord of All Worlds, the Endpoint, as also the First Point, of All Life?

The strongest, most persistent retort to literalist notions of Allah comes from the rapt attention and insights of Sufi masters. They, along with their devotees, take their inspiration from *al-asma al-husna*, Allah's Beautiful Names, and they also confront and reject the Wahhabi worldview from their own spiritual treasury.

Consider the Sufi effort to expand the core of Islamic devotion to an inclusiveness that at once embraces Indian spirituality yet rejects Salafi repudiation of all nonliteral approaches to Allah/God. It comes from Scott Siraj al-Haqq Kugle. An American, a Muslim, and a Sufi, Kugle is also a scholar, and in a recent book he evokes many of the themes explored above: devotion to the Word and to the world, acknowledging Allah as transcendent, beyond human knowing, yet so close as to be part of the body. Kugle focuses on five spiritual exemplars who exceeded the boundaries of their temporal context. One was particularly prescient. Hajji Imdadullah not only performed the hajj or pilgrimage to Mecca, as his name implies, but also embodied, as his name further suggests, *imdad Allah*, the support of Allah, his own agency as Allah's instrument for the current age.

Hajji Imdadullah was a Chishti master living in what Kugle calls a *barzakh* era. It was late nineteenth-century North India. Though the British dominated South Asia, seeds of change had been planted even before the Mutiny of 1857. The Mughal Empire, after more than three hundred years of rule, was in sharp decline. Commerce ruled, yet it was commerce that originated from Europe not Asia. As the East India Company expanded from a trade network into a military force, it reduced the Mughal emperor to a vassal; it also reduced Muslims to a disempowered minority in a non-Islamic and rapidly globalizing polity.

Because he lived at a time of political transition and societal uncertainty, Hajji Imdadullah focused on inner, spiritual revolution. His own strategy prioritized the heart as the seat of all emotions and also all outcomes, "allowing the heart to reveal its deeper nature as the wellspring for God's presence in the world."[13] His instrument was a training manual: *The Brilliance of Hearts*. The hierarchy of leader and disciple permeates its pages, yet its focus on immersive remembrance of Allah reflects an intense mixture of psychological insight and anatomical training peculiar to the Chishti Sufi tradition. It draws on its own lineage of past masters, including its initial Indian emissary, Muʿinuddin, and the Mughal paragon, ʿAbdul Quddus Gangohi. But it is Hajji Imdadullah who recasts their teaching in a modern idiom.

The goal for Imdadullah remains the same as that announced by Muʿinuddin, his thirteenth-century precursor: "To bring the body into harmony with the cosmos, allowing the ego to dissolve into union with God."[14] For Imdadullah, however, the goal of self-purification and harmony with the cosmos was not an end goal but instead an intermediate step to a higher goal. That higher goal was twofold: performing the *sunna*, the Muhammadan model, while obeying the outer law, or *shariʿa*, since its requirements encompassed both the individual believer and the collective good of the Muslim community.

Indeed, the outcome of all these spiritual techniques for Imdadullah was "to accelerate the spiritual disintegration of the self to erase the will and achieve union with God, allowing the performance of *sunna*."[15] By prioritizing *sunna* over solitude, Imdadullah reinterpreted the spiritual mandate of his Chishti predecessors, yet he maintained their reliance on sainthood as the key to both sanctity and *sunna* observance. On this critical point he departed from the practices that were advocated by his fellow Muslim, Wahhabi contemporaries. For the latter, most Sufis were deemed to be unbelievers, and all saintly devotion condemned as tomb worship, itself a form of idolatry.

The critical locus of difference between Sufis and Wahhabis, however, is their view of the body. The central figure of Wahhabi belief is their eponymous founder, Ibn ʿAbd al-Wahhab. Though Ibn ʿAbd al-Wahhab did not condemn the Sufi vision of God's nature, human nature, and ascetical practice, he was obsessively fixated on the human body as the source of all temptation, evil, and idolatry. Looking at actions instead of intentions (*niyya*), he attributed the crassest motives to all dependence on bodily practices or human exemplars. The Prophet Muhammad was stripped of any link to the Light of Lights, as the martyr of love Shihabuddin Suhrawardi would have it. Instead of the Perfect Man of Sufi reflection, Muhammad became the storehouse, conduit, and announcer of God's Word. The disembodied Prophet becomes, in Kugle's words, "nothing more for the Wahhabis than a mere megaphone for God's speech; they cannot see the human body as an assembly of the signs of God."[16]

In effect, Wahhabis are Arab Cartesians. Notes Kugle: "For while Descartes attempted to gain distance from the body in order to achieve intellectual certainty, the Wahhabis sought religious certainty and, along the way, abdicated intellectual clarity (by decrying the body). Both are united in the drive for certainty, committing ideological violence against the body in order to banish it as a source of moral doubt and ontological ambiguity."[17]

These are not mere differences in outlook among pious Muslims. The ideological brinkmanship of the Wahhabis also fuels more extreme expressions, and often acts of violence, that privilege *jihad* as a monolithic reflex of Islamic loyalty. So much so that in the aftermath of the Cold War, observes Kugle, "al-Qaeda, the Taliban, and other splinter groups of Wahhabi-inspired militants express this ideology's most violent inner drive. These radicals who cannot or will not engage in military *jihad* engage in cultural *jihad* by prohibiting body images in other ways: suppressing women, denouncing Sufis, or reviling as idolatry technologies of visual communication (like photography, cinema, and television)."[18] *Jihad*, no longer a metaphor of self-perfection, becomes an instrument for endless warfare.

Conclusion

Let us admit that we cannot avoid warfare, both physical and metaphysical, in the name of Allah. Battles over the Thing, the Absolute, the One are lengthy and limitless. The skirmishes are far from over. The greatest danger of these ongoing skirmishes is that both Muslims and non-Muslims will be debarred from the power of Allah. It will not matter whether Allah is presented in the unadorned Arabic of the original revelation, or mediated, then transformed through intense reflection on that name, or one of its ninety-nine facets, as it has been in the history of Islamic spirituality. That outcome will be a loss, not just for Muslims but for all humankind.

And so what are the guideposts, and the takeaway message, from our engagement and struggle with multiple practices that focus on Allah? No matter how intense or persistent our quest, it hinges on a single question: what are we to make of Allah? Who *is* Allah? The question remains as haunting, its answer as elusive, at the end of this quest as at the outset. What we have reviewed, examined, analyzed, and projected are but the fragments of a millennial odyssey. It encompasses the history of Islam and beyond. It echoes the shifts and challenges of human society across time and place, from the seventh century to the twenty-first century, from Arabia to Asia, Africa and now America. It also reflects varied groups within Islam, many mainstream and respected, but also others marginal, questioned or even rejected by the majority of Muslims.

And so instead of one overarching conclusion we have three possible conclusions. Let us call them sociological, existential, and skeptical, each with their distinctive perspective and discrete audience.

The *sociological* approach focuses on persons: WHO seeks to connect with Allah, and WHY? In the resources scanned and the sources cited above, we find mostly urban men of culture, education, and wealth, enjoying public acclaim during, as also after, their lifetime. The champions of Allah include the heroes of Islam: Al-Ghazali, Ibn ʿArabi, Rumi, Hajji Imdadullah. The voices of women, especially radical revisionist women like Nawal El Saadawi and Shirin Neshat, are few and recent. One could argue that their impact today, like that of the Brethren of Purity from the eleventh century, affects only a handful of skeptics, but will not they too linger as part of the larger legacy of Islamic creativity across centuries? Dissident artists like Arahmaiani and M. F. Husain continue to invoke Allah. They see themselves in the image of the Thing, the Absolute, the One, even if it is not the image imagined or embraced or acceptable to their coreligionists. It is Allah on the edges or at the margin. Each end heralds a new beginning. The quest has amplified without exhausting the Thing. Its power remains Absolute, for It persists as the One, beyond knowing yet ever inviting us to know. "To Allah we belong, and to Allah we are ever returning" (Q 2:156).

The second conclusion veers to the experience of the process, the search itself. It is an *existential* process. It focuses on WHAT is linked to Allah, and HOW? Its advocates dwelling in the mystery of the Name. Allah exceeds the Name, even as the Name itself becomes a focus of attention on Allah as immeasurable force, the source of life and death, good and evil, hope and despair. Smell the bouquet, hear the echo, see the rainbow, join the feast, and feel the fire—of Allah, Khoda (a Persian word for God), and Tanri (a Turkish word for God). All the senses, not just the mind or intellect, attune to the beyond which is also within, so much so that one cannot speak of Allah without first feeling the spark within, either as the second-person You in English or as the third-person *hu* "He/Him" in Arabic. Mirror, mind, moment are not goals but goads: how are we to see Him/*hu* in the mirror, how to imagine Him/*hu* in the mind, and how to feel Him/*hu* in each moment, the present moment, neither past nor future, beyond birth and rebirth, the Eternal Now? This is the mainstream Muslim quest for Allah, the Sufi search for the Beloved. It parallels the quest for a cosmic *qibla* (at once daily focus and final vista) in every religious tradition or spiritual path.

Yet neither the sociological assessment nor the existential response will satisfy the *skeptic*. The skeptic may be a believer or unbeliever but she never ceases to ask: WHERE is Allah, and WHEN does the quest end? At the least, she asserts, there is no supreme name for God. Allah, like Adonai or God, Khoda or Tanri, Om or Om Shanti Shanti Shanti, may not exist or may exist but only as Being—infinite, timeless, and unknowable. To the extent that He is a Being, His ipseity (that is, who He is at His core self) goes beyond description, beyond naming. The Thing is ever more, and always other, than what is named the Thing, the Absolute, the One. It appears as an ethereal image traced by jinns but not by "real" people. It resides in the *barzakh*, not in heaven or hell nor on earth or in the sky but at the margins of each and within each simultaneously. Unthinkable, untraceable, it has no true Name since any name, whether God or Adonai or Allah or Allat, confines Him/Her/It. At best there are a surfeit of names for Allah, at least ninety-nine, though likely many more. All pale beside the infinite reality—Allah simply "is"; all the Names that we devise or use are mere artifacts. Fickle humans remain mortal, finite, and feeble; they cannot truly conceptualize the eternal, the immortal, the infinite. The Unseen persists as the Unknown and the Unknowable. The Thing and the Name elide but never equate. The search is endless, the goal unattainable. Neither patience nor piety satisfies. Only loyalty and love endure. Only they can—and *inshallah* they will—prevail.

Notes

Bruce B. Lawrence, conclusion to *Who Is Allah?* (Chapel Hill: University of North Carolina Press, 2015), 163–81. Copyright © 2015 by the University of North Carolina Press. Used by permission of the publisher.

1 I am here echoing without fully engaging the project of Mohammed Arkoun, an Algerian semiotician. Steeped in Francophone culture and a longtime professor at the Sorbonne, Arkoun elaborated in numerous writings that he called applied Islamology. At its heart was the task of critiquing "the ideological function of orthodoxy" in search of the Unthought/Unthinkable as a historical, and not merely a philosophical, project. See Mohammed Arkoun, *Rethinking Islam: Common Questions, Uncommon Answers* (Boulder, CO: Westview, 1994), 47. For a magisterial analysis of Arkoun, comparing his legacy with that of other Muslim modernists, see Carool Kersten, *Cosmopolitans and Heretics: New Muslim Intellectuals and the Study of Islam* (New York: Columbia University Press, 2007), 198–209.

2 Kenneth M. George, "No Ethics without Things," *Journal of Religious Ethics* 44, no. 1 (2016): 51–67; but see also his "Ethics, Iconoclasm, and Qur'anic Art in Indonesia," *Cultural Anthropology* 24, no. 4 (2009): 589–621.

3 Kenneth M. George, *Picturing Islam: Art and Ethics in a Muslim Lifeworld* (Oxford: Wiley-Blackwell, 2010). On the inset between pages 46–47 he includes these two Qur'anic chapters, along with other calligraphic representations, done in marble paste, gold leaf, and acrylic on canvas.
4 The commentary here is excepted from the "artist's statement" that accompanied a group exhibit of exiled Iranian women artists, titled *Labyrinth of Exile*, and shown at the UCLA Fowler Museum of Cultural History (June 25–September 18, 1994). I have paraphrased the syntax slightly in order to underscore the point about connecting literature to art.
5 See Bill Chappell, "Egyptian Author Sentenced to Prison for Book 'Where Is God?,'" June 12, 2013, http://www.npr.org/blogs/thetwo-way/2013/06/12/191091018/egyptian-author-sentenced-to-prison-for-book-where-is-god.
6 See Nawal El Saadawi, *The Dramatic Literature of Nawaal el-Saadawi: God Resigns and Isis* (London: Saqi, 2012).
7 For more on this painting and the artist's cosmopolitan creativity, see Lawrence, "All Distinctions Are Political, Artificial: The Fuzzy Logic of M. F. Husain," *Common Knowledge* 19, no. 2 (2013): 269–74.
8 To explore more about the Malaysian controversy on the Christian use of Allah, see Abhrajit Gangopadhyay, "Priest's Use of 'Allah' Brings Malaysia Sedition Probe," *Wall Street Journal*, January 8, 2014, http://online.wsj.com/news/articles/SB10001424052702303848104579308180235121604.

   Especially disturbing is the survey cited in the last paragraph of this article: "On the specific use of the word 'Allah,' a recent survey by the University of Malaya's Centre for Democracy and Elections showed that 77% of 1,676 citizens surveyed in peninsular Malaysia believe that Muslims should have exclusive right to use the word 'Allah,' while only 11% supported non-Muslims using the word." What is not said here is that all those surveyed were Malay Muslims, not Chinese or Indians or Malay Christians, so politicians loyal to Malay Muslim constituents will continue to feel justified using Allah as an exclusive moniker for Islamic loyalty.
9 Abdullah Yusuf 'Ali, *The Holy Qur'an: English Translation and Commentary (with Arabic Text)* (Lahore: Kashmiri Bazaar, Shaikh Muhammad Ashraf, 1934).
10 See Imad-ad-Dean Ahmad, "On the New Revised Edition of Yusuf Ali's Qur'an Translation," American Muslim, http://theamericanmuslim.org/tam.php/features/articles/ book_review_on_the_new_revised_edition_of_yusuf_alis_quran_translation (accessed December 4, 2012).
11 Excerpted from the preface to Yusuf 'Ali's translation of the Qur'an at http://www.institutealislam.com/the-holy-quran/preface-to-the-first-edition-1934/ (accessed May 15, 2020). Though many references to the Yusuf 'Ali edition, recycled and modified by Amana, have now disappeared from the internet, it is still available at http://www.sacred-texts.com/isl/quran/00101.htm (accessed May 15, 2020).
12 See Ziauddin Sardar, *Reading the Qur'an: The Contemporary Relevance of the Sacred Text of Islam* (Oxford: Oxford University Press, 2011), 49.

13 Scott Kugle, *Sufis and Saints' Bodies* (Chapel Hill: University of North Carolina Press, 2007), 222.
14 Kugle, *Sufis and Saints' Bodies*, 238.
15 Kugle, *Sufis and Saints' Bodies*, 258.
16 Kugle, *Sufis and Saints' Bodies*, 287.
17 Kugle, *Sufis and Saints' Bodies*, 287–88.
18 Kugle, *Sufis and Saints' Bodies*, 290.

TWENTY-FIVE

The Future of Islamic Studies: Bruce B. Lawrence Interviewed by Ali Altaf Mian | 2018

AM: Your recent scholarship has produced several accessible texts for undergraduate students and the general readership, including *The Qur'an: A Biography* [2006]. These texts are great pedagogical resources and I am intrigued to know the backstory, so to speak, of this shift in your work from specialized knowledge production to general surveys.

BL: Sure. Before *The Qur'an: A Biography*, I had never thought of myself, nor had others thought of me, as a scholar of the Qur'an. I've been engaged with a range of issues that affect Islam and Muslims in global history, and Islamic civilization, but the Qur'an had never been a specific focus of either my research or my writing, until *The Qur'an: A Biography* came out.

Actually I was contacted maybe around 2002, so it's fair to say that maybe for almost two decades I've been thinking more specifically about the Qur'an than at any prior period in my life. The book was commissioned for a series on Great Books from Atlantic Books based in London.... Surprisingly, they had picked only two works of scripture: the Bible and the Qur'an. So they contacted me. I at first said no, but then when I asked my wife, she said, "You know you've always referred to the Qur'an, you always engage it whenever you travel somewhere, you always have a copy of the Qur'an in your bag, so why not take this as an excuse to do a general book on the Qur'an?" Her response made me hesitate. Eventually I said okay, maybe it would be a better way to think differently about Islam post-9/11.

More than simply engaging 9/11, I wanted to gain a further perspective—at once more helpful and more hopeful—on Islam across the ages. I found myself writing *The Qur'an: A Biography* at the same time that I was editing *Messages to the World*, a collection of the speeches of Osama bin Laden. So it was a kind of juggling act, a healthy balance between this one very dark book, which talked about Bin Laden, and then this other, which uses the Qur'an as the basis for revisiting and rethinking moments—decisive moments, what Braudel would call "hinge moments"—in the history of Islam. So finally I decided to do it, not because it was on my agenda, but because a publisher had asked me, my wife convinced me, and then the political circumstances encouraged me to do this.

AM: What I really admire about *The Qur'an: A Biography* is its use of biographies to show how people from a range of ideological orientations approached the Qur'an. The book places "human lives" at the center of the reception history of the Qur'an, and is in this way akin to the genre of biography, both the biography of a text but also how readers' responses to scripture are mediated by their historical and social location. This seems like a powerful way to deflect the reductionism that surrounds Islam as a political object in our post-9/11 culture.

BL: Yes. I'm glad that you found a riposte to political reductionism in the three selections from *The Quran: A Biography* that are included in this reader. They highlight how looking at individuals and thinking about how they use the Qur'an gives you a distinctive window into its meaning. It's deeper than reading a *tafsir* [commentary] or thinking yourself about a fresh or updated translation of the text itself. For instance, the W. D. Mohammed selection, for me, was a natural one to include because I knew him personally and greatly admired him as a leader.

Back in 1985 I had been privileged to be part of a conference in Morocco, where he and I were the only two American representatives for a very large gathering in Fez, Morocco. I came to know him personally there as well as to engage his work. Along with another Duke colleague, C. Eric Lincoln, we later invited W. D. Mohammed to Duke and there did an interview with him for Living History. So I knew him both abroad and at home long before I contemplated writing *The Qur'an: A Biography*. When I got the chance to write this book, I said, "You know, one of the crucial things about W. D. Mohammed is not just his role in the Nation of Islam, or what became The Mosque Cares, he also deeply thought of the Qur'an as a book that spoke to him as an African American seeking new forms of knowledge. So he takes a seemingly obvious phrase, *rabb al-ʿalamin*, which everyone translates as 'the Lord of all worlds' or 'the Lord of the universe,' and he looks at the basic structure of the word *ʿalam* and says well, *ʿalam* or *world* has the same root as the word *ʿilm* or *knowledge*, so for me, as an African American, what this really means is that the Qur'an opens up the invitation to explore '*all* worlds of knowledge.'"

Now you can read all the commentaries you want, you can see classical, modern, Arabic, and Persian commentaries, but you will seldom find this translation. Never before have I seen this translation, or this commentary, for the key phrase, first qualifying Allah. It also occurs in *al-Fatiha* or the Opening, which is the one chapter of 114 chapters in the Qur'an that must be used in ritual prayers by Muslims. So to me that was simply a light bulb—here is this man, he's famous, or infamous, he's well known for many things, but until I wrote this chapter about him in *The Qur'an: A Biography*, few had thought to place him in the galaxy of those who engage and interpret the Qur'an, not just with local interests, but also with broad understanding of the Qur'an as a pivotal resource.

AM: And you have actually looked at both: those who engage with the Qur'an as insiders, but also those who engage with the Qur'an as outsiders. And it seems that, methodologically speaking, what's important for you, as a historian of religion, is to examine the vast reception of the text—in terms of both identification and disidentification. Here I'm thinking of the chapter on Robert of Ketton. Perhaps you could speak about the different biographical sites where you examine receptions of the Qur'an? What sort of methodological impulse guides you as a historian of religion to look at not only a community's reception but also external engagements?

BL: Yes. Thank you for that question. I like the way you framed it: to look not just at internal but also at external responses to the Qur'an. So one of the reasons that Robert of Ketton stood out for me was because he read the Qur'an as an enemy of Islam but one intent on seeing its development as a text with a set of commentaries within Sunni and Shiʿi communities.

What Robert of Ketton did, and it's kind of remarkable to read it, is to combine opposite reflexes. In the introduction he says as many bad things as possible about both the book and the man, about the Qur'an and the Prophet, but then you read the actual translations and there's a kind of lightness of spirit and a recurrent clarity of thought. There's a sense in which Robert—though an enemy of Islam who believed that the Qur'an was not revealed but was instead a humanly performed and then transcribed text—nonetheless sees benefit in it. Robert produces a more than sympathetic translation; he actually does a translation where he's also looked at commentaries along with his own translations.

As I show in my chapter, he reflects certain commentaries that shape how he understood the Qur'an as he did. This is an example, if you will, of an enemy—certainly someone who is trained to think about Islam in a negative way—reading the Qur'an, attempting to translate it, and feeling an engagement, even an empathy with his subject, through deep reflection and inter-textual labor.

AM: I want to return to W. D. Mohammed for a moment, and to see him as an exegete who was not constricted by the long history of Qur'anic exegetical tradition but could innovatively, and faithfully, take the Qur'anic text and generate new meanings. This resonates with your own generation of new meanings, as in the way you deploy lyrical language to talk about the Qur'an.

BL: One of the ways in which I do that toward the end of *The Quran: A Biography* is one I've thought about whenever writing a book: who are the antecedents and mentors—those people to whom you are deeply indebted and need to recall? Beyond my wife and partner, miriam cooke, to whom I'm indebted for many, many things, the notion of approaching the Qur'an as an *English* masterpiece and then actually writing this book on *The Qur'an: A Biography* was inspired by Ibrahim Abu Nab. Ibrahim was a journalist, a literary scholar, but also a lover of the Qur'an.

When I met him in Jordan, in Amman, back in the late 80s, he immediately understood my own engagement with the Qur'an. He insisted that we do some translation together. I protested: "I have never translated the Qur'an; I don't know how to do that." But he persisted. "Well, let's just take some time and look at a couple of *suras*." And so we did, but then he said, "Well, instead of looking at particular *suras*, let's just look at one phrase. Let's look at the *basmala*." And I produced translations that I'd frequently heard, such as the Beneficent, the Merciful, the Compassionate, the Kind. "You know, any one of those is fine," I suggested. "No." Again, he declared: "No." Then he explained: "You know, because you have a knowledge of literature and poetry, that when you hear *Rahman* and *Rahim*, you hear the echo of one in the other. *Rahman* and *Rahim* come from the same root in Arabic, so if one is going to render not just the meaning but the sound of these terms in English, there has to be something that is as it were a kind of interweaving, or a kind of mutual force from both words in English, that gives you the sense of this beautiful sequence in Arabic *Rahman* and *Rahim*." "Now, of course," he immediately added, "when I have a similar conversation with people in Jordan they will reply at once, 'Well, you can't translate the Arabic so it doesn't matter what you say in English. As long as people know the Arabic, give it any word you want in English, and they'll know that the true meaning is only found in *Rahman* and *Rahim* in Arabic.'" With a smile, he quipped: "Well, I don't accept that. If one's going to translate, one has a loyalty not just to the language of origin, but to the host language—the language into which you are introducing new concepts with lyrical value." We agreed on the foundational principle that you must translate not just the meaning, but the echo, or the force of Qur'anic Arabic, into whatever language you are translating: French, German, Latin, or, in our case, English.

Yet after six hours, we came up with two different options: the one that he liked and favored was to think of God as mercy. I preferred compassion, as "In the name of God, Full of Compassion, Ever Compassionate." So we agreed to disagree. Years later, the memory of that evening hovers over me. Unfortunately Ibrahim Abu Nab died in the early 1990s, but his influence persists. He inspired me to think carefully and critically and also empathetically about the English speaker/listener who will not know Arabic, but for whom this will be the first sense that she or he has of Qur'anic Arabic. And so the translation I currently favor is "In the name of God, the All Merciful, Ever Merciful." Yes, I've come back to mercy. But either way, whether you choose mercy, compassion, grace, or beneficence, you have to use the same word for both of these adjectives or attributes of God in translating the *basmala* into English.

AM: I remember one of the first questions I asked you as a graduate student at Duke was, Dr. Lawrence, how have you always been able to make your work interdisciplinary? You said that the secret lies in engagement with others—the key is to be in dialogue with others. You've mentioned some of your interlocutors, for example, Dr. cooke and Ibrahim Abu Nab. I also know that your trip to India in the 1970s was a major shifting point in your scholarly career. Could you shed some light on the transformation of your thinking at the Aligarh Muslim University in the 1970s?

BL: It is difficult, perhaps impossible, to do justice to the impact of my many trips to India, beginning with the sojourn in Aligarh at the Nizami villa in Dodhpur from 1974 to 1976. There I was also attached as a visiting scholar to the Department of History at Aligarh Muslim University. Professor Khaliq Ahmad Nizami was the doyen of medieval Indian and early Sufi studies at Aligarh Muslim University. At his invitation, I came to India for one year, and stayed for two.

During that time Nizami sahib, as he was known to me and others, served as Indian ambassador to Damascus, and so he arranged for me, along with my family, to stay in the Nizami villa, which he had just built but not yet occupied. Each week I made new friends. I explored the Urdu language. I learned about Indo-Persian. I was lucky to have tutorials with Professor Waris Kirmani at his home. He lived not far from the Nizami villa, in Dodhpur. Additionally, I traveled throughout India. I went to Rajasthan. I paid my respects to the tomb of Muʿinuddin Chishti in Ajmer. I also traveled to Hyderabad and Gulbarga, for a visit to the tomb shrine of Sayyid Muhammad Gesu Daraz. The closest, and most frequent, trip was to Delhi. There I visited the shrines of two other Chishti masters, Qutbuddin Bakhtiyar Kaki, and also the foremost of the early Chishti giants, Nizamuddin Awliyaʾ, also known as Mahbub-e Ilahi, the beloved of God. It was perhaps due to the proximity I felt to this saint, Shaykh Nizamuddin, that I shifted from my initial academic pursuits. I had received formal training with interests in *kalam*, *falsafa*, and history, the "high" stratum of Islamic intellectual production, but after India, and because of Nizamuddin, I began to focus on the everyday spirituality of Sufism. I became immersed in a dizzying cast of characters, both lofty and mundane. I engaged an array of vernacular literature, often in Indo-Persian. I tried to make sense of the works to which I had been exposed time and again.

Invited to give lectures at Patna at the Khoda Bakhsh Library, I found myself writing what was to become my first book on Sufism: *Notes from a Distant Flute: The Extant Literature of Pre-Mughal Sufism* [1978]. I also fulfilled a promise to Professor Nizami and later produced an English translation of Shaykh Nizamuddin's everyday conversations. They are known as *malfuzat* and were recorded by one of his disciples, Amir Hasan Sijzi: *Morals for the Heart* [1992]. What I have scarcely noted in these and subsequent publications is the intense personal engagement

I found with the material I was studying. I kept a regular diary during those years. I updated that same diary during subsequent visits to India.

In summer 1980 after a Thursday evening of *sama'* [ritual music] at the tomb of Nizamuddin in Tuqhluqabad, Delhi, I wrote: "How can I begin to describe the effect this slab of marble and its residents have on me? I come back from Nizamuddin *dirtied* and *washed*. How could I not be dirtied, stepping into freshly formed mud puddles, making my way through that tattered alley, lined with collapsing shops and ragged, wire-thin people (including the beggar girls who chorused me with "mujhe khana chahiye" [I must eat] all the way back from the Shaykh's tomb). So yes, I was dirtied but I was also washed—by the purity of feeling that flowed from those moments I strode before his flower-decked marble resting place, trembling with thanks for the two weeks just passed since I first visited him on coming to Delhi. I gave thanks for a new sense of purpose. I gave thanks, too, for patience with those who demand constant attention, those who need to be not just tolerated but even loved despite themselves. And so many others also deserved, and received, my thanks. High on that list were those who form a chain of light, sustaining me by their prayers and friendship. But above all, thanks were due to the source of light, to that saintly ascetic by whom I have the privilege of being inspired to give thanks and to count slowly life's passage. One reflection recurs. If saints can overcome the barrier between life and death, can they not also collapse other walls, walls between rich and poor, walls between *afrangis* [foreigners] and Hindustanis [local Indians], walls between the proud and the humble, as also the walls between those remembered and those who remember them? Of Rumi, Talat Halman once said: 'He belonged less to Turkey than to humankind.' And the same could/should be said of Shaykh Nizamuddin. I cannot count the ways that my life—personal and professional, at home and abroad—has been shaped by his pervasive *baraka*. It has marked my life continuously since the early 1970s."

AM: Thank you for this rich reflection. You are also a keen reader of an American historian, Marshall Hodgson, and you also started engaging with him in the 1970s. How does Hodgson's methodology and his message still reverberate in Islamic studies today?

BL: I don't know that I ever would have discovered Hodgson without the other side of *baraka* from Shaykh Nizamuddin. If every saint is marked by holiness, the benefit of that quality is not singular but dyadic. Does not every saint possess within himself (or herself) both *jamali* [uplifting] and *jalali* [terrifying] qualities? It is a trope of Indian Sufi lore that Nizamuddin embodied the divine *jamal* or beauty while his contemporary, the other major disciple of Baba Farid Ganj-i Shakar, ʿAlaʾuddin Sabir of Kalyar sharif (north of Delhi), projected the divine *jalal* or terror, but that judgment, in my view, is too simplistic and dichotomous. Each saint is more complex, and a more nuanced view sees their lives as braided, their traits linked. The challenge is to discern the extent to which one or the other trait has been most celebrated, sometimes in subsequent legend, often in the testimony of their own disciples. For me the *jalali* dimension of Shaykh Nizamuddin was my own illness, not just the constant stomach upset and diarrhea of Delhi but also the longer-term hepatitis A.

An onset of hepatitis at the end of my time in India left me so weak that I was bedridden after returning to the United States in summer 1976. I had strict instructions: lots of rest and only one book to read. I settled on volume one of Marshall Hodgson, *The Venture of Islam*. It was a new book. I had heard about it just as it came out in 1974, the year I left for India. I never read it before summer 1976. While in bed I consumed volume one, then volume two, and finally, by the end of the summer, volume three. I did recover from my bout of hepatitis A but I never recovered from Hodgsonitis. Hodgsonitis?! Yes, it is my neologism, a backhand compliment to Hodgson, himself the master coiner of neologisms. Hodgsonitis is an affliction well known to those who have spent time with his quirky, original, and beguiling read of the Islamic world. Hodgson himself calls that world by a new name: Islamdom, and its legacy, Islamicate civilization. Islamicate civilization, for Hodgson, becomes a chapter in world history. It is no longer an Orientalist fantasy nor an isolated Arabian military expansion and certainly not a lost remnant of Western expansionism. I read, and reread, Hodgson's *The Venture of Islam*. His expansive, empathetic approach to Islam and its legacy moved me to teach differently.

In spring 1978 I began teaching a course titled "Introduction to Islamic Civilization." I divided it into two parts: the Formative Period of Islamic Civilization, followed by the Modern Phase of Islamic Civilization. I offered it nearly every year till my retirement from Duke in 2010. Hodgson's three volumes were at once the anchor of analysis and centerpiece for pedagogy.

Decades later, in 2014, I returned to Aligarh Muslim University. I was invited by the History Department to reflect on Hodgson vis-à-vis other global historians. I elected to frame him with two other notable masters of the craft. One was Ibn Khaldun, the fourteenth-century North African polymath; the other was Richard Bulliet, the twenty-first-century doyen of Iranian and global history at Columbia University. What made Hodgson the heir of one and precursor of the other was his ability to ground abstract categories in empirical evidence. Hodgson bridged these two giants. Like them, he underscored the distinct character of regions as nodes of culture but also, even more, as vectors of religious loyalty and practice, values and norms. The local did not exclude the universal, nor the latter diminish the former. While each religion, including Islam, has a universal scope encompassing all races, languages, and cultures, it is still the case that each cosmopolitan/metropolitan site frames the character and sets the tone of religious life according to its own rhythm, using its own resources. It is too easy to collapse Islam into narrow abstracts—religion or politics—and to limit it to one region: the Middle East. For Islamicate civilization, moreover, the core region is not the Middle East but the Indian Ocean. The Indian Ocean rather than MENA—the Middle East and North Africa—has given Islam its particular civilizational shape. It is the Indian Ocean that has made Islamicate civilization a vital, pivotal category for historical and contemporary analysis. Through its presence out there, way out there, in the Indian Ocean, Islam has become, and remains, a pan-Asian cultural agent. It influenced—and continues to influence—the beliefs and practices of millions of Asians. The compass moves east, from Central to South Asia, and then further east to Southeast Asia. While there are other pan-Asian religions—Hinduism to the far south, Buddhism to the Far East—none spans the southern rim of the Asian continent to the extent that Islam does.

I could expand on this Hodgsonian insight at length, but let me just end by citing two other authors and two more books. In the recent work of Garth Fowden [*Before and After Muhammad: The First Millennium Refocused* (Princeton, NJ: Princeton University Press, 2013)] and also Shahab Ahmed [*What Is Islam? The Importance of Being Islamic?* (Princeton, NJ: Princeton University Press, 2016)], we have two twenty-first-century historians who embrace Hodgson's geopolitical vision. Fowden recasts Late Antiquity with Islam as integral to the Eurasian hinge zone. Ahmed, for his part, reimagines the middle period (the fourteenth to the nineteenth centuries) from Balkans to Bengal as the crux of Islamicate effervescence.

Hodgson might demur on the scale and scope of both studies, yet he would applaud the epistemic boldness and moral mission of their respective authors. I would argue that we can understand each of them more fully and apply their theses more broadly because of Hodgson. *The Venture of Islam* still remains a beacon for scholars and students of Islam over forty years since its 1974 publication.

AM: And it seems that Hodgson's work not only is historically rigorous but also attends to the ethics and politics of scholarship. I'm interested to hear your thoughts about this issue. What responsibilities do contemporary scholars of Islam have to Muslim textual traditions, but also to the global Muslim community and to each other?

BL: Yes, it has to do with how one sees one's self, not just in the academy, but also in public life at large in post-9/11 America. That fateful morning I was listening to a lecture on Islamic art when the first plane hit the World Trade Center building. The lecturer, a Muslim scholar from the United Kingdom, stopped. He wanted to end the lecture but I insisted he continue. The second plane hit, and he stopped again, announcing: "I am afraid that Muslims are major actors in this horrific event; I cannot continue." That was Azim Nanji from the Isma'ili Institute in London. He, of course, was right, and as a result he had to wait another week before he could take a transatlantic flight home to London.

Life was never the same. We never recovered from the horror of that moment, but I remain grateful that another Muslim scholar had just come to Duke as a colleague of mine: Professor Ebrahim Moosa. For me Ebrahim was a huge resource but also a constant benefit for my own work after 9/11. When there was this constant drumming of people saying, "Who are these terrorists? What do they do?," I could say, "Well, this is my view," but I could also say, "This is my colleague, Ebrahim Moosa. Dr. Moosa, who himself is a trained imam, has experienced Islam not only textually, but personally in Asia. He came from India, but also lived in South Africa. Actually he was a citizen of South Africa but worked and studied in South Asia, then taught in the United States, first at Stanford, and later, when I knew him, at Duke." So to me it was extremely important, in that moment in my life and in that moment in our history as Americans, that I was able to have a colleague such as Ebrahim Moosa and actually, if one looks at the beginning of *The Qur'an: A Biography*, I give credit to lots of people for reading it and giving me feedback, but I also mention among them Ebrahim Moosa because he was able to say what sounded authentic. I can still recall the time when we were first discussing how broadly relevant I thought were the Dome of the Rock, the *qubbat as-sakhra,* in Jerusalem and the Taj Mahal in Agra—at first he said, "Well, are you sure you can justify those as expressions of the Qur'an?" And the more we talked about it, the more he gave me his own personal reflection on each of those chapters. That feedback was critical; he helped me get the tone right. Even though these are not books but monuments, Ebrahim's reflections made the tone of those chapters and what followed seem much more engaged, sedimented in a broad-gauged Muslim spirituality.

AM: You have just refreshed my memory that there are chapters in *The Qur'an: A Biography* that are about monuments. And so your view of the biographical is not restricted to human personages but extends to the historical buildings and monuments erected by historical personages.

And so would it be fair to say that you see the Qur'anic text unfolding not only in books, in the lives of people, but also in architectural forms and in material remains? I don't know if you want to take that up as a question but it's an observation on my part and it's fascinating methodologically speaking because it inspires a historian of religion like myself to search for inscription beyond the written word, to look for instances where textuality meets materiality in the traces that remain.

BL: One of the things that evolved in my own thinking was how someone who was trained to think philologically about texts—in my case they were texts in Arabic but also in Persian, and later in Sanskrit—to think of all the ways in which these different texts reflect a certain academic knowledge that presupposes a correct understanding of the origins of words and more. First of all, how does one look at the etymology of words, etymological discourse, and then the whole production of particular forms of argument based on not just etymology but also usage? The rigorous way in which one thinks about words has to be connected with people and the ways in which people bring their frames of knowledge, as also their own set of interests, to looking at texts. Beyond that insight, the buildings and the monuments themselves really fascinate me because each one of them is also in its own way a text.

What really fascinated me with the Dome of the Rock, and I hadn't realized it until I did the book, is that it is also the first, or at least the oldest extant, text of the Qur'an since the manuscripts that were produced in the seventh century are no longer with us. The earliest versions of the Qur'an from later centuries have been printed and reprinted, written and rewritten, in different places, but the earliest enduring text of the Qur'an that we have is not in print, but in rock; it's not in a book, it's in the Dome of the Rock. And so to me it's really fascinating to see how those sections of the Qur'an were performed. That both makes the Qur'an a more vibrant book, but also brings up the question that many people raise, "So how does the Qur'an engage Christians and Jews?" You're talking about ethics, and here we see the ethics of having this new building in a very old city, because by the time the Muslims arrived there in the seventh century, Jerusalem was already an old city, old from the period of early Jewish history, and then, of course, remodeled or rethought in terms of Christian history from the fourth century on, when Constantine commissioned building of the Church of the Holy Sepulchre. So the fact that there is a Muslim monument that's not actually a mosque, but more of a memoriam marking a particular place, makes that edifice alluring. There is, of course, a mosque next to the Dome of the Rock, but the Dome of the Rock itself is a memoriam rather than a mosque, and it's a memoriam of one spot, this rock that's supposed to be the rock of ages, though which age is still a matter of debate.

It could be the rock on which Abraham almost sacrificed Isaac or Ishmael, depending on your view; it certainly can be the rock that was supposed to be near the tomb of Jesus; and it's also the rock on which the Prophet Muhammad is said to have alighted, then ascended to heaven. So this is a really important rock that has been encased in what is now known as the Dome of the Rock. But what's equally important for the Qur'an is the scripture, the writings around its border, that talks about how important Jerusalem is and how important Jesus is. Jesus becomes a prophet of Islam through the Qur'an, and so the Qur'an memorializes Jesus along with Muhammad, and earlier prophets, in this ancient Jerusalem structure. It is that influence and that aspect of what you might term the "material expression" of literary antecedence and influences—that is to me very important.

AM: Yes, it is not beyond textuality per se, but what I meant was a textuality irreducible to the codex.

BL: I agree: it's a textuality that goes beyond writing on paper; it can also be inscription in stone, echoing Tagore's dictum: "The language of stone surpasses the language of man."

AM: Let us briefly address the ethics of interfaith dialogue. Your work draws attention to those authors who model for us careful modes of interfaith dialogue, but then there are scholars who have recently pointed out the limitations, but also the resourcefulness of the Abrahamic, for example. You've highlighted, or your work takes up, how Muslims and Christians can navigate this politicized landscape in a very careful way so that one is not painting a religious tradition in the hegemonic terms of another tradition but rather observing, and preserving, a careful balance between the identity of a religious tradition as it encounters another religious tradition. I'm thinking, for example, about Sandow Birk's *American Qur'an*. Does Birk have anything to say about the politics of interfaith engagement, what to do and what to avoid?

BL: Well, I'm glad you mention Sandow Birk. It's important to say that in the same way I never imagined writing a book on the Qur'an as a biography, I certainly did not think about doing a sequel on Qur'an translations, *The Koran in English: A Biography* [2017], my most recent book. It is also fair to say, when thinking about translation, I was always doing this in a linguistic register: as I mentioned with the *basmala*, how does one take words that are so densely evocative in Arabic as are the words *rahman* and *rahim*, or even the word Allah—how does one take those, as it were, and find a counterpart in English that may not capture all the nuance but at least projects an elevated tone so that one gets a feeling of the original, or the first language, which is Arabic for the Qur'an?

Among the things about Sandow Birk that really surprised me was that he did something that no other translator of the Qur'an has ever done. Instead of simply translating the Qur'an, he transcribed it. In English it is no longer the Qur'an but the Koran, in my view. Birk took the entire Koran, all 6,236 verses in English, and thought about each one deliberately in the text of each chapter or *sura*, but also in the sweep of an entire book—beginning in chapter 1 or *sura* 1, that is, *al-Fatiha*, and going all the way until the 114th chapter [*an-Nas*]. And then saying, "Here is my effort to transcribe in English what most other people had always transcribed in Arabic."

So, for instance, the Emperor Aurangzeb has been lauded and also challenged as one of the major Muslim Mughal rulers of premodern India. But consider Emperor Aurangzeb as a devout believer: one of the things that he did was to write, in his own hand, the entire Qur'an, and he felt that this act of reproducing it in Arabic was a certain kind of spiritual exercise that enabled him, and also elevated him, in his practice as a Muslim. Now Sandow Birk is not a Muslim, and he makes it clear that he is not. He says that he is not even a man of faith, which is kind of hard to believe after reading *American Qur'an*. Despite the fact that Birk says he is not a man of faith, he undertakes a practice that's identified with very intense Muslim rulers and skilled calligraphers, those who transcribe the whole of the Qur'an in Arabic. He transcribed the entire text. As a non-Muslim, nonbeliever, he transcribes the whole of the Qur'an not from right to left in Arabic all the way through, but going from left to right in English all the way through until the end.

AM: It seems that if he is someone who inhabits interfaith dialogue in a productive manner, then ethical engagement with the "religion of the other" requires a certain crossing or traveling, inhabiting a liminal space in which one participates.

BL: That is beautifully said. The aspect of Sandow Birk that is critical is his distance from conventional religion. He may not have a creedal base or liturgical practice in the conventional sense; he's not a Protestant or a Catholic, he's not a Christian or a Jew, he's not a Unitarian or a Scientologist, so he doesn't assert, "Oh this is like so-and-so," approaching something else. But he does have a religion; his religion is that each human being is responsible for his or her own destiny and has to use the resources... not only the skill set but also the community, the people in one's family or larger neighborhood; one has to use both those personal and professional resources to better humankind.

So Birk is really espousing a notion of responsibility for others. In his own work he is trying to bring forward those people who are either forgotten or misunderstood or marginal to life in twenty-first-century America. And he did this earlier. He's only around fifty years old and he had made such efforts before 9/11, but when 9/11 happened he suddenly realized the group that's most marginal, least understood, and most at risk, in twenty-first-century America, are Muslims. And he didn't take an interest in Islam or Muslims as someone engaged in interfaith dialogue, but rather as someone who was very much aware of all the drama and all the media as well as political consequence of 9/11.

So one of the things he did was to think about Islam through the eyes of different Muslims whom he knew, at the same time that he also traveled around the world to different places. When he would go to a place where he would be surfing, because he likes to surf, he would ask,

"Is there anything here that relates to Islam or Islamic history?" At one point he was in Dublin, and it was a rainy day and someone said, "Well, if you're interested in Islam you ought to go to Chester Beatty." This was in 2005, and so he went to Chester Beatty. Suddenly he saw all these Qur'ans along with illuminated Celtic Bibles. There they were: Celtic Bibles and Mamluk Qur'ans under the same roof, and he saw how different people had been transcribing but also erasing and changing sacred texts for centuries. So it wasn't as if it was a polished text, it wasn't a kind of neat errorless, immaculate text; it was continually in process and correction. And he thought, "That's the kind of thing I can do. Maybe I should think about doing the Qur'an but I can't do it in Arabic, I'll do it in English." So he goes and buys his own copies of the Qur'an in English, and starts to think about how he would transcribe them but also add border images. And immediately as soon as he thought of what images to include he thought of the text as having representation in American life.

So this project starts from a conscientious American citizen, thinking about Islam after 9/11, and trying to think about it with fresh eyes. His form of dialogue is not to go out and say, "Let me talk to a bunch of Muslim imams or let me go find out someone who's an expert. No, let me dig into it myself. Let me see what this Qur'an stuff is all about." And then he thinks about the images that suggest themselves by the Qur'anic discourse mirroring a voice beyond. He can't exhaust it, but what he does is to defamiliarize it so that something that seems to exist only in seventh-century Arabia might also be something that one might see in twenty-first-century America.

Take moon exploration: there's a chapter in the Qur'an called *al-Qamar*, "the moon," and Birk does the American landing on the moon as one of the expositions there that relates it to an American context. Also, when it comes to the whole question of 9/11, there's a Qur'anic chapter called *Al-Dukhan*, which is "smoke." He shows the Twin Towers burning and says this is the way in which an American might relate to it. But he does find humor as well, at the end, for instance, when he talks about *al-Falaq*, "the daybreak," he says, "The daybreak, whatever it meant in Arabia, for me today it means going with my surfboard out to the California coast." So he takes everyday scenes, he takes historical moments, he takes lunar landings, he takes morning surfings, and he frames these as a kind of commentary. They become pictorial commentary on each of these large frames from the Qur'an that he puts together in a huge volume. So it's textual, it's pictorial, it's interpretive, but, above all, it's contemporary. So this is a new form, in my view, a new form of the Qur'an in translation, which I call the "graphic Koran," using the English spelling of Qur'an, because it's not exhaustive, it picks out certain elements, it gives you a sense of them, and it allows you to enter and then to move wherever you want to move in your own imagination.

AM: Yes, this is a very productive mode of engaging with a scriptural tradition in the post-9/11 context. We have seen many faith-based communities in the United States turn to interfaith dialogue, so to speak, with a hope and a belief that interfaith dialogue will do some of the reparative work between Christians, Muslims, and Jews and others in the post-9/11 American context, but what I am hearing from you in highlighting people like Sandow Birk or M. F. Husain, someone else whom you've engaged a lot, is that we have to be really careful as we engage with a tradition other than ours so as not to reinforce our own doctrinal or taken-for-granted presuppositions; neither should dialogue fossilize the other tradition. Instead, it should undo our own identity in the face of the heterogeneity of the other: instead of trying to territorialize or capture its subjects, we are relating to them, and engaging with them, promoting a genuine conversation.

BL: Yes, and that begins with a conversation with one's self. One of the things Birk tries to do, which is like interfaith dialogue but very different, is to say that while interfaith dialogue is very productive, and one should have as much of it as possible, most of the frame for interfaith dialogue is going back to texts and saying, "Well, let's see. The Qur'an says this. Now let's just take one chapter—let's just take the chapter of Joseph. Well, there's a Joseph story that's there in the Hebrew Bible so let's see how we compare the Qur'anic Joseph with the Israelite Joseph and see if the two match or which is different." And while all of these are interesting exercises and you get some deeper sense of the complexity of this character, a very important character, a prophet, named Yusuf or Joseph, it doesn't really help you think of circumstances today.

What Sandow Birk does is to eschew those sorts of backward-looking commentary, and do a side step, or, if you will, a forward commentary, that says, "Think about how maybe the story of Joseph plays out in American life today. What would be the equivalent?" He introduces, for instance, an imagined scene from the CDC [Centers for Disease Control], where folks from various backgrounds are held in detention, and another of Mexican migrants being frisked by a border patrol in Texas or Arizona. In both cases the reader/viewer can imagine Joseph-like figures from twenty-first-century America. You can see the people who are imprisoned or under arrest as representative of some of the issues and circumstances that face Americans, whether Jewish or Christian or Muslim, whether white, black, or Latino. So it's the difference between dialogue that is getting it right, convincing but not converting the other, and imagining yourself as the other. This is a critical shift. Birk's strategy is to say straight up, "I want you to think about how the Joseph story is not just Jewish, Christian, or Muslim, but how it's also American."

AM: You say that his work is an artistic adaptation. There's adaptation, but a certain mode of, we could say, graffiti transcription, and certain citational poetics, but all in the background of 9/11. So how did 9/11, the event, place the Qur'an in the limelight as an object that would facilitate representations about Muslims?

BL: If one looks at the previous sixteen years, 2001 to now, one could say that the Qur'an comes up again and again. I, for instance, was teaching with my wife and colleague, miriam cooke, in Indonesia during early 2006, and there was the whole question about caricatures of the Prophet Muhammad and then the Qur'an burnings that happened in spring 2006. So the crucial question that came up again and again was: how does the person of the Prophet Muhammad or the sacrality of the Qur'an evoke part of what identifies as a Muslim difference in a Muslim outlook—not just in the twenty-first century but more emphatically since 9/11—as a mark of distinction between Muslims and non-Muslims?

Birk sees that same process and says, "Well, maybe beyond satirizing or burning, there's also engaging, and one can engage the Qur'an not only by looking at commentaries, but also by looking at other events that align with the Qur'anic message, without suggesting that they exhaust that message." So the word that I use not only in this book but I use it elsewhere is *barzakh*.... Instead of talking about compatibility or conversion, saying, "I can be both Muslim and Christian, or Jewish and Christian and Muslim, or, in the case of Sandow Birk, I can be both a pagan, or nonbeliever, and also a firm believer," I believe it's healthier to think about this image that comes from the Qur'an itself, which is the image I prefer to use: *barzakh*. When I mention the term *barzakh*, everyone says, "Oh, yeah that's in the Qur'an. It's somewhere in *Surat ar-Rahman* [Q 55:19–20] and it means something like a barrier or a buffer." And I say, "Well, actually *barzakh* has a geographic meaning elsewhere in the Qur'an. It's the water, it's two levels of water: it's salt water and fresh water. And the two of them come together, but neither one becomes the other because the fresh water would be lost and the salt water would be diminished [Q 25:53]." And so what I really think is crucial is to say, "How can there be *barzakh* moments where there's a meeting, and there's a benefit of that meeting because both parties can exist together and both reinforce each other, and yet, crucially, neither one has to change the other?" To use this wonderful phrase we heard recently from Pope Francis, "If all you're doing in religious dialogue is looking for proselytism, you're engaging in, and furthering, solemn nonsense." The counterpoint to solemn nonsense, in my view, is to have engaged sensibility of two traditions without moving or altering one in favor of the other. That is, or should be, counted as a sacred act, a genuine dialogue.

AM: Yes, and I think that studying *The Qur'an: A Biography* or *The Koran in English: A Biography*—both the 2005 text and the 2017 text—would really help people who aspire to engage with the Muslim tradition. I still want to ask you specifically about violence.

Do you think that there's a certain violence, representational or epistemic violence, done to Islam and Muslims by letting the political events of the last thirty or forty years translate Islam through the prism of the Qur'an in ways that might make more sense in a post-Reformation Christianity where the defining feature of Christianity is the Bible? Are we seeing this heightened awareness of the pivotal role of the Qur'an because, historically speaking, it's been a very important facet of Muslim moral law and ethics as well as creativity and culture, but not the exclusive one? The role of other discourses internal to Islam—Sufism and philosophy and legalism and other modes of spirituality, in addition to *hadith* and advice literature—have they been ignored or disregarded? All of these other channels of knowledge and axes of authority are also there, to be discovered and recovered, understood and applied.

So what I am trying to ask is: does one do a disservice to the longer history and heterogeneity of Muslim faith and practice by looking at the Qur'an as the pivotal access or entry point to Islam?

BL: Well, I really like your question, and I agree with the tone of hyperscripturalism that is there, pervading and sustaining this whole project of looking too narrowly at the Qur'an. Sandow Birk would also agree that it stems from an underlying notion of epistemic violence. We face the danger of reappropriating the past in terms of a lens from the present, a presentist bias, and that introduces an epistemic violence. The presentist bias sees a whole tradition defined by its initiatory or foundational text, rather than by myriads of other influences and activities and individuals who are not bound up with or loyal to that text in the same way this conversation implies.

So one of my arguments in *The Koran in English* is to say that it's really difficult to think of the Qur'an in a pioneering, exploratory or expansive, additive way—as a kind of additive rather than foundational element in Muslim life—because of the Protestant emphasis on the Bible: it becomes not just the basis but the sole resource for religion. If everybody just had enough access to it, and could understand the Bible on its own terms, goes the argument, they would then become a perfect Christian [or] at least an enabled Christian who could lead a better life than someone else without that understanding of the Bible.

So this overdetermined view of scripture, hyperscripturalism is what I would call it, underlies some of this fascination with the Qur'an, and you have to say, and I do say, and I believe that Sandow Birk would also concur, "It's not an emphasis that is historically replicated or justified, but since we live in the present moment, even when we understand this epistemic violence, we can't counter it by simply denying it. We have to counter it by offering a broader vista of the present." I totally agree that the Qur'an in history does not have the exclusionary role that it seems to have in defining and projecting Muslim identity in the twenty-first century.

Birk, who is, by his own standards, neither a believer nor a philosopher, but an artist, and also an activist, is trying to make people think broadly about how beautiful the Qur'an is as a book of sayings, a code of ethics. He is really a lot closer to the medieval view of the Qur'an, as Navid Kermani said, and I take Kermani to be a very important thinker about Islam: "If you read the Qur'an and you want to memorize and recite it, you have just re-created another form of the text. But if you want to understand it and apply it, you take particular dicta, particular sayings in the Qur'an, particular verses and then make them a linchpin for your ethical behavior." So Birk in a way not only talks about something called the *qibla* but also displays it. For instance, whether in Los Angeles or in

Pittsburgh or as he's also now doing it in Eugene, Oregon [January 2017], namely, when he offers a display of pages from *American Qur'an* he also includes the image of a *qibla*, a point of orientation, in order to demonstrate how the Qur'an itself is a hall of worship and requires an orientation. The orientation frames certain verses from the Qur'an that make it a kind of visual focal point, a specific orientation. It gives you a kind of center of attention around which you can then look at all of these other pages, but you're always drawn to something that says, "Here is the Qur'an itself and it's always saying to be just and to be fair, to mark your words, all guidelines taken from the Qur'an, all in English, but here it is given to you as if it were a kind of distillation, a ready summation, rather than a vast expansion of its multiple meanings."

AM: The work of Sandow Birk is indeed inspiring, but let me shift gears. We are living increasingly in times of extreme uncertainty as to what the future holds for us as a collectivity, at least in present-day America. What resources do academics have in this moment? But also what are the responsibilities of public intellectuals, academics, engaged citizens in terms of reaffirming human rights, gender equality, pluralist citizenship, public reason, and the nonintervention of the state in religious affairs?

BL: Yes, well, like anyone who is listening or reading about this in 2018 and beyond, we seem to have reached a watershed where the democratic process has yielded, as the result of a set of leaders, where it's very difficult to see how public reason—along with affirmation of human rights and gender parity and opportunity for all people—is going to survive. Will we witness a total breakdown of American institutions and also America's standing, however liminal and however reduced, in the world at large?

I don't have an answer to those questions, but I do know that the affirmation of Muslims as citizens, and what it means to be an American-Muslim citizen, will continue to be important, and it will always be important because it will bracket not only Muslims and non-Muslims together, but also immigrant Muslims with indigenous Muslims. Those Muslims who are coming over from Syria to the United States along with those who have been here not only from the Middle East, but North Africa and also South Asia, but also those Americans, African Americans and other Americans who become Muslim—all of them are part of the American Muslim community.

So one of the things that will happen now, even more, is the Muslim community will be seen as an essential element of American pluralism, even more than it was before the election of Donald Trump. That's not necessarily a hopeful thing in the short term for Muslims. I read the other day about a mosque in Texas being burned down. Even as I shudder to think of that un-American act of destruction, I am preparing myself for more headline episodes like this: "Attack on Muslims." Do I want to see that? No. But do I feel that we have to be prepared for it? Yes. However, I hope the response to it, the increasing response of more and more Americans, not just Muslims but also those who support pluralism in general, and Muslims as part of the plural public square in America, is this: we have to stand up for those rights; we have to advocate for them in local communities through our representatives, through our senators, through all in authority. Whenever there is something really bad and it seems just a really bad, dangerous time, I say, "What is it that's good?" And I think what is good about it is at least the hope, the seed of hope, that people will recognize how core these values are, and they don't just play out against Mexicans, as important as Mexicans are, or Latin Americans, but also against people from Asia and Africa and the Middle East who are Muslim, who are also being denied entry or being harmed because they want to be American residents and/or American citizens in the twenty-first century.

So that's one thing. The other thing that is really important is the alliances that are fostered between people of goodwill, whatever their background, and that Muslim voices are heard in their midst. To give one example of something that has happened, which I hope will grow, and by the time this book is published, be more evident, is people like Khizr Khan, who nobody knew about before the Democratic convention back in July 2016. Yet Khizr Khan together with his wife, Ghazala Khan, have suddenly became icons for immigrants and for Muslims, affirming their American constitutional right, that everybody has their place in the American public square if they agree to abide by all the rules to be citizens as the Khans have. So, for instance, Khizr Khan came to Duke University in the spring of 2017 as part of an initiative that I supported, saying, "It's one thing for Bruce Lawrence to speak about Muslims; it's another thing for Khizr Khan to do it." So Khizr Khan is from Pakistan; lived in the Gulf; trained at Harvard Law School; works in Charlottesville, Virginia; is speaking throughout the country not against Trump per se; instead, he's talking on behalf of citizens' rights and the opportunities to be a full participant in American society, affirming that fighting for America is as much a duty for any American Muslim as it is for any American Christian or Jew or Buddhist. So that all three of his sons, he has three sons, all of them joined ROTC. We now know about Khizr Khan because his one son who stood up, volunteered, and went off to Iraq was killed by a roadside bomb, protecting his fellow soldiers. That makes Khizr Khan a gold star father. And he is no less a gold star father because he is a Muslim American immigrant gold star father than are others who have lost children in war. It doesn't justify the war; it doesn't mean that the war will finally achieve its aims, but it does mean that those who are American, those who agree to be citizens and to serve in the military, deserve respect and deserve to have the support of other people due to their service.

I imagine that the future will not be easy, it will not be smooth, it will not be happy in all regards, but there is, at least in my understanding of citizenship, an opportunity for those of us who advocate holism, public reason, a larger opportunity for citizenship to be for people of faith as well as for people who are secular. For me, this is and will remain an ongoing *jihad*—what Bennabi calls *jihad fikri*, an intellectual *jihad* that we will carry on well into the twenty-first century, beyond Trump.

AM: What you just said is really relevant, that the political climate has ushered in an epoch that will press us to not take human rights and our values in this country for granted, but we must struggle for them, and how freedom requires extensive and ongoing struggle. We have to reaffirm these values through the struggle, a struggle that will engender a more just society.

BL: Yes, and there is one thing I want to add to that, something so important but often overlooked: the impact of social media. Social media are held up and both promoted and derided with equal force because they are pervasive. You can't get around it; every one of us uses it even when we claim we don't. But one of the things that's really evident is that social media by themselves don't produce change; they can be an instrument for change, but they themselves don't produce the change. What I admire is that there are young people, by young now I mean people under thirty, millennial rather than simply those from Generation Y. Millennials are understanding for themselves both the benefits and the limits of social media. More and more of them are engaged in thinking, "Oh, if Muslims are under attack just because they're Muslims, that is un-American and we have to stand up for them."

So the fact that younger people, and not just isolated groups, but cohorts of people are seeing Muslim rights as human rights in twenty-first-century America, this gives me a lot of hope. I often sign my email messages "a prisoner of hope," and so like Sandow Birk, I too identify with the prophet Joseph in twenty-first-century America.

AFTERWORD

Yasmin Saikia

When Bruce Lawrence asked me to write the afterword to this volume, I readily accepted. It is a great honor for me to contribute to this reader. Bruce Lawrence is a prolific writer, an omnivorous reader, a rigorous thinker, and an erudite teacher. His scholarly profile confirms his authority in the field of Islamic studies. He has written more than half a dozen monographs, edited several volumes, contributed chapters to several outstanding edited books, published numerous journal articles, translated foundational Islamic texts and Sufi poetry, and remained active in debates and discourses on social and political themes on Islam. Theory, translation, and analysis blend together to create Bruce Lawrence's unique scholarly voice. But Bruce Lawrence is much more than his scholarship. His colleagues, students, and friends admire him for his deep compassion and the openness he brings to the study of Islam and Muslims. Even after forty-five years of intense study and writing on Islam, Bruce Lawrence still continues to find new themes to explore, and the joy of this discovery he readily shares with colleagues through his frequent publications. Each new publication spurs novel discussions on Muslims for better understanding and appreciation. Bruce Lawrence has a remarkably curious mind and a genuinely open heart.

His scholarship on Islam and Muslims crosses multiple borders. It traverses many sites and time periods, geographies and cultures. He has been tackling ideas that have theological and historical significance as well as contemporary political relevance. Using investigative methods that address Islam's multiple trajectories, his work speaks across diverse fields, such as religious studies, history, philosophy, media studies, and art history. The multiple levels of his contributions provide a crucial nursery of ideas that are evident in many recent works; his students and admirers, myself included, have been inspired by him to engage in an open conversation on themes that have contemporary relevance as the basis of investigating Muslim communities and lived Islam. He has led the way in creating a new space for appreciating the humanity of Muslims and humanizing discourse about Islam.

Yet the task of writing this afterword did not come easy. I was in a quandary how to craft an afterword to a reader of Bruce Lawrence's immense and awe-inspiring scholarship. Ali Mian has done a remarkable job of sifting, selecting, and reproducing a selection of his essays in one book. The reader, however, does not exhaust Lawrence's scholarship. Bruce Lawrence never tires in asking new questions and seeking uncharted areas of exploration on Islam and Muslims. I suspect he might even open a new discussion on the published essays that appear in this reader since he does not hesitate to rethink his own approach; for him, the quest is more important than the outcome. My concern in writing the afterword is more a sign of appreciation than closure because I know that academic language cannot capture the energy and force of his thinking and articulation. Nonetheless, once I had accepted the task, I also knew I could offer a distinctive voice, contributing to the conversation on Lawrence's capacious scholarship. Bruce and I have been talking for almost two decades and though our conversations will continue, my connection with Bruce is not limited to academic discussions. Hence, I want to reflect here a little more personally on what Bruce has meant to me as a mentor and sojourner in the study of Islam and Muslim communities.

Let me begin with a short story about this journey. I share with Bruce an immense love and reverence for Hazrat Nizamuddin Awliya', perhaps the most famous Sufi saint buried in Delhi, India. Long before I met Bruce, during one of my trips to India, an elderly Muslim gentleman approached me and asked if I knew Professor Bruce Lawrence. I politely replied in the negative because I did not know Bruce then. The elderly man encouraged me to meet him, because, in his words, "he is a special person." He also advised me to read his books on Islam because his scholarship "flows from his heart and his mind."

Several years later, in 1999, I did meet Bruce when I joined the University of North Carolina at Chapel Hill as a brand-new assistant professor. Bruce was the first to welcome me to the South Asian studies academic community in the Triangle. We immediately became friends; over the years our friendship has grown. A decade later, when I was leaving UNC to take up a new position at Arizona State University, Bruce retired from Duke University. In his retirement speech, he shared multiple stories of his research journey, the places he went to study, the challenges and discoveries, the multilayered conversations with a variety of people that became the stuff of his books; his life reflects the rich and wholesome life of a sojourner. But, he also recalled only one person as his steadfast guiding light in this eventful journey. For him, this friend is Hazrat Nizamuddin Awliyaʾ. At that moment it became clear to me that the voice of the elderly man I had heard in India was the voice of Nizamuddin Awliyaʾ; it was he who led me to Bruce Lawrence. We were brought together by the saint to share our academic journeys and an enduring friendship. I am richer because of that confluence. My reading of Bruce Lawrence's scholarship and writing this afterword, therefore, combine intellectual with personal reflections.

The traditional approach in Islamic studies has focused on philology and textual analysis of Arabic texts. This approach privileges Islam in its fixity as an Arab religion emphasizing the foundational history of the religion in the seventh century, the Prophet Muhammad, and the Qurʾan. The *hadith* literature, Islamic moral law as well as legal theory, and ritual practices are additional areas of interest. One of the current trends in Islamic studies, however, is to shift the focus to contemporary issues of politics and political discourses, movements, organizations, ideology, and leaders. Some scholars of political Islam see the violent dispersal of religion as an Islamic agenda serving as a tool for emphasizing the clash of civilization narrative. The underlying theme is of Islam and Muslims as disconnected from the ideals of democracy, liberty, and tolerance, deemed to be the cherished values of Western civilization. Lawrence does not neglect the textual approach in order to observe and analyze political Islam. He weaves together both perspectives by engaging the study of texts alongside political discourses generated by Muslims and about Muslims. He shows Islam to be much more than an Arab religion; it is embedded in multiple local environments, in Asia, Africa, Europe, and even the United States. The conversations produced by Muslims reinforce connections rather than encourage separation from non-Muslims. Lawrence's scholarship provides a bridge that joins different strands of knowledge, and he personally embraces the variety of Muslims and the ways they know themselves and express their sense of "us."

To connect texts with people, he carefully unpacks and investigates linkages of discourse to practice, across time and space. He calls these linkages Muslim networks, which are pious but also public systems of exchanges and institutions facilitating the coming together of people and ideas. He has analyzed a vibrant spectrum of linkages. Muslim networks draw the outside world inward into its own sphere of exchanges and circulation, while these networks also serve as nodes embedding Muslims in their own local and regional contexts. Textual knowledge of the religion circulates through lively networks while Muslims reinforce their attachment to faith and rituals by localizing Islam to suit their local cultures and needs. Lawrence finds a variety of networks crisscrossed throughout the Muslim world—in Asia, the Gulf countries, Turkey, Africa, the Middle East, Europe, and the United States. We learn from his study of networks the pervasive but often opaque continuities and discontinuities between past and present forms of Islamic aspirations. Since Muslim networks themselves varied from different spaces and from person to person, Islam appears in Lawrence's "thick description" as a religion with a foundational basis in the Qur'an accepted by all groups and individuals who profess the Islamic faith, at the same time that the culture and politics of being Muslim are subject to change in different spatial and temporal settings. The fluid, adaptive character of Islam, as well as its textual sources brimming with ambivalence and ambiguity, allows for a range of diverse interpretations but also misinterpretations.

The division between who Muslims are and how they are perceived is heightened in the post-9/11 world. There is a double consciousness regarding Muslims that is central to understanding Islam in Lawrence's approach. He is not surprised that laypeople and even scholars repeatedly ask the problematic question of Muslims' place or lack of it in the "civilized" world. For such questioners, everything that Muslims do seems to stem from, or lead to, an ideology of violence; some tend to make a random connection between Islam and violence as a root principle of the religion. Lawrence does not side-step this concern; instead he takes a politically and ethically responsible position to demonstrate what is wrong when we continue to view Islam in isolation as a standalone religion and Muslims as a monolithic community. He draws on diverse factors, including politics, culture, and economy, to develop a multi-axial approach for telling the story of Muslim experiences historically. He shows how Islam became a powerful force connecting and positively transforming the premodern and modern world. He underscores how external conditions of power in the colonial and postcolonial periods inhibited Muslim development and demanded subjugation. Anxiety and rage were the outcomes. He argues that the focus on Muslim rage is misplaced because rage is not an Islamic injunction but reflects responses to inequalities and factors such as race, gender, ethnicity, history, class, and other contingent issues that shape Muslim lives; it is these that must be addressed if we are to move beyond mythologizing Muslim violence and instead understand Muslims in their complex, present conditions. This honest look at Muslim communities is a very powerful intervention in Islamic studies.

The weaving together of different tangents of Islam—theological, anthropological, historical, political, communitarian, and technological—creates a fresh rethinking of Marshall Hodgson's provocative idea of Islamdom and Islamicate civilization as elaborated in *The Venture of Islam* (1974). In Hodgson's and

Lawrence's descriptions, the Islamicate *oikumene* is integral to world history. It is an extensive cosmopolitan civilizational project shaped by interactions and exchanges creating dynamic energy in the expansive space of Islamdom. The evolving space of Islamdom has been marked by inclusivity and fluidity. Islam created the possibilities for this adaptation from its inception. They persist till today, in numerous contexts. Lawrence enables us to understand the Islamicate not as an artifact of the past or Islamdom as Oriental imagery but to rethink in our times the shifting landscapes of global Islam and what Islamicate cosmopolitanism can offer us today. In Lawrence's vision, we see order, forward-thinking movement, and vitality in Islamdom. The Islamicate *oikumene* contributes to modifying and improving the behavior of people, encouraging them to receive and share with others. In the Islamicate *oikumene*, there are no walls closing off possibilities, but rather the promise of expansion and growth. This is a very different perspective from the one that vilifies and paints the picture of marginalized Muslims operating in clandestine spaces plotting and executing terrorism in order to destroy Western civilization. Lawrence confidently presents the Islamicate *oikumene* as a humanizing project, one that has embraced reform and produced new opportunities for a variety of people and cultures. Neither subterranean nor destructive, the Islamicate *oikumene* is at once open and proactive.

In parts I, II, and VI in the reader, we are presented with the story of several nuanced moments from Islamicate history. In the precolonial period, it appears that reception to new ideas and change was often the norm, while Muslim resistance is more pronounced in the postcolonial environment. With a steadfast determination, Lawrence examines the stories of both plurality and resistance, taking the reader from the outside to the insiders' views of what Islam means and what Muslims experience. The "signature story" of Islam for Lawrence is the story of connections and adaptations. He demonstrates how this story has been superimposed with a new signature story of violence and disconnect, one that seeks to denigrate or destroy the Islamicate ecumene. But he does not dwell too much on the downside. Instead, he calls our attention to the long record of events and exchanges that created and sustained the connections of Muslims with a variety of different others, forging an Islamicate cosmopolitan spirit.

Lawrence's approach is friendly, frank, and generous but it is also probing and critical. Trained by Franz Rosenthal, a renowned historian of early and medieval Islamic texts, Lawrence delves into the text of the Qur'an for a deep evaluation of concepts that guide Muslims; he lays bare the meanings and uses of this text in different contexts. This has been one of his sustaining passions in early as well as recent publications. His erudition in textual study of the Qur'an has been expressed in a particularly evocative and creative engagement with the concept of Allah. He does not limit himself to conceptual readings of the Qur'an, but fearlessly translates as well as engages the translations produced by others in order to show the living presence of the Qur'an. In his narrative prose one detects the nuance of poetry and also the inner meanings of Sufi mystical thoughts. Lawrence steps outside the comfort zone of mainstream readings of the Qur'an to look into various alternative readings, including the negative uses of the text, which mushroomed in the post-9/11 world. Lawrence notes the sense of Muslim alienation in the contemporary period, seeking expression in the manipulative use of the Qur'an and disruptive violence in consequence. He engages these new interpretations in a very provocative essay that appears in part IV, namely his introduction to *Messages to the World: The Statements of Osama bin Laden.*

The multivalence study of the Qur'an in different time periods, its ceremonious and unceremonious uses in different places and by a variety of people, Lawrence argues, allows for appreciating the immense possibilities that inhere in the text itself. Muslim rethinking and reimagining of solutions drawn from the Qur'an for addressing social, political, and religious issues is more than reflexive defensiveness; it is evidence of adaptive creativity. This study of the multi-sited engagements with Islamic texts in the context of their use is a demanding methodology. It requires patience to delve into the sites of religious discussions as well as everyday life, on streets and in mosques, in rhetoric and in poetry, and to come up with a reading that is always in process, assembled and dismantled by numerous actors. Lawrence's scholarly reach expands the emphasis from the subject matter in the texts to its entire mode of production and presentation by different audiences and interpreters. We see this in several essays presented in parts I, IV, and V. All these interpretations circulate in different networks of Muslim communities, as he shows in part V. It is Muslim networks that produce the frame for an Islamic cosmopolitanism crossing vast distances and connecting the everyday with ritual and dramatic experiences. This granular study of networks transforms Lawrence from a textual scholar into an ethnographer; text and context come together in multiple sites of exchanges, producing adaptations that have been ongoing in precolonial, colonial, and postcolonial times. He delves further into the micro and intimate issues of the performance of Muslimness, never casting aside the notion of a lively Islamicate spirit evident till today.

Lawrence is not unmindful of the towering figures, "the big men," in Islamic history. But the big men to whom he pays attention are neither rulers nor politicians nor traditional theologians. In his approach, the scientist Abu Rayhan

Muhammad ibn Ahmad al-Biruni, the social scientist Ibn Khaldun, and the educational reformer Sayyid Ahmad Khan become representatives of Islamicate vibrancy and dynamism. They share the characteristics of plurality, inclusivity, and a willingness to adapt and change, opening Muslim pathways for advancement and progress. Lawrence's admiration of these men, and analysis of their republic of letters, creates a memory of Muslim contribution to global humanism.

But what of the local? How does Islamic humanism incorporate local vernaculars of coexistence in different contexts? This is one of the sustained questions in Lawrence's numerous publications; it is also evident in several of the essays in the reader. In undertaking to answer this question, he returns to the lived dimensions of everyday Islam. Muslims' ideas and experiences become intimately accessible to us. Muslim ethics pervades several essays in parts IV and V, offering a wide variety of voices. It is a democratic and compassionate understanding of plurality. The intimacy with people and places that Lawrence shares is offered as an invitation to join in these encounters and to engage the creativity of Islamicate cosmopolitanism. Four essays deserve special mention. In the essays "Muslim Engagement with Injustice and Violence," "AIDS Victims and Sick Women: Qur'an as Prescription for Mercy," "W. D. Mohammed: Qur'an as Guide to Racial Equality," and "A Metaphysical Secularist? Decoding M. F. Husain as a Muslim Painter in Exile," we come face to face with the "visible inside" of Muslim ethics. We see ordinary Muslims producing hope in their individual and collective futures despite the violent rhetoric that engulfs them. The lived internal spaces of Muslims are embedded in the emotional choices made, determining how Muslims view their own religion and ritual in local cultural settings. It is a space of human relationships, at once fraught and rewarding. Lawrence encourages us to see Muslims as fellow travelers on the pathway of cultural creativity and civilizational comity. What emerges through his gaze is a rich and textured analysis that shows the intersectional connections shaping Muslim and non-Muslim lives. Just as his work gives form to a new historical consciousness on Islam, so does it cross the boundaries of understanding Muslim lives in our contemporary world.

Muslim agency is an especially important theme in Lawrence's scholarship. Connectivity and interconnectedness with the rest of the world are foundational to his framework for understanding Muslims. At the same time, Lawrence is astutely aware of the places where and the instances when Muslim agency is denied. He is deeply concerned about Muslim marginalization and subjectivity generated from within and outside, because the erosion of agency produces anger. Sometimes this anger can be productive, as he argues in the essay on Sayyid Ahmad Khan. Anger helped Sayyid Ahmad to fight against injustice; using the tool of dialogue, he increased the power of Muslim voices for self-representation and contributed to community solidarity as well as national development. But anger can also be destructive in Muslim lives. In the essay on Osama bin Laden, Lawrence details the rhetoric of violence transforming some Muslims to believe in death and paradise as the reward for violent martyrdom.

By including the voices of a wide variety of Muslims, Lawrence has made the study of Islam democratic, and the themes he addresses are pursued by his students such as Omid Safi, Scott Kugle, Zia Inayat Khan, Kecia Ali, Rob Rozehnal, Hina Azam, Jamillah Karim, and Ali Mian among others. Equally, there are many others who have benefited from not only his attentive approach to details in the Muslim world but also his personal support and enthusiastic encouragement of their work. This becomes evident in chapter 25 of this reader, where Lawrence opens the space for a new visually oriented scholarship heralded by Sandow Birk's creative mode of transcribing the Qur'an. The future of Islamic studies, as Lawrence says, is to show the way forward in the acceptance of the plurality of thinking and the different ways of presenting it, which is an Islamic way of being at once particular and universal. The recurrent emphasis on developing a multiplicity of interpretations is a generous outlook; it is much needed for encouraging new vistas in the field of Islamic studies. Nor does the hope of plural voices fragment the study of Islam. Rather, the shift to open dialogue and creative forms of engagement can enable the next generation of scholars to develop frameworks for critical analysis that foster intellectual positioning about the persistent value of Islam and the creative role of Muslims in the twenty-first century.

Bruce Lawrence is a productive, pioneering scholar of both Islam and Muslim communities. His authorial voice was not developed in solitary study confined to academic spaces in the United States. Instead, as he recalls in the interview with Ali Mian, his scholarship, like his life, is on the move. It is a product of enduring friendships with Muslims in various places; he blends his voice along with many other Muslim voices to produce harmony in thought and spirit, like a musical composition. His friendship with the doyen of Indo-Muslim history, Professor Khaliq Ahmad Nizami, was one key turning point. Lawrence came from a world vastly different from Professor Nizami's. In the mid-1970s when Lawrence, a non-Muslim and a product of American academia, met Professor Nizami, a devout Muslim and an established historian of Muslim India, the distance between them dissolved on the shared common ground of interest in Muslim culture. It bound them together. Even today, Bruce Lawrence is fondly remembered in the Nizami household and they cherish the time he lived with them. The intellectual and personal hospitality that the Nizami family showered on him opened new pathways of friendship with other Muslims. The Chishti Sufi saint Nizamuddin Awliya' and the Chishti brotherhood in Delhi and Ajmer led him further into the depths of Islam and the study of Sufism. Lawrence's circle of Muslim friends kept on expanding as he journeyed on various paths throughout the Islamicate *oikumene*. M. F. Husain, the dissident Indian artist who lived in exile in Qatar; Sheikha Cemlanur Sargut in Istanbul, Turkey; Dr. Shahina Khatib and Abdul Ghafoor Parekh in Nagpur, India; W. D. Mohammed of the American Society of Muslims; Ibrahim Abu Nab of Amman, Jordan; and several others became his trusted interlocutors and companions. He learned from them and reciprocated their friendship with his own, searching together for ideas and knowledge that bridge rather than reinforce the borders of our universe. He poured the intensity of his compassionate understanding of Muslims and Islam into a vast scholarship that took shape as he sojourned with his many friends.

The Bruce B. Lawrence Reader: Islam beyond Borders brings together several of his essays written over four decades and combines them in one volume. It offers an opportunity to discover a range of possibilities, to appreciate the contingencies that inform and shape Islam and Muslim lives, and to find the deep connections between the past and the present. People, places, books, discourses, and texts share lived experiences; together they forge the narrative of hope that can bring people closer in the future. Here we find the pathway to understanding Islam and Muslims with compassion and openness, fueled by goodwill and driven by hope. Bruce Lawrence's scholarship is from the heart. That is his legacy, and it will endure.

BRUCE B. LAWRENCE'S WRITINGS

1970

(Trans.) "Ömer Seyfettin: Love's Wave" [from Aşk Dalgası]. In *Modern Islamic Literature from 1800 to the Present*, edited by James Kritzeck, 87–96. New York: Holt, Rinehart and Winston.

1973

"Shahrastani on Indian Idol Worship." *Studia Islamica* 38:61–73.

1975

"*Afzal al-Fawa'id*—A Reassessment." In *Life, Times and Works of Amir Khusrau Dehlavi*, edited by Zoe Ansari, 119–31. New Delhi: National Amir Khusrau Society.

"The *Lawa'ih* of Qazi Hamid ad-din Nagauri." *Indo-Iranica* 28:34–53.

1976

"Al-Biruni's Approach to the Comparative Study of Indian Culture." In *Biruni Symposium*, edited by E. Yarshater, 27–47. New York: Columbia University Press. Also published in *Studies in Islam* 15 (1978): 1–13.

Shahrastani on the Indian Religions. Foreword by Franz Rosenthal. The Hague: Mouton.

"The Use of Hindu Religious Texts in al-Biruni's *India*, with Special Reference to Patanjali's Yoga-Sutras." In *The Scholar and the Saint: Studies in Commemoration of Abu'l Rayhan al-Biruni and Jalal al-Din al-Rumi*, edited by P. J. Chelkowski, 29–48. New York: New York University Press.

1978

"Al-Biruni and Islamic Mysticism." *Hamdard Islamicus* 1:53–70.

Notes from a Distant Flute: The Extant Literature of Pre-Mughal Indian Sufism. London: Iranian Academy of Philosophy.

1979

"Mystical and Rational Elements in the Early Religious Writings of Sir Sayyid Ahmad Khan." In *The Rose and the Rock: Mystical and Rational Elements in the Intellectual History of South Asian Islam,* edited by Bruce B. Lawrence, 61–103. Durham, NC: Duke University Programs in Comparative Studies on Southern Asia and Islamic and Arabian Development Studies.

An Overview of Sufi Literature in the Sultanate Period, 1206–1526 A.D. Patna, India: Khuda Bakhsh Oriental Public Library.

(Ed.) *The Rose and the Rock: Mystical and Rational Elements in the Intellectual History of South Asian Islam.* Durham, NC: Duke University Programs in Comparative Studies on Southern Asia and Islamic and Arabian Development Studies.

"Thematic Antecedents for the Sufi Poetry of the Sultanate Period." In *Studies in the Urdu Ghazal and Prose Fiction,* edited by Muhammad Umar Memon, 61–95. Madison: University of Wisconsin.

1980

"Healing Rituals among North Indian Chishti Saints of the Delhi Sultanate Period." *Studies in History of Medicine* 4:119–34.

1981

"The Chishtiya of Sultanate India: A Case Study of Biographical Complexities in South Asian Islam." In *Charisma and Sacred Biography,* edited by Michael A. Williams, 47–67. Chico, CA: Scholars.

"Sufism and the History of Religions." *Studies in Islam* 18:119–52.

1982

"ʿAbd al-Qader Jilani." *Encyclopaedia Iranica* 1:132–33.

"ʿAbd al-Qoddus Gangohi." *Encyclopaedia Iranica* 1:138–40.

"Islam in India: The Function of Institutional Sufism in the Islamization of Rajasthan, Gujarat and Kashmir." In *Islam in Local Contexts,* edited by Richard C. Martin, 27–43. Leiden: Brill.

1983

"Abu Bakr Tusi Haydari." *Encyclopaedia Iranica* 1:265.

"Abu Eshaq Kazaruni." *Encyclopaedia Iranica* 1:274–75.

"The Early Chishti Approach to Samaʿ." In *Islamic Society and Culture: Essays in Honour of Professor Aziz Ahmad*, edited by M. Israel and N. K. Wagle, 69–93. New Delhi: Manohar. Also in *Sacred Sound: Music in Religious Thought and Practice*, edited by J. Irwin, 93–110. Chico, CA: Scholars, 1983.

1984

"Ahmad Rodawlavi." *Encyclopaedia Iranica* 1:653–54.

"Akbar al-Akhyar." *Encyclopaedia Iranica* 1:711–12.

"The Diffusion of Hindu/Muslim Boundaries in South Asia: Contrasting Evidence from the Literature and the Tomb Cults of Selected Indo-Muslim Shaykhs." In *Identity and Division in Cults and Sects in South Asia*, ed. Peter Gaeffke and David A. Utz, 125–32. Philadelphia: Department of South Asia Regional Studies.

"Early Indo-Muslim Saints and Conversion." In *Islam in Asia*, edited by Yohanan Friedmann, 1:109–45. Jerusalem: Hebrew University Press.

"The Fundamentalist Response to Islam's Decline: A View from the Asian Periphery." In *Islam in the Modern World*, edited by J. Raitt, 11–40. Columbia: University of Missouri.

(Ed.) *Ibn Khaldun and Islamic Ideology*. Leiden: Brill.

"Ibn Khaldun and Islamic Reform." In *Ibn Khaldun and Islamic Ideology*, edited by Bruce B. Lawrence, 69–88. Leiden: Brill.

1987

"Fatehpur Sikri as an Intellectual Center." *Marg* (Special Issue: Akbar and Fatehpur Sikri) 38, no. 12:84–92.

"Muslim Fundamentalist Movements: Reflections toward a New Approach." In *The Islamic Impulse*, edited by Barbara Freyer Stowasser, 15–36. London: Croom Helm.

"Religion, Ideology and Revolution: The Problematic Case of Post-1979 Iran." In *The Terrible Meek: Revolution and Religion in Cross-Cultural Perspective*, edited by Lonnie D. Kliever, 60–92. New York: Paragon.

"The Sant Movement and North Indian Sufis." In *The Sants: Studies in a Devotional Tradition of India*, edited by Karine Schomer and Hew McLeod, 359–73. Delhi: Motilal Banarsidass.

1989

Defenders of God: The Fundamentalist Revolt against the Modern Age. San Francisco: Harper and Row. Reissued with a new preface: Columbia: University of South Carolina Press, 1995.

1990

"Can Sufi Texts Be Translated? Can They Be Translated from Indo-Persian to American English?" *Islamic Culture* 64:25–46.

"Reconsidering 'Holy War' (Jihad) in Islam." *Islam and Christian-Muslim Relations* 1:261–68.

1991

"Holy War (Jihad) in Islamic Religion and Nation-State Ideologies." In *Just War and Jihad: Historical and Theoretical Perspectives on War and Peace in Western and Islamic Traditions*, edited by John Kelsay and James Turner Johnson, 141–60. New York: Greenwood.

"The Islamic Idiom of Violence: A View from Indonesia." *Terrorism and Political Violence* 3:82–100. Reprinted in *Violence and the Sacred in the Modern World*, edited by Mark Juergensmeyer. London: Cass, 1992.

1992

"Muslim Women and Islamic Fundamentalism." AMEWS (Association of Middle Eastern Women's Studies) Newsletter 7 (May): 1–5.

(Trans. and annot.) *Nizam ad-din Awliya: Morals for the Heart (Conversations of Shaykh Nizam ad-din Awliya Recorded by Amir Hasan Sijzi)*. New York: Paulist. Reissued with a new foreword by Zia Inayat-Khan. Manchester, UK: Beacon, 2017.

1993

"Biography and the 17th Century Qadiriyya of North India." In *Islam and Indian Regions*, edited by Anna L. Dallapiccola and Stephanie Zingel-Ave Lallemant, 1:399–416. Stuttgart: Steiner.

1994

"Honoring Women through Sexual Abstinence: Lessons from the Practice of... Shaykh Nizam ad-Din Awliya." In *Festschrift für Annemarie Schimmel*, edited by Maria Eva Subtelny. *Journal of Turkish Studies* 18:149–62.

"An Indo-Persian Perspective on the Significance of Early Persian Sufi Masters." In *Classical Persian Sufism: From its Origins to Rumi*, ed. Leonard Lewisohn, 19–32. London: Khaniqahi Nimatullahi.

"Rethinking Islam and Violence." *Middle East Affairs Journal* 2:2–22.

"Tracking Fundamentalists and Those Who Study Them: A Sequel to Sadik al-Azm, 'Islamic Fundamentalism Reconsidered: A Critical Outline of Problems, Ideas and Approaches.'" *South Asia Bulletin* 14:41–50.

"Woman as Subject/Woman as Symbol: Islamic Fundamentalism and the Status of Women." *Journal of Religious Ethics* 22:163–85.

1995

"Enough Said: Trying to Build Cultural Bridges Instead of Shoring Up Ideological Walls." *Actes du colloque: Revue de la faculte des lettres et ds sciences humaines* 11:233–45.

"Islam in South Asia." In *The Oxford Encyclopedia of the Modern Islamic World*, edited by John Esposito, 2:278–84. New York: Oxford University Press.

Towards a History of Global Religion(s) in the 20th Century: Parachristian Sightings from an Interdisciplinary Asianist. Tempe: Arizona State University Department of Religious Studies.

1996

"Fundamentalism and the Future in the Islamic World." In *The Muslim Almanac: A Reference Work on the History, Faith, Culture and Peoples of Islam*, edited by Azim A. Nanji, 459–63. New York: Gale.

1997

(With miriam cooke) "Muslim Women: Between Islamic Norms and Human Rights." In *Religious Diversity and Human Rights*, edited by Irene Bloom, J. Paul Martin, and Wayne L. Proudfoot, 313–31. New York: Columbia University Press.

1998

"From Fundamentalism to Fundamentalisms: A Religious Ideology in Multiple Forms." In *Religion, Modernity and Post-Modernity*, edited by David Martin, Paul Heelas, and Paul Morris, 88–101. Oxford: Blackwell.

"Religious Studies: Islam." In *India's Worlds and U.S. Scholars*, edited by Joe Elder, Ed Dimock, and Ainslie Embree, 489–500. New Delhi: Manohar and American Institute of Indian Studies.

Shattering the Myth: Islam beyond Violence. Princeton, NJ: Princeton University Press. Special Millennium edition: Karachi: Oxford University Press, 2000.

"Transformation." In *Critical Terms for Religious Studies*, edited by Mark C. Taylor, 334–48. Chicago: University of Chicago Press.

1999

The Complete Idiot's Guide to Religions Online. Indianapolis: Alpha.

"The Eastward Journey of Muslim Kingship: Islam in South and South-East Asia." In *The Oxford History of Islam*, edited by John Esposito, 395–431. New York: Oxford University Press.

"Muslim Networks in the Information Age: Women, Human Rights and Transnational Civil Societies." *Brown Journal of World Affairs* 6:177–89.

"Veiled Opposition to Sufis in Muslim South Asia: Dynastic Manipulation of Mystical Brotherhoods by the Great Mughal." In *Islamic Mysticism Contested: Thirteen Centuries of Controversies and Polemics*, edited by Frederick de Jong and Bernd Radtke, 436–51. Leiden: Brill.

2000

(Coed. with David Gilmartin) *Beyond Turk and Hindu: Rethinking Religious Identities in Islamicate South Asia.* Gainesville: University Press of Florida.

(With Marcia Hermansen) "Indo-Persian Tazkiras as Memorative Communications." In *Beyond Turk and Hindu: Rethinking Religious Identities in Islamicate South Asia*, edited by David Gilmartin and Bruce B. Lawrence, 149–75. Gainesville: University Press of Florida.

2001

"God On Line: Locating the Pagan/Asian Soul of America in Cyberspace." In *Religion and Cultural Studies*, edited by Susan L. Mizruchi, 236–53. Princeton, NJ: Princeton University Press.

"The Jihad after the Tragedy." September 24. http://groups.colgate.edu/aarislam/blawrenc.htm.

2002

"Allah On-Line: The Practice of Global Islam in the Information Age." In *Practicing Religion in the Age of the Media: Explorations in Media, Religion, and Culture*, edited by Stewart M. Hoover and Lynn Schofield Clark, 237–53. New York: Columbia University Press.

"Conjuring with Islam II." *Journal of American History* 89:485–97. Also published in *History and September 11th*, edited by Joanne Meyerowitz, 175–90. Philadelphia: Temple University Press, 2003.

New Faiths, Old Fears: Muslims and Other Asian Immigrants in American Religious Life. New York: Columbia University Press.

(With Carl W. Ernst) *Sufi Martyrs of Love: The Chishti Order in South Asia and Beyond.* New York: Palgrave Macmillan.

2003

"Christians, Muslims, Terrorists: The Crescent and the Cross since 11 September 2001." *Anglican and Episcopal History* 72:435–50.

"Islamicate Civilization: The View from Asia." In *Teaching Islam*, edited by Brannon M. Wheeler, 61–74. New York: Oxford University Press.

2005

"Al-Biruni." In *Encyclopedia of Religion*, 2nd ed., edited by Lindsay Jones, 2:954–55. Farmington Hills, MI: Macmillan Reference.

(Co-authored with Marilyn Robinson Waldman) "Al-Nubuwah." In *Encyclopedia of Religion*, 2nd ed., edited by Lindsay Jones, 10:6733–39. Farmington Hills, MI: Macmillan Reference.

"Al-Shahrastani." In *Encyclopedia of Religion*, 2nd ed., edited by Lindsay Jones, 12:8267–68. Farmington Hills, MI: Macmillan Reference.

"Approximating *Saj'* in English Renditions of the Qur'an: A Close Reading of *Sura* 93 (*al-Ḍuḥā*) and the *Basmala*." *Journal of Qur'anic Studies* 7:64–80.

Introduction to Ibn Khaldun, *The Muqaddimah: An Introduction to History*, translated by Franz Rosenthal, abridged by N. J. Dawood, vii–xxv. Princeton, NJ: Princeton University Press.

"Khanagah." In *Encyclopedia of Religion*, 2nd ed., edited by Lindsay Jones, 8:5117–18. Farmington Hills, MI: Macmillan Reference.

(Ed. and intro.) *Messages to the World: The Statements of Osama bin Laden.* Translated by James Howarth. London: Verso.

(Coed. with miriam cooke) *Muslim Networks from Hajj to Hip Hop.* Chapel Hill: University of North Carolina Press.

2006

The Qur'an: A Biography. New York: Atlantic Monthly Press, 2006.

2007

(Coed. with Aisha Karim) *On Violence: A Reader.* Durham, NC: Duke University Press.

"The Shah Bano Case." In *On Violence: A Reader*, ed. Bruce B. Lawrence and Aisha Karim, 262–67. Durham, NC: Duke University Press.

2008

(With Scott Kugle) "Competing for Loyalty: Strategies for Survival at Chishti *Dargahs* of Delhi in the 21st Century." *Journal of the Henry Martyn Institute* 27:110–26.

"Scripture, History, and Modernity: Readings of the Qur'an." In *Muslim Modernities: Expressions of the Civil Imagination*, edited by Amyn B. Sajoo, 25–50. London: Tauris.

2009

Islam in the Public Square: Minority Perspectives from Africa and Asia. Youngstown, OH: Youngstown State University.

"Networks of Solidarity." In *A Companion to the Muslim World*, edited by Amyn B. Sajoo, 107–32. London: Tauris.

2010

"Afterword: Competing Genealogies of Muslim Cosmopolitanism." In *Rethinking Islamic Studies: From Orientalism to Cosmopolitanism*, ed. Carl W. Ernst and Richard C. Martin, 302–23. Columbia: University of South Carolina Press.

"Islam in Afro-Eurasia: A Bridge Civilization." In *Civilizations in World Politics: Plural and Pluralist Perspectives*, edited by Peter J. Katzenstein, 157–75. London: Routledge.

"Modernity." In *Key Themes for the Study of Islam*, edited by Jamal J. Elias, 245–62. Oxford: Oneworld.

"Sufism and Neo-Sufism." In *The New Cambridge History of Islam*, vol. 6, *Muslims and Modernity: Culture and Society since 1800*, edited by Robert W. Hefner, 355–84. Cambridge: Cambridge University Press.

2011

"The Cosmopolitan Canopy of East Maritime SE Asia: Minority Citizenship in the Phil-Indo Archipelago." *Comparative Islamic Studies* 7:67–104. Reprinted in *East by Mid-East: Studies in Cultural, Historical and Strategic Connectivities*, edited by Anchi Hoh and Brannon Wheeler, 67–104. Sheffield, UK: Equinox, 2013.

"The Late Shaikh Osama bin Laden: A Religious Profile of al-Qaeda's Deceased Poster Child." *The Muslim World* 101:374–89.

"A Metaphysical Secularist? Decoding M. F. Husain as a Muslim Painter in Exile." In *Barefoot across the Nation: Maqbool Fida Husain and the Idea of India*, edited by Sumathi Ramaswamy, 253–73. New York: Routledge.

"Osama bin Laden—The Man and the Myth." In *The Leader: Psychohistorical Essays*, edited by Charles B. Strozier, 119–34. New York: Springer.

"Polyvalent Islam in the Public Square." *Middle East Journal* 65:133–42.

2012

"Muslim Cosmopolitanism." *Critical Muslim* 2:19–39.

(Coed. with Lindsay Jones and Robert M. Baum) Marilyn Waldman Robinson. *Prophecy and Power: Muhammad and the Qur'an in the Light of Comparison*. Sheffield, UK: Equinox.

2013

"'All Distinctions Are Political, Artificial': The Fuzzy Logic of M. F. Husain." *Common Knowledge* 19:269–74.

"Citizen Ahmad among the Believers: Salvation Contextualized in Indonesia and Egypt." In *Between Heaven and Hell: Islam, Salvation, and the Fate of Others*, edited by Mohammad Hassan Khalil, 288–311. Oxford: Oxford University Press.

"Islam: Unbound and Global." In *Islam in the Modern World*, edited by Jeffrey T. Kenney and Ebrahim Moosa, 209–30. Abingdon, UK: Routledge.

"Muslim Engagement with Injustice and Violence." In *The Oxford Handbook of Religion and Violence*, edited by Mark Juergensmeyer, Margo Kitts, and Michael Jerryson, 126–52. New York: Oxford University Press.

2014

"Al-Biruni: Against the Grain." *Critical Muslim* 12:61–71.

"Genius Denied and Reclaimed: Hodgson's *The Venture of Islam*." *Los Angeles Review of Books*, November 11.

(With Dereje Feyissa) "Muslims Renegotiating Marginality in Contemporary Ethiopia." *The Muslim World* 104:281–305.

2015

Who Is Allah? Chapel Hill: University of North Carolina Press.

2016

"Minority Matters: Perspectives from the Indian Ocean." In *Muslim Minorities in Europe and India: Politics of Accommodation of Islamic Identities*, edited by Anwar Alam and Konrad Pedziwiatr, 3–49. New Delhi: New Century.

2017

The Koran in English: A Biography. Princeton, NJ: Princeton University Press.

2018

"Islamicate Cosmopolitanism from North Africa to Southeast Asia." In *Challenging Cosmopolitanism: Coercion, Mobility and Displacement in Islamic Asia*, edited by Joshua Gedacht and R. Michael Feener, 30–52. Edinburgh: Edinburgh University Press.

2019

Afterword to *Sufism East and West: Mystical Islam and Cross-Cultural Exchange in the Modern World*, edited by Jamal Malik and Saeed Zarrabi-Zadeh, 273–84. Leiden: Brill.

"Exegeting Peace from Nagpur." In *People's Peace: Prospects for a Human Future*, edited by Yasmin Saikia and Chad Haines, 85–100. Syracuse, NY: Syracuse University Press.

2020

"Commentary on Part IV: Sufism in Indian National Spaces." In *The Politics of Islam in South Asia and Beyond*, edited by Katherine Pratt Ewing and Rosemary R. Corbett, 227–32. New York: Columbia University Press.

Foreword to *The Gospel According to Sayyid Ahmad Khan (1817–1898)*, part 3, edited and translated by Christian W. Troll, Charles M. Ramsey, and M. Basharat Mughal, vii–xii. Leiden: Brill, 2020.

"Popular Culture and the Qur'an: Classical and Modern Contexts." In *The Oxford Handbook of Qur'anic Studies*, ed. Mustafa Shah and Muhammad Abdel Haleem, 578–91. Oxford: Oxford University Press.

"A Shaykh for All Occasions." In *Words of Experience: Translating Islam with Carl W. Ernst*, ed. Ilyse R. Morgenstein Fuerst and Brannon M. Wheeler. Bristol, UK: Equinox, 2020.

INDEX

ʿAbd al-Rahman, ʾAʾisha, 353
Abdel Haleem, Muhammad, 356, 362, 366–67
Abdel Rahman, Omar, 31
Abduh, Muhammad, 44
ʿAbdul ʿAziz, Shah, 145, 148, 153, 199
ʿAbdul Ghani, Shah, 145, 147–48
Abdulhamid II (sultan), 200
ʿAbdul Hayy, 146, 150
ʿAbdul Qadir, Shah, 146
Abraham (prophet), 276, 420
Abu Bakr, 91, 281
Abu ʿInan Faris, 61, 335
Abu-Lughod, Janet, 67
Abu Nab, Ibrahim, 352, 372, 412–13, 440
Abu Saʿid, Shah, 147
adab (cultural and behavioral refinement), 6, 9, 126, 128, 188
adab al-rihla (travelogues), 335–56
Adam, 84, 116, 220, 371
Adas, Michael, 55
Afaq, Shah Muhammad, 145
Afghanistan, 104, 182, 263–66, 269–71, 300, 308, 322
African American Muslims, 20, 209, 306, 314, 316, 327, 330–31
Ahmad-i Jam, Shaykh, 170–71, 182
Ahmadiyya, 371
Ahmed, Shahab, 417–18
AIDS, 21, 306, 345, 438
Ajami, Fouad, 247–48
Ajmer, 335, 414, 440
ʿAla al-Dawla, Muhammad, 104
ʿAlaʾuddin Sabir of Kalyar Sharif, 416
Alberuni's India (Biruni), 109–12
Alevis, 371
ʿAli, Abdullah Yusuf, 400–401

Al-i Ahmad, Jalal, 39–40, 65
Aligarh Muslim University, 3, 101, 141, 145, 414, 416–17
ʿAli, Mawlana Mamluk, 147
Ali, Monica, 355–56
Al-Jazeera, 97, 262, 298–99, 301
Allah Resigns at the Summit Meeting (El Saadawi), 398
All India Muslim Personal Law Board, 258
Al Thani, Shaykh Hamad ibn Khalifa, 379–80
America: Americanness, 20, 310–13, 318; Christians in, 237, 238, 246; citizenship and immigration, 20, 430; contemporary, 314, 318–20, 422–23, 425, 428–29, 431; Euro-America, 19, 97, 192, 240, 249; future of, 315; modern, 31; Muslims' experiences after 9/11, 305; during 1960s, 98; nineteenth-century, 80; North, 38, 47, 66, 203, 297, 317; pluralist, 250; Protestant, 247; South, 39; Sufism, 191, 210–13
American Qurʾan (Birk), 3, 421–22, 428
Anatolia, 85, 121, 199, 200, 285–87, 339
Al-Andalus, 40, 124, 335, 341
Anderson, Benedict, 18
Anderson, Jon, 129
Annales school, 63
anthropologists, 31, 82, 111–12, 236
Appadurai, Arjun, 320
Apter, David, 247
ʿ*aql* (reason), 61
Arabia, 47, 78, 91, 382, 385, 404, 423; colonialism and, 19, 268; networks, 333, 334–36; Ottomans and, 285; Prophet and, 191, 281; seventh-century, 18, 179, 191, 275–76, 371, 423; southern, 124; traders from, 67; Wahhabism and, 180, 231, 266, 292. *See also* Saudi Arabia
Arabic language, 61, 68–69; alphabet, 348; Qurʾanic, 21, 74, 353, 413

Arabs: Cartesians, 403; conquest of, 91; French colonialism and, 194; W. D. Mohammed on, 328–30; pagan, 130; pre-Muslim, 115, 193; and racial profiling, 308–9
Arahmaiani, 352, 396–97, 405
Arberry, A. J., 354, 356, 363–64, 368
Aristotle, 10, 58, 68, 105, 108
Arkoun, Mohammed, 248, 372
Arnason, Johann, 54
ʿasabiyya (group feeling), 12, 60, 80, 101, 129–30, 136, 139
Asad, Talal, 71, 341
Ashkenazi Jews, 242
Asoka the Munificent, 68
Ataturk, Kemal, 84–86, 200, 206
Atlas of the Islamic World since 1500 (Robinson), 94
Aurangzeb, 421–22
authenticity, 14, 45, 72, 204, 208, 241, 245, 370
authority, 34, 153, 177, 185, 188, 191, 197, 237, 240; absolute, 281; canonical, 166; colonial, 195; of the court, 183; divine, 68, 184; extra-scriptural, 270; God as, 282; intellectual, 106; Islamic, 204; judicial, 338; of W. D. Mohammed, 327; Ottoman, 285; personal, 280; political, 70, 287; Qurʾanic, 269; religious, 14, 176, 182, 193, 267, 297; royal, 127, 288–89; secular, 288; Shahrastani and, 117; Sufis and, 208, 212; of Tradition, 12
Avicenna (Ibn Sina), 10, 100, 104–5, 108–9
Ayodhya, India, 259
al-Azhar University (Cairo, Egypt), 263–64, 398
Azurda, Mufti Sadruddin, 145, 148
ʿAzzam, ʿAbdullah, 263, 266

Baba Farid Ganj-i Shakar, 179, 184, 416
Babri mosque (Ayodhya, India), 259
Badr, Battle of, 279, 393–94
Baghdad, Iraq, 78, 178, 284–87, 299, 340
Baghdadi, Khalid, 200
Baha'is, 294
Balakot, Battle of, 149–50. *See also* Shahid, Muhammad Ismaʿil; Shahid, Sayyid Ahmad
Balkans, 206, 286–88, 291, 417
Bangladesh, 32, 47, 202, 203, 255, 257, 296, 322, 355
al-Banna, Hasan, 202
Barelwis, 204, 211
Barr, James, 244
barzakh (liminal space between this life and the hereafter), 87, 222, 346, 347, 402, 406, 425–26

basmala (Qurʾanic formula), 220, 351, 353, 358, 362–63, 366–68, 372, 412–13, 421
battles. *See specific battles*
Bayazid, 287
Bayly, Christopher, 94
Beautiful Names (of God), 185, 193, 219, 220–22, 347, 377, 402
beauty, 81, 168–71, 222, 224, 239–40, 351, 416
Bedil, ʿAbdul Qadir, 166
Bell, Derrick, 311
Bell, Richard, 357
Bennabi, Malek, 430
Bentham, Jeremy, 236
Bhagavadgita, 111
Bible, 142, 242, 328–29, 409, 423, 424, 426–27
bidʿat (innovation), 149, 151–52, 154, 199
Bilal ibn Rabah (companion), 388, 393, 398–99
Bilgrami, Akeel, 391
Bin Laden, Osama, 17–18, 230, 439, 262–72, 298–302
Birk, Sandow, 2, 421–22, 423–28, 431, 439
al-Biruni, Ahmad, 10–11, 79, 99–100, 114; and Aristotle, 105, 108; on Hindu tradition, 109–12; and Ibn Sina, 104–6; life of, 103–4, 108; as mathematician, 106–7; on pharmacology, 107; and al-Razi, 108; works of, 108
al-Bishri, Tariq, 44
Bloch, Marc, 16, 237
Blumenberg, Hans, 244, 252
Bohras, 379
Bolshevik Revolution of 1917, 202, 206–7
borders, 1, 22, 280, 295, 311, 336, 432, 440; contested, 297; creedal, sectarian, or linguistic, 95; discursive and territorial, 10; geographical, 26, 311; of India, 104; mental, 72; postcolonial, 296; temporal and spatial, 161; territorial and cultural, 20
Borkenau, Franz, 54
Bose, Sugata, 67
Boullata, Issa J., 353–54, 363
Bradstreet, Anne, 166
Braudel, Fernand, 54, 55, 56, 238, 410; Fernand Braudel Center, 64–65
Brethren of Purity, 379, 405
Brick Lane (Monica Ali), 355, 362
Brink-Danan, Marcy, 83
Bruns, Gerald, 235
Buddhism, 32, 36, 67–68, 92, 238, 307, 417
Bulliet, Richard, 25, 70–71, 417
Bunt, Gary, 343
Burhanuddin "Gharib," 182–83, 186

Burke, Jason, 299
Burmese Days (Orwell), 56
Bush, George W., 265, 301, 321
Byzantine empire, 26, 75, 79, 85–86, 92, 280, 283, 286, 288

Cairo, Egypt: as cosmopolitan center, 78, 80; and transregional epistemic communities, 61
caliphate, 18, 78, 87, 127, 129, 162, 272, 288, 302, 330
Canfield, Robert, 69
capitalism, 7, 41–42, 57, 63–66, 73, 297
Casanova, José, 34
Case for Islamo-Christian Civilization (Bulliet), 70
Cassirer, Ernst, 235
Catholics, 315, 422
Caucasus, 200–201, 206–7
censorship, 397–98
Central Asia, 56, 68, 88, 287; Sufism in, 102, 181, 199–200, 205–7
Central Intelligence Agency (CIA) (United States), 263–64, 267
Chadwick, Owen, 234
Chalabi, Deena, 376, 388, 390–91
Charles V (king), 288, 290
Chatterjee, Partha, 391
Chaudhuri, K. N., 56, 67
China, 56, 64, 79, 296, 313, 337, 339, 342
Chishti, ʿAbdur Rahman, 186
Chishti, Muʿinuddin, 180, 182, 403, 414
Chishti Sufi order: formation, 181–84; historiography, 179–80; Lawrence on, 14, 414; literature and practices of, 184–89; neo-Sufism and, 213–14; Nizami branch, 144, 182; Sabiri branch, 149; Sufi poetry, 162; Tablighi Jamaʿat and, 204; women and, 188
Chittick, William, 400
Christianity, 13, 32, 36–37, 382, 426; Bible Belt, 16; and Islam, 40, 70, 92, 377–80; Jacobite Christians, 109; Protestant, 233, 244, 249
Chronology of Ancient Nations, The (Biruni), 109
Cisse, Hassan, 209
citizenship, 93, 430; Bin Laden and, 264; cultural, 310, 315–18, 325; Indian, 257; Jewish, 83; Muslim, 2, 19–20, 305–6; pluralist, 428
civilization: Arab, 382; and barbarian "others," 57; Biruni on, 106; Christian, 246; clash of, 33, 97, 434; comparative analysis of, 54; definition of, 5, 26, 54–55, 57; European/Western, 40–41, 57, 436; Hodgson on, 65–67, 90–91; Ibn Khaldun and, 57–61, 92, 101, 126–36; Islamic(ate), 3, 11, 54, 62–63, 70–73, 90–91, 93, 96, 99, 126, 166, 176–78, 334, 336, 340, 343, 351, 377, 379, 391, 409, 416, 435; networked, 336, 340; Wallerstein on, 63–65
Civilization 1914–1917 (Duhamel), 56
civilizational discourse, 25, 54–58, 60, 62–63
civilizing mission (*la mission civilisatrice*), 55, 57, 178, 198
civil society, 37, 57, 72, 315–16, 319, 321
class, 20, 93, 289, 296, 312, 338, 339; Biruni and, 111; Lawrence and, 8, 33; middle class, 33, 39, 57, 247, 296; modernity and, 39; movement, 192, 201; Muslims and, 189, 247, 250, 435; prejudice of, 329–21; slavery and, 41; in Turkey, 47, 82
Cleary, Thomas, 303, 357–58, 361, 364
Clinton administration, 265
coincidentia oppositorum, 374, 380, 390
Cold War, 31, 90, 98, 404
Coleridge, Samuel Taylor, 235, 236
colonialism: Bin Laden's critique of, 268–69; and domination, 66; European, 231, 293; legacy of, 36, 297; and Muslim history, 42–45, 47, 71; and neo-Sufism, 194, 198; violence of, 7; in Wallerstein's model, 64
common good, 249, 319
communalism, 258–59
communication, 88, 212–14, 342; languages and, 165, 337; modern, 72, 198, 204, 211, 262, 292; oral, 136, 337; visual, 404
communism, 41–42, 206, 265
compassion: as Divine Attribute, 220–21, 347, 366–67; as methodology, xi, 1–2, 6, 9, 11, 22, 440; translation of, 368–73, 412–13
Confucianism, 92
connectivity, 1–2, 8, 21, 438
consensus, 12, 44, 54, 86, 128–30, 249, 259
cooke, miriam, 5, 11, 129, 306, 333, 412, 413, 414, 425
Corm, Georges, 47
Cornell, Vincent, 62
cosmopolitanism, 3, 4, 5–6, 59, 67, 99, 213; as analytical lens, 6; Jewish, 82–83; in Istanbul, 84–88; Islamicate, 71, 93, 438; Muslim, 9–11, 22, 25–27, 78–89, 124, 336
Crapon de Crapona, Pierre, 354
creation, 16, 110, 116–17, 187, 237, 328, 331, 399
creation science, 241, 245
creativity, 239–40, 395, 405, 426, 438
Criminal Procedure Code of 1973 (India), 260
Crusades, 18, 31, 85, 230, 284; crusaders, 26, 150, 283, 299, 338

INDEX 453

culture: assimilation, 311, 315, 317; cross-culturalism, 34; norms, 17, 65, 255; relativism, 8

Dale, Stephen, 58
Dallal, Ahmad, 105–6
Dalmia, Yasodhara, 386
Damascus, Syria, 125–26, 138, 414
dan Fodio, ʿUsman, 198
dar al-Islam (the domain of Islam), 42, 199, 284, 297, 336, 340
Dard, Khwaja Mir, 144
Darqawiyya Sufi order, 197
Dawood, N. J., 356
Defending the Land of the Muslims Is Each Man's Most Important Duty (ʿAzzam), 266
Delhi, India, 61, 78; Baghdadi and, 200; Ibn Battuta and, 340; Ilyas and, 203; Lawrence and, 414; Nizamuddin Awliyaʾ and, 162, 180, 433, 440; riots in, 258; Shahid and, 199; Sir Sayyid and, 143–49
delusionary escapism, 8, 34
democracy, 22, 47, 309; American, 300; ideals of, 434; Indian, 260; liberal, 37; parliamentary, 294
Deoband movement, 204, 211
Desert Fox (military operation), 298–99
Desert Storm (military operation), 264
Devji, Faisal, 95
diaspora, 14, 209, 309
Dihlawi, ʿAbdul Haqq, 186
Dinawari, ʿUlu, 182
Diouf, Mamadou, 209–10
divans (poetry collections), 224
diversity, 65, 316; of Islam, 2, 334, 343; of Istanbul, 88; of scripture, 242; of transcendence, 391; of worldviews, 306
Divine Attributes and Essence, 220, 222
divine revelation, 41, 331, 362, 366
divorce, 72, 255–57, 260, 372
Dome of the Rock, 22, 419–20
Donner, Fred, 281
doubling, 171, 316
Duhamel, Georges, 56
Dunn, Ross, 339–40

East India Company, 402
ecumene. See *oikumene*
Egypt, 247, 290; British, 44, 268; conquest of, 288; festivals of Sufi saints in, 213; forces of, 196; French invasion of, 268, 291; fundamentalists in, 246; prerevolutionary, 42; reformers in, 294; Sunnis in, 238, 240; Tahrir Revolution, 397–98; today, 397–98; and Yom Kippur War, 263
Eisenstadt, Shmuel, 55, 65
elites, 80, 321, 327; Aryan, 69; cosmopolitan, 126; Euro-American Christian, 36, 315; fundamentalists, 237, 240–41, 246, 249, 251; Indian, 100; indigenous, 44–45, 233–34; intellectual, 204; Muslim, 45–46, 48, 250, 257, 294–95; ruling, 292; Sufi-oriented, 193; urban, 55, 84
Enduring Freedom (military operation), 265
Enlightenment, 58, 235–36, 244; equality and, 79; European, 242; fundamentalism and, 233, 251; Hodgson and, 95; Judaism and, 249; post-, 61, 245
Eoyang, Eugene, 162, 167, 176
Ernst, Carl W., 14, 162
Europe, 2, 20, 30, 287, 310, 401, 402, 434–35; civilization of, 40–41, 56; and colonialism, 19, 33, 43, 46–48, 55, 66, 71, 94, 194, 231, 234, 237, 250, 291–97; M. F. Husain and, 383–87; Islam and, 95–97, 212–13; Istanbul and, 80–82; Jews and, 242, 245, 249; Muslims in, 32, 341–42; nationalism in, 38; Ottoman empire and, 287–90; terrorism in, 269; Turkey and, 39; Wallerstein on, 64
evangelicals, 241, 244
Eve, 220
expansionism, 231, 311, 416
extremism, 16, 42, 238, 245

Faiz, Faiz Ahmad, 167, 381
Fakhry, Majid, 361, 366
Falwell, Jerry, 244
Fanon, Frantz, 66
Faraʾidis, 192, 199, 201, 293
Faridi, Shahidullah, 204–5
Farrakhan, Louis, 32, 305–6, 327–28
al-Faruqi, Ismaʿil, 162, 177–78
Faruqi, Ziyaʾ al-Hasan, 167–68
Fethullahcilar movement (Turkey), 206
Fihrist (Ibn an-Nadim), 114
Foda, Farag, 398
Fowden, Garth, 417
Fox, Richard, 46
Francis (Pope), 426
Fukuyama, Francis, 33, 93
fundamentalism, 4, 259; cultural, 317; Indian-style, 259; Islamic, 29, 39, 229, 242–43, 291, 294; Jewish, 242; modernity and, 16–17; as religious ideology, 233–52
futuh (conquests), 282

Gabriel (Jibril) (archangel), 185, 331
Gadamer, Hans-Georg, 235
Gandhi, Indira, 257–58
Gandhi, Mahatma, 71
Gandhi, Rajiv, 258, 260
Gangohi, ʿAbdul Quddus, 184, 403
Gangohi, Rashid Ahmad, 204
Gellner, Ernest, 38
gender: complementarities, 222; inequities, 31–32, 229, 247, 261, 352, 428, 435; law and, 17; perspectives of, 93
Gesu Daraz, Sayyid Muhammad, 414
Ghalib, Mirza, 381
al-Ghazali, Abu Hamid, 149, 392, 405
al-Ghazali, Ahmad, 172
Ghazi, Osman, 286
Ghulam ʿAli, Shah, 143, 145, 147–49, 154, 200
Giacometti, Alberto, 376
Giddens, Anthony, 238
Gibbon, Edward, 177
Gibb, H. A. R., 242
Gospel, 381
governance, 67–69, 255, 295
Gramsci, Antonio, 66
Grunebaum, Gustave von, 97
Guevara, Che, 230, 272
Guha-Thakurta, Tapati, 380, 390
Gujarat, 110
Gulbarga, 414
Gulen, Fethullah, 206
Gulf War (1990), 299
gunpowder empires, 18–19, 284–90
Gush Emunim, 245, 250

Habermas, Jürgen, 49
hadith (prophetic utterance or action): Ibn Khaldun and, 12, 128, 134, 139n22; religious authority and, 191, 426
Haeri, Shaykh Fadhlalla, 222
Hagar, 276
hajj. *See* pilgrimage (hajj)
hakimiyya (divine lordship), 42
halakha (Jewish ritual law), 237
Hali, Altaf Husayn, 143, 148
al-Hallaj, Mansur, 170
Halman, Talat, 415
Hamallah, Shaykh, 195
Hamka, 208
Haramayn, 196, 198, 201, 203, 208. *See also* Holy Land

Harwani, ʿUsman, 180
hegemony, 234; Hindu, 258; modernist, 17, 233, 239–40, 251; Mughal, 180, 292; political, 113; Western, 55, 66, 93, 263, 237
hierarchy: as cultural stratification, 55; Harranian, 116; Islamicate civilization and, 26, 62, 69, 75n28, 101, 337–38; Ottoman, 200; Tusi on, 288
Hijaz, 195–96, 199, 207, 288, 292, 335
hijra (exodus), 59, 74, 135, 277
Hillenbrand, Carole, 283–84
Hinduism: Biruni and, 11, 109–12; and fundamentalism, 258–59; M. F. Husain and, 22, 391; Lawrence's and, 4; pan-Asian, 67; Shahrastani on, 113–20
hip hop, 334–35, 342
History of Islamic Societies, A (Lapidus), 94
HIV/AIDS, 346
Hobsbawm, Eric, 234
Hodgson, Marshall G. S., 5, 8–9, 16, 19; on Great Western Transmutation (GWT), 229; on Islamicate civilization, 26, 63, 65–67, 78; and Lawrence, 415–18, 435–36; life of, 90; on Persianate culture, 68–70; reception of, 94–98; on Sufi orders, 178, 181; as world historian, 27, 47
Hofstadter, Douglas, 239–40
Hollinger, David, 318
Holy Land, 264, 270, 284. *See also* Haramayn
Hourani, Albert, 336
Hujwiri, ʿAli, 186
humanism, 1, 8, 9, 10, 33, 35, 251, 334
humanities, 8, 26, 33, 35
Hunain, Battle of, 280
Hungary, 242, 288
Huntington, Samuel, 33, 70, 93
Husain, M. F., 22, 352, 374–406, 424, 438, 440
Husain, Shah Fida, 148
Husain ibn Ali, 237
Husayn, Taha, 353
Hussein, Saddam, 264, 295
hybrid language, 165–66, 173

ibn ʿAbd Allah, Muhammad Ahmad (the Sudanese Mahdi), 196–97, 274
ibn ʿAbd al-Wahhab, Muhammad, 192–93, 231, 292–93, 403
Ibn ʿArabi, 194, 197, 211, 220–24, 347, 405
Ibn ʿAtaʾ Allah, 222
Ibn Battuta, 21, 61–62, 69, 306, 335–42
ibn Hanbal, Ahmad, 135

INDEX 455

ibn Hayyan, Jabir, 379
ibn Idris al-Fasi, Ahmad, 196–97
ibn Ishaq, Hunayn, 108
Ibn Juzayy, 61, 335
Ibn Khaldun: on civilization, 57–62; Hodgson and, 92; as jurist, 99, 101–2, 129–31; life of, 124–25; and *Muqaddimah*, 125–36; and Muslim network, 335–36
Ibn Sina (Avicenna), 10, 100, 104–5, 108–9
Ibn Taymiyya, 18, 270, 284, 285
identity: cosmopolitan, 81; cultural, 93; ethnic, 36, 83, 310; Muslim, 30, 71–73, 202, 204–5, 207, 213, 285, 293, 306, 310, 334, 342–43, 385, 427; national, 44, 245; politics of, 257; racial, 305; religious, 88, 259–61, 421; secular, 390
ideology, 16, 56; American, 311, 313, 315; civilizing mission as, 55; empire and, 290; fundamentalism as religious, 233–52; Islam and, 7, 32, 45, 142, 193, 196, 211, 287, 404, 434; nationalism as, 42; networked, 20, 332; new media and, 213; secularism as, 72
Idris (king), 197
ijazas (certificates of competency), 339
Ilyas, Mawlana Muhammad, 203–4
imagination: artists and, 399, 402; critical reflection and, 41–42; methodology and, 1, 6, 9, 13, 23; translation and, 174
Imdadullah Muhajir Makki, Hajji, 149, 158n29, 204, 402–3, 405
immigrants: Arab to Andalusia, 124; Asian Muslim to the United States, 2, 305, 307–22; as threat, 97
Immigration and Naturalization Act of 1965 (United States), 213
Inada, Lawson Fusao, 312–13, 318
India, 39, 192; anticolonialism in, 19, birth of, 202; Biruni in, 104–12; buildings in, 61; Chishti order and, 180–82, 185; colonial, 13, 46, 101, 195, 400; fundamentalist interpretations in, 17; healers in, 348; M. F. Husain and, 374–92, 398; Ibn Battuta in, 336–38, 341–42; Lawrence and, 414–18; migrations, 309, 311, 314, 322; modernity and, 56; Mughal, 143–44, 285, 291; Muslims/Islam in, 20, 95, 294; Parliament, 257–60; Persianate Turks in, 69; precolonial, 101; Shah Bano case in, 31–32, 230, 255–61; Shahrastani and, 100, 113–20; Sir Sayyid and, 141–45; Sufism in, 102, 161–63, 199, 202–3, 213, 285, 293; Supreme Court, 256–57; world civilization in, 90
India (Biruni), 10, 114
Indian Ocean: as centerpiece of Islamicate civilization, 67, 292, 337, 417

indigenous/immigrant, 124, 305, 428
Indonesia: Dutch in, 71, 195; Islamic scholars from, 207; Muslims in, 56; Sufism in, 208
Information Age, 161, 163, 210, 214, 269, 300, 306, 342
Ingushetia, 200
International Women's Decade (1975–1985), 256
interfaith dialogue, 372, 421–24
Inter-Service Intelligence Agency (ISI) (Pakistan), 263–64
introspection, 218
Iqbal, Muhammad, 331, 381
Iran, 19, 47, 71, 86, 114, 310; Afghans in, 292; economy of, 247; Muslims in, 238, 240, 250, 296; nationalism, 42; 1979 revolution, 2, 38–39, 96, 97, 202, 237, 242–43; reformers in, 294; Safavid, 285, 289; Sufis and, 188; war with Iraq, 297, 352
Irano-Semitic languages, 91, 96
Iraq: American occupation, 272; Bin Laden and, 299; UN sanctions and, 269; war with Iran, 297, 352
Isaac/Ishmael, 276, 420
Isfahan, 61, 62, 69, 104
Islamicate civilization: as bridge, 71; Hodgson on, 63, 416; Ibn Khaldun on, 131; periods of, 90–92; self-replication, 61; traits of, 55; world history and, 62, 64
Islamic law (*shariʿa*): consensus, 129; Ibn Khaldun and, 129; Muslim Personal Law, 256, 258; Shah Bano Case and, 257; scholars as guardians of, 340
"Islam in Afro-Eurasia: A Bridge Civilization" (Lawrence), 9, 54–73
Islamism (political Islam), 7; Bin Laden and, 230; and colonialism, 291; and media, 205, 229; and modernity, 3; Qutb and, 42; radical, 271; as religious fundamentalism, 17, 27; varieties of, 231; and violence, 18, 434
Islamization, 84, 206
islam noir (Black Islam), 71, 195
Islamoğlu, Huricihan, 92, 95
Islam: The Misunderstood Religion (Qutb), 41
Israel: Bin Laden on, 270, 300; Jewish fundamentalism in, 237–38, 240, 242, 245–47, 250, 252
Istanbul, 26–27, 61, 62, 80–88

jahiliyya (ignorance), 42, 122, 276, 297
Jakarta, Indonesia, 334
Jalalabad, Afghanistan, 264–65
Jamaʿat-i Islami, 203
Jan-i Janan, Mirza Mazhar 144–45, 147

Jarrahi Sufi order, 214
Jaspers, Karl, 55
al-Jazaʾiri, ʿAbdul Qadir, 198
Jeffrey, Arthur, 364
Jerusalem, 272, 283–84, 288, 419, 420
Jews and Judaism: American, 315; Anglo-Saxon Protestant norm and, 315; Bin Laden on, 270; European, 242; fundamentalism, 233, 237, 240, 245; *haredi*, 241; Turkish, 83
jihad (divinely sanctioned war), 17–18; Bin Laden and, 230, 263–66, 269–72; of Ibn Taymiyya, 18; intellectual, 430; in Islamic history, 230–31, 281–86, 297–302; modern, 297–98; nineteenth-century, 199–201; of Sayyid Ahmad Shahid, 192; and social transformation, 19; of Al-Hajj ʿUmar Taal, 198; Wahhabis and, 404
Jinnah, Muhammad ʿAli, 205
jinns (invisible beings), 345, 406
Joseph (prophet), 424–25, 431
Judaism. *See* Jews and Judaism
Juergensmeyer, Mark, 38–39
justice: ʿ*adl*, 172; early Islam and, 277; imperial dispensation of, 69; racial, 20; reciprocal obligations and, 338; rule of, 42; Sayyid Qutb on, 42; social, 206, 270, 293; Tusi and, 288–89
Justice Department (United States), 308, 414

Kabir, Ananya Jahanara, 380
Kalimullah, Shaykh, 144
Kant, Immanuel, 49, 317
Kapferer, Bruce, 33
Kapur, Geeta, 386
Karta, Neturei, 245, 350
Keaton, Buster, 386
Kemal, Mustafa, 84–87
Kermani, Navid, 427
khabar (event), 12, 58, 128, 131–36
Khan, Ghazala, 429
Khan, Khizr, 429–30
Khan, Mawlana Rashiduddin, 146
Khan, Muhammad Muhsin, 354, 401
Khan, Nusrat Fateh ʿAli ("Dam Mast Qalandar"), 212–13
Khan, Pir Inayat, 213
Khan, Pir Vilayat, 213
Khan, Pir Zia Inayat, 213, 439
Khan, Sayyid Ahmad (Sir Sayyid Ahmad Khan), 10, 12–13, 99, 101, 141–55, 331, 438–39
Khatmiyya Sufi order, 196–98

Khatun, Jahan Malek, 225
Khayyam, Omar, 61
Khomeini, Ayatollah, 31, 371
Khusraw, Amir, 166
King, Martin Luther, Jr., 71
King Abd al-Aziz University, 263
kingship, 67–71, 144
Kippenberg, Hans, 297, 303
Kirmani, Waris, 414
Kitab al-Saydanah (Biruni), 10, 107
Kosovo, Battle of, 287
Kuala Lumpur, Malaysia, 14
Kubra, Najmuddin, 181
Kubrawiyya Sufi order (Kubravis), 181, 206
kufr (unbelief), 192–93, 293
Kugle, Scott Siraj al-Haqq, 402–4, 439
Kurdistan, 200, 295

Lapidus, Ira, 94
Laroui, Abdallah, 37, 133
Lazard, Naomi, 167
Lebanon, 238, 240, 300
Legitimacy of the Modern Age, The (Blumenberg), 253
Lewis, Bernard, 70, 92–93, 267
Lewis, Samuel, 214
lex talionis, 270, 281
Lincoln, C. Eric, 410
Lind, Michael, 318
loyalty: Islamic, 44, 67, 72, 166, 191–92, 194; political, 296; in Soviet Union, 206, 214, 170, 302, 339
Lum, Wing Tek, 312–13

Maʾ al-ʿAynayn, Sayyid, 195
Madan, Tiki, 391
madhhabs (law schools), 193
madrasas (religious schools), 141, 195, 198, 204, 339
maghazi (raids), 282
Maher, Bill, 96–97
Mahmud of Ghazna, 104, 109, 113
Majid, Anouar, 94
majority/minority, 16, 20, 87, 93, 305
Makhsusullah, Mawlana, 146–47
Malaysia, 39, 71, 213, 238, 240, 313, 399
malfuzat (dialogues), 151, 162, 204, 414
Mandaville, Peter, 71–72
Mandela, Nelson, 71
Manicheans, 100, 109
Mann, Michael, 269

al-Mansur, Abu Nasr, 103
Manzikert, Battle of, 286
marabouts, 194–95, 198
Martin, Rabiʿa, 214
Massive Attack (British hip hop group), 212
Mathaf: Arab Museum of Modern Art (Doha, Qatar), 375, 378, 380, 382, 384, 390
Maududi, Sayyid Abuʾl Aʿla, 203, 231
May, Henry, 241
al-Mayassa, Sheikha, 377
Mazdeism, 92
McCarthy, Thomas, 317
Mecca, 78; as cosmopolitan center, 196–97, 199, 333–34, 336; Muhammad in, 277–81
media, 202, 212–13; cyberspace, 320, 334, 343, 398; electronic, 211; internet, 7–8, 21, 210, 241, 262, 306, 320–21, 343, 346–47, 401; Muslims and, 204; new, 21, 262; print, 194, 204, 207, 211–12, 262; social, 8, 430
Medina, 78, 179, 278–79, 336
meditation, 15, 146, 151, 153, 188, 212, 218–19, 347
Mehmet II (Mehmed the Conqueror), 84–87, 287
Messages to the World (Bin Laden), 17, 230, 262–72, 410, 437
Mevlevi Sufi order, 200, 210
Middle East: Bin Laden and, 266; discursive construction of, 91, 310, 417; Western domination of, 268–69, 272
Mignolo, Walter, 83
militancy, 18, 31, 231, 245
Mill, John Stuart, 236
Miller, Flagg, 299
al-Mirghani, Muhammad ʿUthman, 196–98
mobility, 210, 339–40; Muslim, 335; social, 68, 124; transregional, 194
modernity, 15, 238, 317; antimodernism, 243; Blumenberg on, 245–46; and fundamentalisms, 240; Great Western Transmutation (GWT), 47–48, 229; hegemony of modernization, 17, 249; high-tech era, 241, 243; modernism, 238; Muslims and, 19, 46; nationalism and, 37; religious, 16, 229, 305; social, 39; tradition versus 16; Western, 56, 64–65, 192, 210
Mohammed, W. D., 20, 306, 327–32, 410–13, 438, 440
Mongols, 92, 287; in China, 337; Ibn Khaldun and, 125–26; invasions, 91, 231, 270, 284, 286
Moosa, Ebrahim, 418–19
Morals for the Heart (Lawrence), 162, 166–67, 171–73, 414

Morocco, 285, 290, 294–95, 341, 348, 410
Moses (prophet), 346, 348
Mosque Cares, The, 327, 331, 411
Motahhari, Morteza, 252
Moustafa, Ahmed, 398
Mozah, Sheikha, 374, 377, 379–80, 382, 388
Mubarak, Hosni, 265
Mughal empire, 183, 285, 290–92
Muhammad. *See* Prophet Muhammad
Muhammad, Elijah, 327
Muhammad, Hasan (Chishti Sufi master), 179
mujahidin (holy warriors) 149–51, 153–54, 263–64, 270–71, 293, 300–301
Mumbai, India, 374, 376, 391
Muqaddimah (Ibn Khaldun), 10–11, 58, 79, 124–36, 336
Murad I, 286–87
Muridist Insurrection (Russia), 200
Muridiyya Sufi order, 208–9
music, 15, 40, 42: assemblies of (*majalis-i samaʿ*), 182; and cosmopolitanism, 80; festivals, 81; mind and, 239; musicians, 62, 69; *qawwali* music, 212; *samaʿ* (listening to music), 162, 179, 211, 415; Sufism and, 161, 167, 183, 188, 212–13, 227
Muslim American Society, 327
Muslim Brethren/Brotherhood, 42, 202, 298
Muslim League, 204
Muslim networks, 20, 192, 194, 306, 333–43, 434–35
Muslim Networks from Hajj to Hip Hop (cooke and Lawrence), 20, 306, 333–43
Muslim Women (Protection of Rights on Divorce) Act (India), 260
al-Mutanabbi, 340–41
Mutiny of 1857, 155, 402

Nadwi, Abuʾl-Hasan ʿAli, 338
Nagauri, Qadi Hamiduddin, 169
an-Naʿim, Abdullahi, 71
Nandy, Ashis, 391
Nanji, Azim, 418
Naqshbandi Sufi order, 102, 145–46, 148, 196, 214; challenges of, 208; masters of, 181; during nineteenth century, 199–200; saints, 154; in Southeast Asia, 201; during twentieth century, 205–6
Nasir, Muhammad, 144–45, 148
Nasiruddin Chiragh-i Dihli, 179, 184, 185
al-Nasser, Gamal Abd, 42, 263, 297
nationalism: Arab, 42, 44; ethnic (*qawmiyya*), 7, 43; Eurocentric view of, 38; Islam and, 32–33;

mimetic, 295; and nation-state, 33, 39, 72–73, 84, 238–39, 243, 245–46, 248, 250, 296; region-specific (*wataniyya*), 43–44; Turkish, 84
National Salvation Party (Milli Selamet Partisi) (Turkey), 205–6
Nation of Islam, 327–28
Native Americans, 311
Needham, Anuradha Dingwaney, 390
Neshat, Shirin, 352, 397, 405
networks. *See* Muslim networks
Neuwirth, Angelika, 354, 363, 365
Newsweek, 371–72
Niasse, Ibrahim, 209
Nietzsche, Friedrich, 235, 244, 251
Nigeria, 195, 209, 293
Nile-to-Oxus region, 6, 78, 79, 90–91
Niʿmatullahi Sufi order, 214
Nizami, Khaliq Ahmad, 3, 155, 439–40
Nizami, Khwaja Hasan, 203
Nizamuddin Awliyaʾ, Shaykh, 3, 162, 166–69, 171, 179–80, 182, 184–85, 414, 433–34, 440
Notes from a Distant Flute: The Extant Literature of Pre-Mughal Sufism (Lawrence), 414
Nuʿmani, Shibli, 338
Nursi, Badiʿuzzaman Saʿid, 205–6

Obama, Barack, 398–99
O'Fahey, R. S., 194, 202
oikumene (Afro-Eurasian), 19, 61–62; civilizational definitions and, 55; colonialism and, 45; counter-cosmopolitan forces and, 87; Ibn Khaldun on, 79
oil, 47, 263, 295–96, 301
Orientalism, 6, 34, 46, 63, 65
Orientalism (Said), 97–98
Orwell, George, 56
Oslo Accords, 264
Ottoman empire, 18, 26; Naqshbandiyya, 200; and other empires, 62; pan-ethnic identity, 83; violence and, 284–90; Wallerstein on, 64–65

Padri Reform movement, 201, 294
Pakistan, 32, 47; Bin Laden and, 263; birth of, 202; emigration from, 322; fundamentalists in, 246; judiciary in, 255, 257; Muslims in, 238, 240, 296; nationalism, 42; Sufism in, 202–5, 212–13; Tablighi Mission in, 203; Taliban and, 265
Palembang, ʿAbdus Samad, 201
Palestine, 245, 249, 263, 268, 279
Pan-Islamism, 43–44

Park, Robert, 319–20
Partition of India (1947), 202, 380
Pascal, Blaise, 240
Patocka, Jan, 54
Paz, Octavio, 35–36
Pei, I. M., 377, 382
performance art, 396
Persianate culture, 68–69, 93, 95–96
Persians, 68–69, 99, 300
Peshawar, Pakistan, 199, 263–64, 266
philosophers (*falasifa*), 223
Pick, Daniel, 35
Pickthall, Mohammed Marmaduke, 354, 359, 366
pilgrimage (hajj), 333–35, 340–41
Pirous, Abdul Djalil, 397
pluralism, 22, 242, 249, 251; American, 429; ecumenical, 294; legal, 93; religious, 4
poetry, 11–12, 413, 437; Arabic, 21, 124, 230; of love, 224; Persian, 143, 166, 171, 225; in Qurʾan, 351, 354; Sufi, 226–27, 432; translations of, 166–74
politics, 19, 33, 65, 72, 204, 234; civilizational, 58, 70; cultural, 376, 380; democratic, 294, 319; divine, 42–43; geopolitics, 63–64; identity, 257; of interfaith engagement, 421; Islam and, 25, 36, 39, 41, 47, 182, 372, 399, 417, 435; national, 205–6; as research topic, 14, 26, 434; of translation, 13
polyvalence, 20, 69, 126, 305, 316, 319–20, 322
popular culture, 212–13; hip hop, 334–35, 342
Potuoğlu-Cook, Öykü, 82–83
Progressive Patriotic Protestantism, 238
Prophet Muhammad: and African American Muslims, 331; and Allah, 403; death of, 91; in Islamic studies, 434; and Jesus, 388; and law, 134, 255; mission of, 85; and Muslim networks, 333, 339; name of, 84; and Qurʾan, 353–63, 370–73, 388, 420, 425; Sir Sayyid on, 152, 154; and succession, 116, 129; Sufism and, 179–80, 182, 184–87, 191–92, 196–97, 204, 209, 211; and Tradition scholarship, 59; and violence, 230, 270, 275–80, 297, 300

Qadiriyya Sufi order, 181, 194–200, 214
al-Qaʿida, 269, 271, 298, 300, 308; bombings of the 1990s, 202; history of, 263–65; leader of, 230; as violent Islamism, 18
Qajar, 250, 292
Qalandar, Bu ʿAli Shah, 184
Qalandar movement, 183–84
qanun (civil law), 288
al-Qaradawi, Yusuf, 338

al-Qarni, Uways, 184
Qur'an, 2, 22, 191; as Book of Signs, 330–32, 347–48, 370, 372–73; healers and, 353–69; interpretations of, 61; Meccan *suras*, 354; Sufis and, 211; translation of, 3, 21
Qushayri, 223
Qutb, Muhammad, 41–42, 263
Qutb, Sayyid, 42, 231, 263, 271, 297–98, 353
Qutbuddin Bakhtiyar Kaki, 414

Rabbani, Wahid Bakhsh, 204
Rabbuh, Murabbih, 195
race: equality, 310–11, 327, 438; profiling, 305, 309; racism, 305, 311–12, 327, 328, 329, 332
Rafi'uddin, Shah, 146
Rajan, Rajeswari Sunder, 390
al-Rashid, Ibrahim, 196
al-Razi, Muhammad b. Zakariya, 108
religion: Abrahamic, 238, 383, 401; Asian, 67, 307, 417; civil, 243, 245; and civilization, 56, 67, 70; comparative, 99; and Enlightenment, 289, 319; and ideology, 33, 41, 229, 233–52; Islam as, 7, 40–41; and nationalism, 35–37, 39; and pluralism, 4; and politics, 71, 309; popular, 12, 41; practical, 21, 347; religious studies, 1, 23, 319, 432; and violence, 4
remembrance (*dhikr/zikr*), 15, 199, 203, 204, 207, 224, 299, 347
revival, 29, 39, 120, 144, 194, 254, 293–94
Rich, Adrienne, 166
Ridda Wars, 281–83
Ridding, John, 376
Rihla (Ibn Battuta), 61–62, 335
Rings of Wisdom (*Fusus al-hikam*) (Ibn 'Arabi), 220
Robert of Ketton, 411–12
Robinson, Frances, 94
Rorty, Richard, 251–52
Rosenthal, Franz: defining civilization, 5; influence of, 4, 11, 436; translation of *Muqaddimah*, 12, 129, 133
Roy, Olivier, 72
Rudawlavi, 'Abdul Haqq, 184
ruhaniyat (spiritual beings), 115–19
Rumi, Jalaluddin, 161, 163, 213, 225–26, 375, 405, 415
Rushdie, Salman, 258, 371
Russia, 64, 81, 200–201, 206–7, 263–64, 291
Russo-Ottoman War (1877), 205

Saadawi, Nawal El, 352, 398, 405
Saber, Karam, 397–98

Sabians, 100, 115–19
Sadat, Anwar, 247
Sa'di, Muslihuddin, 143, 225
Safavid empire, 18, 62, 91, 231, 250, 284–85, 289–91
Said, Edward, 63, 97
Sa'id, Shah Ahmad, 145, 147
saints: biographical dictionaries, 186; healing, 346–48; Ibn Khaldun on, 346; intercession, 15, 191, 193; Sayyid Ahmad Khan on, 144–46, 148, 152–54; shrines, 177, 183, 206; Sufi websites and, 213
Saladin (Salah ad-din Ayyubi), 31, 267, 283–84
Salafi, 194, 196, 202, 402
Salafiyya (Islamic scripturalism), 294
Samanids, 104
Sambas, Ahmad Khatib, 201
Sammani Sufi order, 201
al-Sanusi, Muhammad ibn 'Ali, 192, 196–97, 293
Sanusiyya Sufi order, 196–97
Satanic Verses, The (Rushdie), 371
Saudi Arabia, 45, 71, 263–64, 292, 295, 400–401
Scheuer, Michael, 267–68
Schlesinger, Arthur, 319
scientific positivism, 206, 245
Scott, James, 66
scripture: Bin Ladin's use of, 267; Biruni on Indic scriptures, 111; fundamentalism and, 237, 242–43; M. F. Husain's use of, 381; Lawrence's understanding of, 410, 420, 427; translation of, 21; violence and, 18
secularism, 22, 26, 72, 202, 205, 248, 390–91
Segal, Robert, 34
Seljuks, 285–86
Sells, Michael, 358, 364, 366
Sen, Amartya, 391
Senegal, 71, 208–10, 333–34
Shackle, Christopher, 168–72
Shahabuddin, Syed, 259–60
Shah Bano, 17, 31–32, 230, 255–61
al-Shadhili, Abu'l-Hasan, 181
Shadhiliyya Sufi order, 181, 196–97, 214
Shahid, Muhammad Isma'il, 145–54, 149–52, 154
Shahid, Sayyid Ahmad, 145–46, 150–51, 154, 192, 199, 293
Shahrastani, 10–11, 99–101, 113–20
Shahrour, Muhammad, 372
Shami, Abu Ishaq, 180, 182
Shamil, Imam, 200–201
shari'a. *See* Islamic law (*shari'a*)
Shari'atullah, Hajji, 199

Shattari Sufi order, 201
Shattering the Myth (Lawrence), 6–7, 29–48
Shi'ism, 285, 294
Shikoh, Dara, 101, 120
Shirazi, Hafez, 225
Shirazi, Zaynuddin, 186
shirk (polytheism), 193, 299
Shouri, Arun, 260, 391
Sijzi, Amir Hasan, 162, 167, 414
Sikhs, 32, 149–50, 199, 258, 293, 307, 322
silsila (chain), 182
Silsilat al-muluk (Sir Sayyid), 144
Singh, K. Bikram, 287, 378–79, 390
Sirhindi, Shaykh Ahmad, 144–45, 148
Sir Sayyid. *See* Khan, Sayyid Ahmad (Sir Sayyid Ahmad Khan)
slavery, 41, 210, 311, 328, 335, 342
social scientists, 1, 35, 63, 251, 334, 438
sociology, 6, 63, 99
Somalia, 264, 270–71, 300
Southeast Asia, 69–70, 201
Spain, 61, 64, 79, 83, 124, 335–36, 341
Spengler, Oswald, 54
Spivak, Gayatri, 34
Steiner, George, 165, 246
stereotypes, 29–30, 96, 309, 317, 401
Subaltern School, 38
Subrahmanyam, Sanjay, 70
Sudan, 46, 195–97, 264–66
Sufi Martyrs of Love (Ernst and Lawrence), 14, 162
Sufi Order International (Inayati Sufi order), 213–14
Sufism: in America, 210–12; and Allah, 402–5; approaches to, 178–79; in Asia, 3, 15, 21, 202; concept of, 14, 161; dervishes, 341; historiography of, 176–89; and iconoclasm, 113; institutional, 14, 161–63, 191, 192; Lawrence and, 2, 414, 426; lore, 416; masters, 185, 219–27, 287, 339, 346–48, 395; music, 212–13; and Muslim networks, 338–39; and mysticism, 12, 437; Neo-Sufism, 15, 163, 190–214; orders, 285; origins of, 181; and poetics, 13, 161–62, 213, 226, 432; and Prophet Muhammad, 191–92; saints, 213, 433; Sir Sayyid and, 13, 102, 146, 155; *zawiyas*, 336
Suhrawardi, Abu Hafs, 148, 169, 181
Suhrawardi, Shihabuddin, 403
Suleiman I, 288–89
Sumatra, 201, 208, 294
sunna, 117, 128–29, 134, 154, 186, 191, 196, 403
al-Susi, 'Abdul Wahhab, 200

al-Suyuti, Jalaluddin, 194
symbolic capital, 66, 211, 315–16
Syria, 86, 182, 263, 284, 288, 371, 428
"systems of knowledge," 106, 330–31, 345

Taal, Ahmadu, 198
Taal, al-Hajj 'Umar (al-Hajj 'Umar al-Futi), 198
Taal, Saydu Nuru, 198
Taba'i al-hayawan (Marvazi), 114
al-Tabari, 367–68, 373
Tablighi Jama'at, 203–4
Tagore, Rabindranath, 420
Taha, Ustadh Muhmud, 197
al-Tahtawi, Rifa'a, 44–45
tajdid. See revival
Taj Mahal, 22, 376, 419
Talbi, Mohamed, 129, 133–34
Taliban, 18, 265, 271, 297, 308, 404
Tamerlane, 79, 91, 101, 125–26, 136, 287
tanzih (transcendence), 222–23
Taqi al-Din al-Hilali, Muhammad, 354, 356, 401
tashbih (immanence), 223
taskhir (reciprocity), 337–38
taswir (rhymed closure), 353
tawhid (divine unity) 193, 293, 382
ta'widh (talisman) 147, 157, 345–48
Taylor, Charles, 317
Teaching Islam (Wheeler), 96
Technical Age, 55, 243, 245–47, 251–52
technology, 211–12, 239, 248, 294, 300, 342
terrorism: Islamophobia and, 93; 9/11 attacks, 2, 7, 90, 96, 230, 265–66, 274–75, 297–98, 305, 410, 418, 422–23, 425; post-9/11, 70, 424, 435; war on, 97–98, 262, 274, 308, 321–22
theocracy, 38–39
theologians (*mutakallimun*), 13, 115, 223, 437
theology, 12, 41, 100, 102, 108, 116, 119, 236
Third World, 35, 66, 93–95, 233, 239–41, 247, 251, 296–97
Tibetan Buddhists, 219
al-Tijani, Shaykh Ahmad, 196, 209
Tijaniyya Sufi order, 195, 197, 198, 208–9, 214
Timurid dynasty, 62, 287
Tolstoy, Leo, 174
Toorawa, Shawkat, 364–67
Torah, 242, 381, 383
Toynbee, Arnold, 54, 58, 125, 177
Tradition (Ibn Khaldun), 59
Trench, Battle of the, 279

tribalism, 80
Trimingham, J. Spencer, 162, 176–78
Tunisia, 39, 86, 294
al-Turabi, Hassan, 264
Turcomans, 286
Turkey, 80, 88, 296, 435, 440; nomads in, 285; post–World War I, 85–86; present-day, 26, 46–47, 371; reformers in, 294; social modernity in, 39; Sufism in, 200, 205–7
Tusi, Nasiruddin, 288

Uhud, Battle of, 279
'ulama' (religious scholars or officials): as guardians of Islamic law, 340; Sayyid Ahmad Khan on, 145–46; religious authority and, 191, 193; Saudi, 264; Shi'i, 250; Sufi-minded, 196
umma (Muslim community), 43, 45, 230, 242, 272, 341, 371; Bin Laden and, 302; decline of, 162, 177–78, 268, 270; formation and expansion of, 187, 276; idea of, 282; networks and, 334–35, 341, 343; Qutb and, 297; twenty-first-century, 343
United Kingdom, 94, 400, 418
United Nations, 33, 264, 269
United States, 311; Asian religions in, 307; Black Muslims in, 327; Christians and, 246, 250; forces of, 294; Hodgson and, 94; immigrants to, 2, 213, 313–22; interfaith dialogue in, 424; Khomeini and, 31; Lawrence and, 416, 418, 439; Muslims and, 70, 428, 434–35, 16; post-1945, 16; racial prejudice in, 312; Sufism in, 214; terrorism in, 265–66, 297–98, 300, 308
Uwaysi initiation, 184

Venture of Islam, The (Hodgson), 90–97
Vietnam, 98, 312–13
violence: Bin Laden and, 268, 298–302; colonialism and, 19, 66, 291–97; epistemic, 427; in gunpowder empires, 284–90; inequality and, 38; Islam and, 3, 6–7, 9, 15, 25–26, 29–32, 43, 230, 255, 275–83, 435, 438, 439; Shah Bano case and, 17; and state sovereignty, 19; structural, 7; Wahhabis and, 404

wadud, amina, 372
Wahhabism: in Arabia, 180; in Delhi, 149; and Egyptian/Ottoman forces, 196; impact of, 192; and the Prophet Muhammad, 192; Shahid and, 199; Sir Sayyid on, 154
Waldman, Marilyn, 45, 91, 96
Waliullah, Shah, 134, 144–49, 153, 194, 196, 199
Wallerstein, Immanuel, 63–66, 70
war: Bin Laden and, 299–301; Hindu prisoners of, 111–12; Islam and, 18, 26, 230, 298; media war, 400; Naqshbandis against Russian forces, 200–201; offensive war (*harb*), 270; Prophet and, 277–79; on terror, 97–98, 262, 274, 308, 321–22; Wahhabis and, 293. See also *jihad* (divinely sanctioned war); *specific wars*
Washington, Booker T., 320
Weber, Max, 54, 56, 65
Welfare Party (Refah Partisi) (Turkey), 205
Wheeler, Brannon, 96
Where Is Allah? (Saber), 397
Whitehead, A. N., 54, 57
Who Is Allah? (Lawrence), 15, 218–27, 352, 395–406
Wilson, John, 240
Wittgenstein, Ludwig, 236
World War I, 48, 56, 86, 195, 205–6, 268, 294
World War II, 48, 90–91, 207, 209, 233, 238, 265

Yasavi Sufi order, 206
Yemen, 124, 184, 197, 263, 278, 379, 391
Yom Kippur War, 263
Young Turk revolt (1908), 202

Zakaria, Rafiq, 260
zakat (alms), 339
al-Zawahiri, Ayman, 264–65
zawiyas (lodges), 194–95, 197, 209, 336, 339
Zawqi Shah, Muhammad, 204–5
Zayn al-akhbar (Gardizi), 114
Zengi, 283–84
Zitzewitz, Karin, 385
Zoroastrianism, 109
Zuhri, Muhammad, 346–47

CREDITS

CHAPTER 1. Bruce B. Lawrence, "Introduction: Islam across Time and Cultures," in *Shattering the Myth: Islam beyond Violence* (Princeton, NJ: Princeton University Press, 1998), 3–29. Copyright © 1998 by Princeton University Press. Reprinted by permission.

CHAPTER 2. Bruce B. Lawrence, "Islam in Afro-Eurasia: A Bridge Civilization," in *Civilizations in World Politics: Plural and Pluralist Perspectives*, edited by Peter J. Katzenstein (London: Routledge, 2010), 157–75. Used courtesy of Taylor & Francis.

CHAPTER 3. Bruce B. Lawrence, "Muslim Cosmopolitanism," *Critical Muslim* 2 (2012): 19–39. Used by permission.

CHAPTER 4. Bruce B. Lawrence, "Genius Denied and Reclaimed: Hodgson's *The Venture of Islam*," *Los Angeles Review of Books*, November 11, 2014, 4. Used by permission.

CHAPTER 5. Bruce B. Lawrence, "Al-Biruni: Against the Grain," *Critical Muslim* 12 (2014): 61–71. Used by permission.

CHAPTER 6. Bruce B. Lawrence, "Shahrastani on Indian Idol Worship," *Studia Islamica* 38 (1973): 61–73. Used by permission.

CHAPTER 7. Bruce B. Lawrence, introduction to *The Muqaddimah: An Introduction to History*, by Ibn Khaldun, translated by Franz Rosenthal, abridged and edited by N. J. Dawood (Princeton, NJ: Princeton University Press, 2005), vii–xxv. Copyright © 1958 and 1967 by Princeton University Press. Reprinted by permission.

CHAPTER 8. Bruce B. Lawrence, "Mystical and Rational Elements in the Early Religious Writings of Sir Sayyid Ahmad Khan," in *The Rose and the Rock: Mystical and Rational Elements in the Intellectual History of South Asian Islam*, edited by Bruce Lawrence (Durham, NC: Duke University Programs in Comparative Studies on Southern Asia and on Islamic and Arabian Development Studies, 1979), 61–103.

CHAPTER 9. Bruce B. Lawrence, "Can Sufi Texts Be Translated? Can They Be Translated from Indo-Persian to American English?," *Islamic Culture* 64 (1990): 25–46.

CHAPTER 10. Bruce B. Lawrence, "What Is a Sufi Order? 'Golden Age' and 'Decline' in the Historiography of Sufism," in *Sufi Martyrs of Love: The Chishti Order in South Asia and Beyond*, by Carl W. Ernst and Bruce B. Lawrence (New York: Palgrave Macmillan, 2002), 11–26. Reproduced with permission of Palgrave Macmillan.

CHAPTER 11. Bruce B. Lawrence, "Sufism and Neo-Sufism," in *The New Cambridge History of Islam*, vol. 6, *Muslims and Modernity: Culture and Society since 1800*, edited by Robert W. Hefner (Cambridge: Cambridge University Press, 2010), 355–84. Copyright © by the Cambridge University Press. Reprinted with permission.

CHAPTER 12. Bruce B. Lawrence, "Allah Remembered: Practice of the Heart," in *Who Is Allah?* (Chapel Hill: University of North Carolina Press, 2015), 84–117. Copyright © 2015 by the University of North Carolina Press. Used by permission of the publisher.

CHAPTER 13. Bruce B. Lawrence, "Fundamentalism as a Religious Ideology in Multiple Contexts" and conclusion, in *Defenders of God: The Fundamentalist Revolt against the Modern Age* (San Francisco: Harper and Row, 1989), 96–101, 227–45. Copyright © Bruce B. Lawrence. Used by permission of the author.

CHAPTER 14. Bruce B. Lawrence, "The Shah Bano Case," in *On Violence: A Reader*, edited by Bruce B. Lawrence and Aisha Karim (Durham, NC: Duke University Press, 2007), 262–67.

CHAPTER 15. Bruce B. Lawrence, introduction to *Messages to the World: The Statements of Osama bin Laden*, edited and introduced by Bruce B. Lawrence, translated by James Howarth (London: Verso, 2005), xi–xxiii.

CHAPTER 16. Bruce B. Lawrence, "Muslim Engagement with Injustice and Violence," in *The Oxford Handbook of Religion and Violence*, edited by Mark Juergensmeyer, Margo Kitts, and Michael Jerryson (New York: Oxford University Press, 2013), 126–52. Used by permission of Oxford University Press.

CHAPTER 17. Bruce B. Lawrence, preface and conclusion, to *New Faiths, Old Fears: Muslims and Other Asian Immigrants in American Religious Life* (New York: Columbia University Press, 2002), ix–xvi, 133–44. Copyright © Columbia University Press. Used with permission of the publisher.

CHAPTER 18. Bruce B. Lawrence, "W. D. Mohammed: Qur'an as Guide to Racial Equality," in *The Qur'an: A Biography* (New York: Atlantic Monthly Press, 2006), 163–71. Used by permission.

CHAPTER 19. miriam cooke and Bruce B. Lawrence, introduction to *Muslim Networks from Hajj to Hip Hop*, edited by miriam cooke and Bruce B. Lawrence (Chapel Hill: University of North Carolina Press, 2005), 1–25. Copyright © 2005 by the University of North Carolina Press. Used by permission of the publisher.

CHAPTER 20. Bruce B. Lawrence, "AIDS Victims and Sick Women: Qur'an as Prescription for Mercy," in *The Qur'an: A Biography* (New York: Atlantic Monthly Press, 2006), 184–92. Used by permission.

CHAPTER 21. Bruce B. Lawrence, "Approximating *Saj*ᶜ in English Renditions of the Qur'an: A Close Reading of *Sura* 93 (*al-Ḍuḥā*) and the *Basmala*," *Journal of Qur'anic Studies* 7 (2005): 64–80. Used by permission.

CHAPTER 22. Bruce B. Lawrence, epilogue to *The Qur'an: A Biography* (New York: Atlantic Monthly Press, 2006), 193–99. Used by permission.

CHAPTER 23. Bruce B. Lawrence, "A Metaphysical Secularist? Decoding M. F. Husain as a Muslim Painter in Exile," in *Barefoot across the Nation: Maqbool Fida Husain and the Idea of India*, edited by Sumathi Ramaswamy (New York: Routledge, 2011), 253–73. Used courtesy of Taylor & Francis.

CHAPTER 24. Bruce B. Lawrence, conclusion to *Who Is Allah?* (Chapel Hill: University of North Carolina Press, 2015), 163–81. Copyright © 2015 by the University of North Carolina Press. Used by permission of the publisher.

www.ingramcontent.com/pod-product-compliance
Lightning Source LLC
Chambersburg PA
CBHW070817250426
43672CB00031B/2754